BUDDHIST ETHICS

BUDDHIST ETHICS

Jamgön Kongtrul Lodrö Tayé

Translated and edited by the
International Translation Committee
founded by the V.V. Kalu Rinpoché

Snow Lion Publications
Ithaca, New York

Snow Lion Publications
P.O. Box 6483
Ithaca, New York 14851 USA
607-273-8519

Printed in Canada on acid-free recycled paper.

ISBN 1-55939-066-2

Library of Congress Cataloging-in-Publication Data

Koṅ-sprul Blo-gros-mtha'-yas, 1813-1899
    [Śes bya mtha' yas pa'i rgya mtsho. English. Selections]
    Buddhist ethics / by Jamgön Kongtrul Lodrö Tayé ; translated
and edited by the International Translation Committee.
        p.   cm.
    Includes bibliographical references and index.
    ISBN 1-55939-066-2 (alk. paper)
    1. Buddhist ethics. 2. Buddhism--China--Tibet. I. International
Translation Committee. II. Title.
BJ1289.K6513 1997
294.3'5--dc21   97-33450
                                                                      CIP

Contents

*Dedicated to the long life
of His Holiness the Dalai Lama*

Foreword

Jamgön Kongtrul Lodrö Tayé was one of the great nineteenth-century figures in Tibet—in learning, in spiritual attainment, and in reputation. He was a master of the ten fields of classical knowledge. With great confidence, respect, and pure vision in the Dharma, he studied, contemplated, cultivated, mastered, and applied the teachings of all schools of Buddhism. In particular, he had a special aptitude for commentary and writing.

In his day, many of the instructions for spiritual maturation and liberation were rarely practiced, widely scattered, and close to extinction. With his special abilities, he collected these rare and fragile transmissions into what are now known as *The Five Great Treasuries*, a collection of more than a hundred volumes.

Of these, the treasury called *The Encompassment of All Knowledge* discusses the path to freedom, describing the three disciplines of ethics, contemplation, and wisdom. It covers the Buddha's teachings from the sutras and tantras, the main commentarial traditions and essential instructions along with such traditional subjects of learning as medicine, art, and linguistics. This work doesn't just touch on one topic here and there but encompasses all areas of knowledge with unprecedented clarity and thoroughness.

The Lord of Refuge, the Venerable Kalu Rinpoché, Rangjung Kunkyab, was the activity manifestation of Jamgön Kongtrul Lodrö Tayé. He felt that in the present times this great treasury was essential for Buddhist practitioners around the globe and he therefore spearheaded the effort to translate this work into English. The present text is the translation of the section of this treasury that deals with the three vows, the essence of the practice and application of what Buddha Shakyamuni taught in the three collections of teaching (Skt. *tripiṭaka*) and the four divisions of Tantra.

For any person, the proper practice and application of these teachings will reduce the negative dimensions of life such as suffering and inappropriate reactions. Equally, the positive dimensions of life, happiness and well-being for oneself and others, will grow and flourish. Ultimately, one will completely stop what is problematic, understand how things are, naturally realize the two aims, and awaken fully into buddhahood.

> Bokar Rinpoché
> Bokar Ngedön Chökhor Ling
> Mirik, India
> April 4, 1997

Introduction

Buddhist Ethics, the fifth book of Kongtrul Lodrö Tayé's ten-part *Encompassment of All Knowledge*, begins with a presentation of the qualifications of both the spiritual teachers who embody the different systems of ethics and their disciples, the trainees of these systems. The text explains the process whereby teachers and disciples establish and cultivate a proper spiritual relationship, which, once it has been established, provides a foundation from which teachers can expound the Buddha's doctrine and disciples can receive the teachings. The author then provides a detailed description of the three major systems of ethics, or vows, within the Buddhist tradition.

In Buddhism, vows are viewed in many ways, depending on the context of the discussion, but generally the ethical systems are designated as three sets of vows, as two sets of vows, or as one all-inclusive vow. The three sets of vows spoken of throughout all divisions of the Buddhist scriptures are those of personal liberation (*prātimokṣa*), of meditative absorption (*dhyāna*), and of the uncontaminated (*anāsrava*) vows. These are essentially identical to the three forms of training on the Buddhist path: the development of morality, meditation, and wisdom. In fact, in order to gain the different types of enlightenment of their systems, proclaimers (*śrāvaka*), solitary sages (*pratyekabuddha*), and bodhisattvas must forsake disturbing emotions and other obstacles on their paths by cultivating an uncontaminated discriminative awareness which is developed by training in wisdom.

This discriminative awareness is grounded in mental quiescence achieved by training in meditation, and mental quiescence is developed on the basis of training in pure morality.

The proclaimers' system speaks of two sets of ethics, each with three vows: the vows of a lay practitioner, novice, and monk (or nun); and the vows of body, speech, and mind. The three vows in the scriptures of the Universal Way (*mahāyāna*) refer to the processes of refraining from the unwholesome, of aiming at acquiring good qualities, and of working for the benefit of all living beings. These are also known as the three trainings, or ethics, of the bodhisattva.

The tantras speak of four sets of ethics, each with three vows. The first set includes the commitments of awakening mind, the vows related to the creation phase, and those related to the completion phase. The second set includes the pledges of the Buddha's body, speech, and mind. The third set, as taught by the great adept Vitapada, consists in not conforming to the practice of accepting what is good and rejecting what is bad with respect to any physical, verbal, or mental action. The fourth set includes the vows of personal liberation, the bodhisattva commitments, and the pledges of the awareness holder (*vidyādhara*).

The tantras also speak of two types of ethics: the common pledges received during the vase initiation of the five awarenesses (of the vase) and the stages of the initiation prior to these; and the uncommon ones received at the time of the irreversible vajra-master initiation. According to a different explanation, the two types of ethics in the tantras refer to the vows related to the creation phase and those related to the completion phase, also known as the outer and inner vows. Moreover, when the tantric adept assumes all the vows of personal liberation, the bodhisattva commitments, and the tantric pledges, he or she maintains these ethics in both their outer and inner aspects.

All of these systems of ethics in the Buddhist tradition, whether presented in a threefold or twofold form, were proclaimed by the Buddha to be contained in a single system of ethics: that of the Perfection of Wisdom. This is clearly stated in the *Condensed Perfection of Wisdom Discourse:*

> Just as the rays of the sun radiating through space
> Dispel all obscurity throughout the firmament,
> The Perfection of Wisdom outshines the other perfections
> All of which are its precepts and are included within it.

Can we call the Perfection of Wisdom a vow or ethic? The answer is found in the same scripture:

> Our Guide taught that it is the lack of clinging to [the concept of]
>   vow or no vow
> That is the true vow or ethic.

Among these various classifications of vows, the three vows that are the subject of this particular work of Kongtrul are the vows of personal liberation (*prātimokṣa*), of awakening mind (*bodhicitta*), and of the awareness holder (*vidyādhara*). These three vows, or systems of ethics, embrace all forms of spiritual practice set forth in the Buddhist doctrine. Their integrated presentation is nonetheless found only in the Way of Secret Mantra. The higher ethics of the bodhisattva and the awareness holder are prescribed in the ways of neither the proclaimers nor the solitary sages, since followers of these ways believe them to be unnecessary for the attainment of their goal of enlightenment. Indispensable to the proclaimers and solitary sages are the personal liberation vows, on the basis of which, once trainees have developed the intention to attain enlightenment, they cultivate mental quiescence and insight and thereby reach their goal.

The awareness holders' ethics are not prescribed in the Way of the Perfections, the path followed by bodhisattvas. Trainees on that path do not disregard the personal liberation vows, however, even though unsurpassable enlightenment can be achieved on the basis of the bodhisattvas' commitment alone. Personal liberation vows must definitely be assumed by bodhisattvas in training, but these vows are enhanced by the altruistic awakening mind characteristic of the Universal Way.

According to the Way of Secret Mantra, the tantric vows are crucial to the attainment of unsurpassable enlightenment, but a yogin must also assume the bodhisattva and personal liberation vows. Therefore, the tantras instruct practitioners to safeguard all three forms of ethics. In fact, the preliminary rite for a tantric initiation includes procedures for the conferral of the personal liberation and bodhisattva vows, while the main part of the initiation includes the conferral of the tantric vows. Moreover, prior to engaging in the phases of creation and completion (the main aspects of tantric observance), the practitioner must affirm the personal liberation and bodhisattva vows. While continuously striving to avoid root infractions of the tantric vows, the yogin must also safeguard the personal liberation and bodhisattva ethics.

To understand the importance of the three forms of ethics on the tantric path, it should be noted that most of the mandala rituals include specific procedures for assuming the three vows. When disciples make a petition in order to receive the vows, with the words "Bestow on me the pledges...," they are requesting the tantric vows. With the words "Bestow on me also awakening mind...," they are requesting the bodhisattva commitments. With the words "Bestow on me also refuge in the Buddha, Dharma, and Sangha...," they are requesting the vows of personal liberation. The three vows are actually assumed as the initiating master proclaims first the tantric vows, as is stated in *Indestructible Peak,* with the words "The pledges of the five families..."; then the bodhisattva vows with the words "In addition, the other fourteen..."; and the personal liberation vows with the words "You should not kill living creatures...."

The *Ritual of Confession* provides clear evidence that the two lower forms of ethics must precede the main part of the tantric path, which consists of the phases of creation and completion. One of the major tantric vows is not to "transgress the Buddha's word"; this pledge addresses the necessity of safeguarding the vows of the two lower systems of ethics as well as the tantric ones. That a yogin must follow all three ethics is also stated by Sakya Pandita, the master of the doctrine:

> [First one] searches for a spiritual master
> And then receives the four initiations.
> One thereby becomes a possessor of the three vows.

and

> Endowed with the three vows
> And the knowledge of the profound points of the two phases....

All of the different forms of spiritual practice taught by the Buddha are encompassed by the three vows: the discipline (*vinaya*) and the common doctrine constitute the training undergone by the proclaimers; the perfections (*pāramitā*) and the common doctrine, the training of bodhisattvas; and the uncommon doctrine, the training undergone by followers of the tantra, or Indestructible Way. The proclaimers' training is summarized in the following citation from the *Personal Liberation Discourse:*

> Do not do any evil,
> Engage in excellent virtue,

And tame your mind:
This is the doctrine of the Buddha.

Here, the trainee first assumes the ethics of renouncing harm to others and the basis of harm, thereby conforming to virtue and rejecting evil. The proclaimers' training pertains to the ethics of personal liberation inasmuch as these ethics are defined as the forsaking of injury to others, along with the basis of injury.

The bodhisattvas' training is summarized in this citation from the *Indestructible Tent*:

Contemplation of the mind
As the indivisibility of emptiness and compassion
Is the supreme doctrine of the Buddha,
Of the Dharma, and of the Sangha.

The bodhisattva first develops compassion and then, using skillful means to realize perfect enlightenment, merges the relative awakening mind with the understanding of emptiness. This method pertains to the bodhisattvas' ethics inasmuch as the bodhisattvas' ethics are defined as the special factor that makes it possible to achieve perfect enlightenment.

The tantric training is encapsulated in the *Indestructible Peak*:

The ripening [initiation] and the liberative path are the supreme
doctrine of enlightenment of the Buddha.

Tantric training falls into two classes: the ripening initiation, which plants a seed in the disciple in order to consecrate ordinary body, speech, and mind as inseparable from and unified with Vajradhara's body, speech, and mind; and the liberative path, which gradually brings that inseparability to an apex. These two pertain to tantric ethics inasmuch as tantric ethics are defined as the ripening and liberative aspects.

I will now mention a few points about each of these three systems. First, the personal liberation vows are defined as the intention, attended by correlated mental factors and grounded in an attitude of renunciation, to forsake both harming others and the basis of harm. If vows lack an underlying motivation of renunciation, they are not true personal liberation vows. Vows assumed with the desire to gain a divine or human condition in the next life are known as a "wish to excel," and ethics maintained out of fear of punishment, sicknesses, demonic forces, and other problems of this life are known as "ethics

to protect one from fear." These are not the ethics of personal liberation, because they lack the spirit that renounces the cycle of existence.

Does this mean that followers of other religions lack correct morality? The answer is found in Vasubandhu's own *Commentary on the
Treasury of Phenomenology:*

> Others do have a valid morality. However, their morality is not
> equal to the ethics of personal liberation, because it is bound to
> conditioned existence and does not lift one eternally from what
> is unwholesome.

In the preceding definition of the personal liberation vow, "harming
others" refers to the seven unwholesome acts of body and speech
(killing, stealing, etc.). "Basis of harm" denotes unwholesome mental
states (covetousness, malice, and bad views) that underlie physical
unwholesome acts. Thus, although there are seven classes of personal
liberation vows, all of them consist in forsaking the ten unvirtuous
acts. Many Tibetan scholars, such as the patriarchs of the Sakyas as
well as Chim Namka Drak, the Great Translator Pang, Butön, and
Kongtrul, agree in defining the personal liberation vows in this way.
The meaning of "intention attended by correlated mental factors" is
explained in the *Compendium of Phenomenology:*

> When a particular virtue is present, other factors such as inten-
> tion, attentiveness, or discriminative awareness will accompany
> it. The predominant factor among these will become the nature
> of that virtue. As a consequence, the other concomitant mental
> factors will also turn into the same nature. In this context [of per-
> sonal liberation], the main factor is intention, but attendant mental
> factors also become the vow.

Does this imply that while a monk is sound asleep or experiencing
violent hatred or absorbed in the state in which [his discrimination]
is interrupted, he does not have vows? The Analysts (*vaibhāṣika*) assert that the vows are form in order to avoid such a conclusion. The
Compendium of Phenomenology says, however:

> The assertion that the vows exist as a potential is indeed the cor-
> rect one. Just as a man still owns money that he has lent to an-
> other with interest even though he does not actually have it in
> hand, [a monk] who has assumed vows through the necessary
> conditions still holds these vows as long as he does not give them
> up, even though the vows may not be manifest at a particular time.

Personal liberation is of two types: that of the proclaimers and that of
the universalists. These types are differentiated with respect to their

focus or goal, that of the first being the attainment of a lesser form of enlightenment for the sake of oneself alone; that of the second, perfect enlightenment for the sake of all living creatures. Personal liberation vows may be received in the proclaimers' ceremony, the universalists' ceremony, or a tantric initiation; therefore, the glorious Sakya patriarchs have declared that the personal liberation vows permeate all three sets of vows.

Second, the ethics of awakening mind of the Universal Way are defined as the special factor for the accomplishment of perfect enlightenment. In terms of focus, there are two awakening minds: one is the simple aspiration to be awakened; the other, the mind that ventures to awaken. As for its nature, awakening mind has both an ultimate aspect and a relative one. Awakening mind correlated with the stages of demarcation of the path yields an awakening mind based on appreciation, an awakening mind of noblest intention, an awakening mind fully matured, and an awakening mind that has forsaken all impediments. Furthermore, twenty-two types of awakening mind are described by examples or metaphors, from "earth-like" up to "cloud-like."

Some scholars assert that the awakening mind of a bodhisattva still on the worldly path is the simple aspiration to awaken and that this aspiration turns into the "venturing mind" once the bodhisattva has gained the first stage of awakening. That is not the case, however, since Shantideva's *Compendium of Trainings* states that the commitment of the venturing mind may be formed by ordinary persons who have not attained a stage of awakening. Other scholars believe that the aspiring mind does not involve a commitment. To sustain their view, they cite the following passage from *Guide to the Bodhisattva's Way of Life*:

> Although the mind that aspires to awaken
> Yields great fruits in cyclic existence,
> An uninterrupted flow of merit does not ensue
> As it does with the venturing mind.

This passage, however, does not imply that the aspiring mind has no commitment; it refers to the simple aspiration unheld or unattended by the vow.

The Sakya patriarchs speak of three aspects of the mind that aspires to awakening: the simple aspiring mind, the actual formation of an aspiring mind, and the safeguarding of the aspiring mind from deterioration. The venturing awakening mind also has three corresponding aspects: the simple venturing mind, the actual formation of a venturing mind, and the safeguarding of the venturing mind from deterioration.

What is the difference between the aspiring and venturing minds? The first is the desire to awaken for the sake of others. The second is the desire to travel the path to awakening for the sake of others. When these two minds arise but are not held by commitment, they are the simple aspiring and venturing minds subsumed under the mental factor of aspiration. Held by the commitment, they become the formation of the aspiring and venturing minds, consisting mainly in the intention to forsake factors incompatible with the awakening mind itself. From this point forward, the essence of all bodhisattva practices is that of safeguarding the aspiring and venturing minds from degeneration. Thus, for the generation of an actual aspiring and venturing awakening mind, the mind must be held by commitment.

Some scholars believe that the aspiring and venturing minds pertain only to the relative awakening mind, not to the ultimate awakening mind. The *Ornament of Realizations*, however, states that all aspects of a bodhisattva's awakening mind are included in the aspiring and venturing minds. When it says, "The formation of the awakening mind for the sake of others...," it provides a general description of awakening mind that embraces both the relative and ultimate ones.

In summary, the bodhisattva commitment is defined as the special factor for realizing perfect enlightenment and as the intention attended by concomitant factors to forsake elements incompatible with awakening mind. The commitment may be assumed in a ceremony in common with the proclaimers' personal liberation vows, in the special ceremony of the universalists, or during a tantric ritual.

Third, the vows of an awareness holder are defined by the venerable Drakpa Gyaltsen in the following way:

> The awareness holder's vows are the blessing of the form of the
> deity or of pristine awareness.

The awareness holder's vows apply to all four sets of tantra. With respect to the three lower tantras, in the yoga with signs, they are the blessing of the form of the deity; and in the signless yoga, the blessing of pristine awareness. In the Highest Yoga Tantra, with respect to the phase of creation, they are the blessing of the form of the deity; and with respect to the phase of completion, the blessing of pristine awareness.

The mandala rites, in accordance with the etymology of the "initiations of the five awarenesses," explain the meaning of "awareness-holder vows": "Awareness" (Tib. *rig pa*) refers to the five pristine awarenesses which are the transformation of the five emotions, such as unawareness. "Holder" (Tib. *'dzin pa*) refers to both the process of actualization and the actualization of the five pristine awarenesses. The "vow" of such an awareness holder is defined as the special skillful means that protects one from objectifying concepts and as an intention (attended by concomitant factors) to forsake incompatible factors.

What does the vow protect? From what does it protect? How does it protect? The Sanskrit term *mantra* (Tib. *sngags*) is composed of *man* for *mano*, "mind," and *tra*, "to protect"; the vow protects the mind. Mind is defined here as the six consciousnesses (or eight, when the last one is subdivided) which arise from the contact of the senses with their objects.

The vow protects the mind from concepts that cause it to cling to the attributes of ordinary appearance or to those of the deity. "Attributes" here are the individual aspects of the objects, and "conception" is the clinging to the reality of these particular aspects.

Protection is effected through the ripening and liberating aspects of the Indestructible Way, which are superior to those of the Universal Way, which in turn are superior to the forms of practice of the lesser spiritual ways.

Tantric vows are assumed in the course of an initiation in two ways: through promise and through ritual. At the time of the preparatory part and entrance to the mandala, one assumes the pledges through a promise. If one does not participate in the main part of the procedure, however, one is not authorized to safeguard those pledges. At the completion of the vajra-master initiation of each of the four classes of tantra, one assumes the main tantric pledges through ritual.

As for the tantric pledges of the Highest Yoga Tantra, those assumed through a promise are similar to those of the lower tantra. Those assumed through ritual are related to the phases of creation and completion. The first are assumed at the conclusion of the vase initiation, since the vase initiation is a precondition for the cultivation of the phase of creation. The pledges of the phase of completion are assumed at the conclusion of the higher initiation, since the three higher initiations are ripening factors for the phase of completion.

Tantric pledges may be assumed in the presence of a master who has attained a stage of awakening or a master who is the physical manifestation of awakening. Generally, however, the disciple is an ordinary person and is initiated by a master who is also an ordinary person; in such a case, the disciple must find a master who possesses the qualifications set forth in the tantras. These are summarized in the *Fifty Verses on Devotion to the Spiritual Master*:

> A genuine spiritual master is steadfast and disciplined,
> Intelligent, patient, honest, and sincere,
> Knowledgeable in the application of mantra and tantra,
> Compassionate, learned in the treatises,
> Master of the ten fields of expertise,
> Proficient in the drawing of mandalas,
> Competent in expounding the Secret Mantra,
> Honorable and upright in all aspects of life.

Please bear these points in mind.

His Holiness Sakya Trizin
Sakya Dolma Phodrang
Dehra Dun, India
June 1, 1996

Translators' Introduction

KONGTRUL LODRÖ TAYÉ AND *THE INFINITE OCEAN OF KNOWLEDGE*

Buddhist Ethics is the translation of Book 5 of *The Infinite Ocean of Knowledge* (*Shes bya mtha' yas pa'i rgya mtsho*), with its root verses *The Encompassment of All Knowledge* (*Shes bya kun khyab*). The author of this major treatise is Kongtrul Lodrö Tayé (Kong sprul Blo gros mtha' yas, 1813–1899), a saint and scholar of the nineteenth century who played a vital role in the revitalization and preservation of Buddhism in Eastern Tibet.

Kongtrul is perhaps best known for his writings: he composed more than ninety volumes on theory and practice according to the Nyingma, Kadam, Sakya, Kagyu, and Bon traditions. His major works are referred to as the *Five Great Treasuries* (*mDzod chen lnga*); the first to be written was *The Encompassment of All Knowledge*, which was followed by *The Kagyu Treasury of Mantra*, *The Treasury of Key Instructions*, *The Treasury of Precious Treasure Teachings*, and *The Special Secret Treasury of Advice*. Because of the unequaled scholarship shown in these works, Kongtrul came to be called Jamgön ('Jam-mgon), "Gentle Protector," which is an epithet of Manjushri, the bodhisattva who symbolizes higher wisdom.

Kongtrul's huge literary output gives the impression that his primary focus was writing. This was not the case; most of his life was spent meditating and teaching. He composed the verses of *The Encompassment of*

All Knowledge, for instance, between periods of meditation while he was living in seclusion at his hermitage, Kunzang Dechen Ösal Ling, in Eastern Tibet. Kongtrul composed this work in response to a request by Ngedön Tenpa Rabgyé, the first Dazang incarnation, who asked that he produce a treatise on the three Buddhist ethics: the vows of personal liberation in the Hinayana system, the commitments of the bodhisattva in the Mahayana, and the pledges (*samaya*) of the awareness holder in the Vajrayana. Kongtrul decided to write a book that not only set out the three ethics, but also contained a full presentation of all aspects of the Buddhist path from the perspectives of these three systems. Indeed, *The Encompassment of All Knowledge* embraces all fields of spiritual knowledge as well as the related secular sciences known at the time of its composition.

Kongtrul presented the finished manuscript of *Encompassment* to Jamyang Kyentsé Wangpo (1820–1892), another outstanding figure in the nineteenth-century renaissance in Eastern Tibet, who, highly impressed, declared the work to be "a treasury of knowledge...the first of your five treasuries." Kyentsé urged him to write a commentary to it. In 1863, Kongtrul composed a three-volume commentary on these root verses, entitled *The Infinite Ocean of Knowledge*, completing it in less than four months. The work was revised a year later with the help of Trashi Özer, the abbot of Pelpung Monastery.

The Encompassment of All Knowledge, together with its commentary *The Infinite Ocean of Knowledge*, has come to be known as *The Treasury of Knowledge*. In Tibetan religious literature, the work stands out as a unique masterpiece embodying the entirety of the theories and methods of implementation of the Buddhist doctrine as it was preserved in Tibet. Its encyclopedic presentation, summarizing history, views, traditions, and spiritual practices, reveals an author with an exceptionally broad intellect and deep experiential understanding, without which qualities the work of presenting in an orderly and insightful fashion the major themes of such a vast literature could not possibly have been carried out.

Although he was officially affiliated with the Kagyu school of Tibetan Buddhism, Kongtrul rarely shows any partiality in his presentation. For the most part, he restricts himself to expounding different views and their implementation, putting them into context and clarifying the underlying rationale. While many authors are only "masters" of the views and practices of their own schools, Kongtrul, with his breadth of knowledge and lack of sectarian bias, demonstrates great generosity toward his readers.

Kongtrul's *The Infinite Ocean of Knowledge* comprises ten books, each of which is four chapters long. The first book, *Myriad Worlds: Buddhist Cosmology in Abhidharma, Kalacakra, and Dzog-chen* (Snow Lion, 1995), with its detailed description of the universe and explanation of the causes of cyclic existence, sets the framework for the entire book. It is, however, the fifth book, translated here as *Buddhist Ethics*, which stands as the backbone or "life pillar" of Kongtrul's work. All of the themes presented before and after rely on its treatment of the three sets of vows: the preceding sections lead up to the formulation of ethics, and the ethical systems provide the bases for the practical implementations that are elucidated in subsequent chapters of *The Infinite Ocean*.

THIS BOOK

The Teacher-Student Relationship

Buddhist Ethics begins with an elucidation of the context for training in ethics: a genuine teacher-student relationship. The first chapter describes the qualifications of both the spiritual teachers who represent the three systems of ethics and their disciples. Kongtrul emphasizes that, in order for the teachings to contribute to one's knowledge and development and ultimately reveal one's primordial condition of enlightenment, a living example, the spiritual master, is essential. Each of the three ethical systems is demonstrated by its own teachers—the monastic preceptor for the Individual Way, the bodhisattva instructor for the Universal Way, and the vajra master for the Tantric Way—who must meet strict qualifications. One master can assume all the various roles of teachers as long as he or she meets all of the requirements for each type of teacher as specified in each system.

To help the aspirant choose a suitable teacher and avoid a bad one, thereby eliminating major perils and obstacles on the path, Kongtrul outlines the knowledge and virtues to look for in a teacher and warns of possible faults. He notes, however, that at the present time it is hard to find an ideal master; therefore, one must work with one who shows more qualities than faults.

Often students seek the perfect master without first determining whether they themselves are qualified disciples. To enlighten naive students, Kongtrul provides a brief description of the qualities disciples must have. He adds that, since in these times good disciples are hard to find, a teacher must accept those who, even though they have faults, are willing to learn and to put into practice the teachings of the Buddha.

To work with a spiritual teacher involves following certain guidelines, such as developing the right motivation; carrying out acts of offering, respect, and service; and, above all, proving for oneself the validity of the teacher's message. Indications that the student is not working with a spiritual guide in a proper way include mixing with bad friends, passing time in an idle way, and showing excessive concern with one's own welfare. Of utmost importance in the teacher-student relationship is the tool of faith, which is said to be the source of all of the student's wholesome qualities.

Kongtrul also discusses the methodology whereby exposition of the doctrine is made meaningful, the qualities and kinds of expertise the teacher needs to demonstrate while instructing disciples, different ways of instructing, and the proper way for disciples to listen to the teaching.

The Three Ethics

Kongtrul then presents in detail the three ethics, or vows: those of personal liberation (*prātimokṣa*), of the awakening mind (*bodhicitta*), and of the awareness holder (*vidyādhara*). These ethical systems are not simply sets of rules; they are primarily the practical applications and outcomes of different Buddhist theories. The three ethics are linked to three different existential choices, or models, proposed in the Buddhist way: the monk or renunciate; the layperson who remains involved in the world while working toward an altruistic awakening; and the tantric adept, a sharp-witted layperson who works toward awakening while enjoying sense pleasures. These choices do not preclude one another; a monk, for example, may embody all three by being simultaneously a renunciate, a bodhisattva, and a tantric adept.

The ethics of personal liberation, which embody the way of renunciation (Tib. *spong lam*) that permeates the Individual Way (*hīnayāna*), serve as the means for securing personal freedom from the cycle of existence by renouncing the causes of suffering. Its precepts are mainly concerned with the physical aspect of existence. Although precepts for lay Buddhists are included, the model of the monk best exemplifies this approach.

The ethics of awakening mind, the path of the bodhisattva, are chiefly concerned with mental disposition. Despite the fact that its points of training are generally explained (in Asanga's works and elsewhere) through examples that relate to the monastic life, this approach remains definitely a Universal Way (*mahāyāna*) that best fits the layperson who is involved in the world.

The ethics of the awareness holder in the Secret Mantra Way (*guhyamantra*) provide the basis for the process of "reawakening" the pristine awareness of great bliss, which is the ultimate nature of the mind. Its approach is grounded in the non-violence and altruism of the previous two "vows," but its special feature is that it is a way of transformation (Tib. *'gyur lam*) rather than one of renunciation. It is mainly concerned with the mind as clear light, which is the underlying nature of being.

Kongtrul's presentation of ethics is connected to the so-called affinity for awakening (*gotra*) and the concordant path that nurtures such affinity. Whereas the goal of the various Buddhist paths is achieving awakening either for one's own or others' welfare, the connecting thread between one's ordinary condition and the state of awakening is the affinity, or potential, for awakening. Hinayana, Mahayana, and Vajrayana define spiritual affinity in different ways.

In the Individual Way, the "exalted affinity" spoken of by the Analysts means a detachment from conditioned existence and worldly possessions characterized by contentedness and few desires. That affinity is nurtured by the personal liberation vows, which are consistent with the attitude of detachment and cause it to blossom into freedom from disturbing emotions, the state of perfect peace of a saint (*arhat*).

In the Universal Way, the affinity is known as the buddha-nature (*tathāgatagarbha*) in its twofold aspect, intrinsic and evolved. The Third Karmapa, Rangjung Dorjé, explains that the intrinsic affinity is the unborn character that is the very nature of the mind, attended by impurities. The evolved affinity is the unceasing radiance of the very empty nature of mind, attended by impurities. The union of the nature of the mind and its radiance is called the "union of the two impure dimensions of enlightenment" (the impure *dharmakāya* and *rūpakāya*, respectively). Nurtured by the bodhisattva commitment in its two aspects, related to the relative and ultimate awakening minds, such twofold affinity blossoms into the two pure dimensions of enlightenment.

In the Secret Mantra, the affinity is said to be the nature of the innate pristine awareness of great bliss. As it is unceasingly present from the level of an ordinary being until buddhahood, it is known also as causal continuity (*tantra*). When such affinity is nurtured by the concordant vows of the two phases of creation and completion of the Highest Yoga Tantra, the method continuity, it blossoms into the state of Buddha Vajradhara, the resultant continuity.

The Ethics of Personal Liberation

The focus of the ethics of personal liberation is to control impulses that lead body and speech to undertake negative actions. Because such actions are always linked to limiting emotional patterns, Individualists, in addition to observing ethics, must train in the discriminative awareness that realizes selflessness in order to attain perfect peace, the state of cessation of such patterns. Furthermore, for that meditation to be stable, mental concentration also must be cultivated. Thus, personal liberation ethics are essentially identical with training in morality, meditation, and wisdom. Although the aim of the monk's vows and other personal liberation vows appears to be restraint from unwholesome physical behavior, it would be misleading to view those vows reductively, because their implicit aim is to overcome limiting mental patterns.

The foundation of these ethics lies in the precepts relating to taking refuge and the four "root," or crucial, precepts that prohibit murder, theft, lying, and adultery. Refuge relates to the Buddha, the Dharma, and the Sangha: the first is understood as the Teacher, the second as the teachings, and the third as the community (here the monastic one in particular). Originally, taking refuge was primarily an expression of faith that distinguished a follower of the Buddha from practitioners of other religions. Refuge marked the beginning of an earnest undertaking of the Buddhist path. In higher forms of Buddhist view and methods of implementation, refuge takes on deeper layers of meaning, and in the ultimate sense means taking refuge in "the buddha within," the realization of the natural and unmodified intrinsic awareness lying within oneself.

The four root precepts prohibit the four actions that would undoubtedly cause suffering for others and also compromise the tranquility of one's mind, thereby destroying one's chance to develop meditation and gain the discriminative awareness needed to uproot cyclic existence.

When the Buddhist community was first being formed, taking refuge in front of the Buddha was all that was needed for one to be accepted as a monk. Gradually, because of the misbehavior of monks and for other reasons, rules were instituted, for the most part limited to a particular temporal and social context. Many were intended not only for the welfare of the monks themselves, but also for the community's internal harmony and external social respectability.

Rules gained more importance; to be a monk became a matter of maintaining specific rules and regulations rather than a matter of freely heading into a spiritual life. Eventually, to enter the Buddhist community, the aspirant needed to assume vows, and vows came to represent a commitment to abide by the entire body of rules. Such vows were not simple promises. Instead, they were "generated" in the candidate through a series of conditions and requisites, such as the abbot, and their primary requirement was an attitude of disengagement from cyclic life.

As the vow developed into an "entity," the identification of its nature became an important matter, which explains the various assertions Kongtrul presents, based on detailed analyses, on the nature of the vow. The conclusions would have little relevance to the keeping of the rules themselves but would definitely be relevant to determining at what point a vow is lost.

Personal liberation vows are basically of two kinds: those that prohibit actions such as killing and lying, which are considered unwholesome for anyone who commits them; and those that prohibit actions such as eating in the evening, which are improper only for monks and nuns. The first kind involves a concept of "natural evil," or "absolute morality," which is probably influenced by the realist philosophical view held by the Analysts, to whom the tradition of personal liberation is undoubtedly connected. That also explains, to some extent, why the personal liberation vow is compared to a clay pot; once broken, it cannot be repaired.

Kongtrul discusses in detail the various classes of personal liberation: the precepts of the purificatory fast and the vows of the layperson, the male and female novices, the female postulant, and the monk. He also briefly examines the series of monastic rites, including confession. The vows of a nun, regrettably, are not included, because, as Kongtrul explains, the ordination of nuns was never introduced into Tibet.

The Ethics of the Mind of Awakening

The focus of the commitments of the mind of awakening is the training to be followed on the bodhisattva path. As these commitments are centered on the awakening mind itself, its causes, nature, varieties (the aspiring and venturing, the relative and ultimate), and so forth are explained in detail before the training itself is described.

The actual cultivation of the awakening mind, attended by specific points of training, is presented from the perspective of the lineage of the profound view, which was inspired by Manjushri and transmitted to Nagarjuna, Shantideva, and others, and the magnificent deeds lineage, which was inspired by Maitreya and transmitted to Asanga, Chandragomin, Atisha, and others.

These two systems are basically the same, and certain aspects of training are common to both. The common training includes the three forms of ethics for the bodhisattva, which are to shun non-virtue, acquire wholesome qualities, and work for the benefit of others, and the implementation of the six perfections: generosity, ethics, patience, effort, meditation, and wisdom.

Nagarjuna's system allows anyone who is willing and sufficiently intelligent to take the commitments of the aspiring and venturing awakening minds simultaneously, either in front of a master or alone in the imagined presence of buddhas and bodhisattvas. As long as one preserves the mind that aspires to awaken, the commitments are not lost. A damaged commitment can be restored in a dream through supplication to the bodhisattva Akashagarbha; the bright trainee restores damaged commitments through the understanding of the unborn nature of things. The points of training are followed according to one's ability, and the commitments are taken for a period as long as one estimates one can safeguard them.

In Asanga's system, only a person who holds one of the seven sets of personal liberation vows is entitled to assume the awakening-mind commitments, and such a person does so gradually (in different ceremonies), first accepting those of aspiration and then, once he or she has gained proficiency, those of venturing. It is recommended that one assume the commitments in the presence of a qualified master. If a major infraction has been committed with great emotional involvement, the commitment is deemed to be lost and must be taken anew. (Here Kongtrul adds an enigmatic note from the great Dzogchen master Longchenpa, which says that the commitment, once it has deteriorated, cannot be retaken more than three times.) The infraction should be confessed in the presence of vow holders. According to this lineage, the trainee must safeguard all of the points of training from the very beginning and must promise to keep the commitments until he or she attains enlightenment, not just for a selected period of time.

Nagarjuna's system seems more lenient and less influenced by monasticism than that of Asanga, whose points of training are more complex. Presumably, differences in the two traditions stem from their different emphases: the profound view lineage stresses the knowledge aspect of the path; the lineage of magnificent deeds, the conduct, or method, aspect.

Historically and psychologically, the bodhisattva's path is halfway between the paths of renunciation and transformation. The peacock whose feathers grow more colorful as a result of eating poison symbolizes the bodhisattva, who remains unpolluted and grows more radiant as his involvement in the world deepens. Accordingly, the *Cluster of Jewels Scripture* says:

> Just as the paddy and cane-sugar fields are nurtured by the ordure of the village, likewise, the sprout of the awakening mind is nurtured by the ordure of the emotions of a bodhisattva.

Such images clearly show that the Universal Way transcends the Individual Way's form of renunciation, which regards "objects of desire...as poisonous leaves." This transcendence of strict renunciation holds the seed of the principle of transformation, which is developed to its fullest extent in tantra.

The Universal Way prescribes a set of personal liberation vows that are not radically different from those of the Individualists. Because Universalists are distinguished for their noble intention of seeking enlightenment in order to serve all living beings, however, there is a fundamental difference in principle between their form of observance and that of the Individualists. Moreover, since the philosophical trends underlying the Universal Way stress the selflessness of phenomena and, in particular, the Centrists speak of the non-reality of all appearances, how could morality, or ethics, in the bodhisattva path be asserted as absolute rather than as a variable factor dependent on conditions? The Universal Way therefore exhibits a flexible approach to the personal liberation vows and goes so far as to say that a bodhisattva may engage in the seven unwholesome actions of body and speech if motivated by love and compassion. As Shantideva says:

> The Compassionate One, in his broad vision,
> Gave permission even for what is prohibited.

Owing to its focus on mental disposition, the ethics of the awakening mind, if damaged, can be renewed or repaired by the bodhisattva, just as a golden vessel can be repaired by a skilled goldsmith.

The Ethics of the Awareness Holder

The awareness-holder pledges of the Secret Mantra Way aim to dissolve the patterns of movement of dualistic conceptions by reawakening, through special means, the blissful pristine awareness that has always existed as the core of being. As this pristine awareness finds its support in the seminal essence, to dissolve the patterns of movement has the sense of blocking the movement or emission of seminal essence, which is the starting point of cyclic existence in a double sense (emission meaning both the beginning of dualistic representations and the conception of a new being in the womb).

The natural "vow," or "reality," in the tantra is that everything is permeated by innate pristine awareness. The "vow" of implementation consists in the phases of creation and completion, which bind dualistic appearances within blissful pristine awareness. The final, resultant "vow" is the spontaneous arising of all subjective appearance as enlightened dimensions and pristine awareness.

Only with a very elastic conception of the term can tantric vows be designated as moral obligations. For that matter, the very purpose of the vows is to overcome the dualistic judgment of good and bad, from the beginning of the path up to realization of the pristine awareness that is at the origin of all phenomena, conditioned or otherwise.

In assuming the vow of tantra, no distinction is made among candidates, who may even be prostitutes or butchers; however, one should be interested in and capable of maintaining the pledges. As a precondition for all subsequent tantric conduct, aspirants must conform to the four great pledges: to believe in the law of cause and effect, to take refuge, to develop the awakening mind, and to be initiated.

Kongtrul discusses the tantric vows according to the traditions of both the ancient and the new tantras. The ancient ones are followed primarily in the Nyingma school of Tibetan Buddhism; the new, in the Kagyu, Geluk, and Sakya schools.

Tantric Pledges in the New Schools

The new schools categorize the tantras into four main classes. Each has its own sets of pledges, which share the single aim of dissolving dualistic conceptions but are distinguished by the use of different and gradually more intensely blissful experiences, ranging from the delight born from looking at a consort to that experienced in sexual union with a consort. All these "vows," or "conducts," are included in pledges concerned with skillful means and those concerned with wisdom, or in the vow of *EVAM*, the single union of bliss and emptiness, the reality that pervades all seasons of being, from the ground up to the fruition of enlightenment. Included within the tantric pledges are some of the vows of personal liberation and other commitments incorporating the spiritual practices of the Way of the Perfections.

In the Highest Yoga Tantra, pledges are interpreted in terms of their provisional and definitive meanings, the creation and completion phases, and their relation to the five or six buddha families. An adept of the phase of creation may perform, for others' welfare, actions prescribed in the provisional meaning which would be strictly prohibited by the personal liberation vows. The hidden, or definitive, meaning of interpretable pledges is largely related to the phase of completion and the various techniques dealing with winds, channels, and semen.

The Highest Yoga Tantra is distinguished from the three lower tantras in that it teaches a deity yoga based on the awareness of the inseparability of oneself as the deity ("symbolic deity," *samayasattva, dam tshig sems dpa'*) and the pristine-awareness deity (*jñānasattva, ye shes sems dpa'*) invited from space. This tantra dispenses with many of the lower tantras' observances related to cleanliness, white foods, and outer purification which involve the concept of a deity different from and superior to oneself.

Because the "binding agent" of dualistic conceptions is the pristine awareness of great bliss, many of the pledges in the Highest Yoga Tantra concern pristine awareness and the outer and inner means for its actualization, such as the action seal, the imaginary seal, and the great seal, or the semen which is the support of the pristine awareness of bliss. The tantric path is deemed the "resultant way," because the practitioner transforms his or her own ordinary body, speech, and mind into the deity's and thereby realizes enlightened body, speech, and mind. The result is buddhahood. For this reason, the pledges are also presented as those of a buddha's body, speech, and mind. Moreover, the spiritual master is the medium through which the enlightened activities of all the buddhas shine; therefore, the most important of the fourteen vital pledges is never to lose respect for one's master. Several other pledges prescribe the proper relationship to the vajra master and vajra siblings.

The prescribed conduct for adepts of the Highest Yoga Tantra who dwell in a state of uninterrupted contemplation prohibits the performance of symbolic hand gestures, building stupas, drawing mandalas, paying homage to masters other than one's own, and other external good deeds, all of which are required by lower tantras. Once practitioners have gained mastery of pristine awareness, they are beyond vows and transgressions, acceptance and rejection, good and bad conduct, and other creations of dualistic thought. For these yogins, the pledge is an "all-embracing observance" that takes place spontaneously.

Numerous methods of restoration of tantric pledges are mentioned, such as the fire ritual, recitation and meditation on Vajrasattva, and so forth. Higher tantric pledges associated with higher initiations are to be restored by understanding the intrinsically pure nature of one's own mind. Tantric pledges, though strict, are likened to a dented vessel that can be restored to its original form through one's own efforts.

Tantric Pledges in the Ancient Schools

In the ancient tantras, the pledges are described in relation to the Mahayoga, Anuyoga, and Atiyoga systems of tantra. The general ones are not radically different from those of the new tantras, while the specific, exceptional, and ultimate ones are flavored by the language and the views of these three inner tantras.

The pledges are classified as those with and those without limits to be observed. Those with limits are associated with compassion and are said to be assumed gradually, in dependence on initiation. Those without limits, which are the very realization of reality, are said to be gained instantaneously, without ritual. The latter are said to be most wonderful and to exceed all others, but practitioners of "weak aspiration," who have not had the realization of reality, are advised to observe the pledges with limits to be observed.

Pledges in the system of Atiyoga, or self-perfection, reflect the "third way"—that of intrinsic freedom (Tib. *rang 'grol*). Included among its general pledges are vows typical of personal liberation and others of a tantric nature, most likely because this system is placed by the Nyingmapas at the peak of (that is, as the result of) nine spiritual pursuits.

Although included within the three inner tantras—Mahayoga, Anuyoga, and Atiyoga—Atiyoga does not belong to the path of transformation. It speaks of the primordial state of being that cannot be polluted by unawareness or actions stemming from unawareness, and is therefore beyond the sphere of purification and the means of purification. It does not involve pure and impure visions, and it is beyond the sphere of transformation and the means of transformation.

The pledges of self-perfection comprise four exceptional pledges. Two are related to the practice of "cutting through," and two are related to the practice of the "direct leap." These do not involve prohibitions; these pledges represent the view and method of implementation of this system. The two pledges of "cutting through" are to realize that all phenomena are primordially non-existent and to drop all clinging to appearances and allow all appearances to flow into the state of reality through the cultivation of natural intrinsic awareness unbounded by the sense of an observer. The two pledges of the "direct leap" are, first, to abandon an external spiritual quest by finding the buddha within oneself through the cultivation of the four visionary appearances out of one's inner radiance, and, second, to dissolve all things into the state of reality through the experiential knowledge that the entire universe is simply one's own natural intrinsic awareness.

In concluding his discussion of the three ethics, Kongtrul provides an extremely terse résumé of the process of spiritual development for individuals following the Individual, Universal, and Secret Mantra ways. These serve as introductions to themes that are developed fully in the later sections of *The Infinite Ocean of Knowledge*.

About the Translation

Kongtrul's systematic and precise style hardly affords any room for a "creative" translation. Nonetheless, for the sake of study and comprehension, a linear translation that closely follows Kongtrul's style may prove more useful to the reader than any attempt to facilitate the reader's understanding by sacrificing accuracy.

Very often, Kongtrul is succinct to the point that a clear understanding of a theme becomes difficult. For that reason, numerous explicatory notes have been added. When it was possible and appropriate to do so, we drew from Kongtrul's own explanations in the latter parts of *The Infinite Ocean of Knowledge*. For certain points, however, explanations found elsewhere were more helpful, and therefore we relied on several authoritative sources. Some of these are recommended by Kongtrul in the text, such as Pema Karpo's *Three Vows* and Dharmashri's *Commentary on the Three Vows*; others were our own choices, such as Tsonapa's *Sunlight Illuminating [Gunaprabha's] Fundamental Summary of Discipline*, and several others contained in the Kangyur and Tengyur.

To clarify difficult points, we have consulted scholars and accomplished masters who patiently answered our questions. Nowadays, however, it is difficult to find masters who embody the knowledge that Kongtrul exhibits in his works and who can confidently unravel very subtle and profound themes. This clearly indicates that much of the ancient knowledge contained in works such as *The Infinite Ocean of Knowledge* is rapidly vanishing and that preservation is urgently needed. It is probably one of the reasons that Kalu Rinpoché asked that this book be translated.

To complete the translation of this part of *The Infinite Ocean of Knowledge* took considerable time and effort, accompanied by the graying of the translators' hair. Although we cannot claim to have undertaken this task solely for the benefit of others, we have not done it for personal profit or fame. While aware that this work could have been carried out more brilliantly by gifted scholars, we feel confident that, because the project was inspired and blessed by the exceptionally noble intention of the venerable Kalu Rinpoché, *Buddhist Ethics* will be of true help to those who wish to make the Buddhist teachings a living experience. Activities that have been initiated with such altruistic resolve may yield results far beyond the estimation of the rational mind. The following story illustrates this point.

The great Indian scholar Chandragomin had composed a treatise on Sanskrit grammar entitled *Chandravyakarana*. Later, while staying at Nalanda, he came across an excellent book on grammar, written in verse, called the *Samantabhadra*, the author of which was Chandrakirti. Chandragomin felt that, in comparison with Chandrakirti's work, his own book was not of much use, so he dropped it into a well. His mystic inspirer, Tara, appeared to him and declared: "You have composed your text with the good intention that it should help others. In future, it will be very useful to intelligent people. Chandrakirti is proud of his scholarship, and thus his work will be of limited use to others. So take your book out of the well!"

He did so. According to legend, those who drank water from that well immediately developed great intelligence, to say nothing of those who studied his work. In accordance with the prophecy, Chandragomin's grammar remains well known even today, whereas that of Chandrakirti soon vanished.

Kongtrul's work provides a clear and masterly exposition of Buddhist ethics, and it is particularly useful in that the three different ethics of the three spiritual pursuits—Hinayana, Mahayana, and Vajrayana—are presented together, allowing the reader to make a comparative analysis. At first, the volume of material may seem overwhelming. Eventually, however, as the material is assimilated, a synthesis of its contents will arise in one's mind in the form of a simple understanding. That understanding will be relevant to all situations in one's life and will guide one on the compassionate path to knowledge.

It would not have been possible to complete such a complex work without the wisdom and support of several great masters. Bokar Rinpoché, senior meditation master of the Kagyu lineage, and Kenpo Lodrö Dönyö have tirelessly shared their knowledge with us, clarifying numerous points throughout the work; the late Tara Trulku Rinpoché elucidated the subject of personal liberation vows; and Jadral Rinpoché, Khetsun Zangpo Rinpoché, Denma Lochö Rinpoché, and Thrangu Rinpoché provided scholarly interpretations on many difficult points concerning the Vajrayana pledges.

Over the course of several years, many persons have participated in the project to translate the entire *Infinite Ocean of Knowledge*. This final version of the translation of the *Buddhist Ethics* section was completed by Elio Guarisco and Ingrid McLeod. Significant contributions at different stages of its preparation were made by Tenpa Kalsang, Ngawang Zangpo, Mathieu Ricard, and Sarah Harding. The end notes were composed by Elio Guarisco. Sincere thanks is due to Susan Kyser of Snow Lion Publications for her editorial work on the final manuscript; to Shawn Woodyard, for his editing of the introduction; to Lydia and Olivier Brunet for their research of the citations; and to the many others who have helped in countless ways.

This translation work has been carried out at the monastery of Kalu Rinpoché in Sonada, West Bengal, where the necessary facilities were provided by Lama Gyaltsen Ratak. Several benefactors have generously supported different aspects of the project.

May this work, in some small way, repay the kindness of our spiritual guide, Kalu Rinpoché.

Chapter I

The Qualities of the Spiritual Teacher and Student

OUTLINE

The Qualities of the Spiritual Teacher and Student

This subject is presented in ten parts: (1) the search for a spiritual guide; (2) the necessity of working with a spiritual guide; (3) spiritual guides and their qualifications; (4) the teacher to ignore and the one to favor; (5) the requirements of the disciple; (6) examining and working with a spiritual teacher; (7) the benefits of working with a spiritual teacher; (8) clearing away impediments to spiritual growth; (9) awakening the faith conducive to spiritual growth; and (10) the methods of teaching and listening to the doctrine.

THE SEARCH FOR A SPIRITUAL GUIDE [I]

> To take advantage of life's leisure and endowments
> Upon approaching the Buddha's teaching, the source of all
>   happiness and well-being,
> First find and then follow a spiritual guide.

The source of our present and lasting happiness and well-being is the precious teaching of the Buddha. Just to hear its name is rare, how much more so to encounter it. Now that the Buddha's teaching is known in this world and you are a human being whose life is replete with leisure and endowments,[1] do not waste this opportunity, for such a life is a wish-fulfilling jewel. In order to make your life fruitful, as you wisely approach [the teaching,] first search for a qualified spiritual guide and then follow his or her guidance impeccably.

The search for a master comprises three preliminary steps: the first [is reflecting upon the uniqueness of the Buddha's teaching] as described in *Interwoven Praises*[2]:

> [Your doctrine is] the sole path, easy to enter;
> It grants supremacy and has no flaw.
> Propitious in the beginning, middle, and end:
> No one has taught a doctrine like yours!

The teaching of the Buddha provides the sole path to liberation. Easily entered, it grants none other than supreme attainment. [The Buddha's doctrine] is flawless [in being the antidote] to attachment and other [emotions]. It is propitious because all stages [of its practice]—first listening, then reflection, and finally making it a living experience—become the seed for the attainment of higher levels of existence and liberation. For these reasons, the Buddha's doctrine represents, in every respect, the source of all happiness and well-being. These features are not found in the doctrines of other teachers, such as that of the seer Kapila,[3] but are exclusive to the teachings of the Buddha. Accordingly, the bodhisattva Shantideva composed this prayer[4]:

> May the doctrine, the only cure for suffering
> And the source of all happiness,
> Be supported and honored
> And endure for long!

The second [step is valuing the precious human life.] The *Reunion of Father and Son Scripture* states[5]:

> Having shunned all of the eight fetters[6] of life
> And found the marvelous endowments so rare to obtain
> Wise ones who have come to have faith in the doctrine of the
>   Joyful One
> Engage in the right spiritual practice.

Only by having faith in and following the Buddha's teaching can we take full advantage of our human lives that are replete with leisure and endowments.

The third step [is considering the need for a spiritual guide]. The *Transcendent Wisdom in Eight Thousand Lines* states[7]:

> A bodhisattva, great being, who wishes to attain ultimate, authentic, and perfect awakening, should first approach, work with, and honor spiritual guides.

What kind of spiritual guide should one look for? The *Collection of Spontaneous Utterances* states[8]:

> **Since by relying on an inferior, one regresses,**
> **On an equal, one stagnates,**
> **And on a superior, one excels,**
> **Keep in touch with a spiritual guide superior to yourself.**

We will not develop any wholesome qualities by working with a spiritual guide who is inferior to ourselves in the areas of ethical, scholarly, and meditative abilities, etc. [On the contrary, the relationship] will prove detrimental in many ways, and we will regress. When the spiritual guide is an equal, of similar abilities to ours, we will stagnate, neither progressing nor regressing. When the spiritual guide has qualities superior to ours, we can excel and attain the desired supreme goal. Therefore, we should always remain close to an individual superior to ourselves, a spiritually advanced master. The same scripture states[9]:

> If you study with a master
> Far superior to yourself in ethics,
> Contemplative tranquility, and wisdom,
> You can even excel him.

THE NECESSITY OF WORKING WITH A SPIRITUAL GUIDE [II]

> **The need for a guide can be determined from scripture, logic, and similes.**

The necessity of working with a spiritual guide can be determined from (1) scriptures, (2) logic, and (3) similes.

Scriptures [A]

There are countless scriptural references to the need for working with a spiritual guide. The *Condensed Transcendent Wisdom Scripture* states[10]:

> Worthy students who respect spiritual teachers
> Should always remain close to learned masters
> Because from them the virtues of the wise spring.

The *Flower Array Scripture* states[11]:

> O child of the universal family, all your virtuous qualities issue
> from your spiritual guide. You can encounter and receive instructions from one only if you have cultivated merit and wisdom for

oceans of eons. Otherwise, to meet a spiritual guide may prove more difficult than coming upon the most rare of gems. Therefore, never tire of honoring your spiritual guide.

Logic [B]

Given that a student wishes to attain the state of an omniscient buddha, the basic premise is that it is necessary for him or her to work with a spiritual guide. The reason is that the individual does not know how to cultivate merit and wisdom or to clear away obscurations. Examples consistent with this proof are the enlightened ones of the three times. The converse can be illustrated by solitary sages[12] and other examples.

Similes [C]

Many similes illustrate [the need for a spiritual guide]. For example, the *Biography of Shri Sambhava* states[13]:

> Spiritual teachers are like guides because they set us on the path of the perfections.

The *Biography of the Lay Practitioner Achala* states[14]:

> Spiritual guides are like escorts because they escort us to the state of omniscience.

The *Flower Array* states[15]:

> Spiritual guides are like ferrymen because they carry us across the river of cyclic life.

SPIRITUAL GUIDES AND THEIR QUALIFICATIONS [III]

This section has two parts: (1) an overview, and (2) an explanation. The first of these has two parts: (1) types of spiritual guides, and (2) their qualifications.

Overview [A]
Types [1]

> **A spiritual guide may be an ordinary human being, a**
> **bodhisattva, a buddha in manifest or enjoyment dimension**
> **Suited to the four phases of the disciple's growth.**

There are four types of spiritual guide: ordinary human beings, bodhisattvas, the manifest dimension of a buddha, and the enjoyment dimension of a buddha. These four are suited to the four phases [of our spiritual growth]. At the beginning of our quest, it is impossible for us to come in touch with buddhas or bodhisattvas who have reached the higher stages of awakening. Therefore, we have to work with ordinary human beings as our spiritual guides.

When the obscurations caused by our previous deeds have cleared, we can meet bodhisattvas on higher stages of awakening.[16] As we reach the highest level of the path of accumulation,[17] we can encounter the manifest dimension of a buddha. Then, as we attain the higher stages of awakening, we can come in contact with the enjoyment dimension of a buddha as our spiritual guide.

At the beginning of our quest, when we are still trapped in the dungeon of our emotions and previous deeds, we cannot consider working with higher spiritual guides because we will not see as much as their faces! We first must seek a spiritual guide who is an ordinary human being. When our path has been illuminated by the light of his or her speech, we will come to meet higher spiritual guides. Therefore, the kindest of all is the spiritual guide who is an ordinary person.[18]

Qualifications [2]

> **Eight, four, or two qualities characterize the teacher who is an ordinary person.**

Since the [latter] three types of spiritual guide do not directly benefit the beginner, it is not necessary to describe their characteristics here.

The spiritual guide who is an ordinary person must possess eight, four, or two specific qualities. The eight are listed in the following verse, which summarizes the treatment of this subject in the *Stages of the Bodhisattva*:

> He or she is ethical and learned,
> Spiritually accomplished, full of compassion and love,
> Fearless, patient, dauntless,
> And eloquent.[19]

The four [qualities] are referred to in the *Scripture Ornament*[20]: being a great teacher by virtue of prodigious learning; having the capacity to clear away doubts by virtue of higher wisdom; speaking words worthy of taking to heart because this teacher's deeds are those of a virtuous person; having the ability to point out the exact nature of both thoroughly polluted and fully pure phenomena.[21]

The two [qualities of a spiritual guide] are erudition and the commitment [to awaken for the benefit of others]. [Shantideva's] *Guide to the Bodhisattva's Way of Life* states[22]:

> Even at the cost of my life,
> I will never forsake my spiritual friend
> Who is knowledgeable in the meaning of the Universal Way
> And who is a supreme follower of the bodhisattva's way of
>   life.[23]

Explanation [B]

This section has two parts: (1) the particular types of teacher, and (2) their respective qualifications.

Particular Types [1]

> **The teacher may be a monastic preceptor, a bodhisattva's instructor, or a tantric master.**

[A disciple] may have three types of teacher—a monastic preceptor, a bodhisattva's instructor, or a tantric master—depending on which of the three sets of commitments he or she has assumed in the teacher's presence. The qualifications of each are explained below.

Individual Qualifications [2]

This three-part section describes the qualifications of (1) the monastic preceptor, (2) the bodhisattva's instructor, and (3) the tantric master.

The Monastic Preceptor [a]

> **The ordaining preceptor, ceremonial master, interviewer, tutor or instructor, and instructor of novices act as the five monastic teachers.**

There are four types of monastic preceptors: the preceptor who presides over the novice and monk's ordination, the ceremonial master, the interviewer who inquires [whether the candidate has] the requisites [for taking monastic vows], and the [monk's] tutor and instructor. Five types [can be counted] if the instructor of male and female novices is added.

The general requirements of the monastic preceptor are mentioned in [Shakhyaprabha's] *Three Hundred Stanzas on the Novitiate*[24]:

> **A monk who is ethical, well-versed in monastic ceremonies,**
> **Compassionate toward the sick, associated with upright monks,**
> **Diligent in helping others spiritually and materially, and able**
> **   to give timely counsel**
> **Is qualified to be a monastic preceptor.**

A monastic preceptor is known by the following qualities: [steadfastness, learning, and helpfulness]. Steadfastness refers to living by ethical discipline; [specifically,] having kept the monastic vows for [at least] ten years. Learning refers to flawless recollection of the monastic ceremonies set forth in the collection of scriptures on discipline. Helpfulness comprises several aspects: caring with benevolence and compassion for students who are sick; keeping company with monks who are upright in that they maintain ethics; being diligent in helping others by giving both instructions and material things; and offering [disciples] timely and pertinent counsel.[25]

In particular, the preceptor [who presides over ordination ceremonies] must possess the four virtues of steadfastness, learning, respectability,[26] and helpfulness. Steadfastness and learning may be considered as a single quality or may be further divided into twenty-one groups of five characteristics each.[27] These characteristics are explained in [Mikyö Dorjé's] *Great Commentary on the Summary of Discipline* and in the works of the eminent Pema Karpo. Helpfulness is said to be of twelve kinds:

> Compassionate and patient, maintaining close ties with
>   upright persons,
> Persevering in the two forms of helpful activity, being of the
>   same gender and view [as the candidate],
> Able to speak, comprehend, and being of sound mind,
> Having a natural human body, and [holding] his usual rank
>   [within the monastic community].

The primary qualifications of the ceremonial master are six: (1) observing monastic vows, (2) being of the same gender as the candidate [for ordination], (3) sharing with the candidate the same view on the discipline,[28] (4) fulfillment of the three basic requisites [knowing

how to speak, comprehending what is said, and being of sound mind],
(5) having a natural human body [i.e., not being an emanation], and
(6) holding his usual rank [i.e., not having been demoted]. In addition to those six qualities, he must be skilled in conducting the ordination procedure.

The interviewer must meet the above six requirements and be proficient in conducting an inquiry to determine potential impediments
for a candidate [wishing to receive ordination].

The tutor, in addition to the six requirements, must be able to instill the sense of pure ethics in his students by explaining the prohibitions and duties [of a monk].

The instructor, in addition to the six requirements, must be qualified to teach by virtue of his clear understanding of the three collections of scriptures.[29]

The Bodhisattva's Instructor [b]

The *Scripture Ornament* states[30]:

> An aspirant bodhisattva should work with a spiritual guide
>   who is self-controlled, tranquil, and has pacified
>   deception,
> Is eminent, diligent, and displays a wealth of transmissions,
> Has realized the nature of all phenomena, is articulate,
> Embodies loving-kindness, and shows no weariness or
>   discouragement.

The instructor of the bodhisattva should meet the following ten
requirements: (1) self-control, i.e., having tamed the "wild horse" of
the mind by the "fine bridle" of training in ethics; (2) mental tranquility, achieved through training in contemplation, using [the tools of]
mindfulness and inspection; (3) pacification of deception, achieved
through the wisdom of discerning reality and grounded in the tranquility of a pliant mind; (4) eminence, i.e., possessed of greatly superior qualities, being neither inferior nor equal to students; (5) diligence, i.e., a constant delight in helping others; (6) a wealth of transmissions gained from extensive study of the three collections of scriptures; (7) supreme realization of the nature of all phenomena gained
through the strength of listening, pondering, and meditating; (8) skillful articulation, i.e., the ability to present the stages of the path in a
way that suits the mental aptitude of the disciple; (9) genuine loving-
kindness, in having the pure motivation to teach out of compassion,

without regard for personal gain or honor; (10) freedom from weariness and discouragement, in never tiring of repeating lessons and showing patience [in the face] of anger.

[Four of these qualifications]—self-control, tranquility, pacification of deception, and realization of the nature of phenomena—are aspects of spiritual accomplishment. Possessing a wealth of transmissions is an aspect of [mastery of] the transmission. Those five, together with eminence, are the six qualities of personal growth. The remaining four are qualities related to caring for others. A teacher who meets these ten requirements is known as an exemplary human being.

> **The bodhisattva's instructor who exhibits twelve qualities such as erudition is an exceptional teacher.**

Exceptional is the instructor of the bodhisattva who exhibits twelve qualities, erudition and so forth, as referred to by the exalted Nagarjuna:

> Remain near an instructor who has these twelve [qualities]:
> Erudition, profound wisdom,
> Disinterest in material gain or possessions,
> An awakening mind, great compassion,
> Patience in enduring hardship, [strength to overcome] weariness or discouragement,
> [A wealth of] oral instructions, freedom through [the practice of] the path,
> And knowledge of the student's affinity and spiritual maturity.

The Tantric Master [c]

> **The tantric master must be steadfast, self-controlled, intelligent,**
> **Patient, honest, and well-versed in the activities related to mantra and tantra.**
> **He or she is compassionate, learned, expert in ten fields,**
> **Proficient in the drawing of mandalas, and skilled in the ways of explaining the Secret Mantra.**

The types of tantric or vajra master will be explained below.

The qualifications of the vajra master are discussed at length [in various works]. As a summary of these, the *Fifty [Verses on Devotion to] the Master*[31] lists fifteen qualifications, six general and nine specific. The six are as follows: (1) steadfastness, by virtue of having an unperturbed body, speech, and mind; (2) self-control, by virtue of meditative training; (3) intelligence or capacity for accurate analysis; (4) patience or restraint from anger (when seeing students' poor conduct); and (5 and 6) honesty and sincerity, i.e., freedom from deceptive ways (hiding one's faults or shortcomings) and artifice (giving a false impression in order to mislead others).

The nine specific qualifications [of the vajra master] are as follows: (1) knowledge of the use of mantras[32] in performing the four charismatic activities,[33] etc.; (2) knowledge of the practices related to tantra,[34] for example, [being able to explain the tantras by means of the] six parameters[35]; (3) loving compassion for others; (4) proficiency in the common treatises[36]; (5, 6, and 7) mastery of the [three sets of] ten fields; (8) proficiency in the drawing of mandalas[37] based on proper performance of familiarization,[38] etc., and mastery of initiation[39] procedures; and (9) knowledge of how to explain the Secret Mantra in the manner appropriate for [disciples] of superior, moderate, and lesser capabilities.

The first set of ten fields of expertise comprises those areas indispensable to the vajra master. The *Tantra of Consecration* states[40]:

> Mandala, contemplation, seal,
> Stance, mantra, seated position,
> Recitation, fire offering,
> Food offering (*torma*), and dissolution.[41]

The second set of ten fields of expertise which concern ritual is taught in the *Indestructible Tent Tantra* and enumerated accordingly in Dombipa's *Ten Essential Points*[42]:

> The victorious ones have specified ten fields of expertise:
> Protection [wheel], conferral of initiation, food offerings,
>   recitation, rite of tearing apart the union,
> [Two] reversals, actualization of the mandala,
> The threatening rite, and departure request.[43]

The third set of ten fields of expertise which are of ultimate significance are elucidated in the *Tantra [of Hevajra] in Five Hundred Thousand [Lines]*[44] and summarized in the *[Means of Accomplishment of the Glorious] Blazing Jewel*[45]:

> Know these ten fields of expertise:
> Vajra, bell, pristine awareness,
> Deity, mandala, fire offering,
> Mantra, colored sands, food offerings, and initiation.

The ten outer fields given in the *Indestructible Nucleus' Ornament* [*Tantra*][46] resemble the [first set] of fields of expertise given in the *Tantra of Consecration*. There is a similar enumeration in the *Summation of Essential Points*. These are presented from the viewpoint of the yoga tantra system.

The father-son transmission from Mikyö Dorjé asserts that the ten secret [or inner] fields of expertise taught in the *Indestructible Nucleus' Ornament*[47]—

> The rites of the two reversals,
> The secret initiation and the initiation of pristine awareness
>   through wisdom,
> The ritual of tearing apart the union [of hostile forces],
> Food offerings, vajra muttering,
> The ritual of accomplishing the fierce act,
> Consecration and actualization of the mandala
> Are the ten secret fields of expertise.[48]

—as well as those found in the *Beholding the Qualities of the Spiritual Master Tantra*,[49] the *Commentary on the Buddhasamayoga*,[50] and the *Cluster of Secret Instructions*[51] are from the standpoint of the Highest Yoga Tantra.

> **From a different perspective, the vajra master owns three**
>   **treasures, has received the entire course of initiations,**
> **Is committed, learned in the tantras, skilled in performing**
>   **rituals, and has produced signs of experience.**

According to the Ancient Translation School of the Secret Mantra, [a qualified vajra master] owns three genuine treasures: (1) the view that realizes the indivisibility of the [relative and ultimate] truths; (2) the contemplation that has reached the culmination of the phases of creation and completion[52]; and (3) the preservation of general and specific pledges. (The three treasures are also explained as expertise in the systems of Mahayoga, the treasure of the creation phase; Anu, the treasure of the completion phase; and Ati[53], the treasure of the view.) [Further, the vajra master] (4) has received the entire course of profound initiations that empower and transform; (5) does not forsake the secret mantra and intentionally nurtures worthy disciples; (6) is learned in the tantras and able to elucidate the meaning of the transmissions; (7) is skilled in composing rituals for the performance of charismatic activity; and (8) has produced the signs of experience derived from the practice of the secret instructions of oral transmissions. In Buddhaguhya's *Sequence of the Path [of the Magical Net]*, such a teacher is called a vajra master who possesses the eight qualities of natural expression.

> **In summary, the vajra master belongs to an authentic lineage,**
> **preserves the pledges, has heard secret instructions,**
> **And has realized the meaning of tantra. A monk is the best of**
> **the three types of vajra master.**

The vajra master's qualifications mentioned above are all included in the following: The vajra master belongs to a lineage of masters who from Buddha Vajradhara to the present time have transmitted maturing [initiations] and liberating [instructions] and have not violated any of the pledges; preserves vows, pledges, and tantric conduct; has received the secret instructions that have been transmitted from one lineage holder to the next; has realized the teachings of the Buddha and their commentaries, and, in particular, the import of the tantras; and has a compassionate and altruistic mind.

Lay vajra masters are said to be lower [in rank] to novice or monk and nun vajra masters unless they have reached stages of awakening. Accordingly, *Vajragarbha's Commentary*[54] states:

> Unless he has attained the stages of awakening,
> A layman is not to be venerated as a [tantric] master, [not even]
>   by a king.
> Someone following the monastic life, who is learned and
>   possesses true knowledge,
> Is to be honored in his place.
> When a layperson who has not reached the stages of
>   awakening
> Is revered [as a vajra master],
> The respect accorded to the Buddha, to his doctrine,
> And to the monastic community will wane.

The novice is superior to the layperson [as vajra master] because he or she is a renunciate, but of junior status when compared to the monk or nun, who is the best [choice for vajra master]. The *Wheel of Time Fundamental Tantra* states[55]:

> Among experts in the ten fields,
> The monk is foremost;
> The novice is average,
> And the layperson is the least qualified.

> Magnificent is the master with the power to evoke in the
>   student
> The adamantine pristine awareness of the state of union.

A magnificent master is one who is able to evoke adamantine pristine awareness of the state of union, i.e., mahamudra,[56] in the disciple's mind, and is therefore a crucial factor [in the attainment] of supreme accomplishment. The primary characteristics of such a master [are referred to] in the *[Wheel of Time] Condensed Tantra*[57]:

> A magnificent master is one in whose mind and speech the face
> of the Buddha is present.[58]

As elucidated in the *Commentary by the Bodhisattva*[59] as the model in the tantric system, a "magnificent master" is a teacher whose speech can instill in the disciple the experiential cultivation of the state of union [pointed out in] the fourth initiation (referred to as the "face" or "entrance" of the Buddha). Such a master, with the state of contemplation[60] present in his or her mind, has the ability to transfer realization in the form of a blessing to the mind of the disciple. Having ascertained [the nature of] mantra, the master has attained the first stage of awakening. Being far superior to any ordinary spiritual teacher, he or she is known as a "magnificent master."

THE TEACHER TO IGNORE AND THE ONE TO FAVOR [IV]

> Avoid a master whose traits are discordant with those of a true
>   teacher;
> But since a fully qualified master is rare, follow the one who is
>   replete with good qualities.

A teacher whose traits are discordant with the characteristics of the [true] master stands outside of the Buddhist doctrine and cannot be taken as a spiritual teacher. Consequently, even though the teacher may be very famous, active, etc., the discriminating student should be aware [of these shortcomings] and detach himself or herself [from the teacher]. This should be done even if a teacher-student relationship has already been formed. If one has not yet formed such a relationship, one should avoid doing so, right from the beginning. Sakya Pandita states[61]:

> Detach yourself from the spiritual teacher
> Who does not conform to the Buddha's teaching.

We should learn how to recognize [bad teachers] from the many descriptions given in the scriptures and then shun them. For example, the *Condensed Tantra [of the Wheel of Time]* states:

> Proud, subject to uncontrollable anger, defiant of pledges,
>   guilty of misappropriation, ignorant [of the doctrine],
> Willfully deceptive of students, having failed to enter the state
>   of supreme bliss, uninitiated,
> A slave to wealth and enjoyments, careless, rude in speech, and
>   obsessed with sexual desire:
> Wise students who wish full awakening should shun such a
>   teacher as they would hell.[62]

Because we are living in a [degenerate] age, we very rarely meet a teacher endowed with all of the necessary qualifications. Since we may never meet such a teacher, we should accept a master who has many good qualities and very few weaknesses. [Pundarika's] *Ultimate Familiarization*[63] states:

> In this age of conflict, spiritual masters will exhibit both faults
>   and virtues;
> Not one is absolutely irreproachable.
> Therefore, examine well even those who excel in virtue
> Before beginning to study with them.

THE REQUIREMENTS OF THE DISCIPLE [V]

This section has two parts: (1) the disciple to favor, and (2) the disciple to ignore; and related points.

The Disciple to Favor [A]

This section has three parts: suitable candidates for (1) monastic life, (2) the bodhisattva's training, and (3) Secret Mantra.

The Suitable Candidate for Monastic Life [1]

> **The suitable candidate for the life of a renunciate must be free from obstacles to assuming the vows.**

A suitable candidate for monastic life, as a general requirement, must be free from the four types of obstacles and unfavorable conditions (explained below) that are incompatible with the monastic ordination. The specific requisites are listed in Shakhyaprabha's *Three Hundred Stanzas [on the Novitiate]*[64]:

In particular, he must respect the instructor, follow an ethical
     code strictly,
Persevere in meditation and study,
Be conscientious, restrained, and patient,
Since a good monk who lives by the monastic discipline is
     known by these very qualities.

A virtuous monk who is capable of living by the monastic code is
known by the following qualities: unfailing respect for the preceptor
and, above all, for the tutor and instructor; the determination to follow strictly the ethical code by forsaking the four conditions that lead
to transgression of the rules[65]; constant effort in meditation and in
studying and recitation [of scriptures]; conscientiousness and a natural restraint in character and behavior; and patience in accepting the
directives of teachers and [in withstanding] others' harm.

The Suitable Candidate for the Bodhisattva's Training [2]

A suitable candidate for the bodhisattva's training is gifted
     with faith, kindness, intelligence,
And the stamina to engage in the bodhisattva's conduct, does
     not seek personal peace,
Is energetic, and delights in hearing about emptiness.

A suitable candidate for the bodhisattva's training should have the
following qualities: faith in the collections of teachings on the Universal Way and in the spiritual guides of that tradition, loving-kindness and compassion toward others, intelligence [capable of] realizing profound and magnificent [doctrines], and the stamina to engage with courage in a vast range of [bodhisattva] practices (such
as the four means of attracting disciples[66] and the six perfections[67]).
This individual is not seeking personal peace and happiness but is
working with joy in order to liberate all sentient beings. He or she is
always energetic and delights in hearing about the profound subject of emptiness. These qualities indicate that the spiritual potential for the Universal Way has awakened. The *Ten Qualities Scripture*[68] states:

The spiritual potential of the wise bodhisattva
Is known by its signs
As fire is indicated by smoke,
And water, by herons.

Also, [Aryadeva's] *Experientialist Four Hundred* states[69]:

> The individual who is impartial, intelligent, and persevering,
> Is referred to as a suitable disciple.

[To explain,] impartiality refers to freedom from bias toward one's own spiritual tradition and a dislike of others' traditions.[70] Intelligence refers to [the capacity to] discriminate between the value of true doctrines and the futility of fallacious ones. Perseverance refers to dedication to the practice of the Universal Way. The disciple who possesses these three qualities will appreciate the excellent virtues of the spiritual guide. The disciple who lacks these qualities will see shortcomings in even the most gifted spiritual guide.

The Suitable Candidate for Secret Mantra [3]

**A suitable candidate for the Secret Mantra is devoted to the
master and is discrete,
Shows great aptitude, lives by the pledges, and perseveres in
the practice.**

A suitable candidate for the Secret Mantra system of ripening [initiations] and liberative [instructions] must fulfill all the qualities [mentioned in the last section]. Furthermore, he or she is deeply devoted to the spiritual master and knows how to maintain secrecy on the profound view and conduct, is free of reservations concerning the Secret Mantra, has great aptitude for understanding reality, and lives by the pledges while persevering in the tantric practice. The *Condensed Tantra of the Wheel of Time*, the *Indestructible Garland* (an explanatory tantra of the Guhyasamaja), and other works discuss these qualifications in some detail.

A tantra of the Ancient Translation School, the *Magical Net*,[71] describes the qualities of the suitable candidate for the way of Secret Mantra in the following way:

> [The disciple] must revere the teacher, be strenuous, be bright
> [in intelligence],
> Honor the pledges, know mantra and seals,
> And possess the necessary resources.

Reverence to the master permits the disciple to be gradually initiated [into the tantra]. Devotion and constancy ensure that the disciple does not forsake listening to and reflection on [the tantras]. A bright and flawless intelligence enables him or her to examine the view to be realized. [In addition,] the disciple must honor the root and branch pledges [of the Secret Mantra], know the significance of mantras and seals, and not be lacking in the necessary resources [for tantric practice].

The Disciple to Ignore [B]

The teacher should ignore a disciple ridden with shortcomings, but accept one who, despite imperfections, is gifted with qualities such as faith.

An individual whose characteristics are opposite to those of a qualified candidate must be ignored. The *Samvara [Tantra]* states[72]:

> Spiritual masters should reject
> Those who have no compassion, are ill-tempered,
> Arrogant, unrestrained, distracted,
> Unreasonable, stupid, or lazy,
> Have no concern for the lives of others,
> Or covet others' possessions.

Nagarjuna's *Five Stages* states[73]:

> Do not teach the graded instructions
> To those who have contempt for, try to deceive, or lack faith in
>   their spiritual masters;
> Are proud of being Mantra practitioners; are arrogant [in that
>   they boast knowledge of the tantras after] having read a few
>   scriptures[74];
> Fall short of having confidence [in the tantras], or have
>   received [only] lower initiations.[75]

A person replete with virtues such as faith and perseverance, despite having imperfections, should be accepted as a disciple even though he or she does not meet all of the necessary qualifications. Accordingly, the *Secret Tantra of the General Ritual of All Mandalas* states[76]:

> Rare to find is a disciple who lives by the commitments,
> Is outstanding in qualities, and has no illness,
> Who comes from a good family,
> Is inspired with faith, and follows the tantric conduct.

> Accept as a disciple someone with the noble traits
> Of faith in the Three Jewels,
> Attraction to the Universal Way,
> And great merit.

Although ugly or uncultivated,
A disciple who shows earnest interest and perseverance
In the Secret Mantra of the joyful ones
Should be encouraged by the wise master to follow that way.

EXAMINING AND WORKING WITH A SPIRITUAL TEACHER [VI]

This section has two parts: (1) mutual examination, and (2) the ways to work with a spiritual teacher.

Mutual Examination [A]

To determine whether they can brave a spiritual relationship, the jewel-like teacher and disciple must first examine each other.

A teacher and disciple who satisfy the necessary requirements are like [rare] jewels. When they first meet, it is crucial for master and disciple to examine each other [to determine whether they can brave] a spiritual relationship. [Ashvaghosha's] *Fifty [Verses on Devotion to] the Master* states[77]:

For neither the master nor the disciple
To damage the commitments,
They must first examine whether they can brave
The teacher and disciple relationship.

Further, the *Essence of the Great Seal* states[78]:

A qualified spiritual master
Should carefully test the student.
Just as a skillful smith will melt the ore
To determine the worth of gold,
Or a [yogin] will check [the signs of] a blissful maiden,[79]
The teacher must assess [the worth of] the student.
To avoid unfortunate consequences
Both the teacher and the student
Must examine well each other's character.

The consequences are particularly unfortunate when a tantric master initiates disciples indiscriminately without first testing them. An unworthy disciple will be unable to honor pledges. This will lead to the ruin of both master and disciple in this life and the next, and their commitments will deteriorate. The master's own spiritual accomplishment will be remote, and he or she will be beset by obstacles.

Similarly, many detrimental results befall a disciple who fails to determine whether a master is fully qualified and receives initiation from anyone at all. He or she is likely to be deceived by a false guide. Thereafter, the disciple will be unable to keep the words of honor [pledged in the presence of the master], and the very source of accomplishment will be destroyed. Led astray on a false path [by a deceptive master], the disciple cannot take advantage of life's leisure and endowments.

The Ways to Work with a Spiritual Teacher [B]

> Those intent on liberation should devote themselves to a
> spiritual guide with offerings and respect, service, and
> spiritual practice.

This section has two parts: (1) motive, and (2) application.

Motive [1]

The *Condensed Transcendent Wisdom Scripture* states[80]:

> Wise [bodhisattvas] highly motivated to seek true awakening
> First vanquish their pride;
> Then, like the sick who rely on doctors for their cure,
> They devote themselves to spiritual guides without wavering.

Accordingly, with an unshakeable intent to seek the true state of awakening, the highest freedom, we should unfailingly revere [our spiritual guides].

Application [2]

Devotion [for the teacher is shown in] three ways. The *Scripture Ornament* states[81]:

> Devote yourself to a spiritual guide
> By making offerings and showing respect, serving, and
> establishing the validity [of the teaching].

Making Offerings and Showing Reverence [a]

Making offerings refers to giving with pleasure presents of food, clothing, and other articles that the master will like. Moreover, it is said that we should even [be willing to] offer our children and spouse, or our own body.

Showing reverence refers to behaving respectfully toward the spiritual master, by prostrating or rising on sight, expressing praise, etc. We should not step on the master's shadow, let alone step over or use without permission his or her clothing, seat, personal articles, boots, or horse; or [show any disrespect toward] the spouse. We should not lie down, slouch, spit or blow the nose in the master's presence, or criticize the master in private, etc. Any form of disrespect must be avoided in all circumstances.

Serving [b]

The disciple should precede an act of service by making prostrations. Then, while performing any daily task (washing, massaging with oil, or drying the teacher's body, etc.), one should be calm and skillful.

Establishing the Validity of the Instructions [c]

The disciple should willingly carry out all the directives of the spiritual master and practice earnestly [in order to ascertain the validity of] the master's instructions in whatever way is appropriate—study, reflection, or meditation. This is the best form of reverence because a true spiritual guide is delighted by the offering of one's spiritual practice and is not [particularly] pleased by gifts, etc. The *Flower Array Scripture* states[82]:

> Don't ever become weary of seeking a spiritual guide.
> Having found one, follow his instructions without neglecting to
>   serve him.
> Consider yourself like the earth, not wearied by any burden.
> Consider yourself a servant, heeding any order.

THE BENEFITS OF WORKING WITH A SPIRITUAL TEACHER [VII]

This section has two parts: (1) reasonings for the need to work with a teacher, and (2) the benefits of working with a teacher as taught in the scriptures.

Reasonings [A]

> The Victorious One said: "By devoting yourself to a spiritual
>   friend,
> You will attain the full, accomplished, unique, and perfectly
>   immaculate path to liberation.
> By trusting me now as your spiritual guide, you will gain
>   freedom from suffering. Consider these reasons!"

The Victorious One, the compassionate teacher, proclaimed [the need to study with a master] with this advice: "By working with a spiritual guide, you will attain the full, accomplished, unique, and immaculate path to liberation.[83] Now, by trusting me as your spiritual guide, you will easily gain freedom from the suffering of existence. Consider these reasons and examples!"

The scriptures state:

> Ananda, it is like this: Spiritual guides and virtuous companions are the fulfillment of the path to liberation.

Letter to a Friend states[84]:

> Reliance on a spiritual guide
> Fulfills one's path to liberation, said the Sage.
> Therefore, devote yourself to a spiritual friend
> As did the many who attained peace by relying on [the
>   Buddha as] their teacher.

The Benefits as Taught in the Scriptures [B]

Many other benefits that accrue from studying with a spiritual guide are taught in the scriptures.

In addition to the above, many benefits of working with a spiritual guide are mentioned in the discourses and tantras. The *Flower Array Scripture*,[85] for example, states:

> Bodhisattvas who are under the guidance of spiritual guides will not fall into miserable forms of life. Able to discriminate good from evil, they do not engage in what is unwholesome. They shun all sources of distraction and escape from the "city" of cyclic existence. They will not contravene the bodhisattva's training and they stand above all worlds. They will not be easily overcome by emotions and previous actions. Therefore, children of the Universal family, always keep these benefits in mind and follow your spiritual guides!

The salient points of the many scriptural references on this subject are summarized in the words of the all-knowing Drimé Özer (Longchenpa)[86]:

> The benefits of devoting yourself to a spiritual master are
>   limitless:
> You embark upon the perfect path, discern what is authentic,
> Cultivate merit and enhance pristine awareness, clear away
>   obscurations, dispel hindrances,
> Attain the stature of a holy person,
> And swiftly reach the city of freedom.

Furthermore, [the scriptures] mention the following benefits: we come closer to enlightenment; the victorious ones are pleased with us; we never lack spiritual guides; we never fall into miserable forms of life; the negative consequences of our past deeds and emotions will not defeat us; our deeds never contradict the bodhisattvas' conduct; and we always bear this conduct in mind. Our positive qualities thereby steadily increase, and we achieve all temporal and ultimate objectives. Furthermore, by revering a spiritual guide, the results of past deeds [that would lead to] miserable forms of life are met and exhausted in this life as the experiences of only slight mental or physical affliction, or even just in dreams. So vast is its merit that to venerate a spiritual guide far surpasses other forms of virtue such as making offerings to an infinite number of buddhas.

On the other hand, if we relate to the spiritual guide in a wrong way, we may be afflicted by many sicknesses and beset by malevolent influences during this life. In future lives, we may experience countless sufferings in miserable existences. We will not acquire any new qualities, and we will lose the qualities we now have. Because of these destructive consequences, the *Vajrapani Initiation Tantra* states[87]:

> O Lord of Secrets! How should the disciple regard the teacher?
> You should think of him as you would the Blessed One, the
> Buddha.

Similar statements are found in the collection of Universalist scriptures and the scriptures on discipline. Thus, we should never form an overly critical attitude toward the spiritual guide but should devote ourselves to him or her with even greater respect than for the Buddha.

The merits of honoring one's spiritual master are inconceivable. As the *Guhyasamaja [Tantra]* says[88]:

> There is far greater merit in venerating a single pore of the
> master's body than in worshiping all the buddhas throughout
> all time and space.

The *Biography of Shri Sambhava Scripture* states[89]:

> By pleasing the spiritual guide, one attains the enlightenment of
> a buddha.

In summary, limitless virtues, manifest [in this life] and in the next, are acquired by venerating spiritual teachers. Merit and pristine awareness are enhanced to their fullest extent; all hindrances caused by adverse circumstances subside; fame and prosperity increase; and enlightenment is swiftly attained.

Generally, anything we do, wholesome or unwholesome, in relation to significant persons such as a spiritual master, preceptor, teacher, sick person, practitioner of the Buddhist teachings, bodhisattva in his or her final existence, exalted proclaimer, exalted solitary sage, or one's own parents yields extremely powerful results. Vasubandhu's *Treasury [of Phenomenology]* states[90]:

> Helping parents or the sick
> Even though they may not be exalted
> And honoring spiritual teachers or bodhisattvas in their final
>   existence
> Are said to yield inconceivable merits.

CLEARING AWAY IMPEDIMENTS TO SPIRITUAL GROWTH [VIII]

This section has two parts: (1) shunning bad friends, and (2) overcoming demonic forces.

Shunning Bad Friends [A]

> **Shun unvirtuous friends who have bad characters, cynical
>   outlooks, and prejudice,**
> **Believe their own view to be the best, are boastful, and dispar-
>   age others.**

It is imperative that we eschew spiritual teachers, instructors, preceptors, students, and companions who engage in unwholesome activities out of worldly concerns since they are not true spiritual friends. We should particularly avoid persons who give the impression of integrity but [in fact] create obstacles to our own attainment of liberation. Similarly, we should forsake those who have bad characters and cynical outlooks; those who are strongly prejudiced, or who consider as best only their own views and doctrines; those who praise themselves and disparage others; those who covertly belittle and thereby reject other spiritual systems; and those who discredit the spiritual guides and friends who are shouldering the burden of other beings' welfare. If we associate with these kinds of people, devoting ourselves to or befriending them, we will become polluted by their faults and our characters will gradually worsen. The scriptures on discipline[91] state:

> Just as *kusha* grass wrapped around rotting fish
> Will soon begin to smell the same,
> A person who associates with bad friends, in time,
> Will certainly come to resemble them.

Therefore, we should always be careful not to associate with bad friends in any circumstances, as stated in the *Great Mindfulness Scripture*[92]:

> The main obstacle to [the cultivation of] any wholesome quality is an unvirtuous friend. Hence, don't associate or converse with such a person or even allow his or her shadow to fall on yourself.

Overcoming Demonic Forces [B]

When working with a spiritual teacher, recognize demonic forces and defeat them with their antidotes.

As soon as a disciple has met a true master who embodies the genuine doctrine and begins to listen to, reflect on, and make a living experience of the instructions, he or she may be beset by demonic forces that block the way. The *Condensed [Transcendent Wisdom Scripture]*[93] states:

> The Buddha's doctrine is a rare gem, but perils lurk close by:
> Disciples of limited capacity who are beginners in the way
> And have not yet discovered this gem's [worth]
> Are provoked by demonic forces who enjoy making obstacles.

The scriptures speak of four general demonic forces (the emotions, etc.[94]). The secret instructions [of masters] refer to eighteen specific demonic forces belonging to three classes (outer, inner, and secret, each comprised of six). These sources also describe at length the causes that can provoke the demonic forces; their forms, their influence, the various signs indicating their presence; and the common and extraordinary means to drive them out.

In the context of our relationship with a teacher, we should recognize the following [mental states as evidence of] demonic forces that will obstruct our path to freedom: an overly critical attitude toward our spiritual guide; lacking the desire to apply ourselves to study and reflection; nurturing the causes of anger, such as creating discord and passing time in idle talk; excessive concern with food and drink, residence, furniture, business, etc.; apathy due to drowsiness, dullness, and laziness; and being overpowered by infatuation and other emotions. As soon as we recognize these negative forces, we must skillfully overcome them by wearing the armor of these antidotes:

faith in and respect for our spiritual master and companions; enthusiasm for study, reflection, and meditation; unwavering confidence in the teaching; and freedom from distractions and unrealistic ideas.

AWAKENING THE FAITH CONDUCIVE TO SPIRITUAL GROWTH [IX]

Moreover, cultivate lucid, trusting, and longing faith.

The awakening of the three kinds of faith is the prerequisite for acquiring any wholesome quality and the single most crucial factor when first embarking on the spiritual path under the guidance of a spiritual teacher. The *Precious Palm Scripture* states[95]:

> First, awaken faith which is like a mother:
> Faith will dispel your doubts, carry you across the river [of
>   cyclic life],
> And direct you to the city of sublime happiness.

The essence of faith is a clear mind focused upon the conduct of forsaking the unwholesome and undertaking virtue. The [scriptures on] phenomenology elucidate the [three] types of faith:

> What is faith? Faith is conviction in the law of causality, the [four] truths, and the Three Jewels. It is longing; it is a clear state of mind.

Thus, [the three kinds of faith are] lucid faith, trusting faith, and longing faith. Lucid faith depends upon the Jewels as its object. It is a clear mind that appreciates the spiritual master and the Three Jewels. Trusting faith refers to belief in action as cause, and its results. Longing faith is the aspiration to attain unsurpassable awakening, which directs us to train on the path with perseverance. [Nagarjuna's *Jewel Garland*] states[96]:

> He who does not forsake the Buddha's teachings out of
>   willfulness,
> Hatred, fear, or confusion,
> Is called a man of faith.
> He is the best candidate for liberation.

To not reject the teachings for reasons of attachment, aversion, or confusion indicates that faith has awakened.

The benefits of faith are infinite: the attitude of a supreme being arises, the eight fetters of life[97] are transcended, etc. When we have faith, the transcendent ones will appear before us and give spiritual teachings. The *Precious Palm Scripture* states[98]:

> The attitude of a great person is formed
> When one has faith in the Victorious One and in his doctrine,
> In the way of life of the bodhisattvas,
> And in unsurpassable awakening.

The *Bodhisattva Section Scripture* says[99]:

> When the buddhas, the blessed ones, have acknowledged a bodhisattva who has constant faith as a worthy recipient for their teachings, they will appear before him and teach him the authentic path of the bodhisattvas.

In summary, faith forms the basis for all positive qualities. Therefore, we should nurture the causes and conditions for its awakening and growth and forsake those that weaken it. Once we have awakened faith, we should make every effort to strengthen it.[100]

THE METHODS OF TEACHING AND LISTENING TO THE DOCTRINE [X]

This section has four parts: (1) the preliminary steps, (2) the main activities, (3) the concluding duties, and (4) the usefulness of teaching and listening to the doctrine.[101]

Preliminary Steps [A]

This section has two parts: (1) the responsibilities of the teacher, and (2) those of the disciple.

The Responsibilities of the Spiritual Teacher [1]

> The teacher prepares for a spiritual discourse by creating a
> congenial setting,
> Dispelling malevolent influences, and maintaining dignified
> composure.

[The spiritual teacher has] three tasks: [(1) creating a congenial setting, (2) driving away malevolent influences, and (3) maintaining dignity].

Creating a Congenial Setting [a]

The scriptures describe at length the procedure for creating the setting. The *White Lotus of the True Doctrine [Scripture]*[102] states:

> In a clean and pleasant environment,
> Wearing fine, tidy, and good-looking robes,
> The teacher should take his place
> On an attractive and slightly raised seat
> Draped with various kinds of elegant cloth.

and

> In the midst of a gathering of attentive disciples,
> Without concern for material gain or prestige,
> He teaches enthusiastically, motivated by loving-kindness.

Driving Away Malevolent Influences [b]

According to the procedure described in the *Questions of Sagaramati Scripture*, the teacher should keep five thoughts in mind[103]:

> Regarding himself as a physician,
> The teaching as medicine,
> The listeners as patients,
> The Transcendent One as the supreme being,
> And wishing that the doctrine last long.

The teacher then recites the charm[104] that prevents the class of malevolent gods from approaching within a radius of one hundred leagues.

Maintaining Dignity [c]

When teaching, the spiritual master does not lie down, slouch or stretch the legs, etc., but behaves as did the Shakya King when turning the doctrinal wheel. He or she avoids verbosity, repetitiveness, speaking in a poor timbre of voice or in a pitch that is high or low, but speaks clearly and distinctly, with an abundance of the melodious qualities [of speech]. While teaching, the master relinquishes any feelings of attachment or aversion and remains absorbed [in the contemplation of emptiness] or in deity meditation, etc., depending on the occasion. Then, with the aspiration to benefit all sentient beings and to guide them to the state of happiness and well-being, the master invokes a rain of teachings to descend on the disciples.

The Responsibilities of the Disciple [2]

> **The disciple makes offerings, behaves respectfully, and values the opportunity.**

The disciple has three tasks: (1) to make suitable offerings, (2) to behave respectfully, and (3) to value the opportunity.

Making Suitable Offerings [a]

The disciple first prostrates by touching the five points [of the body][105] to the ground and then offers pleasing gifts and a vast imagined offering of the entire universe.

Behaving Respectfully [b]

The *Garland of Former Lives of the Buddha* states[106]:

> Sit on the lowest seat,
> Maintaining humble dignity;
> Look [at your teacher] with joy in your eyes;
> Drink in his words like an elixir.
> With reverence, a pure and deeply inspired mind,
> Wholeheartedly bow to [the teacher].
> Then as a patient heeds the physician's advice,
> Respectfully listen to the doctrine.

The disciple does not lie down, slouch, or turn the back to the master, etc., but kneels or sits straight. Behaving respectfully and remaining silent, he or she listens with full attention.

Valuing the Opportunity [c]

The *[Scripture Revealing] the Inconceivable Secrets [of the Transcendent One]* states[107]:

> Rare and brief is the appearance of a buddha here,
> And to be born as a human is extremely difficult.
> But even more exceptional is it to find in this world
> Someone inspired to listen to the teachings.

Now that these [unique] circumstances are present, we should approach the doctrine with sincere interest and joy.

The Main Activities [B]

This section has three parts: (1) the master's discourse, (2) respectful listening on the part of the disciple, and (3) the speaker's and listener's fulfillment of the six perfections.

The Master's Discourse [1]

This section has three parts: (1) the experienced speaker, (2) the teaching methods, and (3) the styles of teaching.

The Experienced Speaker [a]

The speaker must possess three qualifications: (1) expertise, (2) benevolence, and (3) patience.

Expertise [i]

When teaching, the master demonstrates three kinds of expertise

When teaching, the master demonstrates eight qualities. To begin with, he or she is well versed (1) in the subjects, (2) in the presentation, and (3) in skillful conduct.

Expertise in the Subjects [A']

Ideally, the teacher would be learned in all subjects within the entire collection of scriptures. The teacher must at least be proficient in the language, meaning, scriptural references, reasoning, and essential instructions related to the subject being presented. By virtue of these skills, the teacher will thereby be able to resolve students' doubts.

Expertise in Presentation [B']

[A learned presentation comprises three features:] (1) grammatically correct language, (2) coherent delivery (which implies that the teaching is relevant to the subject, moderate in length, and logical throughout), and (3) a melodious voice that pleases the audience. On this subject, the *Scripture Ornament* states[108]:

> The teaching of the Buddha is pure in three ways[109]:
> Eloquent in voice and language;
> Informative, analytic,
> Dispelling doubts, and reiterated;
> [Concise] for those who understand brief instructions,
> And elaborate for those who need lengthy ones.
> The manner [in which it is proclaimed]
> Is free of eight faults:
> Taught with laziness or unclear speech,
> Inappropriate, uncertain,
> Unable to resolve doubts
> Or to confirm the absence [of doubt],
> Taught with weariness, or incomplete.[110]

These are regarded as faults in delivery.
A buddha's teaching is unsurpassable
Because it is devoid of such faults.

Teachings free of these eight faults of delivery are pure in the three ways. Alternatively, the *Principles of Elucidation* states[111]:

[A teacher should] incorporate twenty qualities[112] into any discourse in order to eliminate the eleven faults of expression.

Skillful Conduct [C']

Skillful conduct means that the teacher maintains a demeanor that inspires admiration, by manifesting goodness in body, speech, and mind. Skillful in knowing students' conduct means that the teacher comprehends the capabilities, temperaments, and predispositions of students, and teaches accordingly so that the instructions will be useful to them.

Benevolence [ii]

...two types of kindness

Ideally, the teacher would have the compassionate wish to guide all sentient beings to great awakening. For the instruction to be effective, the teacher must, at the very least, show compassion by teaching out of a desire to help others without concern for material gain and be knowledgeable in the subject to be taught. If the teacher is lacking in altruistic concern and instead is seeking material reward, etc., he or she incurs the moral offense of selling the Buddha's teaching.

Patience [iii]

And three kinds of patience

Three kinds of patience enable a teacher to spiritually nurture disciples: acceptance of hardship or fatigue when teaching, responsiveness to disciples' questions, and tolerance toward and the capacity to meet the challenges of others.

A discourse given by a teacher who embodies the above qualities will prove interesting and appealing to the listeners, and it will be useful. The *Scripture Ornament* says[113]:

The bodhisattva who is eloquent in speech
By virtue of a good intellect, an indefatigable mind, concern
   for others,

Pleasant delivery, and knowledge of proper teaching methods,
With the brilliance of his teachings, shines as the sun of
humanity.[114]

Teaching Methods [b]

This section has two parts: (1) an overview, and (2) a detailed presentation.

Overview [i]

...and includes six elements in the discourse.

The *Synthesis of Phenomenology* states that a spiritual discourse should
include six elements: the subject matter to be known, its import, the
approach to the knowledge [of the subject], finalized knowledge, its
result, and its experience.[115] From another point of view, [the same
text gives] fourteen elements, such as the "grouping of themes."[116]
Some treatises state that a teaching should indicate its purpose and
include a summary [of the subject matter] and the literal meaning [of
the words of the text]. Other treatises state that a discourse should
incorporate two aspects, the general meaning and the details.

A certain master of the Chim clan[117] asserts that a discourse should
present the following [three elements]: an introduction that reveals
the meaning, an explanation of the [main body of the text], and ascertainment with regard to both.

The introduction consists of a synopsis of the [subject treated in
the] text and contains background information concerning the sources,
purpose of the composition, and its subject matter. This prelude will
allow the student to appreciate the meaning of the text.

After the student has gained familiarity with the basic character of
the text through the overall view provided by the synopsis, the explanation [of the main body of the text] is given with clarifications to
dispel uncertainty. Then, through analysis[118] of the explicit and implicit meanings, the student is provided with a good comprehension
of the verbal part [of the text].

The ascertainment [is necessary] because although the student may
have understood the explanations, he or she may still not be able to
respond to others' challenges. Therefore, [the teacher] presents objections based on [possible] misinterpretations of what he or she has
taught by stating, for example, that a particular point is contradictory, redundant, or lacks a due connection. He or she then responds
to these possible objections, thereby dispelling misunderstandings.

Using logic and scriptural references, the teacher eliminates every possibility that [the opponent's] objection is founded. In these ways, the student will ascertain the message of the text.

Detailed Presentation [ii]

> **Alternatively, the teacher first states the general and specific purposes,**
> **Provides two summaries which have six qualities,**
> **And then analyzes the words in terms of object, agent, and action, and their literal meaning.**
> **To facilitate understanding, the speaker clarifies the sequence of words and meaning by illustrating the two types of relationships,**
> **And in response to objections, ascertains the meaning through scriptures and logic.**

The prevalent method of teaching [among learned Tibetan masters] is the one described in the *Principles of Elucidation*. First, the purpose [of the teaching] is stated so that the student has the incentive to listen to and remember what has been taught. Therefore, at the beginning of the discourse, the teacher should outline the benefits of listening to the doctrine (as the general purpose) and the relationship between the special purpose and the specific subject matter to be taught.

Second, two kinds of summary of the contents are given: (1) The general overview (beginning with the statement, "This is the overview of the text") presents the contents in sections. If necessary, [as a support to the summary,] scriptural references and reasoning may be drawn from other sources. Thus, the text is summarized in a way that is accessible and easily remembered. (2) The overview of each topic presents the text as a whole from beginning to end. Major sections are distinguished, their subdivisions classified in a consistent manner, and the divisions and summaries of the supplementary sections explained distinctly.

This style of presentation ensures that the general overview is useful and the specific topics of the text easily understood. These two [qualities] (utility and accessibility counted as one) along with proper words, fluency, conciseness, uniformity, and memorability constitute the six qualities of an effective discourse. In short, a skilled teacher knows how [to deliver] a lecture that is easily understood by and pleasing to both parties.

Third is the analysis of the words. In Sanskrit, the meaning of words is explained in terms of agent, action, and object; in the Tibetan language, in terms of three criteria: what it denotes, the denoting agent, and how it denotes. [To begin the analysis of a text,] its meaning must be discerned through an examination of its words or terms. To do that, the teacher must use his or her expertise in the general descriptions of names, terms, and letters given in phenomenology treatises and in the specialized treatises on grammar and definitions. Once the teacher has provided a detailed and unambiguous explanation of terms, he or she should explain each part of the contents of the text and their meaning without addition, omission, or error.

Fourth is an elucidation of the two kinds of relationship within any text (or discourse)—that between words and that between ideas. The teacher must give clarifications (as in "the former and latter words relate in this way") when words seem unrelated, when their relationship is ambiguous, or when their relationship is clear but contextually obscure. For the relationship between ideas, [the teacher] begins the explanation of the sequence [of words and ideas] by saying, [for example,] "That brief presentation can be elaborated upon in this way..." or [otherwise,] by clarifying [specific details] such as related or incompatible [subjects], what is to be forsaken, the remedy, cause and result, etc.

Fifth is the response to objections. Concerning the difficult points of the text (or discourse), the student may raise questions or objections, such as, "Are not such and such contradictory?" or, "How can this be?" The teacher should then resolve such qualms and ascertain the meaning of the text with arguments consistent with logic and scriptural references.

Styles of Teaching [c]

> For the brightest student, the teacher may explain deep and far-
>   reaching subjects; for the less intelligent, first give easily
>   retained and accessible teachings,
> Then delve into subtle details, connections, and contradictions.
> Another task of the teacher is to encourage dispirited persons
>   and counteract their distraction and apathy.

For the brightest and most capable students, the teacher may explain deep and far-reaching subjects, using precise language and a coherent presentation. For students of limited intelligence and lesser capability, the teacher must present comprehensible subjects in a way pleasant to listen to and in easily retained and accessible language. Once the students have developed their analytical powers to some degree and are able to grasp the relationship between words and their meanings, the teacher may delve into the subtle details of the subject and delineate connections and contradictions.

The teacher should encourage dispirited persons who feel unable to listen to and make a living experience of the teaching, such as obtuse students, the elderly, those who have only a short time to live, or those who are able to study and meditate but feel they have no spare time to do so. The teacher may urge them to reflect upon the life stories of the exalted Shudapanthaka[119] and others or upon sayings such as[120]:

> Develop your mind, even though you may die tomorrow.
> You may not become a sage in this life,
> But, like wealth left in someone's care,
> You can retrieve your learning in the next.

In order to spiritually inspire those who are attached to worldly affairs, or distracted and excited by sense pleasures, the teacher provides illustrations of impermanence and explains the shortcomings of sensual indulgence and the dreadfulness of miserable forms of life. To those subject to drowsiness and apathy, etc., the teacher relates remarkable events [to motivate them] and explains the negative consequences of such states of mind.

Listening with Respect [2]

> **The disciple should eliminate the three defects of a jug, the six improper ways of listening, etc.,**
> **And regard himself or herself as an ill person, [the doctrine] as medicine, and the master as a physician.**

The [Medium Length Transcendent Wisdom] Discourse states:

> Listen with attention, listen closely, and bear in mind [what you hear]! I will teach you.

These words [of the Buddha] indicate the way we should listen [to spiritual instructions] by first eliminating the three defects comparable to those of a jug. To "listen with attention" means to eliminate the defect of being like a jug turned upside down. If we do not perk up our ears when the words of the doctrine are being spoken and instead become self-absorbed due to lack of interest, or because we are distracted by something else, or affected by dullness or drowsiness, it is as if juice were being poured onto an overturned jug.

To "listen closely" means to eliminate the defect of being like a dirty jug. If we listen to the teaching with a mind tainted by emotions, what we have heard will not be useful to us or others, like juice poured into a dirty jug. Therefore, we must eliminate ideas influenced by emotions such as pride or skepticism.

To "bear in mind what you hear" means to eliminate the defect of being like a leaky jug. If we are dispirited when receiving teachings, we will make no effort [to retain] the words [and their] meaning and our listening will be wasted, like juice poured into a leaky jug. Therefore, we must strive to eliminate feelings of inadequacy and listen [carefully].

Accordingly, the *Principles of Elucidation*[121] lists six improper ways of listening, all of which are included within the [previously mentioned] three defects like those of a jug.

> The [six] improper ways of receiving teaching
> Are to listen with pride, skepticism,[122]
> Lacking interest, distracted outwardly,
> With apathy,[123]
> Or with lassitude.

"Etc." in the root verses above refers to additional guidelines given in the same text on how to listen to the teaching: we should listen to the doctrine while using sixteen antidotes to counteract thirteen particular faults[124] and relinquishing six defects: the defect concerning one's [physical and mental] actions, of lack of interest, of irreverence, of [inappropriate] intention, of incompatibility, and of apprehension. (The last two have five aspects each.[125])

When listening to a teaching, we should do so keeping in mind the metaphors found in the *Flower Array Scripture*, such as the following: regarding ourselves as ill, the teaching as the cure for the disease, and the spiritual master as the physician; or ourselves as passengers, the teaching as a ferry, and the master as the ferryman; or ourselves as inexperienced [travelers], the teaching as the conveyance, and the master as the driver.[126]

The Speaker's and Listener's Fulfillment of the Six Perfections [3]

The speaker and the student should practice the six perfections when teaching and listening.

The teacher and the student should integrate the practice of the six perfections with the teaching and listening activities. Generosity is fulfilled by the gift of words of instruction and by the offerings made by the student for the purpose [of requesting instruction]. Ethics is to abstain from what is incompatible with didactic activities. Patience is to overcome discouragement caused by physical or verbal hardships. Diligence is to delight in teaching and listening to the doctrine. Meditation is to focus single-mindedly on the instructions. Appreciative discernment is to analyze the words and the meaning.

Concluding Duties [C]

This section has two parts: (1) the responsibilities of the speaker, and (2) the responsibilities of the listener.

The Responsibilities of the Speaker [1]

> **The teacher concludes the discourse with an apology, dedication, and sealing by contemplation.**

At the conclusion of the discourse, the teacher should perform three noble activities. First is the request that the buddhas excuse any errors he or she has made [in the teaching]. This is accomplished by reciting appropriate words such as the following[127]:

> In the presence of the buddhas
> I openly acknowledge
> Any mistakes I may have made
> Under the influence of unwholesome states of mind.

The second is the dedication, directing the virtue [of teaching] to the goal of awakening by reciting prayers of dedication, such as the following one [from the Buddha's discourses][128]:

> By this merit, may I attain omniscience,
> [And upon defeating the enemy of unwholesomeness,
> May I rescue from the ocean of existence all beings
> Swept by the turbulent waves of aging, sickness, and death].

or these words of Asanga:

> Through the limitless merit I have created
> By expounding the precious doctrine of the Universal Way,
> May all beings become perfectly receptive
> To this true and precious teaching.

The third is to seal the teaching with the state of nonconceptualization. The *Guide to the Bodhisattva's Way of Life* states[129]:

> Generosity that is empty of gift, recipient, and benefactor
> Is called the transcendent perfection.

Accordingly, [the teaching activity] should be sealed with [contemplation on] the nonconceptual wisdom that is free of the limited concepts [of agent, act, and object].

The Responsibilities of the Listener [2]

> **The student makes offerings, recites dedication prayers, and maintains mindfulness.**

As students, we have three tasks: First, we show our appreciation by giving remuneration; remembering [the master's] kindness, we make prostrations and offerings, such as a mandala[130] of thanksgiving.

Second, we dedicate the merits [of listening to the teaching] to the goal of awakening by reciting Asanga's prayer (above), substituting the words "listening to" for "expounding."

Third, we maintain mindful awareness of the words and meaning of the teaching, as advised in Sönam Tsemo's *Gateway to the Doctrine*[131]:

> Mindful of the teaching, go to a solitary place. Without distraction or apathy, reflect continuously on whatever instruction you have received! Read it! Write it! Question your spiritual master on all points about which you have doubts! Make the teaching a living experience and then please your master by showing your appreciation.

The Usefulness of Teaching and Listening [D]

> **Study, reflection, expounding, listening, and upholding the doctrine**
> **Integrated with living experience is said to yield limitless merits.**

The manifold virtues of study of and reflection on the teachings are taught in the *Garland of the Former Lives of the Buddha* and other sources such as the *Analysis of Discipline Scripture*, which states:

> Persons who have listened and reflected extensively earn five benefits: they become learned in the subject of the aggregates, learned in the subject of the experiential elements, learned in the subject of the experiential media, learned in the subject of interdependent origination, and acquire the skill to present these subjects as teachers in their own rights.

The sutras and tantras all proclaim the merits of listening to the doctrine to be inconceivable. Accordingly, the *Principles of Elucidation*[132] states:

> The Blessed One declared that five merits are acquired by listening to the doctrine: by listening, you become learned, and you acquire mastery [of the doctrine]; thereby, your doubts are quelled and your philosophical views are rectified; and by virtue of discriminative awareness, you will gain understanding of the words and the profound meaning [of the teaching].

Among the myriad virtues attributed to teaching the doctrine, the *Inspiring Universal Responsibility Scripture* gives a list of twenty.[133] All of those stem from the following three: teaching is the best way to honor the buddhas; it is the highest gift one can make to others; and by teaching, the teacher's merit increases and he or she gains supernatural knowledge.

The benefits accrued from upholding the doctrine that are mentioned in several [sources] are summarized in the *[Scripture] Revealing the [Inconceivable] Secrets of the Transcendent One*[134]:

> Even if for millions of eons
> The buddhas were to describe
> The merits of preserving the sacred teachings
> [They] could not possibly encompass them all.

The particular merits of expounding the Universal Way or listening to it are described in many scriptures in the following way. In the context of the basis for spiritual life, the merits outshine those of teaching and listening to the doctrine of the Individual Way. In the context of the experiential cultivation of the path, by virtue of these merits, each and every obscuration is overcome. In the context of the fruition, the merits [culminate in] the attainment of complete buddhahood.

[The merits] accrued from spiritual practice done in order to gain realization far surpass even those [mentioned above]. Simply taking seven steps in the direction of a place of spiritual practice while aware of the selfless nature of persons and phenomena is said to yield inconceivable merits. To be concerned only with hearing the teaching without making a living experience of it is utterly meaningless. Therefore, [the Buddha in his] discourses spoke of twenty shortcomings of taking delight only in listening to the doctrine. Nevertheless, to engage in ethical and contemplative disciplines without [sufficient] study

is like a blind person embarking on a journey. Thus, a supremely qualified practitioner is one who both is learned and has made a living
experience of the teaching. Accordingly, the *Scripture Ornament*
states[135]:

> The meditation of the yogi[136] is not fruitless.
> The teaching of the joyful ones is never without value.
> If reality could be perceived simply through learning, then
>   meditation would be without purpose.
> If meditation could be cultivated without study, teaching
>   would be senseless.

The benefits [that result] from integrating learning with living experience are unfathomable, as stated by the exalted Nagarjuna:

> Wisdom is enhanced by study
> And reflection. When both are present,
> Meditation will also develop accordingly.
> With meditation, unsurpassable awakening is attained.

Chapter II
The Vows of Personal Liberation

OUTLINE

5. The Way to Safeguard Vows
   a. Overview
   b. Explanation of the Different Ethics
      i. The Ethical Conduct of the Layperson
         A'. Purificatory Fast Precepts
         B'. Precepts of the Lay Practitioner
      ii. The Ethical Conduct of the Renunciate
         A'. Rules for the Novice
            1'. Transgressions of the Rules
            2'. Related Minor Infractions
            3'. Related Violations of Vows Assumed during the
                [Intermediate] Ordination
         B'. Rules for the Postulant Nun
         C'. Rules for the Monk and Nun
            1'. Accepting a Tutor
            2'. The Actual Training
               a'. Learning What Is Prohibited
                  i'. The Rules of the Monk
                     aa'. Overview
                     bb'. Extensive Explanation
                        1". The Defeating Offenses
                        2". The Partially Defeating Offenses
                        3". The Downfalls that Require Forfeiture or
                            Confession Alone
                           a". Downfalls that Require Forfeiture
                              i". The First Set of Ten
                              ii". The Second Set of Ten
                              iii". The Third Set of Ten
                           b". Downfalls that Require Confession
                               Alone
                              i". The First Set of Ten
                              ii". The Second Set of Ten
                              iii". The Third Set of Ten
                              iv". The Fourth Set of Ten
                              v". The Fifth Set of Ten
                              vi". The Sixth Set of Ten
                              vii". The Seventh Set of Ten
                              viii". The Eighth Set of Ten
                              ix". The Ninth Set of Ten

5. Permissible Transgressions of the Rules
6. Amendment of Downfalls
7. The Criterion for Loss of the Vows
C. The Core of Ethical Conduct
D. Consequences of Neglecting and Merits of Maintaining Ethical Conduct
III. A Synopsis of the Phases of the Path in the Individual Way
1. Formation of the Monastic Community
2. Establishing the Community in the Disciplinary Code
3. Providing the Conditions for Living Comfortably
4. Creating Incentive

The Vows of Personal Liberation

This presentation of the personal liberation system begins with an overview of the three systems of ethics, followed by a detailed explanation of the vows of personal liberation. [It concludes with an appended synopsis of the phases of the path in the Individual Way.]

AN OVERVIEW OF THE THREE SYSTEMS OF ETHICS [I]

> **To follow in the footsteps of saints, bodhisattvas, and buddhas**
> **Is to preserve a threefold morality, the foundation for all good**
> **qualities,**
> **Known as the ethics of personal liberation, of the bodhisattva,**
> **and of the awareness holder.**

Followers of the ancient tradition of our teacher, the unsurpassable King of the Shakyas, should first train in the foundation for all good qualities, the three forms of precious morality established by the Buddha himself. These disciplines contain the essence of the practice of the Buddha's teaching. The *Indestructible Peak Tantra* states[1]:

> When tantric adepts are renunciates,
> They thereby hold all three sets of vows
> Whose nature is the ethics of personal liberation,
> Of the bodhisattva, and of the awareness holder.

Further[2]:

> To live by the three [sets of] vows
> Is said to be the first cleansing.[3]

These three ethical systems are known as the disciplines of the proclaimers (*śrāvaka*), the bodhisattvas, and the transcendent ones; or as the vows of personal liberation, of the bodhisattva, and of the awareness holder (*vidyādhara*). Accordingly, Atisha, the sole lord, has said:

> The first discipline is to train in the footsteps of the saints (*arhat*); the middle discipline, to train in the footsteps of the bodhisattvas of the past; and the Secret Mantra discipline, to train in the footsteps of the buddhas.

EXPLANATION OF THE VOWS OF PERSONAL LIBERATION [II]

This section has four parts: (1) a general discussion of the vows of personal liberation of the proclaimers, (2) the distinctive features of the vows of personal liberation in the Universal Way, (3) the core of ethical conduct, and (4) the consequences [of neglecting] and the merits of maintaining ethical conduct.

The Vows of Personal Liberation of the Proclaimers [A]

This section has six parts: (1) the essential meaning of the vows, (2) the etymology of personal liberation and its other names, (3) distinctions of the disciplines, (4) conferral of vows, (5) the way to safeguard them, and (6) a supplementary discussion.

Essential Meaning of the Vows [1]

This section has three parts: (1) the basis for defining the vows, (2) the definition, and (3) different assertions concerning their nature.

The Basis for Defining the Vows [a]

> **Concern for personal peace motivated by renunciation**
> **Forms the basis for defining the personal liberation vows of the**
>   **proclaimers.**

The basis for the definition of the vows of personal liberation of the proclaimers consists in ethics motivated by concern for one's own peace alone. This concern is not based simply on a desire to be protected from anxiety or a wish to excel, but is an intention to emerge from all aspects of cyclic existence.[4]

The Definition [b]

> **The vows themselves are defined as the intention (as well as concomitant mental factors)**
> **To forsake both injury to others and its basis.**

The vows of personal liberation are defined as the intention (as well as concomitant mental states) to forsake both injury to others and the basis [of injury].

[Karma Trinlepa's] *Chariot of Karma*[5] clarifies the above in stating that "injury" refers to the seven unwholesome deeds of body and speech.[6] "Basis," which generally carries five different meanings,[7] here means motive, and refers to the three unwholesome states of mind[8] that form the impulse [to injure others]. "Both" (in the root verses) indicates that the vows include both the forsaking of injury and its basis.

In brief, all of the seven vows[9] of personal liberation are fulfilled in the forsaking of the ten unvirtuous actions.[10] "As well as concomitant mental factors" signifies that while the intention is the primary factor, its correlated mental factors are also part of the vows.

A different explanation states that "injury to others" refers to the seven unwholesome deeds of body and speech, and "basis," to related or similar deeds.[11] Thus, the vows of personal liberation can be concisely defined as the ethics of forsaking unwholesome deeds of body and speech only. Accordingly, [Purnavardhana's] *Commentary on the Treasury of Phenomenology* states[12]:

> As they discipline body and speech, they are known as vows of personal liberation.

This last interpretation is shared by all experts on the treatises [dealing with this subject]. Therefore, it seems reasonable to regard the former view as reflecting, primarily, the [vows of] personal liberation of the Universal Way and the latter as defining the nature of the [vows of] personal liberation of the proclaimers.

Different Assertions Concerning the Nature of the Vows [c]

> **In the Analysts' view, these vows have form.**

A sketch of the principal assertions concerning the essence of the vows of personal liberation will be provided first, and then these assertions will be expanded upon.

According to the Analysts (*vaibhāṣika*),[13] the vows have form, either perceptible or imperceptible,[14] and are connected to the individual by the "rope" of acquisition.[15] The Traditionalists (*sautrāntika*) hold a different view, stating that [the vows amount to] a complete transformation of the continuum of mind. The Idealists (*cittamātrin*) consider [the vows] to be both the seed and the continuity of the intention to forsake what is unwholesome. For the Centrist (*mādhyamika*) proponents of intrinsic emptiness (Tib. *rang stong pa*), [the vows] consist in the intention (and concomitant mental factors) to renounce [unwholesome deeds]. Stated concisely, the Traditionalists and the higher schools agree that the vows have the nature of consciousness and that they form with an attitude of disengagement [from cyclic existence] serving as their substantial condition, and with the essential elements[16] [for assuming the vows], etc., serving as their cooperative conditions.

[Since the above summary of the main views] is difficult to understand, it will now be explained to some extent. [According to the Analysts,] in the very first moment that the vows of personal liberation are assumed, they have the essence both of perceptible and imperceptible form. [The vows have the essence of perceptible form in that the aspirant, in order to assume them,] relies on the perceptible form of others (the ordaining preceptor, the ceremonial master, etc.[17]). From the second moment onward, as long as the vows have not been violated, they remain with the person [only] as the essence of an imperceptible form. The same criterion applies to the vows regarding the seven virtuous actions that have form (not to murder, etc.): in their first moment, they possess both perceptible and imperceptible forms. Then, from the second moment onward, they exist only as an imperceptible form. Therefore, in consideration of the first moment in which they are assumed, [Analysts] say that [the vows have] both [perceptible and imperceptible] forms.

[Traditionalists] assert that the essence of the vows is simply a transformation from one frame of mind into a new one, for example, the change in the attitude of someone who comes to regard himself as a [Buddhist] lay practitioner, a novice, [or a monk] as a result of undergoing the ceremony in which the respective vows are assumed.

[The Idealists, or] "Proponents of the Aspect of Consciousness" (*vijñānavādin*), as a consequence of their belief in the existence of a fundamental consciousness, assert that physical actions such as those related to the vows [of personal liberation] are of the nature of the mind stream. The Idealists thus maintain [that the essence of the vows is] the continuum of the intention to forsake [unwholesome deeds] and the seed of the propensity [for that intention], which coexists with the fundamental consciousness. This is because (they say), if you were to consider the essence of the vows as just an intention, when the person who has assumed them falls under the sway of distraction, unconsciousness, or similar states, their continuity would be broken. On the other hand, if you were to consider the essence of the vows as a propensity alone, they would not be lost even when violated.

Centrist proponents of intrinsic emptiness, who do not accept the existence of a fundamental consciousness, assert [that the essence of the vows is] the intention (together with its concomitant mental factors) to forsake [unwholesome deeds]. However, Chandrakirti[18] in his *Analysis of the Five Aggregates*,[19] a treatise on the Central Way, considers [the vows] to be imperceptible form, and Lord Drigungpa[20] and Taktsang the Translator[21] stressed the same view with clever arguments.

In brief, most scholars are of the opinion that the vows at the desire realm level (defined as the ethics of abandoning unwholesome conduct, imbued with an attitude of renunciation) have form.

Etymology of Personal Liberation and Its Other Names [2]

Personal liberation is known as morality, virtue, endeavor, and vow.

[The discipline of] personal liberation is known as *prātimokṣa* [in Sanskrit] since it effects the individual's (*prāti*) liberation (*mokṣa*) from cyclic existence.[22] It is also referred to as "morality" (*śīla*) as it gives cool relief from the distressing heat of the emotions and uplifts the nature of body, speech, and mind; "virtue" because it is praised by the wise; "endeavor" since its nature is that of engagement; "vow" by virtue of serving as a dam that blocks moral corruption, and because it restrains body and speech.

Distinctions of Disciplines [3]

This section has two parts: (1) distinctions of disciplines according to the level of existence, and (2) distinctions of personal liberation vows according to the person.

Distinctions of Disciplines according to the Level of Existence [a]

**The vows of personal liberation, meditative absorption, and the
uncontaminated are found within different levels of existence.**

Three categories of discipline are distinguished according to the level
[of existence] where each is found: the vows of personal liberation
within the level of the desire realm; those of meditative absorption
within the level of the form realm; and the uncontaminated vows
within the levels of the exalted ones,[23] the last transcending the three
realms of existence.

The first consists in the ethical conduct of forsaking unwholesome
conduct, which is followed by Buddhists living in the desire realm.
The second is the ethics of gods of the form realm, acquired through
contemplation. The third is the ethics of supramundane beings, which
is derived from uncontaminated wisdom.[24]

According to the Analysts, since the three [ethics] are substantially
incompatible, they cannot coexist in a single mental continuum. Followers of the Universal Way, however, assert that the three ethics can
coexist without contradiction. For example, the vows of personal liberation in the mind of an exalted bodhisattva encompass all three
ethics: the forsaking of unwholesome conduct, the ethics pertaining
to the actual meditative absorption,[25] and the [uncontaminated] ethics that are of the nature of the exalted path.

Distinctions of Personal Liberation Vows according to the Person [b]

**The eight vows, those of the monk and nun, male and female
novices and lay practitioners,
Postulant nun, and the purificatory fast,
Diversified in nature, are condensed into four types. Only
seven meet the necessary requirements.**

The vows of personal liberation are of seven categories when distinguished according to the person: (1) the [vows of the] monk
(*bhikṣu*),[26] (2) the nun (*bhikṣūni*), (3) the male novice (*śrāmaṇera*),[27] (4)
the female novice (*śrāmaṇerikā*), (5) the layman practitioner (*upasaka*),[28]
(6) the laywoman practitioner (*upasika*), and (7) the postulant nun
(*śikṣāmanā*).

Another system separates the vows of the purificatory fast
(*upavāsa*)[29] from those of the lay practitioner and thereby lists eight
categories of vows. These eight categories may be condensed into

four types that differ in nature or substance: from among the renunciate vows, those of the monk and the nun form one type, and the vows of [the postulant nun and] the male and female novice form a second type; from among the lay vows, those of the male and female lay practitioner form a third type, and the purificatory fast [vows][30] form a fourth type. Only seven [of the eight categories] meet the necessary requirements for the discipline of personal liberation. There are two different views [concerning which vows constitute the seven]: one excludes the precepts of the purificatory fast [since they are assumed just for one day]; the other, those of the vows of the postulant nun since this discipline does not last for a lifetime, nor does it last for just one day.[31]

Conferral of Vows [4]

This section has four parts: (1) the various procedures for monastic ordination, (2) the candidate, (3) unfavorable conditions and obstacles, and (4) favorable conditions for the conferral of vows.

Various Procedures for Monastic Ordination [a]

The present-day ceremony of ordination was introduced after the demise of the original one.

In the original procedure for conferring monastic ordination, the aspirant became a monk without any complex ritual. The present-day procedure confers ordination with a considerable amount of ritual. Analysts have recorded ten ways persons became instantaneously ordained as monks and nuns in the original way[32]:

(1) Spontaneously; for example, at the moment the Buddha and solitary sages gained knowledge of the final extinction of the emotions, thereby achieving awakening, they became monks.

(2) By realizing pristine awareness; for example, when the excellent group of five[33] achieved the path of seeing, they became monks.

(3) By being called [by the Buddha], "Come hither, monks!" For example, at the moment [the Buddha called upon] Shariputra[34] and others to come before him, they became monks.

(4) By accepting the teacher; for example, at the moment Mahakashyapa[35] accepted the Buddha as his teacher, he become a monk.

(5) By taking refuge; for example, at the moment the sixty followers of Bhadrasena accepted the triple refuge, they became monks.

(6) By accepting the eight severe precepts[36]; for example, at the moment when Mahaprajapati[37] and others (five hundred women of the Shakya clan) promised to maintain the eight precepts difficult to observe, they became nuns.

(7) By pleasing the Buddha with a [correct] answer; for example, at the moment the Buddha rejoiced after Sudatta answered a particular question, Sudatta became a monk.

(8) By messenger; for example, at the moment Dharmadinna,[38] whose parents prevented her [from becoming a nun], received the ordained community's message of approval brought by the messenger, the nun Utpala, she became a nun.

(9) By an assembly of [at least] ten masters of the discipline in the central region; or

(10) By an assembly of [at least] five masters of the discipline in a remote region, through a four-part formal procedure including proposal[39] that conferred instantaneously the status of monk.

[This ordination] was conferred by an exalted preceptor upon aspirants of pure mind, that is, disciples whose three impediments (of intentional actions, emotions, and fruition[40]) were minimal and whose intelligence, continuum, and faculties were ripened.[41] Once the present-day procedure [of ordination] was introduced, the former method was discontinued.[42] The present method, a four-part procedure, has been [the only one] in use from the time of the passing of the Buddha and his circle [of close disciples] until now. It must be performed by an assembly of ten [monks] in a central region or five in a remote region.

The distinction between a central region and a remote region may be made in terms of geography, in which case, roughly speaking, central India is considered to be the central region,[43] and the regions exterior to be remote regions. In spiritual terms, a central region is an area where the Buddha's teachings as transmission and as spiritual accomplishment[44] are found, and the remote regions are those in which these are not found.

The Candidate [b]

Men or women of the three continents are suitable candidates.

Only men and women of three continents[45] are suitable candidates for any of the eight vows of personal liberation. Accordingly, Guna-prabha's *[Fundamental] Summary of Discipline*[46] says:

> Non-humans and inhabitants of the northern [continent] of Un-pleasant Sound are not eligible candidates for the vows.

Eunuchs and hermaphrodites are also not eligible to assume the vows.

The scriptures on discipline, however, mention that the *naga* Kumaraka observed the purificatory fast on the eighth day of the [lunar] month. Furthermore, the *Stories of Buddha's Former Lives* recounts details of four [animals], such as an "elder" partridge, who observed the purificatory fast.[47] Traditionalists take these accounts literally and thus believe that animals and other beings can assume [the precepts of] the purificatory fast.

Unfavorable Conditions and Obstacles for the Conferral of Vows [c]

In assuming the vows, the candidate must not be bound by five stipulations, and must be free of the four obstacles.

While assuming the vows of personal liberation, the candidate must not make any of the following five stipulations with regard to region, time, situation, persons, and minor rules:

(1) To intend to safeguard the vows provided one is living in a region that has supportive conditions, but not in others;

(2) To intend to safeguard the vows for at least a month or a year, but not longer, thinking that one would not be able to do so;

(3) To intend to maintain the vows in all situations, except in case of war;

(4) To intend to abstain from murder, unless the other is one's enemy;

(5) To intend to keep the major rules, but not the minor ones.

An aspirant who attends the ceremony for monastic ordination with the wish to become a monk (or likewise, a novice) but makes any of these five stipulations will not actually assume the vows, but will at least have participated in something good.

Furthermore, the candidate must be free of the obstacles that would prevent assuming the vows, the obstacles to abiding by them, and obstacles to their meaningfulness, plus obstacles concerning physical appearance, explained, respectively, as follows:

(1) Being a neuter person or one who has committed [any of] the crimes of immediate retribution or other [serious offenses], etc.[48];

(2) Not having the approval of one's [country's] ruler, or of one's parents or guardians, etc.[49];

(3) Not being able to drive away crows [meaning to be less than eight years old], or being incapacitated by [serious] sickness or affliction, etc.[50];

(4) Having blond hair or deformed ears, etc.[51]

These stipulations and obstacles, however, are not considered detrimental factors in assuming the precepts of the lay practitioner or those of the purificatory fast.

Favorable Conditions for the Conferral of Vows [d]

This section has two parts: (1) temporary vows, and (2) vows for life.

Temporary Vows [i]

> **An aspirant who has not gone for refuge cannot assume the personal liberation vows.**
> **The precepts of the purificatory fast are observed for a day and may be conferred by any person holding the precepts.**

The *Treasury of Phenomenology*[52] states:

> Except for the person who has not gone for refuge,
> Anyone may assume [the purificatory fast] vows.

Thus expressed, an aspirant who has not gone for refuge in the Three Jewels[53] cannot receive the precepts of the purificatory fast or, for that matter, any of the vows of personal liberation.

Analysts assert that any of the eight classes of personal liberation vows must be conferred by a monk. However, Traditionalists say that the precepts of the purificatory fast may be taken from anyone who is observing the purificatory fast, either a lay practitioner or a renunciate. Accordingly, the *Brahmana Vyasa Scripture*[54] states:

> ...in the presence of one who has knowledge of the ceremony, whether it be a monk, a brahman, a householder, or a novice.

Also, the *Analysis of Discipline Scripture*[55] mentions that the layman Anathapindika[56] transmitted the precepts of the purificatory fast to a large crowd of people.

In any case, the various perspectives agree that the aspirant must assume the eight precepts of the purificatory fast before dawn in the presence of a practitioner holding the same precepts and preserve them until sunrise of the next day, a period of one full day.

When assuming these precepts for the first time, the aspirant may promise the teacher that he or she will also maintain the precepts on the [days of the] full moon, the new moon, and the eighth day of every [lunar] month. Despite that [promise], each time that aspirant intends to practice the purificatory fast, he or she must assume the precepts anew.

According to the Analysts, making a single promise [to maintain these eight precepts on the various days of the month] allows one to retake the precepts [on the next occasion] even after having eaten.[57] According to the Traditionalists, [this promise] authorizes one to retake the precepts by oneself in front of a representation [of the Three Jewels].

The main part of the ceremony [for the transmission of the precepts of the purificatory fast] involves repeating the words of the preceptor three times while sitting lower than him or her.

Vows for Life [ii]

> **The layperson's precepts, the novice's, and the monk's ordina-
> tion are conferred in their respective ceremonies.**
> **The ceremony for the monk's ordination requires ten essential
> elements.**

The three levels of vows—those of the lay practitioner, the novice, and the monk—are conferred in ceremonies that fulfill the requisites for their respective level. [As to the order,] higher grades of discipline cannot be given unless the candidate has received the lower ones.

The following description of the procedure for the conferral of vows is made in terms of an aspirant who is assuming all three types of discipline. (An independent ceremony must be performed in the case of someone who wishes to follow only the precepts of the lay practitioner or only the novice precepts.)

The vows of a lay practitioner may constitute a "partial discipline" (consisting of one, two, three, or four precepts) or a "perfect discipline" (comprising five precepts as the basis of training). Only the perfect discipline of holding five precepts may be considered as the actual lay practitioner discipline that constitutes two [i.e., male and female] of the eight categories of personal liberation vows.

For the first level, a monk qualified to be the ordaining preceptor for a renunciate asks [the aspirant] questions concerning obstacles to determine whether or not he is suitable to be admitted into the order.[58] Then, as the main part [of the ceremony of the first level],[59] the aspirant accepts the commitments of refuge and the lay practitioner's precepts. As the conclusion, the aspirant promises to follow the training. [The ceremony] for those individuals who are assuming only a partial [lay] discipline (and are not going to become renunciates) is modified to omit the questions concerning obstacles.

To become a novice (the second level), the aspirant participates in the preparatory phase of the ceremony for the interim renunciate.[60] The ceremonial master asks the aspirant questions[61] to determine whether he has any obstacles that could prevent him from being ordained. If the aspirant is free of obstacles, the ceremonial master addresses the members of the monastic community with the request to admit him into the order. Once permission is granted, the aspirant himself entreats the ordaining preceptor to ordain him as a novice.[62] During the course of this preparatory phase of the ceremony, three transformations take place: the aspirant changes his outward appearance, name, and attitude.

For the main part [of the ceremony], the ordaining preceptor entrusts the aspirant to the ceremonial master. With the certainty that the aspirant is free from the four kinds of obstacles that would make him ineligible for ordination and possesses all five favorable conditions, the ceremonial master guides the aspirant, beginning with the refuge [vows], in assuming the novice vows.

At the conclusion of the ceremony, a monk [who is neither the ordaining preceptor nor the ceremonial master] measures the [length of the] shadow[63] and announces the time [of day, month, season, and year] that the novice ordination was received. The teacher states the ten rules of the novice and makes [sure the aspirant] confirms his commitment to maintain them.

The five favorable conditions [for the novice ordination] concern environment, mind continuum, outward appearance, attitude, and ceremony, and are explained, respectively, as follows: (1) [The ceremony takes place] in a land where the Three Jewels are honored and where there are monks qualified to ordain a novice. (2) The aspirant has not already received the ordination, has no residue of old vows obstructing him,[64] and has assumed the lower levels [of discipline]. (3) The aspirant forsakes the attire of a layperson and takes on the threefold aspect of the renunciate: to be shaven, to wear the robes, and to use the begging bowl and the other monastic accessories. (4) The aspirant's attitude is one of renunciation, which permeates his aspiration to become a novice (the underlying causal motive), his awareness of having become [a novice] (the motive of the moment[65]), the freedom from the five unfavorable conditions,[66] and the presence of all three excellent conditions.[67] (5) The refuge ceremony is performed first, following which the aspirant repeats three times the phrases formalizing the novice ordination.

The ordination of a monk[68] (the third level) requires ten essential elements: the Buddha, the doctrine, the monastic community, the preceptor, the teachers, the aspiration to become a monk, the monastic necessities, purity, the proposal, and the ceremony.

The essential element of the Buddha refers to a consecrated image of the Buddha placed [on the shrine].

The essential element of the doctrine refers to the doctrine as spiritual accomplishment, [represented by] the officiating monks' zeal in following the discipline; and the doctrine as transmission, [represented by] the ordination ceremony itself.

The essential element of the monastic community refers to three requirements: The first is a quorum of four [monks] who form the officiating group (excluding the ordaining preceptor). The second requirement is that the monks have the necessary virtues [which means that they must be free of the following defects]: standing rather than sitting; deserving punishment or other disciplinary measures; not attending personally the ceremony but giving their assent to it; not being true monks; responsible for violating the vows; guilty of a crime of immediate retribution; adhering to bad opinions such as that drinking alcohol and other such offenses are not unvirtuous; having been demoted or delegated to menial tasks; being of unsound mind (subject to insanity); not living within the same monastic boundary, but in another; being the opposite sex (a nun); and following another [religion]. The third requirement is that the monks do not behave in two contrary ways: (1) not attending the ordination but [instead simply] giving their assent to it, reporting their purity from downfalls, etc.; or (2) leaving [without permission].

The essential element of the ordaining preceptor is fulfilled by a monk well-qualified in terms of steadfastness and learning, who, moreover, has no lapse of discipline[69] that has been seen, heard of, or suspected by the aspirant.

The essential element of the teachers refers to the ceremonial master who is skilled at performing ceremonies in the midst of the monastic community and the interviewer who is capable of covertly investigating whether the aspirant has obstacles [to ordination] and then informing the inner [circle of the ordaining monks] of the result of his inquiry.[70] To fulfill properly his role, the interviewer must be free of the four biases of intimacy, fear, dislike, and inability to recognize the aspirant's impediments. Intimacy with the aspirant might tempt the interviewer to conceal the aspirant's possible obstacles; fear of him could make him reticent to report them; antagonism could lead him to falsely claim that the aspirant is unfit; and incapacity to determine whether an aspirant is qualified or not might allow the aspirant's unfitness to go unreported.

The essential element of sincere aspiration to become a monk refers to the wish to assume the monk's vows with a spirit of renunciation. [For this aspiration to be fulfilled, the candidate must] be at least twenty years of age, know how to express himself, understand the meaning of words, and be in a sound state of mind.[71] [In addition, he must] not harbor thoughts incompatible with the ordination[72] or make any of the five stipulations, or have already taken these vows.

The essential element of the monastic necessities consists in a complete set of five articles: the three robes of proper measure (either the [robes] already sewn or material suitable [for making them], no [piece being] longer or wider than a cubit); a permissible begging bowl of the prescribed dimensions; a cloth mat and a water strainer.

The essential element of purity refers to the absence of the four kinds of obstacles, and so forth.

The essential element of proposal refers to the request made three times by the aspirant to the ordaining community.

The essential element of the ceremony is a four-part formal procedure including proposal that is conducted in its entirety, without error or confusion [regarding the structure].

The ceremony is arranged in three parts: the preparation, the main ceremony, and the conclusion.

The preparation serves the purpose of assembling the first nine essential elements. The main ceremony begins with the proposal, followed by the monastic community's formal procedure of full ordination. The conclusion consists in the announcement of the time the ordination was conferred in order to determine who is to be shown reverence [based on seniority].[73] Following this, [the ceremonial master] gives [the new monk] eleven instructions on points of discipline as aids to safeguarding the vows and developing the training related to them. Nine of these relate to the focus of training, [the vows] received; the [last] two points relate to the person engaged in the training.[74]

The ceremonies that confer the lay practitioner vows or the novice vows on a woman are essentially the same as those for a man, except for the aspirant being referred to as "the woman known as...," instead of "the man known as...," and the additional questions posed to the woman. The precepts of the postulant nun may be assumed at the age of eighteen in the case of one who has not been married and at the age of ten in the case of a woman who has been married. This ordination is conferred by a group of twelve nuns in a central region, or six in a remote region, through a two-part ceremony including proposal.[75]

After [two years], at the age of twenty (in the former case) and twelve (in latter case), the postulant becomes eligible to receive full ordination. This ordination is conferred in the following manner: The preceptress and the members of the nun's community, in the number previously specified, present the aspirant nun with the three robes, plus an undershirt and an upper robe [to absorb] perspiration, etc.— the attire [of a renunciate]. With the completion of the questions concerning obstacles, the vow for strict observance of celibacy is given.[76] Then the full ordination is bestowed in the presence of [the original group of nuns] augmented by a group of ordaining monks [ten in a central region and five in a remote region]. At the conclusion of the ceremony, the preceptor instructs [the new nun on the twelve] points of discipline, which include the eight defeating offenses, the eight severe precepts, and other rules.[77] However, it should be mentioned that the traditions for the ordinations of the postulant and fully ordained nun were never introduced in Tibet.

The Way to Safeguard Vows [5]

There are two parts to the explanation of how to safeguard ethical conduct: (1) an overview, and (2) an explanation of the different ethics.

Overview [a]

> Ethical conduct is maintained by reliance on others, purity of
>   mind, recognition of incompatible factors,
> Engagement in the training, and relying on the conditions for
>   living comfortably.

Ethical conduct is maintained by five methods: by relying on other individuals [as the external condition], through purity of mind [as the internal condition], by recognizing incompatible factors, through engagement in training, and by relying on the conditions for living comfortably.

First, ethical conduct is maintained by relying on the instructions of learned scholars and following the example of venerable [elder] monks. In particular, as soon a monk or nun has received full monastic ordination, he or she must begin studying under a tutor. (This is briefly explained below.)

Second, purity of mind or intention refers to zeal and conscientiousness in observing precepts and prohibitions, vigilance and mindfulness in examining the state of one's own mind, embarrassment in response to others' [judgment], and shame arising from one's own [conscience].

Third, recognition of incompatible factors means [knowing] the causes for losing the vows,[78] the conditions for damaging the vows,[79] factors [that help] to maintain the vows,[80] and the causes that hinder the mind's clarity.[81] In short, in order to know what the incompatible factors are, one should study, reflect upon, and follow the guidelines given in the scriptures on discipline.

Fourth, engagement in training refers to the observance of the three bases [of confession, rainy season retreat, and lifting of the restrictions].

Fifth, relying on the conditions for living comfortably entails shunning the thirty-six downfalls concerning robes, the twenty-two concerning food, the three concerning monastic articles, and the ten concerning monastic sites and monks' quarters.[82]

The main causes for violating the vows are ignorance [of the rules], irreverence [for the discipline], negligence, and strong emotions. Therefore, as remedies to these, one applies these five methods of maintaining [ethical conduct] and strives to protect one's discipline as one would one's eyes.

Explanation of the Different Ethics [b]
This section has two parts: (1) the ethical conduct of the layperson, and (2) the ethical conduct of the renunciate.

The Ethical Conduct of the Layperson [i]
This has two parts: (1) the purificatory fast precepts, and (2) the precepts of the lay practitioner.

Purificatory Fast Precepts [A']

> **The eight branches of the purificatory fast consist of the four**
>> **basic precepts, abstinence from alcohol, dance, necklaces, etc.,**
> **Luxurious or high beds, and eating after noon;**
> **Ethical conduct, conscientiousness, and disciplined conduct**
>> **encompass these eight.**
> **An individual who observes these precepts for life is known as**
>> **a venerable lay practitioner.**

The eight branches of the one-day purificatory fast consist of the four basic [precepts] to renounce murder, theft, sexual intercourse, and untruth, and [the four precepts] to abstain from drinking alcohol; dancing, etc., and the wearing of necklaces, etc.; using luxurious or high beds [and seats]; and eating after noon.

"Dancing, etc." refers to singing, dancing, and [playing] musical instruments. "Necklaces, etc." refers to the wearing of necklaces, perfumes, jewelry, and cosmetics. "Perfumes" means to perfume one's clothes, etc., in order that they have an agreeable fragrance. "Luxurious" refers to a bed made from precious materials such as jewels, and "high" to a bed being one cubit high or more; [this last rule,] however, does not apply [to the seat being used] when explaining the doctrine.

The four basic precepts are branches of ethical conduct; abstinence from drinking alcohol is a branch of conscientiousness, and the last three are branches of disciplined conduct. In this context, "disciplined conduct" means to renounce one's previous immoral ways as a lay person to engage in the conduct of the purificatory fast. The disciplined conduct of the lay practitioner and of the renunciate should also be understood in the same manner.

To these eight branches, the practice taught by Lord Atisha adds two [precepts]: eating vegetarian food[83] and drinking water [after the noon meal] as a reminder [that one is not supposed to eat afterwards].

Moreover, the purificatory fast allows the lay practitioner to purify and renew his or her vows, while for one who has not assumed layperson's vows, it simply serves as a purificatory fast. Renunciates need not be expressly concerned with the one-day purificatory fast.

The person who observes a life-long purificatory fast is known as a "venerable (*gomi*) lay practitioner."[84] Concerning this, Vasubandhu states:

> The "venerable lay practitioner" discipline is derived from the oral instructions transmitted by the Sthavira,[85] but it does not seem to have been taught by the Joyful One.

References to this [discipline], however, are found in the scriptures of the Universal Way. For example, *Cluster of Jewels* states that Prince Mind of Great Compassion took the eight precepts of the purificatory fast for life. Therefore, in the above words, Vasubandhu must have meant that the scriptures on discipline do not explicitly mention a life-long purificatory fast.

Precepts of the Lay Practitioner [B']

> Lay practitioners are of five types. The first is committed to
>   the Three Jewels
> And abides by the three special and five general precepts.
> The second abstains from one; the third, from some; the fourth,
>   from most;
> And the fifth, from all four root downfalls and alcohol.
> Traditionalists maintain that there is also a celibate lay
>   practitioner.

There are five types of lay practitioner. The first is known as the lay practitioner committed to the Three Jewels. Once he or she has taken refuge, this lay practitioner must follow the six special and five general precepts related to refuge alone, as they are explained by Lord Atisha.[86]

The first three special precepts concern prohibitions: having gone for refuge in the Buddha, a Buddhist must not venerate worldly deities; having gone for refuge in the doctrine of the Buddha, a Buddhist must refrain from injuring others; having gone for refuge in the Buddhist community, a Buddhist must not form close ties with religious extremists.

The other three special precepts concern obligations: the practitioner should regard as if it were the actual Three Jewels [and treat respectfully] any representation [of the Buddha], even just so much as a fragment of a votive image[87]; any symbol of his words, even a single letter; or any symbol of the Buddhist community, even someone wearing as much as a patch of yellow cloth.

The five general precepts are not to renounce the Three Jewels, even for the sake of one's life or country; to put one's trust exclusively in the [Three] Jewels, without seeking worldly means, however great the necessity or importance; to make offerings regularly to the Three Jewels on the prescribed occasions, with a constant appreciation of their qualities; to go for refuge with an awareness of the benefits [of doing so], and to encourage others to do the same; and to prostrate before the buddhas and depictions of them wherever one happens to be.

These precepts are the preconditions not only for the vows of a lay practitioner but also for the purificatory fast and the novice and monk disciplines.

In addition to these, the actual ethical conduct of the lay practitioner includes the four basic precepts [to abstain from murder, theft, adultery, and untruth], plus abstinence from intoxicating drinks, this last vow facilitating the preservation of the former ones.

Depending on the number [of precepts] one promises to follow, there are four types [of lay practitioners]: a lay practitioner who observes one precept alone (to abstain from murder); one who observes some precepts (to abstain also from stealing); one who observes most of the precepts (to abstain also from untruth); and the perfect lay practitioner who follows all five precepts, including forsaking adultery and drinking alcohol.

According to Analysts, when the aspirant receives any of these four precepts, he or she simply vows to be a lay practitioner and subsequently observes one, two, or however many he or she intended to follow.

For Traditionalists, however, this is not the case; they assert that during the ceremony to become a lay practitioner, the aspirant must assume the specific precept or precepts he or she wishes, and observe them thereafter. If, after having assumed all five precepts, the practitioner does not observe them all, his or her ethical conduct will be disrupted.

Traditionalists assert that there is yet another lay practitioner, the celibate lay practitioner, who renounces all forms of sexual intercourse. As implied in these words from the scriptures on discipline[88]:

> Practicing the teachings even while wearing jewelry....

Further, the disciplines of the celibate layperson and the venerable practitioner of the purificatory fast [mentioned above][89] have been explicitly taught in the *Display of Miracles Scripture*. In both cases, since sexual intercourse has been renounced, the practitioner is no longer a householder, but as the [monastic] lifestyle has not been adopted, he or she is not considered a renunciate.

Concerning the lay practitioner who has entered the Secret Mantra, the *Questions of Subahu Tantra* states that he or she must follow all the rules set out in the scriptures on discipline [for the renunciates], with the exception of a few rules prescribed by the Buddha [for monks], such as taking on the attire of a monk, participation in formal monastic ceremonies, and not eating after noon.

The Ethical Conduct of the Renunciate [ii]

This section has three parts: (1) rules for the male and female novice, (2) rules for a postulant nun, and (3) rules for the monk and nun.

Rules for the Novice [A']

> Novices may incur ten transgressions of the rules: violations of
> the eight branches,
> Plus the rule not to accept gold and silver. With the exception of
> thirteen permissible ones,
> The related minor infractions are the same as those of the
> monk.

The ethical conduct of the male or female novice has three parts: (1) transgressions of the rules for the novice, (2) related minor infractions, and (3) related violations of vows assumed during the [intermediate] ordination.

Transgressions of the Rules [1']

The novice vows summarized under ten overt violations of the novice's ethical conduct are taught mainly for the sake of those aspirants who would become disheartened on hearing of many rules [and thus be reluctant to become novices]. Nine of these are the violations prohibited by the eight precepts of the purificatory fast. The extra one is derived from the transgression of the precept prohibiting dancing and wearing necklaces, that for a novice is split into two. The tenth is a rule not to accept gold and silver.

Transgressions of the four basic precepts, although the same as those of the monk, would be only "violations similar to a defeat" for a novice. The other six, failure to abstain from alcohol, etc., are minor infractions to be confessed. These novice rules may be subdivided into thirty-three:

(1-4) The four basic vows (not to murder, etc.);

(5-7) Three related to the rule not to murder: not to kill animals, not to use grass that has insects, and not to use water that contains insects;

(8-19) Twelve related to lying: to abstain from making groundless accusation or accusation for a trivial reason, causing a schism in the monastic community, taking sides, causing a layperson to lose faith, consciously lying, falsely accusing another monk of favoritism, censuring the caretaker of the monastic community, accusing another monk of teaching to get a little food, defaming [a monk] by accusing him of having committed a partially defeating offense, rejecting the discipline out of disdain for it, and covering the [vegetables with] rice when wanting more [vegetables];

(20) One to abstain from drinking alcohol;

(21-23) Three to abstain from dancing, [singing, and music];

(24-26) Three to abstain from wearing necklaces, [cosmetics, and perfumes];

(27-28) Two to abstain from the use of a luxurious bed or a high bed;

(29) One to abstain from eating after noon;

(30) One not to accept gold and silver;

(31-33) Three to safeguard oneself from the three types of deteriorations: [adopting the attire of a layperson, giving up the
monastic attire, and despising the preceptor]. There are
other ways of enumerating the novice rules.[90]

Related Minor Infractions [2']

Except for the permissible transgressions to the rules, any offense that
would be a downfall for the monk is also an infraction for the novice,[91]
though a minor one. Such an infraction can be remedied by privately
reaffirming one's intention to refrain from the act in the future. No
public confession is required.

Accordingly, in his *Luminous Commentary on the Three Hundred Stanzas on the Novitiate*,[92] Shakyaprabha explains in detail how [the novice]
should maintain all of the monks' rules as part of a concordant ethical
conduct. However, the transgressions of thirteen rules for monks are
not even infractions for the novice by virtue of dispensation. In addition (to explain "etc." in the root verses), six other transgressions are
permissible according to Tibetan masters of the discipline. These nineteen permissible transgressions of the monks' rules are as follows[93]:

(1) Keeping extra cloth, (2) being separate from one's robes,
(3) keeping an extra begging bowl, (4) tilling the soil,
(5) Handling precious objects, (6) lighting a fire, (7) resuming
eating, (8) climbing or (9) cutting trees,
(10) Eating what has not been ritually offered and accepted,
(11) urinating or defecating on the grass,
(12) Partaking of food that has been stored, and (13) destroying
seeds.
The six are: (1) retaining [cloth] for more than a month, (2)
storing [any of the three kinds of food], (3) being without
[one's robes] while in seclusion,
(4) [Going to the village] without informing [a senior monk],
(5) withdrawing assent, and (6) sleeping in the same room as
the unordained.

Related Violations of Vows Assumed during the [Intermediate] Ordination [3']

During the intermediate ordination, the novice makes the vows to
relinquish the attire of a layperson, to adopt the monastic attire, and
to respect his preceptor. Renouncing these three by adopting whole-
heartedly the attire of a layperson even for just a day is said to lead to
the loss of ordination.

Rules for the Postulant Nun [B']

The postulant nun observes six basic and six additional rules.

Once the aspirant has been ordained as a postulant nun, in addition to the ten precepts of the female novice, she must observe the [six basic and six additional] rules of that [ordination] for two years. Vishakhadeva states[94]:

> These six basic rules
> Have been prescribed for the postulant nun:
> She should not travel alone,
> Swim across a river,
> Touch a man,
> Sit together with him,
> Conceal downfalls [of other postulants],
> Or arrange a union [between a male and a female].

Further:

> Do not commit these offenses:
> Handling gold,
> Shaving the pubic hair,
> Tilling the soil,
> Cutting grass and other plants,
> Eating what has not been ritually given and accepted,
> And eating food that has been stored.
> These are the six additional rules.

Moreover, it is explained that, with the exception of seven transgressions[95] that are admissible, the postulant nun should preserve the entire ethical code of a nun.

Rules for the Monk and Nun [c']

The first point related to the ethical conduct of the monk deals with the procedure for accepting a tutor.

Accepting a Tutor [1']

As soon as an aspirant has taken the vows of a novice or monk, he should study under a well-qualified tutor and follow correctly the rules until he has acquired the two qualities relating to steadfastness and learning. Steadfastness refers to having preserved full ordination for ten years without interruption, and learning, to erudition possessing the five characteristics.[96]

If the monk or novice is living [in a monastery] with the preceptor who has ordained him, that preceptor will automatically be his tutor, and he does not need to perform the ceremony of accepting him as tutor. If he is not living with his ordaining preceptor, he should search for a monk who is qualified to be a tutor and perform the ceremony of accepting him as such.[97] Then, as the sun rises on the second day, he becomes his tutor.[98]

A tutor is allowed to be the instructor for many monks; however, he cannot accept more than one novice [into his care]. Since it is not permissible [for a monk] to stay with a novice for more than three nights, [a novice] should not stay with the tutor but should reside nearby.

Concerning the way of studying under the tutor, it is said[99]:

> Once he has accepted a tutor, the monk should request permission from his teacher for whatever he wishes to do.

Accordingly, with the exceptions of permitted times or activities (such as prostrating before a nearby stupa, defecating and urinating, or being absent for one day), the monk should not simply act on his own, but should ask his teacher for permission.[100]

The teacher must offer good counsel and give teaching [to the student] in the proper way. Disregard of the reciprocal obligations[101] on the part of the teacher and the monk under his care nullify their tutor and tutored status.

The Actual Training [2']

The actual training is discussed under two headings: (1) learning what is prohibited, and (2) training in the prescribed discipline.

Learning What Is Prohibited [a']

This section has two parts: (1) the rules of a monk, and (2) the rules of a nun.

The Rules of the Monk [i']

(1) An overview, and (2) an extensive explanation.

Overview [aa']

The rules of the monk concern five classes of downfalls.

The prescribed rules for a monk concern [the avoidance of] five classes of downfalls: the class of defeating offenses, the class of partially defeating offenses, the class of downfalls [whose restoration involves forfeiture or confession], the class of offenses that must be individually confessed, and the class of minor infractions.[102]

Extensive Explanation [bb']
This consists of five parts, corresponding to these five classes.

The Defeating Offenses [1"]

> **Sexual intercourse, theft, murder, and lying about one's level of**
>   **spiritual attainment**
> **Constitute the class of defeating offenses.**
> **If the basis, attitude, act, and consummation are all present, the**
>   **ordination is lost.**
> **If one or more aspects are missing, a serious infraction or**
>   **another offense is incurred.**

The class of defeating offenses consists of four acts: (1) *Sexual intercourse* refers to the experience of orgasm arising from the contact made when the penis penetrates any of the three [orifices]—the mouth, anus, or vagina—of a living being, be it male, female, neuter, or animal, or of a corpse with at least half the body.

(2) *Theft* refers to personally stealing, or inducing someone else to steal, another person's possessions of significant value. The measure of significant value in India equals the value of four hundred cowrie shells, or one quarter *karshapana*.[103] To steal an object equal in worth to that [would be the defeating offense]. In Tibet, an object is considered of significant value when it is worth one bushel of barley when there is no famine, or one-half bushel of barley in times of famine. Thus, what has significant value must be determined in the context of each individual country.

(3) *Murder* is to kill, or to induce another to kill, a human being or a foetus in the earliest [or later] stages of development in the womb[104] with a weapon, poison, mantra, or in other ways. [As for inducing another to kill,] the *Treasury of Phenomenology* states[105]:

> In war and similar circumstances, those who share the same
>   purpose
> Bear [the same responsibility] as the one who carries out the
>   action.

(4) *Telling lies about one's level of spiritual attainment*[106] (saying one has qualities superior to human attributes) is to falsely claim that one

has attained high or superior qualities not easily accomplished by a human being. Falsely claiming to be enlightened, to have clairvoyance, to have experienced signs of spiritual accomplishment, to have seen a deity, and other such examples would fall into this category. Vishakhadeva[107] clarifies the meaning of the words "superior to human attributes" (Tib. *mi'i chos bla ma*):

> According to this doctrine, the five types of impediments [to the
> three trainings]
> Are known as human attributes [*mi'i chos*]
> And their cessation is asserted as the superior quality [*bla ma*].[108]

The five impediments [to the three trainings]—longing for objects of desire, ill-will, sleep and drowsiness, excitement and remorse, and reservations [concerning the doctrine]—are the natural tendencies or attributes of ordinary persons.[109] The cessation of those tendencies is "superior" since as a result of their ending, the mental level of higher realms is attained.

A monk who has incurred any of these four offenses and has concealed the fact for even a single moment[110] entirely destroys his ordination. They are therefore known as root downfalls. No remedy can repair these violations and thus they are known as the four "defeats" or the class of defeating offenses.

Various details pertain to the downfalls discussed above and below: the circumstances [that determined the prescription of the rules], the negative effects [of incurring a downfall], the result, the attitude, the deed [transgression], its fulfillment, exceptions,[111] cases in which there is no downfall [even though one has transgressed the rule], the advice regarding them, etc. These details will not be elaborated upon in this work. Bright persons can study these details by referring to the works on this subject by the second buddha in this age of conflict, Butön [Rinchen Drup],[112] and the *Great Commentary on Discipline* by the Eighth [Karmapa, Mikyö Dorjé].[113] Beginners should refer to the *Commentary on the Three Vows* by the great translator Dharmashri,[114] or the *Three Vows* by the venerable Pema Karpo,[115] or that of the master Wönkarma.[116]

What should be noted here is that the presence or absence of four complementary aspects—basis, attitude, act, and consummation—determines whether or not a downfall is an actual defeat. In the case of sexual intercourse, for example, the basis [for the act] refers to any one of the three unimpaired orifices[117] and a healthy and functional male organ.[118] The attitude is lust devoid of any fear or shame. The act refers to [even] the slightest penetration. The consummation refers to the experience of orgasm. The defeating offense itself is incurred when all four aspects are present. The offense is a serious infraction[119] within the [category of] defeats if any one of the aspects is missing. In other words, defeating offenses may be major or minor depending on the number of complementary aspects accompanying the act.

The number of aspects must also be considered in cases of partial defeats and other offenses. If one aspect is missing in a partial defeat, the act is referred to as a serious violation within the [category of] partial defeats. For all other downfalls, if one aspect is not present, the act is a minor infraction.

Simply to have intended to pursue the desire [to commit an offense that would be a defeat] is a minor infraction to be restrained from in the future; in addition to the intention, to pursue the act short of consummation is a downfall of plotting. In the case of insanity, no downfall is incurred. The same applies to other kinds of downfalls. While many details are described [in other texts], those are the main points.

The Partially Defeating Offenses [2"]

> Ejaculation, touching, and speaking of sexual intercourse to a
>   woman, extolling reverence,
> Matchmaking, constructing a hut, or a large dwelling, ground-
>   less, or trivial accusation,
> Causing a schism, taking sides, causing a layperson to lose
>   faith, and defiance
> Constitute the class of partially defeating offenses.
> Any of these offenses is said to leave only a residue of the vows.

Thirteen offenses constitute the class of partial defeats of the monastic community:

> (1) *Ejaculation* means to emit semen through [contact with] a part of one's body such as the fingers, or a part of another person's body, with the exception of the three [orifices] of mouth, anus, or vagina.

(2) *Touching or holding* is to touch the bare skin of a woman[120] motivated by sexual desire.

(3) *Speaking of sexual intercourse* is to use lascivious language with a woman, with words that suggest sexual intercourse, etc., motivated by lust.[121]

(4) *Extolling reverence* means, motivated by sexual desire, to suggest to a woman in glorified terms that sexual intercourse would be a good way to revere oneself.

(5) *Matchmaking* means to cause a previously uninvolved man and woman to engage in sexual intercourse by carrying or having another carry a message between them three times.[122] [Vishakadeva's *Stanzas on the Discipline*] states[123]:

> The sword of the partial defeat
> Will cut off the head
> Of that monk who has united a man and a woman
> Or induced another to do so.

(6) *Constructing a hut* means to build on an improper site,[124] and for oneself, a house that exceeds the prescribed size. The [prescribed] hut must be large enough to stretch the arms when standing; to extend or draw in the arms and legs when sleeping; to take three strides in each direction when moving around, and to easily assume the cross-legged posture. It must not, however, exceed the [prescribed] size of eighteen cubits[125] in length and ten and a half cubits in width.

(7) *Constructing a large dwelling* means to construct on an improper site, and with improper materials,[126] a large house for four monks or more.

(8) *Groundless accusation* means to defame a fellow monk without any of the three [grounds for accusation] of having seen, heard about, or having suspected that he has incurred a defeating offense.[127]

(9) *Accusation for a trivial reason* means to falsely accuse a fellow monk of having committed a defeating offense, justifying this on the basis of a trivial event.[128]

(10) *Causing a schism* means to persist in causing a division in the order, not desisting even though other monks have admonished one three times.[129]

(11) *Taking sides* refers to supporting a fellow monk who is trying to create a schism in the order, not desisting although admonished three times.

(12) *Causing a layperson to lose faith* means to defame the fellow monks who have expelled one [from the boundaries of the monastery] because one's depraved conduct[130] has subverted a lay devotee's faith in the order, and not desisting even though admonished three times.

(13) *Defiance* means not to accept the allegation made by fellow monks when one has incurred a downfall, and persistently refusing to acknowledge [and amend] it in spite of the [triple] admonishments of the monastic community.

These thirteen are called "the class of partial defeats of the monastic community," "of the monastic community" since amendment depends on the community and "partial" [or with remainder] because some trace of the vows' purity remains.[131]

The *Summary [of Discipline]*[132] mentions two undetermined offenses that may occur when a monk lures a woman

> ...into a secluded, sheltered place.

A secluded place refers to a situation where there are no other conscientious friends[133] and that is a sheltered place providing concealment. (1) If this is a convenient place for sexual intercourse, a monk might commit one of three [types of offenses]—a defeat, a partial defeat, or a downfall [requiring confession alone]. (2) If it is not suitable for sexual intercourse, he might commit one of two [types of offenses]—a partial defeat or a downfall [requiring confession alone].[134] These offenses are "undetermined" in the sense that it is uncertain which offense will occur or what will be the outcome.

The Downfalls that Require Forfeiture or Confession Alone [3"]

This section has two parts: (1) downfalls that require forfeiture, and (2) downfalls that require confession alone.

Downfalls that Require Forfeiture [a"]
Downfalls that require forfeiture consist of three sets of ten.

The First Set of Ten [i"]

> **Keeping, being without, retaining cloth, or inducing a nun to**
> **wash robes, accepting, and requesting cloth,**
> **Asking for cloth of a greater measure or value from two donors,**
> **and excessive insistence**

> (1) *Keeping extra cloth* means to keep for more than ten days an
> unconsecrated piece of cloth that is owned by oneself, mea-
> sures one cubit or more, and is not intended for one's robes.
> (2) *Being without* is to be separated from the three robes for more
> than a day.[135]
> (3) *Retaining [cloth] for a month* is to keep a piece of cloth in order
> to make one of the three robes that one is lacking, which is
> between one cubit long and the size sufficient to cover the
> three areas,[136] and which remains unconsecrated for more than
> one month. (The three areas refer to the waist and the two
> areas around the knees.)

The first downfall of keeping unconsecrated cloth for more than
ten days occurs at sunrise on the eleventh day. The same downfall is
accrued by vitiation if one receives a second piece of cloth subsequent
to the first, even though one has [kept] the second piece less than ten
days. Further, if one obtains a stitched monastic robe after first acquiring a piece of cloth [as described in] the downfall of "retaining
for a month," at sunrise on the eleventh day one incurs the downfall
of "keeping [extra cloth] for ten days." Downfalls by vitiation occur
in relation not only to cloth but also to the begging bowl and food.

Concerning the second downfall, to determine whether or not a
monk has incurred the downfall of being without robes, different factors such as boundary, dispensation, and consecration[137] must be taken
into consideration. One should refer to other books [for more infor-
mation] on this point.

> (4) *Having one's robes washed* is to ask a nun who is not a relative
> to wash one's robes. Here, "relative" includes one's kin up
> to seven times removed on either one's mother's or father's
> side.

(5) *Accepting cloth* is to accept cloth sufficient to cover the three areas, when one already has the three robes, from a nun who is not a relative.

(6) *Requesting* is to request cloth as just described from a layperson who is not a relative.

(7) *Requesting more than the permissible* means to request more cloth than the measure [required for] one set of the upper and lower robes, when one lacks the three monastic robes, from a layperson who is not a relative.

(8) *Requesting finer* means to request from a layperson who is not a relative [robe material of] a fine quality, more valuable than that which the layperson had intended to offer.

(9) *Requesting finer quality than two donors have prepared to offer* differs [from the previous downfall] only in that it concerns [robe material] offered by male or female donors separately, [rather than] a common offering from a household.

(10) *Insistence* means to accept a robe after one has insistently asked for it more than three times, and [when undelivered] has made oneself obvious more than three times to the caretaker of the community who has been given [by a patron] precious items [such as gold or silver] to purchase the cloth.[138]

The Second Set of Ten [ii"]

To make a mat with silk, black wool, or more than half black
    wool, making a new one before six years,
Not adding to it a handspan's patch, carrying, and spinning
    wool, handling gold or silver,
Usury, trading

(1) *A silk mat* is to make[139] for oneself a mat out of a valuable material such as silk of at least the measure that covers the three areas.

(2) *A black wool mat* is to make a mat out of only black [sheep's] wool measuring as above.

(3) *A mixture with more than half black wool* is to make a mat [of white and black wool] containing more than half black wool.

(4) *Six years* is to make a new mat while the old one has not been used for [the prescribed period of] six years.

(5) *A handspan* is to use a new mat that has not been sewn with a patch from the old one the length of the Joyful One's handspan.[140]

(6) *Carrying wool on the road* is to walk more than an earshot[141] within a single day while carrying a great load such as wool, motivated by acquisitiveness.

(7) *Having wool washed* is to have a nun who is not a relative wash, spin, or dye wool.

(8) *Handling what is precious* is to handle or induce [another person] to handle gold or other precious substances [that are one's property but] unconsecrated[142] and to consider these as one's own, motivated by acquisitiveness.

(9) *Usury* is to lend gold or other commodities to make a profit or gain interest to a layperson who is not a relative, motivated by acquisitiveness.

(10) *Trading* means to buy and sell [to a layman] other non-precious items such as grain in order to make a profit. In the last two rules, the actual downfall is accrued only if a profit is realized.

The Third Set of Ten [iii"]

...keeping an unconsecrated begging bowl, or requesting an
    extra one, engaging a weaver, improving the weave,
Taking back gifts, using rainy season retreat offerings, being
    separated from the robes, keeping the large rain cloak too long,
Redirecting dedicated offerings, and storing food constitute the
    class of downfalls that require forfeiture.

Two downfalls concern the begging bowl:

(1) *Keeping a begging bowl* is to keep an unconsecrated begging bowl for more than ten days.

(2) *Requesting an extra begging bowl* is to ask for and obtain a begging bowl from a layperson who is not a relative, when one already has an appropriate begging bowl.

Two downfalls concern weavers:

(3) *Engaging a weaver* is to have a weaver who is not a relative make cloth for one's robes without payment or remuneration.

(4) *Improving the weave* means to engage a weaver to make finer and more valuable cloth for one's robes without the consent of the patron who has already agreed to give one a particular quality of robe and has already paid for that.

(5) *Taking back gifts* is to take back an article [such as a robe, begging bowl, etc.] one has given to a fellow monk.

(6) *Using rainy season retreat offerings* means to use the offerings donated by a patron [to be distributed at the conclusion of the retreat] before the retreat ends.

(7) *To be separated from the robes while in seclusion* means to be apart from one's robes for more than seven days when one is living in seclusion.

(8) *Keeping the large rain cloak for too long* is to request and to keep the large rain cloak for more than one month before entering the rainy season retreat or for more than half a month after the conclusion [of that retreat].

(9) *To redirect dedicated offerings* is to take possession of any article that [a donor] has already intended to donate to the monastic community or another monk.

(10) *Storing* is to keep any of the three foods and medicines[143] beyond the prescribed time.

These are referred to as the "thirty downfalls that require forfeiture" because one day before the formal confession of the downfall, the article that is the basis for downfall must be relinquished[144] along with any other requisite articles one has acquired subsequently. Requisite articles acquired subsequently must also be relinquished because a downfall with respect to the latter articles is accrued by vitiation by the former.

Downfalls That Require Confession Alone [b"]
This class of downfalls consists of nine sets of ten.

The First Set of Ten [i"]

Lying, criticizing, slandering, reviving quarrels, teaching a woman,
Reciting the scriptures, revealing lapses, telling the truth,
accusing a steward, reviling the discipline

(1) *Lying* means to consciously tell a lie of a type that would not be classified as a defeat, partial defeat, serious violation, or minor infraction.[145]

(2) *Criticizing* means to speak of the faults of a fellow monk such as his being from a bad family lineage or not having all his faculties intact.

(3) *Slandering* is to calumniate [two or more] fellow monks with the intention to cause discord among them.

(4) *Reviving quarrels* is to rekindle a dispute among monks that had already been settled.

(5) *Teaching a woman* is to teach more than five or six words of the doctrine [from scriptures or commentaries] to a laywoman in private.

(6) *Reciting the scriptures* means to chant verses from the scriptures out of vanity and in a variety of melodies, with someone who is not a monk.

(7) *Revealing lapses in discipline* is to divulge to [a layperson and others] who are not fully ordained that a fellow monk has committed a defeating or partially defeating offense, when one has not been appointed to bring forth the allegation [in the appropriate ceremony].

(8) *Telling the truth about one's level of spiritual attainment* is to declare that one has developed superhuman powers to someone who is not a monk, without a specific necessity.

(9) *Accusing a steward of favoritism* means to falsely accuse of favoritism a monk steward because one is jealous that he has given a worthy monk an article that was the common property of the community.

(10) *Reviling* is to scorn [the monastic discipline] by [saying to a fellow monk, for instance]: "What is the use of these minor rules of discipline?"

The Second Set of Ten [ii"]

...destroying vegetation, censuring the caretaker,
Refusing to comply, leaving the bed outside or grass under the mat, driving out or harassing a monk, poking holes, casting water, laying bricks

(1) *Destroying vegetation* is to cut grass or trees, or to ruin any kind of seed [by touching them] with fire or in other ways, unless they are consecrated.[146]

(2) *Censuring the caretaker* means to censure directly or indirectly through devious slander an honest caretaker of the community.

(3) *Refusing to comply* is to deny the allegation of a downfall that has been presented by a fellow monk so that one can amend it, but to [attempt to] dissuade [one's fellow monks] in various ways.

(4) *Leaving the bed outside* is to leave the communal bedding or seats that one has used where sun, wind, rain, etc. can spoil them.

(5) *Grass under the mat* is to leave the temple without clearing up the grass and leaves that one has spread under the mat.

(6) *Driving out* is to evict another monk from the residence of the community out of anger.

(7) *Harassment by a new monk* means to physically or verbally injure a fellow monk who had taken up residence in the monastery earlier than oneself or to impose upon his space [lit. "crush him under" or "press on him physically"].

(8) *Poking holes* or *making a dent* means to make holes or dents on the soft roof of the monastery by sitting down heavily upon a chair with pointed legs.

(9) *Casting water* means to use water, grass, etc., or to throw water on grass or vice versa, etc., [even] in the interest of others, knowing that they contain living beings.

(10) *Laying bricks* is to lay more than three layers of [unbaked] bricks in one day [when constructing] a monastic building on unstable foundations or without taking precautions to prevent damage in the rainy season.

The Third Set of Ten [iii"]

> Teaching a nun doctrine when not appointed, or after sunset; accusing of teaching for gain; giving to, or making a robe for a nun;
> Walking with or going in a boat with a nun, sitting or standing with a woman, persuading someone to prepare food

(1) *Teaching the doctrine to a nun* is to instruct a nun when one has not been appointed as a nuns' teacher by the community.[147]

(2) *Teaching the doctrine after sunset* is to instruct a nun after sunset in a frightening place, even if one [has been appointed] a nuns' teacher.

(3) *Accusing a monk of teaching to get a little food* means, in a jealous frame of mind, to defame a monk who has been appointed to instruct a nun by insinuating that he teaches for the sake of gaining food, drink, etc.

(4) *Giving a robe* means to give a robe to a nun who is not a relative.

(5) *Making robes* is to have a robe made for a nun who is not a relative.

(6) *Walking together on the road* is to accompany one nun [or more] on the road for more than an earshot.

(7) *Going with a nun in a boat* means to go with a nun in a boat for more than an earshot upstream or downstream.

(8) *Sitting in a secluded and sheltered place* means to sit in a secluded and sheltered place together with an [unaccompanied] woman who is not a relative.

(9) *Standing in a secluded and sheltered place* means to stand in a secluded and sheltered place with a woman who is not a relative.[148]

(10) *Persuading someone to prepare food* means to induce a householder to prepare one's food and beverage through the intermediary of a nun who is not one's relative.

The Fourth Set of Ten [iv"]

**Eating consecutively, or while staying with non-Buddhists,
taking excess, resuming eating, giving leftover food to a monk,
Gathering to eat, eating at inappropriate times, eating stored
foods, foods not given, and good foods**

(1) *Eating consecutively* means to accept alms of food (to be eaten before noon) two or three times in one day from householders who are not one's relatives.

(2) *Eating [while staying with non-Buddhists]* means to stay more than one day at the home of a householder [who is not a relative and who hosts] non-Buddhist renunciates and [on the second day] to accept food from him.

(3) *Taking excess* is to receive more than three [small] begging bowls [of food] at the home of a layperson who is not a relative.[149]

(4) *Resuming eating* is to resume eating an offered and accepted meal after thinking and saying, "I have finished," unless the leftover food has been made permissible [through a ritual].[150] *Standing up after having started*, which means to stand up before the end of the meal [and then to eat the leftovers later], is also comprised by this downfall.[151]

(5) *Giving food to a monk who has finished eating* means to invite a monk who has finished eating to partake of food, saying that the food is "leftover" [i.e., made permissible through a ritual] when in fact it is not. In this case, the downfall is accrued by the monk who gives the food.

(6) *Gathering to eat* is to partake of a meal with [three or more] fellow monks within the same boundary but in a place other than [the communal dining hall], when this action is due to disharmony.

(7) *Eating at inappropriate times* means to partake in the afternoon of foods that are permissible only from dawn to noon.

(8) *Partaking of what has been stored* is to eat any of the three [types of] foods and medicines that remain from previous use or after storing them beyond the permitted time.

(9) *Eating what has not been offered and accepted* is to consume any of the four types of foods and medicines that have not been offered and accepted.[152]

(10) *Asking for good food* means to ask a householder who is not a relative for good foods[153] and to enjoy them freely without the host's invitation to do so, motivated by greed.

The Fifth Set of Ten [v"]

> Using water that contains life, sitting or standing at a place of
>   sexual intercourse, serving food to a naked ascetic,
> Watching, or staying in an army camp, inciting preparations,
>   striking, threatening to strike, concealing a lapse

(1) *Using water that contains life* means to use (wash in, drink, etc.) for one's own purposes water, grass, or wood containing living beings.[154]

(2) *Sitting in the home of those engaging in intercourse* means to sit where a layman and laywoman are engaged in sexual intercourse and to disturb them [with one's presence].

(3) *Standing in the home of those engaging in intercourse* means the same as above except for standing instead of sitting.

(4) *Serving food to a naked ascetic* means to give food to a male or female adherent of another religion when there is no special necessity.[155]

(5) *Watching an army* is to observe an army in a place that is beyond the vicinity of the monastery's boundary.

(6) *Staying in an army camp* is to stay for more than one day [and night] in an army camp, without special necessity [for example, being invited by a king].

(7) *Inciting war preparations* is to handle and prepare weapons, or to incite an army's divisions to take up their strategic positions, without special reason.

(8) *Striking* is to strike a fellow monk or induce another to strike him.

(9) *Threatening to strike* is to prepare to strike a fellow monk.

(10) *Concealing a lapse of discipline* is to consciously conceal, without special necessity, that a fellow monk has incurred a defeating or partially defeating offense.

The Sixth Set of Ten [vi"]

Preventing alms from being given, lighting a fire, withdrawing one's assent, sleeping with the non-ordained, not giving up erroneous views,
Siding with or befriending the expelled, wearing undyed clothes, handling treasures, bathing frequently

(1) *Preventing alms* is to stop [directly or indirectly] a patron from giving food to be eaten before noon to a fellow monk, due to enmity.

(2) *Lighting a fire* is to make a fire unless one has consecrated the occasion or one is ill. In addition, to touch fire embers is a minor infraction, to place firewood on a fire is an actual downfall, and to put hair, etc., [onto a fire] is a minor infraction. To consecrate the occasion,[156] the monk [simply] recollects that the Buddha gave permission to light a fire to perform

religious duties in the interest of the community as a whole, such as [the preparation of colors for] the painting of statues of deities. The scriptures on discipline speak of eleven types of consecration:

> Consecration of robes, begging bowl, precious articles,
> Downfalls,[157] confession, rainy season retreat,
> Lifting of restrictions, medicine, kitchen,
> Donations, and occasions.

(3) *Withdrawing assent* is to have given one's assent to a formal procedure of the monastic community so that no disagreement would arise, and subsequently [after the completion of the formal procedure] to withdraw it.[158]

(4) *Sleeping extra nights with the non-ordained* means to sleep more than two nights in the same room with someone who is not fully ordained.[159]

(5) *Not giving up erroneous views* is to not abandon the erroneous views of disbelieving [the discipline] taught by the Buddha,[160] even after one has been admonished by the members of the community.

(6) *Befriending an expelled monk* is to share [spiritual instructions and material things[161]] with a monk who has been expelled from the monastery.

(7) *Befriending an expelled novice* is as in the former with the difference that this concerns a novice instead of a monk.

(8) *Wearing undyed clothing* is to wear, uncovered, clothing measuring a cubit or more that has not been dyed with one of the three prescribed colors.[162]

(9) *Handling treasures or other precious articles that may cause pride* is to touch with vanity treasures that do not belong to oneself. This includes pearls and other precious gems, items that are considered precious such as conch and drum and other musical instruments, as well as weapons. The downfall is accrued by the simple act of handling treasures even if one does not have the intention to possess them. Wearing ornaments and perfumes, singing, or playing musical instruments in a proud frame of mind are also comprised by this downfall.

(10) *Bathing frequently* is to bathe[163] more than once a fortnight, unless one is ill or during the three months of the hot season.

The Seventh Set of Ten [vii"]

> Killing an animal, causing regret, tickling, playing in water,
> sleeping in the same place as a woman,
> Frightening, hiding, or using without permission the belong-
> ings of fellow monks, defaming a monk, accompanying a
> woman

(1) *Killing an animal* is to intentionally kill any animal, large or small.
(2) *Causing regret* is to sadden a fellow monk by denigrating the benefits of entering the monastic life or by saying that he has not received vows [i.e., he is not actually a monk].
(3) *Tickling* is to tickle a fellow monk with the intention of provoking a reaction.
(4) *Playing in water* is to sport in water frivolously.
(5) *Sleeping in the same place as a woman* is to sleep one night in the same room with a woman [without the presence of a conscientious companion].
(6) *Frightening* is to frighten a fellow monk in various ways out of scorn.
(7) *Hiding* is to hide any of the articles of a fellow monk, such as his robes or begging bowl, out of scorn.
(8) *Using without permission* means to use without his consent a robe [or other monastic article] that one has passed on [for good] to a fellow monk or the robe of a monk with whom one does not share things.
(9) *Defaming* is to intentionally accuse a monk of having committed a partially defeating offense without having seen, heard, or had reason to suspect [that this is the case].
(10) *Accompanying a woman on the road* is to walk with a woman farther than one earshot along a road. As in the case of sleeping in the same room as a woman, a downfall is not accrued if a conscientious companion is present.

The Eighth Set of Ten [viii"]

> Traveling with a thief, conferring full ordination to one under
> age, tilling the soil, overstaying one's welcome,
> Rejecting advice, eavesdropping, leaving without informing,
> being disrespectful, drinking alcohol, going at the inappro-
> priate time

(1) *Traveling with a thief* is to travel more than an earshot with a thief or tax evader as one's companion.

(2) *Conferring full ordination on someone under the age of twenty* is [for an ordaining preceptor] to give higher ordination while knowing [or suspecting] that the aspirant is under the [requisite] age of twenty years from the time of conception.

(3) *Tilling the soil* is to turn up even as much as a handful [four fingers' full] of hard-packed earth, without any special necessity.

(4) *Overstaying one's welcome* means to enjoy [meals] offered by a patron while staying at his house for more days than he indicated, or for more than four months if he has not specified a time limit.

(5) *Rejecting advice* is to regard with disdain advice concerning the monastic discipline given by another monk.

(6) *Eavesdropping* is to listen in secret to the conversations of fellow monks with whom one has a dispute with the intention to increase it.

(7) *Leaving without informing* means to leave one's place during a formal procedure of the community (such as a confession) without informing [or giving one's assent to] one's fellow monks.

(8) *Disrespect* means to disrespectfully refuse to perform a religious duty for which one has been appointed by the monastic community, without politely giving a reason for refusal.

(9) *Drinking alcohol* is to take any kind of intoxicant leading to negligent behavior that could cause others to lose faith [in the doctrine or the order].[164]

(10) *Going to town at the inappropriate time* is to visit the home of a layperson who is not a relative and stay from the afternoon of one day until dawn of the following day [without informing any member of the ordained community].

The Ninth Set of Ten [ix"]

> Wandering into the village, making a visit at night, showing disdain for the rules,
> Accepting a fine needlecase, making a seat with legs, covering a mat with cotton, exceeding the sizes for the mat, the robe for skin rash, the large rain cloak, and the robes
> Constitute the class of downfalls that require confession alone.

(1) *Wandering into the village* means to go to the village and to not return before the mealtime of the community.[165]

(2) *Visiting the royal apartment in the night* means to spend the night in the royal palace [knowing] that the queens are present.

(3) *Showing disdain* means purposefully to disparage the rules of discipline as they are being recited in the *Personal Liberation Discourse* during confession.

(4) *Accepting a needlecase* is to have a layperson who is not a relative make for oneself a needlecase of fine materials.

(5) *Making a seat with legs* is to make a seat [for the monastic community] with legs higher than a cubit.

(6) *Covering the mat with cotton* is to intentionally cover the seats [of the monastic community] with cotton.[166]

(7) *Exceeding the size for the mat* is to use a mat that exceeds the prescribed length or width.

(8-10) *Exceeding the size for the flannel [to relieve] skin rash, exceeding the size for the large rain cloak,* and *exceeding the size for the robes* are self-explanatory.

This class of "downfalls that require confession alone" are called "downfalls" (Tib. *ltung byed*, lit. "leading to downfalls") since these offenses may lead to [rebirth in] lower realms and "[that require confession] alone" (*'ba' zhig pa*) because purification of these downfalls does not require forfeiture, but only confession.

Offenses That Must Be Individually Confessed [4"]

> **Accepting a nun's alms, accepting food served without regard to seniority,**
> **Transgressing the rule not to beg at a household, and eating without checking the forest**
> **Constitute the class of offenses to be individually confessed.**

(1) *Accepting a nun's alms* means to request from a nun who is not a relative the food she has begged for herself [wherever one has met her,] in the village, [near a village, or on the road].

(2) *Accepting food served without regard to seniority* means to accept food at a meal offered by a householder to three or more monks, without correcting the nun in charge of serving, by

saying, "Please serve the food first to the elder monks," when, disregarding the order of seniority, she distributes the food first to the younger monks.

(3) *Transgressing the rule not to beg at a household* is explained in this way: When a patron has become destitute of food and wealth, a rule [not to beg from him] should be instituted [by the monastic community] through formal procedure. Once instituted, monks should not beg for more than, say, a few vegetables from that person. If one begs [for more], this downfall has been committed. Subsequently, [when the patron is no longer destitute,] lifting of this rule is to be done through a ceremony.

(4) *Eating without checking the safety of the forest* means to eat in a secluded and precarious place away from the monastery without having verified its safety, when one has been appointed to do so by the monastic community.[167]

These are called "offenses to be individually confessed" because at the time of purifying the downfall, the monk must confess each of them while showing regret.

Minor Infractions [5"]
This class consists of one hundred and twelve minor infractions:

> **The one hundred and twelve minor infractions**
> **Concern the wearing of robes, decorum,**
> **Sitting, receiving food, manner of eating,**
> **Begging bowl, teaching the doctrine, behavior,**
> **And climbing. Thus, a monk must observe**
> **A total of two hundred and fifty-three rules.**

To facilitate recitation, the rules dealing with minor infractions are here set forth in easily understood verses:

> Ten rules concern the *wearing of robes*:
> (1) Wear the lower robe evenly, not high in one place or low in another.
> Never wear it untidily in any of the following ways:
> (2) Raised up so that it is too high, or (3) trailing so that it is too low,

(4) The bottom edge hanging to one side like an elephant's trunk,

(5) Folding the top like a palm leaf,

(6) Gathered unevenly at the belt like [tying] a sack of grain, or (7) hanging over the top of the belt like a cobra's hood. The upper robes should also be worn (8) even all around,

(9) Not too low or (10) high.

Twenty rules concern *decorum while traveling:*

(1) Control body and speech with mindfulness.

(2) Dress with dignity; (3) limit idle chatter.

(4) Keep eyes from wandering; (5) gaze just a yoke's length ahead.

(6) Don't cover the head; (7) don't hoist the lower robe.

(8) Don't drape the upper robe over both shoulders.

(9) Don't walk with the hands clasping the nape of the neck, or (10) clasped behind the head.

(11) Don't go about jumping, or (12) strutting, or (13) walking only on the heels or (14) on tiptoes.

(15) Don't walk with the hands on hips, elbows extended.

(16) Don't walk with the body bent; (17) don't swing [or wave] the arms while walking.

(18) Don't walk wagging the head, or (19) touching shoulders with others.

(20) Don't walk around holding another's hand.

Nine rules concern *sitting:*

(1) [Don't sit] before the patron or host has invited one to sit.

(2) Don't sit without checking whether or not there are living beings on the seat.

(3) Don't sit down heavily; (4) do not sit with the legs stretched out and the feet crossed,

(5) Don't sit with thighs crossed,

(6) Or with one ankle on top of the other,

(7) Tucking the legs under the seat, (8) with legs outspread,

(9) Sitting with the private parts exposed.
   As ancillary [rules], do not rest cheek in hand,
   Or walk while carrying a mat on the back.

Eight rules concern *receiving food:*

(1) Don't fill to the brim the begging bowl.

(2) Take equal amounts of rice and vegetables.

(3) Accept [food] only if served in the order of seniority.

(4) When accepting food, pay attention to the begging bowl.

(5) Don't hold out the begging bowl before food is offered.

(6) Don't cover [the vegetables] with rice when wanting [more] vegetables,

(7) Or [the rice] with vegetables when wanting more rice.

(8) Do not hold the begging bowl higher than the serving dishes.

Twenty-one rules concern the *manner of eating*:

(1) Don't eat food with poor manners.

(2) Don't eat very large or (3) very small mouthfuls.

(4) Eat in moderation, according to etiquette.

(5) Don't open the mouth before bringing food to it.

(6) Don't speak with the mouth full.

(7) Don't eat making *blah blah* sounds when food is not tasty,

(8) *Yum yum* when tasty, (9) *brr brr* when cold, (10) *phff phff* when hot.

(11) Don't poke out the tongue while eating.

(12) Don't eat rice, etc., a grain at a time.

(13) Don't criticize [the quality of] the food, or (14) chew the food on the right and then the left cheek,

(15) Don't make a smacking sound against the palate, or (16) bite off part of a mouthful of food,

(17) Don't lick food off the hands after wiping the begging bowl, or (18) lick food from the begging bowl.

(19) Don't shake off food that is stuck to the hand.

(20) Don't shake the begging bowl while eating,

(21) Or make the food into the shape of a stupa.

Fourteen rules concern the *use of the begging bowl*:

(1) Don't scorn the begging bowl of another monk.

(2) Don't touch the water container with food stuck to the hands.

(3) Don't toss dishwater at another monk.

(4) Don't throw dishwater into the grounds of a household [without permission].

(5) Don't put leftover food into the begging bowl.

(6) Don't put down the begging bowl on bare earth without a support beneath it, or

(7) [At the edge of] a ravine, or (8) a crevice, or (9) near a slope or steps;

Don't wash the begging bowl in three locations:
(10) [At the edge of] a ravine, or (11) a crevice, or (12) near a slope or steps, or (13) while standing.
(14) Don't scoop water by holding the begging bowl against the current of the river.

Twenty-six rules concern *teaching the doctrine:*
(1) Do not teach standing up to a person who is seated as though sick.
(2) Similarly, do not teach [sitting] to someone lying down, or
(3) A person seated on a high or rich seat.
(4) Do not teach someone when walking behind him, (5) or someone walking in the center [of the road] when you are on the side.
(6) [Do not teach] those with covered heads, (7) clothes hoisted up, or (8) their upper robes draped over both shoulders,
(9) Those with arms crossed holding the neck,
(10) Or hands clasped behind,
(11) Those wearing topknots, (12) hats, or (13) crowns,
(14) Those wearing flower garlands, or (15) silk veils,
(16) Those mounted on elephants, or (17) horses, or (18) those riding in a palanquin, or (19) a vehicle,
(20) Those wearing shoes, (21) those holding staffs, or (22) umbrellas,
(23) Those holding weapons, (24) swords, (25) bows and arrows, or (26) those wearing armor.

Three rules concern *proper behavior:*
(1) Do not defecate or urinate while standing; (2) do not throw feces or urine into water or onto grass;
(3) Don't spit or clean the nose, vomit [or discharge mucus] into water, unless ill.

One rule concerns *moving:*
(1) Don't climb trees taller than a man, unless in danger.

If one transgresses any of these rules, one commits an infraction. Conforming to the proper conduct is all that is required to correct the wrongdoing; thus, they are called minor infractions.

To enhance the laity's appreciation [of the monastic community], when going to the home of a layperson, a monk should keep these rules in mind; his robes should be dignified, and his conduct peaceful and disciplined. Having taken his place, he should sit in a contemplative posture and partake politely of the food and drink. Then, maintaining mindfulness, he should speak of the doctrine in a way appropriate to the occasion.

Thus, the disciplinary code of a monk is made up of a total of two hundred and fifty-three rules that prohibit the five classes of downfalls. These downfalls fall into two categories: naturally unwholesome and unwholesome because of prescription. "Naturally unwholesome" refers to murder and similar acts that would be negative if committed by anyone (laypersons or renunciates). "Unwholesome because of prescription" refers to eating after noon, etc.—[acts] that would not be negative for laypersons but are prohibited for renunciates. Any transgression of the above-mentioned rules is a downfall because by transgressing it, one may be reborn in the lower realms.

The Rules of the Nun [ii']

The nun must observe three hundred and sixty-four rules.

The nun must observe three hundred and sixty-four rules: not to commit the eight defeating offenses that constitute root downfalls,[168] twenty partially defeating acts, thirty-three downfalls involving forfeiture, one hundred and eighty downfalls requiring confession alone, eleven downfalls to be individually confessed, and one hundred and twelve minor infractions. However, since the nun's ethical conduct is not observed in Tibet at the present time, [the subject] will not be discussed here. One wishing to know more [on this subject] should refer to texts [on monastic discipline].[169]

Prohibitions concern that which is incompatible with ethical conduct.

All the above prohibitions concern acts incompatible with ethical conduct. Therefore, one should know what these offenses are and avoid doing them.

Training in the Prescribed Discipline [b']

The scriptures [on discipline] state:

> The entire [monastic disciplinary code] is contained within [seventeen] bases:
> (1) Ordination, (2) confession,

(3) The lifting of restrictions, (4) the rainy season [retreat], and
(5) [rules concerning] the use of leather articles,
(6) Food and medicines, (7) robes, (8) the making and distribution [of the robes],
(9) *Koshambi* (legal procedures in case of disagreements over
formal procedures[170]), (10) formal procedures,
(11) The *Pandulohitaka* (for amending downfalls through
subjugation),[171] (12) [factors concerning] the individual,[172]
(13) Demotion,[173] (14) suspension from confession,[174]
(15) [Rules concerning] monastery sites and monks' quarters,
(16) procedures [for settling] disputes, and (17) procedures [to
resolve] schisms in the community.[175]

The [Sanskrit] word *vastu* (basis) denotes that which provides support for the three trainings [of ethics, meditation, and wisdom].

The first [basis, ordination,] has been presented above. The other
sixteen can be subsumed under five [major bases] of monastic discipline: (1) [confession, rainy season retreat, and lifting of the restrictions
form] the basis for the refinement of the training, (2) [making and distribution of the robes, regulations for robes, the use of leather articles,
and food and medicines form] the basis of the conditions for living
comfortably, (3) the various sorts of ceremonies [form] the basis of
formal procedures, (4) [*Koshambi, Pandulohitaka,* factors concerning the
individual, demotion, suspension, settling disputes, and ways to resolve schisms form] the basis of amendment (purification of failings),
and (5) monastery sites and monks' quarters and the ancillary advice to
abandon two extreme [lifestyles form one] basis.[176]

Refinement of the Training [i']

This section has two parts: (1) a brief presentation, and (2) an extensive explanation.

Brief Presentation [aa']

**The first basis for monastic discipline consists of three methods
for refinement of the training.**

The first of the five major bases consists of the threefold basis for
refining monastic training.

Extensive Explanation [bb']

The extensive explanation is presented under three headings: (1) confession, (2) the rainy season retreat, and (3) lifting of restrictions.

Confession [1"]

> The purification-renewal to develop mental quiescence perfects
> meditation and wisdom.
> Confession to foster harmony should be performed
> Every half month, to increase prosperity, to eliminate misfor-
> tune, and to settle disputes.

Confession (lit. "purification-renewal,") [whose nature is] to regen-
erate the spirit of the three trainings and to purify downfalls, is of
two kinds: (1) purification-renewal to develop mental quiescence, and
(2) confession to foster harmony.

Purification-Renewal to Develop Mental Quiescence [a"]
Purification-renewal to develop mental quiescence [embraces all
stages of practice on the path to liberation]. To accomplish such "renewal," a monk should be of pure morality and have a contented
mind with few desires, the exalted potential for freedom from attachment. He must first learn and reflect upon the collections of scripture, thereby establishing the conditions for entering the path. Then,
having built a meditation hut and appointed a helper,[177] he engages
in the practice to develop mental quiescence,[178] applying the nine
methods of setting the mind.[179] [Once that stage is attained,] the monk
cultivates the discriminating awareness of insight[180] by exercising the
four mindfulnesses[181] and other meditations, [gradually] traversing
the five paths[182] by means of the thirty-seven factors of awakening,[183]
to attain the four kinds of result.[184]

Confession to Foster Harmony [b"]
The *One Hundred Formal Procedures*[185] states:

> Confession to foster harmony[186] consists of five types:
>> (1) confession on the fourteenth [day of the lunar month],
>> (2) confession on the fifteenth,
>> (3) confession to increase prosperity,
>> (4) confession to eliminate misfortune,
>> (5) confession to unify the community.

The great translator Dharmashri[187] states that the first of the five confessions is performed on the following dates:

> On the fourteenth day of the waning moon,
> Of the eleventh, first, third, fifth, seventh,
> And ninth months of the Mongolian calendar.[188]

Concerning the second, confession on the fifteenth day of the month:

> Know [that confession should be performed]
> On the fifteenth day of both the waxing and waning moon;
> Whatever else is stated is erroneous.

To explain, Tsonapa, Jadul,[189] and others consider the beginning of the calendar year to be the first day of the waning moon of the first month of winter (equivalent to the tenth month of the Mongolian calendar) [October-November]. Therefore, they assert that the first confession of the year is held one and a half months later (in the waning moon of the eleventh month of the Mongolian calendar), on the fourteenth of the month of the constellation Pushya.

Butön and others consider the sixteenth of the ninth month of the Mongolian calendar [September-October, as the beginning of the calendar year] and the earlier Tibetan masters such as Chim,[190] the sixteenth of the eighth month [August-September]; the sixth Shamar[191] agrees with Butön. However calculated, "the confessions to be performed on specific days" are to be done on the six fourteenth days, and the eighteen fifteenth days [of the lunar calendar—the days of the full and new moon].

The setting for the confession should be within a boundary defined [with signs in the four directions], the large or small,[192] in a natural place such as a cave, a man-made construction such as a house, or a natural phenomenon such as the shade of a tree. The participants of the confession may be any of the five types of renunciate.

The preparation for the ceremony of confession[193] begins with the monks [examining whether or not they have incurred any downfalls since the last confession; if so,] they confess, promise to restrain from such acts in the future, and "consecrate" the downfalls [in front of a worthy monk].[194]

The monastic community is summoned by [the sound of striking] a *gandi* wood of the right dimensions.[195] [Once the monks are gathered,] the three-part customary rite [of making prostrations, recitation of the Buddha's discourses, and dedication of merits] is performed, and the scripture that praises ethical conduct[196] is recited if it is not possible to propound the doctrine.

[Next are three indispensable preparations:] (1) To purify their minds, the monks [recollect their downfalls in the midst of the assembly and thus are consecrated through a proposal by the ceremonial master]; (2) agreement [on the place for confession or on the boundary is reached through a twofold procedure including proposal];

and (3) for the sake of the community's harmony and so that for those monks unable to attend the ceremony due to sickness and so forth confession may still take place, the elder praises the *Personal Liberation Scripture*,[197] [announces the date for the confession ceremony, and gives advice, while the disciplinarian reports the assent to the ceremony given by those unable to attend.]

During the main part [of the ceremony of confession], an elder recites the *Personal Liberation Scripture*. The ceremony is concluded by the dedication [of merit] and [prayers of] aspiration.

If there are no more than three fully ordained monks in that place, each performs the consecration [of the downfalls] in turn, one in front of the others. If one is alone, one confesses verbally and mentally. At the very least, one should recite the three and a half lines of verse[198] that was the original confession formula [spoken by] the Buddha.

The elder who recites [the *Personal Liberation Scripture*] must be duly qualified. A monk who has been a full member of the order in good standing for more than twenty years is called a regent-like elder. One who has been a full member of the order in good standing for twenty years is a lion-like elder. [Both of these] should be well-versed in the scriptures on discipline and self-reliant [in matters of discipline]. The child-like elder is one who has not learned the scriptures on discipline even though sixteen years have elapsed since he entered the order. The elder who resembles the *karandava* corn[199] is one who has transgressed ethical conduct. Of these four, the former two fulfill [the requirements].

The third, [confession to increase prosperity,] is performed on auspicious occasions such as consecration [of a temple, etc.], or at the occurrence of inauspicious circumstances such as floods, droughts, infestations of rats, parrots, or locusts, or the advent of a tyrannical ruler.

The fourth, [confession to eliminate misfortune,] is performed in order to dispel adversity such as hail, robbers, thieves, sickness, or an epidemic, or to ensure that these do not recur.

The fifth, [confession to unify the community,] is performed in order to reconcile dissensions in the order.

The latter three types of confession (to increase prosperity, etc.) are not performed on fixed dates and therefore the reason for their performance must be stated at the beginning of the ceremony (as the proposal). Except for this point, the procedure is the same as the one for confession held on fixed dates.

Rainy Season Retreat [2"]

**Each of the two rainy season retreats, the earlier and later, lasts
three months.**

The rainy season retreat[200] lasts for three months and is performed
during an earlier or later period. The earlier retreat begins on the first
day of the waning moon of the last of [the three] summer months (the
month of the constellation Alpha Aquiloe[201] [June-July]) with the
monks making the promise [to remain in] retreat for three months.
The later begins on the first day of the waning moon of the first month
of autumn (the month of the constellation Alpha Pegasi,[202] [July-
August]). However, Butön and his followers have said that it is best
to make the pledge of the earlier rainy season retreat on the sixteenth
day of the month of the constellation Antares,[203] [May-June]. The sixth
Shamar makes the same assertion.

In order to create the conditions for a harmonious retreat, [the
monastic community] should do extended[204] preparations to ensure
that quarrelsome monks are excluded from the rainy season retreat
and that monks who are well-versed in the [three] collections of the
scriptures will participate. The temple should be cleaned and [dam-
age repaired] as part of these preparations. The immediate preparations are [done one day before the beginning, on the fifteenth]. A ceremony of confession is first performed, following which [one monk
or several] are appointed to distribute [in order of seniority anointed]
wooden sticks [to reckon the number of participants][205] and to assign
rooms and beds.

On the morning of the sixteenth, under [the prescribed] roofed
dwelling, the monks begin the actual retreat with the promise to follow its rules, made by repeating three times the appropriate formula
in the presence of [an experienced] monk. From that point forward,
the participants are not allowed to remain outside of the boundary of
the retreat from one day to the dawn of the following one without
having received permission. [For the duration of the retreat,] the
monks are required to exert themselves in listening [to the doctrine],
reflecting [on it], and meditating[206] until the retreat concludes with
the lifting of restrictions.

Lifting of Restrictions [3"]

**Timely, untimely, or unexpected lifting of the restrictions
conclude the retreat.**

This section has three parts: (1) timely lifting of restrictions, (2) untimely lifting of restrictions, and (3) unexpected or sudden lifting of restrictions in the case of special necessity.

The timely [lifting of restrictions] is performed on the full moon when the three months of the rainy season retreat have passed. The extended preparations [to be started seven days before this ceremony] are to decorate the temple, to inform the [householders living in the] nearby villages, and to give the concluding discourses on the doctrine throughout the night of the fourteenth, [the evening of the lifting of restrictions]. The immediate preparations take place on the day of the fifteenth: [these include] mutual requests by the monks for pardon [for any faults that occurred during the retreat], followed by reconciliation through a proposal made by the monk appointed [to lift the restrictions]. The main part [of the ceremony] is performed [by each monk kneeling in turn in front of the appointed monk] while holding quitch grass[207] and reciting the appropriate words three times. With this threefold recitation, the restrictions concerning downfalls are lifted. Once done, the appointed monk then lifts the restrictions concerning articles, in order that the donations made by the laity during the rainy season retreat may be distributed [among the members of the order]. As the conclusion, on the day of the sixteenth, the monks travel around the district in order to eliminate excessive attachment that may have developed toward the place [of retreat].

The untimely lifting of restrictions is performed [either on the fifteenth or thirtieth of the lunar calendar] when, through the force of circumstances, [it is necessary to end the retreat] before the three months of the rainy season have passed.

The unexpected lifting of restrictions is performed collectively [with each monk standing before another] [on any day] when the entire monastic community must suddenly disperse, as in the outbreak of war. The same procedure must also be followed when a monk must leave the retreat permanently due to particular circumstances.

If there are no more than four monks, the proposal and the lifting of restrictions may be performed without appointing a monk to preside over the ceremony. If there are no more than three or even just two monks, a permission rite for lifting restrictions [is sufficient]. If there is none other than oneself, one repeats just the main part [of the appropriate formula] three times.

This ceremony to mark the end of the retreat is called "lifting the restrictions" because during the retreat, four [activities] that are potential causes of agitation in the community—allegations of downfalls, punitive measures, distribution of the offerings, and spending one night outside of the boundaries—had been prohibited. With this ceremony, the restrictions [on these activities] are lifted.

Conditions for Living Comfortably [ii']

This section has two parts: (1) robes, and (2) food and medicine.

Robes [aa']

Robes and related articles are discussed under three headings: (1) their making and distribution, (2) regulations, and (3)the use of leather articles.

The Making and Distribution of Monastic Robes [1"]

The making and distribution of robes constitutes a basis of training concerned with conditions for living comfortably.

Robes and medicine are the two conditions for a monk to live comfortably. On the occasion of the making and distribution of new robes, the *kathina* practice[208] is performed. This practice extends over a period of relaxation of rules.[209]

On the day following the lifting of restrictions at the conclusion of the earlier or later rainy season retreat, the new robes made from cloth that has been donated [by the laity] during the retreat to the monastic community as a whole are entrusted to [a monk] who has been appointed through a formal procedure of the monastic community [to protect them].[210]

From that day, the sixteenth day of the month, for up to five months [the period of relaxation of the rules for monks who have participated in the retreat], the robes remain in the care of the [appointed] monk who has received them according to the ceremony of "laying out the robes." The appointed monk must not carry the robes outside the boundaries, or leave them in an unclean building or unsheltered place. From time to time, he must air them, dust them off, and so on.

The *kathina* practice is said to have ten advantages[211]: the monks who participate in it[212] do not incur the three downfalls of "keeping," "being without [the monastic robes]," and "retaining [cloth]," etc. This [aspect of the monastic discipline] was not practiced in Tibet since the relaxation of the rules was prohibited by royal decree.[213]

Regulations for Robes [2"]

> **Robes include prescribed, accessory, and extra garments.**
> **The thirteen prescribed robes should be colored by the appro-**
> **priate dyes.**

Clothing for the monastic way of life is of three types: (1) prescribed, (2) accessory, and (3) extra garments.

The prescribed garments are not to be made from cloth that has been wrongfully procured. The cloth should be neither too poor nor too fine: robes may be made from any of seven appropriate materials[214] such as wool, but not made from unsuitable materials such as camel or goat hair, and must not be shaggy or have fringe. The cloth is not to be colored by any of the eight valuable dyes that are inappropriate for monks' use, but colored instead in one of the three appropriate dyes. [Vishakadeva's *Stanzas on the Discipline*] states[215]:

> Red cochineal, poppy, Bengal madder,
> Red sanders, indigo, vermilion,
> Red lead [minium] and saffron
> Are the eight valuable dyes.

While,[216]

> The appropriate [colors for] dyes
> Are blue, red-ocher, and orange.[217]

Moreover, as a general rule, the cloth [for making robes] must have been cut into pieces. As is said:

> One must not keep cloth that has not been cut.

After having been cut, [the cloth for] any of the thirteen garments is sewn according to the prescribed size. [The thirteen garments are the following:] the patched robe, the upper robe, the skirt, the underskirt, the night underskirt, the sweat cloth, the night sweat cloth, the towel, the gauze for wounds, the flannel for skin rash, the sheet to collect hair when shaving, the mat, and the rain cloak.

The *patched robe* may be one of three dimensions, large, small, and medium. The prescribed size for the large patched robe is three cubits in width and five in length. It may be made with twenty-one, twenty-three, or twenty-five patches [in the length], and four and a half [sections in the width].

The size for the small patched robe is a half cubit less [than the large one] in each dimension. It may be made with nine, eleven, or thirteen patches [in the length] arranged with two and a half sections [in the width].

The medium patched robe's size is in between the sizes of the large and the small patched robe. It may be made with fifteen, seventeen, or nineteen patches [in the length], arranged with three and a half [sections in the width].

The *upper robe* must have seven lengthwise patches and two and a half widthwise sections, but may be any one of the three dimensions prescribed for the patched robe.

The *skirt*[218] has five lengthwise patches and one and a half widthwise sections. Its dimensions are two cubits in width and five in length, or at the very least, large enough to cover the three areas.[219] If this does not suffice due to the body being stout, one square cubit of cloth may be added on. Generally, the term cubit refers to any of three measures—a cubit [measured in relation to] a particle, a cubit [measured in relation to] the hand, or a cubit [measured on] the body; what is meant in this context is the cubit [measured on one's own] body. This is stated in the *Summary of Discipline*[220]:

> The measure of a cubit is two-sevenths of the body's height.

The *underskirt* and *night underskirt* are the same size as the skirt and are worn under it, during the day and at night, respectively.

The *sweat cloth* and the *night sweat cloth* used to absorb perspiration are the same size as the upper robe and are worn under it, during the day and at night, respectively.

The *towel* measures one cubit in length and width; *the gauze for wounds* equals the size of the upper robe; and the *sheet to collect hair when shaving* measures three cubits in length and one and a half in width. The *flannel to relieve skin rash* measures six cubits long and three cubits wide; the *mat* measures three cubits long and two cubits plus six finger-widths wide, and has one and a half widthwise sections.

The *rain cloak* for the rainy season is nine cubits in length and three cubits and eight finger-widths in width.

Accessory garments refers to any pieces of cloth the monk considers valuable that have not been stitched on the model of any of the above thirteen robes, and that are of various types measuring a [square] cubit or more, for example, a piece of silk, brocade, or felt. Included in this category are also [the unstitched material for] hat or belt, etc., that the monk considers part of his robes.

Extra articles refers to clothes sewn on the model of any of the thirteen requisites (the patched robe, for instance) or additional garments, such as a second belt.

Minor articles belonging to the category of prescribed garments are items like a [first] hat, shoes, and a belt; minor articles belonging to the categories of accessory and extra are items [like pieces of cloth], the use of which should be predetermined and the size less than a square cubit. All these articles must be consecrated by their respective rituals.[221]

These are the garments worn by renunciates on a regular basis. The patched robe, however, is worn exclusively by full-fledged monks or nuns on specific occasions such as when prostrating before sacred images, going for alms, listening to or expounding the doctrine, or assembling for a monastic ceremony. The upper robe and the skirt, however, are worn as general daytime apparel. These garments are not intended to increase the monk's pride or other negative emotions, but to remind him of his discipline. When they have become old and can no longer be repaired, they should be [cut into tiny pieces,] mixed with earth, and used to seal the crevices of reliquaries, or for similar purposes.

The Use of Leather Articles [3"]

Leather seat and shoes are permitted in special cases.

Leather may be used in special circumstances. In central India, monks and nuns were given permission by the Buddha to wear leather shoes only when necessary in order not to spoil the monks' quarters; and to sit on, but not sleep on, a leather seat in a place other than the monastery, such as the house of a layman, provided there is no other seat.

In the remote regions, the use of leather shoes and beds is allowed for monks and nuns so that they may protect themselves against cold. However, some stipulations do apply: it is not appropriate to wear studded boots that make noise or fancy ones such as those with many colors or adorned with gold and silver ornaments. The Buddha also permitted the wearing of high boots and hats in regions [like Tibet] where the lakes freeze.[222]

Food and Medicine [bb']

The four types of food and medicine
Are those permissible before noon, within a day, seven days, or
    kept until one is cured of an illness.

The foods and medicines that allow a monk to live comfortably are of four types. The first, *foods that must be consumed before noon*, refers to the five foods and five beverages, etc., that alleviate hunger and thirst and are permissible between dawn and noon, but not after. The five foods are dough-balls, cooked rice, meat, light mash [of flour and ground herbs], and pastry. The five beverages are those made from roots, stalks, leaves, flowers, and fruits.[223]

The second, *beverages permissible within a day*, refers to drinks to alleviate thirst, which once consecrated[224] must then be consumed within the same twenty-four hour period. If some is kept after that time, the fault of storing is incurred. This category includes drinks made from apples, grapes, and dates,[225] etc., as well as the whey from cheese or yogurt, sour gruel[226] (the liquid from cooking rice, millet, wheat, and so on, to which no yeast is added and which is allowed to steep), milk, and tea. These drinks possess the five attributes of containing suitable water,[227] being strained, very thin, very clear, and mud-colored.

The third, *foods taken as medicines that can be kept for seven days*, refers to food items used to alleviate both thirst and illnesses of phlegm, bile, and wind, which once consecrated [as medicines] may be used within seven days. These include raw sugar cane, sesame oil, honey, ghee, sugar [from raw sugar cane or honey], powdered sugar from raw sugar cane, and the fat of fish, pig, bear, and rabbit.[228]

The fourth, *medicines that may be kept for life*, refers to real medicines[229] that cure illnesses [caused by the imbalance] of the three humors, which once consecrated may be kept as long as one lives.[230]

In order not to incur the infractions of "cooking [in a natural] boundary" or that of "a day elapsing,"[231] monks should designate and consecrate a kitchen on the four occasions.[232]

Moreover, monks and nuns are required to regard and partake of foods or medicines in a way that accords with the rules set forth in the scriptures [on discipline].

Formal Procedures [iii']

One hundred and one formal procedures are subsumed under three categories.

The one hundred and one formal procedures of the monastic community fall into three categories:

(1) Twenty-four simple formal procedures composed of a proposal alone, such as the appointment of an interviewer [to check the qualifications of the aspirants wishing to enter the order], for which nothing is said but the proposal itself.

(2) Forty-seven two-part formal procedures composed of a proposal and the procedure itself, such as [requesting] the assent of the community [to the performance of a ceremony] in
a [particular] place, followed by the actual procedure.

(3) Thirty four-part formal procedures composed of a proposal
and the actual formal procedure recited three times, such as
the monk's ordination that involves a request and the ordination formula repeated three times [making a total of four
component parts].[233]

Amendment of Infractions [iv']

This section has three parts: (1) the causes of losing one's vows, (2)
amendment of downfalls, and (3) settling disputes.

Causes of Losing the Vows [aa']

The ordination is lost by returning it, death, wayward views, etc.

There are four causes of loss of the ordination of personal liberation: (1) giving up the ordination following sincere reflection [by explaining that one is doing so] to someone capable of understanding
one's words, (2) death, (3) holding wayward views that deny the law
of causality, etc., and (4) becoming a hermaphrodite or changing sex
three times. The expression, "etc." [in the root verse] refers to this
fourth condition.

Moreover, the ordination is invalid if the person [is aware or] becomes aware later on that he has assumed the monk vows before the
age of twenty, even counting the months in the womb.[234]

> **Scholars disagree on what constitutes loss of vows: some
> maintain that vows and downfalls exist together like a rich
> person with debts.
> Others maintain that committing a root downfall destroys the
> whole ordination.**

There are two different viewpoints concerning the criteria for losing the ordination. Kashmiri Analysts[235] maintain that even if a monk
has incurred a root downfall with concealment, he has not lost his
ordination because they consider it illogical that a violation in one
area constitutes an exhaustive loss of [all] vows. In this case, the individual is still ordained although he has broken his discipline, just as a
man can be rich and yet have debts. Drigung Kyopa,[236] the sixth Sha-
marpa, and others agree with this view.

Traditionalists and the early Tibetan masters maintained that if an individual commits a single root downfall, [the whole ordination] is violated since the defeating offenses are downfalls that destroy the [very] root [of the ordination[237]]. Therefore, that person is no longer a monk or nun, and is like the palm tree [which dies by] cutting off just the top branches.

The assertion that the violation of a single vow cannot destroy the ordination stems from the [Analysts'] view that the essence of the vows has form, which implies that each of the basic precepts (as well as the other precepts) must have a separate form.

On the other hand, if the vows are held to be consciousness, since a separate substance does not exist [for each vow], if one vow is broken, it is logical that all are lost.

> **In particular circumstances, a defeat may not be an infraction
> due to incapacity to maintain the rules or other reasons.**

Although the downfall of a defeating offense may have occurred, there are circumstances when this does not constitute an infraction of the rule per se. As examples, a monk may be unable to maintain [a rule] when he does not have control over the functions of his body and mind, such as dreaming of having sexual intercourse; a newly ordained monk [may break a rule] because he is not fully aware of what the rules are; or a monk might commit murder in a state of insanity.

> **Any type of ordination is destroyed by the violation of the four
> roots.**

All of the eight classes of personal liberation [vows] are the same in that the violation of the four basic precepts destroys the ordination. If there has been concealment of the downfall as well, the violation is very serious.

Amendment of Downfalls [bb']

This section has two parts: (1) amendment of transgressions by confession in the case of a monk willing [to atone for his downfall], and (2) amendment through subjugation in the case of an monk [unwilling to atone for a downfall].

Amendment by Confession [1"]

> **In this case, a layperson must reassume the precepts; novices
> and monks
> Can amend unconcealed downfalls but not concealed ones.**

Partial defeats are amended by demotion and services; downfalls are amended
By forfeiture, confession, and restraint

A layperson who has committed a root downfall must take the precepts again in order to amend the transgression. If a branch downfall
(the drinking of beer and so on) has occurred, confession of the offense
must be made to someone who has maintained the precepts purely.

If a novice or a monk [or nun] has incurred a root downfall and has
concealed the fact, no possibility for amendment exists. The downfall
cannot be repaired in this life, and the novice or monk must be expelled from the order. If a root downfall has occurred but has not
been concealed even for a moment, the novice or monk undergoes
penances to amend the offense. For the rest of his or her life, he or she
is relegated to five menial tasks and is not granted the five privileges
within the monastic community.[238] If a monk incurs a defeating offense but does not conceal it, it is said he may return the vows and
take the ordination again.

A partially defeating offense that has not been concealed must be
confessed before one's fellow monks. The main part of the purification is effected by appeasing services, followed by a ceremony to allow the monk to assume his original status.[239]

A monk who has concealed a partial defeat for more than a day is
demoted to a lower status for the number of days he has concealed
the offense. This is in order to purify the fault of concealment. To
purify the partial defeat itself, the monk must perform appeasing service for the monastic community for six days; if the offender is a nun,
a half month. Finally, the monk or nun is reinstated to his or her original status with a ceremony including proposal [and censoring]. [At
the conclusion of the ceremony], the monk or nun is instilled with the
confidence to resume the original position.

In this context, "to demote" means to degrade in rank; "appeasing
service" means to serve the monastic community by performing
menial tasks, such as cleaning, sweeping, and so on, and to sit at the
end of the row of monks.

The legal procedures in case of disagreement over formal procedures[240] (*Kośāmbī*) and the amendment of downfalls through subjugation (*Pāṇḍulohitaka*) are both extensions of the points just discussed,
since the first allegations originated with the two cases [concerning
the dispute in the city of Koshambi and the bad behavior of the
Pandulohitaka monks].[241]

In the case of a downfall that requires forfeiture, the monk must first forfeit the article that has caused the offense to occur and then must undergo one day of punitive measures. Finally, the downfall is confessed in the presence of a monk who is not stained by a similar offense. A downfall that does not require forfeiture, a downfall to be individually confessed, or a "minor infraction that requires confession" can all be purified by confession alone [in front of a single monk]. A "minor infraction to be refrained from" [one that has not been expressed physically or verbally] is amended by reaffirming one's intention to refrain from it.

For the novice, a "minor infraction that requires confession" is confessed to another monk by specifying [the rule one has transgressed]; a "minor infraction to be refrained from" is amended by reaffirming one's intention to refrain from it.

Amendment through Subjugation [2"]

...if a monk is unwilling to amend, he must be subjugated.

The means of subjugation are imposed when a monk is unwilling to amend his transgressions to the rules because he has a bad character or for other reasons. "Subjugation" (Tib. *nan tur*) means to repress or humble that monk. There are thirteen [ways to subjugate an undisciplined monk], classified in the following way: censoring, surveillance, banishment, ostracism, seven [grounds for] expulsion from the monastery, suspension from confession, and suspension from the lifting of restrictions. When the seven [grounds for] expulsion are counted as one, the ways of subjugation number seven.

"Censoring" means that a monk who [has committed a downfall but negates the allegation made by the monastic community, and instead of confessing] argues back, is given a warning such as, "Stop acting this way; if you persist, you will be expelled from the monastery."[242]

"Surveillance" means that a monk, even one who is self-reliant [in matters of discipline], who has not restored a partial defeat and continually commits it is compelled to take up residence with a teacher [and study the discipline with him].[243]

"Banishment" means that a monk who has caused a layperson to lose faith is required to leave the monastery.[244]

"Ostracism" means social boycott of [i.e. avoiding friendly relations with] a monk who has shown contempt toward a layperson.[245]

"Expulsion" is the penalty applied in these seven cases: when a monk declines to acknowledge the offenses he has committed, when he refuses to confess the offenses he has committed, when he does not give up wrong views [concerning the discipline], when he creates the circumstances for quarrels, when he becomes intimate with or lives with a nun, and when he continues to argue although a point [of doctrine] has been settled.[246]

"Suspension" from communal confession and from the lifting of the restrictions is imposed when a monk cannot be disciplined by means of suspension from [correcting] advice.[247]

"Turning down the begging bowl" is also a way to subjugate undisciplined behavior. However, because this is a penalty against a layperson,[248] it is not counted here.

After an offender has been subjugated in these ways and has made his apology, qualified monks perform the ceremony to accept his apology and to reinstate him.

In the case of uncertainty [as to what offense has been committed], as, for example, when the monk has sat [beside a woman] in a secluded and sheltered place, [that monk] is made to investigate the nature [of the offense].[249]

The following bases for monastic discipline are extensions of the points just discussed:

(1) The basis related to the individual, which involves determining whether or not a downfall can be amended, by analyzing the person who has incurred the fault of concealment and the extent of the concealment (complemented by basis, intent, act, and consummation[250]), etc.;

(2) The basis of degrading a monk in twenty-six ways,[251] such as imposing the penances [for transgression without concealment], demotion, appeasing services, and so on;

(3) The basis of the suspension from confession or basis related to the training concerned with the ways of stating allegations of downfalls seen, heard, or suspected.[252]

Settling Disputes [cc']

Four types of dispute are settled in seven ways.

There are four reasons for which a monk who harbors resentment against someone may provoke [the four types of] disputes:

(1) [Mistaken ascertainment of the nature of things]. This leads to a dispute in order to argue; for example, arguing about the permanence or impermanence of the composite.

(2) [Rejecting advice]. This leads to a dispute in order to avoid disciplinary measures; for example, arguing with the monks imposing suspension from advice, confession, or the lifting of restrictions, and contesting the disciplinary measures themselves.

(3) [Having incurred a downfall]. This leads to a dispute [to exculpate oneself] from a downfall, such as a dispute with the monk who brings forth the allegation of a downfall by refuting the substance of the allegation.

(4) Not giving one's assent to a ceremony of the community (such as confession) due to involvement in any of the above three [forms of] dispute. This leads to a dispute related to monastic duties.[253]

These disputes may come naturally to an end when, for instance, the monk who has caused the disputes dies or his attitude changes.[254] Otherwise, the monastic community may pursue the following seven ways of settling disputes:

(1) For the first [of the above four disputes], the eight types of evidence[255] are used [to reach consensus].

The second dispute is quelled in three ways:

(2) The [same] eight types of evidence are used when there is ground for bringing forth an allegation of a downfall;

(3) The order gives a verdict of purity in consideration of [the monk's clear] recollection through a four-part formal procedure, including proposal,[256] when there is no [ground for bringing forth an allegation];

(4) Or the order gives a verdict [of purity] based on non-derangement to an insane monk[257] through a four-part formal procedure when there is no ground [for bringing forth an allegation].

The third dispute is quelled in three ways:

(5) The monk who does not recognize the [nature of his] downfall is made to analyze the nature of the offense he has incurred[258];

(6) The monk voluntarily acknowledges the allegation[259] once he has recognized the nature of his downfall;

(7) The way comparable to spreading straw[260] is used to bring harmony to the monastic community.

All of these seven ways contribute to the settlement of the fourth type of dispute [since involvement in the first three disputes would prevent a monk from giving his assent to the formal procedure]. The dispute comes to a final conclusion when [the quarreling monk] gives assent for the formal procedures to take place.

Monastery Sites and Monks' Quarters [v']

The monastic sites and monks' quarters at least should accord with the teachings on discipline.

Nowadays, it is rare to find any of the teachings on discipline practiced as they were taught [by the Buddha]. However, it would be good and fitting if at the very least the monastic sites and monks' quarters were to accord with the style described in the scriptures on discipline, since this style was taught by the Buddha himself. Accordingly, monasteries should be built on [legally] undisputed land in a place where there are no dangerous animals or other living beings. The land should not be desolate, not have large salt and soda deposits, be overgrown with thorny plants, and so on.

The prescribed monastery has a main temple of five stories. Within the innermost shrine room stands [an image of] Shakyamuni, the master of the doctrine, with [depictions of] events of his previous lives on the side walls.[261] In the assembly hall, where the one hundred and one formal procedures will take place, are paintings of the great elders.[262] Vajra-bearing yaksha[263] are drawn on the wall at the sides of the door and the design of the five-part wheel of cyclic existence[264] with the [two] verses that encapsulate the truth of the path[265] inscribed on the wall of the portico. A lion-throne for doctrinal discourses stands inside the courtyard, which is encircled by an iron fence.[266] Furthermore, within the monastery, the ten facilities (treasury, dining room, and so on[267]) should be included. The monks' rooms are spacious enough to permit the four basic activities [of standing, sleeping, walking, and sitting]. Two types of reliquary and two kinds of standard adorn the grounds.[268] The caretakers for the maintenance of the buildings are appointed in accordance with [procedures described in] the texts [on monastic discipline].

Supplementary Discussion [6]

The supplementary discussion of related subjects consists of three points: (1) advice to relinquish two extreme lifestyles, (2) a concise formulation of the ethical code, and (3) how the three levels of discipline coexist.

Advice to Renounce Two Extreme Lifestyles [a]

A monk must relinquish the two extreme lifestyles: indulgence and austerity.

Those who have entered the monastic discipline should live comfortably. This implies living in such a way as to renounce the two extreme lifestyles of indulgence and austerity. Indulgence in intense desire for sense pleasures would deplete one's store of merit. On the other hand, austerity would lead to a state of fatigue and dispiritedness, making one unfit for study and meditation.

At the same time, if [wealth] such as clothing worth ten million *karshapana*, or foods of a hundred flavors, or houses of five-hundred stories should come one's way without any effort, one may enjoy these without attachment. However, striving excessively for such wealth will hinder study and meditation. Therefore, one should be content while wearing clothes that are discarded rags, subsisting on alms, and dwelling at the base of a tree, etc. Thus, a monk should maintain the perfect conduct of the twelve ascetic practices. As it is said [in the scriptures on discipline]:

> Subsisting on alms, eating in a single sitting, not taking food
>   after rising from one's seat;
> Wearing the three monastic robes, clothes of rough [sheep's]
>   wool, discarded rags;
> Dwelling in isolated places, at the foot of a tree, roofless abodes,
> In charnel grounds, remaining [day and night] in the sitting
>   posture, and [sleeping] wherever one happens to be.[269]

All food and clothing of a monk, whether fine or poor, must not have been obtained by any of the five wrong means of livelihood.[270]

A Concise Formulation of the Ethical Code [b]

> **If an action accords with those permitted by the Buddha, it is performed; if it does not, it is renounced.**

As recorded in the *Scripture on the Subtle Matters of Discipline*, the Buddha gave the following essential formulation of the monastic discipline [in Kushinagari] as he was about to enter into perfect peace: Any action not specified [by the Buddha] as permissible or prohibited needs to be evaluated with reasoning and then performed or renounced accordingly. [Evaluation is done in this way:] if an action accords with those permitted by the Buddha and is verified to be appropriate, it should be performed without any reservations. For instance, Buddha prescribed the lifting of restrictions ceremony for novices; from this, [one can infer] that novices may also participate in the confession ceremony.

An action that resembles those prohibited [by the Buddha] and is verified to be inappropriate must always be renounced. For example, because a silk mat was prohibited, it is therefore inappropriate to make a mat from a material equal or finer in quality than silk.

How the Three Disciplines Coexist in an Individual [c]

> **Analysts believe that the three disciplines have form and are substantially different;**
> **Centrists assert them to be consciousness, the former transformed into the latter ones.**

Once a person has assumed and is maintaining the three levels of discipline [layperson, novice, and monk or nun] discussed above, in what way do these three coexist? Do these exist each with a different or with an identical essence, or does the former level change into the next?

According to the Analysts who believe [the levels of discipline] to be form, each level exists simultaneously and is substantially different in the mind of a monk who has received them sequentially. They substantiate this view by stating that within the continuum of that monk, each level of discipline exists with a substantially different form because he has received the three disciplines through their respective procedures and he has not lost them through any cause.

According to the Centrists and others who believe the levels of discipline to be consciousness, the levels neither exist simultaneously nor with different natures in the mind of the monk who has received them sequentially. They substantiate this view by saying that if this were the case, three substantially different attitudes of renunciation would exist simultaneously in the sphere of a single primary mind, which is illogical. Moreover, they assert that the levels of discipline are not substantially identical since in a single continuum these three are mutually exclusive. This being the case, [it follows that] in the continuum of a monk, the former levels of discipline transform into the latter ones, becoming increasingly advanced in terms of the essence [of the ethical training], etc. When a layperson receives the vows of novice and then those of a monk, at those times, the former disciplines become the essence of the latter ones. This is comparable to the path of accumulation transforming into the path of preparation, and that path into the path of seeing. Therefore, although a full-fledged monk has received and not damaged the novice ordination, it is illogical to assert that he still has the novice vows. This is because in the continuum of a monk, the three disciplines are neither substantially different forms nor substantially different in the nature of consciousness; neither do the two disciplines [that of a novice and that of a monk] exist simultaneously and with an identical nature [in the mind of a monk].

The Distinctive Features of the Vows of Personal Liberation in the Universal Way [B]

The distinctive features of the personal liberation vows of the Universal Way are explained in seven parts: (1) awakening mind, (2) ceremony, (3) preceptor, (4) candidate, (5) permissible transgressions to the rules, (6) amendment of downfalls, and (7) the criterion for loss of the vows.

Awakening Mind [1]

> **Individualists' vows of personal liberation become Universalists'**
> **If assumed with an altruistic motive to attain enlightenment,**
> **Or even when the mind of awakening arises afterwards.**

The exclusive and extensive procedure for the conferral of Universalists' vows of personal liberation was never introduced into Tibet.

However, [one can still receive such ordination without that procedure] as is indicated in the *Three Hundred Stanzas* [*on the Novitiate*][271]:

> Engendering the glorious intention to reach full awakening is the bestowal of power.

[and in its commentary,] *Luminous*[272]:

> [The intention to reach] full awakening is glorious because it is the seed [that develops into] the enlightened deeds of a Dharma sovereign. Power is bestowed[273] in order to attain that [state].

Accordingly, the proclaimers' personal liberation vows themselves, received with an altruistic intention, form the basis of the characteristics of the Universalists' vows of personal liberation. If at the time of receiving the Individualists' vows, one's objective is to attain full awakening for the benefit of others, the vows become Universalists' vows. This is the case even if this was not one's objective at that time, but one develops the resolve to awaken afterwards.

The Ceremony [2]

> **Universalists' vows are received in the course of proclaimers'**
> **ceremonies,**
> **In special ceremonies such as the one for taking the vows of**
> **purification-renewal,**
> **And in higher rites, the one for the formation of the awakening**
> **mind, the preparatory part of a tantric initiation, etc.**

The Universalists' precepts of personal liberation are conferred in three types of ceremonies:

(1) The Universalists' ceremonies that are undifferentiated from those of the proclaimers' system, which are the ceremonies of the eight classes [of vows], performed according to the proclaimers' system, but received with the attitude of the Universal Way, the resolve to awaken.

(2) Special ceremonies, which include the ceremonies of the past by which Maitreya, Manjushri, and others conferred full ordination on many persons, and the ceremonies of the present day, such as the procedure for taking the precepts of purification-renewal[274] as discussed in the *Amoghapasha* [*Scripture*].[275]

(3) Higher rites, which include the rite for assuming the commitment of the aspiration [for complete awakening], the preparatory part of a tantric empowerment, and other rites, which [among their precepts] confer the vows of personal liberation.

The Preceptor [3]

The preceptor may be a renunciate or a lay practitioner.

The vows common [to both the Individual and Universal Ways] must be received from a duly qualified member of the monastic community. The special precepts such as the purification-renewal (as is discussed in the *Display of Miracles Scripture*) may, however, be taken from a lay practitioner who has the same precepts, not exclusively from an ordained person.

The Candidate [4]

The candidate must fulfill the same qualifications specified for the proclaimers' system;
But anyone ready to make the resolve to awaken is eligible to receive these precepts during special ceremonies.

The candidate who receives any of the Universalists' vows of personal liberation in the course of the ceremony of the proclaimers' tradition must fulfill [the qualifications] described in the proclaimers' system. However, anyone who is ready to form the awakening mind characteristic of the Universal Way is a suitable candidate to receive these types of precepts during the special [Universalists'] ceremonies.

Permissible Transgressions of the Rules [5]

In a case of special necessity, even the seven unvirtuous acts are permissible.

The ethical conduct related to any kind of personal liberation vows received in the course of a common ceremony must be maintained just as it is by the proclaimers unless there is a special necessity for not doing so. This is very important because an unnecessary transgression of the rules of this dual ordination is reckoned as a downfall in the context of the commitments of the Indestructible Way (*vajrayāna*). However, when there is a special purpose—to benefit others, for instance—it is permissible to commit the seven verbal and physical unvirtuous actions that are normally prohibited. Accordingly, the *Guide to the Bodhisattva's Way of Life* states[276]:

> The Compassionate One, in his broad vision,
> Gave permission even for what is prohibited.

For someone performing the purification-renewal of the Universal Way, having taken by himself or herself the precepts in accordance with the special ceremony, the [vows] to be maintained are identical to those of the common purificatory fast.

Amendment of Downfalls [6]

> **Concealed downfalls may be confessed and ordination retaken.**
> **Secondary downfalls are amended by confession, sustained by
>   the four forces.**
> **Downfalls are purified by attitude, not by penances.**

Most of the masters of discipline maintain that a monk cannot retake his vows if he has assumed Universalists' vows in the course of a ceremony undifferentiated from that of the proclaimers and he has committed a defeating offense with concealment. This view is good because it is conducive to strict maintenance [of discipline].

However, Lord Trinlepa[277] and others have stated that a root downfall may be repaired by confession accompanied by regret and by retaking the vows, regardless of whether the downfall was concealed or not. This is possible because these vows have been taken with the altruistic mind of awakening. Moreover, these masters taught that a secondary downfall may be purified by amending it with sincere confession sustained by the four forces.[278]

With regard to the amendment of downfalls, it must be said that if one has strong regret, embarrassment, and shame, all transgressions can be purified. When these [dispositions] are missing, however, downfalls cannot be purified simply by undergoing penances. In consideration of this, it is said [in the *Commentary on the Summary of Discipline*] that a person who has great shame or someone who is a master of the three collections of scriptures may purify all offenses simply by confessing them [in front of a fellow monk, without undergoing disciplinary measures].

The Criterion for Loss of the Vows [7]

> **The vows are lost through wayward views, defeating offenses,
>   or by returning them;**
> **No other condition can destroy them.**

The vows are lost when the root of one's virtue is cut by harboring wayward views, committing a defeating offense, or giving back the ordination. The vows are not lost through any other circumstances (such as death and sex-change) because both offenses and vows [in this system] are asserted to be of the nature of consciousness.

The Core of Ethical Conduct [C]

**In brief, the purport of all the scriptures on discipline is
contained in these words:
Abandon negative actions, cultivate virtue, and discipline the
mind.**

All the above-mentioned ethical codes may be formulated in the following instructions: Renounce all negative actions that are naturally
unwholesome or unwholesome due to [Buddha's] prescription. Cultivate all virtuous and wholesome physical, verbal, and mental qualities. With the remedies of mindfulness and awareness, strive to tame
your mind, which is the root of all virtue and evil and is liable to be
overpowered by thoughts. The point of all the scriptures on discipline is thus summarized in the verses of the original confession[279]:

Commit no evil,
Engage in excellent virtue,
Fully tame your mind:
This is Buddha's teaching.

Consequences of Neglecting and Merits of Maintaining Ethical Conduct [D]

**Violation of ethical conduct bears serious consequences,
While pure ethics serve as the foundation and condition for all
virtue.**

Violation of the ethical conduct to which one has committed oneself
bears very serious [consequences] and hinders the development of
one's spiritual qualities. *Proclamation of the Doctrine Scripture* states[280]:

Whoever damages or destroys his ethics will have no affinity for
a spiritual life for up to ten million lifetimes. He forsakes all happiness and experiences great misery.

The scriptures on discipline list the negative consequences of violating ethical conduct, including the following:

You will never hear the true teaching
And quickly forget what you have learned.
Thus, you will not realize the stages and paths [of awakening].

Even a minor offense can lead to a major consequence. Thus, it is
necessary to follow also the minor rules. Accordingly, the scriptures
on discipline state:

> Whoever lightly regards the doctrine of the compassionate
>   teacher
> And transgresses as much as a minor dictate
> Will be oppressed by misery,
> Just as in cutting down the bamboo thicket
> One also destroys the mango grove.
> Although a subject may have disobeyed his king's laws at
>   various times,
> He may still escape punishment,
> But if one disregards the advice of the Sage,
> One will be born as an animal such as the *naga* Elapatra.[281]

In brief, it is stated in the scriptures that a monk or nun who has transgressed the rules by committing a defeat, partial defeat, serious violation, downfall [involving forfeiture or confession alone], offense that must be confessed individually, or minor infraction, will be reborn in one of the hells from the Hot Hell up to the Reviving Hell, respectively.

On the other hand, a pure ethical conduct serves as the basis and as a condition for the development of all knowledge and spiritual accomplishment [that is the fruition] of all Buddhist paths. Nagarjuna's *Letter to a Friend* states[282]:

> Ethical conduct was proclaimed to be the foundation of all
>   virtue,
> Just as the earth is the foundation of the animate and inanimate.

The *Proclamation of the Doctrine Scripture* lists the many benefits of ethics, for example[283]:

> One who maintains ethical conduct is praised by all.

Vishakhadeva stated[284]:

> Ethical conduct yields magnificent fruit:
> Highest praise, abundance of wealth,
> Birth in the celestial residences of the gods,
> The state of contemplation, and emergence from cyclic existence.

The *Valuable for Monks Scripture* states:

> He who believes in ethics
> Creates boundless merit
> Even during a single day
> And eventually attains the goal of full awakening.

Now that the doctrine is in decline, to preserve a single aspect of ethics for even a day has far greater merit than was accrued through maintaining ethical conduct, pure in all aspects, for incalculable years during the initial propagation of the doctrine. Accordingly, the *King of Contemplations Scripture* states[285]:

> Exceptional is the merit of venerating with faith
> Billions and trillions of buddhas
> For millions of eons equal in number to the grains of sand of the
>   Ganges
> With offerings of food, drinks, parasols, banners, and rows of
>   lamps.
> Nonetheless, far greater is the merit accrued
> By observing a single aspect of ethics for just one day
> In this age when the sacred teachings [on discipline] are coming
>   to an end
> And the [other] doctrines of the Transcendent One are
>   vanishing.

Therefore, those who wish to attain liberation should endeavor to maintain pure ethical conduct.

A SYNOPSIS OF THE PHASES OF THE PATH IN THE INDIVIDUAL WAY [III]

As a supplementary discussion, there now follows a concise description of the phases of the path of personal liberation within the Individual Way. Generally, all subjects concerned with monastic discipline are contained within Asanga's presentation[286] of four points: (1) formation of the monastic community, (2) establishing the community in the disciplinary code, (3) providing conditions for each member to live comfortably, and (4) creating the incentive for others to enter into a life of peace and happiness in the future.

Formation of the Monastic Community [1]

Formation of the community refers to the [Buddha's gathering of] four classes of followers[287] who with faith have become renunciates, leaving home to embrace the homeless life, by receiving the full ordination according to the original or present-day procedure.[288]

Establishing the Community in the Disciplinary Code [2]

Establishing the disciplinary code refers to the expounding of the doctrine by means of the basis of training (the reason for the prescribed ethical conduct, etc.), and by means of renunciation, teaching, subduing, and display of miraculous abilities.[289]

Providing the Conditions for Living Comfortably [3]

[Asanga explains] this subject in five points: The first point concerns the monastic necessities that serve as conditions for a monk to live comfortably. [The Buddha] specified that all monastic necessities must be acquired licitly, without resorting to devious means, and unpolluted by transgressions of the rules [regarding their use]. The monk should use these in a manner that does not succumb to either of the two extremes of indulgence and austerity. The necessities include four types of foods (called "medicines") to be consumed, respectively, before noon, within a day, within seven days, and until one is cured of an illness; the four types of garments (prescribed, accessory, extra, and minor); other prescribed and indispensable monastic articles (begging bowl, water strainer, etc.); living quarters, including the monastery buildings, individual cells, dwellings at the foot of a tree, seats, bed, bedding, etc.

The second point concerns the measures used to discipline a monk whose behavior goes against the Buddha's teaching. This includes dismissal from the order of a monk who has committed a defeating offense that cannot be purified; other disciplinary measures to prevent a monk from perpetuating his misconduct; and amendment of downfalls by testimony, reminders, and the ways to settle disputes.

The third point involves dispelling despair through these fifteen means: [recognizing] the five types of despair, [adopting] the five-limbed conscientiousness, and thinking in five ways that help dispel despair.[290]

The fourth point consists in subduing strong emotional entanglement by observing the five-limbed method to maintain ethical conduct:

    (1) Maintaining [the rules concerning] the conditions for living comfortably (the prescribed food, robes, articles, living quarters);

    (2) Studying with a teacher, that is, obeying the instructions of the tutor, or of the elders, who are masters of the three collections of the scriptures;

    (3) Recognition of factors incompatible with ethical conduct, which is to know the means to eliminate the conditions leading to five classes of transgressions of the rules, regardless of whether they are serious or light;

    (4) Meticulous observance of ethical conduct, which means to attend regularly the confession, the rainy season retreat, and the lifting of restrictions; and

(5) Excellent attitude and application. Excellence of attitude refers to virtues such as faith, compassion, intelligence, mindfulness, alertness, shame, embarrassment, and conscientiousness.[291] These eight attitudes serve as preconditions for an
excellent application of ethical conduct, in which one develops the following six foundations of the training:

(1) the discipline that is indispensable in the beginning,
which means having an excellent attitude;

(2) diligent practice of the four means to prevent the occurrence of transgressions of the rules[292];

(3) elimination of the five factors incompatible with the
training[293];

(4) reliance on the five conducive ones[294];

(5) familiarity with the five topics to be known[295]; and

(6) familiarity with the five factors that foster peace.[296]

In addition, to maintain ethical conduct, a renunciate must possess
the five qualities of a monk who is faithful to his discipline[297] and the
five strengths.[298]

Concerning the way to cultivate ethical conduct excellent in both
attitude and application, the scriptures state:

> Whether you are an elder, a monk or nun of some years stand-
> ing, or newly ordained, you should always consider yourself a
> renunciate and should always consider the Buddha, the Blessed
> One who is your guide, as your protector. [With such consider-
> ations,] set as your goal perfect peace, observe the bases of train-
> ing in discipline just as they were prescribed, and work toward
> the realization of ultimate truth.

The fifth point[299] concerns the abandonment of latent emotions.[300]
To accomplish this, the monk engages in the purification-renewal to
develop mental quiescence, which consists in the practice of [the various stages of] meditation. He first asks a master experienced in meditation [for instructions]. The master makes sure that the beginner is
free of four obstacles and examines well his four conditions.[301] [Once
accepted,] the monk then applies himself to the five points: maintaining and creating the conditions for contemplation,[302] perfect seclusion,[303] intense concentration,[304] removing impediments,[305] and the
cultivation of mental contemplation.[306]

With discriminative meditations, such as the discernment of the aspects of grossness and peacefulness,[307] the practitioner becomes free from the desires related to the worldly paths,[308] and strives in the mental quiescence in which the compositional factors of the body and the three times are analyzed. These discriminative meditations and meditation on the thirty-seven aspects of awakening (including the four forms of mindfulness[309]) lead the practitioner through the eight stages (beginning with the one called "full positive sight"[310]), and the paths of accumulation, preparation, seeing, and meditation.[311]

To expand, there are [four] mental contemplations associated with quiescence,[312] [differentiated with regard to] the nine methods of stabilizing the mind; and four mental contemplations associated with insight, [distinguished according to] four analyses[313]—full analysis of phenomena, etc. Through reliance on these two [types] of single-pointed concentration, one attains the four [types] of mental contemplation, beginning with ever-present distress.[314] At that point, one begins [meditation on] the noble truths: one engages in the mental contemplation of knowledge of their characteristics (individual analysis of the sixteen attributes [of the truths], such as impermanence).[315] [This contemplation,] integrated with study and reflection, effects the traversing of the path of accumulation. Beyond that path, the aspect of meditation that unifies the four truths leads to the stage of appreciation.[316] The mental contemplation based on appreciation[317] effects the traversing of the path of preparation [in its stages,] warmth, peak, receptivity, up to highest quality.[318]

Subsequent to the stage of highest quality, as soon as one focuses on the truth which one previously examined, non-conceptual definitive pristine awareness or direct pristine awareness arises. The impediments that are removed through seeing [this awareness] are thereby eliminated, and one attains the path of seeing, the mental contemplation of thorough isolation.[319]

With the mental contemplation of analysis[320] and mental contemplation of withdrawal or joy,[321] one removes the impediments to be forsaken on the path of meditation and one traverses all the stages of that path of meditation.[322] When the mental contemplation of the final training (adamantine contemplation[323]) arises, one attains arhatship, the complete liberation of mind. At the moment of entering the [contemplation that is the] fruit of the final training, all contamination is exhausted. The three results (stream-enterer, etc.[324]) are likewise attained in the different stages of elimination of the emotions that are removed on the path of meditation.

Creating Incentive [4]

The fourth point concerns [being the incentive for others to enter into a life of peace and happiness]. By preserving pure ethical conduct, those who have become monks and nuns live comfortably, endowed with ten personal benefits. Furthermore, they become the source for abundant happiness and benefit of gods and humans and the cause for the continuance of the doctrine. Thus, their example becomes an incentive for others to enter into the same life of peace and happiness.

Chapter III
The Commitments of Awakening Mind

OUTLINE

The Commitments of Awakening Mind

The ethical system of the bodhisattva is treated in seven parts: (1) the causes of awakening mind; (2) the essence of its commitments; (3) distinctions; (4) the two traditions for the development of awakening mind; (5) training common to both traditions; (6) formation of ultimate awakening mind; and (7) the consequences of damaging the commitments and benefits of safeguarding them. [A synopsis of the phases of the path in the Universal Way forms the conclusion.]

THE CAUSES OF AWAKENING MIND [I]

The causes of awakening mind are discussed in three parts: (1) causes in general, (2) specific factors that contribute to its formation, and (3) the particular [cause according to a] quintessential instruction.

Causes in General [A]

> The ethics of awakening mind in the Universal Way
> Arise from awakened affinity, faith, love, and courage.

To enter the path to enlightenment, the Universal Way, one must first generate an altruistic resolve to awaken and assume its commitments. The formation of this "awakening mind" depends on the following causes: signs of an awakened affinity for the Universal Way, faith in the unfailing sources of refuge [the Buddha, Dharma, and Sangha], loving concern for others, and the courage to endure great hardships [for their sake]. The *Stages of the Bodhisattva* states[1]:

What are the four causes [of the mind of awakening]? The most perfect affinity[2] is the first cause of the spirit of a bodhisattva. The support of the buddhas, bodhisattvas, and spiritual guides is the second cause of the spirit of a bodhisattva. Compassion for others is the third cause of the spirit of a bodhisattva. Fearlessness in facing the lengthy, diverse, intense, and constant misery of existence and the hardships [endured for the sake of others] is the fourth cause of the spirit of a bodhisattva.

Specific Factors that Contribute to its Formation [B]

Awakening mind is formed through the strengths of a friend, cause, effect, path, and familiarization

The specific factors that contribute to the formation of the relative awakening mind in its two aspects[3] are stated in [Maitreya's] *Scripture Ornament*[4]:

Awakening mind is generated through the [five] strengths
Of the friend, cause, root [of virtue], learning, and familiarization with the wholesome.
It is said to be unstable when revealed by others (the strength of the friend)
And stable when born from the latter [four] strengths.

In other words, an awakening mind is formed in dependence upon [one or more of] these five factors: the strength of [i.e., indication by] a spiritual guide (the friend)[5]; the strength of awakened affinity (the cause)[6]; the strength of a nurtured root of virtue (the result)[7]; the strength of study of the scriptures of the Universal Way (the path)[8]; and [the strength of] increased familiarization with what one has learned.[9] An awakening mind formed as a result of the first factor is unstable because it relies upon a friend. One formed as a result of [one of] the latter four factors is stable since it will not be easily damaged in adverse circumstances. The relative awakening mind is formed principally due to [the first factor], the strength of others' [indications].[10]

The Particular Cause according to a Quintessential Instruction [C]

It arises from compassion, which springs from love.

Awakening mind, the intention to attain enlightenment, arises from compassion, the wish that all beings be free of suffering and its root. Compassion arises from the cultivation of love, the essence of which is the wish to give help and happiness to others. Therefore, the cause of all noble qualities is love. This teaching is found in the *Advice to the King Scripture.*

THE ESSENCE OF THE COMMITMENTS [II]

The essence of the commitments consists in the ethical conduct
that forsakes unwholesome deeds of body, speech, and mind,
Motivated by the intention to attain complete awakening for
the sake of others.

The essence of the commitments of awakening mind is defined as the ethics of renunciation endowed with an exceptional scope: the motivation to attain awakening for the sake of others, and the resolve (and its concomitant mental factors) to engage in concordant conduct and to forsake unwholesome thoughts, words, and deeds that are incompatible with one's goal. [Maitreya's] *Ornament of Realizations* states[11]:

> Awakening mind is the intention to achieve
> Complete and authentic awakening for others' sake.

DISTINCTIONS OF AWAKENING MIND [III]

Different aspects of awakening mind are distinguished according to (1) its characteristics, (2) the ways it is formed, (3) differentiation of its stages, (4) similes for awakening mind, (5) its focuses, and (6) its ceremonies.

Characteristics [A]

The aspiring mind is characterized by wish; the venturing
mind, by endeavor.

Two aspects of awakening mind are distinguished on the basis of its principal characteristics: (1) the commitments of the aspiration to awaken, and (2) the commitments of venturing [on the path to awakening].

The first is defined as the ethics of a bodhisattva on the training [stage] of the Universal Way, accompanied by the wish to attain complete awakening for the sake of others. The second is defined as the ethics of a bodhisattva on the training [stage] of the Universal Way, accompanied by the intention to engage in a vast range of virtuous activity that leads to the goal of awakening. Aspiring mind is exemplified by the awakening mind in the continuum of a bodhisattva on [the path of] accumulation or preparation. Venturing mind is exemplified by the awakening mind that exists as the nature of the post-equipoise state of an exalted bodhisattva.[12]

In drawing distinctions between the aspiring and venturing aspects of awakening mind, Damstrasena[13] and other masters explain that the former pertains to the worldly paths,[14] and the latter to the supramundane paths. Abhayakara,[15] Smritijnana,[16] and other scholars maintain that aspiration [corresponds to the awakening minds illustrated by] the first three similes listed below[17] and venturing [corresponds to those indicated by] the other nineteen [similes].

Moreover, Sagaramegha[18] and other masters believe that a mind of awakening formed without relying on a ceremony is an aspiring mind, and one formed during a ceremony is a venturing mind. Lord Atisha[19] and other masters of the magnificent deeds lineage explain that aspiration is the promise to attain the goal of awakening, and venturing is the promise to [create] the causes [leading to this goal]. In addition, some scholars believe that until it has become irreversible, an awakening mind is one of aspiration; once it is irreversible,[20] it is venturing mind.

Shantideva and the masters of the profound view lineage assert that an aspiring awakening mind is simply the formation of the wish to awaken born out of compassion for sentient beings and other positive factors. This may or may not be formalized in a ceremony. The wish to awaken is likened to the desire to set out on a journey. A venturing awakening mind begins with the full acceptance of the mind of aspiration and its commitments and is likened to the actual journey. Simply put, aspiration is the resolve to awaken, and venturing is the acceptance of the commitments of such a resolve. The noble Sakya patriarchs[21] assert that the aspiring and venturing minds are characterized by three aspects each:

> Aspiration, forming the aspiration, and safeguarding the aspiration from degeneration; venturing, forming the venturing [mind], and safeguarding the venturing mind from degeneration.[22]

These masters maintain that aspiration and venturing minds in themselves do not constitute commitments. Commitments are assumed only when these minds are permeated with an indispensable element: the intention to give up what is directly or indirectly incompatible [with their training].

The Ways It Is Formed [B]

> **Awakening mind is approximate or subtle, depending on the way it is formed.**

Two kinds of awakening mind are distinguished according to the ways it is formed: approximate and subtle. An approximate awakening mind arises from an indication [by a spiritual guide], and a subtle one is attained through [the realization of] the fundamental nature of things. Accordingly, Shantipa's *Four Hundred and Fifty Lines Commentary* states[23]:

> A mind of awakening is conceived through indications as long as one has [only] an intellectual understanding of emptiness, but has not yet realized it directly. However, once [emptiness] has been realized, the mind of awakening should be understood to be ultimate [awakening mind].[24]

Differentiation of Stages [C]

> **Its stages are differentiated by appreciation, intention, full maturation, and freedom from all impediments.**

There are four aspects to the formation of awakening mind according to differentiations of the stages of the path. These are set forth in [Maitreya's] *Scripture Ornament*[25]:

> The awakening mind formed on each respective stage
> Is said to be a mind of appreciation,
> Extraordinary intention, maturation,
> And likewise, freedom from all impediments.

During the paths of accumulation and preparation, the awakening mind is formed by appreciation[26]; on the seven impure stages, by an extraordinarily [pure] intention[27]; and on the three pure stages, by maturation.[28] At the stage of a buddha, the awakening mind is one of freedom from all impediments [emotional and those preventing omniscience].[29]

Similes [D]

> Twenty-two similes, earth, gold, moon, etc., are used to distin-
> guish awakening mind with respect to individuals.

Twenty-two aspects of awakening mind are distinguished with respect to [the levels of realization of] the individual or the stages of the
path. These are illustrated by the similes of earth, gold, moon, etc.
Each simile represents an awakening mind accompanied by a particular quality. [Maitreya's] *Ornament of Realizations* states[30]:

> Earth, gold, moon, fire,
> Treasure, jewel mine, ocean,
> Diamond, mountain, medicine, spiritual friend,
> Wish-fulfilling gem, sun, song,[31]
> King, storehouse, highway,
> Conveyance, spring,
> Echo, river, and cloud:
> These are the twenty-two similes [for awakening mind].

The qualities that accompany the twenty-two aspects of awakening
mind[32] are the following: earnest desire, intention, determination,
application, generosity, ethics, patience, effort, meditation, wisdom,
skillful means, strength, aspiration, pristine awareness,[33] clairvoyance,
merit and pristine awareness, factors conducive to awakening,[34] mental quiescence and insight, memory and eloquence, feast of the teachings, sole path, and the awakened dimension of reality.[35]

[As for their correlation with] the stages of the path, the first three
aspects of awakening mind, earnest desire, etc., are found on the three
levels of the path of accumulation.[36] The awakening mind accompanied by application is present on the path of preparation. The ten
aspects accompanied by the ten perfections, from generosity to pristine awareness,[37] are found on the ten bodhisattva stages[38] included in
the paths of meditation and seeing. The next five, from the awakening
mind accompanied by clairvoyance to the one accompanied by memory
and eloquence, are found on the superior path that encompasses the
three pure stages.[39] The last three, beginning with the one accompanied by the feast of the teachings, are present, respectively, during
the initial, actual, and final parts of the tenth stage, known as complete enlightenment, the stage of a saint of the Universal Way.[40]

Earnest desire, which constitutes the foundation for all positive qualities, is likened to earth. To use a syllogism whose pattern is applicable to the other awakening minds, the subject, awakening mind accompanied by the earnest desire to work toward awakening, is comparable to earth in that it forms a foundation for the development of all good qualities.[41]

Focuses [E]

Relative and ultimate awakening minds differ in their focuses.

Two aspects of awakening mind are distinguished in terms of its focus: relative and ultimate. The first [which has the relative focus of sentient beings] consists of the aspiration [to awaken] and the actual venturing [toward that goal]. The second [which has the ultimate focus of emptiness] is the actual ultimate mind of awakening, i.e., the non-conceptual pristine awareness of an exalted being. A facsimile of the ultimate awakening mind may also be found at the beginner's level.[42]

Ceremonies [F]

Awakening mind may be formed in three ceremonies.

The commitments of awakening mind are distinguished according to the ceremonies followed to assume them: (1) awakening mind commitments assumed during the same ceremony for receiving personal liberation vows. This refers to the ceremony for taking personal liberation vows in the system of the Universal Way, as described in the previous chapter which discusses the proclaimers' vows; (2) awakening mind commitments assumed during a ceremony exclusive [to the Universal Way], such as the commitments of aspiring and venturing minds accepted during their respective ceremonies in either the Centrists' or the Idealists' system; and (3) awakening mind commitments assumed in the same ceremony used to receive a tantric empowerment, such as the commitments of awakening mind made during the preparatory part of a tantric initiation and the Secret Mantra pledges made during the main part of an initiation.[43]

THE TWO TRADITIONS FOR THE DEVELOPMENT OF AWAKENING MIND [IV]

This section has two parts: (1) an overview, and (2) a detailed discussion.

Overview [A]

> The exclusive ceremonies are known as the two traditions of
> the pioneers;
> These have been preserved by their followers.

The two ceremonies [to form an awakening mind] exclusive [to the Universal Way] are known as the two traditions of the "pioneers" [Nagarjuna and Asanga[44]]. The later Indian and Tibetan followers of these masters have preserved these as two distinct traditions.

The first ceremony was mystically transmitted by Manjughosha[45] to Nagarjuna, who taught it to his spiritual heir, [Aryadeva[46]]. Subsequently, it was received by the bodhisattva Shantideva,[47] who took it as his regular practice. Lord Punyashri[48] introduced this ceremony [to Tibet], where it became adopted by the Sakya patriarchs.[49] The procedure of this rite accords with Nagarjuna's *Ceremony for the Formation of the Awakening Mind*, Jetari's *Ceremony for the Acceptance of the Sacred Commitments*, and rites based on Shantideva's *Guide to the Bodhisattva's Way of Life* and *Compendium of Trainings*.

The second ceremony was mystically transmitted by the bodhisattva Maitreya[50] to Asanga, who taught it to his brother, Vasubandhu.[51] Subsequently, it come down to the master Chandragomin,[52] who took it as his regular practice. Lord Atisha[53] introduced this ceremony [to Tibet], where it was adopted by the Kadampa[54] and the Dakpo Kagyu[55] schools. Its procedure accords with the rites based on Asanga's *Stages of the Bodhisattva* and Chandragomin's *Twenty Verses on the Bodhisattva's Commitments*.

Many Tibetan scholars believe Nagarjuna to be the founder of Centrism (*mādhyamika*) and Asanga to be the founder of Idealism (*cittamātra*). They therefore refer to those two ceremonies as the Centrist and Idealist traditions for the formation of awakening mind. They regard them as fundamentally different, claiming the one or the other to be the best. However, Lord Daö Shönnu (Gampopa)[56] does not refer [to these traditions] as Centrist and Idealist, and, for that matter, the master Abhayakara[57] does not consider there to be any difference between them. The omniscient Pema Karpo and others hold the same opinion and refute the [former] view using scriptures and reasoning. The illustrious Tsuklak Trengwa[58] and other scholars also agree with Gampopa.

Another ceremony for the formation of awakening mind, which resembles the Centrists' one, originated with the instructions of the greatly accomplished masters Virupa and Naropa.[59] This was handed down to the Sakya masters and now constitutes the procedure for the formation of awakening mind found in the preliminaries of the empowerments of their lineage. Although it stands in its own right, it is not considered to be different from the two ancient traditions of the pioneers.

Detailed Discussion [B]

This section has two parts: (1) awakening mind in the lineage of profound view, and (2) awakening mind in the lineage of magnificent deeds.

Awakening Mind in the Lineage of the Profound View [1]

This section has five parts: (1) assuming the commitments [of awakening mind], (2) honoring them, (3) causes of loss of the commitments, (4) restoration of the commitments, and (5) additional points on the training.

Assuming the Commitments of Awakening Mind [a]

> **In the profound view's tradition, anyone able to articulate ideas**
> **May assume the commitments of the aspiring and venturing**
> **minds at the same time**
> **In the presence of a master or a sacred representation, following**
> **preparatory cultivation of merit and purification of mind.**

According to the tradition of the profound view lineage, a suitable candidate for accepting the commitments of awakening mind is any being who has the capacity to articulate and to understand what is said, as well as the willingness to assume the commitments. One can refer to scriptures [for examples]. The *Flower Ornament Scripture* states that three thousand ocean-dwelling *nagas* were inspired by Manjushri to form [awakening] minds. The *Fortunate Eon Scripture* relates the following event[60]:

The victor Upakantha, as a mayor [in a past life],
Resolved to achieve supreme awakening
When he made a promise not to kill for one day
In the presence of the Transcendent Punyaprabha.

Furthermore, the *Questions of Ratnachuda Scripture* describes how
twenty thousand gods and men made the resolve to attain awakening. The incomparable Gampopa, however, states that in order to form
the awakening mind of aspiration, one must possess an affinity for
the Universal Way, have awakened that affinity, and have sought refuge in the Three Jewels. Moreover, he asserts that in order to receive
the commitments of a venturing mind, in addition to these [two req-
uisites], an aspirant must have assumed one of the seven classes[61] of
personal liberation vows (other than the purificatory fast precepts)
and possess an aspiring awakening mind.

The qualifications of the master [in the presence of whom] one accepts the commitments of awakening mind have been described in
the first chapter of this book in accordance with Shantideva's *Compendium of Trainings* and *Guide to the Bodhisattva's Way of Life*. A person
who cannot find [a qualified master] may accept the commitments
before [an image or other] sacred representation [of the Buddha]. If
even that is not available, one may visualize the buddhas and bodhisattvas in the sky before one and make the commitments by oneself
in their presence.

The ceremony for assuming the commitments [is outlined in this
way]: If the commitments are being made in the presence of a master,
the disciple [offers] an imagined universe[62] and requests [the bestowal
of the commitments]. The preliminary part consists in the purification of one's mind through performance of the seven-branch service[63]
and, in particular, taking refuge in the Three Jewels.

The main body of the ceremony consists in accepting the commitments of the aspiring and venturing minds at the same time [by repeating three times Shantideva's formula:

All the enlightened ones of the past
Have formed awakening minds
And engaged themselves progressively
In the bodhisattvas' training.

In the same way, for the sake of all that lives,
I now form an awakening mind

And will apply myself in stages
To the training of the bodhisattvas.][64]

As the conclusion, the disciple cultivates joy [over having generated an awakening mind by reciting these prayers of Shantideva:

Today my life is fruitful:
Having attained a good human life,
I have been born into the family of the enlightened
And now I have become a buddha's child.
Henceforth, whatever happens,
I shall act in accordance with this line
In order not to sully this noble and faultless family.]

and exhorts others to rejoice [by reciting this verse:

Today, in the presence of all the protectors,
I invite all beings to be my guest
At this feast of temporary and ultimate happiness.
May gods, demigods, and all rejoice.]

In this way, one encourages oneself and others, and then recites [prayers not to forget] the precepts of awakening mind. [The ceremony is completed by] an offering to the master as a token of appreciation. When an aspirant assumes the commitments alone, all parts of the ceremony are performed, except for the beginning and concluding offerings.

It is certainly possible to form at least the essence of an awakening mind by performing the ceremony to assume the commitments by oneself. However, scholars believe that for that mind to be bound by the commitments, the strength of the [spiritual] friend, the strength of the cause, and the other contributory factors [mentioned above] must be present.

Honoring the Commitments [b]
This section has two parts: (1) the root downfalls, and (2) the secondary infractions.

Root Downfalls [i]
The root downfalls are explained in three sections: (1) the fourteen downfalls that apply to acute practitioners, (2) the four downfalls that apply to average practitioners, and (3) the one downfall that applies to obtuse practitioners.

Fourteen Downfalls that Apply to Acute Practitioners [A']

> **Acute practitioners must avoid fourteen root downfalls.**
> **Five of these apply mainly to kings: to steal the Three Jewels'**
> **property, to reject the teachings,**
> **To blame the immoral, to commit deeds of direct retribution,**
> **and to profess wayward views.**

Fourteen root downfalls of the commitments of training are explained in [Shantideva's] *Compendium of Trainings* in accordance with the *Akashagarbha Scripture*. Five of them apply mainly to kings, one applies exclusively to ministers, and eight apply to beginners. The five [downfalls] that apply mainly to kings who are bodhisattvas-in-training are the following[65]:

(1) To steal [or have someone steal] property that has been offered to representations of [the Buddha's] body, speech, and mind,[66] or to the monastic community;

(2) To reject [or cause someone to reject] the teachings of the Universal or Individual ways [by saying that they are not the words of the Buddha or that they are not the means to attain liberation];

(3) To harm someone who wears the attributes of a monk, regardless of whether he maintains the vows purely or is an immoral monk[67];

(4) To commit any of the five evil deeds of direct retribution, i.e., matricide, patricide, murder of a saint, causing a schism in the monastic community, or out of malice, causing a buddha to bleed; and

(5) To profess nihilistic views claiming that actions do not bring results and that there are no future lives, and engaging in unvirtuous types of behavior [or encouraging others to do so].

> **Five downfalls apply mainly to ministers: the first four are the**
> **same as those prohibited for kings,**
> **And the fifth is to plunder a town.**

The five root downfalls that apply mainly to ministers who are bodhisattvas-in-training include the first four root downfalls for a king, plus plundering of a town and the like.[68]

To plunder [a town] comprises five kinds of ravage: of a village (inhabited by four castes[69]); a town (inhabited by eighteen kinds of artisans[70]); a county (an area that includes several towns); a province (an area consisting of several counties); or a country (an area consisting of several provinces).

> **The eight root downfalls that apply to beginners are to teach emptiness to the untrained,**
> **To cause another to give up the intention to awaken, to make someone abandon the Individual Way,**
> **To assert that the Individual Way does not conquer emotions, to praise oneself and belittle others,**
> **To falsely claim realization of emptiness, to cause a king to inflict a fine and then accept stolen property as a bribe,**
> **To disrupt meditation or to give the possessions of a contemplative monk to one who merely recites scriptures.**

The eight root downfalls [that apply mainly to] beginner bodhisattvas are as follows[71]:

(1) To teach the profound subject of emptiness to those who are of limited intellect or to those who are untrained [in the Universal Way], causing them to be intimidated [by the Universalists' doctrine] and thereby to lose faith in it.[72]

(2) To cause someone to give up the intention to become fully enlightened and to enter the way of the proclaimers or solitary sages when that individual is already following the Universal Way, by declaring that he or she is not able to practice the six perfections and other aspects [of the Universal Way].

(3) To advise someone with an affinity for the Individual Way to abandon that path and then cause him or her to enter the Universal Way[73] without special necessity to do so.

(4) To believe and to cause another to believe, without any special necessity, that by following the Individual Way, one cannot conquer the emotions.[74]

(5) To praise oneself when one is not worthy and to belittle others when they do not deserve it, for the sake of wealth and honor.[75]

(6) To [falsely] claim, for the sake of wealth and honor, to have attained [direct] realization of profound [emptiness] by saying that one has understood profound truth and to incite others to meditate to achieve the same goal.[76]

(7) To cause a king or other person in a position of power to inflict a fine on a Buddhist monk by slandering him. If as a

result the monk steals property of the Three Jewels in order to bribe oneself [the instigator] and one accepts it, one incurs this downfall. If one gives the property to the king, both [instigator and king] incur this downfall.

(8) To cause a good monk to abandon mental quiescence or other forms of spiritual practice by imposing unfair punishment on him, or to deprive a contemplative monk[77] of his life necessities and to give these directly or indirectly to a monk who merely recites scriptures. If the recipient is an accomplice to one's act, he or she also incurs this downfall.

These are the fourteen downfalls that apply to acute practitioners, five for kings, one exclusive to ministers, and eight for beginners.

Four Downfalls that Apply to Average Practitioners [B']

**Downfalls for average practitioners are to give up awakening mind,
Be ungenerous, angry, or hypocritical.**

Four [downfalls] apply mainly to average practitioners. These are stated in the *Compendium of Trainings*, based on their presentation in the *Skill in Means Scripture*[78]:

To abandon one's awakening mind;
Not to give alms to mendicants
Out of strong attachment and avarice;
Not to forgive
But to strike others in anger
Even though they try to please one;
And to present false teachings as the Buddha's teachings
Motivated by an emotion or in order to please others.

One Downfall that Applies to Obtuse Practitioners [C']

An obtuse practitioner must at least maintain the aspiration to awaken.

Having entered the Universal Way, an obtuse practitioner must, at the very least, maintain the aspiration [to awaken]. Accordingly, the *Advice to the King Scripture* states that all precepts are fulfilled in this alone. To abandon one's [aspiration] is a very serious root downfall for any bodhisattva, whether acute, average, or obtuse. The *Condensed Transcendent Wisdom Scripture* states[79]:

Though [a bodhisattva] may have tread the path of the ten
    virtues[80] for ten million eons,
If his goal shifts to becoming a solitary sage or a saint,
His ethics deteriorate and his commitments are lost.
Such a setback is far more serious than the defeating offense [of
    a monk].

Secondary Infractions [ii]

**The secondary infractions number eighty: twenty-four stem
from disinterest in others' happiness or suffering;
Sixteen stem from neglecting to accomplish greater goals.
Each may be incidental or continuous.**

The *Compendium of Trainings* lists eighty secondary infractions. Of
these, twenty-four stem from disinterest in others' happiness and indifference to their suffering. The two basic infractions in this category
are (1) failing to relieve the physical suffering or sorrow of others
when able to do so, and (2) failing to provide physical comfort or
happiness.

These two basic infractions are divided into four to distinguish the
physical and mental aspects of suffering or happiness:

(1) failure to relieve the physical suffering of others when able
    to do so,
(2) failure to relieve their sorrow,
(3) failure to provide them with physical comfort, and
(4) failure to instill them with happiness.

These are further divided to draw a distinction between the present
and future:

(1) failure to relieve in the present others' physical suffering or
    (2) sorrow,
(3) failure to provide them in the present with physical comfort
    or (4) happiness,
(5) failure to work so that others will be free in the future of
    physical suffering and (6) sorrow, and
(7) failure to work so that in the future they will have comfort
    and (8) happiness.

These eight are further divided to distinguish [failures to act]
in three ways to relieve others' sufferings and provide them with
happiness:

(1) failure to make an effort in order to relieve in the present others' physical suffering or (2) sorrow, or (3) in order to provide them in the present with physical comfort, and (4) happiness, etc., up to (8) to provide for their future happiness;
(9) failure to seek out the causes and conditions that would relieve in the present others' physical suffering, etc., up to (16) so that in the future they will have happiness; and
(17) failure to apply the remedial means to relieve in the present others' physical suffering, etc., up to (24) so that in the future they will have happiness.

Sixteen infractions stem from neglecting to accomplish [greater goals]. The two basic infractions (for these sixteen) are (1) failing to work even in the slightest to relieve great physical suffering, and (2) failing to work even in the slightest to relieve intense sorrow.

These two are divided to distinguish between present and future lives:
(1) failure to work even in the slightest to relieve in this life great physical suffering or (2) intense sorrow, and
(3) failure to work even in the slightest to remove [what would be the cause] in future lives of great physical suffering or (4) intense sorrow.

These are further divided to draw a distinction between oneself and others:
(1) failure to work even in the slightest to relieve one's own great physical suffering in this life or (2) others' great physical suffering,
(3) failure to work even in the slightest to relieve one's own intense sorrow in this life or (4) others' intense sorrow,
(5) failure to work even in the slightest to remove [what would be the cause] in future lives of great physical suffering for oneself or (6) for others, and
(7) failure to work even in the slightest to remove [what would be the cause] in future lives of intense sorrow for oneself or (8) for others.

The remaining eight infractions are derived from the two infractions of (1) failing to sacrifice [lesser goals] in order to accomplish the greater [goals] of providing solace or (2) affording physical comfort.

These two are divided as above into eight infractions by making the distinctions between [present and future] lives and oneself and others.

For each of these forty infractions, the failing may be incidental or continuous; that further distinction yields a total of eighty infractions.

Causes of Loss of the Commitments [c]

> The commitments may be lost in six ways, such as giving up refuge.
> While a root downfall may damage some aspects of the venturing mind,
> As long as aspiration is present, the commitments cannot be lost.

The illustrious master Tsuklak Trengwa explains the six specific causes of loss of the commitments [of the mind of awakening]:

> The causes for the irreparable loss of awakening mind's commitments
> Are to give up seeking refuge [in the Three Jewels], to renounce the aspiration [for enlightenment],
> To return one's commitments, to adopt wayward views,
> To turn toward [the path of] the proclaimers and solitary sages,
> And to abandon [love for] any being.
> Root downfalls damage and destroy [the commitments];
> The various minor transgressions weaken them.

Lord Trinlepa explains that if any of the root downfalls (described in the *Akashagarbha Scripture*) is committed, some aspects of one's training in the venturing mind will be damaged. However, provided that one has not given up the resolve to awaken for the sake of all beings, the awakening mind of aspiration is not lost. As long as one maintains that aspiration, one's commitments are never damaged beyond restoration.[81]

Restoration of the Commitments [d]

> To restore the commitments, one invokes Akashagarbha and acknowledges the downfall in his presence.
> If the time limit for confession has passed, one restores the commitments using the four forces.

If the commitments of awakening mind have deteriorated because the aspiring mind has been relinquished, they can be restored by assuming them again in a ceremony. The *Akashagarbha Scripture* states that any root downfall may be amended by invoking the bodhisattva Akashagarbha and acknowledging the infraction in his presence when he appears in one's dream.[82] Likewise, [Shantideva's] *Compendium of Trainings* states[83]:

> Openly confess to the bodhisattva Akashagarbha
> [When he appears] in your dreams.

Minor offenses that contradict the precepts of awakening mind should be acknowledged during each of the six periods (three daytime periods and three nighttime). As taught in *A Guide to the Bodhisattva's Way of Life*, acknowledgment may be made by reciting the *Three-Part Scripture*[84] and by strengthening the awakening mind.

The master Krishna[85] taught [a different method for the restoration of commitments] for each of three kinds of practitioners. Superior practitioners [restore their commitments] through understanding the unborn nature of all that exists. Average practitioners do so by invoking the deities of the awareness mantra, [a favored deity, or Akashagarbha, and by confessing in front of them]. Inferior practitioners, because they conceive the downfall as something real, [must restore their commitments] by regretting [the downfall] and openly acknowledging it to another person.[86]

Generally, if one does not amend the downfall by the end of a three-hour period following its occurrence, confession is "overdue," and it becomes an actual downfall. If the time limit for acknowledgment has not passed, the commitments are restored simply by the conscientious [performance] of the means for renewal described above. If the time limit for acknowledgment has passed (for example, if the downfall is left without confession for a number of days), the downfall can be purified by confessing it with the help of the four forces and accepting the commitments again.

The four forces are the following: the force of reliance, which is to take refuge [by repeating the refuge formula called] *Prayer to the Chief Victorious One*[87] or any other one; the force of repudiation, which is to specify the downfall, regretting it intensely; the force of remedial action, which is to employ the six kinds of remedies,[88] such as recitation of recollection mantras (*dhāraṇī*) and other mantras, principally the one-hundred-syllable mantra of the transcendent ones; and the force of renewal, which is to promise not to repeat [the misdeed].

Additional Points on the Training [e]

**One should promise to train in the prescribed practice only to
the extent and for as long as one estimates one can.**

Most of the points of training discussed so far prescribe what actions
should be avoided. Of the points of training that prescribe what should
be practiced, a few will be given below; a full presentation of them is
provided in scriptures on this subject. One should promise to practice these only to the extent one feels capable of and only for as long
as one feels able to, be it a day, a month, a year, this life, or until
awakening. The *Compendium of Trainings* states[89]:

> Assume commitments according to your ability [to honor them].
> To do otherwise would be to deceive all the buddhas, the
> bodhisattvas, and the whole world, including the gods.

Awakening Mind in the Lineage of Magnificent Deeds [2]

Awakening mind in the lineage of magnificent deeds is discussed in
four parts: (1) assuming the commitments of awakening mind, (2)
honoring them, (3) restoration of the commitments, and (4) additional
points on the training.

Assuming the Commitments of Awakening Mind [a]

**In the magnificent deeds tradition, commitments of aspiring
mind are assumed by a holder of one of the seven personal
liberation vows
Before an erudite and competent master who abides by the
same commitments.
The commitments of venturing mind are bestowed only after
the scriptures are studied.
The extensive rite for the venturing mind includes an inquiry
concerning obstacles, etc.**

According to the tradition of the magnificent deeds lineage, a suitable candidate for the commitments of awakening mind must definitely hold one of the seven classes of personal liberation vows. Anyone with obstacles to receiving personal liberation vows would not
be able to assume these commitments.

The spiritual master in the presence of whom the commitments
are assumed must fulfill the qualifications described in the first chapter, which are encompassed by the following four qualities: ideally,

learned in the [three] collections of scriptures, but at least well-versed in the ritual procedure for the bestowal of the commitments; capable of communicating clearly with the aspirant; possessed of undegenerated commitments; loving toward students and capable of nurturing [their spiritual development]. Such a teacher is definitely necessary [for assuming the commitments] and should be searched for unless one's life or chastity would be at risk. If one fails in one's search, the commitments may be made before a representation of the Three Jewels, as stated in *Stages of the Bodhisattva*[90]:

> If it does not entail peril to one's life or chastity, an aspirant should search for a spiritual friend within one league and an earshot.[91] If none is found, the aspirant may accept the commitments alone or before a representation of the Three Jewels.[92]

However, the elder Bodhibhadra[93] and others have stated that the presence of a master is indispensable when renewing commitments that have deteriorated.

The works of Asanga and those of the masters who immediately follow him in the lineage do not clearly set out a ritual for assuming the commitments of the mind of aspiration. The actual ceremony, considered to be a pith instruction transmitted by Maitreya, was later introduced by Lord Atisha.[94]

In this tradition, the commitments of the aspiring mind and venturing mind are assumed in two separate ceremonies. Both procedures comprise [three stages]: (1) [prior to the ceremony itself] the aspirant becoming a "definite candidate" [for the commitments]; (2) the preliminary, central, and conclusive parts of the ceremony; and (3) a description of the nature of awakening mind [its causes, etc.].

The aspirant becomes a definite candidate [by contemplating pertinent advice which transforms his or her attitude so that] he or she gives up adherence to the two extremes [of attachment to cyclic existence and complacency in the peace of liberation], and then develops an earnest interest in generating an awakening mind.

The preliminary part of the ceremony for the commitments of aspiring mind is composed of [the offering of a mandala and] the request [for the bestowal of the commitments] made to the special referent, the master; taking refuge in the special support [the Three Jewels]; and the application of special means, which is the cultivation of merit [by performing the sevenfold service].

The central part of the ceremony consists in assuming the commitments. This is accomplished through one's own strength (an awakened spiritual affinity), the strength of others (discerning the marvelous qualities of complete awakening by [listening to] the master's words), and the strength of application (that gives rise to the [three] attitudes of disengagement from cyclic existence, disenchantment with perfect peace, and earnest interest in awakening mind.)

The ceremony is concluded by rejoicing, receiving instruction in training, and offering the teacher a token of appreciation.[95]

A practitioner who has formed the aspiration to awaken through such ritual should study the scriptures concerning the bodhisattva's training. Later, when the practitioner has developed faith [in the teachings] and the capacity for putting them into practice, he or she may assume the commitments of the venturing mind.

The ceremony for assuming the commitments of venturing mind has three parts: the preliminary, the central part, and the conclusion. The preliminary part of the ceremony consists of a request, the teacher's examination of the candidate's motivation, an entreaty for immediate bestowal [of the commitments], inquiry concerning [possible] obstacles for the candidate, acquainting the candidate with the nature of the training, and inquiry about his or her interest [in the training].[96]

The central part of the ceremony consists in assuming the commitments with a threefold repetition of the promise [to follow the training]. The ceremony is concluded with a supplication [that the aspirant's promise] be acknowledged [by the buddhas and bodhisattvas], an explanation of the merits [of the venturing mind], advice to maintain secrecy, instructions on points of training, and offerings of appreciation.[97]

For the third stage, the description of the nature of awakening mind, the master explains in detail to the beginner bodhisattva the causes, essence, aspects, and benefits of the aspiring mind; and those same details of the venturing mind at the end of their respective ceremonies.

In both traditions, [that of the profound view and this one,] the end of the third recitation of the formula for assuming the commitments marks the point at which the commitments were accepted.

Honoring the Commitments [b]

This section has two parts: (1) a concise statement, and (2) an extensive explanation.

Concise Statement [i]

A practitioner must guard against four root downfalls and forty-six secondary infractions.

A practitioner who has assumed the commitments of the aspiring and venturing minds must avoid four root downfalls and forty-six secondary ones.

Extensive Explanation [ii]

This section has two parts: (1) root downfalls, and (2) secondary infractions.

Root Downfalls [A']

The root downfalls are to praise oneself and belittle others out of attachment to wealth and honor;

Not to give material aid or not to give teachings to the needy out of miserliness;

Not to forgive someone though he has apologized and to strike him in anger;

To abandon the Universal Way and to present false teachings as true Buddhism.

Depending on the strength of involvement, the downfall may be serious, moderate, or light.

The four root downfalls, comparable [in gravity] to the defeating offenses of a monk, are enumerated in [Chandragomin's] *Twenty Verses on the Bodhisattva's Commitments*[98] as a summary of the discussion of the subject in the *Stages of the Bodhisattva*[99]:

To praise oneself and belittle others [who are endowed with wholesome qualities] out of desire for wealth and honor;

To be miserly with one's personal wealth, i.e., not to give spiritual instructions to those who yearn for them or material aid to the needy, the pitiful, the poor, or the destitute;

Not to forgive someone though he has apologized and, in anger, to strike the person with one's hands, sticks, or in other ways;

To disparage and reject the Universal Way as it is presented in the scriptures that expound the bodhisattva's [training], and to delight in and give false teachings while pretending that they are true Buddhism.

The three conditions necessary for these four deeds to be root downfalls are to have assumed the commitments, to be in a normal state of mind, and to be emotionally involved in the act. Depending on the degree of [emotional] involvement, the downfalls may be serious, moderate, or slight. When there is a considerable degree of emotional involvement and all three of these conditions are met, the downfall is comparable to a defeating offense within the proclaimers' system (i.e., for a monk) [since the commitments are destroyed]. If the involvement is moderate, the downfall is comparable to a partially defeating offense; if slight, to a monk's minor downfall. [In the last two cases, downfalls do not destroy the commitments].

To perpetuate the act, feel no shame or embarrassment about it, be pleased with it, and regard it as a good deed [constitutes] great emotional involvement. The involvement is moderate or slight depending on the presence of many or few of such factors.[100] Further distinctions of involvement are made based on the lapse of time before shame arises, how long it lasts, how quickly [one turns away from the infraction], etc.

Secondary Infractions [B']

The explanation of the forty-six secondary infractions[101] has two parts: (1) the thirty-four contradictions to the development of wholesome qualities, and (2) the twelve contradictions to working for others' welfare.

Thirty-four Contradictions to the Development of Wholesome Qualities [1']

This section has six parts: (1) seven contradictions to generosity, (2) nine contradictions to ethics, (3) four contradictions to patience, (4) three contradictions to effort, (5) three contradictions to meditation, and (6) eight contradictions to wisdom.

Seven Contradictions to Generosity [a']

> **The seven contradictions to generosity are not to make offerings, to indulge in desires, not to have respect,**
> **Not to answer questions, not to accept invitations, to refuse gifts, and not to explain the teachings.**

There are seven [contradictions to] generosity:

(1) Not to make offerings to the Three Jewels[102] and (2) to indulge in one's desires[103] are deviations from the generosity of material things.

(3) Not to respect those senior in training[104] and (4) not to answer questions[105] are deviations from the generosity that protects others from fear.

(5) Not to accept invitations to be a guest[106] and (6) to refuse gifts out of anger[107] are deviations that deny others the opportunity to be generous.

(7) Not to give teachings to those who request them[108] is a deviation from the generosity of providing teachings.

Nine Contradictions to Ethics [b']

The nine contradictions to ethics are to reject the immoral, not to observe the rules, to make little effort for others' sake,
Not to commit an unvirtuous deed although permitted, to engage in wrong livelihood, to play out of excitement and agitation,
To wish for a solitary escape from cyclic existence, not to avoid a bad reputation, and not to resort to disquieting methods.

There are nine contradictions to ethics. Four of these deviate principally from accomplishing the welfare of others:

(1) To reject those with corrupted morals[109];

(2) Not to observe rules of morality in order to inspire others' faith[110];

(3) To make little effort to benefit others[111]; and

(4) Not to commit an unvirtuous deed out of compassion when there is a need to do so, even though this was permitted [by the Buddha].[112]

Three deviate principally from accomplishing one's own welfare:

(1) To engage willingly in one of the five means of wrong livelihood[113];

(2) To play games out of excitement, distraction, and agitation[114]; and

(3) To wish to make a solitary escape from the cycle of existence out of desire [for perfect peace].[115]

Two deviate from both one's own and others' welfare:

(1) Not to avoid a bad reputation[116]; and
(2) Not to resort to disquieting methods.[117]

Four Contradictions to Patience [c']

**Four contradictions to patience are to neglect the four obliga-
tions, to reject an angry person,
To refuse apologies, and to give in to anger.**

There are four contradictions to patience:

(1) To neglect the four obligations of a monk (not to respond to
being chided by chiding, to anger by expressing anger, to
being struck by striking back, and to insult by insulting);
(2) Not to work peacefully with people who are angry with one
but instead to reject them[118];
(3) Not to accept someone's sincere apology[119]; and
(4) To give in to anger.[120]

Three Contradictions to Effort [d']

**The three contradictions to effort are to gather followers, not to
overcome laziness, and to delight in meaningless conversation.**

There are three contradictions to effort:

(1) To gather a circle of followers out of desire for wealth and
fame[121];
(2) Not to overcome the various forms of laziness[122];
(3) To delight in entertainment and meaningless conversation
out of attachment.[123]

Three Contradictions to Meditation [e']

**The three contradictions to meditation are not to seek instruc-
tions, not to overcome impediments, and to be attached to the
pleasurable experience of meditation.**

There are three contradictions to meditation:

(1) Not to seek [instructions in] contemplation[124];
(2) Not to overcome the impediments [that hinder] meditation[125]; and
(3) To regard the [pleasurable] experience of meditation as a goal
in itself and to be attached to it.

Eight Contradictions to Wisdom [f']

> **The eight contradictions to wisdom are to reject the proclaimers'
> way, to embrace that way or a non-Buddhist one,
> To prefer its literature, to take no interest in the distinctive
> features of the Universal Way, not to seek the true teachings,
> To praise oneself and belittle others, and to rely on the words
> rather than the meaning:
> These thirty-four contradictions prevent the development of
> wholesome qualities.**

Of the eight contradictions to wisdom, four concern the lesser [spiritual pursuits]:

- (1) To reject the proclaimers' way out of disrespect[126];
- (2) To embrace the proclaimers' way after forsaking the Universal Way[127];
- (3) To study non-Buddhist treatises[128] after forsaking the Universal Way; and
- (4) To prefer the Individual Way or non-Buddhist literature although attaching oneself to the Universal Way.[129]

Four contradictions concern the highest [spiritual pursuits]:

- (1) Not to take interest in the distinctive features of the Universal Way[130];
- (2) Not to seek the true teachings due to pride or laziness, and so forth[131];
- (3) To praise oneself and belittle others[132]; and
- (4) To rely on the words rather than on the meaning of the teachings.[133]

Twelve Contradictions to Working for Others' Welfare [2']

The twelve contradictions to working for others' welfare are divided into two categories: (1) four contradictions to altruism in general, and (2) eight contradictions to altruism in particular cases.

Four Contradictions to Altruism in General [a']

> **Not to help persons in need, not to care for the sick, not to
> relieve others' suffering,
> Not to correct the heedless**

There are four [contradictions to altruism in general]:

(1) Not to help others when it is definitely needed[134];
(2) Not to care for sick persons[135];
(3) Not to relieve others of suffering[136]; and
(4) Not to correct those who are heedless.[137]

Eight Contradictions to Altruism in Particular Cases [b']

**...not to repay kindness, not to relieve pain, not to be
generous,
Not to care, not to comply, not to praise, not to correct,
Not to uplift others: these twelve contradict working
for others' benefit.**

Of the eight contradictions [to altruism in particular cases], six involve the fault of not helping another:

(1) Not to repay the kindness one has received[138];
(2) Not to relieve another's pain[139];
(3) Not to give material aid to someone who asks, even
though one can[140];
(4) Not to take care of one's circle [of students, friends, and
relatives][141];
(5) Not to act in accordance with another's wish[142]; and
(6) Not to praise someone who deserves praise.[143]

Two contradictions involve not taking corrective measures:

(1) Not to discipline a wrongdoer[144];
(2) Not to uplift spiritually, with demonstrations of miracles
or supernatural knowledge, a suitable aspirant.[145]

**Infractions are of three types: emotional, non-emotional,
and without consequence.**

The *Stages of the Bodhisattva* explains that each of the forty-six secondary infractions is considered one of three types: emotional (i.e., committed out of irreverence or complacence[146]); non-emotional (when committed out of forgetfulness or carelessness); and of no consequence (when committed in order to maintain discipline within the monastic community or in a state of mental derangement).[147]

Restoration of the Commitments [c]

> **If a root downfall is committed with great emotional involve-**
> **ment or if the aspiration for awakening has deteriorated,**
> **The commitments are lost and must be reassumed.**
> **Downfalls committed with medium or slight involvement are**
> **confessed before three vow holders or one;**
> **Emotional minor infractions, before one; and non-emotional**
> **minor infractions, with one's mind as witness.**

The *Stages of the Bodhisattva* states that the two causes[148] of loss [of the commitments] are to incur a root downfall with great emotional involvement or to allow one's aspiration for enlightenment to deteriorate. In these cases, a complete breach of the commitments is incurred. [To restore it], one must first acknowledge one's failing and promise not to repeat it and then reassume the commitments in a ceremony. However, the venerable Longchenpa said that this may not be done more than three times.

Downfalls incurred with either moderate or slight emotional involvement [do not constitute loss of the commitments and] are not [actually] defeats but are similar to them.[149] In the case of moderate involvement, one must acknowledge the downfall with a promise to refrain [from it in the future] made in the presence of three or more vow holders[150]; in the case of slight involvement, in the presence of a single vow holder.

Any of the forty-two minor infractions incurred with emotional involvement should be acknowledged in the presence of a vow holder if circumstances allow. Non-emotional minor infractions are purified by acknowledgment [of the failing] in the imagined presence of the buddhas and bodhisattvas, with one's own mind as witness.[151]

The general causes of loss of the commitments have been elucidated above and should be well understood. Although the returning of vows is permitted in the personal liberation system, to return the commitments of the awakening mind would have extremely serious consequences and is therefore absolutely prohibited.

Dying, being reborn, forgetting [one's previous existence], and so on, do not damage one's commitments. The *Stages of the Bodhisattva* states[152]:

> In going from one life to another, a bodhisattva may forget his commitments. He may assume them again many times in the presence of spiritual guides, as a result of which he may recollect his [former] commitments. However, this would not be a case of taking them anew.

Additional Points on the Training [d]

> In this tradition, one must observe all points of training to their
> full extent and until awakening.

Unlike the tradition of the profound view, in this tradition, once one
has assumed the commitments of awakening mind, one must observe
the full range of training in the aspiring and venturing minds. Furthermore, unlike the previous tradition in which one [promises to]
train in the prescribed practice only for as long as one wants, here
one must observe the training from the time the commitments are
assumed until the attainment of awakening. The two systems should
not be confused on these two points.

THE TRAINING COMMON TO BOTH TRADITIONS [V]

The explanation of the training common to both traditions has three
parts: (1) the training in aspiring mind, (2) the training in venturing
mind, and (3) advice on safeguarding the trainings in the aspiring
and venturing minds.

Training in the Aspiring Mind [A]

This section has three parts: (1) the five precepts, (2) the three noble
aspirations, and (3) eliminating the causes of deterioration of the aspiring mind.

Five Precepts [1]

> Common to both traditions are five precepts for the aspiring
> awakening mind:
> Not to reject any being; to ponder benefits; to acquire merits;
> to refine the awakening mind;
> And to shun the four black deeds of deceiving one's master
> or a venerable person, feeling regret for what is not to be
> regretted,
> Being angry at a bodhisattva, and being cunning and deceitful,
> And to undertake the four white deeds in their place.

For the training common to both traditions, first is the training in the
awakening mind of aspiration which consists in the observance of
five precepts:

(1) Not to reject or consider insignificant any being, be it an enemy or a mere insect (the basic precept);

(2) To ponder the benefits of awakening mind by recalling and reciting passages from the scriptures and their commentaries, as did the great Lord Atisha, who was renowned for his sudden exclamations such as "[Awakening mind] saves us from miserable existences!" (the precept of the favorable condition for preserving aspiring mind);

(3) To strive at the cultivation of merit in conjunction with pristine awareness by engaging in the ten virtuous activities,[153] the six perfections, etc. (the precept of the cause that strengthens the awakening mind);

(4) To refine awakening mind by reaffirming one's commitments daily in each of the six [three-hour] periods, cultivating love and compassion, and practicing an oral instruction to develop awakening mind using a technique that is the basis of mind training—exchanging one's own happiness for others' suffering (the precept of the skillful means to develop awakening mind); and

(5) To shun the four black deeds and undertake the four white ones (as the means to give up what weakens the awakening mind or causes one to forget it, and to engage in the opposite).

These four black deeds are explained in the *Questions of Kashyapa Scripture*[154]:

(1) To deceive one's master or other persons worthy of veneration by lying or in other ways;

(2) To feel regret for what is not regrettable (regrettable actions are those that constitute downfalls or unwholesome deeds);

(3) To speak offensive words in anger to someone who has formed an awakening mind; and

(4) To be cunning and deceitful toward someone, whether in substantial or minor ways.

Regardless of whether the offended person is aware or not, or is displeased or not, these four deeds constitute downfalls and are therefore called black. If [one fails to amend any of these acts] before three hours have elapsed, the commitments are lost. Therefore, one must acknowledge one's wrongdoing, and reaffirm the commitments immediately.

As antidotes to the four black deeds, these four white actions should be undertaken:

(1) Not to consciously tell a lie, even to save one's life;

(2) To encourage others to engage in virtuous pursuits and, in particular, to follow the Universal Way,

(3) To see every bodhisattva as the Buddha, and to proclaim his or her virtues; and

(4) To maintain a noble [and altruistic] attitude toward others.

Three Noble Aspirations [2]

One should have the three noble aspirations of goal, skillful means, and marvelous activity

The three aspirations of a noble person are these:

(1) "I shall attain enlightenment for the benefit of all beings" (the aspiration to achieve the goal);

(2) "In order to attain enlightenment, I shall enter the path of awakening" (the aspiration to apply skillful means); and

(3) "I shall fulfill the hopes of all beings" (the aspiration to engage in marvelous activity).

The bodhisattva-in-training should always have the [same] aspirations.

Eliminating the Causes of Deterioration [3]

And eliminate despair, apprehension, and other emotions that cause aspiration to deteriorate.

A practitioner should eliminate the following emotions since they are antagonistic to an awakening mind and cause it to deteriorate:

(1) Despair when thinking of the hardships involved in giving up for altruistic reasons one's children or spouse, or even one's head and limbs; or when thinking of the hardships involved in observing [the bodhisattva's] ethics, making endeavors [for the sake of others], and engaging in the rest of the six perfections;

(2) Faint-heartedness when thinking that having to cultivate all aspects of merit and to enhance pristine awareness over thirty uncountable eons is far too long to bear; and

(3) Apprehension [from knowing that] wherever one is born in cyclic existence, one will not find any vestige of happiness; and, as a result, longing to make a solitary escape from cyclic existence.

Training in the Venturing Mind [B]

The training in the venturing mind is explained in two parts: (1) a concise statement, and (2) an extensive explanation.

Concise Statement [1]

The points of training in venturing mind prescribe both what to avoid and what to practice.
All these points are included in the threefold ethics of restraint, acquiring good qualities, and working for the benefit of others.

The points of training in the venturing mind prescribe both what to avoid and what to practice. These two aspects of training constitute a vast subject that encompasses most disciplines of the Universal and Individual ways. All points of training, however, are included in the three types of ethics: the ethics of restraint from acting in unwholesome ways, ethics aimed at acquiring good qualities, and the ethics of working for the benefit of others.[155] The *Stages of the Bodhisattva*'s treatment of the three ethics is summarized by Lord Daö Shönnu (Gampopa) in the following words[156]:

The first makes our minds calm, the second ripens our minds' qualities, and the third brings all sentient beings to full spiritual maturity.[157]

The Extensive Explanation [2]

This section has two parts: (1) the prescription for what to avoid, and (2) the prescription for practice.

Prescription for What to Avoid [a]

This is presented in two parts: (1) the essence of the prescription, and (2) the points of training in detail.

Its Essence [i]

> **The prescription for what to avoid corresponds to the commitments set out in the two traditions mentioned above.**

The prescription for what to avoid is essentially the ethics of restraining from what is unwholesome. Included in this prescription are the ordinary vows one has taken [as part of] the eight classes of personal liberation, as well as the commitments exclusive to the Universal Way to avoid the root downfalls and secondary infractions explained above in the context of the two traditions of the pioneers [Nagarjuna and Asanga]. Also included is the advice to shun what is incompatible with the commitments of awakening mind as set out in the scriptures of the Universal Way and referred to as "demonic":

(1) The ten unvirtuous deeds;
(2) The eight worldly concerns[158];
(3) The eight opposites of the eightfold noble path[159] (wrong view, wrong thought, etc.);
(4) The five forms of wrong livelihood (flattery, hinting, seeking reward for favor, pretentious behavior, and hypocrisy);
(5) The five unsuitable environments (of butchers, liquor sellers, prostitutes, politicians, and those of evil occupations[160]);
(6) The four causes that undermine virtue (not dedicating merits, inappropriate dedication, regretting one's good deeds, and anger); and
(7) The mixing of contradictory views, cherishing bad friends, professing unwholesome views, and so forth.

The Points of Training in Detail [ii]

> **One should renounce what is naturally unwholesome or unwholesome by prescription except in cases of special necessity,**
> **Impediments to the spiritual maturity of oneself and others,**
> **Pleasures of this life that create suffering in the next, or what causes misery in both,**
> **Deeds that qualify as downfalls, and downfalls-in-disguise**

A practitioner should renounce the following unless there is a special necessity for not doing so:

(1) All deeds that are naturally unvirtuous or unvirtuous by Buddha's prohibition;

(2) Impediments to the spiritual maturity of oneself or others (for example, a monk adopting the lifestyle and apparel of a layperson);

(3) Superficial pleasures of this life that will result in painful experiences in future lives (for example, enjoying food and wealth acquired illicitly);

(4) What leads to misery now and in future lives (for example, making war preparations),

(5) All the downfalls mentioned above; and downfalls-in-disguise.

And undertake what brings happiness in the next life though is painful in the present, what brings happiness in both,
Deeds that do not constitute downfalls, and those that might seem to be downfalls but are not.

A practitioner should engage in what brings great happiness in future lives though it may entail suffering in the present one, for example, withstanding difficulties in seeking the Buddha's teaching and making large offerings to worthy objects; what brings both immediate and permanent happiness, such as observing pure morality; and deeds that do not constitute downfalls, as well as deeds that seem to be downfalls but in fact are not.

Four distinctions apply to deeds categorized as downfalls: In observing the ethics of restraint, to kill someone motivated by hatred [for example] would constitute a downfall (Tib. *ltung ba*); to kill with an altruistic purpose might seem to be a downfall but actually is not (*ltung ba'i gzugs brnyan*); to refrain from killing out of compassion for the object does not constitute a downfall (*ltung med*); and not to kill although it would help another might seem not to be a downfall but actually is (*ltung med gzugs brnyan*).

In observing the ethics aimed at acquiring good qualities, not to give because of miserliness [for example] would be a downfall; to refrain from giving because one has an altruistic purpose in not giving resembles a downfall but is not one; to give with pure intention does not constitute a downfall; and to give in order to harm others might seem not to be a downfall but in fact is.

In observing the ethics of working for the benefit of all beings, not to nurse the sick [for example] would be a downfall; not to nurse the sick in order to accomplish a higher goal resembles a downfall but in fact is not; to lovingly nurse the sick does not constitute a downfall; to renounce a higher goal such as one's own meditation or study to nurse a sick person when there already is a nurse attending to his needs might seem not to be a downfall but actually is one.

All actions done with compassionate concern are without fault.

Twenty Verses on the Bodhisattva's Commitments states[161]:

> When one's action springs from compassionate concern, love,
> Or a virtuous intention, no fault is incurred.

When a person acts from three motives—compassionate concern, love, or virtuous intention—and without any self-interest but solely to help another, no downfall is incurred in doing any of the actions in [the above scheme of] four distinctions unless it entails losing the commitments of awakening mind. In fact, acting in these ways is said to be part of one's training [in awakening mind].[162]

Prescription for Practice [b]

This is presented in two parts: (1) a concise statement, and (2) the practice in detail.

Concise Statement [i]

> **The prescribed practice corresponds to the ethics aimed at acquiring good qualities, which is the practice of the six perfections.**

The prescribed practice for the venturing mind is the ethics aimed at acquiring good qualities. The incomparable Gampopa states[163]:

> The ethics aimed at acquiring good qualities includes, in addition to all the precepts of the bodhisattva's ethics of restraint, everything that serves to cultivate wholesomeness of body and speech in order to attain great enlightenment.

All aspects of training [in the venturing mind] are set forth in great detail in the scriptures and their commentaries. Everything that is prescribed, however, is encompassed by the practice of the six perfections alone.

The Practice in Detail [ii]

This section has three parts: (1) an overall description of the six perfections, (2) the six perfections in detail, and (3) the ethics of working for the benefit of all beings.

Overall Description of the Six Perfections [A']

> **The perfections are described in terms of their number, order, characteristics,**
> **Semantic meaning, divisions, and groups.**

The six perfections are described generally in terms of their number, order, characteristics, semantic meaning, divisions, and groups. First, the perfections number exactly six in view of the goals of higher states and liberation to which they lead: the first three, generosity, ethics, and patience, lead to rebirth in higher states of existence, while the latter three lead to liberation. A different explanation states that by practicing the first three one accomplishes the benefit of others, and the last three, one's own purpose.

The six perfections are presented in a set order, from generosity to wisdom, to reflect their gradual development, as ethics develops from generosity, patience from ethics, and so on. According to another explanation, the order represents degrees of excellence, the lesser presented first and the greater later (ethics being superior to generosity, etc.) or in the sequence of coarse to subtle. In any case, those easier to cultivate are presented first.

The perfections possess four characteristics: they weaken miserliness and other emotions incompatible [with generosity, and so forth]; they are accompanied by pristine awareness which is free of the concepts of act, agent, and object; their function is to fulfill the needs of others; and their result is the maturation of students' minds in accordance with the three spiritual ways.[164]

They are called perfections ["transcendent virtues"] because they transcend all the virtues of worldly beings, proclaimers, and solitary sages, and lead to the perfect state.

Each perfection may be divided into six branches, the generosity of generosity, the generosity of ethics, etc., to make thirty-six branches, which may be further subdivided into one hundred or one thousand.[165]

The perfections may be grouped according to the two cultivations of merit and pristine awareness: generosity and ethics are the means to cultivate merit; discriminative wisdom, the means to cultivate pristine awareness; and the other three, the means to cultivate both merit and pristine awareness. They may also be grouped according to the three types of training: the first three (generosity, ethics, and patience) belong to the training in higher ethics; the fifth (meditation), to the training in meditation; and the sixth (discriminative wisdom), to the training in wisdom; effort accompanies all three trainings.[166]

The Six Perfections in Detail [B']

> Each perfection is threefold: Generosity of material aid, the
> teachings, protection,
> Ethics of restraint, aimed at acquiring good qualities, and
> working for the benefit of others,
> Patience to withstand harm, accept hardships, and fathom
> emptiness,
> Effort that is armor-like, applied to the task, and insatiable,
> Meditation of resting at ease, aimed at acquiring good qualities,
> and focused on the welfare of others,
> Wisdom that is worldly and supramundane, higher and lower,
> Or wisdom that arises through listening, pondering, and
> meditating.

An explanation of four aspects of each perfection—definition, etymology, classifications, and purpose—will not be provided at this point. However, the essential points will be covered.

Generosity is threefold, that of material aid, the Buddhist teachings, and protection. The generosity of material goods includes the "gift" of one's various possessions, "great gift" [of spouse or children], or "highest gift" [of the parts of one's body]. For generosity to be authentic, it must be unpolluted by the four stains of improper intention, gift, recipient, or manner of giving.[167]

The generosity of the teachings is to teach the Universal or Individual ways according to the intellectual ability of aspirants.

The generosity of protection means to save from temporary fear those threatened by rulers, tigers, lions, fire, flood, disease, weapons, etc., and from lasting fear those [who have fallen into lower forms of life or are bound to cyclic existence]. (An alternative system distinguishes the following three forms of generosity: continuous generosity, impartial generosity, and generosity that fulfills the wishes of others.[168])

Ethics is threefold: ethics of restraint from what is unwholesome, ethics aimed at acquiring good qualities, and ethics of working for the benefit of all beings. These three have been explained above.

Patience is threefold: patience in withstanding harmful persons, accepting hardships, and determining reality.

Patience in withstanding harm done by others means not to retaliate for the harm done to one's person or interests. This patience is developed through meditation according to the nine methods[169] taught in Shantideva's *Guide to the Bodhisattva's Way of Life* or by cultivating the five thoughts described in Asanga's *Stages of the Bodhisattva*.[170]

Patience in accepting hardships consists in enduring difficulties, such as fatigue, hunger, and thirst, that one may encounter in the quest for the teachings.[171]

Patience in determining reality means not to be discouraged or intimidated by profound subjects such as emptiness.

Effort is threefold: armor-like effort, effort applied to the task, and insatiable effort.[172] Armor-like effort means to [wear the armor of] endeavor in what is wholesome throughout every single session of practice, with the intention of never relinquishing it until awakening is attained.

Effort applied to the task means never to be indifferent to the three areas [of training]: to overcome one's emotions, to accomplish what is wholesome, and to work for the benefit of all sentient beings. The second of these, effort in accomplishing what is wholesome, is fivefold: ever-active effort, devoted effort, effort unshaken by emotions, effort not deflected by circumstances, and effort without pride.[173]

Insatiable effort means never considering one's virtuous endeavor to be sufficient.

Meditation is of three kinds: meditation through which one rests in a state of ease in the present life, meditation aimed at acquiring good qualities, and meditation of working for the welfare of others.[174]

Meditation through which one rests in a state of ease in the present life refers to the meditative concentration that produces both the approximate and subtle aspects of perfect physical and mental ease.[175]

Meditation aimed at acquiring good qualities has common and exclusive aspects. The common aspect refers to the powers of totalities, masteries, liberations, and so forth[176]; and the exclusive, to the powers that are special qualities of the bodhisattvas only.[177]

The meditation of working for the welfare of others refers to the meditative concentration through which one uplifts others spiritually by demonstrating miracles, using supernatural knowledge, etc.

Wisdom [or discriminative wisdom] is of three types: worldly, lower supramundane, and higher supramundane wisdom, each being progressively superior.

Worldly wisdom refers to learning [derived from study of] the common sciences.[178]

Lower supramundane wisdom refers to the understanding of the four truths [derived from learning, pondering, and meditating on] the tenets of the proclaimers and solitary sages.

Higher supramundane wisdom refers to the understanding of the two types of selflessness [derived from listening, pondering, and meditating upon] the tenets of the Universal Way.

An alternative system distinguishes the following three types of wisdom: the wisdom that arises from listening, from pondering, and from meditating.

The wisdom that arises from listening refers to knowledge of many scriptures and reasonings and comprehension of their meanings.

The wisdom that arises from pondering refers to the elimination of misconceptions about the objects of knowledge gained from a discriminative understanding of the four philosophical systems,[179] the relative and ultimate truths, the definitive message [of the scriptures] and the interpretable one, and other subjects.

The wisdom that arises from meditation refers to the realization of the abiding nature [of reality] which results from meditating on those subjects.

> **When wisdom is present, all five become supramundane perfections.**

One's practice of the six perfections must incorporate six noble components:

(1) A noble foundation, which is to have formed the resolve to awaken;

(2) A noble deed, which is generosity and the other perfections practiced impartially in all their different aspects;

(3) A noble referent, which is to engage in the six perfections for the benefit of all other beings;

(4) A noble means, in which the six perfections are permeated with wisdom free of the concepts of act, agent, and object;

(5) A noble dedication, which is to dedicate the merit thus acquired to the attainment of unsurpassable awakening;

(6) A noble purity, which is to engage in the six perfections as direct remedies to the two types of impediments (emotional impediments and impediments to omniscience).

Of particular importance is the perfection of wisdom. Practice of the first five perfections without non-conceptual wisdom constitutes only worldly good deeds. On this point, the *Condensed Transcendent Wisdom Scripture* states[180]:

> How will a hundred billion blind people
> Find the road, let alone enter a city?
> Lacking wisdom, the other five perfections are blind,
> And without the guide of wisdom, enlightenment cannot be attained.

These perfections become "supramundane perfections" when such wisdom accompanies them.[181]

The Ethics of Working for the Benefit of All Beings [C']

Four means of attraction and other ways are used to benefit others.

Once a practitioner has come to spiritual maturity by following the ethics aimed at acquiring good qualities, he or she should engage in the ethics of working for the benefit of all beings. These ethics include the four means of attracting disciples: generous acts, pleasant speech, suitable teachings, and appropriate behavior:

(1) In order to attract new disciples, the master acts generously by offering gifts that will please them.

(2) Once disciples are attracted, the master uses pleasant speech to draw them closer while giving them teachings on the Buddhist doctrine. In this way, the master instills in them enthusiasm for and appreciation of the teachings, as well as earnest interest in putting them into practice.

(3) The master guides disciples in practicing the teachings suitable to their capabilities. Children must be nourished first with liquid and then [as they grow] with solid foods. Similarly, disciples of different intellectual capacities cannot be spiritually nourished by one instruction alone.

(4) The master behaves in accordance with the teachings in order to be a leading [example] for disciples in their virtuous endeavors and in [their pursuit of] the Buddha's teachings.

The words "other ways" [in the above root verse] indicate that one should also earnestly put into practice the twelve ways [of helping others that are included in the four means of attraction], which are opposite to the twelve contradictions to working for the welfare of others previously mentioned.

Advice on Safeguarding the Trainings in the Aspiring and Venturing Minds [C]

> Awakening mind and its training are safeguarded with mindfulness and discriminating alertness.

Awakening mind should be safeguarded by relying on mindfulness, discriminating alertness, and conscientiousness. Mindfulness means never to forget awakening mind and always to maintain its precepts. Discriminating alertness is to recognize whether or not an infraction [of the precepts] has occurred. Conscientiousness means to be strict in one's observance of proper behavior and avoidance of wrongful acts.

In particular, once one has formed a precious mind of awakening and is engaged in its training, one should strive to preserve, refine, and enhance both this mind and its training. To preserve awakening mind so that it does not deteriorate means to abide in the essence of the aspiring and venturing minds and abide by the precepts conducive to its preservation. To refine awakening mind means to abide by the precepts whereby one shuns all wrong actions and avoids nonconducive conditions. To enhance the virtue [of awakening mind] means to exchange one's own happiness for others' suffering and to abide by the precepts conducive to virtue's enhancement.

To preserve the training means to scrupulously avoid what is prohibited and practice what is advised. To refine the training is to forsake inappropriate actions of body, speech, and mind—purposeless jumping, running, and moving about; excessive, harsh, or divisive words; harboring desire for material gain or fame, and attachment to sleep and mental inertia—and to cultivate peaceful, relaxed, pleasant, and considerate behavior; gentle and moderate speech; and a mind of faith and detachment. To enhance the training is to develop three aspects of the training: pristine awareness, discriminative awareness, and the dedication [of merit].

Furthermore, both awakening mind and its training should be diligently preserved through techniques of mental development, such as making the forty-one [prayers] to cultivate awakening mind as taught in the *Pure Domain* chapter of the *Flower Ornament Scripture*.[182] As well, the following four practices should be undertaken since all aspects of the commitments of the awakening mind are encompassed by them: To give others [one's body, wealth, and virtues, which are] the three bases for generosity, to safeguard awakening mind, to refine it, and to enhance it. Accordingly, the *Compendium of Trainings* states[183]:

> To give away to others one's body and belongings
> And all virtues throughout time,
> And to guard one's awakening mind,
> To refine it, and enhance it.

It is important to understand that a beginner will be primarily concerned with safeguarding [the awakening mind]; a bodhisattva whose practice is based on appreciation,[184] with refining it; those who are on the seven impure levels,[185] with giving [all they have to others]; and those on the three pure levels, with expanding [the awakening mind].

THE FORMATION OF ULTIMATE AWAKENING MIND [VI]

The ultimate awakening mind is discussed under five headings: (1) cause, (2) essence, (3) classification, (4) ceremony, and (5) nature.

Cause [A]

> **A great wave of altruistic deeds is the cause of an ultimate awakening mind.**

The formation of a relative awakening mind serves as the general condition for the arising of an ultimate awakening mind. The specific factors that determine the formation of the ultimate mind are stated by the incomparable Gampopa in the following words[186]:

> It arises from the distinguished factors of scriptures, practice, and realization.

Ultimate awakening mind may arise as a result of learning and pondering the scriptural teachings or realizing it as spiritual accomplishment, or both of these together. It may also arise from a realization awakened in the depths of one's heart through the blessing of a marvelous connection between oneself and a qualified teacher. In all cases, however, the actual cause of ultimate awakening mind is the generation of an immense wave of altruistic deeds.

Essence [B]

Its essence is the pristine awareness of an exalted bodhisattva's equipoise.

The essence of ultimate awakening mind is pristine awareness, the direct realization of the non-conceptual nature of reality. Accordingly, the incomparable physician of Dakpo states[187]:

> What is ultimate awakening mind? It is emptiness endowed with the essence of compassion, clear, unwavering, and free from fabrications of any objectifiable attributes.

Such pristine awareness is an awakening mind existing as the nature of the meditative equipoise of exalted bodhisattvas dwelling on the various stages of awakening. It also exists as the nature of indivisible equipoise and post-equipoise at the buddha's stage.

Classification [C]

It may be divided into the awakening mind of the first stage, and so forth.

Ultimate awakening mind, being in essence emptiness, is not divisible. However, there are many distinctions according to the different ways it arises: awakening mind [that has the nature of] the realization [of reality] gained on the first stage of awakening, and so forth, up to awakening mind at the stage of a buddha.

Ceremony [D]

Some scholars assert that ultimate awakening mind can be formed in a ritual; others deny this.

Lord of the Teachings Jikten Sumgön and his followers believe that ultimate awakening mind can be formed in a ritual and substantiate their assertion with quotations from discourses and tantras.[188] The ultimate awakening mind taught in the tantras can arise in a ceremony; therefore (they say) the one taught in the discourses can be formed in a ritual, just as the vows of personal liberation [can be assumed in a tantric as well as a non-tantric ceremony]. To prove that the Secret Mantra system speaks of the formation of the ultimate awakening mind, they say that in the context of the tantras, the "creative imagination of a vajra standing on a moon,"[189] though it is not called so, is well known to be referring to the formation of the ultimate awakening mind.

The following objection may be raised to their position: One cannot speak of the formation of the ultimate awakening mind in relation to the "creative imagination of a vajra standing on a moon" because this creative imagination, being a technique to train on the path using the aspect [of the resultant buddhahood], does not produce the actual ultimate mind of awakening, but only a facsimile of it.

To this objection, they reply that [if one cannot speak of formation of ultimate awakening mind just because it is not the actual awakening mind that is formed but only a facsimile,] similarly one could not speak of the formation of the commitments of the venturing awakening mind or the generation of other vows as well. However, this is not the case. For example, though the vows of personal liberation are ordinary when initially assumed, they later become genuine when they become imbued with renunciation. Likewise, the commitments of awakening mind initially exist simply as aspects of a virtuous mind. Later, when the bodhisattva actually enters the path of accumulation, the totality of mind and mental states becomes of one nature with the commitments, and, as a result, the genuine aspiring and venturing minds are formed. In the same way, [the ultimate awakening mind of] the non-conceptual pristine awareness [of reality] is initially cognized through a powerful ritual. Later, when the roots of virtue ripen, the continuity of such cognition evolves into a direct realization [of reality, which is ultimate awakening mind].

On the basis of such reasonings, Jikten Sumgön and his followers adopted the system [of performing a ritual for formation of ultimate awakening mind]. Sakya Pandita, however, presents a different perspective on this argument[190]:

> Ultimate awakening mind arises through the power of meditation, not by a ritual. If it were possible [by ritual], ultimate awakening mind would be formed simply by indications, and to call that [ultimate] is not logical.[191] Although it is possible that the Buddha [as cited in the *Hundred Rites of Renunciation and Fulfillment*[192]]

declared "You should form the ultimate awakening mind!" this refers simply to a promise, not to a rite [for the formation of the ultimate awakening mind].

The followers of the outstanding Ngari Panchen also assert that the ultimate awakening mind cannot arise in a ritual.[193]

These two perspectives do not contradict each other. The former view [that of Jikten Sumgön] asserts that the ritual produces a facsimile [of ultimate awakening mind], while the latter [that of Sakya Pandita], that a ritual cannot produce a genuine [ultimate awakening mind]. However, it would be unreasonable to say that the adherents [of Sakya Pandita's view] categorically deny the possibility of ultimate awakening mind arising in a ritual. In fact, the reasons and proofs that validate the statement, "the pristine awareness of the fourth empowerment arises depending just on words," [which these followers are bound to accept] are similar to those that would validate the statement, "ultimate awakening mind arises in a ritual."

Nature [E]

> Ultimate awakening mind possessed of three ultimate aspects
> Is the pristine awareness that directly realizes the sphere of
>   reality.

What is the actual nature of ultimate awakening mind? In the Secret Mantra system, it is considered to be non-dual pristine awareness. The assertions of different masters seem to indicate many levels of subtlety. However, from the perspective of the Way of the Perfections, ultimate awakening mind is awakening mind possessed of three ultimate aspects: absolute dedication, subsequent achievement, and realization,[194] as stated in [Maitreya's] *Scripture Ornament*[195]:

> Because the perfect buddhas have been well honored,
> And merit and awareness have been thoroughly cultivated,
> Because non-conceptual pristine awareness has arisen,
> It is said to be ultimate.

Scholars [of the Universal Way] consider ultimate awakening mind to be the pristine awareness of the direct realization of the selflessness of phenomena, which is naturally present on the first stage of awakening. This pristine awareness arises as a result of honoring the perfect buddhas (the principal condition) while on the path of accumulation; and of cultivating merit and pristine awareness over an incalculable eon (the cause) while on the path of preparation.[196]

THE CONSEQUENCES OF DAMAGING THE COMMITMENTS AND BENEFITS OF SAFEGUARDING THEM [VII]

> To damage awakening mind brings four adverse consequences.
>   To safeguard aspiration reaps eight merits; and venturing
>   mind, two special ones.
> The awakening mind is indeed the source of all temporary and
>   lasting benefits and happiness.

The scriptures state that deterioration of the training in awakening mind leads to unlimited negative consequences. These are summarized in the following four consequences (the first three are general consequences of downfalls; the fourth, specific consequences of a root downfall):

(1) One becomes an object of everyone's scorn because one has broken a promise and thereby deceived the teacher, the Buddha, sentient beings for whose benefit one was working, and oneself, the perpetrator.

(2) Like a king losing his kingdom, one loses one's purpose in life, and consequently all sorts of misfortunes, both immediate and in the long run, befall one.

(3) In the future one will fall into miserable forms of life, from which escape is difficult.

(4) All the virtues one had amassed by forming an awakening mind are nullified; the Three Jewels and the deities [who favor the Buddhist teachings] are deceived, and as a result, one is reborn in one of the great hells. Even though one may have felt some shame or embarrassment, acknowledged one's mistake, and reaffirmed one's commitments, if one has engaged in a downfall, the attainment of the stage of a bodhisattva is greatly delayed.

Similarly, Shantideva says[197]:

> Those who have the power of awakening mind
> But have committed a downfall
> Stay revolving in cyclic existence,
> And are greatly delayed in reaching the [bodhisattva's] stages.

Therefore, from the very beginning, a bodhisattva should make every effort to prevent transgressions to the training.

To safeguard the training in awakening mind brings unlimited benefits, which are summarized in the following ten (eight merits are accrued from safeguarding the mind of aspiration; two, from the venturing mind). The eight are illustrated in the following words of the incomparable Gampopa[198]:

> Preserving the aspiration to awaken brings eight benefits: one enters the Universal Way; one becomes a candidate for the training of a bodhisattva; all evil deeds are uprooted; the seed of unsurpassable awakening is planted; infinite merits are amassed; all buddhas are pleased; all beings are served; and full enlightenment is swiftly reached.

In addition to those, two special merits are accrued from safeguarding the venturing mind:

(1) From the time an awakening mind has first been formed, the flow of merit never ceases, [even when] asleep or careless, thus fulfilling one's own purpose.

(2) The interest of others is accomplished in various ways, by alleviating their misery, working for their well being, etc.

Moreover, each of the six perfections is said to yield its own boundless merits. In short, from now until the attainment of enlightenment, all of one's noble qualities will spring from the precious mind of awakening. Thus, awakening mind is the source of all happiness and well being, now and in the future.

A SYNOPSIS OF THE PHASES OF THE PATH IN THE UNIVERSAL WAY [VIII]

The phases of this path are summarized in Maitreya's *Scripture Ornament*[199]:

> To awaken spiritual affinity, show interest in the teachings,
> Engender awakening mind,
> Practice generosity and the other perfections,
> Bring others to spiritual maturity,[200]
> Enter a faultless state,[201]
> Create buddha fields,[202]
> Attain non-abiding perfect peace,[203]
> And demonstrate the path to supreme awakening.[204]

An awakened affinity for the Universal Way, which forms the basis for all good fortune, is indicated by the qualities of compassion, respect, patience, and delight in the practice of virtue. One who possesses such qualities will show an undivided interest in the teachings and form a connection by seeking refuge [in the Three Jewels], which means to enter the Buddhist path. To engender a supreme awakening mind marks one's entrance to the Universal Way.

Once one has entered the Universal Way, the practice of the six perfections (generosity, etc.) brings one to spiritual maturity. Striving to the best of one's ability, both in the state of equipoise and post-equipoise, at the four means to attract disciples brings others to spiritual maturity.

As a natural consequence of these efforts, one's focus never shifts from spiritual development. Faith, renunciation, meditation, and other forms of virtue are never tired of; enthusiasm increases as naturally as a swan alights on a lotus pond. These signs indicate the start of the journey on the lesser path of accumulation.[205]

Effort is then directed toward the attainment of exalted qualities, such as the abilities [to enter] faultless meditative absorption and to create a buddha field.[206] Gaining some measure of a clear impression of the [sixteen] attributes of the four truths[207] is to achieve the path of accumulation.

The strength of meditation [on the four truths] conjoined with the strength of the cultivation of all aspects of merit produces the realization of the phantom-like nature of the five aggregates.[208] Gradually a clear understanding of phenomenal selflessness is achieved; this is the path of preparation.

The first sight of the essential meaning of the two kinds of selflessness marks one's entrance onto the path of seeing. Further cultivation of special meditative concentrations focused on the [two selflessnesses] previously understood characterizes the path of meditation. Finally, the apex of knowledge and freedom is reached on the path of no more learning.

The correlation between these paths and the bodhisattva's stages of awakening is as follows. On the path of seeing, the bodhisattva attains the pristine awareness of that path and the first stage of awakening simultaneously. On the path of meditation, he or she traverses all stages up to and including the ninth. On the path of no more learning,[209] the bodhisattva enters the oceanic tenth stage (called Cloud of the Teachings).

In summary, the basis for all five paths and ten stages is awakening mind. By relying on ultimate awakening mind, the bodhisattva traverses the five paths using discriminative awareness applied to the meditation on emptiness as the primary cause and the skillful means of great compassion as the contributing condition. By relying on relative awakening mind, the bodhisattva attains the ten stages[210] using the skillful means of compassion as the primary cause and wisdom of emptiness as the contributing condition. To attain the stage of buddhahood is to have reached the end of all paths and attained the dimension of reality and the end of all stages and the form dimensions [of a buddha].[211]

The result of fulfilling all the paths and stages is supreme awakening, which is limited neither to cyclic existence due to great wisdom nor to perfect peace due to great compassion. In supreme awakening, all the qualities of the stage of full enlightenment are spontaneously present, and the marvelous activity of revealing the path to all beings in response to their needs continues until the end of time.

Chapter IV
The Vows and Pledges of Secret Mantra

OUTLINE

1'. The Pledges of Action Tantra
   a'. General Action Tantra Pledges
   b'. Pledges of the Action Tantra Families
   c'. Restoration of the Pledges
2'. Pledges of Conduct Tantra
3'. Pledges of Yoga Tantra
   a'. Pledges of the Five Families Taught in the
       Explanatory Tantras
     i'. Concise Statement
     ii'. Detailed Explanation
       aa'. The Fourteen Injunctions
       bb'. The Fourteen Prohibitions
   b'. Two Main Sets of Pledges Taught in the
       Fundamental Tantras
   c'. Other Enumerations of Pledges in the
       Explanatory Tantras
4'. Pledges of Highest Yoga Tantra
   a'. Extensive Presentation of the Pledges
     i.' Concise Statement
     ii.' Detailed Explanation
       aa'. Conduct
       bb'. Vows of the Highest Yoga Tantra
          1". The Common Vows
          2". The Exceptional Vows
       cc'. Pledges of the Highest Yoga Tantra
          1". Root Downfalls
          2". The Eight Secondary Downfalls
          3". The Twenty-eight Subtle Infractions
          4". The Pledges of the Four Initiations and
             Other Pledges
   b'. Other Ways of Enumerating the Pledges
   c'. The Seriousness of a Transgression and the
       Means to Restore Pledges
     i.' Seriousness of a Downfall
     ii.' Means to Restore Pledges

2. Mantric Vows in the Ancient Tantras
   a. General Presentation of Vows Common to Mahayoga, Anuyoga, and Atiyoga
      i. Concise Statement
      ii. Extensive Explanation
   b. Classification of the Vows of Each System
      i. Pledges of Mahayoga
      ii. Pledges of Anuyoga
      iii. Pledges of Atiyoga
         A'. General Pledges
         B'. Four Exceptional Pledges
   c. Deterioration of Pledges and Their Restoration
      i. Violations
      ii. Means of Restoration

A Synopsis of the Phases of the Path in the Indestructible Way

II. General Points on the Three Ethical Systems
   A. The Number of Sets of Vows Held by One Person
   B. The Way the Three Ethical Systems Coexist in One Person
      1. Concise Statement
      2. Extensive Explanation
         a. The Assertions of Indian Scholars
         b. The Assertions of Tibetan Scholars
   C. The Benefits of Observing Ethics

The Vows and Pledges of Secret Mantra

The ethical system of the awareness holder (Skt. *vidyādhara*) is presented in two parts: (1) the vows of the Secret Mantra [with an appended synopsis of the phases of the path in the Indestructible Way], and (2) general points on the three systems of ethics.

THE VOWS OF SECRET MANTRA [I]

The vows of the Secret Mantra Way are presented in two parts: (1) a concise statement, and (2) an extensive explanation.

Concise Statement [A]

> **The two systems of awareness-holder vows are the new and the ancient.**

There are two distinct systems for the Secret Mantra vows of an awareness holder, the one prevalent in the new schools [originating from] the later translations[1]; and the other prevalent in the ancient school [originating from] the early translations.[2]

Extensive Explanation [B]

This section has two parts: (1) mantric vows in the new tantras, and (2) in the ancient tantras.

Mantric Vows in the New Tantras [1]

These are presented in two parts: (1) a general discussion of the entry into the Secret Mantra, and (2) the mantric vows in detail.

Entry into the Secret Mantra [a]

> **In the system of the later translations, some enter the Secret Mantra gradually; others, straightaway.**

Masters of the later translation schools state that there are two ways of entering the Secret Mantra Way: those with a weak connection to Mantra are led to this way gradually; those whose connection is strong are led to it straightaway.

The former method is explicitly taught in the *Hevajra Tantra* and is an implicit guideline in other tantras as well. Initially [the aspirant] is introduced gradually to [different levels of] conduct. Accordingly, the *Two-Part Hevajra Tantra* states[3]:

> First, bestow the purificatory fast [precepts].
> Then, [teach] the ten areas of training.[4]

Then [the aspirant] is introduced gradually to [different levels of] philosophical views. The same tantra states[5]:

> To disciples [grounded in that training], teach [the philosophy]
> Of the Analysts, and then [in progressive stages],
> That of the Traditionalists, the Experientialists,
> And that of the Central Way.[6]

After learning the views, the disciple enters the levels of the different classes of tantra. The same tantra states[7]:

> Once all levels of mantra are known,[8]
> Teach [the tantra of] Hevajra.

This gradual entry into the classes of tantras has a parallel within the Ancient Translation *Kilaya Wrathful Anger Tantra*:

> First, confer [the vows of] personal liberation
> And explain the doctrine of the proclaimers;
> Then, grant the great vow of the bodhisattva
> And present the teachings of the Central Way.
> Finally, bestow the initiation of the fruition Universal Way[9]
> And teach this fruition tantra.

According to the latter method, disciples who have assumed the ethics of refuge and awakening mind exclusive to the Universal Way can be led [straightaway into the Secret Mantra] by conferring upon them the initiation and the mantric vows.

The Mantric Vows in Detail [b]

This section has seven parts: (1) the essence of the mantric vows, (2) distinctions in the vows, (3) ways to assume the vows, (4) phases in the process of assuming vows, (5) differentiations between the vows of the higher and lower tantras, (6) suitable aspirants for assuming the vows, and (7) the pledges to be honored.

Essence of the Vows [i]

Mantric vows are essentially the resolve, accompanied by its concomitant factors,
To train in methods to experience blissful pristine awareness in order to bind grasping to subject and object and the propensity for movement.
In short, the ethics consist in the discipline of binding body, speech, and mind with skill in means and wisdom.

In the ethical system of the Secret Mantra, the object [of practice] is to bind conceptual grasping to subject and object[10] and the propensity for movement.[11] The binding agent is blissful pristine awareness, which [the practitioner] is committed to "hold" (experience). The essence of mantric vows is the resolve (with its concomitant mental factors) to train in the method [to hold pristine awareness], and the [blessing of] pristine awareness, itself actualized through an initiation.

Although within the four classes of tantras the methods for actualizing pristine awareness differ in profundity, there is no differentiation in the pristine awareness to be experienced. Therefore, despite differences in complexity, the aim of all initiations is said to be [the experience of] blissful pristine awareness.

In short, the ethical system of the Secret Mantra has as its object the binding of body, speech, and mind, and their subtle propensities. Its binding agent is [blissful pristine awareness]. Its vows consist in the resolve (and its seed) to experience [pristine awareness] using special skill in means and wisdom. These vows are assumed anew through an initiation.

In the phrase "the vows of an awareness holder," the term "awareness" refers to the pristine awareness of great, unchanging, and supreme bliss, free from dualistic patterns of thought. One becomes a "holder" of pristine awareness, which is the ground of being that has existed from the very beginning, by virtue of again becoming aware of (reawakening) it.[12] The method to reawaken pristine awareness is [to receive] the blessing of the form of the deity or the blessing of pristine awareness itself: this is what is meant by the term "vows." This method is the specialty of the Secret Mantra.

Moreover, profound bliss is actualized on the basis of the [seminal essence or] element of awakening mind and its stabilization. In the context of the Secret Mantra vows, awakening mind thereby assumes a meaning additional to that held in common with the Way of the Perfections, as stated in [the *Hevajra Tantra*][13]:

> The formation of the relative awakening mind
> Embodies the ultimate awakening mind.

And in the same tantra[14]:

> The relative jasmine-flower-like [seminal essence[15]]
> Is the embodiment of bliss, the ultimate.[16]

For this reason, it should also be understood that the vow of the Secret Mantra is superior [to the others].

Distinctions [ii]

Mantric vows are distinguished according to (1) the actual tantra, the subject matter of tantra; (2) the four classes of tantra, the words of the tantras themselves; and (3) initiatory rituals, the procedures for assuming vows.

Distinctions in the Actual Tantra [A']

> **Three types of vows are distinguished according to subject matter:**
> **The causal tantra's vow to bind all phenomena, form, sound, etc., within innate pristine awareness;**
> **The vow of the tantra of skillful means to bind subtle and gross objectifying thoughts within the creation and completion phases;**
> **And the resultant tantra's vow to bind subjective experience within the nature of the dimensions of awakening and pristine awareness.**

Although there are many ways to enumerate the distinctions of mantric vows, here we will briefly note the three types of mantric vows of the "actual tantra,"[17] the subject matter of tantra. These three types are the vow of causal tantra, the vow of the tantra of skillful means, and the vow of the resultant tantra, and are defined as follows:

The vow of causal tantra is to bind the nature of all phenomena, form, sound, etc., within the state of innate pristine awareness.

The vow of the tantra of skillful means is to bind all subtle and gross forms of thinking that objectify dualistic appearances within the meditations of the phases of creation and completion.

The vow of the resultant tantra is to bind all phenomena arising in one's subjective experience within the essence of the dimensions of awakening and pristine awareness.

The first of these three is a nominal vow; the second two, actual vows.

Distinctions in the Four Classes of Tantra [B']

> **Four classes of tantra teach the actual tantra: Action, Conduct, Yoga, and Highest Yoga tantras.**

Mantric vows are distinguished according to the four classes of tantra that teach [the actual tantra]—the vows of the Action, Conduct, Yoga, and Highest Yoga Tantra.[18]

Action Tantra vows [are defined as] the commitment to experience (hold) blissful pristine awareness which binds conceptual grasping to subject and object and the propensity for movement [through the technique] of using the pleasure [of smiling at a consort] as the spiritual path.

Conduct Tantra vows [are defined as] the identical commitment except that the technique uses the pleasure of gazing [at a consort] as the spiritual path.

Yoga Tantra vows [are defined as] the identical commitment except that the technique uses the pleasure of embracing [a consort] as the spiritual path.

Highest Tantra vows [are defined as] the identical commitment except that the technique uses the pleasure of union [with a consort] as the spiritual path.[19]

These four different techniques serve as antidotes for four subtle and gross forms of conceptual grasping to subject and object to be forsaken in the common spiritual way[20] and four subtle and gross propensities for movement[21] to be forsaken in the exceptional Secret Mantra. Thus, the awareness-holder vows of the four classes of tantra, which are commitments to experience non-dual intrinsic awareness or blissful pristine awareness, are differentiated according to the techniques [used to fulfill their commitments].

Distinctions in Initiatory Rituals [C']

> Three kinds of mantric vows are distinguished according to
> initiatory rituals in which they are assumed:
> The mantra's own personal liberation and awakening mind
> vows assumed during regular confession;
> Vows of divine fortune taken upon entry into the mandala;
> And the creation and completion vows assumed in the main
> part of an initiation.

Three kinds of mantric vows are distinguished according to the initiatory rituals in which they are assumed: the vows assumed during
the preparatory phase; upon entry [into the mandala]; and during
the main part [of an initiation]. These are explained as follows:

(1) The Secret Mantra's own version of personal liberation vows
and commitments of awakening mind are assumed during the regular confession[22] [performed during the preparatory part of an initiation[23]]. The actual mantra vows are assumed when the three places[24]
[of the disciple] are consecrated [as the three vajras]. At this point,
these vows [and even the personal liberation and awakening mind
vows] arise as the essence of mantric vows.

(2) Vows are assumed at the time of the outer entry [into the man-
dala],[25] when the [master] has inquired about [the disciples'] interest[26] and they have responded, and [the symbols of] moon and vajra
have been introduced.[27] Vows are also assumed when pledges are
made at the inner entry,[28] pristine awareness descends,[29] and the deities [of the mandala] are revealed.[30] These together are called the vows
of divine fortune.

(3) Vows assumed in the main part of an initiation include vows of
the three lower tantras received during their respective initiations;
vows related to the creation phase received during the vase initiation[31] of any Highest [Yoga tantra]; and the vows related to the completion phase received in the course of the higher initiations.[32] For the
second, vows related to the creation phase, there are common and
exclusive ones. The vows of the vase initiation common to both Highest Yoga Tantra and Yoga Tantra are assumed with the verbal promise to keep the pledges of the five buddha families made during the
preliminary ritual. The vows of the vase initiation exclusive to the
Highest [Yoga] Tantra are made with the promise not to disrespect
the [vajra] master, etc., at the appended [initiation] given through symbols of auspiciousness.[33]

The vows of the creation phase differ from those of the completion phase in that the former pertains to an experience of blissful pristine awareness that is not actualized, while the latter [pertains to an experience of blissful pristine] awareness that is actualized. Also, the techniques [in the initiatory procedure] employed for assuming the two kinds of vows are different: for the former, pristine awareness is induced indirectly; for the latter, directly.[34]

Ways to Assume the Vows [iii]

> **The vows are assumed with a promise upon entry into the mandala,**
> **Or in their entirety at the end of the initiation.**

Mantric vows are assumed in two ways: (1) by making a verbal promise, and (2) through the initiatory procedure [which involves meditation on the content of the initiation]:

(1) At the completion of the triple recitation for assuming vows done during the preparatory part of an initiation or at the entry [into the mandala], vows have definitely been received. However, the pledges one has promised to honor are not empowered to be preserved until the actual initiation takes place. This is similar to the way that [renunciate vows] become vows to be safeguarded when the monk or novice ordination is performed, despite the fact that during the interim renunciate [phase of the ordination][35] the promise [to abide by the] renunciate vows is made.

How then are mantric vows assumed with a verbal promise? By promising "I will keep these vows and pledges" when assuming the actual mantra vows in the main part of the initiation.

(2) The initiatory procedure [i.e., through meditation on the content of the initiation] is the way the principal mantric vows are assumed. The main mantric vows of each class of tantra are fully assumed once the vajra-master initiation for that class of tantra has been received. In Action Tantra, the vajra-master initiation will come at the completion of the water and diadem initiations; in Conduct Tantra, at the end of the five (water, etc.[36]) initiations; in Yoga Tantra, at the conclusion of the irreversible initiation[37]; and in the Highest Yoga Tantra, at the completion of the four initiations.[38] In short, the vows of mantra are assumed in their entirety at the conclusion of the initiatory rituals of the particular tantra.

An objection may be raised here: "Do the Action and Conduct [tantras] have vajra-master initiations?" Each class of tantra specifies the tasks to be performed by a vajra master, such as conferring initiations, expounding [the tantras], performing consecrations, etc. To perform these tasks, an aspirant must receive the vajra-master initiation; therefore, it is logical that all four classes of tantras must have their own vajra-master initiation. This can also be proven by scriptural references. [For example], the *Vajrapani Initiation Tantra* [a Conduct tantra] states[39]:

> Placing the vajra in the right hand
> And the wheel in the left,
> Say to the disciple,
> "You have now become a vajra master."

The *General Tantra* [an Action tantra] also states[40]:

> To acquire the rank of vajra master,
> The first [initiation] must be well celebrated.

This citation means that the initiations of water and diadem must be conferred on the disciple prior to placing him or her in the rank of a vajra master [through the relative initiation].

Another objection may be raised: "Is it not true that the *Essence of Pristine Awareness* considers the vajra-master initiation a Yoga Tantra specialty?" The *Pristine Awareness* does state this in reference to the [exclusive] irreversible wheel initiation[41] [of the Yoga Tantra]; therefore, its statement does not negate [that Action and Conduct tantras have vajra-master initiations].

Phases in the Process of Assuming Vows [iv]

> **The vows' seeds are planted when the body, speech, and mind**
> **are consecrated;**
> **They are formed with the promise to maintain them and**
> **blessed by the descent of pristine awareness;**
> **The main conferral of initiation brings them to the apex.**

The process of assuming the vows of Secret Mantra begins when the body, speech, and mind of the disciple have been consecrated as the three vajras[42] [in the preparatory ritual] and is completed only at the end of the conclusive initiation given through symbols of the particular class of tantra.

The seeds of the mantic vows are planted with the consecration of the disciple's body, speech, and mind as the three vajras. The vows are formed with the triple repetition to take the vows of the five buddha families. They are blessed by the descent of pristine awareness [upon the outer and inner entry into the mandala, respectively]. They are augmented during the central part of the initiation when the conferral of the initiations of the five buddha families and the conduct[43] initiations consecrates the disciples' five aggregates as the five buddhas (Akshobhya, etc.),[44] and their reality [veiled] by impurities [is consecrated] as Vajrasattva, the sixth buddha. The vows are greatly augmented in the vase initiation when the impurity of adherence to ordinary appearances is cleansed in [the experience of] the world and its inhabitants manifesting as the display of the deities and their supporting mandala. The vows reach their apex in the course of the three higher initiations,[45] which are the supreme ones, when the impurity of considering the deity as real is also cleansed and all aspects of cyclic existence and perfect peace are released into great pristine awareness, the union of bliss and emptiness. This is the point at which the mantric vows of the Highest Yoga Tantra have formed completely and have been fully assumed.

With the conferral of the main initiation of one of the four classes of tantra, disciples also receive the vajra-master initiation that invests them with the authority to give initiations, teach [the tantras], perform consecrations, etc. In the conclusive [initiation] given through the symbols [of auspiciousness], disciples make a succinctly formulated promise three times to maintain the pledges to which a vajra master is bound after these pledges have been extensively illustrated [by the initiating master]. At the end of this triple promise, the mantra vows are fully assumed, and from this point forward, disciples become susceptible to the root downfalls of the specific class of tantra. For this reason, it is said that the vows are fully assumed at the conclusion of the initiation and not before.

Differentiations between the Vows of the Higher and Lower Tantras [v]

> **Mantric vows of the lower tantras are called incomplete or**
> **partially complete;**
> **And those of the higher tantras, fully complete.**
> **Bliss and emptiness, as two or as one, embrace all vows.**

Earlier scholars designated the mantric vows of the lower classes of tantra as incomplete (those of Action and Conduct tantras) or partially complete (those of Yoga Tantra); and mantric vows of the Highest Yoga Tantra, as complete, according to the extent to which the mantric vows are assumed. In short, all vows and pledges are encompassed by two pledges: the ultimate pledge of skill in means, profound bliss, and the relative pledge of wisdom, emptiness comprehensive of all [aspects].[46] All too are embraced by the single vow of *EVAM*, the union of skill in means and wisdom. Accordingly, the *Two-Part Hevajra Tantra* states[47]:

> The vow of all the buddhas
> Existing in the aspect of *EVAM*
> Is the great bliss of *EVAM*
> To be realized through initiation.[48]

Since the vow of *EVAM* pertains to both ground and fruition stages, the Buddha himself called it the great pledge. The *Continuation of the Guhyasamaja Tantra*[49] states:

> It is the vow or pledge
> Taught by One Beyond Worldly Conduct.

And *Manjushri's Magical Net*[50]:

> Our Teacher, guide of beings,
> Realized this one great pledge.

The same is explained in detail in *Samvarodaya* and other tantras.

Suitable Aspirants for Assuming the Vows [vi]

> **Although no discrimination is made with regard to aspirants,**
> **A person unable to safeguard as much as the common vows**
> **Is not to be initiated but may enter the mandala.**

Suitable aspirants for assuming mantric vows are principally human beings, who embody six elements.[51] No discrimination is made on the basis of social status, past actions, etc. Accordingly, the *Sacred Primordial Buddha's Tantra* states[52]:

> A bamboo weaver or other untouchable
> Or even one guilty of one of five deeds of immediate
>   retribution
> Will become awakened in this very life
> By following the conduct of mantra.

[The same tantra] also recounts the story of *nagas* being initiated in the land of Oddiyana.[53] A number of tantras state that since gods, demigods, and other beings are included among the suitable aspirants for tantra, all beings who have faith and interest should be accepted as disciples. However, it is inappropriate to initiate into the Secret Mantra weak-willed individuals who are incapable of safeguarding the common vows, such as the purificatory fast and other personal liberation vows, or the awakening mind of aspiration and other bodhisattva commitments. Nevertheless, in order that the seed of their liberation be planted, aspirants who demonstrate earnest interest, though unfit in other respects, should be led [into the mandala of the deity]. Accordingly, the *Indestructible Peak*[54] states:

> Those who do not assume vows,
> Are untameable, and lack faith,
> Are eligible only for entry into [the mandala].
> [Initiation] is not to be conferred on them.

In addition, the same tantra states[55]:

> As soon as [the mandala] is seen,
> The vows become pure.

The Pledges to be Honored [vii]

This section has two parts: (1) pledges common to the four classes of tantra and (2) the pledges of the individual classes of tantra.

Pledges Common to the Four Classes of Tantra [A']

> **Vows and pledges assumed during the initiation must be
> safeguarded like one's life.
> Four pledges constitute the foundation common to all tantras:
> To maintain correct view, refuge, and awakening mind, and to
> receive the mandala's initiation.**

A person who has received in its entirety an initiation into a great mandala [of the Highest Yoga Tantra] has thereby received all of the vows and pledges of the Way of Indestructible Reality. Even to have simply entered [into the mandala] means that during the forming of the vows, the nominal mantric vows are assumed by verbal promise. Thereafter, a practitioner who engages in the experiential cultivation of the Secret Mantra while safeguarding the vows and pledges just as promised will swiftly gain spiritual attainments. On the contrary, one who forsakes these vows will incur very serious negative consequences in spite of making [great] effort on the path. Therefore, the pledges should be safeguarded like life itself. The *Samvarodaya Tantra*[56] states:

> Should you desire supreme attainment,
> Though you may risk your life
> Or be on the point of dying,
> Always safeguard the pledges.

Of the pledges to be honored, the first to be concerned with are the pledges that are common to all classes of tantras and form their foundations: the "four great root pledges." These prescribe correct view of the conventional, refuge in the Three Jewels, the awakening mind, and initiation into the mandala. The sixty-verse *Guide to Mantra*[57] states:

> Know that for tantra
> The basic pledges are four:
> To have a correct view of the conventional,
> Not to forsake the Three Jewels,
> To safeguard the awakening mind,
> And not to reject the true initiation.[58]

The *Manjushri Fundamental Tantra* states:

> Following a detailed explanation of the four pledges, [the master proclaims:] O heir of the victorious ones! The pledges for entering the marvelous domain of my Mantra [system] are all included in two groups: the foundation and branches. What is the foundation? The foundation is [the pledge] not to reject the initiation [and the other three pledges]. [These form a foundation] because without a correct view, one is not a renunciate; without taking refuge, one is not a Buddhist; without an awakening mind, one is not a bodhisattva; and without initiation, one cannot be called a mantrin.

These four root pledges are indispensable requirements for entering any stage of the path of the four classes of tantra. Thus, they are considered to be pledges common to all classes.

Pledges of the Individual Classes of Tantra [B']

This section has four parts: (1) the pledges of Action Tantra, (2) Conduct Tantra, (3) Yoga Tantra, and (4) Highest Yoga Tantra.

The Pledges of Action Tantra [1']

Scholars provide various presentations of the Action Tantra pledges, some of which have been clearly enumerated within the Action Tantra, and some not. Butön's *General Presentation of the Classes of Tantra* states:

> Lord Atisha's *Summary of Pledges*[59] speaks of thirty root downfalls for the Action Tantra. It must be examined whether or not these are the same as those listed in the *Susiddhi Tantra* beginning with "Wise ones should not be angry [with the mantra, the deity, or the tantric master]."[60]

The *Wheel of Time Tantra* states that each of the four classes of tantra has a set of fourteen root downfalls. Butön identifies the set of [the Action Tantra's] downfalls as the [fourteen] taught in the *Secret General Tantra*.[61]

Ngorchen[62] and other masters consider the first three pledges[63] given in the *[Secret] General Tantra* as general [Action Tantra] pledges; they classify the rest with their subdivisions into thirteen [as Action Tantra pledges] received through initiation.

The omniscient Pema Karpo is of the opinion that [Action Tantra] practitioners must observe thirty pledges and avoid sixteen root downfalls. The thirty pledges consist of the twelve prescriptions for what to practice and eighteen prescriptions for restraint given in the *Susiddhi Tantra* [to be explained below]. The sixteen root downfalls consist of the four transgressions (of the basic pledges given in the *Manjushri Fundamental Tantra*) and the downfall of offending the master, the five deeds of immediate retribution, the five deeds nearly as serious,[64] and harming the Three Jewels[65] as set out in the *Questions of Subahu Tantra*.

Different ways of enumerating, differentiating, and grouping the Action Tantra pledges are found in other works such as Bodong Panchen's *General Presentation of Tantras*[66] and Jampa Lingpa's *Great Mantra Discipline*.[67] All scholars, however, agree that the principal [Action Tantra vows] are those taught in the *General Tantra*.

Action Tantra pledges are discussed under three headings: (1) the general pledges, (2) the pledges of the Action Tantra families, and (3) restoration of the pledges.

General Action Tantra Pledges [a']

> The fourteen general pledges of Action Tantra
> Are to have faith in the Three Jewels and in mantra, to have
>   earnest interest in the Universal Way,
> To be devoted to the supreme field of merits, not to be angry
>   with deities, to make offerings on special occasions,
> Not to venerate other traditions, to honor guests, to be always
>   benevolent,
> To acquire merit, to exert oneself in reciting the mantra and in
>   safeguarding other commitments,
> Not to teach mantras or mudras to those without pledges, and to
>   accomplish the aim of the tantras.

Fourteen pledges of the Action Tantra are given in the *Secret General Tantra*[68]:

(1) To have faith in the common and exceptional Three Jewels[69];

(2) To have impartial and non-judgmental faith in secret mantras, awareness mantras, and recollection mantras[70];

(3) To have an especially earnest interest in the Universal Way, and to adopt its principles;

(4) To be devoted to the four kinds of companions who form the supreme field [of merit]—the master,[71] those who have entered the Action Tantra, those who abide by its pledges, and the followers of the Buddhist teachings;

(5) Not to be angry with one's favored deity if wrathful rites are not effective, or with deities the worship of whom is shared with other practitioners[72] if they do not perform the desired task;

(6) Not to neglect offerings on the appropriate occasions, such as the days of the full and new moon, the eighth of the lunar month, etc.;

(7) Not to venerate the scriptures of other traditions, such as those of extremist teachers, etc.[73];

(8) To offer food, drink, etc., to others without any partiality, [even] unexpected guests;

(9) To be always benevolent toward all creatures;

(10) To augment one's acquisition of merit[74];

(11) To exert oneself at reciting the mantra according to the guidelines given in the *Questions of Subahu Tantra*[75];

(12) To strive to safeguard the pledges of one's own [buddha] family, as well as those of other families[76];

(13) Not to teach mantras or seals[77] to those who have not assumed pledges or those who have allowed them to deteriorate;

(14) To conceal and protect the tantras and mantras, while striving to achieve spiritual accomplishment through study, reflection, and meditation on them.

The thirty vows taught in the *Susiddhi* are presented concisely as follows:

> Take earnest interest in (1) the Three Jewels, (2) the Secret Mantra, and (3) the Universal Way;
>
> Make offerings (4) to the deities on special occasions, and (5) to guests without partiality;
>
> (6) Acquire merit; (7) strive at correct recitation of mantra;
>
> Abide steadily in the pledges of (8) all families and (9) your own particular family;
>
> (10) Guard the tantras and work in order to realize their meaning; (11) remain peaceful in body, speech, and mind[78];
>
> (12) Wash and keep yourself clean[79]: these twelve [pledges] prescribe what to practice.
>
> (1) Do not become angry with the deity or (2) worship other traditions;
>
> (3) Do not practice [tantras] you are not authorized to or (4) invent your own Secret Mantra [practice][80];
>
> (5) Do not perform evil rites[81] or (6) direct tantric activities to the wrong end[82];
>
> (7) Do not bestow [initiation and tantra] on those without pledges[83] or (8) step over [tantric] symbols, etc.[84];
>
> (9) Do not be unrestrained[85] or (10) eat food that is not permitted[86];
>
> (11) Do not forsake loving-kindness[87] or (12) speak before the [tantric recitation] is completed[88];
>
> (13) Do not perform wrathful rites in anger[89] or (14) mistreat yourself[90];
>
> (15) Do not refute others[91] or (16) perpetuate unworthy actions[92];
>
> (17) Do not watch shows[93]; and (18) do not defecate or urinate into water:
>
> These eighteen [pledges] prescribe restraint.

Pledges of the Action Tantra Families [b']

Practitioners must observe the pledges of each family as taught in the respective tantras.

A practitioner is required to follow all the points of conduct specifically prescribed for each of the three Worldly and three Supramundane Families,[94] which form the foundation of the general pledges [of the Action Tantra]. In addition to these, one must observe the pledges of one's own family taught in the corresponding tantras and commentaries. [Ratnakarashanti's] *Jewel Lamp Commentary on Yamantaka, the Black Enemy* states that these pledges are to be preserved also by those who have been initiated into the Yoga and Highest Yoga tantras, not only by Action and Conduct tantra practitioners.

Restoration of the Pledges [c']

> **The means of purifying transgressions include reciting one**
> **hundred thousand of the mantra of one's family**
> **Or the recollection mantra [called the "Unconquerable Vajra]**
> **That Blazes Like Fire," the performance of appeasing fire**
> **offerings, etc.**

A practitioner should first of all understand what the pledges are. With that knowledge, one should then safeguard them in order not to be polluted by major downfalls and minor transgressions. Should transgressions occur, the pledges must be restored immediately. The means of purifying transgressions taught in the *General Tantra* include the recitation of the heart mantra of the deity of one's [buddha] family[95] one hundred thousand times; reciting one hundred thousand times the recollection mantra called "Unconquerable Vajra That Blazes Like Fire"[96]; or the performance of the same number of appeasing fire offerings.[97] "Etc." [in the root verses] refers to the restoration [of pledges] by repeated entry into the mandala.[98]

Transgressions incurred in the daytime must be purified [by acknowledging them] within the same night, and those incurred at night, [before dawn] of the following day. Accordingly, the *Susiddhi* states[99]:

> Careless failings in the day
> Should be acknowledged that same night;
> And failings at night, the next dawn.

Pledges of Conduct Tantra [2']

> **Conduct Tantra's pledges are fourteen: to refrain from the ten**
> **unvirtuous deeds, not forsake the sacred doctrine,**
> **Not give up one's awakening mind, not be miserly, and not**
> **harm others.**
> **The means of restoration of the Action Tantra's pledges also**
> **apply to the Conduct and Yoga Tantra.**

In the Conduct Tantra, there are fourteen distinct pledges that apply to all tantras in this class. These are enumerated in the *Vairochana-abhisambodhi Tantra*[100] as follows: [1-10] To refrain from the ten unvirtuous deeds (three of body, four of speech, and three of mind) and instead to continuously practice the ten virtues; and [11-14] to avoid the four root [downfalls] of forsaking the sacred teachings,[101] giving up the awakening mind, being miserly [by refusing to give] spiritual instruction or material aid, and inflicting harm on others. These fourteen all pertain to actions that should be avoided.

Specific pledges apply to each of the families of the Conduct Tantra and are taught in the different tantras of these families. The points of conduct prescribed in these pledges must be observed; if one fails to do so, the pledges must be restored. The means of restoration of the pledges explained for the Action Tantra also apply to these pledges of the Conduct Tantra, as they do for pledges of Yoga Tantra, which will be explained below.

Venerable Pema Karpo presents a distinct classification of the Conduct Tantra pledges. Three pledges pertain to the training: (1) the vow of the "mind of entering" [assumed] in order to enter the great pledge; (2) the vow of the "abiding mind" once one has entered the great pledge; and (3) the vow of the "mind of involvement," bringing others to the great pledge once one has mastered it.[102] The fourteen pledges mentioned above are considered to be the fourteen root downfalls for practitioners who are renunciates. The four root downfalls plus sexual misconduct, murder, theft, untruth, and wayward views are considered pledges applying to lay practitioners.

What is the difference between the shunning of the ten unvirtuous deeds in this context and the shunning of them by the proclaimers, solitary sages, worldly people, and non-Buddhists? The difference is significant, because proclaimers and solitary sages do not possess [the special] skillful means and wisdom [taught in the Conduct Tantra].[103] Worldly people and non-Buddhists observe [a wholesome conduct] induced by their grasping to the [self as] real. On the other hand, practitioners who have formed awakening minds and are possessed of skill in means and wisdom are able to freely engage in wholesome forms of conduct with the understanding of the sameness of all things, without [this conduct] being induced by such grasping.

Pledges of Yoga Tantra [3']

This section has three parts: (1) the pledges of the five families taught in the explanatory tantras; (2) the two main sets of pledges (the pledges of the five classes of deities and the ten root downfalls) taught in the fundamental tantras; and (3) other enumerations of pledges in the explanatory tantras.

Pledges of the Five Families Taught in the Explanatory Tantras [a']

These pledges are presented in two parts: (1) a concise statement, and (2) a detailed explanation.

Concise Statement [i']

Yoga Tantra pledges consist of fourteen injunctions and fourteen prohibitions.

For the Yoga Tantra [pledges], earlier scholars condensed the main points of the extensive discussion in the *Indestructible Peak*, an explanatory tantra, into two groups of pledges: fourteen pledges prescribing what should be practiced [injunctions] and fourteen prescribing restraint [prohibitions].

Detailed Explanation [ii']

These pledges are presented in two parts: (1) the fourteen injunctions, and (2) the fourteen prohibitions.

The Fourteen Injunctions [aa']

Injunctions related to the five families are to take refuge in the Three Jewels, commit oneself to the vajra, bell, and master, Practice the four generosities, uphold the three ways, and make offerings.

I have taken refuge in the Three Jewels,
The Buddha, his teachings, and the community...

With these words, the vows are proclaimed. Aspirants are then examined for their suitability to receive [initiation]. Those found suitable enter the mandala and recite

Just as the protectors throughout the three times...

up to

...and set all beings in the state of perfect peace.[104]

With the triple repetition of these phrases, the fourteen defeating transgressions are forsworn, and the fourteen branch [pledges] that are injunctions are fully assumed. The mantric vows are thereby taken according to ritual, which is the way the pledges are first assumed. These pledges taken in this way, the fourteen injunctions, are all condensed into the following pledges of the five families[105]:

(1) To take refuge in the Three Jewels comprises the three pledges of the [transcendent] family of Vairochana;

(2) To commit oneself to the vajra seal, the bell seal, and the [vajra] master are the three pledges of the vajra family [of Akshobhya][106];

(3) To be generous with spiritual teachings, material things, protection, and love are the four pledges of the jewel family [of Ratnasambhava];

(4) To maintain the outer (Action and Conduct) tantras; the secret (Yoga) tantra; and the three spiritual ways [of the proclaimers, solitary sages, and bodhisattvas] are the three pledges of the lotus family [of Amitabha];

(5) To make offerings is the single pledge of the action family [of Amoghasiddhi].

The correspondence of the pledges with these particular families can be explained as follows: Vairochana represents the family of the enlightened body of the transcendent ones. This physical dimension is the foundation for acquiring all good qualities of which taking refuge in the Three Jewels constitutes the root.

Akshobhya represents the family of enlightened mind, which is indivisible emptiness and compassion. One commits oneself to these two aspects, which are symbolized by the vajra and bell, and to the vajra master who reveals their meaning.

Ratnasambhava represents the family of enlightened quality, which, like a wish-fulfilling jewel, provides the source of all that is desirable. Likewise, the four kinds of generosity fulfill the hopes and desires [of all beings].

Amitabha represents the family of enlightened speech from which originate the eighty-four thousand aspects of the teachings. These eighty-four thousand aspects are all included in the three spiritual ways: the outer way [of proclaimers and solitary sages], the inner way [of bodhisattvas], and secret way [of mantric practitioners].

Amoghasiddhi represents the family of marvelous activity, the essence of which is to venerate the buddhas and to work for the benefit of all beings. Both of these tasks are accomplished by making offerings as much as possible.

The Fourteen Prohibitions [bb']

> The prohibitions are not to forsake the Jewels and the awakening mind,
> Not disrespect the deity, mantra and seals, and master, not step over sacred objects,
> Not eat wrong foods, not divulge the secrets, not forsake mantra and seals, not harm others, not delight in the Individual Way,
> Not despair, not forsake the training, and not engage in what is unwholesome:
> These five families' pledges are the main pledges taught in the explanatory tantras.

The fourteen pledges that are prohibitions are as follows:
  (1) Do not renounce the Three Jewels;
  (2) Do not forsake the awakening mind;
  (3) Do not disrespect deities;
  (4) Do not criticize mantra and seals[107];
  (5) Do not disrespect the master;
  (6) Do not step over the master's seat, etc., or over the weapons, ritual implements, or insignias of deities;
  (7) Do not eat the wrong food[108];
  (8) Do not divulge the secret pristine awareness[109];
  (9) Do not forsake the practice of mantra and seals[110];
  (10) Do not harm others;
  (11) Do not delight in the Individual Way;
  (12) Do not be discouraged in the face of difficulties encountered in working for the benefit of others;
  (13) Do not forsake training in the six perfections;
  (14) Do not engage in what is unwholesome.

These prohibitions, which prescribe fourteen points of restraint, [together with the above injuctions,] are known as the pledges of the five families, and are the main pledges taught in the explanatory tantras.

Two Main Sets of Pledges Taught in the Fundamental Tantras [b']

The sets of pledges given in the *Glorious Paramadya* and other fundamental tantras should be learned from other sources.

In the interest of brevity, the pledges taught in the *Summation of Essential Points*,[111] the *Glorious Paramadya*, and other fundamental tantras of this class will not be discussed at length here and should be learned from other sources. However, we shall supplement the root verses with a few explanatory words. The *Summation of Essential Points* gives the following set of pledges related to the five classes of deities:

(1) The pledge of the transcendent family [of Vairochana] is to cultivate the two aspects of awakening mind and then earnestly work to augment them. Thus, the pledge of the transcendent family is to be intensely compassionate by strengthening one's mind of awakening, being affectionate, and uplifting others, etc., without succumbing to the discouragement felt by proclaimers who reject objects of desire, viewing them as sources of pain.

(2) The pledge of the vajra family [of Akshobhya] is to perform rites while feigning wrath in order to awaken malicious and untameable beings;

(3) The pledge of the lotus family [of Amitabha] is to do whatever is of benefit to others, manifesting as the great seal of the deity's body, and the other [seals[112]], from within the understanding of emptiness, the ultimate [truth];

(4) The pledge of the jewel family [of Ratnasambhava] is to give away daily whatever material things, many or few, that others desire;

(5) The pledge of the action family [of Amoghasiddhi] is naturally fulfilled in the altruistic nature of the activities [of the above four pledges].

The *Glorious Paramadya Tantra* enumerates ten pledges to shun the following ten root downfalls:

(1) To forsake the aspiring mind;

(2) To forsake the venturing mind;

(3) To reject the contemplation of moon and vajra,[113] [the symbols] of the formation of the two kinds [of awakening mind differentiated with respect to] the two truths;

(4) To deprecate and reject the Buddhist scriptures;

(5) To forsake the practice of the teachings;

(6) To ignorantly criticize the teachings;

(7) To mortify with asceticism one's body and mind which have been blessed by meditations upon the four seals;

(8) To renounce vajra and bell,[114] yoga, and pledges;

(9) To forsake the four seals and remain [caught in] ordinary [appearances and grasping];

(10) To abandon the vajra master.

The *Indestructible Source*[115] mentions an additional (the eleventh) downfall: to divulge the secrets [of tantra] to the spiritually immature.

Other Enumerations of Pledges in the Explanatory Tantras [c']

Explanatory tantras teach the pledges of the five families,
general pledges, and pledges given in the concise
proclamation.
The general root pledges are to shun the fourteen defeats
for a bodhisattva.
The branches are the ethics of restraint from the four root
offenses and from drinking alcohol;
The ethics aimed at acquiring good qualities by devoting
oneself to authentic masters, etc.;
And the ethics of working for others by giving up four
incompatible attitudes.
Not to disrespect gods, etc., and other common vows are
assumed as part of those given in the concise proclamation.
The vows to be safeguarded by all are taken with a promise,
While the vows not to commit the ten downfalls, etc., are
assumed through initiation.

The explanatory *Indestructible Peak Tantra's* presentation of the vows that are proclaimed and assumed [in the course of an initiation] seems to be the framework for the vows common to both the [Yoga and] Highest [Yoga tantras]. According to that tantra, there are three categories of vows: the pledges of the five families, the general pledges, and the concise form of the pledges that are proclaimed.

The pledges of the five families are the injunctions explained above [from this same tantra].

The general pledges comprise both root and branch pledges (these will be simply introduced here as they will be discussed in order below). The root pledges are to avoid the fourteen defeating offenses for a bodhisattva found in the *Akashagarbha Scripture*.[116] The branch pledges consist in observing the three forms of ethics: of restraint from unwholesome deeds; the ethics aimed at acquiring good qualities; and the ethics of working for others' welfare.

To explain these three forms of ethics, the first is to observe, at the very least, what is indispensable: the four root precepts of a lay person plus the vow not to drink alcohol, which are given in the proclamation of vows beginning with the words: "Do not take the life of other creatures...,"[117] etc.; and the vow to renounce all unwholesome deeds unless done to benefit others. The second form of ethics is to devote oneself to true masters, honor true practitioners of yoga (indicated by the "etc." [in the root verses]), and engage in the ten virtuous deeds of the Universal Way (identical in nature to the six perfections). The third form is to give up the four attitudes that are incompatible with the Universal Way: aspiring to the lesser ways, neglecting to work for the benefit of others, renouncing cyclic existence, or being attached to the state of perfect peace.

The pledges assumed in the proclamation of the concise form of vows are the following:

(1) Not to disrespect gods, demigods, yakshas,[118] etc.;

(2) Not to step over the symbols of the vajra, etc.;

(3) Not to step over the master's seat, or over the weapons, ritual implements, or the insignias of deities.

Further, since the vows of the lower [systems] are included in the higher, the vows in common with the Way of the Perfections and with the Action and Conduct tantras are also to be preserved [as part of this last category of vows].

Venerable Pema Karpo classifies Yoga Tantra vows into the three groups[119] of root pledges, branch pledges, and pledges concerning application:

(1) The root pledges are the fourteen injunctions related to the five buddha families and the fourteen pledges that prohibit downfalls that are counteractive to the injunctions.

(2) The branch pledges are [the four root precepts, etc.,] mentioned [in the *Indestructible Peak Tantra*] beginning with the words: "Do not take the lives of other creatures."

(3) The pledges of the five deities [found in the fundamental tantras] are the pledges that apply to the practice.

Enumerations of the downfalls and pledges of the Yoga Tantra are extremely numerous, and therefore it is not possible to encompass them here. The vows to maintain all the precepts (the fourteen injunctions, the fourteen prohibitions, etc.) are said to be assumed with a verbal promise, while the vows not to commit the [four] root downfalls and other infractions are assumed through the initiatory procedure involving contemplation [on the content of the initiation]. The means of restoration of these pledges and vows are those mentioned above, as well as those given in the *Essence Ornament of the General Procedure for All Secrets* explained below.

Pledges of Highest Yoga Tantra [4']

This section has three parts: (1) an extensive presentation of the pledges, (2) other ways of enumerating the pledges, and (3) the seriousness of a transgression and means of restoring pledges.

Extensive Presentation of the Pledges [a']

These pledges are presented in two parts: (1) a concise statement, and (2) a detailed explanation.

Concise Statement [i']

> **Highest Yoga Tantra prescribes three disciplines: conduct, vows, and pledges.**

Disciples who have assumed the vows in the course of an initiation of the Highest Yoga Tantra have three [kinds of discipline] to maintain: vajra conduct, the vows of the buddha families, and the root and branch pledges.

Detailed Explanation [ii']

This section has three parts: (1) conduct, (2) vows prescribing what to practice, and (3) pledges prescribing restraint.

Conduct [aa']

> **Each tantra presents its special forms of conduct.**
> **The *Guhyasamaja Tantra* teaches the conduct of the five**
> **families and four pledges to be interpreted.**

In our discussion of the vows of the Highest [Yoga Tantra], the first part concerns conduct. Conduct (Tib. *brtul zhugs*) is defined as the transforming (*brtul*) of ordinary activity and thoughts and the entering (*zhugs*) into the mode of Vajrasattva's body, speech, and mind. Each of the tantras presents its own special system [to effect this transformation].

The *Glorious Guhyasamaja* states that the conduct of the creation phase is to rely on the five nectars [in order to fulfill] the pledges of the three vajras: human flesh, the [pledge of] vajra body; excrement and urine, the [pledge of] vajra speech; and semen and blood, the [pledge of] vajra mind; or, alternatively, to rely on the five nectars as the pledges related to the five families. In the completion phase, the conduct is to train in the techniques aimed at dissolving the five aggregates [symbolized by] the five nectars[120] into the state of clear light. Four pledges to be interpreted are presented in the fourth chapter of [the *Guhyasamaja*] *Tantra* with the words:

> Any being who ends life,
> Who delights in lying,
> Covets the wealth of others,
> Or constantly engages in sexual union....[121]

A yogin or yogini who has reached the creation phase will actually resort to these [forms of conduct] when these would benefit others. For a meditator abiding in the completion phase, these are enacted in the following ways:

(1) To end life means to block the energy winds[122];
(2) To lie means to impart the teachings while understanding the levels of interdependent arising [of phenomena];
(3) To steal means to actualize the buddha's pristine awareness by relying on a consort;
(4) To indulge in sex means to experience the very nature of reality.

The beginner should maintain these pledges or forms of conduct by aspiring [to be able to engage in them in the future] and by creating the conditions to actually enact them.

The Chakrasamvara tantras speak of twenty-two modes of pure conduct and eight concerning the awareness-woman.

Most of the earlier masters state that the phrase "twenty-two modes of pure conduct" found in the Chakrasamvara tantras is a reference to the conduct [common to all Highest Yoga tantras] of avoiding the fourteen root downfalls and the eight serious branch downfalls (which are explained below). The exceptional conduct taught in these tantras comprises the following:

(1) Worship on the tenth day of the lunar month;
(2) Hand offering[123];
(3) Worship through the definitive meaning of the four vajras[124];
(4) Practice of the four seals[125];
(5) Ritual feast of heroes and yoginis;
(6) Symbolic behavior[126];
(7) The eight exceptional pledges [concerning conduct with an awareness-woman].

The first, worship or offering made on the tenth day of the lunar month, includes making offerings of young virgins or women who bear the signs [of being yoginis[127]], the outer offerings, the major or minor food offering (*torma*) rituals, etc. The last, [eight pledges concerning conduct with an awareness-woman], are pledges to abandon the following downfalls:

> To fail to remember the conduct of the left; to unite [with the tantric consort] out of desire alone;
> To discriminate [between oneself and others]; to lose interest [in tantra];
> To fail to rely on a tantric consort; to leave the tantric consort;
> To let one's tantric activity deteriorate; to feel revulsion toward pledge substances.

These are explained as follows. (1) To fail to remember the conduct of the left[128] daily in the four periods of the day and night and to fail to apply it during the special occasions of ritual feasts, hand offerings, etc., constitutes this downfall.

(2) To unite with a tantric consort simply out of desire for a woman and to experience [bliss] dispersing [with the emission of the seminal

essence] constitutes this downfall. One should unite with a consort to [enhance] experiential understanding, to receive or confer an initiation, [to use the seminal essence for preparing] the elixir [of long life], or as the pledge substance, and other similar purposes.

(3) To discriminate between self and others by failing to remember throughout the four periods of day and night to foster a non-conceptual mind while resting in the state of sameness within the empty nature of all phenomena constitutes this downfall.

(4) To lose respect for this path due to becoming attracted to other spiritual pursuits or to have reservations born from a fault-finding attitude so that one's enthusiasm for the practice of tantra does not increase constitutes this downfall.

(5) To fail to rely on a tantric consort when one has the ability to control the seminal essence[129] and to sustain the blissful state cognizing emptiness constitutes this downfall.

(6) To leave the tantric consort or action seal before one has stabilized and mastered the blissful pristine awareness or before one has achieved the results of the tantric activities and other experiential means constitutes this downfall.

(7) To let one's tantric activity deteriorate, i.e., to allow emission of seminal essence, unless done for the sake of conferring the secret initiation or other special purposes, constitutes this downfall. Therefore, when training in the descent and reversal of the jasmine-flower[-like] seminal essence by means of [union with] a consort, a practitioner should not emit the seminal essence, but should hold it firmly at the crown of the head.

(8) To feel revulsion toward and to refuse [the pledge substances] and to fail to nourish oneself with the olibanum [blood], camphor [seminal fluid], fragrant water [urine], etc., from the vagina of an awareness-woman constitutes this downfall.

These are known as the eight aspects of conduct for practice with an awareness-woman because they are required to be the main focus of the practice for adepts who have reached the stage of taking recourse to the experiential means of the three emissaries: the mantra-born, the field-born, and the innate.[130]

> **Fourteen conducts are enumerated in the *Tent Tantra*; nine, in the *Unsurpassable Tantra*.**

The *Indestructible Tent Tantra* enumerates the following fourteen conducts that are the focus of practice for beginners:

(1) Not to renounce the Jewels; (2) to observe the pledges;

(3) To hold vajra and bell and (4) the [tantric] scriptures on the crown of one's head;

(5) To perform fire, (6) mandala, (7) and consecration rituals;

(8) To give *torma* to elemental spirits; (9) to exert oneself at recitation and meditation;

(10) To impart the teachings to one's disciples; (11) to attract disciples by means of loving-kindness;

(12) To acquire merits [by venerating] the victorious ones; (13) to offer water to Jambhala;

(14) To cast votive images, build reliquaries, or do other good deeds.

Nine forms of tantric conduct are given in the *Unsurpassable Chakrasamvara Tantra*:

(1) Daily service[131];

(2) Making offerings[132];

(3) Secret and concealed tantric activities[133];

(4) Reliance on the emissaries of awareness[134];

(5) Mantra recitation[135];

(6) Devotion to [one's master], the field [of merit][136];

(7) Tantric activities involving conduct[137];

(8) Listening and reflecting [on the tantras] as activities related to learning;

(9) Making the blessing stable as the activity related to practice.

The *Wheel of Time Tantra* prescribes twenty-five modes of conduct.

Five consist in refraining from the four root offenses and from drinking alcohol.

The *Wheel of Time Tantra* prescribes the twenty-five modes of conduct of Vajrasattva. The first five are to refrain from the four root offenses and from drinking alcohol, as specified in the words: "Forsake harm, untruth...," etc.[138]:

(1) Not to harm means to abstain from inflicting injury on any being, from [killing] an insect to murder of a human or a human fetus, and to give up the motives for inflicting injury;

(2) Not to lie means not to speak any untrue words, from lies in jest to false claims to spiritual attainments;

(3) Not to engage in adultery means to abstain from sexual relations with an inappropriate partner, such as another's spouse, whether or not one has taken the vow of celibacy;

(4) Not to engage in theft means not to steal even the husk of a sesame seed, not to mention another's valuable possessions;

(5) Not to drink alcohol means to renounce all kinds intoxicants as they attract obstacles [to one's practice]. However, drinking alcohol for the sake of observing the pledges or as means to gain experiential understanding is not prohibited.

Transgressions of these five points of training for the lay practitioner are called the five extreme ill deeds as they are definitely unwholesome and serve as conditions for the worsening of one's nature.[139]

The remaining twenty modes of conduct are imparted to those disciples who wish to follow them and who are able to renounce [the five extreme ill deeds].

> Twenty consist in abstaining from the five related ill deeds of gambling, eating impure food, reading perverse subjects,
> Making sacrifices for ancestors, and extremist religious practices;
> Five murders of killing an animal, child, man, woman, or destroying reliquaries;
> Five kinds of enmity toward friends, leaders, the Buddha, the Buddhist community, or a trustworthy person;
> Five desires related to form, sound, smell, taste, and sensation.
> These modes of conduct form the foundation of all vows and pledges.

[The remaining twenty modes of conduct consist in] refraining from five ill deeds related [to the extreme ones], five murders, five kinds of enmity, and five desires. The five related ill deeds, [so-called because] they waste one's time and destroy one's virtues, are the following:

(1) Gambling, which means to play dice;

(2) Eating impure food, which refers to eating the meat [of an animal] that has been killed for consumption or profit, or similar foods. This is an ill deed in that it involves ways of livelihood incompatible with the [Buddhist] teachings;

(3) Reading perverse subjects, such as stories of war, robbers, and rulers;

(4) Performing sacrifices for ancestors, which refers to the Vedic custom of worshiping ancestors and similar customs, or making sacrifices of cattle thinking that by doing so one [will be born in] a higher form of life;

(5) Following barbaric religious practices, i.e., following the practices of extremists' religions [such as eating the meat of animals that one has killed oneself].

The five murders, which are here listed separately from "not to harm..." (above) to refute [the belief] that these qualify as [legitimate] spiritual conduct,[140] are the following:

(1) To kill any animal (such as a cow);

(2) To murder a child;

(3) To murder a man;

(4) To murder a woman;

(5) To destroy a reliquary (which includes the killing of a monk or destroying statues and images of the Three Jewels).

The five types of enmity are to bear malice toward the following persons:

(1) Friends who help one in worldly or spiritual matters;

(2) Persons worthy of respect in those two fields, such as leaders, elders, etc.;

(3) The Buddha, who is the teacher of gods and humans;

(4) The Buddhist community;

(5) Masters who are worthy of one's trust.

The five desires refers to attachment to visual form, [sounds, smells, tastes,] and physical sensations. These five desires are completing factors for intentional actions, which lead one into further existences.

These last groups of five [as they appear in the *Wheel of Time*] are expressed as prohibitions (Do not kill..., etc.) and are therefore points of conduct that prescribe restraint. Together, these twenty-five serve as the foundation of all other pledges and vows.

These twenty-five modes of conduct must definitely be assumed prior to receiving initiation [into the Wheel of Time tantra]. This is not necessarily the case with the other forms of conduct mentioned above. However, they have been placed in this beginning section [on the tantric vows] for convenience, and because, for most initiations, in order just to enter the mandala, one must assume one or another of these forms of conduct, even if one does not attend the main part of the rite.

Vows of the Highest Yoga Tantra [bb']
These vows, which prescribe what to practice, are presented in two parts: (1) the common vows, and (2) the exceptional vows.

The Common Vows [1"]

> **The common vows are those of the five families, or the six:**
> **For the Akshobhya family, to keep the seals and master;**
> **For the jewel, to practice the ten kinds of generosity; for the**
>   **wheel, to rely on ten foods;**
> **For the sword, to make offerings; for the lotus, to maintain**
>   **vows of retention;**
> **For Vajrasattva, to cultivate a mind of awakening. These have**
>   **both provisional and definitive meanings.**

In some tantric systems, the term "vow" is used to denote the moral prescription for what to practice, and "pledge," the moral prescription for restraint. Others reverse the definitions, and yet others consider them to be synonymous. Although these different ways of defining "vow" and "pledge" are not contradictory, for convenience in this discussion, the terms are used according to the first definitions.

The etymology of the [Tibetan] word *sdom pa* (vow), *sambara* [in Sanskrit], is "to bind." [In this context,] "vow" means to bind ordinary body, speech, and mind, as well as their propensities, to the essence of the four vajras[141] by special means and wisdom.

The general and specific vows of the five families common to [the Yoga and Highest Yoga] classes of tantras have been explained above. Now we shall discuss the pledges of the six buddha families taught in the *Glorious Wheel of Time Tantra*. These have both provisional and definitive meanings.

First, the provisional meanings will be given. For the five-pronged vajra family of Akshobhya, the pledges are explained as follows. The vajra (enlightened mind), emptiness; the bell (enlightened speech), great compassion; and the seal (enlightened body), the deity's form, are the "secrets"[142] of [ordinary] body, speech, and mind. From the beginning of time, these three have been the very essence of Akshobhya (Immovable), never other than the enlightened body, speech, and mind of all the transcendent ones: this is the pledge of the ground. The three pledges to "hold" [vajra, bell, and seal] means to recognize, in accordance with one's level of experiential understanding, that body, speech, and mind are the three vajras and to maintain this recognition in one's meditation. These [three pledges] are linked to the substantial cause [for the actualization of enlightened body, speech, and mind]. The vajra master serves as the main contributory condition [in actualizing these]; therefore, the pledge never to be transgressed is to devote oneself to him or her in all the ways appropriate to the relationship. The pledge to "hold" the master means to see him or her as one's chief, that is, to rely on the master while shattering one's pride. As symbols [of these pledges], a tantric adept carries a vajra and bell (endowed with the proper characteristics), performs symbolic hand gestures, wears the five symbolic bone ornaments,[143] etc.

For the jewel family of Ratnasambhava (Source of Jewels), the pledge is to train in the ten kinds of generosity[144]:

> To give jewels, iron, copper, oxen, horses,
> Elephants, young maidens, land,
> One's spouse, and one's own flesh
> Are the ten kinds of gifts.

Beginners should give what they are able, and aspire to be able to give [in the future] what they are reluctant to give now.

For the wheel family of Vairochana (Illuminator), the pledges are to eat the five meats and five nectars,[145] etc., and other foods appropriate for yogins:

> Since they enhance camphor,[146]
> Always consume meat
> And especially alcohol.

For the sword family of Amoghasiddhi (Unfailing Accomplishment), the pledge is to acquire merit by making all kinds of offerings to the supreme ones, such as flowers, etc., to the buddhas and bodhisattvas.[147]

For the lotus family of Amitabha (Measureless Light), the pledge is to abide in pure conduct. In relation to the first seven [Wheel of Time] initiations,[148] this means to refrain from adultery. In the higher initiations, pure conduct refers to the "vow of no emission," which consists in the non-emission of seminal essence even when engaging in sexual intercourse with [an ordinary] woman.

For the single-pronged vajra family of Vajrasattva (Adamantine Being),[149] the pledge is to preserve the awakening mind, the union of non-objectifying compassion and emptiness[150] which is the pristine awareness that cognizes the ultimate.

Next are presented the definitive meanings. The Akshobhya family pledge of the vajra of enlightened mind is to train in order that one's mind be made the immutable bliss. The pledge of the bell of enlightened speech is to train in order that one's speech be made the invincible sound of speech.[151] The pledge of the seal of enlightened body is to train in order to make one's body an empty image.[152] The pledge of the master is the same [as described above], although practitioners [at the level of the completion phase,] due to their superior experience and realization, feel a stronger devotion for the vajra master.

For the family of Ratnasambhava, the pledge is to bind the ten winds[153] within the central channel.

For the family of Vairochana, the pledge is to prevent emission of [seminal essence] which is the pure essence of the five aggregates and of the five sense organs.

For the family of Amoghasiddhi, the pledge is to ignite, by warmth or passion, the fire of inner heat[154] so that the [body's] seminal essence melts [and descends], and to reverse its flow and thereby saturate the aggregates, elements, sense organs, and their objects with bliss.

For the family of Amitabha, the pledge is to transform the bliss arising from the melting of the seminal essence into the immutable bliss, relying on the great seal of the empty image.[155]

For the Vajrasattva family, the pledge is to cultivate the indivisibility of immutable bliss[156] and emptiness endowed with the supreme aspects.[157]

A practitioner on the creation phase trains in [the methods relating to] the provisional meanings of these pledges; and the completion phase practitioner, the definitive meanings.

In general, all aspects of the Secret Mantra paths are intended to be included in the three cultivations [of merit, ethics, and pristine awareness]. The jewel family pledge of generosity and the action (sword) family pledge to make offerings serves to cultivate merit. The pledge of the wheel family serves as the cause for the cultivation of ethics and the lotus family pledge serves as the actual cultivation of ethics. The five-pronged vajra and single-pronged vajra [family pledges] serve to cultivate pristine awareness. All mantric vows and pledges are thereby encompassed by these three cultivations.

The sequence [in which the pledges of the six families have been set out] corresponds to the course of experiential understanding, and therefore one should engage in the practice of them in exactly that order. The procedure is as follows:

Having entered this tantra [of the Wheel of Time], for the seal pledge [of the Akshobhya family], one dissolves conceptual grasping to the ordinary appearance of the body [into emptiness] and assumes the deity's form. For the bell pledge, one dissolves grasping to the ordinary manifestation of speech [into emptiness] and assumes the [deity's] mantra. For the vajra pledge, one dissolves ordinary thoughts [into emptiness], and whatever thoughts arise, dwells in that very nature [of emptiness]. These [three] are known as pledges that pertain to consciousness because they [involve the imaginative] conceptual process.

Then, having been introduced in the course of the initiation to [the ordinary] body, speech, and mind as the three vajras [body, speech, and mind] of a buddha, and having carried this [identification] into the meditation, one [trains in order to fulfill the definitive meanings of Akshobhya's] three pledges pertaining to pristine awareness. [For the pledge of the seal,] one actualizes the body as the real empty-form[158]; [for the bell's pledge,] the speech as the real self-reverberating sound (*nāda*) of indestructible speech; and [for the vajra's pledge,] the mind as the real profound bliss.

The most important contributory condition for preserving both [the pledges pertaining to consciousness and those pertaining to pristine awareness] is the vajra master, who is the principal medium through which the marvelous activity of all the buddhas shines. Therefore, one must devote oneself to a vajra master because through such a relationship ignorance is directly overcome. Devotion to the master is the aorta of all the paths of Secret Mantra, and therefore one should never waver from or feel above it: this is known as the Akshobhya (Immovable) pledge.

The pledge of Akshobhya applied to one's meditation is the remedy for ignorance, the root of cyclic existence. However, to overcome craving, which is the force that propels one into new lives, one trains in non-attachment by giving away the ten external objects of desire[159] [thus fulfilling the pledge of Ratnasambhava]. To use the mind of non-attachment in one's meditation, the body must be made fit for the practice of generosity: one observes the ten pledges that prescribe nourishing oneself with the ten foods.[160] Since these pledges serve as the condition for the achievement of an unpolluted physical aggregate of form, and for the "illumination" of objects by means of the five specially endowed supernatural knowledges,[161] they are known as pledges of Vairochana (Illuminator).

Then, on the basis of non-attachment and physical pliancy, one works toward the realization of the master as the embodiment of all the transcendent ones using the yoga of the inseparability of one's body, speech, and mind [with those of the vajra master]. This realization requires the three cultivations [of merit, ethics, and pristine awareness].

[To fulfill the pledge of the sword family,] one acquires merit by making offerings. Since merit serves as the condition for the attainment of the form dimension [of awakening] on the basis of which a buddha swiftly accomplishes the benefit of all beings, this is known as the pledge of the swift and supreme horse[-like] family of Amoghasiddhi (Unfailing Accomplishment).

[To fulfill the pledge of the lotus family,] one cultivates ethics by holding and not emitting [the seminal essence]. As this is the condition for the attainment of a buddha's boundless luminosity, it is known as the pledge of Amitabha (Measureless Light).

[To fulfill the pledge of the vajra family,] a practitioner enhances pristine awareness by cultivating awakening mind. Since the awakening mind is a single-pointed absorption on emptiness and compassion, it is known as the [single-pronged vajra family] pledge of Vajrasattva (Adamantine Being).

The presentation of the sequence and explanation [of the pledges] given here is exclusively in terms of the definitive meaning and differs from that of the condensed tantras which are mainly given in terms of the provisional meaning.

The Exceptional Vows [2"]

> The exceptional vows are these: for the vajra family, to take life;
>   for the sword family, to lie;
> For the jewel, to steal wealth; for the lotus, to abduct the
>   women of others;
> For the wheel, to eat meat and drink alcohol; and for the curved
>   knife, to be generous and not to disrespect women.
> Practitioners should engage in the evident or hidden
>   meanings of the pledges according to their levels of spiritual
>   accomplishment.

The exceptional pledges of the six families, with both evident and hidden meanings, are set forth [as follows] in the *Sacred Primordial Buddha's Tantra*.

In terms of the evident or provisional meaning, the pledge of the [Akshobhya] vajra family is to take the lives [while liberating the minds] of evil beings who are not tameable in peaceful ways by setting oneself in the immovable (*akṣobhya*) concentration and separating [them from their guardians]. Evil beings include persons who throughout their lives commit serious acts such as the five deeds of immediate retribution and persons who qualify as one of ten recipients.[162]

In the hidden or definitive meaning, to take life means to direct the vital energies that normally flow in the right (*rasanā*) and left (*lalanā*) channels into the central one (*avadhūti*). The immobility of these vital energies in the central channel ultimately stabilizes the winds and mind in the crown of the head, which causes the seminal essence to ascend. This occurs in reality on the twelfth stage of awakening.[163] As a similitude, the beginner trains in holding the seminal essence in the upper [focal point of energy].

In terms of the provisional meaning, the pledge of the [Amogha-siddhi] sword family is to speak untruth in order to turn away from false doctrines those who have fallen onto erroneous paths and who, even if told the truth, would not believe it.

In the definitive meaning, to speak untruth is to proclaim the enlightened speech which encompasses all [languages] and exists in the nature of an invincible and innate sound at the heart.[164] The enlightened speech teaches the unreality and non-abiding nature of all phenomena and in this sense does not speak of the truth of dualistic and limited phenomena, but speaks of their untruth. The innate sound is heard in reality on the fifth and sixth stages of awakening. As a similitude, the beginner, as the means to hear the invincible and innate sound, cultivates [the yoga of] "withdrawal."[165]

In terms of the provisional meaning, the pledge of the [Ratnasam-bhava] jewel family is to steal the possessions of others who crave wealth and are fettered by greed in order to save them from taking rebirth as starving spirits. Once stolen, for the sake of acquiring merit, the goods should be donated to others.

In the definitive meaning, to steal others' possessions means to steal the jewel-like immutable bliss from Vajrasattva. The place from where the immutable bliss is taken is the throat, where bliss and empty form are made inseparable. The immutable bliss is actually achieved on the eighth level. As a similitude, the beginner trains in the means for its achievement.

In terms of the provisional meaning, the pledge of the [Amitabha] lotus family is to abduct the women of others who crave and are attached to women in order to save them from rebirth as animals.

In the definitive meaning, to abduct the women of others means to actualize the great seal of empty form. The great seal of empty form is attained in reality on the ninth and tenth levels. As a similitude, the beginner trains in the means for its achievement.

In terms of the provisional meaning, the pledge of the [Vairochana] wheel family is to eat meat and drink alcohol in order to shatter arrogance about one's social status and personal pride.[166] To eat meat refers to eating the five meats (known as lamps), and [includes] the five nectars.

In the definitive meaning, to eat meat and drink alcohol means to reverse and stabilize at the navel the pure essence of feces, urine, and semen. In this stabilization, alcohol symbolizes innate pristine awareness; the five meats symbolize the five sense organs; the five nectars, the five buddhas[167]; and their "excellent objects," the five transmuted sense objects. The stabilization of the pure essence of feces, etc., occurs in reality on the fourth stage of awakening. As a similitude, the beginner trains in the branches of withdrawal and contemplation.[168]

In terms of the provisional meaning, the pledge of the [Vajrasattva] curved knife family is to give away one's own body, the greatest act of generosity, and to never disrespect women, so that one's practice with an action seal will yield attainments.

In the definitive meaning, to give is to stabilize the seminal essence at the genitals' focal point of energy. The stabilization is effected by keeping the vow of celibacy, i.e., non-emission of the seminal essence which is the cause of immutable bliss,[169] while churning in the lotus of space (vagina of the consort). The seminal essence is stabilized in reality at the genitals on the first stage of awakening. As a similitude, the beginner trains in stabilizing the adamantine bodhichitta[170] at the same place by exercising control over [winds],[171] and in giving away one's body along with one's children, spouse, etc.

The pledges of the six families taught here with an interpretable double sense, hidden and evident, are applicable to individual practitioners depending on their levels of capacity, that is, depending on whether one is an accomplished yogin [yogini] or one who has not yet gained powers. (An "accomplished yogin" has attained the five supernatural knowledges and other feats by practicing the branch of contemplation.[172]) Accordingly, [the tantras] say that unaccomplished yogins who lack supernatural knowledge should not attempt the wrathful rite of liberating, etc., but may perform pacifying, enriching, domineering, or summoning [rites]. Therefore, these pledges are to be maintained in accordance with levels of spiritual attainment: accomplished practitioners should actually engage [in the hidden meaning of the pledges]; beginners observe it imaginatively.

[With regard to the three cultivations mentioned above, the Vajra-sattva pledge of] giving one's body, etc., is said to be aimed at acquiring merit; not disrespecting women, at the cultivation of ethics; and [the Vairochana pledge] of eating the five nectars, etc., at the cultivation of pristine awareness.

The second victorious one, Karmapa Rangjung Dorjé, in his *Ocean of Pledges*, presents the following exceptional vows that apply to the [Highest Yoga] tantras:

> These are the exceptional Highest [Yoga Tantra] vows:
> For the vajra family, the excellent pledge is to take the lives
> Of winds, concepts, and ten recipients;
> For the jewel family, to steal
> Wealth, women, and the Universal Way
> And to accomplish the benefit of self and others;
> For the lotus family, the excellent pledge
> Is to rely on female consorts
> And the action, teachings, pledge, and great seals;
> In the action family, to speak untruth
> Is to proclaim perfect peace to be
> The unreality of oneself and others;
> In the wheel family, the pledge is to enjoy
> The five meats, alcohol, and [sense] objects.
> To safeguard [these vows] in their outer, inner, and secret levels
> Is the highest conduct.

Pledges of the Highest Yoga Tantra [cc']

These pledges, which prescribe restraint, are presented in four parts: (1) the root downfalls, (2) the eight secondary downfalls, (3) the twenty-eight subtle infractions, and (4) an ancillary explanation of the pledges of the four initiations and other pledges.

Root Downfalls [1"]

> **Highest Yoga pledges prescribe avoidance of fourteen root downfalls:**
> **To disrespect one's spiritual master; transgress the Buddha's teachings; be angry at one's spiritual companions;**
> **Abandon love; lose the awakening mind; disparage the teachings;**
> **Disclose secrets; abuse one's own aggregates; disbelieve what is pure in nature;**

> **Love the wicked; apply discursive thought to transcendent**
> **reality; cause believers to lose faith;**
> **Not accept pledge substances; and disrespect women.**

The Sanskrit *samaya* (Tib. *dam tshig*) (pledge) has ten meanings:

> *Samaya* means sameness, stipulation,
> Demonstrated conclusion, excellence,
> Rule, repetition, detailed presentation,
> Sign, occasion, and language.

In the context of mantric pledges, *samaya* should be taken to mean a stipulation or a rule accepted with one's word of honor that is not to be transgressed, etc. If practitioners transgress pledges and do not restore them, the transgressions become the root cause for their fall into the hell of Unceasing Torture or another hell; thus, they are called root downfalls. The fourteen root downfalls are explained as follows:

(1) *To disrespect one's vajra master* means to upset a spiritual master, or to abuse or be contemptuous of him or her in any way, physically, verbally, or mentally, such as striking, criticizing, slandering, or harboring wrong views about him or her. The object of the offense is a spiritual master, of which there six kinds:

> Those who bestow pledges, teach the tantric meditation,
> Expound [the tantras], reveal secret instructions,
> Confer initiation, or perform [charismatic] activities
> Are said to be the six kinds of masters.

Of these [six], the principal ones [in the context of this downfall] are the masters who have initiated one [into the tantra], expounded the tantras, or revealed secret instructions. Of particular significance is the "glorious spiritual master" who points out the pristine awareness of transcendent reality.

For the downfall to be complete, six factors must be present:

(1) The master being an authentic one;
(2) Knowing that the offense will displease [him or her];
(3) Offending the master directly with actions or words;
(4) Done not for others' sake or similar purposes;
(5) Done for selfish motives;
(6) Having no interest in purifying the offense.

If the offended master has conferred initiation, taught the tantra, and revealed secret instructions, the downfall is serious; if the master has performed two of these, or only one, the downfall is correspondingly less serious. These and other distinctions are drawn.

(2) *To transgress the Buddha's teachings*, in its general sense, means to transgress what was taught by the Victorious One. To disrespect and reject the teachings, even when due to lack of understanding of them, qualifies as this downfall. To reject the teachings of the Universal Way constitutes a defeat; to be averse to other teachings of the Buddha that do not appeal to one is a serious violation; to reify or depreciate minor [aspects of the teachings] constitutes a minor failing.

The particular sense of this downfall is to defy one's vajra master's advice to give up unwholesome ways, such as the ten unvirtuous deeds, and to do such deeds in secret. For [this sense of] the downfall to be complete, six factors must be present:

(1) The master being an authentic one;
(2) Knowing that the offense will displease the master;
(3) Committing the offense physically or verbally without the master knowing;
(4-6) And the last three factors of the first downfall.

(3) *To be angry at one's spiritual siblings* means, out of anger, to speak of any fault of a spiritual sibling, or to strike or otherwise inflict any sort of injury on him or her, physically, verbally, or mentally, regardless of whether the recipient of the harm is senior or junior in the training.

The term "spiritual siblings" generally includes all Buddhists. Closer [in terms of spiritual bond] are persons who have formed an awakening mind in the Universal Way. Of particular significance are vajra brothers and sisters who have entered the Secret Mantra and assumed its vows; and above all, those vajra siblings with whom one has received in their entirety the four initiations from the same master.

For the downfall to be complete, six factors must be present:

(1) The object of the offense being an actual spiritual sibling[173];
(2) Knowing that one's anger will displease the sibling;
(3) Expressing the anger with actions or words;
(4-6) And the last three factors of the first downfall.

Spiritual siblings are categorized in other ways. Jnanapada [for example] enumerates five types[174]; the *Wheel of Time*, seven,[175] in which are included all sentient beings as "distant siblings." However categorized, downfalls that are incurred in relation to the latter types (the closest) are progressively more serious.

(4) *To abandon love* means to make the resolve never to help a particular being, whatever the circumstances, and thereby give up the intention to lead him or her to awakening. One's love for someone may be abandoned in the following four ways [listed] in order of the speed of restoration:

> (1) Love abandoned [briefly], like the time it takes for a drawing on water [to disappear];
> (2) For longer, like the time for a drawing on sand [to disappear];
> (3) For even longer, like the time for a crack in the ground to be sealed by rain;
> (4) [Forever,] like a shattered stone or fruit that has fallen to the ground and can never be repaired.[176]

Some mention only the latter two ways of abandoning love as the basis of this downfall. The essential point [in qualifying as a downfall] is that the love is not subsequently restored.

For the downfall to be complete, three factors must be present:

> (1) The object being any sentient being;
> (2) The intention never to help him or her;
> (3) Having no interest in purifying the offense.

(5) *To lose the jasmine-flower-like awakening mind* means to emit the seminal essence, the support [for bliss]. Pundarika's *Great Commentary* [on the *Wheel of Time Tantra*] explains the nature of the downfall in these terms:

> The fifth root downfall is incurred when, lacking an understanding of immanent reality, one engages in union [with a consort] for the sake of using the ensuing bliss as a means to work toward awakening, but in doing so [overcome by desire or out of disregard for tantric vows] loses the seminal essence.

All spiritual accomplishments are rooted in the relative and ultimate awakening minds.[177] From these, the two dimensions of a buddha are realized. The seed of the attainment of the form dimension of awakening is the relative awakening mind, which is the jasmine-flower-like awakening mind (*bodhicitta*) itself. Therefore, to lose this awakening mind constitutes a downfall.

For the downfall to be complete, three factors must be present:

> (1) To be one who has not yet realized immutable bliss-reality by means of great wisdom;
> (2) To lose the seminal essence and experience a transitory bliss, [while engaging in union] as a means to attain awakening;

(3) To lose the seminal essence other than for the special purposes of using it as the substance for the secret initiation, or
as means to [experience] bliss during the conferral of the
wisdom initiation to others, or to make nectar pills.[178]

(6) *To disrespect spiritual teachings*, in its general sense, means to disparage [one's own or] other religions out of desire for personal gain.
To disparage the scriptures of the Universal Way is a serious violation; the Individual Way, a minor offense; and non-Buddhist religions,
a minimal offense. However, [the tantras] state that if one shows disrespect toward non-Buddhist traditions with the intention of spiritually inspiring their adherents [to follow the Buddhist path], one not
only does not incur this downfall, but actually acquires merit.

The particular sense of this downfall is in the context of Buddhist
tenets. The Way of the Perfections and the Secret Mantra are causally
related to one another in that the first is the cause and the second the
result. In the first of the three cycles of teachings, [the Buddha] taught
[on the subject of] the realization of personal selflessness and the unreality of generic images of apprehended objects. In the second, he
taught [on the subject of] the realization of the ineffable, inconceivable, and indescribable empty nature of all phenomena. In the third,
he taught [on the subject of] the realization of the clear-light nature of
mind as a way of teaching [ultimate reality] and on the realization of
the self-experienced intrinsic awareness as the essence of meditation
practice. The four tantras [teach these realizations] in a similar way,
up to the last [the Highest Yoga Tantra] that teaches [the ultimate
truth] as the identical flavor of *EVAM*, the union of bliss and emptiness. Ultimately, all teach but one reality. A downfall is incurred when
one disparages the profound transcendent wisdom [as taught in the
Way of the Perfections] which forms the very heart of the definitive
meaning in Mantra, holding it to be inferior to the transcendent wisdom [taught in the Mantra Way].

For the downfall to be complete, three factors must be present:

(1) To disparage the transcendent wisdom that is the definitive
meaning of Mantra by believing it to be inferior to the transcendent wisdom [taught] in the Secret Mantra and to actually say so;

(2) To believe that such disparaging words are well-founded;

(3) To act not for the sake of uplifting those who adhere only to
the Way of the Perfections.

(7) *To disclose secrets to immature persons* means to reveal the secrets of profound bliss to someone attracted exclusively to the proclaimers' way or similar ways who has not been ripened by initiation and who would become apprehensive or disdainful of such secrets.

For the downfall to be complete, four factors must be present:

(1) The person having an affinity for the proclaimers' or the solitary sages' ways being spiritually immature and becoming frightened or disdainful upon hearing the secrets;
(2) To disclose the secrets of profound bliss to that person;
(3-4) And the last two factors of the first downfall.

Regarding this downfall, Darika[179] states that to disclose the secrets of profound bliss creates obstacles to gaining supreme attainment; and to disclose the general secrets of Mantra, obstacles to gaining common attainments.[180]

There are four types of spiritually immature persons (impeded in one of four ways) to whom secrets should not be revealed. [Beginning with the most] immature, these are as follows:

(1) Persons concerned with the affairs of this world only, who hold virulent wayward views toward the teachings and are immature in that they lack the cause [for Secret Mantra practice];
(2) Spiritual extremists who believe in the [reality of a] self;
(3) Proclaimers who are weary of cyclic existence;
(4) Solitary sages who do not have the incentive to help others (these last three lack the conditions for Secret Mantra practice).

Higher [teachings] should be kept increasingly more secret the more immature the person.

(8) *To abuse one's own aggregates,* in its general sense, means to despise one's own body. The aggregates, elements, and experiential media of oneself or of others should not be despised because they are the form dimension of awakening although veiled by impurities.

In its particular sense, this downfall means to believe the body to be the principal source [of suffering] and engage in forms of self-mortification, such as injuring it with weapons, burning it with fire, or otherwise abusing it through fasting and other austerities. Abuse of the body constitutes a downfall because in receiving the vase initiation,[181] one has been introduced to the aggregates, etc., as the nature of various buddhas. Once introduced in this way, one can increase the [experience of] bliss by offering the aggregates the delight of sensory pleasures, and with bliss as the support, actualize the pristine awareness of reality.

For the downfall to be complete, four factors must be present:

(1) To know the body and the other aggregates to be of the nature of various [buddhas];

(2) To consciously abuse them;

(3-4) And the last two factors of the first downfall.

Many classes of tantras prescribe the purificatory fasting practice; would this practice not be a downfall? In [the context of] tantra, the purpose of fasting is not to abuse the body but to purify it in order to please a deity, or to supplement inner cleansing. Therefore, this practice of fasting not only is not a downfall, but greatly aids [the practitioner's spiritual growth].

(9) *To disbelieve what is pure in nature*,[182] in its general sense, means to misconceive relative truth (while to misconceive ultimate truth would constitute the eleventh root downfall), which is the interdependent arising of all phenomena, being mere appearance without intrinsic reality, like [the reflection of] the moon on water. For example, to contend that statements such as "sentient beings [can] become buddhas" or "buddhas, although without concepts, are replete with knowledge" are self-contradictory [is to incur this downfall].

In its particular sense, this downfall means to fail to appreciate or to harbor doubts about emptiness [as described in statements such as] "the overall meaning of reality is emptiness," etc., or to pursue similar mental fabrications.

For the downfall to be complete, four factors must be present:

(1) The pure nature of emptiness being the object [of one's doubts];

(2) Having the underlying attitude of non-appreciation with the ensuing mental fabrications;

(3-4) And the last two factors of the first downfall.

(10) *To have love for the wicked*, in its general sense, means to show affection for evil beings, such as demons, religious extremists, or arrogant challengers [of the teachings], who are untameable by loving-kindness.

In its particular sense, this downfall means to hypocritically feign love for another person and thereby deceive him or her. The downfall is mainly concerned with feigning love for a tantric consort. For [this sense of] the downfall to be complete, four factors must be present:

(1) The object being another sentient being, and particularly a tantric consort;

(2) Feigning love with gentle words while feeling aversion toward him or her;

(3-4) And the last two factors of the first downfall.

The general sense of this downfall is failure to annihilate [and liberate the minds of] evil beings by implementing wrathful rites (as prescribed above in the exceptional Akshobhya pledge). Here, however, the downfall has been specified [as feigning love for a tantric consort] because it must pertain to what is incompatible with the third initiation [the pristine-awareness-through-wisdom initiation, i.e., a consort].

(11) *To apply discursive concepts to transcendent reality,* in its general sense, means to reify or depreciate that which is beyond designations and to draw sophistic conclusions about existence, non-existence, both, or neither, not understanding that the entirety of all phenomena is simply reality as it is and reality itself is the nature of all phenomena.

In its particular sense, this downfall means to conceptualize or have doubts about immutable bliss, the nature of the body, speech, and mind of the buddhas, which transcends all mundane examples, is nameless, etc.; and about emptiness inclusive of all the appearing forms of "she" who bestows the bliss.[183]

For the downfall to be complete, four factors must be present:

(1) The object being everlasting and immutable bliss;

(2) Conceiving reality to be different from immutable bliss;

(3-4) And the last two factors of the first downfall.

(12) *To cause believers to lose faith,* in its general sense, means to destroy someone's faith [in the Buddhist teachings]. To turn a faithful practitioner away from the Secret Mantra constitutes a defeat; to turn from their respective paths faithful followers of the [Buddha's] discourses or the proclaimers' way is a serious violation; and to turn the faithful away temporarily [from these spiritual pursuits] is a minor offense.

In its particular sense, this downfall means to disrespect and, out of jealousy, [attempt to] destroy the faith of a person of purity who inwardly dwells in the pristine awareness of reality but whose outward conduct is unorthodox.

For the downfall to be complete, four factors must be present:

    (1) The object being a pure person [i.e., yogin];
    (2) To speak words out of jealousy to undermine the person's faith;
  (3-4) And the last two factors of the first downfall.

(13) *To fail to accept the pledge substances* means to have doubts about and to refuse the pledge substances during any tantric activity due to feeling that one must adhere to monastic forms of conduct, etc., [or considering these substances to be impure]. "Pledge substances" refers to the outer and inner five meats, five nectars, etc.,[184] and "tantric activities" refers to ritual feasts, celebrations of heroes and heroines,[185] and other tantric gatherings.

For the downfall to be complete, four factors must be present:

    (1) The occasion being a tantric activity;
    (2) Refusing to partake of the pledge substances;
  (3-4) And the last two factors of the first downfall.

(14) *To disrespect a woman* means to speak disparagingly to a woman out of disrespect.[186]

For the downfall to be complete, four factors must be present:

    (1) The object being a woman;
    (2) To say disparaging words to her out of disrespect;
  (3-4) And the last two factors of the first downfall.

The general sense of each root downfall given here accords with the Highest Yoga Tantra's well-known standard explanations on the subject. The particular sense is as it appears in the *Wheel of Time Tantra*. The *Indestructible Nucleus' Ornament Tantra*,[187] the *Red Yamari Tantra*, and the *Black Yamari Tantra*[188] also list fourteen root downfalls, while the *Indestructible Tent Tantra* gives only thirteen.[189]

Manjushriyashas divides each of the fourteen root downfalls according to six aspects—object, intention, action, occasion, fault, and frequency—to a total of eighty-four, and further subdividing these according to [degrees of] seriousness—heavy, medium, and light—to yield two hundred and fifty-two aspects of the awareness-holder's ethics.[190]

The Eight Secondary Downfalls [2"]

> Eight secondary downfalls are to rely on a consort without
> pledges,
> Quarrel at ritual feast, accept nectar from an unsuitable consort,
> Not teach when appropriate, answer questions perversely,
> Stay in the home of a proclaimer, boast of being a tantric
> practitioner although ignorant,
> And proclaim secrets to the unsuited. There are many other
> ways to enumerate secondary downfalls.

Eight secondary downfalls are related to the fourteen root downfalls:

(1) To rely on an awareness-woman who has no pledges (either because she has not been initiated or has violated them), who cannot keep secret [the practice], lacks faith in oneself, and does not possess the necessary qualifications.[191] This downfall applies principally to the lay tantric practitioner.

(2) To quarrel at times of tantric activities; for example, to argue over seating order, food, or drink during a ritual feast. This includes to argue in the course of mandala rituals, fire rituals, consecrations, etc.

(3) To accept the outer and inner nectars of the pledges[192] from a shameful consort or one who has not been specified in the tantras [i.e., an ordinary consort who is not fully qualified].

(4) To fail to reveal tantric instructions to sincere disciples who request them, either because they are poor or due to one's unwillingness to share one's knowledge.

(5) To fail to answer questions on the teachings directly but to respond with playful banter, or to explain the discourses, for instance, in response to a request for [teaching on] the Secret Mantra.

(6) To stay more than one week in the home of a proclaimer[193] who has contempt for the Universal Way.

(7) To boast of being a tantric practitioner when one is ignorant of the outer, inner, and alternative levels of the Secret Mantra[194] and of the yoga of union [of wisdom and means], and knows only outer rites and procedures of the creation phase.

(8) To disclose secrets in disregard of the stipulation to give personal instructions[195] only to jewel-like disciples, collective instructions to the sandalwood-like and the other [three types of disciples],[196] and teaching on the common principles [of the Universal Way] to disciples unsuited [to tantra].

The *Indestructible Nucleus' Ornament Tantra* enumerates six secondary downfalls: the first, second, fifth, sixth, and eighth as above, plus to show secret [articles].[197] Various other [secondary downfalls] are found here and there in the tantras, and therefore it is difficult to make a definitive enumeration of all of them. Indian masters have also presented these downfalls in various ways. The source for the above list is [Rangjung Dorjé's] *Ocean of Pledges*, itself based on Manjushri-yashas's works.[198] The Great Lord of Jonang [Taranatha],[199] in his work known as *Elimination of Errors*, explains eight [secondary downfalls] in accordance with Garbhapada's work[200]:

(1) To enjoy practice with a consort
Who has no pledges;
(2) To quarrel at a ritual feast;
(3) To expound other teachings
To disciples with faith [in the tantras];
(4) To stay more than seven days in the home
Of someone proud to be a proclaimer;
(5) To disclose secrets to unqualified disciples
Who are not sufficiently prepared;
(6) To teach the physical seal[201]
To disciples who lack the necessary skill in the seals;
(7) To perform mandala rituals [such as an initiation]
Without first completing proper service, etc.;
(8) To transgress the precepts of the Individual and
    Universal ways
Without having a special [altruistic] purpose.

Some scholars say that the secondary downfalls number nine, the ninth being to use symbolic behavior[202] without a specific purpose.

The Twenty-eight Subtle Infractions [3"]

The subtle infractions include fifteen concerning charismatic activity and seven branches.

The first fifteen of the twenty-eight subtle infractions are downfalls in the performance of charismatic activity. These are explained by the master Shura[203] as follows:

(1) To reject the deity on which the flower [tossed into the mandala] has fallen and to favor another[204];

(2) To let a day and a night pass [without engaging] in the creation and completion [phases] of one's deity[205];

(3) To be attracted to [and worship] non-Buddhist deities[206]; (4) to view the [mandala, the deity, and other forms of the] creation phase as real;

(5) To confer [full] initiation on disciples when one has not been fully initiated oneself;

(6) To teach profound subjects for the sake of worldly gains;

(7) To deprecate [and fail to follow] the ethics of lower spiritual pursuits [and minor pledges]; (8) to give a contrived image of oneself [as spiritually accomplished] for the sake of gain;

(9) To engage in [appeasing] charismatic activities, [etc.,] without having gained the necessary power; (10) to pass the time [meant for practice] in meaningless distractions;

(11) To fail to take care of others though able to; (12) to be attracted to [and to follow] lesser forms of spiritual conduct [that of the proclaimers and so forth];

(13) To desire material goods[207]; (14) to fail to discipline those who violate their pledges; and

(15) To engage prematurely in tantric activity[208]: these are the fifteen.

The seven branch subtle infractions are to fail to do the following:
(1) Devote oneself to an authentic master[209];

(2) Examine whether a disciple has the qualifications [to enter the Mantra];

(3) Cause no harm to others while accomplishing one's desires[210];

(4) Refrain from making personal use of the property of the Three Jewels[211] [or of the master or vajra siblings]; (5) engage in what benefits others;

(6) Seal one's [merit] by dedication[212]; and (7) be skillful in the transference [of consciousness[213]].

The six mistakes are these: (1) To have doubts about [the view and conduct of] the Secret Mantra;

(2) To teach the three ways[214] simultaneously, rather than [according to the] levels [of the disciples];

(3) To act as a tantric master without [expertise] in the ten fields[215];

(4) To lack skill in the ways to investigate demonic forces;

(5) To fail to examine [whether one has transgressed the root and secondary] pledges;

And (6) to fail to acknowledge minor infractions.

All these add up to twenty-eight subtle infractions. The Red and Black Yamari tantras list four other secondary downfalls:

(1) Do not wander [into the village] begging [out of desire];

(2) Do not abandon the tantric meditation;

(3) Do not discontinue the recitation of secret mantras; and

(4) Do not fail to rely on the pledge's [substances], etc.[216]

The Pledges of the Four Initiations and Other Pledges [4"]

The tantras give numerous classifications of the pledges, the pledges of the four initiations, etc.

Various ways of classifying the pledges are presented in the tantras, for example, the different pledges for each of the four initiations taught in most of the mandalas related to the fundamental and explanatory Chakrasamvara [tantras]. In particular, the instructions on the Path and its Fruition[217] present different pledges for each of the four initiations.

For the vase initiation,

(1) the pledge of equipoise is [to cultivate] the creation phase;

(2) the pledge of post[-equipoise] conduct is to practice the three realities[218];

(3) the pledge of sustenance is [to eat] the pills made with the five meats and five nectars;

(4) the pledges to be safeguarded are the twenty-two root and secondary mantric vows[219];

(5) the pledge not to be separated from is to hold vajra and bell.

For the secret initiation,

(1) the pledge of equipoise is to engage in the control of the breath and channels[220];

(2) the pledge of post[-equipoise] conduct is [to rest in] self-existing pristine awareness[221];

(3) the pledge of sustenance is [to nourish oneself with] emptiness and clarity;

(4) the pledge to be safeguarded is [to shun] all that hampers self-existing [wisdom] and [its] wind;

(5) the pledge not to be separated from is [to work with] either gentle or forceful breath [control].

For the pristine-awareness-through-wisdom initiation,

(1) the pledge of equipoise is to meditate on the mandala[222];

(2) the pledge of post[-equipoise] conduct is [to rest in] the innate [pristine awareness of bliss][223];

(3) the pledge of sustenance is [to nourish oneself with] bliss;

(4) the pledge to be safeguarded is not to allow the six losses of seminal essence[224];

(5) the pledge not to be separated from is [to rely on] an actual or imaginary consort.

For the fourth initiation,

(1) the pledge of equipoise concerns the "three [vajra] waves"[225];

(2) the pledge of post[-equipoise] conduct is [to rest in the] utterly pure reality;

(3) the pledge of sustenance is [to nourish oneself with] the bliss-emptiness of great bliss;

(4) the vow to be safeguarded is [to overcome] the two impediments,[226] in particular those that hamper the attainment of omniscience;

(5) the pledge never to be separated from is [to rely on] an actual *padmini* [lotus-like consort] or an imaginary consort.[227]

These pledges are honored in four ways: first by assuming them correctly; by recollecting them again and again; by having [at least] a single [meditative] experience; and by having a special respect for the vajra master. It is said that failure to fulfill the first means losing the pledges that would draw one out of the suffering of cyclic existence. Failure to fulfill the latter three ways means loss of pledges resulting in a delay in one's spiritual progress.

"Etc." [in the root verse] refers to pledges taught in other tantras, for example, the *Samputa Tantra*'s pledges of the enlightened body, speech, and mind:

> The pledge of vajra body
> Is not to despise, even if unaware [of reality],
> The body of a male or female

Which is born from many actions.
The pledge of vajra mind
Is not to torment others in any way
Or to demean one's mind
With a net of discursive thoughts.
The pledge of vajra speech
Is to speak gently
And not utter harsh words
Out of sheer jealousy.[228]

To elaborate, the pledge of the vajra body is never to disrespect the body of any being, male or female, of the six classes because each possesses the nature of the body of enlightenment. The pledge of the vajra mind is not to cause distress to oneself or another by instigating feelings of guilt, etc., because all sentient beings possess the nature of enlightened mind. The pledge of the vajra speech is never to speak harsh words but always gentle ones that please and do not upset others, because all beings have the nature of enlightened speech. These pledges are taught with consistency in many tantras such as the *Indestructible Nucleus' Ornament Tantra*.[229]

The *Chakrasamvara Fundamental Tantra* presents eight special pledges:

(1) Not to allow the movement of bodhichitta (loss of the seminal essence). Bodhichitta is the seed of desire-realm [bliss] gained from relying on an action seal; the seed of form-realm [bliss], from relying on an imaginary seal; and the seed of the fruit which is the enlightenment of the great seal.[230] Thus, not to lose the seminal essence serves as the cause for all powerful attainments.

(2) To cultivate [or safeguard] the pledge,[231] which means to cause the sixteen [aspects of] bliss to gradually arise at the throat, heart, navel, and genital focal points of energy by using the passion of the wisdom-woman.

(3) Not to unite with the emissary of another buddha family after having discarded the consort of one's own buddha family if one's purpose is that of gaining only outer attainments.[232]

(4) To attain the undivided state at the end of the full moon,[233] which means to fulfill the pledges related to the four seminal essences of the four focal points of energy by resting in the state of the indivisibility of emptiness and innate bliss.

(5) To shun the waning phase of the moon,[234] which means not to lose [the seminal essence] that has the nature of the sixteen joys through the bliss of emission.

(6) To churn [or follow] the female conduct[235] (the conduct of the transcendent Samantabhadri[236]), which means always to accomplish with joy the many ways to benefit others.

(7) To maintain chastity at the face of the vajra,[237] which is to always maintain the ethics of not emitting [the seminal essence].

(8) To draw [the seminal essences] up the central channel[238] which means to draw up and to stabilize at the crown focal point of energy the seminal essences that have flowed down to the tip of the secret place by reversing them and experiencing the joys in the ascending order.

[Vajrapani's] *Eulogy-Commentary on the Chakrasamvara Tantra*[239] explains these eight pledges in detail and states the benefit of safeguarding them in these words:

> A practitioner who at all times cultivates the eight [special] pledges will swiftly gain the attainment of the great seal.

In addition to these, there are many classifications of the different minor pledges presented in the tantras. However, the principal ones are included in those explained above.

Other Ways of Enumerating the Pledges [b']

Mikyö Gawa asserts that all pledges are included in the four pledges related to the four initiations:
The pledges to be safeguarded, of sustenance, of conduct, and not to be apart from.

The omniscient Mikyö Gawa asserts that all the vows and pledges of the Highest Yoga Tantra are included in four pledges related to the four initiations. These are enumerated briefly as follows:

(1) The vows of the vase initiation are comprised by the "pledge to be honored": to observe the general and specific pledges of the five families, and not to commit the fourteen root downfalls and eight secondary ones.

(2) The vows of the secret initiation are comprised by the "pledge of sustenance": to partake of the five meats and the five nectars.

(3) The vows of the pristine-awareness-through-wisdom initiation are comprised by the "pledge of conduct": the special pledges, to liberate [evil] beings, etc.

(4) The vows of the fourth initiation are comprised by the "pledge not to be apart from": to wear the attire of Heruka and to rely on a wisdom-woman.

> **Pema Karpo presents the pledges of restraint from root downfalls, the pledges of practice of the six families,**
> **And the pledges related to practice, which form the three groups of pledges prescribing ritual articles,**
> **Pledges prescribing enjoyments, and pledges of equipoise and post-equipoise.**

The omniscient Pema Karpo presents the pledges concerning the fourteen root and secondary downfalls to be avoided, the pledges of the six families to be practiced, and the common and special pledges relating to application[240] which are grouped into three categories:

(1) the pledges prescribing use of ritual articles, for example, to keep ritual articles such as images, volumes [of the tantras], and symbolic ornaments[241];

(2) the pledges prescribing enjoyments, such as to enjoy the five meats, five nectars, five drinks, and five types [of consorts][242];

(3) the pledges of equipoise, such as the four pledges to be interpreted[243]; and the pledges of post-equipoise, such as the twenty-five modes of conduct [taught in the *Wheel of Time Tantra*], the fourteen [modes of conduct taught] in the *Indestructible Tent Tantra*, and other post-equipoise pledges.[244]

> **The victorious Rangjung Dorjé states that all pledges are included in four pledges.**

In his *Ocean of Pledges*, the omniscient and victorious Rangjung Dorjé states:

> The Three Jewels and inner and outer awakening mind;
> Perceived and perceiver; outer and inner conditions;
> Activity of annihilation and liberation;
> All pledges are included in these.

All pledges are condensed into these four pledges: not to renounce the Three Jewels or the outer relative and inner ultimate awakening minds; not to harbor doubts about the purity of the object perceived and the perceiver; to rely on the outer and inner conducive conditions; and not to neglect the activity of annihilation and liberation at the proper time.

All of these pledges are encompassed by two categories: prohibitions and injunctions.

All the pledges that have been presented fall into two categories: prohibitions, which are prescriptions for restraint; and injunctions, prescriptions for what to practice. The first includes root downfalls, secondary downfalls, and the modes of conduct. The second includes the vows of the five families and the pledges of the higher initiations.

Six modes of conduct are taught in *Tent Tantra* for practitioners who have reached the stage of warmth.

The *Indestructible Tent Tantra* prescribes six modes of conduct to be performed by a practitioner who has achieved a stable state of contemplation and has attained the pristine awareness of experiential warmth[245]:

Do not perform symbolic hand gestures.
Do not build reliquaries [or cast votive images].
Do not bow to the [representations of the] exalted three vajras
    [i.e., body, speech, and mind of the buddhas].
Do not draw mandalas, or do other outer rituals.
Do not do these even in your dreams.
Honor your tantric master, [his lineage,] and [spiritual] siblings,
But do not pay homage to other teachers.

Practitioners who have perfected pristine awareness are beyond codes of behavior.

A practitioner who has attained a deep level of realization and has perfected pristine awareness has transcended all the creations of dualistic thought, concepts of vows and transgressions, codes of behavior prescribing what to do and what not to do, proper and improper conduct, and so on. For this adept, all pledges are inherently observed in the "pledge of the great observance."

The Seriousness of a Transgression and the Means to Restore Pledges [c']

This section has two parts: (1) the seriousness of a downfall, and (2) means to restore pledges.

Seriousness of a Downfall [i']

> **A defeat occurs when there is motivation, recognition, pursuing, separation,**
> **Lack of regret, non-deranged state of mind, and overdue acknowledgment.**
> **If some completing factors are missing, the infraction may be a serious transgression, downfall, or a minor infraction.**

The root downfalls qualify as actual tantric defeats when seven factors are present:

(1) The offense being motivated by a negative emotion;

(2) Recognition of the object [basis of the infraction];

(3) Having pursued the wrongdoing with physical action or words;

(4) Having engaged in the main part of the particular downfall; this is referred to as "separated" [since the action must be separated from its antidote by a period of three hours to be considered completed].

(5) To be pleased and to have no regret;

(6) To be in a non-deranged state of mind [when committing the downfall];

(7) To let one, or [at the most] three, years pass while the master is still alive without acknowledging the downfall.

When six factors are present, but the deadline for acknowledgment has not passed, the offense is called a downfall and is equivalent in seriousness to a partial defeat in the monastic code. To have engaged in the very cause of the downfall but without having allowed the deadline for acknowledgment to pass and with one of the other factors missing is equivalent to a serious transgression in the monastic code. To have engaged in the very cause of the downfall but without the deadline having passed and with more than one of the other factors missing is equivalent to a downfall [that requires forfeiture or confession alone] in the monastic code. To have pursued the wrongdoing with physical action or words in the absence of all the other factors is equivalent to a minor infraction in the monastic code. One also incurs minor infractions when one transgresses the pledges due to not recollecting them.[246]

The eight secondary downfalls are classified as serious transgressions, downfalls, or minor infractions depending on [the presence of many or few of] the seven completing factors.

The *Essence Ornament of the General Procedure for All Secrets*[247] states that in certain cases transgressions of the pledges may seem to be downfalls but in fact are not: when done for a greater purpose, such as seeing that others would benefit; when observing a pledge would cause an obstacle [for one's life]; when one has received permission to do so [from a master or favored deity]; or when unable [to keep the pledges] because of illness, etc.

A different explanation, which is essentially the same as the explanation given above, specifies the following five factors (person, object, attitude, enactment, and conclusion) that complete a downfall:

(1) the person, a holder of [previously] unviolated pledges;
(2) the object, one's vajra master, for example, and recognition of the object;
(3) the attitude, feeling no shame in transgressing the pledge, not trying to avoid the downfall, and afterwards being pleased and having no regret about it;
(4) the enactment, to engage in the actual transgression;
(5) the conclusion, the consummation of that act.

The factors that lead to transgressions are stated in the *Dakinisamvara Tantra*[248]:

> Six factors lead to the violation of pledges:
> Ignorance [of the pledges], heedlessness,
> Overwhelming emotions, irreverence,
> Forgetfulness, and weak mindfulness.

Practitioners who strive to overcome these factors will naturally honor their pledges.

In general, all the pledges of Secret Mantra are very strict and require extreme caution. In particular, it is imperative not to disrespect one's vajra master. To do so, even while honoring all other pledges, is like cutting the root of a tree.

Means to Restore Pledges [ii']

The *Essence Ornament* teaches twenty-five means of restoration.

It is imperative that pledges be restored if a downfall has been incurred. The general means of restoration are as follows: [In the Wheel of Time tantra,] one who has received only [the first] seven initiations[249] must recite thirty-six thousand mantras for each deity of the mandala and then retake the seven initiations with the intention never to transgress the pledges again. One who has received the uncommon vase and secret initiations must retake the initiation after having applied the means of restoration indicated by the vajra master. The *Essence Ornament of the General Procedure for All Secrets*[250] lists twenty-five means of restoring the pledges:

(1) Confession to [the deities who form] the field of merit; (2) purification with the mantra and gesture of separating the hands [taught in Yoga Tantra];

(3) Ablutions with the outer [water of the vase of the initiation] and the inner [receiving of the initiations of the five buddha families from the deities in the sky]; (4) burning the seed syllables [at the navel] with the fire of inner heat;

(5) Contemplation in the state of non-origination [of the three roles]; (6) taking the four outer [initiations from the master] and inner [self-]initiations;

(7) Acknowledgment before a [tantric feast gathering or another] gathering [of practitioners after the offerings have been done]; (8) making confession while expressing great remorse before a consecrated representation [of the enlightened body, speech, and mind];

(9) Offering the mandala [plus wealth and merits, and then confessing to the three representations]; (10) building reliquaries of the joyful ones [or votive images];

(11) Purification by means of [the elaborated] appeasing fire [rituals or the ritual of Vajradaka]; (12) performing vast offerings of *torma*;

(13) Reciting the mantra of one's favored deity; (14) cultivating profound contemplation [quiescence and insight];

(15) Saving the lives of beings; (16) reading the discourses and the tantras;

(17) Devoting oneself to the master; (18) performing profound self-initiation [after completing recitation of Samayasattva's mantra];

(19) Reciting the one-hundred-syllable mantra of the joyful ones [in front of or while circumambulating a stupa of great blessing]; (20) repeating recollection mantras [that are praised for their purificatory effectiveness] on the auspicious occasions [of the eighth and fifteenth of the lunar month];

(21) Reciting the confession of infractions [the *Three-Part Discourse*] in the six periods [of the day and night]; (22) performing the meditation and recitation of the mantra of Vajrasattva;

(23) Cultivating mystic union with the three vajras [the seed
syllables *OM, AH,* and *HUM* at the forehead, throat, and
heart] of the vajra master [while visualizing oneself in a
deity's form];
(24) Performing the yoga of the glorious seminal essence; and
(25) [performing] the subtle yoga.[251]

Fire ritual, recitation of mantra, meditation, ritual feast, etc.
Are the means to purify downfalls, transgressions, violations,
and ruptures.
Any downfall, regardless of its seriousness, can be purified if
acknowledged before three hours have elapsed.

Of the special means of restoring pledges, all of the higher and lower
tantras emphasize the fire ritual for purifying wrong deeds, in particular, the fire ritual of Vajradaka[252]; the meditation and the recitation of the mantra of one's favored deity; and actual ritual feasts or
similar celebrations of heroes, [heroines,][253] etc. Since these are all
outstanding means of restoration, they should be engaged in with
increasing energy and for a greater number of times depending on
whether the transgression is a deterioration, a violation, or a rupture.

To elaborate, transgressions become increasingly serious the longer
the delay before taking remedial measures. [The different types of]
transgressions are designated as follows: (1) infractions not amended
within a period; (2) contraventions; (3) deteriorations; (4) violations;
and (5) ruptures. An infraction not amended within a period is a transgression that has not been remedied within three hours (one of the
six periods of day and night). A contravention is a transgression that
has not been remedied within the same day. A deterioration is a transgression that has not been remedied within a month. A violation is a
transgression that has not been remedied within a year. A rupture is a
transgression that has not been remedied within two, or three, years.

If, within three years of the occurrence of a transgression, one acknowledges it sincerely and perseveres in applying [the means of
purification], one can rise above it. However, after more than three
years have elapsed, the transgression becomes irreparable and the
perpetrator will certainly be reborn in hell. Hence, one must strive to
prevent downfalls occurring in the first place, arresting them with
the remedies of mindfulness and discriminative alertness. If a downfall does occur, regardless of its seriousness, it can be purified if one
acknowledges it before three hours have elapsed.

> Meditation and recitation of the mantra of Vajrasattva and
>   Samayavajra,
> Initiation, and self-initiation are the best means for purification.

The principal means to remedy transgressions acknowledged within
a period of three hours are the meditation and the recitation of the
mantras of Vajrasattva and Samayavajra,[254] practices which are both
easy and very effective. To receive an initiation or to perform by oneself the ritual of entering into the outer and inner mandalas are the
most effective means of restoration since they are related to that very
purpose [purification]. Therefore, tantras repeatedly state that nothing
is more worthwhile than to exert oneself at these practices at all times.

The first step is to first verbally acknowledge the downfall before a
gathering [of practitioners] or a [sacred] representation; the second,
to perform self-initiation or retake the initiation; and finally, to apply
the methods to purify wrong deeds. This is the procedure followed
by all great vajra holders.

> Higher pledges are restored through self-blessing and the view.

[According to the *Wheel of Time Tantra,*] those who have received all
of the special higher initiations[255] cannot purify transgressions of the
pledges by simply using the common means employed to purify negative deeds in general. Pledges must be renewed in the following ways:
meditation on the creation phase whereby merit is cultivated; the
stages of self-blessing (such as the subtle [yoga and the yoga] of the
seminal essence)[256] whereby ethics is cultivated; enhancement of the
blissful pristine awareness [ensuing] from the melting [of the seminal essence]; and constant equipoise in the view free of the concepts
of the three spheres—agent, act, and recipient [whereby pristine
awareness is cultivated]. In other words, the pledges assumed in the
course of the vase initiation [and those assumed in the secret initiation or those in the initiations of lower tantras] can be restored by the
means indicated by the spiritual master, but [the pledges of the higher
initiations of the Highest Yoga Tantra] must be restored by [realiza-
tion of] the perfect purity of one's own mind.

Mantric Vows in the Ancient Tantras [2]

The presentation of the vows according to the Ancient Translations
of the Secret Mantra has three [parts]: (1) a general presentation of
the vows common to Mahayoga, Anuyoga, and Atiyoga; (2) a classification of the vows of each system; and (3) deterioration of the pledges
and their restoration.

General Presentation of Vows Common to Mahayoga, Anuyoga, and Atiyoga [a]

This section has two parts: (1) a concise statement, and (2) an extensive explanation.

Concise Statement [i]

> **In the tradition of the Ancient Translations, the pledges**
> **common to the spiritual ways of skill in means**
> **Are the general pledges, the particular, and the exceptional**
> **ones.**

The long tradition of the Ancient Translations enumerates nine spiritual ways.[257] The vows most widely known and common to the three higher ways [Mahayoga, Anuyoga, and Atiyoga] are of three types, the general, particular, and exceptional pledges. These are taught in the *Yoga of General Cleansing*, the *Union of Joyful Ones, Peaceful Tantra*, and other tantras.

The etymological definition of pledge (Tib. *dam tshig*) is "an oath that is firm and hard to transgress." Thus, as has been explained above [in the new tantras], pledge refers to an oath that must be preserved just as it has been made and not transgressed or allowed to deteriorate. Pledge also means "strict" in consideration of [the strict consequences of] observance or its transgression. The *Condensed Heruka Tantra*[258] states:

> It is said that by not transgressing it, one becomes a supreme
> (*dam*) being;
> By transgressing it, one will burn (*tshig*) [in hell].

Extensive Explanation [ii]

> **The general pledges are the limits to be observed in the**
> **personal liberation precepts, awakening mind commitments,**
> **and the pledges of the three outer tantras.**
> **The particular pledges are the root pledges of body, speech,**
> **mind, and awakening mind, and**
> **The secondary pledges of the five to practice, five not to**
> **renounce,**
> **Five to accept, five to recognize, and five to integrate.**
> **Practitioners should safeguard and engage in the provisional**
> **and definitive meanings of these pledges**
> **In accordance with circumstances. The exceptional pledges**
> **concern familiarization and attainment practice.**

General pledges common [to the three systems] refers to the limits to be observed as prescribed by the personal liberation precepts, the awakening mind commitments, and the pledges of the three outer classes of tantra [Action, Conduct, and Yoga tantras]. The particular pledges are the root pledges related to the body, speech, mind, and awakening mind of a buddha, and the five sets of five secondary pledges—the five to practice, the five not to renounce, the five to accept, the five to recognize, and the five to integrate. The exceptional pledges are twenty pledges that must be honored especially during familiarization and attainment practices.[259]

[The general pledges have been explained above.] Of the particular pledges, the root pledge of the body of a buddha is to guard one's relationships with the vajra master and spiritual siblings. There are six masters to be honored, as stated in Lilavajra's *Shimmering Light on the Pledges*[260]:

> Masters who are teachers of all, who lead [one to the
>   teachings], initiate, and [bestow] pledges,
> Restore infractions, open one's mind,
> Or transmit secret instructions.[261]

In what way each should be honored is illustrated by corresponding examples[262]:

> Regard them more highly than these:
> The king of your country, your uncle, father, or mother,
> Your own eyes, or your heart.

In particular, as stated in the *Union of Joyful Ones, Peaceful Tantra*, one should regard the three masters who initiate, explain the tantra, and transmit secret instructions more highly than, or at least equal to, the Buddha, or as a fourth Jewel. Without hypocrisy, one should honor masters by doing, through actions, words, and thoughts, whatever pleases them and by following their every directive.

Moreover, [as stated in Lilavajra's *Shimmering Light*,[263]] one must maintain spiritual bonds with the four [types of] siblings:

(1) [All sentient beings,] one's general siblings;
(2) [All Buddhists,] distant siblings;
(3) [All Buddhists who follow the same conduct and view,] close siblings;
(4) [Mantra practitioners with whom one shares the same tantric master, initiation, etc.,] intimate siblings.

One should honor spiritual siblings while showing loving concern for them, and must never forsake them, particularly the latter three who have entered the authentic path, and even more so, intimate siblings, knowing that these relationships are increasingly significant in that order.

The root pledge of the speech of a buddha is to recite the three kinds of incantation, to practice the four seals, and to make offerings, as stated in the *Shimmering Light*[264]:

> To recite the root, generation, and action mantras,
> And apply the four [seals]: the seal of the pledge, action seal,
>   seal of the teachings,
> And the two awakened dimensions [as the] great seal.

In applying oneself to the three kinds of incantation[265] and the four seals, the best effort would be a practice that never ceases, like the current of a river [done without distraction in the day and night meditation sessions]; a moderate effort, a practice carried out [uninterruptedly in the four or six periods] of the day of the new moon [and other special days]; and a minimal effort, a practice of not neglecting the monthly or annual performance of [ritual feast and] food offerings (*torma*) on [special] days.

The root pledge of the mind of a buddha is not to proclaim the ten secrets to those without pledges or those who have violated them, or to ordinary people. The ten secrets are enumerated in the *Shimmering Light*[266]:

> Profound view, outrageous conduct,
> The deity's name and mantra, and signs of accomplishment:
> These are the four general secrets.

And:

> Engage in tantric practice while keeping [four] transitional secrets:
> The place [of gathering], the time, one's companions, and the
>   ritual articles.

These are the four general and four transitional secrets. The remaining two are innermost secrets: The secrets worthy to be kept are the exceptional mantric conduct and the substances of the pledges,[267] and what is unfit to be seen or heard, such as the bad behavior of one's spiritual siblings. Entrusted secrets concern instructions, etc., that the vajra master or spiritual siblings have sealed as secret by command.

The root pledge of awakening mind consists in the pledge of the view, the realization of the abiding nature of [reality], the indivisibility of the [two] superior truths[268] which transcends the [mind's] experiential domain. To fulfill this pledge, one must train in the aspiring and venturing aspects of awakening mind. To train in the mind of aspiration is to focus on the result, which is actualized without abandoning or attaining anything. To train in the venturing mind is to actualize the result by bringing all one's experiences onto the path as pure vision. [This is possible] since all experiences of one's body, speech, and mind, and their domains, which are expressions of the pristine awareness present within oneself, never transcend the seals of the deity's body, speech, and mind.

Of the secondary particular pledges, the five pledges prescribing what to practice have both provisional and hidden meanings. To fulfill the provisional meanings, one engages in sexual union, release, theft, speaking untruth, and speaking outrageously, provided these are done without selfish motives, but as skillful means, and to benefit others. The hidden meanings of these pledges are as follows:

(1) Release means to sever the life of dualistic thoughts with self-experienced pristine awareness;

(2) Theft is to steal the seminal essence (bliss) from the queen (consort)[269];

(3) Union is to achieve immutable bliss through the bliss experienced in melting [the seminal essence] while uniting [with a consort];

(4) Speaking untruth is to say that living beings are [already] liberated from the apparent yet non-existent cycle of existence;

(5) Speaking outrageously is to speak without inhibitions from an inexpressible state of spiritual accomplishment.

To fulfill the provisional meanings of the five pledges that prescribe what not to renounce, one does not renounce the five poisons of negativity [emotions] just as they are[270] as proclaimers [who regard them as enemies] do, but engages in them with skill in means. This is because these five poisons serve as a direct path to liberation and because their nature is primordially that of the five pristine awarenesses.

To fulfill the hidden meanings, one does not renounce the five perfect poisons:

(1) The stupidity that does not differentiate between what to practice and what to refrain from and that is impartial in its view since all things are perfect in the state of sameness;

(2) The attachment that is the affection developed from non-objectifying great compassion for living beings who lack realization of the view;

(3) The hatred that subdues misconceptions with self-experienced pristine awareness;

(4) The pride that does not descend from the heights of the view that realizes the sameness [of phenomena];

(5) The jealousy that does not accommodate dualistic views or conduct in the vast expanse of sameness.

One must not renounce these five, [but should accept them] with the skillful means to experientially cultivate the state of inner realization.

To fulfill the provisional meanings of the five pledges that prescribe what to accept, one accepts the five nectars [of the pledge's substances]:

(1) the great fragrant solids [feces],

(2) fragrant water [urine],

(3) blood,

(4) flesh,

(5) vajra dew [semen].

These five must not be rejected but instead should be accepted [without concepts of clean or dirty] because they are the nature of reality itself, and by virtue of their very essence and potency and through consecration, these are special substances used to gain attainments.

To fulfill the hidden meanings, one binds and does not lose the pure essences of the five aggregates.

To fulfill the five pledges that prescribe what to recognize, one must recognize the following (since all phenomena exist primordially as enlightenment):

(1) the five aggregates as the five male transcendent ones;

(2) the five elemental properties as the five female transcendent ones;

(3) the five sense organs and their five consciousnesses as the male bodhisattvas;

(4) the five sense objects as the female bodhisattvas;

(5) the colors [associated with] the five families as the five pristine awarenesses.

All conceptual representations of these five sets of five phenomena should be recognized as the mandala of pristine awareness and its dimensions[271] with the wisdom that cuts through misapprehension [of the nature of these phenomena].

To fulfill the five pledges that prescribe what to integrate, one must, having gained an experiential understanding of the five pledges that prescribe what to recognize, persevere in the means to correctly effect the integration of this understanding within one's mind.

[The pledges prescribing] what to recognize are pledges of the view. Once those are realized, one observes [the pledges prescribing] what to integrate, which are pledges of meditation. The three [groups of pledges prescribing] what to practice, what not to renounce, and what to accept, in the context of their provisional meanings, are mainly pledges of conduct. Therefore, in a state of equipoise, these pledges should be observed according to their hidden (definitive) meanings. [The three groups of] pledges [according to their provisional meanings] are to be safeguarded or practiced respecting their order of progression and evaluating their [individual] applicability according to circumstances. [Here, "circumstances" refers to] time (for example, whether or not one has reached certainty through realization of the view) and place (whether one is living in solitude or attending social gatherings).

Of the exceptional pledges, the twenty pledges concerning familiarization [and attainment] are presented in symbolic language in the *Union of Joyful Ones, Peaceful Tantra*, beginning with [the words] "Do not destroy the throne of the king of wild animals."[272] Their injunctions are as follows:

(1) Not to inflict harm on the body of the vajra master or disobey his or her words;

(2) Not to engage in sexual union with the consort of one's master;

(3) Not to hinder believers in their acquiring of merit[273];

(4) Not to use the property of the Three Jewels or the learned, or drink intoxicating beverages;

(5) Not to engage in sexual union with the spouse of a vajra sibling;

(6) Not to rely on a consort who lacks the appropriate signs;

(7) Not to use improper pledge substances;

(8) Not to criticize the qualities of learned persons;

(9) Not to divulge the secret teachings to immature disciples;

(10) Not to abandon a qualified consort or a worthy disciple;

(11) Not to be separated from [the union of] bliss-emptiness, or the male-female [union], its symbol;

(12) Not to quarrel with spiritual siblings or [the master's] spouse, even in jest;

(13) Not to partake of the food left over by others;

(14) Not to covet the master's seat;

(15) Not to disrupt one's own or another's meditational retreat;

(16) Not to let contemplation fall under the sway of dullness or excitement;

(17) Not to interrupt [mantra] recitation or rituals with ordinary words;

(18) Not to transgress the seals, which are the symbols of the initiation,[274] or forget their symbolism;

(19) Not to disturb the yogin's mandala,[275] or return the curse of those [who have broken their pledges];

(20) Not to neglect to revere the master with the utmost respect.

Classification of the Vows of Each System [b]

This section has three parts: the pledges of (1) Mahayoga, (2) Anuyoga, and (3) Atiyoga.

Pledges of Mahayoga [i]

> The *Magical Net*, the source tantra of Mahayoga,
> Presents five root pledges: not to forsake the unsurpassable, to honor the master,
> Not to interrupt mantra and seal practice, to be kind to siblings,
> And not to divulge the ten secrets; and ten secondary pledges,
> Five not to renounce and five not to reject.
> Those are divided into three hundred and sixty that can be subdivided indefinitely.

The *Vajrasattva's Magical Net*,[276] the source scripture for the eighteen great classes of Mahayoga tantra, presents five root [pledges]:

(1) Not to forsake the unsurpassable;

(2) To honor the master with devotion;

(3) Not to interrupt [the practice of] the three [kinds of] mantra and the four seals;

(4) To be kind to spiritual siblings;

(5) And not to divulge the ten secrets.[277]

To elaborate, the first [pledge], not to forsake the unsurpassable, means to maintain one's body, speech, and mind within the bounds of the deity's seals of body, speech, and mind by realizing the superior truth: ultimate and relative awakening minds as the inseparability of appearance and emptiness. The remaining four are as described above.

The ten secondary pledges [taught in the same tantra] are the five pledges that prescribe what not to renounce (the five poisons) and the five that prescribe what to accept (the five pledge substances).

The *Subtle and Extensive Pledges*[278] and other texts give detailed classifications of three hundred and sixty pledges. First, the five root [pledges] are each divided into two by differentiating them in terms of skill in means and wisdom. Added to these are the one hundred and fifty pledges which result from a subdivision into thirty of each of the five root pledges. To these are added two hundred further pledges derived from subdividing each of the ten secondary pledges into twenty. Thus, it is impossible to enumerate all pledges because each can be elaborated upon indefinitely to provide a pledge to counteract every discursive thought. The *Secret Nucleus* states[279]:

> Pledges are equal in number to all the discursive thoughts to be calmed
> Of all beings within the three existences
> And throughout the ten directions of the six worlds of beings.[280]

**By virtue of their sevenfold greatness, states Rongzom,
Mahayoga's pledges are superior
To the pledges of lower tantras and to the commitments of the
Universal Way.**

Rongzom Pandita[281] states that the awakening mind commitments are superior to the [personal] liberation vows of the proclaimers by virtue of possessing seven great qualities, such as a vast scope. In turn, the higher pledges [of Mahayoga] are superior to the commitments of the Universal Way and the pledges of the lower tantras due to sevenfold greatness. In his *Precious Jewel Commentary*,[282] Rongzom elucidates [the seven exceptional qualities of Mahayoga pledges]:

> Since [the pledges] bear the seal of Samantabhadra, good qualities are spontaneously accomplished without effort. Powers and blessings are especially exalted since the great gods, principal ones in the world, and their retinues of *mamos* and sky-farers[283] come to regard one as a sacred being, worthy of worship. The compassion of all buddhas and bodhisattvas, who regard one as their child and close vajra sibling, brings swift blessings. One's domain is exalted since it is concordant with the experiential domain[284] of the Transcendent One. One enjoys freedom from all fear and anxiety since all phenomena exist in the buddha field of Samantabhadra.[285] All pledges prescribed in terms of hinted or

definitive meanings are gathered in the natural expression of spontaneous accomplishment. Even if transgressed, there are means to restore them. By virtue of these seven and other limitless qualities, these [pledges] are exceptional.[286]

Pledges of Anuyoga [ii]

> **Anuyoga presents nine general pledges which are encompassed by two:**
> **The pledge of reality with no limits to be observed;**
> **And the pledge of compassion with limits.**

The sixty-sixth chapter of the *General Scripture That Gathers All Intentions*[287] presents nine sets of general pledges of Anuyoga:

(1) Four pledges crucial to all important [Anuyoga] scriptures. These are four pledges to purify completely one's body, speech, mind, and perceptual range.

(2) Twenty-eight pledges in common with the other tantras. The root pledges are the three pledges of vajra body, speech, and mind. The secondary pledges are the five pledges prescribing what to practice, the five to renounce, the five to accept, the five to recognize, and the five to integrate, as explained above.

(3) Four superior pledges. These pledges concern the perfect realization of the abiding nature of reality:

> *(1)* The pledge to perfectly realize that all pledges, in their ultimate nature, are free of transgression or deterioration, and are therefore without limits to be observed;
> *(2)* The pledge to perfectly realize that the expressions of all vows and pledges transcend the forms of dualistic clinging and are therefore all-pervasive simplicity;
> *(3)* The pledge to perfectly realize that all vows and pledges are encompassed by the single expanse of the mind's nature;
> *(4)* The pledge to perfectly realize that all vows and pledges are naturally pure and spontaneously fulfilled in the state that does not stray from the inconceivable realm of reality.

(4) Twenty-three pledges prescribing conduct. The sixty-fourth chapter [of the *General Scripture That Gathers All Intentions*] illustrates this set of pledges through analogies, such as the fox, the centaur, and the thoroughbred. These pledges and the meanings of their analogies are explained by the Great Nub Sangyé Yeshé[288] and others as follows:

(1) [The pledge to be] like the fox who, when caught in a trap, will escape with its paw torn off, without regard for its life. This pledge prescribes the conduct (Tib. *brtul zhug*), which is the means to overcome (*brtul*) all unfavorable conditions and enter (*zhug*) into the power of the pledges, whereby the yogin [or yogini] guards the pledges, even at the cost of life itself.

(2) The pledge to be like the centaur who is aware of everything as he, with unfettered speed, circles the globe in an instant. This pledge prescribes the unfettered conduct whereby the yogin applies discriminative wisdom to the general and individual characteristics of all that is knowable.

(3) The pledge to be like the thoroughbred who takes each step with great impressiveness. This pledge prescribes the conduct whereby the yogin overcomes idleness and perseveres in dance, symbolic gestures, and yantra yoga,[289] with a disciplined body.

(4) The pledge to be like the intoxicated elephant who destroys every enemy he meets without discrimination. This pledge prescribes the conduct whereby the yogin destroys the four enemies of view and action[290] with the knowledge that cyclic existence and perfect peace are indivisible.

(5) The pledge to be like the fearless tiger whose aggressive instincts are fierce, brave, and terrifying. This pledge prescribes the conduct whereby the yogin, possessed of the powerful conduct of fearless contemplation that realizes the abiding nature of reality, performs the rites of liberation fiercely, bravely, and aggressively for the ten recipients,[291] as was done for the liberation of Rudra and the transfer of his consciousness.

(6) The pledge to be like the great garuda who soars effortlessly through the sky, seeing all phenomena without especially looking. This pledge prescribes the conduct whereby the yogin, with the proper view, realizes the indivisibility of the expanse of phenomena and pristine awareness and, out of that realization, acts freely and effortlessly.

(7) The pledge to be like the bear who terrorizes and overpowers whatever it focuses upon without hesitation. This pledge prescribes the conduct of yoga whereby the yogin, with certainty in the view and conduct, performs without hesitation the rites of annihilation.

(8) The pledge to be like gold at the bottom of the ocean which never changes. This pledge prescribes the conduct whereby the yogin is of a firm and unchanging mind, able to maintain secrecy of the profound truth while cultivating it experientially.

(9) The pledge to be like the dumb mute who makes no distinction between what to accept and what to reject. This pledge prescribes the conduct whereby the yogin perfects the wisdom that realizes selflessness through the equipoise which makes no distinction between cyclic existence and perfect peace.

(10) The pledge to be like the unmoving Mount Meru. This pledge prescribes the conduct of skillful means whereby the yogin relies on the remedies of unchanging faith in and respect for teachers and spiritual friends and contemplation unmoved by torpor or excitement.

(11) The pledge to be like the vast and open sky which accommodates everything without acceptance or rejection. This pledge prescribes the conduct whereby the yogin acts hospitably and open-mindedly toward sibling yogins, and with the view and conduct of the great identity, accommodates all spiritual ways and everything within cyclic existence and perfect peace.

(12) The pledge to be like a thunderbolt which shatters whatever it strikes. This pledge prescribes the conduct whereby the yogin unimpededly destroys all enemies and hindrances through the fierce kind of contemplation.

(13) The pledge to be like Vajrapani who vanquishes all those who profess wayward views. This pledge prescribes the conduct whereby the yogin confidently performs meditation on wrathful [deities] and conquers all obstacles.

(14) The pledge to be like the raven who looks out for both predator and prey simultaneously. This pledge prescribes the conduct of skillful means whereby the yogin always strives to observe simultaneously both conduct and restraint [according to] the outer and inner pledges.

(15) The pledge to be like the elephant who plunges into water unconcerned about whether he is soaked. This pledge prescribes the conduct whereby the yogin, possessed of certainty in the view and action of the great identity, acts without the duality of renunciation and acceptance; or, alternatively, performs the conduct of four charismatic activities without discriminating among those to be affected [by these activities].

(16) The pledge to be like the friendless lion who lives without companions. This pledge prescribes the conduct whereby the yogin renounces bad companions who are detrimental to the view and meditation, and protects view and meditation while dwelling in solitude.

(17) The pledge to be like the pair of ducks who happily keep company with each other without ever parting. This pledge prescribes the conduct whereby the yogin keeps company with skillful means without ever parting from it, thereby setting others in the happiness of liberation out of compassion and loving-kindness.

(18) The pledge to be like the magician who creates illusions. This pledge prescribes the conduct whereby the yogin meditates and teaches while knowing the aggregates, elements, and experiential media to be the apparitional mandala of the victorious ones, and creates illusion through skill in means.

(19) The pledge to be like the pig who eats everything regardless of whether it is clean or filthy. This pledge prescribes the conduct whereby the yogin, in a state of equanimity, uses the five pledge substances without discrimination.

(20) The pledge to be like the jackal who loves wanton killing. This pledge prescribes the conduct of skillful means whereby the yogin, with a compassionate attitude cultivated in view and action and by means of inner realization, liberates those who hold wayward views and transfers their consciousnesses to an uncorrupted [realm], thus bringing to perfection the two cultivations [of merit and pristine awareness].

(21) The pledge to be like lightning which swiftly illuminates everything in a flash. This pledge prescribes the conduct whereby the yogin perseveres so that his own and others' aims are swiftly fulfilled through experiential cultivation of the path.

(22) The pledge to be like the vulture whose discipline is to shun killing. This pledge prescribes what appears as outrageous conduct in that it does not conform to the [disciplines of] other spiritual ways, but is in fact conduct whereby the yogin, acting in accordance with the great identity, observes pledges and purifies transgressions.

(23) The pledge to be like the conscientious king who rules over his kingdom and protects his subjects, [cherishing them] more than himself. This pledge prescribes the conduct whereby the yogin, who perseveres in the means to experience and realize the indivisibility of the expanse [of reality] and pristine awareness as profound bliss, rules over the "kingdom" of conducts, protects living beings by realizing all phenomena as self-arisen, and purifies transgressions in their own ground.

It is said that these conducts, of benefit to oneself, others, and oneself and others together, should be practiced all at once by adepts of superior intelligence.

(5) Twenty pledges concerning attainment. These are taught [in the *General Scripture That Gathers All Intentions*] beginning with the following words: "Do not destroy the throne of the king of wild animals" (Do not inflict harm on your master's body or disrespect his or her words), etc. Their meaning is essentially the same as the twenty exceptional pledges mentioned above.

(6) Four pledges concerning the continuity of the path of conduct. The symbols of a vajra, armor, dagger, mystic staff, etc., illustrate the following pledges:
   (1) To forsake sleep that cuts off the life of contemplation;
   (2) To forsake alcohol;
   (3) To communicate with the symbolic language of Secret Mantra;
   (4) To vanquish idleness.

(7) Five pledges to renounce the five evils, which are the five demonic forces that interrupt the continuity of the conduct of yoga:
   (1) To renounce discursive thinking;
   (2) To renounce laziness;
   (3) To renounce entertainment;
   (4) To renounce harsh language;
   (5) To renounce wrath.

(8) Four pledges to conquer the four enemies. These pledges are as follows:
   (1) To conquer the enemy of the creation of an artificial view, meditation, or conduct;

(2) To conquer the enemy of the immorality of being unorthodox in conduct while having an inferior view;

(3) To conquer the enemy of transgressing root and secondary
pledges;

(4) To conquer the enemy who steals the results [of spiritual prac-
tice] with complacency and idleness.

(9) One pledge of the view. This pledge is to realize that the world is
the utterly pure realm Superior[292]; sense pleasures, the utterly pure
offerings; one's entourage, the utterly pure mandala of deities; and
one's own emotions, utterly pure and profound pristine awareness.

All these pledges are encompassed by two: the pledge of reality for
one of instantaneous [realization], in which there are no limits to observe; and the pledge of compassion for one who proceeds gradually,
with limits to be observed. Accordingly, the *General Scripture That Gathers All Intentions* states[293]:

> That for which there is nothing to observe
> Is the highest pledge of reality.

And[294]:

> This pledge is most wonderful
> Since it exceeds all,
> But all those of weak aspiration
> Should observe the different limits.

Pledges of Atiyoga [iii]

> **The general Atiyoga pledges are outer, inner, and secret pledges
>   relating to a buddha's body, speech, and mind;
> Each divided thrice yields a total of twenty-seven.
> The exceptional pledges relate to non-existence,
> Naturalness, spontaneous accomplishment, and oneness.**

In Atiyoga, the system of the Great Perfection, there are two categories of pledges: (1) general pledges, and (2) exceptional pledges.

General Pledges [A']

Three root pledges are the pledges of the body, speech, and mind of a
buddha, each having three pledges on the outer, inner, and secret levels. Each [of the nine] is divided into three to yield a total of twenty-
seven pledges.

(1) The outer pledges relating to the body of a buddha are these:

> Not to steal;
>
> Not to engage in sexual misconduct;
>
> Not to kill.

The inner pledges are these:

> Not to disrespect one's parents, vajra brothers and sisters, or one's own body;
>
> Not to disrespect the teachings, or other individuals;
>
> Not to despise or abuse one's own body through beating or extreme asceticism.

The secret pledges are these:

> Not to threaten to strike tantric brothers and sisters, or mock their ornaments;
>
> Not to strike one's tantric consort or be mischievous toward the master's consort;
>
> Not to step on the shadow of the master or be irreverent (in actions or words) in his or her presence.

(2) The outer pledges relating to a buddha's speech are these:

> Not to lie;
>
> Not to slander others;
>
> Not to revile others.

The inner pledges are these:

> Not to rebuke or slander those who impart the teachings;
>
> Not to rebuke or slander those who ponder the content of the teachings;
>
> Not to rebuke or slander those who meditate on the abiding nature [of reality].

The secret pledges are these:

> Not to have contempt for or transgress the words of tantric brothers and sisters,
>
> The words of the master's consort or his or her close attendants, or
>
> The master's teachings.

(3) The outer pledges relating to a buddha's mind are these:

> Not to be malicious;
>
> Not to be envious;
>
> Not to hold wayward views.

The inner pledges are these:

> Not to be unconscientious (the mistaken conduct);
>
> Not to fall under the sway of dullness, excitement, and deviant impediments[295] (the mistaken meditation);
>
> Not to adhere to the extremes of eternalism or nihilism (the mistaken views).

The secret pledges are these:

> To cultivate in every part of the day the view, meditation, and action;
>
> To practice deity yoga;
>
> To cultivate mystic union with the master[296] and love for tantric brothers and sisters.

Four Exceptional Pledges [B']

The twofold pledge of "cutting through" (Tib. *khregs chod*),[297] posited in relation to the essence of primordial purity (Tib. *ka dag*), is the pledge to liberate oneself from grasping to the reality of ongoing phenomena by realizing that, as illustrated by the eight similes of illusion,[298] everything that manifests as the environment and inhabitants is primordially non-existent; and to liberate projected appearances in the state of reality by cultivating unsupported, utterly natural intrinsic awareness not entangled in the tension of grasping at [the concept of] an observer.

The twofold pledge of "direct leap" (Tib. *thod rgal*), posited in relation to the natural expression of spontaneous accomplishment (Tib. *lhun grub*), is the pledge to disengage oneself from an outer spiritual quest, confident in the realization that buddhahood is to be actualized within oneself through continuous experiential cultivation of the four visionary appearances of spontaneous accomplishment,[299] which are the manifestation of the [inner] radiance of the five[-colored] light; and to arrive in the kingdom of the primordial exhaustion of [phenomena into] reality through the confident realization that all occurrences and manifestations—thoughts, events, feelings, circumstances, and ongoing appearances—are solely natural pristine awareness.

Deterioration of Pledges and Their Restoration [c]

This section has two [parts]: (1) violation of pledges, and (2) the means of restoration.

Violations [i]

> Transgressions are of five types: major deteriorations, root and
> secondary, violations by association, and indirect ones.
> Not to confess these brings misfortune and life in the Hell of
> Unceasing Torture.

The rupture of a pledge, which is caused by letting the [maximum]
deadline [for confession] pass, and the other types of transgressions
have been described above.[300] In addition, the *General Scripture That
Gathers All Intentions* explains five types of transgressions:

(1) Major or total deterioration that occurs [when one commits
a transgression] with strong emotional involvement and in
relation to a crucial object, commits it continuously, or lets
the deadline [of three years without restoration] pass,
whereby it becomes a rupture;

(2-3) [Downfalls] due transgressions of root and secondary
[pledges];

(4) Violation by association, which is the minor infraction incurred by befriending someone who has transgressed his or
her pledges;

(5) Indirect violation, the minor infraction incurred by appearing to agree with someone who is transgressing his or her
pledges.

It is extremely important that all of the pledges that have been discussed, once assumed, are honored and not allowed to deteriorate. If
it happens that a pledge is transgressed, it is essential to perform immediately the confession rituals methodically, as they appear in the
tantras, transmissions, and secret instructions. Not to acknowledge a
transgression brings all sorts of misfortune in this life, and in the next
life one is reborn in the great Vajra Hell of Unceasing Torture, not to
escape from it so long as the sky exists. The *Secret Moon Essence* states:

> Buddhas and bodhisattvas
> Do not bestow blessings
> On one who has violated vows and pledges;
> Even if he were to offer
> Incense, flowers, or other things,
> They would not accept them.
> Killed by enemies, poison, or disease,
> He will be reborn in hell.

And Indrabhuti's *Jnanasiddhi*[301] says:

> He who does not keep the pledges
> Experiences the misery
> Of body, mind, and virtues degenerating,
> Dies in no time,
> And thereafter comes upon the sufferings
> Of hell for one billion years.
> Taking another rebirth,
> He will became an untouchable, a wretch,
> A deaf person, or a mute.

The many tantras of both the Ancient and New traditions unanimously agree that these, and others, are the consequences of violating the pledges.

Means of Restoration [ii]

> **The proclaimers' vows, like a clay pot, once broken cannot be repaired;**
> **The awakening mind commitments, like gold or silver, can be restored;**
> **The tantric pledges, like a dented vessel, are restored by the practitioner's strength.**

When is it possible to restore a vow that has been transgressed? All the tantras and transmissions state that if a monk has incurred a defeat with concealment, the [transgressed] vow, like a broken clay pot, cannot be repaired. An awakening mind commitment that has been transgressed is like a cracked gold or silver vase which can still be soldered by a blacksmith. A violated vow or pledge in this Secret Mantra system is likened to a dented golden vessel, which can be straightened out by the practitioner's own strength.

> **Pledges are restored through action, precious substances,**
> **earnest desire, contemplation, and reality.**
> **The *Great Cleansing* can purify all transgressions.**

The *General Scripture That Gathers All Intentions* lists five methods for restoring pledges:

(1) To renew the pledges through action in the case of a serious transgression is to perform one hundred and thirty thousand times, or more, according to the seriousness, the fire offerings or recitation of the mantra [of one's deity].

(2) To renew the pledge through precious substances is to offer, without any sense of loss, one of the [five] gems[302] appropriate

to the family whose pledge one has transgressed to a master who is of the caste (untouchable, menial, or another caste) that corresponds to the buddha family whose pledge one has transgressed, while regarding the master as the embodiment of the five buddha families.

(3) To renew the pledge with earnest desire means to confess one's failing with intense regret and shame in a state of clear and longing faith.

(4) To renew the pledge in a state of contemplation means to confess one's failing with the four forces,[303] and while doing so, to imagine that one's negativity and impediments are purified by light rays radiating from the three places of the receptacle [object of refuge].[304] In this technique, one imagines all negativity is consumed by the fire of contemplation, all darkness is dispelled by light emanating from awakening mind, [impediments] are washed away by great waves of altruistic deeds, and so forth.

(5) To renew the pledge by [understanding] transcendent reality means that "through great discriminative wisdom, all [karmic] imprints are understood to be without intrinsic reality," as is stated in *All-Gathering [Awareness]*.[305] Thus, the perfect means to purify negativity is to cultivate discriminative wisdom that does not objectify the three spheres.

A special means consists in applying the threefold renewal taught in the quintessential instruction of the *Great Cleansing Yoga* called *Emptying the Depths of Hell*.[306] Externally, this involves confession and restoration through ritual feast; internally, the basis of one's body [i.e., the aggregates]; and on the secret level, the state of pure presence (Skt. *bodhicitta*). It is said that to perform this [practice] on the fifteenth, thirtieth, and eighth [days of the lunar month] will purify all pledges that one has transgressed. Therefore, it is a method most worthy of committing oneself to.

A SYNOPSIS OF THE PHASES OF THE PATH IN THE INDESTRUCTIBLE WAY

The master Subhagavajra[307] enumerates five procedures to be followed:

> An individual possessed of great fortune
> Forms an awakening mind, assumes its commitments,
> And receives initiation in the presence of a holy master;

He then observes [the pledges]; learns the nature [of tantra];
Purifies his mind; and engages in purificatory conduct:
These, in essence, are the five procedures.

The first of the five is the initiatory procedure, which effects the maturation [of one's mind]. The initiation, gateway to the Secret Mantra, is received when two causes and four conditions are fulfilled. These are the two causes:

(1) The concomitant cause, to be an individual possessing the six elements[308] of the adamantine body that is flawless and has channels, seminal essences, and energy winds, and to have awakened the affinity for the mind of awakening, the causal continuity (tantra) that is without beginning or end;

(2) The contributory cause, fulfilled by the master's correct performance of the construction of the mandala and the actualization and worship [ritual], after having engaged in purification through the familiarization practice, etc.

These are the four conditions:

(1) The causal condition of being a worthy candidate for initiation (who belongs to one of the five classes of disciples such as lotus-like[309]);

(2) The principal condition of there being a qualified master to confer the initiation, who has expertise in the ten outer and inner essential fields [of the tantras[310]], and who has mastered contemplation;

(3) The objective condition of the impeccable coordination of substances, mantra, seals, and contemplation [in the initiatory ritual];

(4) The immediate condition of the maturation [of the disciple's mind stream], effected by the initial stages of vase initiation, etc., and by the progressive conferral of the later initiations.

The second [of the five procedures to be followed] is the procedure of observing the pledges received in the course of an initiation in order to protect the maturation of one's mind. The "life force" of the initiation refers to the individual pledges taught in the Action, Conduct, and Yoga tantras, and especially the modes of conduct, vows, root pledges, and secondary pledges, [the pledges concerning] sustenance, and [the pledges] to be safeguarded as taught in Highest [Tantra] with provisional, definitive, and covert intentions. These should be guarded like one's life and according to one's level of spiritual accomplishment.

The third is the procedure of learning the nature of tantra by listening to the master's teachings. To learn the nature of tantra means to gain knowledge of the actual tantra (the subject matter of tantra) by studying the teachings of the tantras (as they are expressed in words) with a spiritual master who applies the four styles[311] [of tantric explanation]; and to develop discriminating wisdom free of confusion that experientially cultivates that knowledge.

The fourth is the procedure of purifying one's mind, which leads to the attainment of awakening. The purification of the mind and its habitual tendencies is effected in the following way: for a practitioner of the Secret Mantra, the principal aim of all the tantric activities is to nurture the seed or potential for awakening. This seed serves as the primary cause for attaining perfect awakening, the realization of one's objective, and the foundation for the accomplishment of others' objectives. The two liberating phases [of the tantric path] that uproot the three impediments[312] connected with the propensities of the four states[313] serve as contributory conditions. In order to transform everything into the path of awakening, the view to be realized is taken as the foundation.

In the three lower tantras, one endeavors in deity yogas called "with signs" and "without signs" or the signless yoga of reality.[314] In the Highest [Yoga Tantra], one meditates on the stages of creating the supporting [mandala] through the three contemplations,[315] the four branches of familiarization and attainment practice,[316] or the six branches of the visualization,[317] etc. At the end of these practices, one accomplishes the charismatic work of a tantric master, such as recitation and meditation, making food offerings (*torma*), consecration and fire rituals, etc. Subsequent [to the creation phase], one cultivates the completion stage, reaching perfection in the supported [mandala, i.e., the deities,] through the practice on the side of the appearance [of the deity's form[318]], on the side of emptiness,[319] and the union of these two[320]; or the practice of self-consecration,[321] the mandala circle,[322] and profound indestructible yoga.[323]

The fifth is the procedure of virtuous conduct, which is to engage in the means to perfect the purification of mind. The conduct related to skill in means consists of the "all-shaking *avadhuti*" conduct intended for a beginner; the "ever-perfect" conduct intended for an advanced practitioner; and the conduct "victorious in all quarters"[324] intended for an accomplished practitioner. Alternatively, the conduct is presented as "using desire"[325] and "training and enjoying desires"

associated with the complex, unelaborated, or utterly simple conducts.[326] [To engage in these forms of conduct] enhances [the realization of] the two phases, and one consequently progresses through
the four [stages of spiritual development] of the individual.[327]

On the three [stages, small, middling, and great,] of the path of
accumulation, one gains the common attainments[328] and an enhanced
vividness [of the visualization of the coarse and subtle aspects of the
mandala]. Following that, on the "stage of warmth" of the path of
preparation, one consolidates the pristine awareness of bliss and
emptiness [resulting] from the wind and mind dissolving into the
central channel. On the "peak" [stage of the path of preparation], one
experiences an uninterrupted vision of the circle of deities of the mandala and attains the [deity's] dimension [that manifests vividly] in
the absence of conceptualizations.[329] On the stage of "receptivity," of
the same path, one's manifest eighty natural conceptualizations[330]
[temporarily] cease. Enhancing pristine awareness, which has the
power to link up to the path of seeing, one reaches the "highest quality" [stage of the path of preparation]. Following this, one practices
wandering in the great outer power places,[331] and with respect to the
inner [power places], one dissolves channels, winds, and seminal essences into the central channel, reaching the provisional result of the
twelve stages. As a result of the proximate cause [of the elaborate,
non-elaborate, and simple conduct], one attains the ultimate result of
the stage of buddha, the union that requires no more learning,[332] the
state of Vajradhara endowed with the sevenfold features of [male and
female deity] facing each other,[333] the great lordliness over the inconceivable mystery, the highest and eternal state.

These phases of the path that begin with the three systems of ethics are presented in the form of a synopsis in order to be easily understood. They are discussed in detail in latter parts of this treatise [*The
Infinite Ocean of Knowledge*].

GENERAL POINTS ON THE THREE ETHICAL SYSTEMS [II]

This section has three [parts]: (1) the number of sets of vows that may
be held by one person, (2) the way the three systems coexist in one
person, and (3) the benefits of observing ethics.

The Number of Sets of Vows Held by One Person [A]

A person may hold one, two, or all three sets of vows, etc.;
These vows are distinguishable.

An individual who has assumed the personal liberation vows of the Individual Way is a "holder of one set of vows," since he or she holds only those vows but not the vows of the higher two systems of ethics. Someone who has assumed the commitments of awakening mind is a "holder of two sets of vows" because the personal liberation vows of the Universal Way and the awakening mind commitments are identical with respect to their essence. A practitioner who has assumed the mantric pledges is a "holder of all three sets of vows" since prior to that he or she must have assumed the personal liberation vows and awakening mind commitments as well.

To elaborate, the three systems of ethics upheld by a monk who is a tantric practitioner exist with identical nature. However, they can be conceptually distinguished in the following way: the discipline of renunciation [of a monk who is a tantric practitioner], in so far as it implies forsaking harmfulness and its [underlying] basis, comprises the [personal] liberation vows. In so far as [such discipline] is accompanied by an altruistic intention, it comprises the awakening mind commitments. In so far as it is accompanied by the skillful means of making the result [buddhahood] the path, it comprises the Secret Mantra pledges.

"Etc." [in the root verses] refers to individuals who have assumed the three sets of vows in stages, or those who have first assumed one of the two higher vows and subsequently assumed personal liberation vows.

The Way the Three Ethical Systems Coexist in One Person [B]

This section has two parts: (1) a concise statement, and (2) an extensive explanation.

Concise Statement [1]

Indian scholars differ from Tibetan scholars in their assertions
On how all three sets of vows coexist in one person.

An individual may successively assume the three sets of vows—personal liberation, awakening mind, and mantra—and thereby possess all three sets. In this case, how do these three ethical systems coexist in one person? Indian and Tibetan scholars differ in their many assertions on the way the three coexist.

Extensive Explanation [2]
This section has two parts: (1) the assertions of Indian scholars, and (2) the assertions of Tibetan scholars.

The Assertions of Indian Scholars [a]

> **Abhayakara says that the vows are similar in that they share an attitude of restraint**
> **But are distinguished by their forms. The great scholar Vibhutichandra asserts**
> **That the higher vows outshine the lower, while remaining distinct.**

Six assertions generally [prevalent] in India are presented in the *Key to the Initiation*[334]:

(1) The assertion that the personal liberation vows serve as the foundation for awakening mind commitments, and these as the foundation for mantric vows;
(2) The assertion that the lower vows are refined and enhanced by receiving the higher ones;
(3) The assertion that the vows are identical in nature but diversified in that the personal liberation vows are outer vows; the awakening mind commitments, inner; and the mantra vows, secret.
(4) The assertion that the vows are cumulative in that higher ones contain the lower ones;
(5) The assertion that the vows are graded since by receiving the higher ones the lower ones are transformed [into the higher];
(6) The assertion that the vows coexist but are unmixed, each being a complete system in its own right.

Of these, the assertion of Abhayakara and that of Vibhutichandra are most widely known in Tibet at present. Abhayakara asserts that just as various pieces of gold jewelry share the same nature by virtue of being made of gold, but differ in form—a crown, an anklet, a bracelet, etc.—

the three ethical systems share the same nature of being [rooted in] an attitude of restraint, but differ in form. Vibhutichandra's *Stream of Light on the Three Vows*[335] states that the three ethical systems are like the stars, the moon, and the sun, respectively. The higher ones outshine the lower ones, which become hidden. However, each of the three ethical systems has a different essence.

The Assertions of Tibetan Scholars [b]

> **The incomparable Gampopa and his followers state that the three ethical systems**
> **Are each of a different essence and should be preserved as prescribed.**
> **Faced with dilemma, the higher system takes precedence;**
> **Transgressions of the lower vows are thereby overcome; their qualities are contained in the higher.**
> **The systems differ in the way vows are assumed and lost.**

Gampopa states:

> [The three ethical systems are] each of a different essence. These must be observed just as prescribed. If faced with a dilemma, the higher takes precedence. The demerit of transgressing a lower vow is outshined by the merit of [observing] the higher. The qualities [of the lower systems] are contained in the higher.

To elaborate, the three kinds of ethical systems differ in their scriptural origins, preceptors, phases, motivations, ceremonies, precepts, causes of loss of vows, benefits of observing vows, possibilities of restoring damaged vows, etc. Therefore, each is of a distinct essence. The form of each is [to prescribe] restraint from what is unwholesome and to cultivate the remedial correct view. Thus, the three are all of the same nature in being [based on] an attitude of restraint, and all three therefore exist for the same purpose: to serve as remedies [for negative emotions and other impediments]. The vows that pertain to the circumstances one encounters, whether these involve forsaking an action or applying a remedy, should be observed just as they are set out in their respective systems.

If faced with the dilemma, for example, of partaking of the pledge substances at a tantric feast and thus transgressing the discipline of personal liberation or not partaking of them and thus transgressing the tantric conduct, [the observance of] the higher discipline should take precedence. This is so because if one violates the personal liberation vows with a special attitude, [i.e., the mind of awakening,] or with the skill in means [taught in the Secret Mantra], no fault is incurred. The demerit of transgressing lower vows is outshined [by the merit of observing the higher]. Not only is there no failing or downfall incurred from the transgression [of a lower vow], but also the great benefits from observing higher ethics are accrued. Thus, the qualities [of the lower systems] are contained in the higher. These points were asserted by Gampopa and his followers,[336] who include the learned and accomplished masters of the four major and eight minor Kagyu schools,[337] and especially the omniscient and victorious Seventh [Karmapa,] Chödrak Gyatso.

> **The venerable Drakpa, the omniscient Longchenpa, and others**
> **Assert that the individual identities of the ethical systems are**
>   **unmixed; each is complete in prescribing both restraint and**
>   **requirements.**
> **The essence of one vow changes into the next; thus, the quali-**
>   **ties of the higher contain the lower.**
> **Special conduct makes them compatible with each other.**
>   **One should observe the most important in any given**
>   **circumstance.**

The venerable uncle Drakpa Gyaltsen and his nephew[338] of the Sakya school, the omniscient Longchen Rabjampa, and others such as the great translators Rinchen Zangpo, Rongzom Chözang, and their followers make these assertions: (1) the individual identities of the ethical systems are unmixed; (2) each is complete in prescribing restraint and requirements; (3) the essence of one vow changes into the next; (4) the qualities of the higher contain those of the lower; (5) special conduct makes them compatible with each other; (6) in any given circumstance, the most important is observed.

To elaborate, the three ethical systems differ in their preceptors, ceremonies, benefits, etc. Therefore, their individual identities are unmixed. However, the three sets of ethical systems have identical aims with respect to what is to be refrained from and what is required: to relinquish ordinary emotions and to release the fetters of the emotions. Thus, each system is complete in its prescriptions of what to restrain from and what is required.

In the manner of [extracting] copper from copper ore and then preparing with it the elixir that transforms poor metals into gold, if the personal liberation vows are imbued with the awakening mind which is the distinguishing feature of the Universal Way, [they become Universal Way] vows, and if accompanied by the special skill in means and wisdom, they become mantric vows. Thus, one essence changes into the next.

In following the higher ethical systems, the restraints and requirements [in the lower systems] are included in the restraints and requirements of the higher system. The qualities [of the higher system] are thereby contained in the lower.

Therefore, although certain [higher] vows may seem to be incompatible [with lower ones], such is not the case by virtue of their view and special conduct of skill in means.

Moreover, one should observe [the vow] that is most significant in any given situation. The great scholar Pema Wangyal states[339]:

> The wise give this advice: when amid a group of people, or
>   when a deed would be naturally unvirtuous,
> The lower vows [of the proclaimers] should have precedence.
>   When no selfish desire is involved, [physical and verbal
>   unvirtuous acts are permitted].
> When engaged in tantric activities, or living in solitude, mantric
>   vows [are most important].
> If there is no dilemma about which one to follow, guard all
>   without mixing them.
> Faced with a dilemma, weigh the act in terms of restraint and
>   requirement.

The Gedenpas assert that the three sets of ethical systems are distinct and that each one is the foundation of the next.
Each of these assertions is substantiated by scriptural references and reasonings.

According to the followers of the Riwo Gedenpa,[340] the three ethical systems are distinct in their styles since each has its own way to assume vows and its own causes of deterioration. [When higher vows are assumed,] the lower [vows] become branches of them, as when a sapphire is placed in a clean jug filled with limpid water, the water reflects the color of the jewel. Thus, the higher system has as its foundation the lower one.

All of the [above] assertions seem to be substantiated by scriptures and reasonings drawn from the different ethical systems.

The Benefits of Observing Ethics [C]

> A supreme vajra holder endowed with the three sets of vows
> who perseveres in practice
> Will attain the rank of Vajradhara in one lifetime and in the
> same body.

A vajra holder possessed of three sets of vows, supreme among all mantric adepts, or anyone who has entered the door of the Secret Mantra and who safeguards the pledges and perseveres in the experiential cultivation of the path, will attain the state of Vajradhara in a single lifetime, in the same body. This statement is found again and again in the tantras. Accordingly, the venerable Rangjung [Dorjé] says:

> By maintaining the pledges, the best adept
> Will accomplish the state of Vajrasattva in one lifetime,
> And through aspiration alone, will perfect
> All common attainment without impediments.

By honoring one's pledges, even those who are not able to apply themselves to practice will attain spiritual accomplishment before long, as stated in the *[Secret Treasury of the Dakini] Tantra*[341]:

> Whoever abides in the vows and pledges
> But, hindered by past deeds, cannot practice now
> Will [certainly] attain realization in another life.

Root Verses from
The Encompassment of All Knowledge

To take advantage of life's leisure and endowments
Upon approaching the Buddha's teaching, the source of all
    happiness and well-being,
First find and then follow a spiritual guide.
Since by relying on an inferior, one regresses,
On an equal, one stagnates,
And on a superior, one excels,
Keep in touch with a spiritual guide superior to yourself.
The need for a guide can be determined from scripture, logic,
    and similes.
A spiritual guide may be an ordinary human being, a bodhisattva,
    a buddha in manifest or enjoyment dimension
Suited to the four phases of the disciple's growth.
Eight, four, or two qualities characterize the teacher who is an
    ordinary person.
The teacher may be a monastic preceptor, a bodhisattva's instructor,
    or a tantric master.
The ordaining preceptor, ceremonial master, interviewer, tutor or
    instructor, and instructor of novices act as the five monastic
    teachers.
A monk who is ethical, well-versed in monastic ceremonies,

Compassionate toward the sick, associated with upright monks,
Diligent in helping others spiritually and materially, and able to
    give timely counsel
Is qualified to be a monastic preceptor.
An aspirant bodhisattva should work with a spiritual guide who
    is self-controlled, tranquil, and has pacified deception,
Is eminent, diligent, and displays a wealth of transmissions,
Has realized the nature of all phenomena, is articulate,
Embodies loving-kindness, and shows no weariness or
    discouragement.
The bodhisattva's instructor who exhibits twelve qualities such as
    erudition is an exceptional teacher.
The tantric master must be steadfast, self-controlled, intelligent,
Patient, honest, and well-versed in the activities related to mantra
    and tantra.
He or she is compassionate, learned, expert in ten fields,
Proficient in the drawing of mandalas, and skilled in the ways of
    explaining the Secret Mantra.
From a different perspective, the vajra master owns three treasures,
    has received the entire course of initiations,
Is committed, learned in the tantras, skilled in performing rituals,
    and has produced signs of experience.
In summary, the vajra master belongs to an authentic lineage,
    preserves the pledges, has heard secret instructions,
And has realized the meaning of tantra. A monk is the best of the
    three types of vajra master.
Magnificent is the master with the power to evoke in the student
The adamantine pristine awareness of the state of union.
Avoid a master whose traits are discordant with those of a true
    teacher;
But since a fully qualified master is rare, follow the one who is
    replete with good qualities.
The suitable candidate for the life of a renunciate must be free from
    obstacles to assuming the vows.
In particular, he must respect the instructor, follow an ethical code
    strictly,
Persevere in meditation and study,
Be conscientious, restrained, and patient,

Since a good monk who lives by the monastic discipline is known
by these very qualities.

A suitable candidate for the bodhisattva's training is gifted with
faith, kindness, intelligence,

And the stamina to engage in the bodhisattva's conduct, does not
seek personal peace,

Is energetic, and delights in hearing about emptiness.

A suitable candidate for the Secret Mantra is devoted to the master
and is discrete,

Shows great aptitude, lives by the pledges, and perseveres in the
practice.

The teacher should ignore a disciple ridden with shortcomings, but
accept one who, despite imperfections, is gifted with qualities
such as faith.

To determine whether they can brave a spiritual relationship, the
jewel-like teacher and disciple must first examine each other.

Those intent on liberation should devote themselves to a spiritual
guide with offerings and respect, service, and spiritual practice.

The Victorious One said: "By devoting yourself to a spiritual friend,

You will attain the full, accomplished, unique, and perfectly
immaculate path to liberation.

By trusting me now as your spiritual guide, you will gain freedom
from suffering. Consider these reasons!"

Many other benefits that accrue from studying with a spiritual
guide are taught in the scriptures.

Shun unvirtuous friends who have bad characters, cynical outlooks,
and prejudice,

Believe their own view to be the best, are boastful, and disparage
others.

When working with a spiritual teacher, recognize demonic forces
and defeat them with their antidotes;

Moreover, cultivate lucid, trusting, and longing faith.

The teacher prepares for a spiritual discourse by creating a congenial
setting,

Dispelling malevolent influences, and maintaining dignified
composure.

The disciple makes offerings, behaves respectfully, and values the
opportunity.

When teaching, the master demonstrates three kinds of expertise,
two types of kindness,
And three kinds of patience; and includes six elements in the
discourse.
Alternatively, the teacher first states the general and specific
purposes,
Provides two summaries which have six qualities,
And then analyzes the words in terms of object, agent, and action,
and their literal meaning.
To facilitate understanding, the speaker clarifies the sequence
of words and meaning by illustrating the two types of
relationships,
And in response to objections, ascertains the meaning through
scriptures and logic.
For the brightest student, the teacher may explain deep and far-
reaching subjects; for the less intelligent, first give easily retained
and accessible teachings,
Then delve into subtle details, connections, and contradictions.
Another task of the teacher is to encourage dispirited persons and
counteract their distraction and apathy.
The disciple should eliminate the three defects of a jug, the six
improper ways of listening, etc.,
And regard himself or herself as an ill person, the doctrine as
medicine, and the master as a physician.
The speaker and the student should practice the six perfections
when teaching and listening.
The teacher concludes the discourse with an apology, dedication,
and sealing by contemplation.
The student makes offerings, recites dedication prayers, and
maintains mindfulness.
Study, reflection, expounding, listening, and upholding the
doctrine
Integrated with living experience is said to yield limitless merits.

To follow in the footsteps of saints, bodhisattvas, and buddhas
Is to preserve a threefold morality, the foundation for all good
qualities,
Known as the ethics of personal liberation, of the bodhisattva, and
of the awareness holder.

Concern for personal peace motivated by renunciation
Forms the basis for defining the personal liberation vows of the
  proclaimers.
The vows themselves are defined as the intention (as well as
  concomitant mental factors)
To forsake both injury to others and its basis. In the Analysts' view,
  these vows have form.
Personal liberation is known as morality, virtue, endeavor, and vow.
The vows of personal liberation, meditative absorption, and the
  uncontaminated are found within different levels of existence.
The eight vows, those of the monk and nun, male and female
  novices and lay practitioners,
Postulant nun, and the purificatory fast,
Diversified in nature, are condensed into four types. Only seven
  meet the necessary requirements.
The present-day ceremony of ordination was introduced after the
  demise of the original one.
Men or women of the three continents are suitable candidates.
In assuming the vows, the candidate must not be bound by five
  stipulations, and must be free of the four obstacles.
An aspirant who has not gone for refuge cannot assume the
  personal liberation vows.
The precepts of the purificatory fast are observed for a day and
  may be conferred by any person holding the precepts.
The layperson's precepts, the novice's, and the monk's ordination
  are conferred in their respective ceremonies.
The ceremony for the monk's ordination requires ten essential
  elements.
Ethical conduct is maintained by reliance on others, purity of mind,
  recognition of incompatible factors,
Engagement in the training, and relying on the conditions for living
  comfortably.
The eight branches of the purificatory fast consist of the four basic
  precepts, abstinence from alcohol, dance, necklaces, etc.,
Luxurious or high beds, and eating after noon;
Ethical conduct, conscientiousness, and disciplined conduct
  encompass these eight.
An individual who observes these precepts for life is known as a
  venerable lay practitioner.

Lay practitioners are of five types. The first is committed to the
Three Jewels
And abides by the three special and five general precepts.
The second abstains from one; the third, from some; the fourth,
from most;
And the fifth, from all four root downfalls and alcohol.
Traditionalists maintain that there is also a celibate lay practitioner.
Novices may incur ten transgressions of the rules: violations of the
eight branches,
Plus the rule to not accept gold and silver. With the exception of
thirteen permissible ones,
The related minor infractions are the same as those of the monk.
The postulant nun observes six basic and six ancillary rules.
The rules of the monk concern five classes of downfalls.
Sexual intercourse, theft, murder, and lying about one's level of
spiritual attainment
Constitute the class of defeating offenses.
If the basis, attitude, act, and consummation are all present, the
ordination is lost.
If one or more aspects are missing, a serious infraction or another
offense is incurred.
Ejaculation, touching, and speaking of sexual intercourse to a
woman, extolling reverence,
Matchmaking, constructing a hut, or a large dwelling, groundless,
or trivial accusation,
Causing a schism, taking sides, causing a layperson to lose faith,
and defiance
Constitute the class of partially defeating offenses.
Any of these offenses is said to leave only a residue of the vows.
Keeping, being without, retaining cloth, or inducing a nun to wash
robes, accepting, and requesting cloth,
Asking for cloth of a greater measure or value from two donors,
and excessive insistence,
To make a mat with silk, black wool, or more than half black wool,
making a new one before six years,
Not adding to it a handspan's patch, carrying, and spinning wool,
handling gold or silver,
Usury, trading, keeping an unconsecrated begging bowl, or requesting an extra one, engaging a weaver, improving the weave,

Taking back gifts, using rainy season retreat offerings, being
   separated from the robes, keeping the large rain cloak too long,
Redirecting dedicated offerings, and storing food constitute the
   class of downfalls that require forfeiture.
Lying, criticizing, slandering, reviving quarrels, teaching a woman,
Reciting the scriptures, revealing lapses, telling the truth, accusing a
   steward, reviling the discipline, destroying vegetation, censuring
   the caretaker,
Refusing to comply, leaving the bed outside or grass under the mat,
   driving out or harassing a monk, poking holes, casting water,
   laying bricks,
Teaching a nun doctrine when not appointed, or after sunset;
   accusing of teaching for gain; giving to, or making a robe for a
   nun;
Walking with or going in a boat with a nun, sitting or standing with
   a woman, persuading someone to prepare food,
Eating consecutively, or while staying with non-Buddhists, taking
   excess, resuming eating, giving leftover food to a monk,
Gathering to eat, eating at inappropriate times, eating stored foods,
   foods not given, and good foods,
Using water that contains life, sitting or standing at a place of
   sexual intercourse, serving food to a naked ascetic,
Watching, or staying in an army camp, inciting preparations,
   striking, threatening to strike, concealing a lapse,
Preventing alms from being given, lighting a fire, withdrawing
   one's assent, sleeping with the non-ordained, not giving up
   erroneous views,
Siding with or befriending the expelled, wearing undyed clothes,
   handling treasures, bathing frequently,
Killing an animal, causing regret, tickling, playing in water, sleeping in the same place as a woman,
Frightening, hiding, or using without permission the belongings of
   fellow monks, defaming a monk, accompanying a woman,
Traveling with a thief, conferring full ordination to one under age,
   tilling the soil, overstaying one's welcome,
Rejecting advice, eavesdropping, leaving without informing, being
   disrespectful, drinking alcohol, going at the inappropriate time,
Wandering into the village, making a visit at night, showing
   disdain for the rules,

Accepting a fine needlecase, making a seat with legs, covering a
     mat with cotton, exceeding the sizes for the mat, the robe for
     skin rash, the large rain cloak, and the robes
Constitute the class of downfalls that require confession alone.
Accepting a nun's alms, accepting food served without regard to
     seniority,
Transgressing the rule not to beg at a household, and eating with-
     out checking the forest
Constitute the class of offenses to be individually confessed.
The one hundred and twelve minor infractions
Concern the wearing of robes, decorum,
Sitting, receiving food, manner of eating,
Begging bowl, teaching the doctrine, behavior,
And climbing. Thus, a monk must observe
A total of two hundred and fifty-three rules.
The nun must observe three hundred and sixty-four rules.
Prohibitions concern that which is incompatible with ethical
     conduct.
The first basis for monastic discipline consists of three methods for
     refinement of the training.
The purification-renewal to develop mental quiescence perfects
     meditation and wisdom.
Confession to foster harmony should be performed
Every half month, to increase prosperity, to eliminate misfortune,
     and to settle disputes.
Each of the two rainy season retreats, the earlier and later, lasts
     three months.
Timely, untimely, or unexpected lifting of the restrictions conclude
     the retreat.
The making and distribution of robes constitutes a basis of training
     concerned with conditions for living comfortably.
Robes include prescribed, accessory, and extra garnments.
The thirteen prescribed robes should be colored by the appropriate
     dyes.
Leather seat and shoes are permitted in special cases. The four
     types of food and medicine
Are those permissible before noon, within a day, seven days, or
     kept until one is cured of an illness.

One hundred and one formal procedures are subsumed under three
    categories.
The ordination is lost by returning it, death, wayward views, etc.
Scholars disagree on what constitutes loss of vows: some maintain that
    vows and downfalls exist together like a rich person with debts.
Others maintain that committing a root downfall destroys the
    whole ordination.
In particular circumstances, a defeat may not be an infraction due
    to incapacity to maintain the rules or other reasons.
Any type of ordination is destroyed by the violation of the four roots.
In this case, a layperson must reassume the precepts; novices and
    monks
Can amend unconcealed downfalls but not concealed ones.
Partial defeats are amended by demotion and services; downfalls
    are amended
By forfeiture, confession, and restraint; if a monk is unwilling to
    amend, he must be subjugated.
Four types of dispute are settled in seven ways.
The monastic sites and monks' quarters at least should accord with
    the teachings on discipline.
A monk must relinquish the two extreme lifestyles: indulgence and
    austerity.
If an action accords with those permitted by the Buddha, it is
    performed; if it does not, it is renounced.
Analysts believe that the three disciplines have form and are
    substantially different;
Centrists assert them to be consciousness, the former transformed
    into the latter ones.
Individualists' vows of personal liberation become Universalists'
If assumed with an altruistic motive to attain enlightenment,
Or even when the mind of awakening arises afterwards.
Universalists' vows are received in the course of proclaimers'
    ceremonies,
In special ceremonies such as the one for taking the vows of
    purification-renewal,
And in higher rites, the one for the formation of the awakening
    mind, the preparatory part of a tantric initiation, etc.
The preceptor may be a renunciate or a lay practitioner.

The candidate must fulfill the same qualifications specified for the
proclaimers' system;
But anyone ready to make the resolve to awaken is eligible to
receive these precepts during special ceremonies.
In a case of special necessity, even the seven unvirtuous acts are
permissible.
Concealed downfalls may be confessed and ordination retaken.
Secondary downfalls are amended by confession, sustained by the
four forces.
Downfalls are purified by attitude, not by penances.
The vows are lost through wayward views, defeating offenses, or
by returning them,
No other condition can destroy them.
In brief, the purport of all the scriptures on discipline is contained
in these words:
Abandon negative actions, cultivate virtue, and discipline the
mind.
Violation of ethical conduct bears serious consequences,
While pure ethics serve as the foundation and condition for all
virtue.

The ethics of awakening mind in the Universal Way
Arise from awakened affinity, faith, love, and courage.
Awakening mind is formed through the strengths of a friend, cause,
effect, path, and familiarization;
It arises from compassion, which springs from love.
The essence of the commitments consists in the ethical conduct that
forsakes unwholesome deeds of body, speech, and mind,
Motivated by the intention to attain complete awakening for the
sake of others.
The aspiring mind is characterized by wish; the venturing mind, by
endeavor.
Awakening mind is approximate or subtle, depending on the way it
is formed.
The stages are differentiated by appreciation, intention, full
maturation, and freedom from all impediments.
Twenty-two similes, earth, gold, moon, etc., are used to distinguish
awakening mind with respect to individuals.
Relative and ultimate awakening minds differ in their focuses.

Awakening mind may be formed in three ceremonies. The exclusive
  ceremonies are known as the two traditions of the pioneers;
These have been preserved by their followers.
In the profound view's tradition, anyone able to articulate ideas
May assume the commitments of the aspiring and venturing minds
  at the same time
In the presence of a master or a sacred representation, following
  preparatory cultivation of merit and purification of mind.
Acute practitioners must avoid fourteen root downfalls.
Five of these apply mainly to kings: to steal the Three Jewels'
  property, to reject teachings,
To blame the immoral, to commit deeds of direct retribution, and to
  profess wayward views.
Five downfalls apply mainly to ministers: the first four are the same
  as those prohibited for kings,
And the fifth is to plunder a town. The eight root downfalls that
  apply to beginners are to teach emptiness to the untrained,
To cause another to give up the intention to awaken, to make
  someone abandon the Individual Way,
To assert that the Individual Way does not conquer emotions, to
  praise oneself and belittle others,
To falsely claim realization of emptiness, to cause a king to inflict a
  fine and then accept stolen property as a bribe,
To disrupt meditation or to give the possessions of a contemplative
  monk to one who merely recites scriptures.
Downfalls for average practitioners are to give up awakening mind,
Be ungenerous, angry, or hypocritical.
An obtuse practitioner must at least maintain the aspiration to
  awaken.
The secondary infractions number eighty: twenty-four stem from
  disinterest in others' happiness or suffering;
Sixteen stem from neglecting to accomplish greater goals.
Each may be incidental or continuous.
The commitments may be lost in six ways, such as giving up refuge.
While a root downfall may damage some aspects of the venturing
  mind,
As long as aspiration is present, the commitments cannot be lost.
To restore the commitments, one invokes Akashagarbha and
  acknowledges the downfall in his presence.

If the time limit for confession has passed, one restores the commitments using the four forces.

One should promise to train in the prescribed practice only to the
extent and for as long as one estimates one can.

In the magnificent deeds tradition, commitments of aspiring mind
are assumed by a holder of one of the seven personal liberation
vows

Before an erudite and competent master who abides by the same
commitments.

The commitments of venturing mind are bestowed only after the
scriptures are studied.

The extensive rite for the venturing mind includes an inquiry
concerning obstacles, etc.

A practitioner must guard against four root downfalls and forty-six
secondary infractions.

The root downfalls are to praise oneself and belittle others out of
attachment to wealth and honor;

Not to give material aid or not to give teachings to the needy out of
miserliness;

Not to forgive someone though he has apologized and to strike him
in anger;

To abandon the Universal Way and to present false teachings as
true Buddhism.

Depending on the strength of involvement, the downfall may be
serious, moderate, or light.

The seven contradictions to generosity are not to make offerings, to
indulge in desires, not to have respect,

Not to answer questions, not accept invitations, to refuse gifts, and
not to explain the teachings.

The nine contradictions to ethics are to reject the immoral, not to
observe the rules, to make little effort for others' sake,

Not to commit an unvirtuous deed although permitted, to engage
in wrong livelihood, to play out of excitement and agitation,

To wish for a solitary escape from cyclic existence, not to avoid a
bad reputation, and not to resort to disquieting methods.

Four contradictions to patience are to neglect the four obligations,
to reject an angry person,

To refuse apologies, and to give in to anger.

The three contradictions to effort are to gather followers, not to
overcome laziness, and to delight in meaningless conversation.
The three contradictions to meditation are not to seek instructions,
not to overcome impediments, and to be attached to the pleasurable experience of meditation.
The eight contradictions to wisdom are to reject the proclaimers'
way, to embrace that way or a non-Buddhist one,
To prefer its literature, to take no interest in the distinctive features
of the Universal Way, not to seek the true teachings,
To praise oneself and belittle others, and to rely on the words rather
than the meaning:
These thirty-four contradictions prevent the development of
wholesome qualities.
Not to help persons in need, not to care for the sick, not to relieve
others' suffering,
Not to correct the heedless; not to repay kindness, not to relieve
pain, not to be generous,
Not to care, not to comply, not to praise, not to correct,
Not to uplift others: these twelve contradict working for others'
benefit. Infractions are of three types: emotional, non-emotional,
and without consequence.
If a root downfall is committed with great emotional involvement
or if the aspiration for awakening has deteriorated,
The commitments are lost and must be reassumed.
Downfalls committed with medium or slight involvement are
confessed before three vow holders or one;
Emotional minor infractions, before one; and non-emotional minor
infractions, with one's mind as witness.
In this tradition, one must observe all points of training to their full
extent and until awakening.
Common to both traditions are five precepts for the aspiring
awakening mind:
Not to reject any being; to ponder benefits; to acquire merits; to
refine the awakening mind;
And to shun the four black deeds of deceiving one's master or a
venerable person, feeling regret for what is not to be regretted,
Being angry at a bodhisattva, and being cunning and deceitful,
And to undertake the four white deeds in their place.

One should have the three noble aspirations of goal, skillful means,
    and marvelous activity;
And eliminate despair, apprehension, and other emotions that
    cause aspiration to deteriorate.
The points of training in venturing mind prescribe both what to
    avoid and what to practice.
All these points are included in the threefold ethics of restraint,
    acquiring good qualities, and working for the benefit of others.
The prescription for what to avoid corresponds to the commitments
    set out in the two traditions mentioned above.
One should renounce what is naturally unwholesome or
    unwholesome by prescription except in cases of special necessity,
Impediments to the spiritual maturity of oneself and others,
Pleasures of this life that create suffering in the next, or what causes
    misery in both,
Deeds that qualify as downfalls, and downfalls-in-disguise;
And undertake what brings happiness in the next life though is
    painful in the present, what brings happiness in both,
Deeds that do not constitute downfalls, and those that might seem
    to be downfalls but are not.
All actions done with compassionate concern are without fault.
The prescribed practice corresponds to the ethics aimed at acquiring
    good qualities, which is the practice of the six perfections.
The perfections are described in terms of their number, order,
    characteristics,
Semantic meaning, divisions, and groups.
Each perfection is threefold: Generosity of material aid, the teachings,
    protection,
Ethics of restraint, aimed at acquiring good qualities, and working
    for the benefit of others,
Patience to withstand harm, accept hardships, and fathom
    emptiness,
Effort that is armor-like, applied to the task, and insatiable,
Meditation of resting at ease, aimed at acquiring good qualities,
    and focused on the welfare of others,
Wisdom that is worldly and supramundane, higher and lower,
Or wisdom that arises through listening, pondering, and meditating.
When wisdom is present, all five become supramundane perfections.

Four means of attraction and other ways are used to benefit others.
Awakening mind and its training are safeguarded with mindfulness
and discriminating alertness.
A great wave of altruistic deeds is the cause of an ultimate
awakening mind.
Its essence is the pristine awareness of an exalted bodhisattva's
equipoise.
It may be divided into the awakening mind of the first stage, and
so forth.
Some scholars assert that ultimate awakening mind can be formed
in a ritual; others deny this.
Ultimate awakening mind possessed of three ultimate aspects
Is the pristine awareness that directly realizes the sphere of reality.
To damage awakening mind brings four adverse consequences. To
safeguard aspiration reaps eight merits; and venturing mind,
two special ones.
The awakening mind is indeed the source of all temporary and
lasting benefits and happiness.

The two systems of awareness-holder vows are the new and the
ancient.
In the system of the later translations, some enter the Secret Mantra
gradually; others, straightaway.
Mantric vows are essentially the resolve, accompanied by its
concomitant factors,
To train in methods to experience blissful pristine awareness in
order to bind grasping to subject and object and the propensity
for movement.
In short, the ethics consist in the discipline of binding body, speech,
and mind with skill in means and wisdom.
Three types of vows are distinguished according to subject matter:
The causal tantra's vow to bind all phenomena, form, sound, etc.,
within innate pristine awareness;
The vow of the tantra of skillful means to bind subtle and gross
objectifying thoughts within the creation and completion phases;
And the resultant tantra's vow to bind subjective experience within
the nature of the dimensions of awakening and pristine awareness.

Four classes of tantra teach the actual tantra: Action, Conduct,
    Yoga, and Highest Yoga tantras.
Three kinds of mantric vows are distinguished according to initiatory
    rituals in which they are assumed:
The mantra's own personal liberation and awakening mind vows
    assumed during regular confession;
Vows of divine fortune taken upon entry into the mandala;
And the creation and completion vows assumed in the main part of
    an initiation.
The vows are assumed with a promise upon entry into the
    mandala,
Or in their entirety at the end of the initiation.
The vows' seeds are planted when the body, speech, and mind are
    consecrated;
They are formed with the promise to maintain them and blessed by
    the descent of pristine awareness;
The main conferral of initiation brings them to the apex.
Mantric vows of the lower tantras are called incomplete or partially
    complete;
And those of the higher tantras, fully complete.
Bliss and emptiness, as two or as one, embrace all vows.
Although no discrimination is made with regard to aspirants,
A person unable to safeguard as much as the common vows
Is not to be initiated but may enter the mandala.
Vows and pledges assumed during the initiation must be
    safeguarded like one's life.
Four pledges constitute the foundation common to all tantras:
To maintain correct view, refuge, and awakening mind, and to
    receive the mandala's initiation.
The fourteen general pledges of Action Tantra
Are to have faith in the Three Jewels and in mantra, to have earnest
    interest in the Universal Way,
To be devoted to the supreme field of merits, not to be angry with
    deities, to make offerings on special occasions,
Not to venerate other traditions, to honor guests, to be always
    benevolent,
To acquire merit, to exert oneself in reciting the mantra and in
    safeguarding other commitments,
Not to teach mantras or mudras to those without pledges, and to
    accomplish the aim of the tantras.

Practitioners must observe the pledges of each family as taught in
the respective tantras.

The means of purifying transgressions include reciting one hundred
thousand of the mantra of one's family

Or the recollection mantra [called "Unconquerable Vajra] That
Blazes Like Fire," the performance of appeasing fire
offerings, etc.

Conduct Tantra's pledges are fourteen: to refrain from the ten
unvirtuous deeds, not forsake the sacred doctrine,

Not give up one's awakening mind, not be miserly, and not harm
others.

The means of restoration of the Action Tantra's pledges also apply
to the Conduct and Yoga Tantra.

Yoga Tantra pledges consist of fourteen injunctions and fourteen
prohibitions.

Injunctions related to the five families are to take refuge in the
Three Jewels, commit oneself to the vajra, bell, and master,

Practice the four generosities, uphold the three ways, and make
offerings.

The prohibitions are not to forsake the Jewels and the awakening
mind,

Not disrespect the deity, mantra and seals, and master, not step
over sacred objects,

Not eat wrong foods, not divulge the secrets, not forsake mantra
and seals, not harm others, not delight in the Individual Way,

Not despair, not forsake the training, and not engage in what is
unwholesome.

These five families' pledges are the main pledges taught in the
explanatory tantras.

The sets of pledges given in the *Glorious Paramadya* and other
fundamental tantras should be learned from other sources.

Explanatory tantras teach the pledges of the five families, general
pledges, and pledges given in the concise proclamation.

The general root pledges are to shun the fourteen defeats for a
bodhisattva.

The branches are the ethics of restraint from the four root offenses
and from drinking alcohol;

The ethics aimed at acquiring good qualities by devoting oneself to
authentic masters, etc.;

And the ethics of working for others by giving up four incompatible
attitudes.

Not to disrespect gods, etc., and other common vows are assumed
    as part of those given in the concise proclamation.
The vows to be safeguarded by all are taken with a promise,
While the vows not to commit the ten infractions, etc., are assumed
    through initiation.
Highest Yoga Tantra prescribes three disciplines: conduct, vows,
    and pledges.
Each tantra presents its special forms of conduct.
The *Guhyasamaja Tantra* teaches the conduct of the five families and
    four pledges to be interpreted.
The Chakrasamvara tantras speak of twenty-two modes of pure
    conduct and eight concerning the awareness woman.
Fourteen conducts are enumerated in the *Tent Tantra*; nine, in the
    Unsurpassable Tantra.
The *Wheel of Time Tantra* prescribes twenty-five modes of conduct.
Five consist in refraining from the four root offenses and from
    drinking alcohol.
Twenty consist in abstaining from the five related ill-deeds of
    gambling, eating impure food, reading perverse subjects,
Making sacrifices for ancestors, and extremist religious practices;
Five murders of killing an animal, child, man, woman, or
    destroying reliquaries;
Five kinds of enmity toward friends, leaders, the Buddha, the
    Buddhist community, or a trustworthy person;
Five desires related to form, sound, smell, taste, and sensation.
These modes of conduct form the foundation of all vows and
    pledges.
The common vows are those of the five families, or the six:
For the Akshobhya family, to keep the seals and master;
For the jewel, to practice the ten kinds of generosity; for the wheel,
    to rely on ten foods;
For the sword, to make offerings; for the lotus, to maintain vows of
    retention;
For Vajrasattva, to cultivate a mind of awakening. These have both
    provisional and definitive meanings.
The exceptional vows are these: for the vajra family, to take life; for
    the sword family, to lie;
For the jewel, to steal wealth; for the lotus, to abduct the women of
    others;

For the wheel, to eat meat and drink alcohol; and for the curved
knife, to be generous and not to disrespect women.
Practitioners should engage in the evident or hidden meanings of
the pledges according to their levels of spiritual accomplishment.
Highest Yoga pledges prescribe avoidance of fourteen root
downfalls:
To disrespect one's spiritual master; transgress the Buddha's
teachings; be angry at one's spiritual companions;
Abandon love; lose the awakening mind; disparage the teachings;
Disclose secrets; abuse one's own aggregates; disbelieve what is
pure in nature;
Love the wicked; apply discursive thought to transcendent reality;
cause believers to lose faith;
Not accept pledge substances; and disrespect women.
Eight secondary downfalls are to rely on a consort without pledges,
Quarrel at ritual feast, accept nectar from an unsuitable consort,
Not teach when appropriate, answer questions perversely,
Stay in the home of a proclaimer, boast of being a tantric
practitioner although ignorant,
And proclaim secrets to the unsuited. There are many other ways to
enumerate secondary downfalls.
The subtle infractions include fifteen concerning charismatic
activity and seven branches.
The tantras give numerous classifications of the pledges, the
pledges of the four initiations, etc.
Mikyö Gawa asserts that all pledges are included in the four
pledges related to the four initiations:
The pledges to be safeguarded, of sustenance, of conduct, and not
to be apart from.
Pema Karpo presents the pledges of restraint from root downfalls,
the pledges of practice of the six families,
And the pledges related to practice, which form the three groups of
pledges prescribing ritual articles,
Pledges prescribing enjoyments, and pledges of equipoise and post-
equipoise.
The victorious Rangjung Dorjé states that all pledges are included
in four pledges.
All of these pledges are encompassed by two categories: prohibitions
and injunctions.

Six modes of conduct are taught in *Tent Tantra* for practitioners who
   have reached the stage of warmth.
Practitioners who have perfected pristine awareness are beyond
   codes of behavior.
A defeat occurs when there is motivation, recognition, pursuing,
   separation,
Lack of regret, non-deranged state of mind, and overdue
   acknowledgment.
If some completing factors are missing, the infraction may be a
   serious transgression, downfall, or a minor infraction.
The *Essence Ornament* teaches twenty-five means of restoration.
Fire ritual, recitation of mantra, meditation, ritual feast, etc.
Are the means to purify downfalls, transgressions, violations and
   ruptures.
Any downfall, regardless of its seriousness, can be purified if
   acknowledged before three hours have elapsed.
Meditation and recitation of the mantra of Vajrasattva and
   Samayavajra,
Initiation, and self-initiation are the best means for purification.
Higher pledges are restored through self-blessing and the view.
In the tradition of the ancient translations, the pledges common to
   the spiritual ways of skill in means
Are the general pledges, the particular, and the exceptional ones.
The general pledges are the limits to be observed in the personal
   liberation precepts, awakening mind commitments, and the
   pledges of the three outer tantras.
The particular pledges are the root pledges of body, speech, mind,
   and awakening mind, and
The secondary pledges of the five to practice, five not to renounce,
Five to accept, five to recognize, and five to integrate.
Practitioners should safeguard and engage in the provisional or
   definitive meanings of these pledges
In accordance with circumstances. The exceptional pledges concern
   familiarization and attainment practice.
The *Magical Net*, the source tantra of Mahayoga,
Presents five root pledges: not to forsake the unsurpassable, to
   honor the master,
Not to interrupt mantra and seal practice, to be kind to siblings,

And not to divulge the ten secrets; and ten secondary pledges,
Five not to renounce and five not to reject.
Those are divided into three hundred and sixty that can be
subdivided indefinitely.
By virtue of their sevenfold greatness, states Rongzom, Mahayoga's
pledges are superior
To the pledges of lower tantras and to the commitments of the
Universal Way.
Anuyoga presents nine general pledges which are encompassed
by two:
The pledge of reality with no limits to be observed;
And the pledge of compassion with limits.
The general Atiyoga pledges are outer, inner, and secret pledges
relating to a buddha's body, speech, and mind;
Each divided thrice yields a total of twenty-seven.
The exceptional pledges relate to non-existence,
Naturalness, spontaneous accomplishment, and oneness.
Transgressions are of five types: major deteriorations, root and
secondary, violations by association, and indirect ones.
Not to confess these brings misfortune and a life in the Hell of
Unceasing Torture.
The proclaimers' vows, like a clay pot, once broken cannot be
repaired;
The awakening mind commitments, like gold or silver, can be
restored;
The tantric pledges, like a dented vessel, are restored by the
practitioner's strength.
Pledges are restored through action, precious substances, earnest
desire, contemplation, and reality.
The *Great Cleansing* can purify all transgressions.
A person may hold one, two, or all three sets of vows, etc.;
These vows are distinguishable. Indian scholars differ from Tibetan
scholars in their assertions
On how all three sets of vows coexist in one person.
Abhayakara says that the vows are similar in that they share an
attitude of restraint
But are distinguished by their forms. The great scholar
Vibhutichandra asserts

That the higher vows outshine the lower, while remaining distinct.
The incomparable Gampopa and his followers state that the three
ethical systems
Are each of a different essence and should be preserved as
prescribed.
Faced with dilemma, the higher system takes precedence;
Transgressions of the lower vows are thereby overcome; their
qualities are contained in the higher.
The systems differ in the way vows are assumed and lost.
The venerable Drakpa, the omniscient Longchenpa, and others
Assert that the individual identities of the ethical systems are
unmixed; each is complete in prescribing both restraint and
requirements.
The essence of one vow changes into the next; thus, the qualities of
the higher contain the lower.
Special conduct makes them compatible with each other. One
should observe the most important in any given circumstance.
The Gedenpas assert that the three sets of ethical systems are
distinct and that each one is the foundation of the next.
Each of these assertions is substantiated by scriptural references
and reasonings.
A supreme vajra holder endowed with the three sets of vows who
perseveres in practice
Will attain the rank of Vajradhara in one lifetime and in the same
body.

Abbreviations

AS	*Akashagarbha Scripture (Ākāśagarbhasūtra; Nam mkha'i snying po'i mdo)* (Toh. 260).
CBS	Kanai Lal Hazra, *Constitution of the Buddhist Sangha.* Delhi: B.R. Publishing Corporation, 1988.
CD	Asaṅga, *Compendium of Discipline (Vinayasaṃgraha; 'Dul ba bsdu pa)* (Toh. 4040).
CFVD	*Commentary on the Fifty Verses on Devotion to the Master (Gurvārādhana-pañjikā; Bla ma'i bsnyen bkur gyi dka' 'grel)* (author unknown) (Toh. 3722).
CNPTV	Karma Ngedon Nyingpo, *Commentary on [Ngari Panchen's] Three Vows.* Edited by Dudjom Rinpoche. Burbin Monastery, Kalimpong.
CSO	Sthiramati, *Commentary on the Scripture Ornament (Sūtrālaṃkāra-vṛttibhāṣya; mDo sde rgyan gyi 'grel bshad)* (Toh. 4034).
CT	Śāntideva, *Compendium of Trainings (Śikṣāsamuccaya, Śikṣāsamuccayakārikā; bsLab pa kun las btus pa, bsLab pa kun las btus pa'i tsig le'ur byas pa)* (Toh. 3939, 3940).
CTHSN	Śākhyaprabha, *Luminous Commentary on the Three Hundred Stanzas on the Novitiate (Mūlasarvāstivādiśrāmaṇerakārikāvṛttiprabhāvati; 'Od ldan/ 'Phags pa gzhi thams cad yod par smra ba'i dge tshul gyi tshig le'ur byas pa'i 'grel ba 'od ldan)* (Toh. 4125).
CTVBC	Śāntirakṣita, *Commentary on the Twenty Verses on the Commitments of Awakening Mind/ Bodhisattva's Commitments (Saṃvaravimśakavṛtti; sDom pa nyi shu pa'i 'grel pa)* (Toh. 4082).
Dg.K.	Dergé Kangyur (sDe dge bka' 'gyur): Dergé edition of the Tibetan canonical collection of sutras and tantras.

Dg.T.   Dergé Tengyur (sDe dge bstan 'gyur): Dergé edition of the Tibetan canonical collection of commentarial treatises.

EC   Vajrapāṇi, *Eulogy-Commentary [on the Chakrasamvara Tantra]* (*Lakṣābhidhānāduddhṛtalaghutantrapiṇḍārthavivaraṇa; bsTod 'grel/mNgon par brjod pa 'bum pa las phyung ba nyung ngu'i rgyud kyi bsdus pa'i don rnam par bshad pa*) (Toh. 1402).

ERD   Mañjuśriyaśas, *Explanation of Root Tantric Downfalls* (*Vajrayānamūlāpattiṭīkā; rDo rje theg pa'i rtsa ba'i ltung ba'i rgya cher bshad pa*) (Toh. 2488).

ESO   Vasubandhu, *Explanation of the Scripture Ornament* (*Sūtrālaṃkāravyākhyā; mDo sde'i rgyan gyi bshad pa*) (Toh. 4026).

GBL   Śāntideva, *Guide to the Bodhisattva's Way of Life* (*Bodhisattvacaryāvatāra; Byang chub sems dpa'i spyod pa la 'jug pa*) (Toh. 3871).

HFP   Guṇaprabha, *One Hundred Formal Procedures* (*Ekottarakarmaśataka; Las brgya rtsa gcig pa*) (Toh. 4118).

IBTS   *Khas grub rje's Introduction to the Buddhist Tantric Systems*. Translated by F.D. Lessing and Alex Wayman. Delhi: Motilal Banarsidass, 1978.

IK   Naropa, *Iniziazione Kalacakra*. Translated by Raniero Gnoli and Giacomella Orofino. In Italian. Milan: Adelphi Edizioni SPA, 1994.

IOK   Kongtrul Lodrö Tayé, *Infinite Ocean of Knowledge* (*Shes bya mtha' yas pa'i rgya mtsho*). 3 vols. Beijing: Bod mi rigs dpe skrun khang, 1983.

JOL   Gampopa, *Jewel Ornament of Liberation* (*Dam chos yid bzhin nor bu thar pa rin po che'i rgyan*). Rumtek, Sikkim: Dharma Chakra Centre, 1974.

KT   Tenzin Gyatso, the Fourteenth Dalai Lama, *The Kalachakra Tantra, Rite of Initiation*. London: Wisdom Publications, 1985.

ME   Jeffrey Hopkins, *Meditation on Emptiness*. London: Wisdom Publications, 1983.

NG   *rNying ma rgyud 'bum* (*Collected Tantras of the Ancient Tradition*). 36 vols. Edited by Dilgo Khyentse Rinpoche. Thimpu, Bhutan, 1975.

NKG   *rNying ma bka' ma rgyas pa* (*Collected Transmitted Precepts of the Ancient Tradition*). Edited by Dudjom Rinpoche. Kalimpong, India, 1982.

NSH   Dudjom Rinpoche, *The Nyingma School of Tibetan Buddhism: Its Fundamentals and History*. 2 vols. Translated by Gyurme Dorje and Matthew Kapstein. Boston: Wisdom Publications, 1991.

PS   Asaṅga, *Proclaimers' Stages* (*Śrāvakabhūmi; Nyan thos kyi sa*) (Toh. 4036).

SB   Asaṅga, *Stages of the Bodhisattva* (*Bodhisattvabhūmi; Byang chub sems dpa'i sa*) (Toh. 4037).

SD   Guṇaprabha, *Fundamental Summary of Discipline* (*Vinayasūtra; 'Dul ba'i mdo*) (Toh. 4117).

SID   Vol. 1 of Panchen Sönam Drakpa, *Sun Illuminating the Discipline with Reasons and Scriptures (So thar tshul khrims kyi pad tshal rgyas byed pan chen bsod grags kyis mdzad pa'i 'dul ba'i legs bshad lung rigs kyi nyi ma).* 2 vols. Woodblock print. (Treats the first basis of the monastic discipline, ordination, and monks's rules.)

SID 16   Vol. 2 of Panchen Sönam Drakpa, *Sun Illuminating the Discipline with Reasons and Scriptures (So thar tshul khrims kyi pad tshal rgyas byed pan chen bsod grags kyis mdzad pa'i 'dul ba'i legs bshad lung rigs kyi nyi ma).* 2 vols. Woodblock print. (Treats the last sixteen bases of monastic discipline.)

SIRD   Vol. 1 (sTod cha) of Tsonapa, *Sunlight Illuminating the Root Summary of Discipline ('Dul ba mdo rtsa'i rnam bshad nyi ma'i 'od zer legs bshad lung gi rgya mtsho).* 2 vols. Woodblock print.

Toh.   *A Complete Catalogue of the Tibetan Buddhist Canons.* Edited by Ui, Suzuki, Kanakura, and Tada. Sendai, Japan: Tohoku University, 1934.

TV   Pema Karpo, *Extensive Commentary on the Three Vows (sDom gsum rgya cher 'grel pa/ sDom pa gsum gyi rgyan ces bya ba'i rgya cher 'grel ba).* Vols. Nga and Ca of the *Collected Works of Pema Karpo.* Edited by Acharya Shedup Tenzin and Lama Dhondup Tharchen. Thimpu, Bhutan, 1991.

f., ff.	folio(s)
p., pp.	page(s)
trans.	translated by
vol., vols.	volume(s)

Notes

Unless otherwise indicated, all references to works included in the Tohoku catalogue (A Complete Catalogue of the Tibetan Buddhist Canons, edited by Ui, Suzuki, Kanakura, and Tada [Sendai, Japan: Tohoku University, 1934]) are to the Dergé edition of the Tibetan bKa' 'gyur and bsTan 'gyur.

Chapter I: The Qualities of the Spiritual Teacher and Student

1. Leisure (*dal ba*) refers to freedom from eight fetters of life that impede full spiritual growth: being born as a hell being, as a starving spirit, as an animal, in a barbarian land, or as a long-living god; holding wayward views, being born in a period when there is no Buddha, and being stupid.

Endowments (*'byor ba*) are given as ten: To be born as a human being; to live in the "central country" (where the Buddha's doctrine is known); to possess all senses; not to have committed acts of immediate retribution (such as killing one's parent, etc.); to have faith in the Buddha's teaching (these first five conditions depend on oneself); the appearance of a Buddha in our world; the promulgation of the doctrine; the continuation of the doctrine; the presence of followers of the doctrine; and facilities for the practice of the doctrine (these latter five conditions depend on others.)

See Gampopa's *Jewel Ornament of Liberation* (henceforth cited as *JOL*) (*Dam chos yid bzhin nor bu thar pa rin po che'i rgyan*) (Dharma Chakra Centre: Rumtek, Sikkim, 1974), ff. 8b1-9b6.

2. Matricheta and Dignaga, *Interwoven Praises* (*Miśrakastotra; sPel mar bstod pa*) (Toh. 1150), f. 187b5-6.

3. Kapila (Kapila, Ser skya): the founder of the ancient Indian philosophical school of the Samkhyas.

4. Shantideva, *Guide to the Bodhisattva's Way of Life* (*Bodhisattvacaryāvatāra; Byang chub sems dpa'i spyod pa la 'jug pa*) (hereafter cited as *GBL*) (Toh. 3871), f. 40a3-4.

5. *Reunion of Father and Son Scripture* (*Pitāputrasamāgamanasūtra; Yab dang sras mjal ba'i mdo*) (Toh. 60). Citation has not been found in this scripture.

6. The eight fetters of life (*mi khom brgyad*): the opposite of the eight kinds of leisure (see note 1).

7. *Transcendent Wisdom in Eight Thousand Lines* (*Aṣṭasāhasrikāprajñāpāramitā; 'Phags pa shes rab kyi pha rol tu phyin pa brgyad stong pa*) (Toh. 12), f. 216a7-b1.

8. *Collection of Spontaneous Utterances* (*Udānavarga; Ched du brjod pa'i tshoms*) (Toh. 326), f. 231b4.

9. Ibid, f. 231b4-5.

10. *Condensed Transcendent Wisdom Scripture* as found in *Collected Scriptures and Dharani* (*mDo sngags gsung rab rgya mtsho'i snying po mtshan gzungs mang bsdus*) (Dharamsala: Bod gzhung shes rig khang, 1976; second edition, 1977), vol. sMad cha, f. 14a6-7.

11. *Flower Array Scripture* (*Gaṇḍhavyūhasūtra; sDong po bkod pa'i mdo*) (Toh. 44). Citation not found.

12. Solitary sages (*pratyekabuddha, rang rgyal*) aspire to achieve only personal liberation, not the omniscience of a buddha (*sarvajñāna, thams cad mkhyen pa*), and therefore this reasoning does not apply to them. Buddhas, however, have had to rely on spiritual guides to reach their goal of complete buddhahood.

13. *Biography of Shri Sambhava* (*dPal 'byung gi rnam thar*) (Toh. 44), vol. A, f. 286a5.

14. *Biography of the Lay Practitioner Achala* (*dGe bsnyen ma mi yo ba'i rnam thar*) (Toh. 44), vol. A, f. 36b3.

15. *Flower Array Scripture*, vol. A, f. 286a6-7.

16. Higher stages of awakening (*sa chen po*) of a bodhisattva refers to the three pure stages of awakening (*viśuddhibhūmi, dag pa'i sa*): the eighth (called "Gone Afar"), ninth ("Immovable"), and tenth ("Cloud of Dharma") stage, which immediately precede the stage of a buddha.

17. See chapter II, note 182.

18. This section is compiled from chapter three of Gampopa's *JOL*, f. 17a3-b4.

19. Asanga enumerates these eight qualities according to the Individual Way as follows:

> (1) ethical (*tshul khrims ldan*): restrained (observes the personal liberation vows) and shows earnest interest in the path that vanquishes passions and leads to perfect peace.
>
> (2) learned (*mang du thos*): able to recall many teachings, and having heard, investigated, and comprehended them, able to expound them.
>
> (3) accomplished (*rtogs pa*): possesses a perfected knowledge of conventional and ultimate reality and has attained the level of a saint; thus, able to impart teachings in miraculous ways.
>
> (4) full of compassion and love (*snying brtse ldan*): wishes welfare and happiness for others and desires their spiritual accomplishment.

(5) dauntless (*skyo ba med*): exhibits no weariness in teaching the four circles of disciples, is learned, without laziness, and enthusiastic.

(6) patient (*bzod ldan*): abides by the monk's obligations (i.e., not to respond to scolding with scolding, etc.); accepts the blame for others' harm, neither fighting with others nor holding grudges; regards abuse and unpleasant words as helpful; and withstands all suffering, even in face of death.

(7) fearless (*mi 'jigs*): is never apprehensive, is able to speak without hesitation and to teach with eloquence without ever forgetting the point, and is unafraid of what is intimidating.

(8) eloquent (*tshig gi bya ba ldan pa*): speaks with words that become well-known, are pleasant and sweet, clear and comprehensible, meaningful, without contradictions, self-reliant, and incontrovertible.

From Asanga's *Proclaimers' Stages* (*Śrāvakabhūmi; Nyan thos kyi sa*) (henceforth cited as PS) (Toh. 4036), ff. 52a7-53b7. For an interpretation of these qualities according to the Universal Way, see H. Guenther's translation of *JOL* (*The Jewel Ornament of Liberation* [Berkeley: Shambhala, 1971]), p. 34 and p. 37, notes 14 and 15.

20. Maitreya's *Scripture Ornament/ Ornament of the Scriptures of the Universal Way* (*Mahāyānasūtrālaṃkārakārikā; Theg pa chen po'i mdo sde'i rgyan zhes bya ba'i tshig le'ur byas pa*) (Toh. 4020), f. 16b6. Kongtrul paraphrases the words of the *Scripture Ornament*, elaborating slightly.

21. For an elaboration of these qualities, see Vasubandhu's *Explanation of the Scripture Ornament* (henceforth cited as ESO) (*Sūtrālaṃkāravyākhyā; mDo sde rgyan gyi bshad pa*) (Toh. 4026), f. 181b3-6, which elucidates the *Scripture Ornament's* section on teaching; and Sthiramati's extensive *Commentary on the Scripture Ornament* (henceforth cited as CSO) (*Sūtrālaṃkāravṛttibhāṣya; mDo sde rgyan gyi 'grel bshad*) (Toh. 4034), vol. Mi, ff. 226b-227b. A brief summary of their treatment of the four qualities follows:

(1) For a qualified teacher to be very learned (*mang du thos pa*) means that having heard the doctrine from the buddhas, bodhisattvas, or spiritual guides, he or she becomes the receptacle who holds the vast range (*rgya che ba*) of the entire Buddhist teachings and is therefore a great teacher able to illuminate every aspect of the doctrine.

(2) Having gained not an inferior or mediocre but a higher wisdom, the qualified teacher has cut through uncertainty as to the general and specific characteristics of phenomena and is therefore able to dispel others' doubts (*the tshom spong ba*).

(3) The qualified teacher performs the deeds of a saintly person, follows an ethical code, avoids unvirtuous actions, and is therefore worthy of respect and his or her words worthy to be heard (*gzung bar 'os pa*). A teacher is an authentic spiritual guide if he or she is able to uplift to the path of virtue persons who engage in evil deeds such as killing, by explaining to them the doctrine.

(4) The qualified teacher points out the two natures (*de nyid gnyis*), that of the thoroughly polluted (*kun nas nyon mongs pa*) and of the fully pure (*rnam par byang ba*). Thoroughly polluted is any phenomenon pertaining to the first two truths of suffering and the cause of suffering. Fully pure refers to any phenomenon

pertaining to the last two truths of cessation and the path. According to a different explanation, the first nature refers to the conventional reality and the second to ultimate reality.

22. *GBL*, f. 14a5.

23. This section is compiled from Gampopa's *JOL*, chapter three, ff. 18b3-19a5.

24. Shakyaprabha's *Three Hundred Stanzas on the Novitiate* (*Āryamūlasarvāstivādi-śrāmanerakārikā; gSum brgya pa/ 'Phags pa gzhi thams cad yod par smra ba'i dge tshul gyi tshig le'ur byas pa*) (Toh. 4124), f. 73b3-4.

25. In his own commentary on the stanza cited in the root text above, Shakhya-prabha states that a preceptor who has disrupted his ethical conduct (i.e., has incurred an infraction of one of the four root vows of a monk, etc.) is spiritually lifeless and will be detrimental to his students. A preceptor who adheres to the rules but does not know the procedures related to the monastic discipline is not qualified to instruct his fellow monks when they become afflicted by emotions. A preceptor who does not care for the sick, who lacks true benevolence toward the students, or a preceptor who does not live with monks who are observing the rules will not live peacefully; like a sandalwood tree entwined by a snake, he will be prey to great anxieties. A preceptor who has pure ethics, knows the monastic practices, is compassionate, and lives among pure monks is like a lotus in a vast lake. By living next to him, his students will increase their virtuous qualities. On the contrary, if the preceptor does not fulfill the requirements, his students, like seeds planted in salty soil, will be ruined. (*Luminous Commentary on the Three Hundred Stanzas on the Novitiate* [henceforth cited as *CTHSN*] [*Mūlasarvāstivādiśrāmanerakārikāvṛttiprabhāvati; 'Phags pa gzhi thams cad yod par smra ba'i dge tshul gyi tshig le'ur byas pa'i 'grel pa 'od ldan*] [Toh. 4125], ff. 155b6-156a4.)

26. Tsonapa states that respectability (*btsun pa*) refers to the quality of a fully ordained monk who has not been stained by a defeating offense and who shuns deeds that are unwholesome by nature. (*Sunlight Illuminating the Root Summary of Discipline* ['*Dul ba mdo rtsa'i rnam bshad nyi ma'i 'od zer legs bshad lung gi rgya mtsho*] [henceforth cited as *SIRD*], f. 66a7).

27. The twenty-one groups with five characteristics each are as follows:

> A monk of ten years' standing (*lo bcu*), knowledgeable (*'dzin*), learned and erudite (*mkhas*),
> Logical (*rig*), illuminating (*gsal*), capable of making others understand (*'dzin 'jug*),
> Trained (*slob*), inspiring others to train (*slob 'jug*), [skilled in] two aspects (*rnam gnyis*),
> Perfect in two ways (*phun sum tshogs pa gnyis*), [skilled in] three aspects (*rnam pa gsum*),
> [Embodying the qualities of] the stages of training (*slob*), and the stage of no more learning (*mi slob*), knowledgeable of the event (*byung shes*) [that led to the establishment of a particular rule],
> Self-reliant as a tutor (*gnas 'cha'*), self-reliant in entrusting his monks to other tutors (*'char 'jug*), and knowledgeable of the transgressions (*ltung shes*).

To explain:

(1) a monk of ten years' standing (*lo bcu*) or more, capable of assisting the sick or arranging assistance, skilled in dispelling remorse and changing the views of unvirtuous monks, and able to eliminate any dissatisfaction on the part of his students with their living quarters or to arrange for this to be done;

(2) knowledgeable (*'dzin*), never forgetting the scriptures on discipline, the discourses, or the scriptures on phenomenology; being learned in that he knows many treatises, and ethical in that his morality never becomes corrupted;

(3) learned and erudite (*mkhas*), the ability to discriminate among the various interrelated points of the scriptures on discipline, the discourses, and the scriptures on phenomenology, and learned and ethical in this aspect;

(4) logical (*rig*) regarding the scriptures on discipline, the discourses, and the scriptures on phenomenology (through reasoning derived from direct perception, inference, and scriptural authority), and learned and ethical in this aspect;

(5) illuminating (*gsal*), able to convey understanding of the scriptures on discipline, the discourses, and the scriptures on phenomenology (through reasoning and scriptural authority), and learned and ethical in this aspect;

(6) capable of making others understand (*'dzin 'jug*) the scriptures on discipline, the discourses, and the scriptures on phenomenology (by virtue of possessing true knowledge of them), and learned and ethical in this aspect;

(7) trained (*slob*) in ethics, meditation, and wisdom superior to those of other religious systems, and learned and ethical in this aspect;

(8) capable of inspiring (*slob 'jug*) others to train in ethics, meditation, and wisdom, and learned and ethical in this aspect;

(9) skilled in the two aspects (*rnam gnyis*) of being trained in the superior conduct (as taught in the discipline scriptures) governing walking, sitting, reclining, and standing; and trained in the four scriptures on discipline, and the personal liberation discourse (which forms the basis of training), and learned and ethical in this aspect (the first aspect);

(10) and capable of inspiring others to train in superior conduct, discipline, and personal liberation, and learned and ethical in this aspect (the second aspect);

(11) perfect in two ways (*phun sum tshogs pa gnyis*): perfect in the three types of faith, in ethics (of shunning naturally unwholesome deeds and those forbidden by Buddha's prescription), learning, generosity, and wisdom (discerning general and particular characteristics of phenomena) (the first way);

(12) and perfect in ethics (by virtue of knowledge of the discipline), single-pointed concentration, wisdom, liberation, and the vision that

knows liberation (the second way);

(13) skilled in three aspects (*rnam pa gsum*): mindful (*dran pa dang ldan pa*) (of physical sensations, mental events, etc.), and learned, ethical, enthusiastic, and wise in this aspect (the first aspect);

(14) having inner composure (*nang du yang dag par bzhag pa*) (not being physically over-active or mentally distracted), and learned, ethical, enthusiastic, and wise in this aspect (the second aspect);

(15) and contemplative (*mnyam par bzhag pa*) (free of torpor and excitement), and learned, ethical, enthusiastic, and wise in this aspect (the third aspect);

(16) embodying the qualities of ethics, concentration, wisdom, liberation, and the vision of the pristine awareness of liberation found on the uncontaminated stages of training (*slob*);

(17) embodying the qualities of ethics, concentration, wisdom, liberation, and the vision of the pristine awareness of liberation found on the uncontaminated stage of no more learning (*mi slob*);

(18) knowledgeable of the event (*byung shes*), the causal emotion, and the reason for the establishment of each rule, the prescription, subsequent amendments, dispensations, and strict prohibitions;

(19) self-reliant (*gnas 'cha'*) in deciding the tutorship and activities of his monks by virtue of his being knowledgeable with respect to what constitutes an obstacle (actions such as killing) and what does not constitute an obstacle to becoming a saint; being a skillful teacher able to explain and make others understand these two; acting in accordance with his teaching so that his morality inspires others to shun unwholesome deeds and engage in wholesome ones; and able to entrust his tutored monks to other qualified teachers if he relocates permanently;

(20) in addition to the first four aspects of point 19, self-reliant in entrusting his monks to other tutors (*'char 'jug*) when staying temporarily in another place or even staying in the same place but undergoing some disciplinary measures;

(21) knowledgeable of what does and what does not constitute a transgression to the rules (*ltung shes*) by virtue of understanding all aspects of the monastic discipline, able to discriminate between minor and serious transgressions, and proficient in reciting the large personal liberation discourse.

(Pema Karpo's *Extensive Commentary on the Three Vows* [henceforth cited as *TV*] [*sDom gsum rgya cher 'grel pa*], vol. Nga, ff. 19b-23b6, in the *Collected Works of Pema Karpo* [*rGyal dbang 'brug pa kun mkhyen pad ma dkar po'i gsung 'bum*]; and Tsonapa's *SIRD*, ff. 66a2-82b6.)

28. Shakhyaprabha states that the ceremonial master must share with the candidate the same view (*lta ba mthun pa*) on discipline. For example, both must regard a particular transgression to the rules (such as drinking alcohol) to be a transgression, i.e., both must view that which interferes with the monastic training

as detrimental to spiritual growth. Conversely, if, for example, the aspirant believes that killing a fetus is not a basis for incurring a downfall, his view is discordant (*lta ba tha dad*) with that of the ceremonial master. (*CTHSN*, f. 155b3).

29. The three collections or divisions of the Buddhist scriptures (*tripiṭaka, sde snod gsum*) (lit. "three baskets"): the scriptures on discipline (*vinayapiṭaka, 'dul ba'i sde snod*), the discourses (*sūtrapiṭaka, mdo sde'i sde snod*), and the scriptures on phenomenology (*abhidharmapiṭaka, mngon pa'i sde snod*).

30. Maitreya's *Scripture Ornament*, f. 25b2-3.

31. Ashvaghosha, *Fifty Verses on Devotion to the Master* (*Gurupañcāśikā; Bla ma lgna bu pa*) (Toh. 3721), f. 10a6-7.

32. See the *Commentary on the Fifty Verses on Devotion to the Master* (*Gurvārādhana-pañjikā; Bla ma'i bsnyen bkur gyi dka' 'grel*) (Toh. 3722) (author unknown) (henceforth cited as *CFVD*), ff. 19b7-20a1.

33. Charismatic activities (*karma, phrin las*): actions based on pristine awareness performed to enhance one's own or others' spiritual scope. Although such activities may be unrestricted in number and mode, they are conventionally classified as four types: appeasing (*śantika, zhi ba'i las*), enriching (*pauṣṭika, rgyas pa'i las*), domineering (*vaśika, dbang gi las*), and destroying (*ābhicārika, drag po'i las*).

34. See *CFVD*, f. 20a1. See also Kongtrul's *Infinite Ocean of Knowledge* (*Shes bya mtha' yas pa'i rgya mtsho*) (Beijing: Bod mi rigs dpe bskrun khang, 1982) (henceforth cited as *IOK*), vol. II, pp. 707-708.

35. Kongtrul enumerates the six parameters (*ṣatkoṭi, mtha' drug*) used for expounding and understanding the tantras as follows: the definitive meaning (*nitārtha, nges don*), the hinted or provisional meaning (*neyārtha, drang ba'i don*), the interpretable or twilight language (*saṃdhabhāṣā, dgongs pa can*), the non-interpretable or non-twilight language (*nāsaṃdhabhāṣā, dgongs pa can ma yin pa*), the literal or standard terminology (*yathāruta, sgra ji bzhin pa*), and the non-literal or coined terminology (*nāyathāruta, sgra ji bzhin pa ma yin pa*) (*IOK*, vol. II, pp. 719-720). See also A. Wayman's *The Buddhist Tantras: Light on Indo-Tibetan Esotericism* (New York, 1973; rpt. Delhi: Motilal Banarsidass, 1990), pp. 128-133.

36. *CFVD*, f. 20a2-3, states that "common treatises" refers to twelve kinds of treatises on the following twelve subjects: social customs (*chos*), logic (*rtog ge*), meanings (*don*), grammar (*sgra*), dance (*gar*), dietetics (*ro bcud*), evaluation of the qualities of things (*yongs su brtag pa*), love-making (*'dod pa*), medicine (*gso ba*), astrology (*rtsis*), arts (*bzo ba*), and consciousness (*rnam par shes pa*).

37. *Maṇḍala* (*dkyil 'khor*, lit. "circle around a center") refers here to the drawing made with powdered colors to symbolize the circle comprising the deity, his or her manifestations, and the divine palace, their residence.

The term mandala has, however, various meanings. Abhayakaragupta cites the *Hevajra Tantra's* statement "Mandala means seizing the essence" to define mandala in the following way: it denotes the gathering of the deities who are the nature of compassion and wisdom, as well as the divine mansion that is their support. The essence referred to in "seizing the essence" or "holding the essence" is the great bliss which is the inseparability of emptiness and compassion.

Mandala are of three kinds: the mandala of the awakening mind (in its two-fold aspect of relative awakening mind or the seminal essence which is the basis for the secret initiation, and ultimate awakening mind, the basis for the fourth initiation), of the *bhaga* (or "lotus" of the consort, the basis for the pristine awareness through wisdom initiation), and of the body (this last is not an actual mandala).

The progenitor of all mandala is the inseparability of emptiness and pristine awareness, free of all mental fabrications. This mandala embodies all forms of deities who are of the nature of bodhichitta, indivisible emptiness and compassion. Externally, this is represented by a mandala of powdered colors or a painted textile, also called a mandala. (*Cluster of Secret Instructions* [*Saṃpuṭa-tantrarājaṭikāmnāyamañjari; Man ngag snye ma/ dPal yang dag par sbyor ba'i rgyud kyi rgyal po'i rgya cher 'grel pa man ngag gi snye ma*] [Toh. 1198], ff. 82b4-83b6.)

The physical body is called a mandala as it is the place where bodhichitta (indivisibility of emptiness and compassion) is seized. In the body, bodhichitta is in the form of the letter *HAM* at the crown of the head, the basis of great bliss, the essence. That essence, which is indivisibility of emptiness and compassion, is the unsurpassable mandala (f. 212a5-7).

See Kongtrul's detailed discussion and classifications of mandala in *IOK*, vol. II, pp. 660-666; and Pema Karpo's *Three Vows* (*TV*), vol. Ca, ff. 102b6-7a3.

38. According to the *CFVD*, f. 20b2-5, the drawing of the mandala (*dkyil 'khor 'bri ba*) involves several activities: purifying the outer and inner ground and taking possession of it; striking interferences with the three-blade dagger in order to eliminate them; sealing the cardinal and intermediate directions; preparing the deities; applying lines of measure and colored sands; completing the ritual of the vase and actualizing the mandala. Proper performance of familiarization (*bsnyen pa*) means to have practiced the deity yoga and related rites.

39. Initiation (*abhiṣeka, dbang bskur ba*). According to Kongtrul, *abhiṣeka* is derived from *seka* meaning to scatter or sprinkle (*gtor ba*). Just as an environment is cleansed by sprinkling water, the pure nature of the mind will emerge when the mind's impediments or impurities (*sgrib pa*) are "cleansed by sprinkling," i.e., eliminated. Another term for initiation, *abhiṣikta*, is derived from *ṣikta* meaning to pour. The initiation is like pouring the potential for pristine awareness into the clean vessel of a pure mind. Fusing these two etymologies, initiation comes to have the meaning of "purification through pouring and sprinkling," i.e., by pouring and sprinkling pristine awareness onto a candidate purified through the common (bodhisattva's) commitment, a pure seed is planted in the fundamental consciousness (*kun gzhi*), etc., and the candidate is thereby made fit.

According to another etymology, *abhiṣeka* means to authorize. Just as a king is authorized to assume his throne through a ceremony of investiture, the candidate through the four initiations—vase, secret, pristine awareness through wisdom, and word initiation—is authorized to practice, respectively, the phase of generation (*bskyed pa'i rim pa*); the *caṇḍāli* (*gtum mo*) or inner heat; the circle of the *maṇḍala* (*dkyil 'khor gi 'khor lo*), i.e., the action seal (*karmamudrā, las rgya*) and, as an auxiliary, the imaginary seal or pristine awareness seal (*jñānamudrā, ye rgya*); and the great seal (*mahāmudrā, phyag rgya chen po*). He or she is further authorized to hear and teach the tantras and engage in activities to accomplish the common and uncommon attainments.

Initiations from a temporal perspective are three: the initiation of the causal preparation (*smin byed rgyu'i dbang*) of the candidate; the initiation of the experiential path (*nyams su len pa lam gyi dbang*), including the self-initiation and principally the experiential cultivation of the subject matter of the initiation until the final result is reached; and the initiation of the result (*'bras bu'i dbang*), i.e., the supreme initiation called the great light (*'od zer chen po'i dbang*) which must precede the attainment of enlightenment (*IOK*, vol. II, Book VI, chapter IV pp. 656-660).

For an example of the initiation procedure, see Tenzin Gyatso, the Fourteenth Dalai Lama, *The Kalachakra Tantra, Rite of Initiation for the Stage of Generation*, edited and translated by Jeffrey Hopkins (London: Wisdom Publications, 1985) (hereafter cited as *KT*).

40. *Tantra of Consecration* (*Supratiṣṭhatantrasaṃgraha; Rab gnas kyi rgyud*) (Toh. 486). Citation not found.

41. According to the *CFVD*, f. 20a, mandala (*dkyil 'khor*) are of three kinds: the body, speech, and mind mandala. Contemplation (*ting nge 'dzin*) is divided into the initial training, the triumphant mandala, and the triumphant ritual act. The seal (*phyag rgya*) is divided into two, the hand seal (gesture) and inner (i.e., mental) seal. The stance (*stangs stabs*) is of many types, such as the "network of bees" (*bung ba'i dra ba*), one of the two stances of a single foot (*rkang gcig gi rkang stabs*). See Kuladatta's *Compendium of Activities* (*Kriyāsaṃgraha; Bya ba bsdus pa*) (Toh. 2531), f. 288b7.

Mantra (*sngags*) is of three types: secret, awareness, and recollection. [Seated] posture (*'dug stangs*) refers to the lotus, vajra, wrathful, and bodhisattva positions. Recitation (*bzlas brjod*) comprises the wrathful muttering, vajra muttering, muttering connected with emanations, and muttering connected with blocking energies. Fire offering (*sbyin sreg*) refers to the four types in connection with the appeasing, enriching, domineering, and destructive activities. Worship (*mchod pa*) and food offerings (*gtor ma*) refer to outer, inner, and secret offerings. Dissolution (*slar bsdu*) refers to the ritual of requesting the departure of the pristine awareness mandala and the dissolution of the visualized mandala.

42. Dombipa, *Ten Essential Points* (*Daśatattva; De kho na nyid bcu pa*) (Toh. 1229), f. 37a3.

43. The ten, according to Dombipa, are as follows:

> (1) The wheel of protection (*srung ba*) refers to meditation on the ten-spoked wheel upon which reside ten wrathful deities.
>
> (2) The initiation (*dbang bskur*) refers to the conferral of the four initiations: the vase, secret, pristine awareness through wisdom, and fourth initiations.
>
> (3) Foods offerings (*gtor ma*) refers to offerings to the worldly protectors.

(4) Recitation (*bzlas*) refers to recitation of mantras and the related visualization of the purification of beings.

(5) The rite of separation (*dgar ba*) refers to the fierce act of annihilating evil beings who perpetuate unwholesome deeds.

(6) The first reversal (*bsgom pa'i phyir bzlog pa*) of expelling through meditation refers to dispatching interfering forces through visualization and mantra.

(7) The second reversal (*bris pa'i phyir bzlog pa*) of expelling through drawings refers to the preparation of a drawing of a wheel of wrathful spokes with mantras to be worn around the neck.

(8) Actualization of the mandala (*dkyil 'khor sgrub pa*) refers to the merging of the actual mandala with the mandala of colored sands.

(9) The threatening rite (*bsdigs sbyor*) refers to the fierce ritual (associated with Buddha Akshobhya) of striking the dagger when the attainments from one's own practice are delayed in order to threaten the buddhas or deities and get their attention forcefully.

(10) Requesting the departure (*gshegs su gsol ba*) refers to the meditation in which the pristine awareness mandala returns to the buddha fields, after which the colored sand mandala is gathered into a container and thrown into a river that flows to the ocean.

(Dombipa's *Ten Essential Points*, ff. 37a–41a.) Dombipa gives *dgar ba* (rite of separation) as the fifth essential point and *bsdigs pa'i sbyor ba* (rite of threatening) as the ninth, while Kongtrul has *bsgom pa* (meditation) and *sdig sbyong* (purification of evil actions), respectively.

44. *Tantra in Five Hundred Thousand [Lines]* (*rGyud 'bum lnga'i dgongs pa*) refers to one of the two original (and no longer extant) tantras of Hevajra, the other being the *Tantra in One Hundred Thousand Lines* (*rGyud 'bum ba*). The *Means of Accomplishment of the Blazing Jewel* mentioned here is a sadhana of the Hevajra class of tantras.

45. Prajnendraruchi, *Means of Accomplishment of the Glorious Blazing Jewel King of Tantras* (*Ratnajvalasādhana; Rin chen 'bar ba zhes bya ba'i sgrub pa'i thabs*) (Toh. 1251), f. 214a5-6.

46. *Nucleus' Ornament/ Indestructible Nucleus' Ornament Tantra* (*Vajrahṛdayā-laṃkāratantra; rDo rje snying po rgyan gyi rgyud*) (Toh. 451), f. 58a4. The ten outer fields (first set of ten) are enumerated in this tantra as follows:

> Mandala, contemplation, seal,
> Stance, seated position, and recitation,
> Fire offering, worship, ritual,
> And dissolution.

These fields are explained in Tsongkapa's *Commentary on the Fifty Verses on Devotion to the Master: Fulfilling the Aspirations of Disciples* (*Bla ma nga bcu pa'i rnam bshad slob ma'i re ba kun skong*) (vol. Ka of the *Collected Works of Tsongkapa*, f. 8a4-8b1) as follows:

(1) Mandala refers to the form and formless mandala;

(2) Contemplation refers to the three contemplations, the initial union of the deity yoga, [the triumphant mandala, and the triumphant act];

(3) Seal refers to the various seals of the deities;

(4) Stance refers to five stances—the left leg drawn in and the right leg extended, the reverse, the shanks of the legs held straight, legs apart mimicking the wings of a bird, and the soles of the feet together. (See Anandagarbha's *Illumination of Reality* [*Sarvatathāgatatattva-saṃgrahamahāyānābhisamayanāmatantratattvāloka-karīnāmavyākyā; De bzhin gshegs pa thams cad kyi de kho na nyid bsdus pa theg pa chen po mngon par rtogs pa zhes bya ba'i rgyud kyi bshad pa de kho na nyid snang bar byed pa*] [Toh. 2510], vol. Li, f. 254b2-5);

(5) Seated position refers to the vajra posture, etc.;

(6) Recitation refers to the [meditation on the] deity in conjunction with various styles of repetition of mantra;

(7) Fire offering is of four kinds, [appeasing, etc.];

(8) Worship consists of offerings and praises to the deity;

(9) Rituals refers to protection, invitation of the deities, etc.;

(10) Dissolution refers to the concluding act of requesting the deity to depart.

47. f. 58a3-4.

48. Tsongkapa (f. 8b1-2 of his *Commentary on the Fifty Verses on Devotion to the Master*) states that the ten outer fields of expertise apply to the vajra master of the three lower tantras and the inner or secret fields are primarily characteristic of the vajra master of the Highest Yoga Tantra. He explains the inner fields in the following way (f. 7b5-8a4):

(1 and 2) The two reversals consist of the rite of turning away negative forces [a] through contemplation of the ten wrathful deities, etc., and [b] through the drawing of [protective wheels] that are then worn by the practitioner around the neck;

(3 and 4) [Knowledge of] the secret initiation and the pristine awareness through wisdom initiation implies knowledge of the vase and the word initiations;

(5) Tearing apart the union [of body and mind] means to drive away the guardians of the enemies of the doctrine and then to implement destructive rituals, [i.e., by the power of concentration in order to terminate the power of enemies];

(6) Food offerings (*bali, gtor ma*) refers to offerings to the [worldly] protectors;

(7) Vajra muttering refers to the mental and verbal vajra recitation;

(8) The ritual of accomplishing the fierce act means that if the adept has been initiated, abides in the pledges and commitments, has practiced according to the prescribed means of attainment (*sādhana*) for eighteen months or more and has had no results, he may strike the dagger to call upon the deities [to bestow attainments];

(9) The consecration refers to the blessing [of temples and so forth];

(10) Actualization of the mandala entails creation of the mandala of the deities in front, veneration, entering into the mandala, and receiving initiation and permission.

49. *Bla ma'i yon tan yong bzung gi rgyud.* Not identified.

50. *Commentary on the Buddhasamayoga (mNyam sbyor 'grel pa)*: The Dg.T. lists several commentaries to the *Buddhasamayoga Tantra (Śrī Sarvabuddhasamā-yogaḍākinījālasambara; dPal sangs rgyas thams cad dang mnyam par sbyor ba mkha' 'gro ma sgyu ma bde ba'i mchog)* (Toh. 366): two commentaries by Pramuditavajra (Toh. 1659, 1660), one by Anandagarbha (Toh. 1662), one by Indrabhuti (Toh. 1661), and one by Shantimitra (Toh. 1663), as well as other works on the sadhana. It is unclear to which text Kongtrul is referring.

51. This text (Toh. 1198) by Abhayakaragupta is also a commentary on the *Buddhasamayoga Tantra* (Toh. 366).

52. The two phases that comprise the path of the Highest Yoga Tantra (*uttaratantra, bla med rgyud*).

The phase of creation (*utpattikrama, bskyed rim*): *krama* means phase; *utpatti* denotes artifice (*bcos ma*). In this phase, meditation is based on artifice or creation by thoughts (*rtog pa*). For this reason, it is referred to as a phase of imagination (*brtags pa'i rim pa*) or yoga of artifice (*bcos ma'i rnal 'byor*). Its special feature is the imagined creation of the mandala, in which the adept assumes the form of the main deity, modelled on the outer creation of the universe and inner experiences of death, the intermediate state, and rebirth. The purpose of this phase is to purify ordinary appearances and clinging to ordinary appearances. The essence of this phase is emptiness, appearance, and bliss represented by the form of oneself as the deity.

The completion phase (*niṣpannakrama, rdzogs rim*): *niṣpanna* denotes ultimate (*yongs su grub pa*) and natural (*rnal ma*). In this phase, the adept cultivates what is already fully present and for which nothing is created anew. He or she shifts the focus of practice to the subtle level of body and mind to effect the actual experience of innate wisdom. Thus, this phase is defined as extraordinary pristine awareness that has arisen from the entering, abiding, and dissolving of mind and energy-winds into the central channel, as well as the causes and result of this awareness (Kongtrul's *IOK*, vol. III, pp. 159-160). For a modern explanation of the creation phase, see H. Guenther's *The Creative Vision* (Novato, CA: Lotsawa Publications, 1987).

53. Mahayoga, Anuyoga, Atiyoga: the three sets of inner tantra in the Ancient Tradition (*rNying ma*), the outer being Action, Conduct, and Yoga tantras.

For a discussion of the characteristics of the outer and inner tantras, and in particular the relation between the three inner tantras, the phase of creation, the phase of completion, and the view, see H. Guenther's *The Creative Vision*, pp. x-xv.

54. *Vajragarbha's Commentary (rDo rje snying 'grel)* is the title used by Tibetan authors to refer to the *Commentary That Epitomizes the Hevajra [Tantra] (Hevajra-piṇḍārthaṭīkā; Kye'i rdo rje bsdus pa'i don gyi rgya cher 'grel ba)* (Toh. 1180) and is so called as it was composed by Vajragarbha (rDo rje snying po). It is part of the

Trilogy of Commentaries by Bodhisattvas (*Byang chub sems 'grel skor gsum*), the other two being the *Stainless Light Commentary on the Kalachakra* by Pundarika and the *Commentary That Epitomizes the Condensed Tantra of Chakrasamvara* by Vajrapani, referred to by Tibetan authors as *Vajrapani's Eulogy-Commentary* (*Phyag rdor bstod 'grel*) (Toh. 1402).

The passage cited here does not appear in that commentary. However, it appears in Pundarika's *Stainless Light* (*Vimalaprabhā*) (Toh. 1347), vol. Da, f. 91a4-5.

55. This verse is cited in Pundarika's *Stainless Light* (Toh. 1347), vol. Da, f. 91a3-4. The *Wheel of Time Fundamental Tantra* is not extant; however, fragments are found in the *Wheel of Time Condensed Tantra* (Toh. 362); Sekoddeśa's *Summary of the [Kalachakra] Initiation* (*dBang mdor bstan pa*) (Toh. 361); Pundarika's *Stainless Light*; and Naropa's *Commentary on the Summary of the Kalachakra Initiation* (Toh. 1351).

56. The state of union (*yuganaddha, zung 'jug*): From a general tantric perspective, the state of union refers to the indivisible merging of innate great bliss (the means) and clear light (emptiness). In particular, it is the indivisible merging of the relative and ultimate truths: the relative truth of the stage called "self-blessing" in which the adept's body appears as the illusory body of the deity and the ultimate truth which is the mind entering the state of reality through the experience of clear light.

In the context of the Kalachakra Tantra, at the level of experiential cultivation, the state of union results from the branch of contemplation (*ting nge 'dzin gyi yan lag*, one of the six yogas of the Kalachakra tantra phase of completion). The union consists in the blending of the known and the knower. The known is the perceived mind, the supreme emptiness endowed with all aspects. The knower is the perceiving mind, the pristine awareness of immutable great bliss. This union is also referred to as the inseparable union of emptiness and compassion; the union of clear light and illusory body in this system refers exclusively to this.

This union is also the nature of the ground of being and the nature of the pristine awareness resultant at enlightenment.

In this discussion, great compassion, clear light, and changeless bliss have the same meaning. They constitute the means aspect and are generally regarded as relative truth. Emptiness, illusory body, and the dimension of emptiness possessing all aspects have the same meaning. They constitute the wisdom aspect and are generally regarded as ultimate truth (Kongtrul's *IOK* vol. III, Book VIII, chapter IV, pp. 219-220).

Mahāmudrā (*phyag rgya chen po*) or great seal: In the tantras, "great seal" generally denotes the final result of the tantrika's endeavor. In consideration of its ever-present nature throughout the ground, path, and result, mahamudra is also explained in terms of the path that leads to such a result, as well as the ground of being or natural condition of the individual and everything that exists. In this context, it is equivalent in meaning to the state of union just explained.

For a discussion of mahamudra as a system of meditation that combines the sutra and tantra perspectives, see Pema Karpo's explanation of four phases of mahamudra meditation as presented in *Meditation Differently*, trans. H. Guenther (Delhi: Motilal Banarsidass, 1992).

57. Toh. 362, f. 113a1-2.

58. Pundarika states that the face of the Buddha symbolizes pristine awareness (*ye shes*). The presence of pristine awareness in the mind of the magnificent master means that he or she has gained a personal experience of it (*rang gis nyams su myong ba*). For pristine awareness to be present in the speech means that at all times, he or she is able to communicate it to others (*Stainless Light Commentary on the Kalacakra Tantra*, Toh. 845, f. 388a6-7). On this last point, see Naropa, *Iniziazone di Kalacakra*, edited and translated by Raniero Gnoli and Giacomella Orofino (Milan: Adelphi Edizioni, 1994), pp. 248-250. See also Naropa's *Commentary on the Summary of the [Kalachakra] Initiation (Paramārthasaṃgrahanāmasekoddeśaṭīkā; dBang mdor bstan pa'i 'grel bshad don dam pa bsdus pa zhes bya ba)* (Toh. 1351), ff. 258a1-7.

59. *Commentary by the Bodhisattva (Byang chub sems dpa'i 'grel pa): The Stainless Light/Great Commentary on the Kalachakra (Vimalaprabhā; Dri ma med pa'i 'od/Dus 'khor 'grel chen)* by Pundarika (Toh. 845 or Toh. 1347). Part of the *Trilogy of Commentaries by Bodhisattvas* (see note 54).

60. State of contemplation (*ting nge 'dzin gyi yan lag*) here refers to the last of the six branches of yoga (*sbyor ba yan lag drug*) of the Kalachakra Tantra.

61. Sakya Pandita's *Analysis of the Three Vows (sDom pa gsum gyi rab tu dbye ba'i bstan bcos)* in the *Collected Works of Sakya Kunga Gyaltsen (Sa pan kun dga' rgyal mtshan gyi gsung 'bum)*, vol. III, p. 88a1-2, published by Bod ljongs bdo yig dpe rnying dpe skrun khang, China, 1992.

62. Toh. 362, f. 58a4-5. Commenting on these lines, Pundarika states: "The master may be proud for various reasons such as his erudition, wealth, or power; his proficiency in the ten fields of expertise; his attainments on the spiritual path or his appearance. He may feel proud when meeting lowly people, or be overly self-effacing when in contact with superior people. A student who has gained a good knowledge of the path should shun a proud teacher who lacks compassion.

"'Defiant of pledges' means that the teacher makes a public display of certain secret pledges that worldly persons would view as distasteful. 'Guilty of misappropriation' refers to a teacher who uses for himself the properties of monastic communities or spiritual masters or the articles intended for worship. 'Ignorant of the doctrine' refers to a teacher who has not received instructions on the true doctrine. Likewise, a master who 'willfully deceives authentic disciples,' i.e., lies to them, should be shunned. An 'uninitiated' master who has 'failed to enter the state of supreme bliss' is one who teaches a tantra without having received the initiation. 'Slave to wealth and enjoyment' means one who is always craving mundane possessions. 'Careless' is one who does not set himself in meditation but is distracted by drinking alcohol, etc. 'Obsessed with sexual desire' is one who is desirous of the pleasure of sexual union. To forsake such teachers is the rule of the Transcendent One" (*Stainless Light*, Toh. 1347, vol. Da, f. 90a7-b5).

63. Pundarika's *Ultimate Familiarization (Paramārthasevā; Don dam pa'i bsnyen pa)* (Toh. 1348), f. 4b2-3.

64. f. 73b3.

65. The four conditions that lead to transgression of the rules: unawareness (*ma rig pa*), unconscientiousness (*bag med pa*), disrespect for the rules (*ma gus pa*), and overwhelming emotions (*nyon mongs mang po*).

66. The four means of attracting disciples (*catuḥsaṃgrahavastu, bsdu dngos bzhi*): generosity (*dāna, sbyin pa*), pleasant speech (*priyavacana, snyan par smra ba*), purposeful activity (*arthacaryā, don spyod pa*), and consistency between words and deeds (*samānavihārā, don mthun pa*).

67. The six perfections (*sadparamita, pha rol tu phyin pa drug*): generosity (*dāna, sbyin pa*), ethics (*śīla, tshul khrims*), patience (*kṣānti, bzod pa*), diligence (*vīrya, brtson 'grus*), meditation (*dhyāna, bsam gtan*), wisdom (*prajñā, shes rab*).

68. *Ten Qualities Scripture* (*Daśadharmakasūtra; Chos bcu pa zhes bya ba'i mdo*) (Toh. 53), f. 167b7.

69. Aryadeva's *Experientialist Four Hundred* (*Catuḥśatakaśāstrakārikānāma; bsTan bcos bzhi brgya pa zhes bya ba'i tshig le'ur byas pa*) (Toh. 3846), f. 13a5.

70. Chandrakirti defines impartiality (*gzu bor gnas pa*) as not being attached to oneself or what is within one's own sphere of activity, and not turning one's back on others or what belongs to others' sphere of activity. Partiality would make the mind polluted with emotions and unfit for the bodhisattva's training. (*Commentary on the Experientialist Four Hundred* [*Bodhisattvayogācāracatuḥśatakaṭīkā; Byang chub sems dpa'i rnal 'byor spyod pa bzhi brgya pa'i rgya cher 'grel pa*] [Toh. 3865], f. 183b.)

71. *Magical Net Tantra*, also called *Secret Nucleus/ Secret Nucleus of the Magical Net* (*Guhyagarbhamayajalatantra; gSang ba snying po de kho na nyid nges pa/ dPal gsang ba snying po sgyu 'phrul drva ba*) (Toh. 834), f. 206a.1-2.

72. *Samvara Tantra* (*Mahāsaṃvarodayatantrarāja; sDom 'byung/ bDe mchog 'byung ba zhes bya ba'i rgyud kyi rgyal po chen po*) (Toh. 373), f. 286b7-287a1.

73. Nagarjuna's *Five Stages* (*Pañcakrama; Rim pa lnga pa*) (Toh. 1802), f. 48a1-2.

74. Nagabodhi describes as arrogant the follower of the tantras who does not attend public teachings due to pride, but reads the tantric scriptures in his home and then thinks, "I know all about the tantras" (*Jewelled Garland*, a commentary on Nagarjuna's *Five Stages* [*Rim pa lnga pa'i bshad pa nor bu'i phreng ba*], Toh. 1840, f. 83a7-b1). On this point, see also Krishnasamayavajra's *Revealing the Difficult Points of the Five Stages* (*Pañcakramapañjikā; Rim pa lnga'i dka' 'grel*) (Toh. 1841), f. 176a2-3.

75. Interpretation of this last point differs among commentators on Nagarjuna's *Five Stages*. Nagabodhi's *Jewelled Garland* (f. 83b2) states that the disciple who has received only lower initiations (*dbang bskur dman pa*) is one who has not been properly initiated (*dbang bskur yang dag ma thob pa*). Lakshminkara's *Elucidation of the Five Stages* (*Pañcakramavṛttārthavirocana; Rim pa lnga'i don gsal bar byed pa*) (Toh. 1842), f. 183b6, explains that not having been properly initiated means that the aspirant has received only the vase initiation, but not the higher—the secret, pristine-awareness-through-wisdom, and word initiations.

On this point, Krishnasamayavajra (*Revealing the Difficult Points of the Five Stages*, f. 176a4) states that having received lower initiation means not to have been initiated at all.

76. *Secret Tantra of the General Ritual of All Mandalas* (*Sarvamaṇḍalasāmānya-vidhīnāmaguhyatantra; dKyil 'khor thams cad kyi spyi'i cho ga gsang ba'i rgyud*) (Toh. 806), f. 145a7-145b2.

77. f. 10a5-6.

78. *Essence of the Great Seal* (*Mahāmudrātilakanāmamahāyoginītantrarājādhipati; Phyag rgya chen po'i thig le zhes bya ba rnal 'byor ma chen mo'i rgyud kyi rgyal po'i mnga' bdag*) (Toh. 420), f. 66b6-7.

79. *bDe ldan bu mo*, a maiden who possesses happiness, i.e., a consort.

80. *Condensed Transcendent Wisdom Scripture*, in *Collected Scriptures and Dharani*, vol. sMad cha, f. 20b3-4.

81. Maitreya's *Scripture Ornament*, f. 25b4.

82. The first line is found in vol. A, f. 283b4-5; second line, not found; third and fourth lines, f. 286b1-2.

83. Literally, "pure conduct" (*brahmacarya, tshangs spyod*): in this case, referring to the path of liberation. See *Nagarjuna's Letter*, trans. Geshe Lobsang Tharchin and Artemus B. Engle, Dharamsala: Library of Tibetan Works and Archives, 1979, pp. 94, 95.

84. Nagarjuna's *Letter to a Friend* (*Suhṛllekha; bShes pa'i spring yig*) (Toh. 4182), f. 43b3-4.

85. These phrases as cited by Kongtrul are excerpts from a longer passage and are not found consecutively or in the same order in their original source. See Toh. 44, vol. A, ff. 284b3-286b1.

86. The citation is found in Longchenpa's *Treasury of Wish-fulfilling Jewels* (*Theg pa chen po'i man ngag gi bstan bcos yid bzhin rin po che'i mdzod*) published by Yeshé De project, Odiyana, USA 1991.

87. *Vajrapani Initiation Tantra* (*Vajrapāṇybhiṣekatantra; Lag na rdo rje dbang bskur ba'i rgyud chen po*) (Toh. 496), f. 141b3-4.

88. *Guhyasamaja Tantra* (*Sarvatathāgatakāyavākcittarahasyaguhyasamāja-nāmamahākālparāja; De bzhin gshegs pa thams cad kyi sku gsung thugs kyi gsang chen gsang ba 'dus pa zhes bya ba brtag pa'i rgyal po chen po*) (Toh. 442), f. 143a7-b1.

89. f. 284b5.

90. Vasubandhu's *Treasury of Phenomenology* (*Abhidharmakoṣakārikā; Chos mngon pa'i mdzod kyi tshig le'ur byas pa*) (Toh. 4089), f. 15b1-2.

91. Scriptures on discipline (*vinayagama, 'dul ba'i lung*) refers to these four *vinaya* scriptures: *Basic Scripture* (*Vinayavastu; 'Dul ba gzhi*) (Toh. 1); *Analysis of [Discipline]*

Scripture (Vinayavibhaṅga; 'Dul ba rnam par 'byed pa) (Toh. 3); *Scripture on the Subtle Matters of Discipline (Vinayakṣudrakavastu; 'Dul ba phran tshegs kyi gzhi)* (Toh. 6); and *Sublime Scripture on Discipline (Vinaya-uttaragrantha; 'Dul ba'i gzhung bla ma)* (Toh. 7).

92. *Great Mindfulness Scripture (Saddharmasmṛtyupasthāna; Dam pa'i chos dran pa nye bar gshag pa)* (Toh. 287), f. 241b7.

93. In the *Collected Scriptures and Dharani* edition, vol. sMad cha, f. 12a4-6.

94. The four kinds of demonic forces (*catvārimāra, bdud bzhi*): the demonic force of the aggregates (*skandhamāra, phung po'i bdud*), of the emotions (*kleśamāra, nyon mongs pa'i bdud*), of the "lord of death" (*mṛtyupatimāra, 'chi bdag gi bdud*), and of the "child of the gods" (pride) (*devaputramāra, lha'i bu'i bdud*). These four, however classified or differentiated, comprise all possibilities of interference on the path of one's spiritual growth.

In *Questions of Sagaramati Scripture (Sāgaramatiparipṛcchasūtra; Blo gros rgya mtshos zhus pa'i mdo)* (Toh. 152) (ff. 31-33), the Buddha gives a lengthy explanation of how these demonic forces may be conquered:

> The demon of the aggregates is conquered by understanding the illusory nature of phenomena, by comprehending the truth of suffering and the nature of suffering of all composite phenomena, by dedicating to the attainment of omniscience the merits accrued by practicing generosity untainted by emotion, and by maintaining ethics detached from the desire for worldly forms of life.
>
> The demon of the emotions is conquered by understanding emptiness, by forsaking the source of suffering, by comprehending the transient nature of all composite phenomena, by dedicating to omniscience the merits accrued from generosity that is not bound by attachment to one's body, and by maintaining ethics permeated by the understanding of selflessness.
>
> The demon of the lord of death is conquered by understanding non-birth and non-arising, by actualizing the truth of cessation, by understanding that all phenomena are selfless, by dedicating to omniscience the merit accrued from generosity imbued by the knowledge that wealth and possessions are impermanent, and by maintaining ethics able to free oneself from old age and death.
>
> The demon of the child of the gods is conquered by eliminating all reifications constructed by pride, by meditation on the path, by understanding that nirvana is peace, by dedicating to omniscience the merit of generosity performed with great compassion in order to set others in the state of freedom from suffering, and by maintaining ethics for the sake of turning those who violate ethics to higher forms of morality.

95. *Precious Palm Scripture (Ratnolkānāmadhāraṇisūtra; dKon mchog ta la la'i gzungs zhes bya ba'i mdo)* (Toh. 145), ff. 63b7-64a1.

96. f. 107a4-5.

97. See note 6.

98. f. 63b6.

99. *Bodhisattva Section Scripture* (*Bodhisattvapiṭakanāmasūtra; Byang chub sems dpa'i sde snod ces bya ba'i mdo*) (Toh. 56). Citation not found.

100. This section is compiled from *JOL*, ff. 12b4-14b4.

101. These sections (with some variations that include additions, elaborations on certain points, and abbreviated sections) are compiled from Butön's *History of Buddhism* (*Bu ston chos 'byung*) (Beijing: Bod kyi shes rig dpe skrun khang, 1988).

102. *White Lotus of the True Doctrine* (*Saddharmpuṇḍarikasūtra; Dam pa'i chos pad ma dkar po*) (Toh. 113). The first five lines (with three lines of the original scripture omitted) are found on f. 86a4-6. The words of Kongtrul and those of the original are slightly different. Kongtrul may have simply summarized the explanation of the scripture on this point in his own verses. The remaining three lines of this citation are not found in the scripture, but summarize the meaning of the subsequent verses of the *White Lotus*.

103. f. 111b4-5.

104. This charm is found on f. 111b1-3 of the *Questions of Sagaramati Scripture*. The Tibetan translation is found on p. 42 of the Beijing edition of Butön's *History of Buddhism* (*Bu ston chos 'byung*); the English translation appears in *The Jewelry of Scripture of Bu-ston* (translated by Eugene Obermiller; 1931; rpt. Delhi: Sri Satguru, 1987), p. 75, line 15.

105. A full prostration touching the head, arms, and legs to the ground.

106. Aryashura, *Garland of Former Lives of the Buddha* (*Jātakamālā; sKyes pa'i rabs kyi rgyud*) (Toh. 4150), ff. 125a1-3.

107. *Scripture Revealing the Inconceivable Secrets of the Transcendent One* (*Tathāgatā-cintyaguhyanirdeśa; De bzhin gshegs pa'i gsang ba bsam gyi mi khyab pa bstan pa*) (Toh. 47), ff. 119a7-120b1.

108. Maitreya's *Scripture Ornament*, f. 17a2-4.

109. According to Vasubandhu, the Buddha's teaching is pure in these three ways: in terms of voice and language; the manner of teaching; and the students to whom it is taught—those who require only a brief synopsis and those who need a detailed explanation (*ESO*, ff. 183b-184a).

110. Vasubandhu states that weariness (*skyo ba*) means that the manner of teaching lacks enthusiasm after being presented repeatedly. Incomplete, i.e., not exhaustive (*ser sna*, lit. "miserly") means that the full range of meaning is not revealed (*ESO*, f. 184a4-5).

111. Vasubandhu's *Principles of Elucidation* (*Vyākhyāyukti; rNam par bshad pa'i rigs pa*) (Toh. 4061), f. 63b5-6. Vasubandhu himself cites this line from the scriptures on discipline.

112. The twenty qualities that counteract the eleven faults of speech:

> (1) discerning the proper occasion (*dus*), i.e., comprehending whether the student is interested and whether he or she is worthy of being taught. This counteracts the fault of teaching those who are not receptive (*snod ma yin pa la brjod pa'i skyon*) in that they attend the teaching but show improper behavior.
>
> (2) teaching accurately (*bsgrim pa*) and without carelessness. This counteracts the fault of giving incomplete explanations (*brjod pa yongs su ma rdzogs pa'i skyon*).

The following three elements counteract the fault of interrupted sequence (*brjod pa bar chad pa'i skyon*):

> (3) following a systematic order (*go rim*) beginning with the subjects that should be taught first, such as generosity, etc.; otherwise, with the ultimate and sublime topics;
>
> (4) setting the context (*mtshams sbyar*) in consideration of the scripture that is to be explained;
>
> (5) responding to questions in accordance (*rjes su mthun pa*) [with the inclinations of listeners] by making categorical statements.

The following three elements counteract the fault of not making the explanation intelligible (*brjod pa go bar mi byed pa'i skyon*):

> (6) making the teaching pleasing (*dga' bar bya ba*) to those who have faith;
>
> (7) arousing the interest (*'dod par bya ba*) of newcomers who have reservations about following the doctrine;
>
> (8) giving satisfaction (*spro bar bskyed*) to listeners who are still uncertain about entering the doctrine.

The following two elements counteract the fault of causing others to disrespect [the doctrine] (*brjod pa mchod par mi 'gyur ba'i skyon*):

> (9) not gratifying (*spro ba mi bskyed pa*) [those who lead an immoral life];
>
> (10) not abusing the listeners (*mi smad pa*) who may become discouraged.
>
> (11) being logical (*rig pa*), i.e., not contradicting valid cognition. This counteracts the fault of giving an incorrect meaning (*don 'thad pa med par brjod pa'i skyon*).
>
> (12) following a sequence (*'brel ba*) by connecting previous topics to later ones counteracts the fault of teaching deep subjects to those of inferior intelligence (*spyod yul ma yin pa brjod pa'i skyon*).
>
> (13) keeping the discourse unmixed with other subjects (*ma 'dres pa*), i.e., keeping to the theme, counteracts the fault of teaching with a distracted mind (*rnam par g.yengs nas brjod pa'i skyon*).
>
> (14) teaching what is wholesome (*chos dang ldan pa*), i.e., concordant with what is virtuous and suited to the audience. This counteracts the fault of teaching meaningless subjects (*don med pa dang ldan pa brjod pa'i skyon*).
>
> (15) being in harmony with the circle of one's students (*'khor ji lta ba bzhin*).

This counteracts the fault of giving unsuitable teaching (*mi 'tsham par brjod pa'i skyon*).

The following elements counteract the fault of teaching out of self-interest or tainted motivation (*nyon mongs pa can gyi bsams pas brjod pa'i skyon*):

(16) benevolent love (*byams pa'i sems*) that wishes the welfare of listeners;

(17) altruism (*phan pa'i sems*), i.e., wishing students to overcome their emotions;

(18) compassion (*snying brtse ba'i sems*) that wishes all others (whether they are virtuous, vicious, or neutral) to be free from suffering;

(19) free of interest in gain, honor, or praise (*rnyed pa dang bkur sti dang tshigs su bcad pa la mi brten pa*);

(20) neither praising oneself nor denigrating others (*bdag la bstod par mi bya zhing gzhan la smad par mi bya ba*) out of jealousy or in order to be regarded as worthy of respect.

(Vasubandhu's *Principles of Elucidation*, ff. 63a-64a). See also Butön's *History of Buddhism* (*Bu ston chos 'byung*), pp. 36-37.

113. Maitreya's *Scripture Ornament*, f. 17b3.

114. Vasubandhu's *ESO* (f. 186) explains that this citation enumerates five conditions that result in the teacher "shining like the sun": a good intellect (*blo bzang*) so that what one teaches is incontrovertible; indefatigability (*skyo ba med ldan*) in teaching repeatedly; concern for others (*brtse ba can*) free from desire for material things; pleasant delivery (*snyan par rab grags*) of useful words; and knowledge of the proper teaching methods (*cho ga bzang shes ldan pa*), teaching in accordance with [the different capacities of] students.

115. The six elements of teaching (*rnam par bshad pa'i sgo drug*):

(1) the subject to be known (*parijñeyavastu, yongs su shes par bya ba'i dngos po*), for example, the aggregates (*skandha, phung po*), the experiential elements (*dhātu, khams*), or the experiential media (*āyatana, skye mched*);

(2) its import (*parijñeyārtha, yongs su shes par bya ba'i don*), consisting in the transient (*anitya, mi rtag pa*), suffering (*duḥkha, sdug bsngal ba*), and selfless (*anātma, bdag med*) nature of the subject (aggregates), and so forth;

(3) the approach to knowledge (*parijñopaniṣad, yongs su shes par bya ba'i rgyu*), consisting, for example, in ethics (*śīla, tshul khrims*) and watching the mind at the door of the senses (*dbang po'i sgo bdams pa*), etc.;

(4) the nature of knowledge (*parijñasvabhāva, yongs su shes pa*) of the thirty-seven factors conducive to enlightenment (*byang chub kyi chos*), the four introspections (*dran pa nye bar bzhag pa bzhi*), etc.;

(5) the result of finalized knowledge (*parijñāphala, yongs su shes pa'i 'bras bu*), i.e., the state of liberation or enlightenment;

(6) its experience (*tatpravedanā, de rab tu shes pa*), i.e., the wisdom attained at liberation.

These six are listed in Asanga's *Synthesis of Phenomenology* (*Abhidharma-samuccaya; mNgon pa kun las btus pa*) (Toh. 4049), f. 117b5-6. For further details, see Jinaputra's discussion in his *Explanation of the Synthesis of Phenomenology* (*Abhidharmasamuccayabhāṣya; Chos mngon pa kun las btus pa'i bshad pa*) (Toh. 4053), f. 105a5-7. See also *Le Compendium de la Super-Doctrine (Philosophie)* (*Abhidharma-samuccaya*) *d'Asanga*, trans. Walpola Rahula (Paris: Publications de l'École Française d'Extrême-Orient, 1980), pp. 178-179; and the Beijing edition of Butön's *History of Buddhism* (*Bu ston chos 'byung*), p. 39.

116. Reading fourteen (*bcu bzhi*) in place of twelve (*bcu gnyis*). Fourteen elements (*mukha, sgo*) used in teaching:

(1) Grouping the themes (*vyākhyāsaṃgrahamukha, rnam par bshad pa bsdus ba'i sgo*): stating the reason a particular discourse was delivered by the Buddha (*mdo sde 'byung ba'i dgos pa*), the meaning of its words (*tshig gi don*), the connections or context (*mtshams sbyar*), intention of the scripture (*dgongs pa*), the incongruencies (*brgal*), and the response to the incongruencies (*lan brjod pa*).

(2) Focusing on the themes (*vastusaṃgrahamukha, dngos po bsdus pa'i sgo*) encapsulated in the sayings (*gāthā*) of the Buddha. For example, one cites, "Do not commit evil, practice virtue, and discipline the mind: this is the Buddha's doctrine," and then comments on these lines in terms of the three trainings.

(3) Presenting both major headings and minor details (*aṅgopāṅgamukha, yan lag dang nye ba'i yan lag gi sgo*): mentioning first the general terms and then explaining the details. For example, when discussing the leisures and endowments of the precious human life, one begins by stating, "Five conditions depend on oneself, and five conditions depend on others," and then successively explains each of the two sets of conditions with five sentences each (see note 1).

(4) Following a sequence from the lower to the higher (*uttarottara-nirhāramukha, gong nas gong du mngon par bsgrub pa'i sgo*): providing orderly explanations from the simpler to the complex or lower to higher; as in the case of the aggregates, explaining first the body, then feeling, etc., or as another example, stating, "Through enthusiastic effort, close application of mindfulness develops; through mindfulness, the mind enters the state of equipoise; and thereby the ultimate is realized just as it is."

(5) Using the method of exclusion (*pratikṣepamukha, spong ba'i sgo*): exclusion of the opposite of the topic in question. The doctrine itself, as method, is to be discarded once the shore of perfect peace has been reached; even more so, what does not conform to the doctrine should be rejected.

(6) Transforming the meaning of words (*akṣarapariṇāmamukha, yi ge yongs su bsgyur ba'i sgo*): changing the usual connotation of words by using them as technical terms of the doctrine.

(7) Describing the corrupted and the uncorrupted and the conditions that lead to each (*nāśānāśamukha, chud za ba dang chud mi za ba'i sgo*): for example, the scriptures say that "corrupted" refers to attachment to outer things (house, spouse, etc.) and inner things (the five aggregates). Uncorrupted means freedom from excessive attachment to these. To remain unrenunciate serves as a cause for the corruption of attachment. To become a renunciate and to work to end one's impediments, etc., leads to the uncorrupted state of detachment.

(8) Defining types of persons (*pudgalavyavasthānamukha, gang zag rnam par gzhag pa'i sgo*) for whom a certain discourse is intentionally taught. Individuals are of two types, ordinary and exalted (the latter have perceived the truth; the former have not). To the first type belong individuals who are negative, slightly positive, and exceedingly positive. Among exalted individuals belong persons who abide in one of the four results (of stream-enterer, once-returner, non-returner, and saint), the first three of whom are trainees, and the last one having reached the path of no more learning.

(9) Defining the divisions (*prabhedavyavasthānamukha, rab tu dbye ba rnam par gzhag pa'i sgo*): through analyses based on quadruple formulas, such as existence, non-existence, both existence and non-existence, and neither existence nor non-existence.

(10) Using methods (*nayamukha, tshul gyi sgo*): this consists of six methods: pointing out the very nature of phenomena, experience, discourses' explanations, excluding the two extremes of existence and non-existence, the inconceivable perfection of a Buddha, and consideration of the six elements (i.e., the subject matter to be known, its import, the approach to knowledge, etc.).

(11) Teaching finalized knowledge (*parijñādimukha, yongs su shes pa la sogs pa'i sgo*): pointing out the manner of engaging in each of the four exalted truths. The truth of suffering is to be understood; the truth of the source of suffering is to be abandoned; the truth of cessation is to be attained; and the truth of the path is to be practiced.

(12) Pointing out the force and weakness of terms (*balābalamukha, stobs dang stobs ma yin pa'i sgo*): for example, in teaching the twelve links of interdependent arising, evaluating each link, noting that if one is omitted, the sense is no longer comprehensible.

(13) Reiterating (*pratyāhāramukha, bzlas te brjod pa'i sgo*): using repetition of and elaboration on one particular word or sentence.

(14) Verifying (*abhinirhāramukha, mngon par bsgrub pa'i sgo*): through analyses, using the quadruple (*mu bzhi*) formula with respect to each term used in the discourse.

(Asanga's *Synthesis of Phenomenology* [Toh. 4049], ff. 117b6-118a1; and Jinaputra's *Explanation of the Synthesis of Phenomenology* [Toh. 4053], ff. 105a6-109a3.)

See Walpola Rahula's translation of *Synthesis of Phenomenology* (pp. 179-180) and Obermiller's translation of *The Jewelry of Scripture of Bu-ston* (p. 70).

117. Chim Namka Drak (mChims nam mkha' grags): A Tibetan scholar who lived at the beginning of the twelfth century and was an important link in the transmission of the *Treasury of Phenomenology*. Author of the *Ornament of Phenomenology: Commentary on the Treasury of Phenomenology* (*mNgon pa mdzod kyi 'grel bshad mngon pa'i rgyan*).

118. Reading *dpyod* for *spyod*.

119. Reading *bstan* for *brtan*. Shudapanthaka (Śūdapanthaka, Lam phran bstan): one of the sixteen saints (arhats), the direct disciples of the Buddha. Born into the brahmin caste, he was a man of very dull intellect. Although he had been taught the *vedas*, he could not understand them. Later in his life, Mahapanthaka (Lam chen bstan) (another of the sixteen saints), ordained him as a Buddhist monk and tried, to no avail, to teach him four verses of the doctrine. Finally, in despair, he led him out of the monks' quarters and left him on a small road (*lam phran*). One day Shudapanthaka met the Buddha, who instructed him to clean the monks' temple, and while doing so, to repeat the words "sweeping away the dust; sweeping away stains" (*rdul spang dri ma spang*). Through the Buddha's miraculous powers, as he swept, the dirt immediately returned just as before. After some time had passed in unsuccessful efforts to clean the temple, Shudapanthaka suddenly understood the meaning of the words that the Buddha taught him. Holding the broom, he declared to his fellow monks that sweeping away dust meant cleaning not the dust of the earth, but the impurities caused by one's emotions—desire, hatred, and ignorance. He came to understand the nature of things as they are, eliminated his obscurations, and became a saint.

Later, the Buddha sent Shudapanthaka to give a lecture in a nunnery. The nuns were offended, thinking that the Buddha had sent them a stupid monk. Enraged, they erected a high teaching throne for him that lacked a staircase by which to mount it. Shudapanthaka mounted the throne miraculously and delivered a talk of unprecedented significance. He was then declared by the Buddha to be the best of his saintly disciples. Legend says that he dwells invisibly at Vulture's Peak (Bihar) surrounded by sixteen hundred saints.

120. Sakya Pandita's *Excellent Sayings* (*Legs par bshad pa rin po che'i gter zhes bya ba'i bstan bcos*) vol. I, p. 216, lines 12-13 in the *Collected Works of Sakya Kunga Gyaltsen* (Beijing: Bod ljongs bdo yig dpe rnying dpe bskrun khang, 1992).

121. Vasubandhu's *Principles of Elucidation*, f. 65b4.

122. Skepticism (*ma dad pa*): this is explained as an emotionally based, overly critical scrutiny of the teaching and the teacher. These points are discussed by the third Kamtrul (*Khams sprul Nga dbang kun dga' bstan 'dzin*) (1680-1728) in *Foundations of Mahamudra Precepts* (*Phyag rgya chen po lhan cig skyes sbyor gyi sngon 'gro'i khrid yig*), vol. I, f. 22b3 (printed at the Hansa Plate Process, Daryaganj, New Delhi).

123. A sense of heaviness, sleepiness, or inertia affecting the student when listening to the teaching.

124. Vasubandhu's *Principles of Elucidation* (f. 64a6-b2) lists thirteen faults of listening:

> (1) Disturbing the speaker who is intent [on teaching] by showing inappropriate behavior (*spyod lam gyi skyon*);
> (2) Listening with pride (*'gying ba'i skyon*) due one's own high caste, etc.;
> (3) Having no real interest (*don du mi gnyer ba'i skyon*) in listening;
> (4) Feeling aversion due to disagreeing in opinion (*gzhan gyi phyogs byed pa'i skyon*);
> (5) Having no consideration (*mchod par mi 'gyur ba'i skyon*) for the teacher;
> (6) Listening with the intention to challenge and disprove (*sun phyin pa'i skyon*) the speaker;
> (7) Lacking respect (*rim gro mi byed pa'i skyon*) for the value of the doctrine and the teaching of it;
> (8) Having contempt (*brnyas pa'i skyon*) for the doctrine, considering it to be irrelevant, or having disdain for the teacher, finding faults with his ethical code, caste, appearance, words, or the way he expounds the doctrine;
> (9) Disparaging the teacher with abusive words (*smod pa'i skyon*);
> (10) Being motivated by desire for gain and honor (*rnyed pa dang bkur sti 'dod pa'i skyon*);
> (11) Not listening (*mi nyan pa'i skyon*) attentively due to distraction, and being plunged into mental dullness;
> (12) Lacking the right apprehension (*legs par yid la mi byed pa'i skyon*), i.e., misunderstanding the intention of the discourse itself;
> (13) Lacking full discernment (*rab tu yid la mi byed pa'i skyon*) due to feeble motivation [to understand], and making little effort.

See also *Butön's History* (*Bu ston chos 'byung*), pp. 40-41.

125. The *Principles of Elucidation* (ff. 64b6-65a3) lists the six defects in listening:

> (1) The defect concerning one's actions (*las kyi skyon*) refers to the fault of physical action, i.e., improper behavior; the fault of not exerting body and speech in the study of the doctrine; and the fault of disposition, i.e., disinterest.
> (2) Lack of interest and (3) irreverence [are both self-explanatory].
> (4) The defect of inappropriate intention (*bsam pa'i skyon*) refers to the wish to incite arguments (*gzhan la klan ka btsal ba*) or trying to escape challenges.
> (5) The defect of incompatibility (*mi mthun pa'i skyon*) has five aspects: (a) lack of respect due to thinking that the doctrine does not bring about liberation; (b) being critical due to thinking that the words of the doctrine are irrelevant; (c) disrespect due to thinking of the shortcomings of the teacher's discipline, words, or delivery; (d) being scornful due to thinking of the humbleness of the caste of the

teacher; (e) self-deprecation due to thinking that one does not have the capacity to understand and accomplish the aim of the teaching. (6) The defect of apprehension (*'dzin pa'i skyon*) has five aspects: (a) misunderstanding (*log par 'dzin pa*), (b) failing to clearly apprehend the meaning (*don mi 'dzin pa*), (c) misinterpreting the words (*tshig 'bru mi 'dzin pa*), (d) not understanding the explanation (*brda sprod pa mi 'dzin pa*) (i.e., not apprehending the essential meaning, not understanding the intended meaning, and not understanding the literal meaning), and (e) not apprehending the entirety (*ma lus mi 'dzin pa*) of the contents.

See also the Beijing edition Butön's *History of Buddhism* (*Bu ston chos 'byung*), p. 41.

126. Reading *nyan pa* for *mnyan pa*.

127. From the *Prayer of Maitreya* (*Āryamaitrīpraṇidhānarāja, 'Phags pa byams pa'i smon lam gyi rgyal po*). See the *Collected Scriptures and Dhāraṇi*, vol. sTod cha, f. 337b2.

128. *bSod nams 'di yis thams cad gzigs pa nyid / thob nas nyes pa'i dgra rnams pham byas te / rga nad 'chi ba'i rlabs chen 'khrugs pa yi / srid pa'i mtsho las 'gro ba 'don par bgyi.*

129. GBL, f. 201a6.

130. A symbolic offering of the universe modelled on ancient Indian cosmology.

131. *Collected Works of Sönam Tsemo*, vol. II (Nga), f. 270a6.

132. Vasubandhu's *Principles of Elucidation*, f. 116b4-5.

133. The twenty benefits of teaching the Buddhist doctrine without expectation of material goods or honor as reward (*zang zing med pa'i chos kyi sbyin pa rnyed pa dang bkur sti mi 'dod par chos kyi sbyin pa gang yin pa de'i phan yon nyi shu*) taught in the *Inspiring Universal Responsibility Scripture* (*Adhyāśayasañcodana; Lhag pa'i bsam pa bskul ba'i mdo*) (Toh. 69), f. 131b1-5, are as follows:

> One becomes mindful (*dran pa dang ldan par 'gyur ba*), intelligent (*blo gros dang ldan par 'gyur ba*), wise (*blo dang ldan par 'gyur ba*), steadfast (*brtan pa dang ldan par 'gyur ba*); one becomes possessed of wisdom (*shes rab dang ldan par 'gyur ba*), and realizes supramundane wisdom (*'jig rten las 'das pa'i shes rab rjes su rtogs par 'gyur ba*); attachment decreases (*'dod chags chung bar 'gyur ba*), hatred weakens (*zhe sdang chung bar 'gyur ba*), ignorance diminishes (*gti mug chung bar 'gyur ba*), demonic forces find no opportunity to disturb one (*bdud kyis de la glags mi rnyed par 'gyur ba*); the buddhas take care of one (*sangs rgyas bcom ldan 'das kyis dgongs par 'gyur pa*), non-humans protect one (*mi ma yin pa rnams de la srung bar 'gyur ba*), deities increase one's radiance (*lha rnams de la gzi byin skyed par 'gyur ba*), malignant creatures do not have a chance to cause one harm (*mi mdza' ba rnams kyis de la glags rnyed par mi 'gyur ba*), close friends do not desert one (*de'i mdza' bshes rnams mi phyed par 'gyur ba*), one's words are trusted (*tshig btsun par 'gyur ba*), one becomes fearless (*des mi 'jigs pa 'thob par 'gyur ba*), one experiences mental happiness (*yid bde ba mang bar 'gyur ba*), one

becomes worthy of being praised by the wise (*mkhas pas bsngags par 'gyur ba*), one's teaching will be worthy of recollection (*de'i chos kyi sbyin pa de yang rjes su dran par bya bar 'os par 'gyur ba*).

134. *Scripture Revealing the Inconceivable Secrets of the Transcendent One*, ff. 130b7-131a1.

135. Maitreya's *Scripture Ornament*, f. 16b4-5.

136. Sthiramati's extensive *CSO*, vol. Mi, f. 225a6, states that meditation here refers to the practice of mental quiescence (*zhi gnas*) and insight (*lhag mthong*) after having listened to and pondered the doctrine, which leads to the attainment of the dimension of reality (*dharmakāya*).

Chapter II: The Vows of Personal Liberation

1. *Indestructible Peak Tantra* (*Vajraśekharamahāguhyayogatantra; gSang ba rnal 'byor chen po'i rgyud rdo rje rtse mo*) (Toh. 480), f. 199b4-5.

2. Ibid, f. 200a7.

3. Cleansing (*khrus*), i.e., purification: This is the first of four purifications mentioned in the *Indestructible Peak Tantra* (f. 200a). The other three are purification by confession, expressed in the form of a supplication, etc.; purification by binding, which seals one's body, speech, and mind to those of the deity; and purification by water.

According to Buddhaguhya, purification or cleansing is of four types: by the three vows, by confession and supplication, by "the releasing of the symbolic gesture" (*phyag rgya dgrol ba*), and by water. To perform the releasing of the symbolic gesture (*mudrā, phyag rgya*), one first imagines the five fingers of the right hand as the five buddhas and the five fingers of the left as the five consorts, unites the hands with the middle fingers extended and touching each other at their tips, and then releases the gesture by separating the hands. This gesture of release symbolizes the purification of unwholesome actions. (*Guide to the Purport of the Tantra* [*Tantrārthāvatāra; rGyud kyi don la 'jug pa*] [Toh. 2501], ff. 36b3-37a2.)

4. Tsonapa distinguishes three forms of ethics according to their motives: ethics based on anxiety (*'jigs skyob gyi tshul khrims*) for which the preservation of morality is motivated by fear of lacking means of livelihood, having a bad reputation, not being praised, etc., or fear of punishment or being born into lower forms of life; ethics based on the wish to excel (*legs su smon pa'i tshul khrims*) for which the safeguarding of morality is based on attachment to wealth and honor; and ethics based on an intention to emerge from cyclic existence (*nges 'byung gi tshul khrims*) for which the safeguarding of morality is to attain liberation from cyclic existence based on a correct view of the law of causality. (*Sunlight Illuminating the Root Summary of Discipline* [*'Dul ba mdo rtsa'i rnam bshad nyi ma'i 'od zer legs bshad lung gi rgya mtsho*] [henceforth cited as *SIRD*], f. 15b4-6).

5. Karma Trinlepa's *Chariot of Karma*. According to Tenga Rinpoché, an extensive

presentation of the three ways—the Individual, Universal, and Secret Mantra ways. Text not located. See also note 277.

6. Three unwholesome deeds of body and four of speech: murder, theft, and sexual misconduct; falsehood, slander, harsh words, and idle gossip.

7. The five meanings of basis (*gzhi*) are cause or motive (*rgyu*), condition (*rkyen*), close place (*nyer gnas*), preliminary (*sngon 'gro*), and place (*gnas*). (Sönam Tsemo's *Presentation of the Sets of Tantras* [*rGyud sde spyi'i rnam par gzhag pa*] [woodblock print, Gangtok, Sikkim, Ngor Monastery], f. 11a1.)

8. Envy, malice, and wayward views.

9. See the section below entitled "Distinctions of Personal Liberation Vows according to the Person."

10. The seven mentioned in note 6, plus envy, malice, and wayward views.

11. Tsonapa explains that the principal unwholesome deeds prohibited by the vows are the seven naturally unwholesome (*rang bzhin gyi kha na ma tho ba*) deeds of body and speech, while drinking alcohol and so forth are the related deeds unwholesome by Buddha's prescription (*'khor bcas pa'i kha na ma tho ba*) (SIRD, ff. 18b7-19a3).

12. Purnavardana, *Commentary on the Treasury of Phenomenology* (*Abhidharma-koṣaṭīkālakṣanānusāriṇī; Chos mngon pa'i mdzod kyi 'grel bshad mtshan nyid kyi rjes su 'brang ba*) (Toh. 4093), vol. Chu, f. 26a5. Pema Karpo points out that the discipline of personal liberation comprises vows that serve to control unvirtuous behavior of body and speech, but includes no vows concerning mental action. Consequently, moral transgressions related to personal liberation vows pertain only to physical and verbal acts. (*Extensive Commentary on the Three Vows* [*sDom gsum rgya cher 'grel pa/ sDom pa gsum gyi rgyan ces bya ba'i rgya cher 'grel ba*], vols. Nga and Ca of the *Collected Works of Pema Karpo* [Thimphu, Bhutan: Acharya Shedup Tenzin and Lama Dhondup Tharchen, 1991] [henceforth cited as *TV*], vol. Nga, f. 5a6-b3.)

13. Analysts (*vaibhāṣika, bye brag smra ba*): followers of one of the four trends of Buddhist philosophical thought (*siddhānta, grub mtha'*), the others being the Traditionalists (*sautrāntika, mdo sde pa*), Idealists (*cittamātrin, sems tsam pa*), and Centrists (*mādhyamika, dbu ma pa*).

Analysts derive their name and also their tenets from the *Great Detailed Exposition* (*Mahāvibhāṣā*), a compendium of the class of phenomenology (*abhidharma, mngon pa*). They could also be called "Atomists," since one of their major beliefs is in the existence of partless and indivisible atoms, as well as partless and indivisible moments of consciousness. For the Analysts, these phenomena, being partless and indivisible (therefore subject to neither material destruction nor division through analysis), are held to be ultimate truths, as opposed to anything that is an aggregation of particles or moments, which they consider to be conventional truths. Both truths, conventional and ultimate, are real for the Analysts, who therefore, in terms of Buddhist philosophy, stand as "Realists" (*bhāvavādin, dngos por smra ba*). Theirs is a philosophy expounded mainly by adherents of the Individual Way and no doubt characterized the tenets of the original schools of Buddhism in India.

Traditionalists are so called because their assertions are based mainly on the scriptures that record the word of the Buddha. Though Traditionalists are Realists, the Traditionalist followers of reason differentiate themselves from Analysts by negating the substantial status of conceptually imputed phenomena and by propounding a finer concept of conventional and ultimate truth. For them, a phenomenon able to produce an effect (*arthakriya, don byed nus pa*) is ultimate truth, and one not able to do so is a conventional truth. Traditionalists were followers of the Individual Way, but their tenets may have been the spark that originated the finer thought of the Universal Way.

Idealists, whose system was pioneered by Asanga, are so called because they assert that all phenomena are of the nature of the mind that perceives them. For this reason, they are also called "Proponents of the Aspect of Consciousness" (*vijñānavādin, rnam rig smra ba*). The lack of substantial duality between observer and observed is for them the subtle selflessness of phenomena, the ultimate truth. This view provided the support for the experientialist approach to meditation; for this reason, they are also called "Experientialists" (*yogācārin, rnal 'byor spyod pa*). This approach, however, led them to overemphasize perception or mind and to attribute to the mind a true or ultimate status. A branch of the Idealists, which follows the scriptures, also subscribes to the belief in a fundamental consciousness (*ālayavijñāna, kun gzhi rnam shes*) as the storehouse of cumulative imprints of actions and as the person itself. Idealists are followers of the Universal Way, and their tenets, along with those of the Centrists, are said to have formed the conceptual frame of reference for the tantric systems.

Centrists, whose system was pioneered by Nagarjuna, are so called because they follow the "center" (*madhya, dbu*) or "middle way" which does not fall into the two extremes of negating conventional reality and asserting the true existence of phenomena. They advocate the complementarity of the two truths, the conventional as the dependent arising of phenomena and the ultimate as the emptiness of true status of everything that exists. Centrists are subdivided into "Dogmaticists" (*svātantrika, rang rgyud pa*) and "Consequentialists" (*prasaṅgika, thal 'gyur pa*), the former advocated by Bhavaviveka and the latter by Chandrakirti, Shantideva, etc. Their main difference lies in their analyses of whether or not a phenomenon has an "essence." The former asserts that it does, but does not say what it is exactly. The latter asserts that when a phenomenon is analyzed, nothing is found that can be said to constitute the phenomena itself. Consequentialists assert that everything is just a name, a mere imputation of the mind, and nothing ever has any true existence, even conventionally. The tenets of Centrists represent the prominent part of the Universal Way philosophy, as well as the view based on which tantric practice is performed. (From the verbal teachings of Geshé Rabten. For a comprehensive discussion of these philosophies, see Hopkins's *Meditation on Emptiness* [London: Wisdom, 1983], henceforth cited as *ME*.)

A distinction exists between the view of Centrist proponents of intrinsic emptiness (*rang stong pa*) and that of Centrist proponents of extrinsic emptiness (*gzhan stong pa*). This distinction, found only within the Tibetan traditions, is one that Kongtrul expressly adheres to in his writings. The former view asserts that all things are empty of their own essence (*rang stong*); such emptiness, a mere negation (*med dgag*), is the ultimate truth. The latter asserts that the ultimate nature is naturally perfect, devoid of any stain, and therefore not empty of its own nature. Phenomena are considered deceptions that manifest adventitiously as the fabrication of duality. They do not exist in reality; therefore, the relative is empty of its nature. Phenomena are extraneous to ultimate reality, and therefore the ultimate is empty of extraneous natures (*gzhan stong*). The masters of the Jonangpa school were the main apologists of the second view. See Dharmashri's *Commentary on the Three Vows* (*sDom 'grel/ sDom pa gsum rnam par nges pa'i 'grel pa legs bshad ngo mtshar dpag bsam gyi snye ma*) (Chorten Monastery edition, Deorali, Gangtok, Sikkim, published by Dodrup Chen Rinpoché) f. 185a5.

14. Perceptible form (*rnam par rig byed kyi gzugs*) refers to form that arises as the object of sense perception. Imperceptible form (*rnam par rig byed ma yin pa'i gzugs*) refers to form for the mental consciousness only, not perceived by others.

15. Acquisition (*prāpti, thob pa*): The Sarvastivadin view on the element ensuring the link between an action and its results. On this point, Analysts assert that the person who assumes vows is like an elephant, and the vows, the elephant's load. The load is tied to the elephant by the rope of the anomalous factor (*viprayuktasaṃskāra, ldan min 'du byed*) of "acquisition." When a cause for losing the vows is present, the rope of acquisition is cut, and the load of the vows falls to the ground; in other words, the person becomes vowless (Tsonapa's *SIRD*, f. 138b2).

16. See section below entitled "Vows for Life," which explains the ten essential elements for the monk's ordination (such as the ordaining preceptor and so forth).

17. Pema Karpo adds that "perceptible" refers also to physical and verbal acts done during the ceremony of ordination such as prostrations and reciting the refuge formula (*TV*, vol. Nga, f. 31a).

18. Chandrakirti (Candrakirti, Zla ba grags pa): a saint and scholar of the sixth century. Born in south India, he became an elucidator of Nagarjuna's thought and an eminent teacher of the Centrist viewpoint and the Universal Way. He is renowned for his *Guide to the Middle Way* (*Madhyamakāvatarābhāṣya; dBu ma la 'jug pa*) (Toh. 3682); *Lucid Exposition: A Commentary on [Nagarjuna's Fundamental Text on] Wisdom* (*Mūlamadhyamakavṛttiprasannapadā; dBu ma rtsa ba'i 'grel pa tshig gsal*) (Toh. 3860); and *Luminous Lamp* (*Pradīpodyotana-nāma-ṭīkā; sGron ma gsal bar byed pa*) (Toh. 1785), a commentary on the *Five Stages*, a tantric work by Nagarjuna.

19. In *Analysis of the Five Aggregates* (*Pañcaskandhaprakaraṇa; Phung po lnga'i rab tu byed pa*) (Toh. 3866), f. 242b3-4, Chandrakirti states: "Imperceptible form belongs to the mental sense-field, cannot be shown, is unobstructed, and is comprehended by mental consciousness alone. Examples of imperceptible form are the [personal liberation] vows, the opposite of the vows, and that which has the nature of a virtuous or unvirtuous continuity pertaining to a class in between [i.e., neither vows nor the opposite of vows]."

20. Drigungpa ('Bri gung pa), a reference to Drigung Kyopa ('Bri gung skyob pa) (1143-1219), the foremost disciple of Pakmodrupa and founder of the Drigung Kagyu school.

21. Taktsang (sTag tshang lo tsa ba Shes rab rin chen), a scholar and translator of the Sakya school, born the year Tsongkapa composed his *Tantric Stages* (*sNgags rim chen mo*) (1405). He became a vehement critic of Tsongkapa.

22. Pema Karpo says that *mokṣa* refers to liberation, which is the transcendence of suffering, and *prāti* (individual) to the causes that lead to the transcendence of suffering, such as the vows of a monk, etc. (*TV*, vol. Nga, f. 4b2).

   Tsonapa discusses three etymological intepretations for *prātimokṣa*: (1) as "vows of individual liberation," where *prāti* is individual and *mokṣa*, liberation. They are called vows of individual liberation because they lead to liberation only the individual person who safeguards such ethics, not anyone else who is not following that system of ethics; (2) as "vows of initial liberation," where *prāti* is initial and *mokṣa*, liberation. They are called vows of initial liberation because in the first moment these vows are assumed, one is liberated from being a vowless person; (3) as "vows as means to attain liberation," where *prāti* is means in the sense of being a "condition" for liberation (*mokṣa*). *Prātimokṣa* [translated here as "personal liberation" according to the usual Tibetan rendering of the term] has undergone two distinct but not unrelated phases of evolution of meaning. Originally, the term simply indicated a confession of faith almost equivalent to *dharma* or doctrine. The principles indicated in the advice "Do not do any evil deeds, practice all kinds of virtue, and control your mind: this is the Buddha's doctrine" formed the original *prātimokṣa* or "bond" for the emergent monastic community, which initially was just another sect of religious wanderers. Later, with the need for and the gradual emergence of a monastic code of discipline, the term referred to a basic list of rules (described in the *Personal Liberation Discourse*). The list was recited at the bimonthly assembly that began as an occasion to preach the doctrine and only later became more of a confession ceremony. This likely occurred after the Buddha's demise around the time of the first Buddhist council. These two concepts of *prātimokṣa* at different phases of its evolution are closely linked since both represent principally a bond for the community. In the beginning, the bond reflected the essence of the doctrine; in the second phase, the bond was expressed more in rules, and the scope of the concept expanded to include a ritualized confession. We can therefore conclude that this term originally meant "bond that leads to freedom" (*SIRD*, vol. sTod cha, f. 12a3-6).

23. Exalted ones (*ārya, 'phags pa*): those who have perceived the truth and are thus exalted compared to other worldly beings. This includes individuals on levels of realization from the path of seeing to final enlightenment.

24. For a discussion of the latter two types of ethical conduct, see Gendun Drubpa's *Commentary on [Vasubandhu's] Treasury of Phenomenology* (*mDzod kyi thar lam gsal byed*) (Sarnath, Varanasi: Pleasure of Elegant Sayings Printing Press, 1973), pp. 215-220.

25. Actual meditative absorptions (*bsam gtan dngos bzhi*) refers to the four meditative concentrations of the form realm and the four absorptions of the formless realm. For a discussion of this subject, see Lati Rinpochay's *Meditative States in Tibetan Buddhism* (London: Wisdom Publications, 1983).

26. Pema Karpo provides an etymological definition for the Tibetan term *gelong* (*dge slong*) (monk), which translates the Sanskrit *bhikṣu*, as a virtuous person who "begs" (*slong*) for alms and seeks the "virtue" (*dge*) of perfect peace (*TV*, vol. Nga, f. 28a3-5).

27. Tsonapa defines the Sanskrit term *śrāmaṇera* as "the person whose eyes shed tears." Just as the person who sheds tears can see things close by but not in the distance, the novice is allowed to hear the discipline intended for him (close by) but not the discipline and ceremonies of the monks (distant). In the common language, the novice is known as *cilu* (servant) because he cannot handle the responsibilities of being a teacher (*SIRD*, f. 39b1-3).

28. The Tibetan term *dge bsnyen* which translates the Sanskrit *upāsaka* is etymologically explained as "being close to" (*upā, bsnyen*) "virtue" (*saka, dge ba*).

29. Gendun Drubpa, the First Dalai Lama, states that the purificatory fast vows are not differentiated in terms of male and female holders of these vows because they last just one day (*Commentary on Vasubandhu's Treasury of Phenomenology*, p. 215). See also Tsonapa's *SIRD*, f. 11b2.

30. See Gendun Drubpa's *Commentary on Vasubandhu's Treasury of Phenomenology*, p. 215.

31. A female novice must receive the postulant nun's vows and observe them for two years before she can receive full ordination as a nun.

Atisha states that eight types of personal liberation vows are spoken of in the scriptures on discipline taught by the Buddha himself, as well as in those composed by saints, such as *Entering Pristine Awareness* (*Ye shes la 'jug pa*) and the *Great Detailed Exposition* (*Bye brag tu bshad mdzod chen mo*). However, the noble Asanga, in the chapter on ethics in his *Stages of Yogic Practice* (*Yogacaryabhūmi, rNal 'byor spyod pa'i sa*), states that there are only seven types, and this cannot be doubted. The practitioner of the purificatory fast is excluded from the eight since a one-day observance of vows is not a true ascetic practice and does not involve restraint from desires for any great length of time. (*Commentary on the Lamp for the Path* [*Bodhimārgapradīpapañjikā; Byang chub lam gyi sgron ma'i dka' 'grel*] [Toh. 3948], ff. 259b3-260a3.)

32. These cases are recorded in Vishakadeva's *Garland of Flowers* (*Me tog phreng rgyud*, Toh. 4123) and Vishesamitra's *Summary of Discipline* (*'Dul ba bsdus pa*, Toh. 4105), and in the commentaries on the phenomenology (*abhidharma*) class of teachings.

33. The excellent group of five (*lnga sde bzang po*): the first five disciples of the Buddha: Ajnata Kaundinya, Vashpa, Ashvajit, Mahanama, and Bhadrika.

34. Shariputra and Maudgalyayana were the Buddha's two most outstanding

disciples. Shariputra excelled in wisdom, and Maudgalyayana, in miraculous powers. Both were teachers in their own right who used to tutor students sent to them by the Buddha.

According to Tsonapa, the Buddha conferred the status of monk by calling "Come hither, monks!" to those aspirants who were capable of attaining the path of seeing in the same life, had already attained it, or were in their last existence before becoming saints (*SIRD*, f. 29b6-7).

35. Mahakashyapa (Mahākāśyapa, 'Od srung chen po): a chief disciple of the Buddha, who became the first patriarch after the teacher passed away. To Mahakashyapa is attributed the formulation of the phenomenology (*abhidharma*) section of the Buddhist canon in its archaic form.

36. Eight severe precepts (*lci ba'i chos brgyad*): To receive ordination from monks; to await announcement of the proper date for the fortnightly confession from monks; to participate in the rainy season retreat near a place where monks are also in retreat; to attend the ceremony of lifting of restrictions (imposed during the rainy season retreat) in an assembly of both monks and nuns; to serve respectfully both monks and nuns if one has transgressed any of these eight precepts; not to reveal the corrupted morals of monks; not to reproach a monk; to behave respectfully (prostrating and so forth) toward the community of monks, including prostrating before a newly ordained monk. (Gunaprabha's *One Hundred Formal Procedures* [henceforth cited as *HFP*] [*Ekottarakarmaśataka, Las brgya rtsa gcig pa*] [Toh. 4118], f. 139a2.)

37. Mahaprajapati (Mahāprajāpati, sKye dgu'i bdag mo): the sister of the Buddha's mother, who raised him after his mother died. Upon her insistence and with the intercession of Ananda, Buddha's cousin, the Buddha consented to having nuns enter the order.

38. Roerich reconstructs the Sanskrit as *Dharmadatta:* George N. Roerich, trans., *The Blue Annals* (Calcutta, 1949; 2nd ed. Delhi: Motilal Banarsidass, 1976), p. 33.

39. Four-part formal procedure including proposal (*gsol ba dang bzhi'i las*): one request (*gsol ba*) and three repetitions of the appropriate formula (*brjod pa*).

40. Impediment of intentional action (*las kyi sgrib pa*): an impediment derived from having committed one of the five actions of immediate retribution (killing one's father, etc.). Impediment of fruition (*rnam smin gyi sgrib pa*): being born as a hell being, hungry ghost, or animal. Emotional impediment (*nyon mongs pa'i sgrib pa*): having strong negative emotions that impede the attainment of liberation in the present lifetime.

41. Three spiritual maturities (*smin pa gsum*): of intelligence (*shes rab*), which refers to the intelligence to discern the meaning of the four truths or emptiness; of continuum of mind (*rgyud*), which means having a pure stream of mind with few obscurations; and of faculties (*dbang po*), which means being a person of highest capabilities.

42. Pema Karpo explains that Buddha entrusted his monks with the responsibility of performing ordination according to the original procedure (*sngon gyi cho ga*) after a certain person who wished to enter the Buddhist order died while being led by a monk to the place where the Buddha was residing. The original ceremony did not require a preceptor or a tutor who would later instruct the new monk. This meant, however, that new monks might remain untrained and act contrary to the principles of the doctrine. As a result, this form of ordination became an object of derision by non-Buddhists. Furthermore, a certain monk who was sick and was without attendants to help him as he approached death requested help from the Buddha. Thus, at that time (six years after his attainment of enlightenment) in order that his disciples could gather followers and in order that sick monks could have [novices] as attendants to help them, the Buddha gave permission to the monastic community to perform the present-day ordination (*da lta'i cho ga*) with an abbot and a teacher among the officiating assembly (*TV*, vol. Nga, f. 6a3-b3).

The original ceremony was simple in that all it required was a group of monks, in front of whom the candidate would offer prostrations while respecting the order of seniority, then kneel and make a threefold request to be admitted into the order. Upon acceptance by the assembly (thus completing the four-part formal procedure including proposal), the aspirant would instantaneously become a monk (f. 6b2-3). The present-day ceremony is performed methodically by a group of monks, some of whom act as preceptor and teachers, unlike the original in which there was no such differentiation of position.

Tsonapa notes that sporadic use of the former ordination occurred even after the present method was introduced. For instance, on the point of passing into perfect peace, the Buddha ordained Subhadra (Rab bzang) as a monk by calling, "Come hither, monk!" (*SIRD*, f. 30a2-3).

43. Gunaprabha states that the central region or country, i.e., the Gangetic basin, is the territory bordered by the following: "To the east, the thicket of sugar cane of Sharkara (Li kha ra) outside the city of Pundravardhana (in the ancient districts of Malda and Dinajpur); to the south, the Ganges (Chu glung) at the south of Sharavati ('Dam bu can); to the west, the region known as Stuna (Ka ba) near the town of the same name; and to the north, the Ushira hill range." (*Fundamental Summary of Discipline* [*Vinayasūtra; 'Dul ba'i mdo*] [henceforth cited as *SD*] [Toh. 4117], f. 74a6.)

44. Buddha's teachings as transmission (*lung gi chos*) refers to the twelve classes of the Buddhist scriptures. Buddha's teachings as spiritual accomplishment (*rtogs pa'i chos*) refers to all that is encompassed by the truth of the path and of cessation.

45. The first three of the four continents in ancient Indian cosmology: Majestic Body (*Pūrvavideha, Lus 'phags po*), Land of Jambu (*Jambudvīpa, 'Dzam bu gling*), Bountiful Cow (*Aparagodānīya, Ba glang spyod*), and Unpleasant Sound (*Uttarakuru, sGra mi snyan*). See Kongtrul's *Myriad Worlds: Buddhist Cosmology in Abhidharma, Kalacakra and Dzog-chen*, translated and edited by the International

Translation Committee (Ithaca: Snow Lion Publications, 1995).

46. *SD*, f. 11b5.

47. The four animals are the partridge, rabbit, monkey, and elephant. It is said that in a previous life the Buddha incarnated as a partridge, and together with a rabbit, monkey, and elephant, took the vows of the purificatory fast that resulted in prosperity and harmony in the area where they lived. Thus, the four animals came to be known as the four harmonious brothers (*mthun pa spun bzhi*) and together form a symbol of harmony. They are often depicted standing one on top of the other to signify respect for elders.

48. Tsonapa divides this first obstacle to assuming the vows (*sdom pa skye ba la bar du gcod pa*) into four categories: (1) eighteen aspirants are unfit to assume the vows because of their bodies (*lus kyi rten ma yin pa*): emanations (from other worlds), ten types of neuter persons, persons who have changed gender three times, who have poisonous sex organs (in that whoever has intercourse with them dies instantly), who have no sex organ, eununchs, animals, non-humans, and inhabitants of the continent of Unpleasant Sound; (2) ten aspirants cannot assume the vows due to impediments caused by deeds (*las sgrib kyi dbang gis*) performed in this life: thieves, religious extremists, persons guilty of any of the five crimes of immediate retribution, persons who have violated a nun, who have concealed a root downfall, or who have been monks before; (3) four aspirants are unfit because of the time and situation (*gnas skabs kyi dbang gis*): aspirants below the permitted age, who still wear lay attire, who do not wear renunciate attire, or who are unwilling to forsake the causes leading to disciplinary measures; (4) five aspirants are unfit because of their disposition (*bsam pa'i dbang gis*): individuals who hold extremist religious views, who lack the natural wish to become a renunciate, or who have no freedom because they are overpowered by strong attachment, anger, or ignorance (*SIRD*, f. 83a2-b1).

49. Gunaprabha mentions that permission should be asked of parents if they live within seven days of travel from the place where the monastic ordination will be conferred. If the parents live further away, permission should be asked of the monastic community (*SD*, f. 4a4).

50. Being affected by a contagious disease such as leprosy or a serious bronchial disorder, or being subject to amnesia, etc., would burden the monastic community and impede the aspirant in making full use of the teaching for his spiritual development. These conditions do not, however, exclude him from the unordained practice of the Buddhist teaching. For a list of diseases that make a person ineligible for ordination, see Gunaprabha's *HFP*, f. 107b.

51. Refusal of admission into the order to persons with mutilation or deformation was means for the community to ensure the laity's respect for the Buddha's doctrine and to defend itself from the intrusion of persons who were seeking only food and shelter.

Certain physical traits mentioned in the scriptures that made one ineligible for monastic life were linked to social and temporal circumstances; blond hair, for example, was extremely rare at the time of the Buddha. Today, blondness would not disqualify an aspirant. For a long list of the physical traits that make a person ineligible for ordination, see Gunaprabha's *SD*, ff. 4b7-5a5.

On this point, Karma Ngedön Nyingpo states that the last two conditions (to be free of obstacles to meaningfulness and of appearance) are imposed principally to cultivate the laity's respect for the doctrine, but are not major obstacles in becoming a renunciate. (*Commentary on [Ngari Panchen's] Three Vows*. Edited by Dudjom Rinpoche, Kalimpong [henceforth cited as *CNPTV*], f. 21a1.)

52. Vasubandhu's *Treasury of Phenomenology* (*Abhidharmakośakārikā; Chos mngon pa'i mdzod kyi tshig le'ur byas pa*) (Toh. 4089), f. 12a2.

53. The Three Jewels: Buddha (the teacher), Dharma (his doctrine), and Sangha (his followers).

54. *Brahmana Vyasa Scripture* (*Brāhmaṇavyāsasūtra; gNas 'jog pa'i mdo*) (Toh. 333), f. 264a6.

55. *Analysis of Discipline Scripture* (*Vinayavibhaṅga; 'Dul rnam 'byed*) (Toh. 3), vol. Ca.

56. Anathapindika (mGon med zas sbyin), lit. "he who gives alms to the helpless": a lay devotee of the Buddha known by this name because of his generosity.

57. These precepts are normally taken before sunrise and before any food has been taken.

58. The aspirant is asked whether he is a non-Buddhist, younger than fifteen, unable to scare away a crow although he is fifteen (or able to scare away a crow although not yet seven years old), a slave, in debt, has his parents' permission, (if not,) has parents living far away, is sick, has violated a nun, is a eunuch or hermaphrodite, a ghost, an animal, adheres to non-Buddhist views, has committed crimes with immediate retribution, is mutilated, belongs to an unworthy family, has changed sex three times, is a female who resembles a man, or is from some other continent (world), and so forth (Gunaprabha's *HFP*, ff. 101a6-b5).

59. Gunaprabha states that after the inquiry, the aspirant first prostrates before a representation of the Buddha and then to the preceptor. He then kneels in front of the preceptor with folded hands and recites three times the verses of taking refuge, as well as promising to maintain the five lay precepts for life. With the acknowledgment of the preceptor and of the aspirant, he receives the precepts (*HFP*, ff. 101b4-102b1).

60. Interim renunciate (*bar ma rab byung*): the preparatory part of the novice ordination consisting of an address with request, an entreaty, and three transformations, performed when the aspirant is in the interim stage of having assumed the lay practitioner's vows, but is not yet a novice.

61. These questions (the same as those mentioned in note 58) are asked only once to a person who is assuming both the lay precepts and the novice vows in the course of one ceremony. However, in the course of the ceremony for becoming

a full-fledged monk, a new set of questions [appropriate for that ordination] is asked, once by a monk appointed to be the interviewer (*gsang ston*), once by the ceremonial master (*las kyi slob dpon*), and once by the ordaining preceptor (*mkhan po*). The interviewer does not participate in the novice ordination since this role is fulfilled by the preceptor (Gunaprabha, *HFP*, f. 106b3).

62. The aspirant kneels in front of the preceptor, and with folded hands, asks him three times to become his preceptor and tutor and to grant him admission into the order. At the end of this formal request, the preceptor verbally expresses his assent. Following this, a tuft of the aspirant's hair (that had been left un-shaven) is cut, the aspirant is made to wash, and the preceptor gives him the alms bowl and the yellow robes. Then, by taking refuge in front of the preceptor and expressing his will to become a novice, the aspirant promises to abandon the lay attributes and adopt those of a renunciate. After a further request, he is granted the vows of novice and expresses his determination to safeguard them (Gunaprabha, *HFP*, ff. 102b7-104a7).

63. This refers to determining the time of the ordination (the year, season, month, first or second part of the month, date, part of the day or night, and hour) by measuring the shadow cast by the sun upon a small, square, pyramid-like wooden device. For details, see Dharmashri's *Commentary on the Three Vows* (Chorten Monastery: Gangtok, Sikkim), ff. 37b1-38a6.

64. This refers to having broken one's vows and kept secret the violation.

65. In discussing this point, Tsonapa defines the attitude of renunciation (*nges 'byung gi bsams pa*) as the intent focused upon the state of perfect peace in which all cyclic states are transcended; the underlying motive (*rgyu'i kun slong*) as the attitude prior to assuming the vows; and the motive of the moment (*dus kyi kun slong*) as the attitude simultaneous with assuming the vows (*SIRD*, f. 15a1-b).

66. The five stipulations mentioned above.

67. Tsonapa states that the excellent conditions are the intentions to relinquish the attire of a layman (*khyim pa'i rtags spang ba nyams pa*), to adopt the attire of a renunciate (*rab tu byung ba'i rtags blang ba nyams pa*), and to put forward the request to became a renunciate to the teacher (*bla mar gsol ba gdab pa nyams pa*) (*SIRD*, f. 45b7).

68. Tsonapa's *SIRD* explains the etymology of the term "ordination of a monk" (*upasaṃpanna, bsnyen par rdzogs pa*) as follows: *rdzogs pa* denotes a state utterly free of potential for harm, that has the nature of perfect peace; *bsnyen* means "to be close to," that is, to come close, with one's whole mind, to the state of perfect peace.

69. In this context, lapse of discipline refers mainly to defeating and partially defeating offenses.

70. The questions are asked by the interviewer in private (away from the assem-bly of ordaining monks). The questioning of a novice who wishes to become a full-fledged monk includes all the questions asked of the aspirant for novice

ordination, as well as others. He is asked, for example, Are you a man? Have you the male sex organ? Are you twenty years old? Do you have the three robes and the begging bowl? Are your parents alive? Do you have your parents' permission? If your parents are dead, are you, by any chance, a slave? etc. See Gunaprabha's *HFP,* ff. 106b6-107b5.

71. Pema Karpo states that the person becoming a monk must not be under the effect of an intoxicant, in a confused state of mind, naked, etc. (*TV,* vol. Nga, f. 27b4).

72. According to Pema Karpo, to know that the preceptor is not a monk, or to intend to reject him afterwards, are thoughts incompatible with the ordination (*TV,* vol. Nga, f. 27b2).

73. Pema Karpo states that those to be shown reverence are renunciates of the same gender and senior to oneself in ordination; those to whom there is no need to show reverence are the laity, monks junior to oneself in ordination, nuns, and those monks who even though senior to oneself have been demoted or are undergoing disciplinary measures (*TV,* vol. Nga, f. 33a3-4).

74. Eleven instructions on points of discipline (*gdams ngag bcu gcig*):

(1) The instruction on right lifestyle free of the two extremes of indulgence and harsh asceticism: (a) to wear discarded rags as one's clothes (or whatever one is given, provided it is made of coarse material); (b) to live on alms (or whatever has been offered to oneself or to the monastic community as a whole); (c) to live under trees (or wherever a dwelling has been provided); and (d) to partake of the residues of broths as food (or when given by others, sugar cane, sesame oil, honey, powdered sugar, or other medicines prepared from roots, stalks, leaves, flowers, or fruits).

(2) The instruction on right morality: to eschew the four defeating offenses—sexual intercourse, theft, murder, and untruth—that are the most serious transgressions of morality for a monk.

(3) The instruction on the four duties of a monk: not to respond to being chided by chiding, to anger with anger, to being hit by striking back, or to abusive words with abusive words.

(4) The instruction on the favorable conditions for the training: to remember that the vows of a monk, the highest aspiration, have been assumed with the fulfillment of the excellent conditions of the preceptor, teachers, monks, and ceremony.

(5) The instruction on example: to observe the same discipline as the monk who is in his first day of monastic life, even if one is a monk who has maintained ordination for one hundred years.

(6) The first instruction on the right outlook: to respect one's preceptor who is of utmost importance to oneself, considering him as a father. The preceptor, from his side, will have to consider his student as his son and help him in times of illness, and so forth.

(7) The second instruction on the right outlook: to have respect for saintly

monks, elders, new monks, as well as those who are one's regular companions in the discipline.

(8) The actual instruction on the right outlook: to learn the scriptures and become expert in the subjects of the aggregates, the experiential elements, the experiential media, interdependent origination, and in what is proper and improper behavior; to understand what one does not know, to realize what what one has not yet realized, etc.

(9) The instruction on what a monk should be concerned with after being ordained: to listen to the detailed description of the disciplinary code given in the *Personal Liberation Discourse* recited at each bimonthly confession and to become proficient in this code by learning it from the preceptor, the teacher, or others.

(10) The instruction on the training: to have respect for the Buddha's doctrine and particularly for the training in discipline.

(11) The instruction on the root of all discipline subsequent to the monk's ordination: to maintain conscientiousness, the means to attain the state of perfect peace.

(Gunaprabha's *HFP*, ff. 110b3-116b1; Pema Karpo's *TV*, vol. Nga, ff. 33b5-34a2; and Tsonapa's *SIRD*, ff. 57b6-61a7.)

75. The request and a repetition of the appropriate formula.

76. Concerning the vow of strict observance of celibacy (*tshangs spyod la nye bar gnas pa'i sdom pa*), Gunaprabha states that the bestowal of this vow constitutes the intermediate part of the nun's ordination. In the first part, her request to become a nun is forwarded to the abbess with a report on whether she is free from obstacles to her ordination (not having received permission from family or husband, being pregnant, etc.). The second part of the ceremony consists of her request for vows of strict observance of celibacy, which is forwarded to the abbess along with a report confirming that she will abide by such a vow (determined from further questioning), and the final agreement by the abbess which signals the conferral of the vow. In the third part, she is fully ordained by a group of both monks and nuns. An extensive explanation of the rules for nuns concludes the ceremony (*HFP*, ff. 122b6-141a2).

Pema Karpo mentions that a woman cannot receive this vow if she has any of the following five obstacles: having both the male and female organ or having neither; menstruating continuously or having no menstruation (including women below twelve and above fifty); having no feeling in the vagina, etc.; and having been a nun before (*TV*, vol. Nga, f. 35a5).

77. Eleven of the twelve points of discipline are the same eleven instructions for the monks (see note 74), except that there are eight (not four) defeating offenses for a nun, and the instruction to live under a tree is omitted in order to safeguard her vow of celibacy. The twelfth point consists in the instruction concerning the eight severe precepts (see note 36). For a detailed discussion of the nun's vows, see Gunaprabha's *SD*, ff. 50a3-56b7.

78. The causes for losing the vows (*sdom pa gtong ba'i rgyu*). See the section with this name (below).

79. Asanga discusses ten conditions for damaging the vows (*sdom pa nyams pa'i rgyu bcu*):

(1) To have assumed the monastic vows for improper reasons and not in order to seek one's liberation;

(2) Weak observance of the ethical code (lack of shame, remorse, etc.);

(3) To have regret for what is not a fault;

(4) Carelessness (not remembering what the transgressions to the rules are, not acting in accordance with the doctrine, perpetuating one's mistakes, etc.) and laziness;

(5) To have the wrong aspiration, such as wishing to be born as a god by maintaining the vow of celibacy, to gain profit or honor for oneself, or to cause others to gain them, etc.;

(6) Corruption of the monastic style of life by allowing one's conduct, daily activities, and cultivation of virtue to degenerate;

(7) Degeneration of one's means of livelihood by becoming over-desirous, lacking contentment, craving clothes, food, medicines, dwelling, and bedding, etc.;

(8) To fall into either of the two extremes, the extreme of luxury—by being attached to good food, etc.—or the extreme of asceticism—by practicing extreme forms of asceticism, such as sleeping on a bed of thorns or in ashes, burning oneself, staying in water, standing on one leg, etc.;

(9) To think that by simply observing morality and discipline one will attain liberation;

(10) To allow the ethics one has promised to observe to degenerate by being careless, to have no regard for monastic life, and to be immoral or evil, like a rotten tree.

(*Proclaimers' Stages* [*Śrāvakabhūmi; Nyan thos kyi sa*] [henceforth cited as *PS*] [Toh. 4036], ff. 16a3-21b2.)

80. Asanga discusses this point as follows: as soon as an impulse to act with body, speech, and mind arises, a monk must examine the nature of the act, by reflecting on whether the action would be harmful or useful to himself and others. If harmful, the monk ponders the unpleasant consequences that would ensue; if useful, the favorable results. Having understood that an action would be harmful, he should avoid it; seeing that it would be useful, he should perform it. In the same way, he should investigate his past actions, and if he realizes that he has done something improper, should confess it in front of a wise and saintly fellow monk. Day and night, the monk should follow a positive course (*PS*, ff. 22b7-23b7).

81. Causes that hinder mind's clarity (*sems rab tu dang ba la gegs byed pa'i rgyu*): sleeping, overeating, remaining in the sun, etc.

82. See below, the section called "Conditions for Living Comfortably."

83. Lit. the three white foods (*zas dkar gsum*): milk, curd, and butter; the expression is to be understood in a broader sense as to eat vegetarian food.

84. Tsonapa says that one is called venerable (*gomin, btsun pa*) because although one has assumed layman's vows, as an indication of a life-long determination to maintain them, one wears the attire of a renunciate (*SIRD*, f. 38b7).

85. *Sthavira* (*gnas brtan pa*): one of the four original schools of the Individual Way, which derives its name from *sthavira*, meaning elder monk.

86. This a reference to Atisha's *Commentary on the Lamp for the Path*, f. 245b2-4. For an explanation of the nature of the refuge, see *Instruction on Taking Refuge* (Skt. *Saraṇagamanadeśanā; sKyabs su 'gro ba bstan pa*) (Toh. 3953), also by Atisha.

87. Votive image (*tsa tsa*) in the shape of a miniature reliquary or moulded image.

88. The full verse is cited in Pema Karpo's *TV*, vol. Nga, f. 7b, as follows:

Practicing the teachings even while wearing jewelry,
He abides in the pure vow of chastity.
Renouncing injury to all elemental spirits,
Yashas is a brahmin, a virtuous practitioner, and a monk.

(*rGyan gyis brgyan bzhin du ni chos spyad de / Dul zhing yang dag sdom pa tshangs spyod la / 'Byung po kun la chad pa spangs pa ni / De ni bram ze dge sbyong dge slong yin.*) These words (from the discipline scriptures) were spoken by the Buddha with reference to one of his disciples, Yashas (Yaśas, Grags pa), when he perceived the truth while wearing lay clothing.

89. Tsonapa says that the venerable person who observes a life-long purificatory fast (*bsnyen gnas*) (mentioned above) is an actual lay practitioner (*dge bsnyen*) (*SIRD*, f. 38b7).

90. Sönam Drakpa provides the more common list of thirty-six novice rules prohibiting the following: (1-4) the four types of killing, (5) theft, (6) sexual intercourse, (7) untruth, (8) groundless accusation or accusation for a trivial reason, (9) causing a schism in the monastic community, (10) taking sides, (11) causing a layperson to lose faith, (12) consciously telling a lie, (13) accusing a monk of favoritism, (14) censuring the caretaker, (15) accusing a monk of teaching for a little food, (16) accusing a monk of having incurred a partial defeat, (17) disparaging the discipline, (18) covering rice with vegetables to get more rice [or vice versa], (19) drinking alcohol, (20) singing, (21) dancing, (22) playing music, (23) wearing jewelry, (24) wearing cosmetics, (25) using perfumes, (26) wearing necklaces, (27) using luxurious beds, (28) high beds, (29) luxurious seats, (30) high seats, (31) eating after noon, (32) accepting gold, (33) accepting silver, (34) adopting the attire of a layperson, (35) giving up the monastic attire, and (36) despising one's preceptor. (*Sun Illuminating the Discipline with Reasons and Scriptures* [*So thar tshul khrims kyi pad tshal rgyas byed pan chen bsod grags kyis mdzad pa'i 'dul ba'i legs bshad lung rigs kyi nyi ma*] [henceforth cited as *SID* for vol. I and *SID16* for vol. II] [*SID*, f. 150a5-b1]).

91. Concerning "related minor infractions" (*phyogs mthun nyes byes*), Shakhya-prabha states that during the ordination, a novice promises not to commit murder and so forth, to renounce the lay lifestyle, to adopt the renunciate's attire,

and to accept his preceptor. What are infractions related to these (*phyogs mthun*)? To use an example, a novice has taken the vow not to have sexual intercourse; related precepts would be not to ejaculate, not to use sexual language, etc. Even though the novice has not specifically assumed those precepts, they are implied in his discipline, and he should refrain from violating them. Thus, they are called "related." Infractions related to murder would be to fail to eliminate potential causes of aggression, to be violent, to engage in a battle, to strike someone, to cause regret in someone, etc. Infractions related to theft would be to appropriate offerings donated to the community, to sit on a seat that is not intended for oneself, to hide another's possessions for a joke, etc. (*Commentary on the Three Hundred Stanzas on the Novitiate* [*Mūlasarvāstivādiśrāmaṇera-kārikāvṛttiprabhāvati; 'Od ldan/ 'Phags pa gzhi thams cad yod par smra ba'i dge tshul gyi tshig le'ur byas pa'i 'grel ba 'od ldan*] [Toh. 4125] [henceforth cited as *CTHSN*], ff. 75b7-76a5).

92. Ibid.

93. The thirteen appear in *CTHSN*, f. 76a7-77b1.

94. Vishakadeva, *Stanzas on the Discipline/ Garland of Flowers* (*Vinayakārikā; 'Dul ba tshig le'ur byas pa/ Me tog phreng rgyud*) (Toh. 4123), f. 45b5-7.

95. The seven admissible transgressions for a postulant nun (*dge slob ma'i gnang ba'i nyes med bdun*) are listed in Pema Karpo's *TV*, vol. Nga, f. 244b2:

> For the postulant nun, to keep [an extra begging bowl and robes],
> To be separate [from the monastic robes], to light a fire,
> Resume eating, damage seeds,
> [Urinate or] defecate in a place where there is green grass,
> Or climb trees [do not constitute transgressions].

96. See chapter I, note 27, point 3.

97. The ceremony for accepting a tutor is simple: The candidate kneels before the teacher with his two hands touching his feet and asks the teacher three times: "Venerable One, please heed me. I ask you to take me, known as (so and so), as your student." The teacher replies positively, and after the third recitation, the teacher states, "That is the skillful way!" The student replies, "Yes, indeed!" thus concluding the rite (Pema Karpo's *TV*, vol. Nga, f. 37b1-2).

98. This does not mean that a novice must live in the same quarters or area as the tutor, but rather that he is entrusted to his spiritual care (Gunaprabha's *SD*, f. 8b2-3).

99. Gunaprabha's *SD*, f. 3a4.

100. The new monk cannot go further than forty-nine fathoms (*'dom*) from his quarters without asking permission from his teacher (*SD*, f. 3a4). Tsonapa (*SIRD*, f. 62a6-7) states that if the new monk lives within the same boundary as his tutor, he should seek his advice three times a day; if at a distance of an earshot, once a day; if at a distance of five or six earshots, once every five or six days, etc.

101. Pema Karpo includes among the various obligations of the student the following: having respect for and serving the teacher, procuring begging bowls and robes for him, helping the sick, dispelling regret caused by having committed a transgression, renouncing opinions contrary to the doctrine, willingly undergoing disciplinary measures when one is at fault, etc. The obligations of the tutor include instructing the disciple, turning him away from bad friends who have let their ethics degenerate, inspiring him to practice the wholesome (which means to engage in study and meditation and to rise above moral transgressions), helping him to engage in right livelihood, imposing on him disciplinary measures only when necessary, and being patient with worthy disciples, etc. (*TV*, vol. Nga, ff. 40b1-43a6).

102. According to Tsonapa, the defeating offenses (*pham pa*) deserve serious punishment; the partial defeats (*lhag ma*) (lit. "with remainder") can be purified by ritual while openly confessing to one's fellow monks; the downfalls [that require forfeiture or confession alone] (*ltung byed*) and the offenses that must be individually confessed (*so sor bshags par bya ba*) can also be purified in the same way as the partial defeats; the minor infractions (*nyes byas*) are downfalls that do not belong to the above four classes (*SIRD*, f. 146a6-b4).

103. *Kārṣāpaṇa*: a coin or weight of fluctuating value used in ancient India. According to the *Summary of Discipline*, one *karshapana* was worth twenty *masaka* (a tiny red and black bean weighing about an eighth of a gram) of gold. A quarter *karshapana* was therefore equal to five *masaka*, which during a period of no famine was worth five bushels of [dry] barley (Dharmashri's *Commentary on the Three Vows*, ff. 57b2-58a2).

104. On this point, Tsonapa states: A fetus in its nineteenth week of development onward is called a human being (*mi*) as it has already formed all the sensory organs. A fetus in its eighteenth week or less is called a forming human being (*mir chags pa*). Both are considered human beings (*mir gyur ba*).

To murder a human being is a defeat (*pham pa*), since a human is the basis for (i.e., could become the embodiment of) the Three Jewels and the three types of ethics (vows of personal liberation, vows of meditative absorption, and uncontaminated vows). To murder a non-human (a god) amounts to a serious violation (*sbom po*), since non-humans can be the basis for only two of the three Jewels and only two types of ethics. In fact, among the gods, there are many saints who embody the Jewels of the community and of the doctrine and live by the ethics derived from contemplation and uncontaminated wisdom. To kill an animal is a downfall [that requires confession alone] (*ltung byed*), since animals are neither the basis for the Three Jewels nor for the three types of vows (*SIRD*, ff. 195a3-196b3).

105. Vasubandhu's *Treasury of Phenomenology*, f. 13b4.

106. Lit. "claiming to have qualities superior to human ones" (*mi'i chos bla mar smra ba*).

107. Vishakadeva's *Stanzas on the Discipline*, f. 25b5-6.

108. Reading *kyi* for *kyis* (line two).

109. Tsonapa states that ill-will and longing for the objects of desire are primarily impediments when training in ethics; sleep and drowsiness are primarily impediments to the training in meditation; and having reservations about the doctrine is an impediment to the training in discriminative awareness (*SIRD*, f. 205a5-7).

110. Shakhyaprabha states that an offense with concealment is incurred when the monk who has committed the defeat harbors, even for a single moment, the intention to conceal it. Thus, intention is the primary factor in an offense with concealment; otherwise, a non-concealed offense would be an impossibility since it is unlikely that after a single moment the offender could find someone to confess to (*CTHSN*, f. 125b3).

111. According to Tsonapa, an exception (*sel ba*) is a case in which the defeat or another downfall does not occur because the object (for example, stolen goods) does not fulfill the condition of worth, etc., because one is not in a normal state of mind (i.e., is in a deranged state of mind), or because the action itself [is not completed] (*SIRD*, f. 166b4).

112. Butön Rinchen Drup, called "Second Buddha" (Kun mkhyen gnyis pa bu ston chos rje) (1290-1364): a scholar and translator, as well as an authoritative master of the Kalachakra Tantra. He was a major editor of the *Tibetan Canon of Buddhist Teachings* (*bKa' 'gyur* and *bsTan 'gyur*). At least eight works related to monastic discipline (*vinaya*) are found in his collected works.

113. The Eighth Karmapa, Mikyö Dorjé (Mi bskyod rdo rje) (1507-54): a scholar, prolific writer, and accomplished meditator of the Kagyu school, contemporary of Tsongkapa. His *Great Commentary on the Discipline* (*'Dul tika chen po*) is also known as *Illumination of the Discipline* (*'Dul ba nyi ma'i dkyil 'khor*), its full title being *A Detailed Commentary on the Vinayasutra and Buddhist Monastic Discipline* (*'Dul ba mdo rtsa ba'i rgya cher 'grel spyi'i don mtha' dpyad dang bsdus don sa bcad dang 'bru yi don mthar chags su gnyer ba bcas 'dzam bu'i gling gsal bar byed pa'i rgyan nyi ma'i dkyil 'khor*). Reproduced from prints of the Pelpung (Dpal spungs) blocks, New Delhi, 1973, by the Sixteenth Karmapa.

114. Dharmashri, the Great Translator (Lo chen dharma śri) (1654-1717): the younger brother of the famous Terdak Lingpa of the monastery of Mindroling, ordained as a novice by the Fifth Dalai Lama, and an important master in the transmission of the discipline (*vinaya*) and Ancient Tradition (*rNying ma*) teachings.

The commentary on the vows (*sdom 'grel*) referred to here is Dharmashri's *Commentary that Ascertains the Three Vows: The Wish-fulfilling Cluster of Corn of Good Explanations* (*sDom gsum rnam par nges pa'i 'grel pa legs bshad ngo mtshar dpag bsam gyi snye ma bstan bcos*), which is a commentary on Ngari Panchen Pema Wangyal's *Treatise that Ascertains the Three Vows* (*sDom gsum rnam par nges pa'i 'grel pa*).

115. Pema Karpo, the all-knowing Drukpa ('Brug pa kun mkhyen Pad ma dkar po) (1527-1592): an eminent scholar of the Drukpa Kagyu school and author of *The Three Vows* (*sDom gsum*) (*TV*).

116. Wönkarma (dBon karma) (also known as Karma Ngelek): nephew (*dbon*) of the Eighth Tai Situ, Chökyi Jungné (Si tu chos kyi 'byung gnas). His commentary is called *The Essential Bountiful Vase of the Three Vows* (*sDom gsum rnam par bstan pa nyer mkho'i bum bzang*) (Dergé, Tibet: dPal spungs thub bstan chos 'khor gling Monastery).

117. According to Tsonapa, unimpaired (*ma nyams pa*) organ refers to the organ of a living person or of a human corpse not affected by a disease such as leprosy (*SIRD*, f. 154b1-2). See also Shakyaprabha's *CTHSN*, ff. 121b7-123a2 and Pema Karpo's *TV*, vol. Nga, ff. 56b5.

118. Tsonapa states that this means not having a disease such as one causing impotency that prevents the experience of orgasm (*SIRD*, f. 154b7).

119. Serious infractions (*sbom po*): infractions that occur only in relation to defeating and partially defeating offenses. (Tsonapa's *SIRD*, f. 141a3).

The word "serious" (*sbom po*, lit. "gross") indicates that the offense is not a major one since the complementary branches are not all present, and yet it is a serious transgression.

120. According to Tsonapa, this implies that to touch the nails, the teeth, and the hair of a woman are not partial defeats but related serious violations (*sbom po*) (*SIRD*, f. 215b2).

121. With regard to this rule, Tsonapa states that the monk's words should clearly refer to sexual intercourse and not just allude to it in unclear terms (in which case, the offense would be a related serious violation and not a partial defeat). For example, the suggestion might be stated as a direct request (*gsol ba*) ("Lady, come! Let's make love.") or an indirect one (*nye bar gsol ba*) ("When a woman and man make love, it is pleasurable. If we were to make love, it would also be pleasurable.") (*SIRD*, ff. 217b3-218b1).

122. Tsonapa explains that to act as an intermediary has three phases: first, the monk suggests to a person that he or she engage in sexual relationship with another; next, the monk conveys the same suggestion to the prospective partner; finally, the monk receives the answer from this last person and conveys it to the first person. This partial defeat is incurred even if the monk does not actually carry the last message, but the first person comes to know of it by other means (*SIRD*, ff. 221b7-222a1).

123. f. 13a5.

124. Improper site (*gzhi ma dag pa*) is the abode of other small creatures (*srog chags phra mo'i gnas dang ldang pa*), a disputed site (*rtsod pa dang bcas pa*), or one that is ill-suited (*brtsam du mi rung ba*). To explain, the place for the building of a monk's dwelling must not (1) be the permanent abode of small creatures, snakes, or other kinds of animals; (2) be owned by a king, a householder, a non-Buddhist, or used by nuns for their rainy season retreat; or (3) be next to a strong flowing river or an underground deposit of water, etc., which can result in death [due to the instability of the land]. Before building, the monk must first ask permission

of the community. The suitability of the site for a hut or other dwelling is subject to the judgment of the monastic community, who will inspect the place or appoint a monk to do so. (*SIRD*, ff. 133b7-136b1; and Gunaprabha's *HFP*, ff. 141a2-144a1).

125. Cubit (*khru*): the length measured from the elbow to the tip of the outstretched middle finger.

126. Materials acquired in an illegal way.

127. Tsonapa clarifies that "having heard" (*thos*) means that the monk who brings forth the accusation of a defeating act should actually have heard the sound made by one of his fellow monks engaged in sexual intercourse (for example). To make a false accusation by reporting the words of a third person who has said that a certain monk has committed a defeating offense would constitute a related serious violation but not a partial defeat. The same applies for having seen (*mthong*) or having suspected (*dogs*). If a monk, believing another's words, lies by saying "I personally have seen," or having simply a suspicion, says, "I have seen," he incurs the partial defeat (*SIRD*, f. 240a1-b6).

128. Tsonapa explains the difference between "groundless accusation" and "accusation for a trivial reason." In the first case, the monk bringing forth the accusation clearly states the agent-action relationship: "I have seen the monk (so and so) incur (such and such) a defeating offense." In the second case, the agent-action relationship is not stated clearly, as in "I have seen the monk (so and so) and the nun (so and so). I have seen the act of sexual intercourse."

The event that led to the prescription of this rule occurred in Rajagriha. Two monks, Suhrit (mDza' bo) and Salé kye (Sa las skyes), had made an accusation without relating agent and action against the monk Vasumallaputra (Gyad bu nor) and the nun Utpali after having seen two deer copulating. Seeing the two deer copulating was the trivial (*bag tsam*) reason (*SIRD*, ff. 240b7-241a5).

129. The circumstance that led to the institution of this rule was a schism that developed at the time of the Buddha in the monastic community at Rajagriha in Bihar caused by Devadatta, Buddha's cousin.

The partial defeat of causing a schism involves taking up an incorrect doctrinal view, converting other monks to this view, and thereby creating a division in the community. A schism can take place only in our continent (world), Jambudvipa, within the boundaries of a monastery, and in a place where the Buddha is not residing. Furthermore, the monks involved in the schism must not number less than nine (counting the monk causing the schism); must be ordinary monks (who have not seen the truth), four on the correct side and four on the non-doctrinal side; must be monks who have pure morality; and must be wise in the three classes of scriptures (otherwise, they could not be taken seriously). Moreover, a schism could not occur when the Buddha had just attained enlightenment, before he attained it, or after he had passed away (unless one of his two outstanding disciples was still alive).

Differentiation must be made among the different forms of schism, "causing dissension in the community" (*dge 'dun dbyen*), "causing a schism that is a deed of immediate retribution" (*dbyen gyi mtshams med*), and "the partial defeat of causing a schism" (*dbyen gyi lhag ma*). The first is a neutral phenomenon (neither virtuous nor unvirtuous) of disharmony among the monks. The second involves an actual schism in the community [and is caused by a monk] through lying. This schism results in a birth in the hell of Unceasing Torture for the monk who has caused it. The third is a partial defeat that is incurred when the offender does not desist after having been reprimanded three times by fellow monks. This form of schism may be incurred by a monk or a nun (but not by a newly ordained monk who has recently begun his training). The schism need not actually take place (if it does take place, the schism would be considered the second type).

Some scriptures state that after the demise of the Buddha, the conditions necessary for these three forms of schism no longer applied. Nevertheless, a monk who causes a division within the community incurs a serious violation (*SID*, ff. 95a4-97b6). As for the unwanted consequence of a schism, it is said that as long as a schism in the community is not resolved, the followers of the Buddhist doctrine living in one great third-order thousand world-system, the buddha-field of a single buddha, will not attain any of the five experiential paths (*SID16*, f. 82a2-5). See also Dharmashri's *Commentary on the Three Vows*, ff. 61b3-5; 118a6-5; and Pema Karpo's *TV*, vol. Nga, ff. 114a3-116a1.

130. Tsonapa explains this as follows: causing a lay devotee to lose faith as a result of one's bad behavior or by proclaiming the faults of other monks and then defaming the monks who have expelled oneself on this account, saying, "They have expelled me because of their desire, anger, or stupidity" (*SIRD*, ff. 251b3-252a2).

131. As an alternative interpretation, Tsonapa states that "defeats of the monastic community" (*dge 'dun lhag ma*, lit. "with remainder in the monastic community") are so called because the monk who incurs one is not expelled from the monastic community (as is the monk who has incurred a defeating offense), but still remains part of it (*SIRD*, f. 149b7).

132. Gunaprabha's *SD*, f. 40a3.

133. Tsonapa's defines conscientious friend (*khrims grogs*) as a friend who prevents a monk from incurring a downfall and who is not non-human, mute or stupid, insane, a hermaphrodite, or blind (*SIRD*, f. 213b3-5).

134. According to Tsonapa, a "convenient place for sexual intercourse" implies that the monk stays with a woman closer than the length of a bow (a fathom) on a seat that is fit for copulation. If the monk is not closer than a fathom to the woman or on a seat unfit for sexual intercourse, he may incur only a partial defeat (touching a woman) or a downfall (sitting with a woman) (*SIRD*, f. 141a5-6).

135. Tsonapa states that although classed among the downfalls that require forfeiture, in this case no forfeiture is required (*SIRD*, f. 263b1).

136. A piece of cloth sufficient to cover the three areas when one is seated in the cross-legged position.

137. Tsonapa notes that if the monk has left the robe within the same boundary, the downfall is not incurred; if the monk is living in solitude, is old or sick, etc., he may be excused from the rule of "to be separate from the three robes" for a day; and if the robes are not consecrated, to be separated from them is not a downfall (*SIRD*, f. 313b6).

138. All three (the patron, the person who carries the money, and the caretaker in this case) must be male laypersons. If any one of them is a monk, the insistence becomes a minor infraction (*SIRD*, f. 295a3-5).

139. "To make" also implies to commission someone to make (*SIRD*, f. 299a2). This applies also to the infractions of similar types listed below.

Silk and black wool were prohibited because at that time they were expensive and difficult to obtain. Silk, in addition, had to be made by sacrificing the lives of many larvae.

140. One and a half cubits as measured on a medium-sized man.

141. One earshot (*rgyang grags*) is a measure of five hundred bow-lengths, one bow being four cubits (*SIRD*, f. 302b2).

142. The consecration of a precious substance that a monk has acquired or donated, and which is to be used for a virtuous purpose, is to be done through a three-part ceremony: (1) Before the monk makes use of a precious item to buy robes or other things, he should think that it does not belong to him, but that it belongs to the householder who has donated it. (2) He entrusts it to the caretaker of the community who is a lay practitioner or a novice, making him accept that he (the caretaker) now owns it. (3) When the monk needs to use the precious substance to buy something, the consecration is done by first placing it in front of another monk. If that monk is an elder, the monk requesting the consecration prostrates to him. After that, both stand up and raise their hands over the substance, and the monk repeats three times after the elder the appropriate formula of consecration (*SIRD*, ff. 304b6-305b1).

143. See below section "Conditions for Living Comfortably: Food and Medicine" for the types of permissible food and medicine.

Kongtrul here mentions only three types, excluding the fourth, because such medicines are consecrated for life. Thus, once consecrated, they may be kept even after the monk has recovered from his illness without incurring the downfall of storing. If unconsecrated, the permitted time for any of the four types of food and medicine expires within the next of the four periods of the day and night in which they have been acquired. See Dharmashri's *Commentary on the Three Vows*, f. 69a1-6.

144. Sönam Drakpa mentions that the article is relinquished (*spang*) by separation (*'bral*), i.e., putting it in another place (the house of another monk, for example). Relinquishment is of two types, temporary (*re shig spang ba*) and permanent (*gtan du spang ba*). When a monk possesses more than one extra begging bowl, he should put them permanently into the custody of any of the five types

of ordained persons; when he has taken back gifts he had given to a fellow monk, he should return them permanently to that monk. With the exception of these two, all other articles relinquished prior to confessing one of these thirty downfalls are relinquished temporarily (for one day) (*SID*, ff. 106b6-107a).

145. Lying that constitutes a defeat means making a false claim to high spiritual attainment. Lying that constitutes a partial defeat would be, for example, a groundless accusation [to a fellow monk of having incurred a defeat when he has not]. Lying that is a serious violation would be teaching a false doctrine to a gathering of monks. Lying that falls into the category of minor infractions would be, for example, knowing that one has incurred a downfall, but remaining silent during the confession ceremony when the elder who recites the *Personal Liberation Scripture* asks three times, "Are you pure [free of downfalls]?" (*SID*, f. 118b1-6).

146. Tsonapa states that a monk is allowed to cut vegetation and use seeds if the rite of consecration of these has been done and it is for a permitted purpose. A permitted purpose would be the building of an image or statue of the Buddha or a stupa, or for the sake of the doctrine or monastic community. The same exception applies to tilling the soil and lighting a fire. The consecration (*rung ba byed pa*) of vegetation or seed must be done by a novice or a layperson as monks are not permitted to do this rite (*SIRD*, ff. 334b1-338a6).

147. To be appointed as a teacher of nuns, a monk must fulfill sixteen qualifications: respectability (not having incurred a defeat or partial defeat and being conscientious in that he has forsaken unwholesome deeds such as killing animals); steadfastness (twenty years of standing as a monk); learning (knowledge of the three collections of the scriptures); and thirteen qualities of helpfulness (the twelve explained in the first chapter of this work in the discussion of the qualifications of the monastic preceptor, plus not having previously been appointed as a nuns' teacher and then removed from that position). A monk with these qualifications is appointed to be the nuns' teacher within the boundary of his monastic community; qualified fellow monks perform the appropriate ceremony during the confession ceremony of the fifteenth of the lunar month (*SIRD*, ff. 349a1-351a1).

148. Tsonapa states that the woman in question here is a nun. If a monk stands alone with a woman who is not a nun, he incurs a minor infraction, not this downfall (*SIRD*, ff. 355b1-356a1).

149. To eat more than two middle-sized begging bowls of food constitutes this infraction (*CNPTV*, f. 38b6). Dharmashri specifies that to eat more than a full large-sized begging bowl, two medium-sized, or three small-sized begging bowls is to incur this infraction (*Commentary on the Three Vows*, f. 74b3-4).

150. Leftover food is made permissible (*lhag por byed pa*) through a three-part ritual: (1) The monk washes his hands, and after having ritually accepted the food, makes a request to a fellow monk (who has not left the meal and is within the boundary of the monastic residence) to make it permissible. That fellow monk eats two or three morsels of it. (2) The fellow monk then says, "It is yours. Go!" (3) The fellow monk hands over the food to the one who has requested it to be made permissible, who then gets up and leaves (*SIRD*, ff. 362b5-363a).

151. "Standing up after having started the meal" is also part of the downfall since it may be the cause for resuming eating (*SIRD*, f. 360b4).

152. See below, section "Conditions for Living Comfortably: Food and Medicine" for the four types of permissible food and medicine.

The ritual is as follows: With the intention of allowing the offering and acceptance (*byin len*) of the food, the monk stands up, raises his hands with the palms facing upward, and accepts the food with the awareness that this is being donated by the novice or layman who is offering the food in front of him. No other rituals are involved (*SIRD*, f. 373b6-374).

153. Gunaprabha states that "good foods" (*zas bsod pa*) refers to milk, curds, ghee, butter, oil, honey, sugar, fish, and dry meat, which are not permissible unless one is ill or one has been offered them (*SD*, f. 38a2).

154. The difference between the rule prohibiting use of water that contains living beings and the rule prohibiting casting and using water that contains living beings (the ninth of the second set of downfalls to be individually confessed) is that, in the former case, the rule prohibits the use of such water for one's own sake, and the latter prohibits the use or casting of such water for the sake of both oneself and the monastic community (*SIRD*, ff. 336b6-337b6).

155. Tsonapa specifies the conditions that would constitute "special necessity": if the ascetic is one's relative; if he could be converted to Buddhism; or if he is sick. If the ascetic is begging, the monk should ask him or her to put the begging cup on the ground; if he refuses to do so, he should not be given food. The main purpose of this rule is to prevent adherents of other religions from receiving more veneration than the Buddhist monks themselves. Since the laity has offered the food to the monks, if the monks then offer it to adherents of other religions, the laity may consider non-Buddhist faiths to be superior (*SIRD*, f. 379a4-b6).

156. Consecration (*byin rlabs*): within the scriptures on discipline, this term does not have the connotation of "blessing" or "making sacred" but instead indicates a "ritualized act" or "thought," the aim of which is to make the monk aware of the disadvantages of transgressing a particular rule, or of permission given in certain cases.

157. Consecration of downfalls (*ltung ba'i byin rlabs*): a part of the rite for purification of downfalls (*ltung ba'i phyir bcos*). This consists in a ceremonial request alone made in order that (1) the ripening effect of the downfall does not increase; (2) the power decreases by being counteracted by the antidote; and (3) the monk is eligible to participate in the monastic ceremonies, confession, etc.

158. The initial assent is given to the ceremonial master who is officiating at a ceremony, whether it be related to the monastic community in general, the ordination of a new monk, or a ceremony related to the doctrine. For this to be a downfall, the assent must be withdrawn once the formal procedure has been completed (*SIRD*, ff. 380b6-381a1).

159. Not fully ordained (*bsnyen par ma rdzogs pa*) includes monks who have incurred a defeating offense with concealment, or have been demoted because of

incurring a defeat without concealment. For the offense to occur, the place must be roofed and walled (*SIRD*, ff. 389b6-390a1).

If a monk has to sleep with an unordained person, he should do so at a distance of eight and half cubits in order to avoid this downfall (*CNPTV*, f. 40a5).

160. Erroneous views (*sdig pa'i lta ba*) refers to not believing that what the Buddha declared to be obstacles to the discipline are in fact obstacles [for example, believing that drinking alcohol or eating after noon is not an infraction of the rules] (Pema Karpo's *TV*, vol. Nga, ff. 189b6-190b1).

Tsonapa points out that "erroneous view" does not mean "wayward view" (*log lta*), which would constitute a condition for losing the vows in their entirety (*SIRD*, f. 391a2).

161. According to Gunaprabha, this means to give spiritual instructions to a monk who has been expelled from the monastery because of his erroneous views, or to use his belongings, accept his service, or sleep in the same area. This does not apply if he is sick or has given up his erroneous view or the other causes that led to the expulsion (*SD*, f. 42a2).

162. The three prescribed colors are blue, red, and orange. Dharmashri adds that this downfall is incurred when one wears white clothing. If one wears black or variegated clothing, or clothing dyed with one of the precious dyes, only a minor infraction is incurred.

163. This refers to bathing the entire body in a pool. Washing parts of the body is permissible.

164. Tsonapa specifies that for this downfall to occur the monk does not need to reach the point of intoxication; not even as much as the tip of a blade of grass of alcohol is permitted for monks (*SIRD*, f. 409b1).

165. Gunaprabha states that the monk who commits this offense has arranged for the community to receive alms from a patron and has not given authorization that the food be distributed if he himself is late, and that as a result, the food is not distributed to the other monks until his arrival (*SD*, f. 47a4).

166. Pema Karpo states that some monks would place cotton under the communal seats in order to make them more comfortable, an improper practice because the robes of other monks sitting on these seats would become covered with cotton lint (*TV*, vol. Nga, ff. 215b3-216a3).

167. To eat food outside the monastery (in a place that is an earshot or more from a village) or in a solitary place without checking whether accepting food would entail danger of thieves, etc., for the donor or one's fellow monks. The downfall is incurred when one has been appointed to investigate the safety of the place and has eaten without performing this duty (*TV*, vol. Nga, f. 220a1-b1).

168. The eight defeats of a nun (*dge slong ma'i pham pa brgyad*):

> Sexual intercourse, theft, murder, untruth,
> Touching, lying with, concealing, and preventing readmission.

The first four are the same as the four defeats of a monk. Touching comprises object, intention, and act. The object is a sexually able male. The intention is the desire to engage in sexual intercourse. The act is to touch, fondle, or caress him with any part of her body from the knees upward.

Lying with a man also involves object, intention, and act. The object, as before, is a sexually able male. The intention is the desire to engage in sexual intercourse. The act is to lie with the male in a place that is fit for intercourse and where they cannot be interrupted.

Concealing comprises object, intention, and act. The object is another nun who has incurred any of the eight defeats. Intention refers to the decision to conceal the fact. The act is to conceal the other nun's defeat while being aware that she has incurred it. The consummation of the act occurs if the defeat is concealed for a day and night.

Preventing readmission also comprises object, intention, and act. The object is a nun who has been expelled from the monastery who wishes to request forgiveness and readmission. The intention is to impede that nun's re-entry. The act is to prevent the nun from asking forgiveness of the community. The consummation of the act is not to allow her to undertake the necessary steps for asking forgiveness (Pema Karpo's *TV*, vol. Nga, f. 244a).

169. For an explanation of the nuns' rules, see Gunaprabha's *SD*, ff. 50a3-56b6.

170. Sönam Drakpa states that the basis of legal decisions to deal with disagreements over formal procedures of the order (*adhikarana, las dbye ba'i gzhi*) is called *Kośāmbī*, from a disagreement over formal procedures that occurred at the time of the Buddha among the monks of the city of Koshambi. A similar incident occurred among the monks of Shravasti (*SID16*, f. 2a-b1).

171. According to Sönam Drakpa, the basis for amendment of downfalls through subjugation (*nan tur gyi phyir bcos kyi gzhi*) is called *Pāṇḍulohitaka* (*dmar ser can*, lit. "clad in orange") from the designation given to a group of quarrelsome monks who persisted in evil behavior (at the time of the Buddha) and were subjected to this method in order to amend their offenses (*SID16*, f. 2b1-2).

172. Sönam Drakpa states that the basis dealing with the duration of concealment of a partial defeat (*dus dang dus ma yin pa bsdud pa'i 'byung ba'i gzhi*) is called the basis of the individual (*pudgalā, gang zag*) because it is in relation to a particular individual that the length of time a partial defeat has been concealed is reckoned (*SID16*, f. 2b1-2).

173. The basis of degrading (*sa gzhan na gnas pa*) a monk is called the basis of demotion (*spo ba'i gzhi*) because a different (lower) status (*sa gzhan*) is imposed as a disciplinary measure on the offending monk, who must then perform the tasks of one who has been demoted (*spo ba spyod pa*), as well as appeasing services (*mgu pa spyod pa*) (*SID16*, f. 2b3-4).

174. In Sönam Drakpa's explanation, the basis related to the training (*yongs su spyod pa'i gzhi*) is called suspension from confession (*gso sbyong gzhag pa*) because at the time of an allegation of a downfall, if the alleged monk does not comply with the advice to amend his downfall, he is not allowed to participate in the confession ceremony of the monastic community. If that suspension does not succeed in subduing him, the monk is suspended from the lifting of the

restrictions ceremony that marks the end of the rainy season retreat (as well as being suspended from [further] advice). The last two suspensions (from the lifting of restrictions ceremony and receiving further advice) are included within the basis of suspension from confession (*SID16*, f. 2b5-6).

175. The basis for resolving schisms in the community (*dge 'dun dbyen rnams bsdus pa*) is also known as the basis concerned with the ways to resolve schisms concerning the "wheel" (*'khor lo dbye ba'i gzhi*), "wheel" referring here to the Buddha's doctrine (*SID16*, f. 8b5). Dharmashri states that schism differs from disagreement over formal procedures (see notes 170 and 240) in that the schism is caused by monks who split the monastic community as a result of which a part of the monastic community comes to follow a teacher other than the Buddha and a path other than the path taught by the Buddha. The previous case of the disagreement occurs when monks who profess ideas contrary to the doctrine perform a different ceremony within the same boundary (*Commentary on the Three Vows*, f. 118a4-6).

176. Ordination is the basis concerned with the ceremony of assuming the monk's vows. Nine bases—numbers 2, 3, 4, 5, 6, 7, 8, 10, and 15 of the above list—are concerned with safeguarding the rules. Seven—numbers 9, 11, 12, 13, 14, 16, and 17 of the above list—concern amending downfalls.

177. According to Pema Karpo, the duties of the helper of a meditating monk (who must be duly appointed by the monastic community) are to sprinkle the hut with water, sweep, spread fresh cow urine, prepare the seat, and so forth (*TV*, vol. Nga, f. 258a1-4).

178. Mental quiescence (*śamatha, zhi gnas*): a state of concentration reached upon the attainment of a special bliss characterized by physical and mental pliancy, on which basis the meditator can unwaveringly analyze reality. See Hopkins' *ME*.

179. Nine methods of setting the mind (*sems gnas pa'i thabs dgu*). See note 312. See also *ME*, pp. 80-90.

180. Insight (*vipaśyanā, lhag mthong*): a form of analytical introspection applied to gain realization of the ultimate nature of things and thereby overcome one's emotions.

181. Four mindfulnesses (*dran pa nye bar gzhag pa bzhi*): modes of discriminative awareness applied in understanding the emptiness of body (*lus*), feelings (*tshor ba*), mental processes (*sems*), and mental contents (*chos*).

182. The five paths (*lam lnga*) of accumulation, preparation, seeing, meditation, and no more learning. The paths of accumulation (*tshogs lam*) and preparation (*sbyor lam*) are the stages at which the understanding of reality is conceptually cultivated through study and reflection. The path of seeing (*mthong lam*) denotes the point at which a direct and contemplative sight of emptiness is gained. This leads to the path of meditation (*sgoms lam*) at which stage one repeatedly enters the contemplation on emptiness in order to remove intellectual and emotional impediments that prevent the dawn of universal knowledge on the path of no more learning (*mi slob lam*).

183. Thirty-seven factors leading to awakening (*byang phyogs so bdun*):

(1-4) the four applications of mindfulness (note 181);

(5-8) the four perfect abandonments (*yang dag pa'i spong ba bzhi*): (a) to renounce all that is unwholesome in oneself, (b) to prevent all that is unwholesome from arising in oneself, (c) to strengthen the virtuous qualities one already has, and (d) to develop virtuous qualities one does not have;

(9-12) the four bases for miracles (*rdzu 'phrul gyi rkang pa bzhi*): concentrations marked by will, perseverance, intention, and analysis;

(13-17) the five powers (*dbang po lnga*): confidence, effort, mindfulness, concentration, and wisdom (these mark the preparatory stages that lead to direct knowledge of reality);

(18-22) the five strengths (*stobs lnga*) (these are the same as the five powers and mark the climax stage prior to direct knowledge of reality);

(23-29) the seven factors conducive to enlightenment (*byang chub kyi yan lag bdun*): mindfulness, investigation of the nature of things, effort, joy, pliancy, concentration, and equanimity (these mark the actual vision of reality);

(30-37) the eightfold exalted path (*'phags lam yan lag brgyad*): (1) the right way of seeing, (2) the right way of expressing that vision in thoughts, and (3) in words, (4) the right way of exerting oneself in that vision, (5) the right livelihood, (6) the right mindfulness in attending the vision, (7) the right concentration on the vision, and (8) the right way of expressing the vision in actions.

184. Four results (*'bras bu bzhi*): the state of stream-enterer (*rgyun zhugs*) attained simultaneously with the direct perception of reality which dawns on the path of seeing; the state of once-returner (*phyir 'ong*) attained with the removal of most of the innate emotions of the desire realm; the state of non-returner (*phyir mi 'ong*) attained when all innate emotions linked to the desire realm are eliminated; and the state of the saint (*dgra bcom pa*) who has fully overcome all types of emotions linked to all three realms of existence, including the form and formless ones. See *ME*, pp. 106-109.

185. Gunaprabha's *HFP*, f. 210a5-6.

186. The confession to foster harmony is performed in order to engage in the three trainings in ethics, contemplation, and discriminative awareness, which are necessary for all types of renunciates. In particular, it is performed to refine the monks' ethics; to keep their practice of the doctrine pure in that during the confession they awaken virtuous minds; and to prevent their being stained by the fault of not confessing lapses in discipline. The purification-renewal related to the development of mental quiescence is performed to practice the trainings of contemplation and discriminative awareness (*SID16*, f. 3b2-3). According to Dharmashri, the first is performed to prevent the arising of what would cause impediments in this life, and the second, to cleanse oneself of impediments created in previous lives (*Commentary on the Three Vows*, f. 90b2-3).

187. This citation paraphrases those of Dharmashri in his *Commentary on the Three Vows* (f. 91a6-b3).

188. The Mongolian (Hor) calendar, equivalent to the Tibetan one, originated in 1207 when the Tibetan region of Minyak (known in Chinese as Hsi-hsia) was conquered by Genghis Khan. To commemorate this event, the day of victory was declared to be the first day of the calendar year. Henceforth, this calendar became widely accepted throughout Tibet.

189. Tsonapa (mTsho sna pa) and Jadul (dGe bshes Bya 'dul ba 'dzin pa) (1091-1167): Both were important masters in propagating the monastic tradition in Tibet. See *Blue Annals*, pp. 80, 304, and 321.

190. See chapter I, note 117.

191. Chökyi Wangchuk, the Sixth Shamar (Zhwa dmar drug pa Chos kyi dbang phyug), was renowned for his scholarship. The Shamar incarnation lineage begins with Drakpa Sengé (Grags pa seng ge), a disciple of Rangjung Dorjé (Rang byung rdo rje), the Third Karmapa (1284-1338). He became known as Shamar (lit. "red hat") when he was given a red crown by the king of Hor.

192. Sönam Drakpa specifies that the large boundary surrounds an area with a radius of two and a half leagues. The small boundary surrounds an area large enough for the monks to gather with a bow-length's space to spare (*SID16*, f. 7a4).

193. According to Sönam Drakpa, the preparatory part of a confession rite has six parts: (1) An image of the Buddha is set up with offerings, a four-part ritual offering is made to those gods who favor the doctrine, and the *gandi* wood is struck to summon the monks. (2) Downfalls are purified through confession, restraint, and consecration. (3) Temple duties, sweeping and so forth, are performed. (4) The night before the confession, teachings on the doctrine are given; if that is not possible, the *Proclamation of the Doctrine Scripture* is recited. (5) The disciplinary monk distributes sticks to determine the number of participants and receives the requests to be excused by those who are unable to attend the confession. (6) The monks offer flowers and request the elder to recite the *Personal Liberation Scripture* (*SID16*, ff. 18b4-19a1).

194. See note 157.

195. Sönam Drakpa describes the *gandi* wood as a plank made of red or white sandalwood, Ashoka wood, etc., measuring 84 finger-widths in length, six fingers in width, and two in thickness. The ends are shaped like the mouth of a frog. It is struck with a pestle of wood shaped like the head of a mongoose and twelve fingers long (*SID16*, f. 16a4-6).

196. This refers to the *Pure Ethics Scripture* (*Śilasaṃyuktasūtra; Tshul khrims yang dag par ldan pa'i mdo*) (also called *Proclamation of the Doctrine Scripture; Chos bsgrags kyi mdo*) (Toh. 303), f. 127a2-b7.

197. *Personal Liberation Scripture* (*Prātimokṣasūtra; So sor thar ba'i mdo*) (Toh. 2).

This scripture lists the context for the prescription of the rules, the defeats, the partial defeats, the undetermined offenses, and the summary of rules.

198. Commit no evil,
Engage in excellent virtue,
Fully tame your mind:
This is the Buddha's teaching.

For a longer form of this original formula, see *The Buddha's Philosophy: Selections from the Pali Canon* by G. F. Allen (London: George Allen and Unwin Ltd., 1959), p. 144.

199. Tsonapa explains this simile as follows: When sprouts of corn (*kāraṇḍava; sred da*), which resemble barley sprouts, are planted together with barley, they will harm the barley's growth. Likewise, the corn-like elder, meaning an elder with corrupted morality, resembles in attire the pure elders, but his faults will contaminate those who associate with him (*SIRD,* f. 116a6).

200. Pema Karpo states that the Buddha instituted the three-month rainy season retreat when his monks became the objects of criticism by non-Buddhists who claimed that Buddhist monks wandering around during the rainy season were crushing insects (which were far more numerous during that season than others) and therefore were not maintaining their vows not to kill (*TV* vol. Nga, f. 271a6-b3).

201. Alpha Aquiloe (*gro shun/ gro bshin*): the month that corresponds to the sixth month of the Mongolian calendar, beginning on the sixteenth of that month (*CNPTV,* f. 45b1).

202. Alpha Pegasi (*khrums stod*): the constellation by which is named the month that corresponds to the seventh month of the Mongolian calendar, beginning on the sixteenth of that month.

203. Antares (*snron*): the constellation by which is named the month that corresponds to the fourth month of the Mongolian calendar.

204. These preparations are made ten or fifteen days before the start of the retreat (Gunaprabha's *SD,* f. 61a6).

205. Gunaprabha states that an anointed stick (*bskus pa'i tshul shing*) is first offered to the Buddha or an image of him. The rest of the sticks are distributed to the monks in order of seniority who accept the sticks as a sign of joyful acceptance of the rules of the retreat. The sticks are then collected, made into a bundle, and attached to a pillar of the temple where they are kept until the end of the retreat, when they are again counted to verify the number of monks who have attended the retreat (*SD,* f. 61a7-b5).

206. Sönam Drakpa states that there are six commitments of the rainy season retreat: to remain in the place one has promised to; not to cause disputes during the retreat; to endeavor to listen, ponder, and meditate on the doctrine; not to do

repair work on monastery buildings; to remain in retreat for the specified time; and not to cross the boundary.

Disruption of the retreat occurs if a monk wanders beyond the boundary without permission and does not return until dawn of the following day. If a monk needs to go beyond the boundary for a virtuous purpose, he should be consecrated to do so. Consecration lasts for seven days. If special permission has been given, the monk is allowed to stay out for up to forty days (*SID16*, f. 26a6-b4).

207. Quitch grass (*dūrvā, ram pa*) (*Agropyron repens*): a grass used as a medicine in the ayurvedic tradition, and as substance of offering in fire ritual. The many knots of the grass are considered an auspicious symbol of longevity.

According to Sönam Drakpa, both monks (the one for whom the restrictions have to be lifted and the one appointed to lift them) hold the ends of the blade of quitch grass or kusha grass. Kusha grass is a symbol of humility: just as the kusha bends without resistance, the monk bends in humility for being allowed to perform according to the doctrine what otherwise would be a downfall (*SID16*, f. 29a6-b1).

208. According to some scholars, *kathina* (lit. "hard") refers to the particular stock of cotton given by the faithful laity to the monks for their robes. Dharmashri, however, states that *kathina* means stable (*gtan pa*) and stretched (*sra rkyang*) and is the term used for the wooden slab to which the newly made robes are secured (*Commentary on the Three Vows*, f. 97b1-2).

The *kathina* practice comprises the making of the new robes (cutting the pieces, stitching, washing, dyeing, and drying the robes all in the same day), their distribution to the monks within the boundaries of the monastery, the actual ceremony of laying them out, and their subsequent storage for the five-month period of the relaxation of rules that follows the monsoon season retreat. Tibetan commentaries refer to this practice as the "laying out of the robes on the wooden slab" (*chos gos sra brkyang 'ding ba*).

As a preparation for the "laying out" ceremony, the monks bless the new robes, gather within the boundary, and with a two-part procedure including proposal, give assent to the ceremony for laying out the robes. With a proposal, they appoint a monk to lay out the robes, and once this is done, they entrust the robes to him. If the material has not been cut, stitched, etc., the appointed monk makes sure that this is done.

As for the actual ceremony which takes place on the sixteenth, the appointed monk, in the midst of the monastic community, recites three times the formula for the laying out of the robes. Then, holding the wooden slab, he stands in front of each monk in turn (in order of seniority) and informs him that he is going to lay out the robes, while the monk shows his approval.

The robes are spread out neatly and tightly, firmly secured on the wooden slab, and stored in the same general area as the rainy season retreat has taken place. The monk especially appointed for this task watches over these robes for the duration of the holiday period.

One of the purposes of *kathina* was to provide incentive to the monks to undertake the rainy season retreat (those monks who did not stay in retreat were not allowed to participate and share the offerings distributed during the ceremony). Another purpose served was that the downfalls of "keeping," "being separated from," and "retaining cloth" did not apply to monks participating in the ceremony. Moreover, the ceremony allowed the sponsors of the community to create merit through their generous gifts to the monks (*SID16*, f. 31a3-5).

For details of this practice, see *Constitution of the Buddhist Sangha* (henceforth cited as *CBS*), Kanai Lal Hazra (Delhi: Motilal Banarsidass, 1988). For an interpretation of the purposes of this ceremony, see *Discipline, The Canonical Buddhism of the Vinayapitaka*, John C. Holt (Delhi: Motilal Banarsidass, 1981), pp. 134-137. See also Pema Karpo's *TV*, vol. Nga, f. 282.

209. To make it easy to acquire one's robes and for the donor to create merit, some of the monks' rules (with the exception of those concerning defeats, partially defeating offenses, and naturally unwholesome actions) were relaxed. During the *kathina* practice, ten infractions to the monks' rules did not apply to monks who had participated in the rainy season retreat for the full period: (1) keeping extra cloth (*gos lhag 'chang ba*); (2) being separate from the three monastic robes (*'bral ba*); (3) keeping cloth for a month (*zla 'jog*) (these first three being the first, second, and third, respectively, of the thirty downfalls that require forfeiture); (4) eating consecutively (*yang yang za ba*), which is the first of the fourth set of downfalls requiring confession alone; (5) eating separately (*'dus shing za ba*), the sixth of the fourth set of ten downfalls requiring confession alone; (6) going to the village without informing (*ma smras ba grong du 'gro ba*), the first of the ninth set of downfalls requiring only confession; (7) requesting cloth (*gos len pa*), the sixth of the first set of downfalls that involve forfeiture; (8) using rainy season retreat offerings (*rnyed pa thun mong du 'gyur ba*), the sixth of the third set of ten that involves forfeiture; (9) keeping unconsecrated pieces of cloth (*byin gyis ma brlabs pa'i gos dum 'chang ba*) that have not been cut for one of the three robes; (10) wandering about the countryside without the upper robe (*snam sbyar med par ljongs rgyu*) or being separated from the robes while in seclusion (*dgon pa'i 'bral ba*), seventh of the third set of downfalls involving forfeiture. (Gunaprabha's *SD*, f. 65b1-2; and Pema Karpo's *TV*, vol. Nga, f. 286a3-5).

210. Pema Karpo specifies which monks are not entitled to receive the offerings of robes, etc., during this ceremony: a monk who holds wayward or evil views, has committed a defeating offense, has been expelled from the monastery due to being quarrelsome, has taken a side against the doctrine, or has participated in a rainy season retreat elsewhere (*TV*, vol. Nga, f. 286b4).

211. "Ten advantages" refers to exemption from the ten rules concerning robes, etc., advantages in the sense that a monk does not incur any downfalls related to these rules.

212. This refers to any monk who has been part of the rainy season retreat and has participated in the ceremony of entrusting the monastic robes made at the end of the retreat for safeguarding during the holiday period.

213. The tradition of relaxing the rules in the *kathina* practice was abolished in Tibet at the "time of the three," the preceptor, master, and king (*mkhan slob chos*

gsum), the preceptor being Shantarakshita, the master, Padmasambhava, and the king, Trisong De'utsen (730-800). The relaxation was later revived by the Kadampa Geshé Kokyimpa (Ko khyim pa), soon to disappear again (*CNPTV,* f. 45b).

214. Vishakhadeva mentions seven appropriate materials for the monks' robes (*rgyur rung ba bdun*): wool (*bal gos*), hempen cloth (*śa na'i ras*), Bactrian fabric (*nyi 'og gi gos*), cotton (*ras gos*), linen (*zar ma'i ras*), quality *kotamba* wool (*go tam ba'i ras*), and wool made from [the inner bark of] the *dakula* plant (*du gu la'i ras*). (*Stanzas on the Discipline,* f. 17a3).

215. Ibid., f. 18a2.

216. Ibid., f. 18a1.

217. Dyes considered valuable (*tshon chen brgyad*) (and therefore not permissible): red cochineal (*rgya skyegs*), poppy (safflower) (*le brgan rtsi*), Bengal madder (*Rubia manjith*) (*btsod*), red sanders (*Caesalpinia sappam*) (*rma shing rtsi*), indigo (*mthing shing*), vermilion (cinnabar) (*mtshal*), red lead (minium) (*li khri*), and saffron (*gur gum*). Permissible dyes include: blue (*Delphinium cashmirianum*) (*sngon po*), red-ochre (red chalk) (*btsag*), orange (*ngur smrig*). Shakhyaprabha states that "orange" refers to any orange dye extracted from leaves, flowers, or fruits. Blue can be of any type (*CTHSN,* f. 150a2).

218. Skirt (*mthang gos*) refers to the lower robe or *shamtap* (*sham thabs*).

219. Skirt must cover waist and knees in cross-legged position.

220. *SD,* f. 23b6.

221. Sönam Drakpa states that the consecration of cloth intended for robes or the robes themselves (*chos gos byin gyis brlab*) is done in order not to incur the downfalls of "keeping" and "retaining" and to avoid the minor fault of not consecrating the robes. The robes are consecrated in front of a qualified fellow monk or by oneself if there is no other monk. Prescribed accessory garments that are larger than one cubit and extra articles are to be consecrated through a three-part ritual: First, the monk offers prostrations to the fellow monk. For the main part, the monk recites three times the appropriate words addressed to the other monk, thereby consecrating the cloth. To conclude, the fellow monk says, "That is the method!" to which the monk replies, "Excellent!"

Minor garments, such as hat and belt, that are not the size of a square cubit may be possessed after mentally examining them. Prescribed garments should be considered as one's own; extras, as belonging to others; and accessory garments, as belonging in common to oneself and others.

Extra garments are allowed only in certain cases, such as illness or infestation by lice (*SID16,* ff. 41b1-42b3).

222. Under no circumstances may a monk use the leather of elephant, tiger, lion, horse, or donkey (Dharmashri's *Commentary on the Three Vows,* f. 102a4-5).

223. According to Gunaprabha, in the first category, the five foods (*bza' ba lnga*) are dough-balls (*zan*), cooked rice (*'bras chen*), light mash (*lde gu*), meat (*sha*), and pastry (*khur ba*); the five beverages (*bca' ba lnga*) are drinks made from roots (*rsta ba*),

stalks or trees (*sdong bu*), leaves (*lo ma*), flowers (*me tog*), and fruits (*'bras bu*). Cooked rice includes all kinds of cooked cereals. Meat and fish may be eaten following the specifications given by the Buddha, which include the way the meat is acquired, the place, etc. Each of these foods denotes a whole class of foods that are included within permissible foods. However, the Buddha specified certain foods not to be eaten, such as the flesh of elephant, horse, snake, fox, monkey, as well as birds who eat human flesh and worms; elephant and human milk should also not be drunk by monks (*SD*, f. 77a7-b1). Shakhyaprabha lists the five foods as cooked barley, pastry cooked in oil, cooked rice, fish, and meat (*CTHSN*, f. 144a2).

224. According to Sönam Drakpa, only the latter three types of foods and medicines are to be consecrated, provided that they belong to oneself and are permissible foods. Foods to be used within a day and foods and medicine to be kept until one is cured of an illness may be consecrated only for monks who are ill. Foods to be kept for seven days may be consecrated for the disciplinary monk, the monk managing the affairs of the monastery, or a monk who is embarking on a journey and needs provisions. These are consecrated in the presence of a qualified monk, or if no monks are available, by the monk himself. First, he adds some permissible water to the food or medicine item. Then, if the food is the type that is permissible for a day, the requesting monk exclaims three times, "O Venerable One, pay attention to me! Consecrate this food of mine, the monk (so and so), to be permissible within a day." At the end, the qualified monk states, "This is the method," to which one replies, "Excellent." The other two types of foods are consecrated in the same way (*SID16*, ff. 46b1-50a1).

Dharmashri states that no consecration is specified for foods permissible before noon since the consecration of these foods will not prevent the downfall of storing them (*Commentary on the Three Vows*, f. 104a3-4).

225. Apple (*ku shu*), grape (*rgun 'brum*), and dates (*'bra go*).

226. Buttermilk (*dar ba*), curd whey (*zho kha chu*), sour gruel of rice, etc., in a state of natural fermentation (*tsab mo*).

227. Tsonapa says that suitable water (*rung chu*) is added to avoid the minor infraction of "not adding suitable water" and to observe the rules concerning what is permitted to be consumed and what is not (*SIRD*, f. 338b6).

Shakhyaprabha states that water was declared suitable to be used in foods or drinks if ascertained to be pure in three ways: drawn from a well or spring; strained by oneself, or given by a monk who knows for certain the water has been strained or by the monastic community who knows for certain; and left to sit for a day (*CTHSN*, f. 85b2).

228. See Shakhyaprabha's *CTHSN*, ff. 144b4-145a1, for details on these medicines.

229. According to Sönam Drakpa, these refer to five principal herbal medicines and five secondary ones. The five principal medicines are medicinal roots, stalks, branches, flowers, and fruits. Examples of roots include sweet flag (*shu dag*) and white aconite (*bon dkar po*); of stalks, sandalwood and heart-leaved moonseed

(*sle bres*); of branches, malabar nut tree (*ba sha ka*) and *Picra fel-terrae* (*nim pa*); of flowers, *Malabar nut tree, Picra fel-terrae, Schisandra sphareandra* (*dha ta ki*, or *da tri ga*), and naga tree (*klu shing*); and of fruits, chebulic myrobalan (*a ru ra*), beleric myrobalan (*ba ru ra*), emblic myrobalan (*skyu ru ra*), black pepper (*na le sham*), and long pepper (*pi pi ling*).

Examples of each of the five secondary medicines are asafoetida (*shing kun*), etc., potential-transforming medicines ('*gyur byed*), rock salt (*rgyam tshwa*), etc., dung from calves fed on breast milk, etc., and toxic medicines (*dug gi sman*) (*SID16*, f. 45a2-b3).

230. The three humors of Tibetan medicine: wind (*anila, rlung*), bile (*pitta, mkhris pa*), and phlegm (*kapha, bad kan*). The imbalance of one, two, or all three humors is said to cause illness.

231. Sönam Drakpa specifies that the infraction of cooking within the boundary (*mtshams btsod kyi nyes byas*) means to touch raw food with fire (to make it permissible to cook) with the intention to cook it within the boundary of the monastic community or in the vicinity but in a spot other than the appropriate kitchen.

The infraction of one day elapsing (*zhag lon gyi nye byas*) is to leave for one day (until night) food within the boundary of the community or in the vicinity but in a spot other than the kitchen (*SID*, 129a5-b3).

232. The monastic kitchen is called "house that makes permissible" (*rung khang*) because it allows the monks to cook raw food and keep food for a day, activities that would otherwise be infractions (Dharmashri's *Commentary on the Three Vows*, f. 105a2). The kitchen, located within the monastery or in its vicinity, must be consecrated on four different occasions: (1) When initially laying bricks for the walls, the monks, or the steward alone, must consecrate the kitchen by thinking and saying: "This ground is becoming the kitchen of the monastic community." (2) At any appropriate time during construction of the walls, a large number of monks consecrate the kitchen by saying: "O Venerable Ones, be in agreement that this ground is becoming the kitchen of the monastic community." (3) Once the kitchen building is completed and when one resident monk is present, the kitchen is consecrated by the monks with a two-part procedure including proposal. (4) The kitchen is consecrated by newly arrived monks when none of the previous resident monks is there, by saying simultaneously: "This place is the kitchen of the monastic community" (Pema Karpo's *TV*, vol. Nga, f. 300a2-b5).

According to Sönam Drakpa, the space designated as the monks' kitchen must be within the boundary of the monastery, the monks who together designate the space should all have the right to use the kitchen, it should not be the temple or a house needed by the other monks, it must have a roof, and it must not have been designated as the kitchen before. The rite to designate the kitchen may be performed by the monastic community as a whole or by the monk who manages the affairs of the monastery, who does so by saying three times: "May this place be fit for the monastic kitchen." This constitutes the rite (*SID16*, ff. 50a6-52a1).

233. For a description of these ceremonies, see *CBS* on *sanghakamma*, pp. 102-149. See also *SID16*, ff. 52a5-62b1.

234. This implies that if the candidate is unaware that he is less than twenty during the ordination ceremony, the ordination is valid. This ordination lasts as long as he is not aware of what his real age was at the time of ordination.

235. Atisha attributes this view to Sarvastivadin discipline masters. See *Commentary on the Lamp for the Path* (*Byang chub lam gyi sgron ma'i dka' 'grel*) (Toh. 3948), f. 262b6-7.

236. See note 20.

237. According to Pema Karpo, the Traditionalists assert that any defeating offense is necessarily a concealed one. Analysts state that the intention to conceal is not a complementary factor to the defeat, since in the case of sexual intercourse, for example, it is impossible to experience orgasm and the intention to conceal the act simultaneously, and that after the defeat has occurred, the intention to conceal it is not a complementary branch (*TV*, vol. Nga, ff. 48b4-49a1).

238. Gunaprabha lists the five menial tasks (*dman pa'i spyod pa'i lnga*) as follows: in the morning, the demoted monk should rise before all other monks and open the doors of the temple, etc.; when spiritual instructions are given, fan the other monks; sound the *gandi* stick to summon the community to the assembly hall at the appropriate times, prepare their seats, and burn incense, etc.; in the evening, wash the feet of the monks, etc.; engage continuously in wholesome activities and sit at the end of the row of monks.

The five privileges (*khyad par gyi spyod pa'i lnga*) are to be honored along with one's fellow monks; to befriend other monks, which means live in the same house, place one's bedding in the same area, etc.; to bring forth an allegation about another monk with pure status; to inflict disciplinary measures on a fellow monk; and to travel with another monk (*SD*, f. 87a3-b1). Dharmashri's *Commentary on the Three Vows* notes that only if the monk becomes a saint (*arhat*) may his original status be fully restored (f. 114b2).

239. Sönam Drakpa mentions one exception: an outstanding monk who is shameful and who upholds and understands the discourses, the discipline, and the phenomenology classes of teachings can purify a partial defeat by just confessing it in front of a single monk, without having to be demoted, do appeasing services, or be expelled from the monastery (*SID16*, f. 71b4-6).

240. Sönam Drakpa specifies that legal procedures in cases of disagreement over formal procedures (*las dbye ba'i gzhi*) are applied when a group of [at least four] monks professes ideas contrary to the doctrine with the intention of performing different formal procedures.

Such disagreements involve the basis, intent, action, and consummation. The basis is a division occurring in one of the three continents (worlds) (Unpleasant Sound is not included since the Buddha's doctrine is not found there) and within the same monastic boundary. The number of monks within that boundary number eight or more. The monks are ordinary (not exalted) and worthy to perform ceremonies. The monks causing the division profess ideas contrary to the discipline while knowing these do not conform to the monastic code.

The intention comprises an unmistaken apprehension of the matter in question and an unabated wish to create different formal procedures based on grasping to ideas contrary to the doctrine while knowing these not to conform to the monastic code.

The act consists in the performance of different ceremonies.

The consummation refers to the completion of the major parts of the formal procedure (*SID16*, f. 79b6-80b5).

Dharmashri states that the procedure for quelling such disagreement consists in first having the monks who profess ideas contrary to the doctrine admit that they have incurred a downfall that has to do with creating a schism in the monastic community and then applying subjugating measures, etc., that will remove the causes of the disagreement. As an internal support for the remedial measures, the monks should always conform to the four duties of a monk (not to respond to being chided by chiding, etc.). As an external support, the monks who have created the division should apologize. A ceremony to accept the apology is then performed and the monks are asked to perform a confession for the sake of harmony. Once this is done, both sides of the community perform the confession to promote harmony (*Commentary on the Three Vows*, f. 118a2-4).

241. See note 171.

242. See the comprehensive discussion on this subject in *CBS*, p. 125.

243. See *CBS*, p. 126, section "Nissayakamma."

244. See *CBS*, p. 126. Sönam Drakpa makes the further point that if after the disciplinary measures of censuring, surveillance, banishment, and ostracism, the monk still persists in his behavior, he must be expelled from the monastery (*SID16*, f. 64a1-2).

245. See *CBS*, p. 126. This is imposed on the monk until his attitude has changed.

246. See *CBS*, p. 127.

247. The suspension from further advice (*gdams ngag gzhag pa*) means that the community ceases trying to make the monk aware of an offense he has committed. This happens after the community has brought forth the allegation, has tried to make him acknowledge his offense, etc., but the monk has refused to admit his guilt and becomes insubordinate.

248. When a layperson, without basis, accuses a monk of having committed a defeat or shows contempt toward him, the monastic community may decree the penalty called "turning down the begging bowl" through a formal procedure. A monk is appointed to inform the layperson of its decision. If the layperson apologizes to the offended monk, the community may remove the penalty upon the layperson's request. If not, the penalty entails that monks do not visit or stay in that household, do not accept offerings or beg from him or her, and do not teach the doctrine to members of that household. Thus, the order penalizes the layperson by not giving him the privilege of acquiring merit by giving alms to the monks. (Gunaprabha's *SD*, f. 86a3 and Pema Karpo's *TV*, vol. Nga, ff. 311b4-312a).

249. Pema Karpo states that in this case, the monastic community asks a trust-worthy laywoman about the behavior of the monk, that is, whether he was walking, standing, sitting, or lying at the secluded place. If the monk acknowledges this type of infraction, he is made to confess accordingly. If the monk refuses to comply, he is subject to disciplinary measures: through a fourfold formal procedure, he is made to analyze the nature of his offense, which is a form of punishment used to humble the monk (*TV*, vol. Nga, f. 313a5-b1).

250. Sönam Drakpa states that here basis (*gzhi*) refers to the actual offense (a partial defeat since a concealed defeat cannot be remedied) of which the monk recognizes the nature without any doubt. The intent (*bsam pa*) means that the monk is not in a deranged state when he conceals the downfall and has an unwavering intention not to reveal it. The act (*sbyor ba*) consists in not revealing the offense and does not need to be enacted physically or verbally. The consummation (*mthar thug*) consists in concealing it until the first moment of dawn of the next day (*SID16*, f. 76a1-6).

251. Twenty-six ways of degrading a monk (*gzhan na gnas pa nyer drug gi spyod pa*):

  (1-3) demoting three times (*spo ba spyod pa gsum*) (demotion for a concealed partial defeat; re-demotion for a similar transgression while demoted; and a further demotion for a similar transgression while re-demoted);

  (4-6) imposing appeasing services three times (*mgu ba spyod pa gsum*) (appeasing service for an unconcealed partial defeat; reassignment to appeasing service for a similar transgression while doing appeasing service; and further appeasing service for a similar transgression while reassigned to appeasing service);

  (7-9) the threefold status of a demotee (*spo ldan gsum*) (having gone through the period of demotion but not yet reinstated to one's original status; having gone through redemotion but not yet reinstated; and having gone through further demotion but not yet reinstated);

  (10-12) the threefold status of appeasing services (*mgu ldan gsum*) (having gone through appeasing service but not yet reinstated to one's original status; having gone through reassignment to appeasing service but not yet reinstated; and having gone through further appeasing service but not yet reinstated);

  (13-16) censoring (*bsdigs pa*), surveillance (*smad pa*), banishment (*bskrad pa*) and ostracism (*phyir 'gyed pa*);

  (17-23) expulsion in the seven cases (*gnas dbyung bdun*);

  (24) expulsion of a novice (*dge tshul bsnyil ba*);

  (25) enforcing a monk to analyze the nature of downfalls (*ngo bo 'tshol ba*);

  (26) imposing penance [for downfalls that have not been concealed] (*bslab pa sbyin pa*).

These demotions, appeasing services, etc., are imposed temporarily on a monk or a nun who has incurred a partial defeat. Both demotion and appeasing services involve performing the five menial tasks and being prohibited from enjoying the five privileges (mentioned above). For details, see Sönam Drakpa's *SID16*, ff. 76b-77b6 and Pema Karpo's *TV*, vol. Nga, ff. 307a3-309a4.

252. Sönam Drakpa explains that the purpose of this basis is to make a monk recollect a downfall that he previously did not recall, and once recollected, to confess it and thus purify his morality.

The allegation is brought forth by a qualified monk in private (or in the presence of the whole community if the infraction was committed in its midst) when a monk exhibits degeneration in terms of his morality, view, rituals, and livelihood, degeneration that can be seen, heard, or suspected with an ordinary consciousness. The monk who brings forth the allegation should first consider whether he himself is qualified to do so; should analyze whether the substance of the allegation, the person toward whom it is made, and the time are appropriate or not; should have developed mindfulness and discriminative vigilance and have a compassionate disposition.

If the monk in question does not listen when admonished with gentle speech and in other ways, he incurs the partial defeat of defiance. If he continues in his defiant attitude, he is subjugated by censoring. If that does not work, he is expelled from the monastery. Alternatively, the means of subjugation are used on him from the start. If these do not work, the monk is suspended from further advice, from the possibility of attending the confession, and from the lifting of the restrictions. If these means do not work, he is expelled from the monastery (*SID16*, ff. 78a6-79b5).

253. Pema Karpo's *TV*, vol. Nga, f. 316a1-5.

254. Change in attitude occurs when the monk engaged in the dispute becomes humble or the distinguished qualities of discriminating awareness and compassion arise in him (Dharmashri's *Commentary on the Three Vows*, f. 119b5).

255. The eight types of evidence (*mngon sum brgyad*):

   (1) evidence from discussion between challenger and challenged monks (*rgol phyir rgol gnyis kyis mngon sum*): the members of the order reach agreement through discussion based on logic and scriptures;

   (2) evidence of neutral testimonies (*gzu bo'i mngon sum*): for example, if the dispute does not subside based on previous evidence, impartial monks (who are self-reliant in spiritual and material matters) are appointed;

   (3) the evidence of four monks (*dge 'dun gyis bzhi po'i mngon sum*): if the second type of evidence fails, the settling is effected by four monks who are well-acquainted with the matter of the dispute;

   (4) authoritative evidence (*gsal ba'i mngon sum*): the last evidence failing, the task of settling the dispute is entrusted through a ceremony to four or more learned monks whose qualities are more outstanding (*gsal ba*) than the previous ones;

   (5) a more authoritative evidence (*gsal ba'i gsal ba'i mngon sum*): the previous evidence failing, these monks, by means of a ceremony, appoint four other learned monks (more outstanding than the previous four) to settle the dispute;

(6) evidence of another monastic community (*dge 'dun gzhan gyi mngon sum*): the previous one failing, these last monks entrust the monk causing the dispute to the previous four; these in turn entrust him to the four previous ones; and these, to the impartial monk originally appointed to settle the dispute. This monk then entrusts the quarreling monk for three months to another section of the monastic community to settle the case;

(7) the evidence of a master repository of the three collections of the scriptures (*sde snod 'dzin pa'i mngon sum*): the previous failing, a master of the three collections of the scriptures who is acknowledged by all as ideal is entrusted with the monk for six months to solve the dispute;

(8) evidence of a powerful elder (*gnas brtan mthu dang ldan pa'i mngon sum*): the last failing, the quarreling monk is returned to the impartial monk who entrusts him for an indefinite length of time to a powerful elder, whose word cannot be trangressed by any other monk, for settlement of the dispute.

If the eight types of evidence fail to settle the dispute, it is then settled by the "way of the majority" (*gang mang gis zhi ba*): sticks are distributed to determine on which side is the majority of monks; a verdict based on the opinion of the majority is then pronounced (Sönam Drakpa's *SID16*, ff. 83b4-85b2). See also the discussion in Pema Karpo's *TV*, vol. Nga, ff. 316b-318b4.

256. This method is applied to these three cases: (1) a dispute arising from a groundless accusation (*gzhi med pa'i rtsod pa*), an allegation of a downfall that the monk has not incurred; (2) a dispute based on an unrelated allegation (*gzhi gzhan rjes su sgrub pa'i rtsod pa*), an allegation of a downfall other than the one the monk has committed; and (3) a dispute stemming from an allegation of a downfall that does not require confession (*phyir bcos la mi ltos pa'i rtsod pa*) since the downfall has already been amended.

A verdict of purity (*dag pa sbyin pa*) is a pronouncement by the community that the monk has not incurred a downfall. This verdict takes into consideration whether or not the monk (who has been asked to recall whether he has incurred a downfall) is generally of a clear mind and good memory. If he is and he does not recollect having incurred the downfall, he is to be considered pure. The verdict consists in stating: "This monk, who has a good memory, is without fault since he does not recall having incurred such and such a downfall." This verdict based on recollection (*dran pas 'dul ba sbyin pa*) is pronounced by the monastic community in the appropriate ceremony preceded by the request made by the monk himself. In this way, disputes arising in these cases are quelled. (Sönam Drakpa's *SID16*, f. 85b4-6; Pema Karpo's *TV*, vol. Nga, ff. 118b4-119a4).

257. In the case of an allegation of a downfall committed in a state of derangement, the monastic community gives a "verdict based on non-derangement" (*ma smyos pas 'dul ba sbyin pa*). This means to pronounce in the appropriate ceremony a verdict of purity through a four-part formal proposal, such as stating, "This monk is without fault since he did not incur the downfall in a state of

non-derangement." Thus, the allegation becomes meaningless and the dispute arising from it subsides (Sönam Drakpa's *SID16*, ff. 85b6-86a1).

258. When a monk does not recognize the nature of his downfall (*ltung ba'i ngo bo 'tshol ba*), the monastic community will impose on him, through a four-part formal procedure, the disciplinary measure of analyzing the nature of the downfall in order to make him aware (*SID16*, f. 86a5-6).

259. A dispute between two monks only, the one who brings forth the allegation and the accused, is pacified when the monk is made to accept the allegation (*khas blangs pas zhi ba*), is willing to refrain from repeating the offense in the future, and confesses it (Pema Karpo's *TV*, vol. Nga, ff. 119b1-120b5).

260. A dispute that involves the entire monastic community is settled in the "manner of spreading straw" (*rtsa bkram pa lta bu'i zhi ba*). Pema Karpo explains that the monks dwelling in different places assemble in order to pacify the cause of the dispute. When they first come together, they bow in respect to each other (likened to the spreading of straw so that the tips touch reciprocally) and in this way restore harmony in the community (*TV*, vol. Nga, f. 320b1). As an alternative reason for the designation "manner of spreading straw," N. Dutt notes that as this method is used to suppress all discussion concerning the dispute, it is comparable to covering mud with straw. "This method is adopted when there is the likelihood that the matter of dispute, if discussed in an open assembly, will give rise to questions that might impair the well-being of the order." The monks prostrate to each other and then proceed to amend the downfall by ceremony; thus, the dispute is settled without discussion. (*Early Monastic Buddhism* [Calcutta, 1941-45], vol. 1, p. 309.)

261. For example, the episode when as a prince he gave his body to a tigress.

262. Likely a reference to the sixteen arhats, the principal disciples of the Buddha.

263. *Yakṣa*: a class of beings said to be both benevolent and malevolent, who may be propitiated to serve the spiritual practitioner.

264. The wheel of cyclic existence (*srid pa'i 'khor lo*), commonly depicted at the entrance to a Tibetan temple, is a circle grasped by the hands, legs, and mouth of a monster who symbolizes the transitory nature of life. The inner core of the circle depicts a pig, a cock, and a snake, the three animals that symbolize, respectively, ignorance, attachment, and hatred, the three driving forces that lead beings into cyclic existence. A circle surrounding the inner core is painted half white, half black, to represent the wholesome and unwholesome actions that determine a person's good and bad migrations. The main central part of the circle, divided into six sections, represents the six realms of existence—the gods, demigods, humans, starving ghosts, animals, and hell beings. In the outer rim of the circle, twelve representations are seen that symbolize ignorance and the other links of interdependent origination in the chain of cyclic existence. Above the drawing, on the left, is the moon which symbolizes the state of perfect peace of a Buddha and on the right, a Buddha pointing his finger at it, symbolizing the means to attain perfect peace.

265. A reference to these lines from the scriptures on discipline (*vinaya*):

Follow the path of virtue, shun the unwholesome,
And enter the Buddha's doctrine.
Like an elephant in a potter's shed,
Skillfully conquer the Lord of Death.

The conscientious person
Who follows the path of discipline
Will conquer the cycle of births
And put an end to suffering.

266. See *Gateway to the Temple* by Thubten Legshay Gyatsho, trans. David Jackson, Bibliotheca Himalayica, series III, vol. 12 (Kathmandu, Nepal: Ratna Pustak Bhandar, 1979).

267. See Pema Karpo's *TV*, vol. Nga, ff. 321a6-322a2 and *CBS*, p. 89, under "Residence and Articles of Furniture."

268. Two types of reliquary (*SID16*, f. 88a4): shrine-shaped (*gtsang khang can nyid*) and pillar-like (*ka ba lta bu*).

Two types of standards: possibly the domed-shaped standard (*rgyal mtshan*) adorned with small bells on the top ring and the bell-shaped standard (*gan ji ra*).

269. Tsonapa states that these ascetic practices are the antidotes to the following, respectively: (1) attachment to good food, (2-3) gluttony, (4-6) attachment to having many clothes of fine quality, (7) attachment to mundane involvements, (8-9) attachment to owning houses, (10) attachment to both dwelling and companionship, (11) attachment to sleep, and (12) attachment to bedding (*SIRD*, f. 60a5-7).

270. Flattery, hinting, seeking reward for a favor, pretentious behavior, and hypocrisy.

271. Shakyaprabha's *Three Hundred Stanzas on the Novitiate* (*Āryamūlasarvāstivādiśrāmaṇerakārikā; gSum brgya pa/ 'Phags pa gzhi thams cad yod par smra ba'i dge tshul gyi tshig le'ur byas pa*) (Toh. 4124), f. 63b2.

272. *CTHSN*, f. 75b2.

273. Bestowal of power (*dbang skur*): not in the sense of tantric empowerment, but as power that transforms the personal liberation vows through the force of the awakening mind.

274. Vows of purification and renewal (*gso sbyong*): to purify negativity and restore virtue. The eight precepts of the purificatory fast in the Universal Way (including not eating meat) are assumed, motivated by awakening mind, in front of a person, ordained or lay, who observes the personal liberation rules, or before an image of the Buddha or other sacred representation. The ceremony for assuming these precepts consists in repeating three times the promise to follow the practices of the buddhas and bodhisattvas of the past.

275. *Amoghapasha Scripture* (*Amoghapāśahṛdayasūtra; Don yod zhags pa'i snying po'i mdo*) (Toh. 682): a scripture associated with a form of Lokeshvara, standing on a

lotus, with four faces and eight arms, holding in the right hands a vajra, a sword, a hook, and a bow; in the left, a bell, a trident, a lasso, and an arrow.

276. *GBL*, f. 13b2.

277. Karma Trinlé Choklé Namgyal (Karma phrin las phyogs las rnam rgyal): A renowned scholar, disciple of the Seventh Karmapa, Chodrak Gyatso (Chos grags rgya mtsho), and master of the Eighth Karmapa, Mikyö Dorjé (Mi bskyod rdo rje).

278. Four remedial forces: the force of repentance is to regret unwholesome deeds; the force of turning away from what is unwholesome is the resolve not to repeat unwholesome acts; the force of remedial application is to pursue various forms of virtue in order to purify unwholesome imprints; and the force of reliance is to take refuge in the Three Jewels, form the mind of awakening, confess the unwholesome, etc. These forces are compared respectively to feeling regret for having ingested poison, resolving not to ingest it again, taking medicine to cure the effect of the poison, and following the advice of the doctor who prescribes the medicine (Dharmashri's *Commentary on the Three Vows*, ff. 220b5-221b4).

279. *GBL*, f. 20b1.

280. The actual title of this scripture is *Possessing Pure Ethics Scripture* (Toh. 303), f. 127a6.

281. The *nāga* Elapatra (E la 'dab): When the Buddha was residing at Rishipatana, the naga Elapatra came to visit him in the form of a universal monarch surrounded by his court. The Buddha's disciples were impressed by him and envious of his position. The naga paid homage to the Buddha and sat beside him. However, the Buddha reproached the naga, saying that he had taken an inferior birth because he had transgressed the monastic code laid out by Kashyapa, the previous Buddha. He told him not to deceive his monks, and to go away and return later in his real form.

The following day, the naga returned in his true form of immense size. Each of his seven heads had an *ela* (pomegranate) tree growing on it with thousands of insects swarming around. Countless flies lived on each tree and foul-smelling pus and blood oozed from his body. He prostrated to the Buddha and sat at his side.

The Buddha then told his disciples that this horrible-looking creature was the real form of the universal monarch they had envied the day before. He explained to them that at the time of Buddha Kashyapa, this being had been a monk. While this monk was living under an *ela* tree, one day he struck his forehead on a branch; enraged, he cut down the tree, an act that Buddha Kashyapa had prohibited; as a result of his action, the monk was reborn as a naga. (Gelong Sönam Lha'i Wangpo's *The Jewel Lamp Illuminating the Cluster of Gems of Parables* [dPe chos rin chen spungs pa'i gsal byed rin po che'i sgron me'am gtam brgyud rin chen phreng mdzes] [Dharamsala: Department of Religious and Cultural Affairs], pp. 114-117.)

282. Nagarjuna's *Letter to a Friend* (Suhṛllekha; bShes pa'i spring yig) (Toh. 4182), f. 41a2-3

283. *Possessing Pure Ethics Scripture*, f. 127b1.

284. *Stanzas on the Discipline*, f. 2a4-5.

285. *King of Contemplations Scripture* (*Sarvadharmasvabhāvasamatāvipañcita-samādhirājanāmamahāyānasūtra; Chos thams cad kyi rang bzhin mnyam pa nyid rnam par spros pa ting nge 'dzin gyi rgyal po zhes bya ba theg pa chen po'i mdo*) (Toh. 127), f. 128a6.

286. This discussion is taken from Asanga's *Compendium of Discipline* (*Vinaya-saṃgraha; 'Dul ba bsdu pa*) (Toh. 4040) (henceforth cited as *CD*), which includes topics treated extensively in his *Stages of the Bodhisattva* (*Bodhisattvabhūmi; Byang chub sems dpa'i sa*) (Toh. 4037) (henceforth cited as *SB*). The fifth point, the abandonment of latent emotions, is drawn from his *Proclaimers' Stages* (*Śrāvakabhūmi; Nyan thos kyi sa*) (Toh. 4036) (henceforth cited as *PS*), except for the mentioning of the stages such as the full sight of the positive.

287. The followers of the Buddha distinguished as four classes (*'khor rnam pa bzhi*): monk, nun, male lay practitioner, and female lay practitioner.

288. See Asanga's *CD*, f. 5a2-3.

289. See Asanga's *CD*, f. 5a3-4.

290. Five types of despair (*'gyod pa*) refers to five thoughts that arise when one commits a transgression: (1) "With this kind of start, my observance will always be faulty"; (2) "The other monks and the gods will belittle me for this"; (3) "The Teacher (Buddha) and the wise men following the pure life will surely condemn me"; (4) "From here to the border regions, I will be known as an evil-doer, and [everyone] will talk about me indecently"; (5) "With this unvirtuous beginning, I will be reborn in the bad destinies after leaving this body" (Asanga's *CD*, f. 9a7-b).

Five-limbed conscientiousness (*bag yod pa'i skabs lnga/ yan lag lngas bsdus pa'i bag yod/ yan lag lnga dang ldan pa'i bag yod*): conscientiousness that (1) puts an end to past transgressions; (2) puts an end to future transgressions; (3) puts an end to present transgressions; (4) learns what should be done from previous mistakes; and (5) puts all these points together and henceforth acts accordingly.

Five thoughts that dispel despair (*'gyod ba sel ba*): (1) "The Blessed One has taught a doctrine that has both a foundation and a way of deliverance; therefore, there surely is a means of rising up from downfalls"; (2) "Because I have not yet learned that transgressions are committed due to ignorance, irreverence, negligence, and strong passions, I should understand the nature of these causes, abandon them, and develop their opposites, knowledge...up to respect"; (3) "I now generate the resolve to awaken with a sincere and noble intention so that I will not go on failing"; (4) "I have now properly confessed my failings in the presence of learned and pure persons"; (5) "I have entered the religious life and am following the well-spoken teaching on discipline, and to give in to despair when I go against its training is not proper. The Blessed One condemned the stream of despair by enumerating the obstructions it creates. Now, knowing that despair is the factor causing obstacles for me, it is neither right nor proper for me to indulge in it and not to rid myself of it" (Asanga's *CD*, f. 9b).

See also Bodhibhadra's *Revelation of the Difficult Points of the Twenty Verses on the Commitments of Awakening Mind* (Bodhisattva-saṃvaraviṃśakapañjikā; *Byang chub sems dpa'i sdom pa nyi shu pa'i dka' 'grel*) (Toh. 4083), ff. 187b5-188a1.

291. In the Beijing edition of *IOK*, *shes pa* (knowing) replaces *bag yod pa* (conscientiousness) of the Pelpung edition (*dPal spungs thub bstan chos 'khor gling*, 1844).

292. Four means to prevent the occurrence of transgressions to the rules: (1) to maintain restraint by [watching] the doors of the senses; (2) to observe moderation in food; (3) to persevere in meditation in the first and latter parts of the night instead of sleeping; (4) to be mindful in one's behavior (Asanga's *CD*, f. 9a3).

293. Asanga's *Compendium of Discipline* lists the five factors incompatible with the training (*bslab pa dang mi mthun pa'i chos lnga*): (1) to be subject to obstacles (*bar du gcod pa*); (2) to construct a similitude of the true teaching (*dam pa'i chos ltar bcos pa*); (3) to befriend evil persons (*sdig pa'i grogs po*); (4) to be a fool with strong passions (*glen zhing nyon mongs pa mang ba*); and (5) to have a meagre accumulation of merits from previous lives (*sngon gyi tshogs stobs chung ba*).

To explain: (1) to be subject to the five types of obstacles—obstacles to the practice of higher ethics, to the practice of higher concentration, to the practice of higher wisdom, to good destinies, to receiving offerings, to life, and to everyday activities; (2) to teach a false and mistaken doctrine and have others practice it; (3) to have an evil friend who is heedless, whose conduct is unwholesome, and who induces one to view inferior characteristics as good qualities and virtues; (4) to be an inferior person and stupid fool with strong passions; (5) to be one who in past lives has not cultivated faith and other wholesome qualities, who therefore has inferior faith and so forth in the present life, and who is unable to meditate although striving to attain perfect peace in this life (*CD*, ff. 12a3-13a1).

294. The five factors conducive to the training (*bslab pa dang mthun pa'i chos lnga*): (1) proper ordination (*legs par mngon par 'byung ba*), which means to receive monk's ordination with the right motivation to attain perfect peace and with the desire to train in the proper discipline, and not to escape a debt, etc.; (2) complete familiarity (*yongs su 'dris ba*) which refers to familiarity with the scriptures that present discourses, discipline, and phenomenology, beginning with the knowledge of what does and what does not constitute an offense and the means to rise from transgressions to the rules; (3) examination (*so sor rtog pa*) during the three periods of the day as to whether one's observance of the rules is proper; for example, seeing that one's observance was good in the morning, to be joyful and to train likewise throughout the day and night; (4) meditation on the remedy (*gnyen po sgom pa*) which means not simply boasting of being moral but to actually engage in the remedy for attachment and the other passions; and (5) conviction (*dad pa*) that offenses will bear their results in future lives and the wish to avoid these results.

Ordination is the basis for the other four. Familiarity prevents transgressions to the rules due to ignorance. Examination prevents transgressions due to heedlessness. Meditation on the remedy prevents transgressions due to strong passions. Conviction prevents transgressions due to irreverence (Asanga's *CD*, f. 15a1-2).

295. Five topics to be known (*yongs su shes pa'i chos lnga*): entities (*dngos po*), transgressions to the rules (*ltung ba*), types of person (*gang zag*), accepting of material offerings (*rdzas blang ba*), and causes of harm (*gnod pa*). These are explained in the following way:

> (1) entities refers to the aggregates, experiential elements, experiential media, twelve links of interdependent arising, and proper and improper behavior;
>
> (2) transgressions to the rules include the cause (of a transgression, desire or hatred), instigation (by body, speech, or mind), the entity (an animate or inanimate object of the transgression), the deed (doing what is not proper or not doing what is appropriate), and consummation (having reached the point at which the action is complete and irreversible);
>
> (3) types of person refers to differences among individuals in terms of ethics, social status, attainments, who is qualified to bring forth an accusation against another monk, etc.;
>
> (4) accepting material offerings refers to rules about accepting offerings that are related to transgressions involving forfeiture, distributing the articles of a monk who because of his immoral conduct has been expelled in order to bring peace to the community, etc.;
>
> (5) causes of harm in this life means to worry that after death others will inflict injury of various forms on oneself; to strive greatly for life's necessities out of avarice and not true need; to engage in means of livelihood that involve mortification of the body, such as cutting off one's limbs (in order to beg); to engage in actions that injure the body, such as starving one's body, putting oneself into fire, or jumping off cliffs, believing that one will attain higher rebirths as a result; self-mortification with the intention of realizing the ultimate, not knowing the right path to such realization (Asanga's *CD*, ff. 18b4-21a6).

296. Five factors that foster peace (*nye bar zhi ba'i chos lnga*): (1) peace by associating [with others] in a gentle way (*des shing 'grogs na bde ba nyid*); (2) abandonment (meditation) (*spong ba*); (3) branches of abandonment (*spong ba'i yan lag*); (4) veneration (*bsnyen bkur*); and (5) settling quarrels (*rtsod pa*). These are explained in the following way:

> (1) the first comprises six factors that foster peace;
>
> (2) abandonment consists of the four "wheels" of gods and humans: mental quiescence and insight which make one become a supreme god among gods and a supreme human among humans; these are like the wheels of a chariot without which the chariot cannot move;
>
> (3) the branches of abandonment or meditation are five: conviction in the spiritual goal one has set about to achieve; speaking with one's teachers straightforwardly as if one were speaking to oneself; mental energy; physical energy; and the capacity to discriminate between the well-spoken [words of the Buddha] and misleading doctrines;

(4) the fourth is reverence for the teacher who provides instruction on discipline and meditation and instills wisdom in oneself, reverence for the teaching, etc.;

(5) the fifth concerns the seven ways of settling disputes previously described (Asanga's *CD*, ff. 15b1-18a).

297. Five qualities of a monk who is faithful to his discipline (*dge slong 'dul ba'i bslab pa la brtson pa'i chos lnga*): (1) perfect morality (*tshul khrims phun sum tshogs pa*), (2) perfect view (*lta ba phun sum tshogs pa*), (3) perfect activities (*cho ga phun sum tshogs pa*), (4) perfect livelihood (*'tsho ba phun sum tshogs pa*), and (5) freedom from quarrels and disputes (*phan tshun 'thab pa dang rtsod pa med pa*).

These are explained in the following way: (1) having neither a weak discipline nor an overly strict one, etc.; (2) elimination of the view that holds perishable aggregates to be the self, the views that hold to the extremes (of eternalism or nihilism), and wayward views (denying causality, etc.); and not holding these erroneous views as supreme, or perverse ethics and modes of conduct as superior; (3) expertise in everyday activities, in wholesome activities, and in modes of conduct that do not contradict worldly customs or the monastic discipline, etc.; (4) freedom from illicit forms of livelihood; and (5) avoidance of quarrels and disputes motivated by anger, grudges, etc. (Asanga's *CD*, f. 21a6-b).

298. Five strengths (*stobs lnga*) : (1) the strength of practice (*sbyor ba'i stobs*), (2) strength of intention (*bsams pa'i stobs*) (to purify transgressions to the rules), (3) strength of understanding (*rtogs pa'i stobs*) the discipline, (4) strength of knowledge (*shes pa'i stobs*) of the discipline, and (5) strength of abiding (*gnas pa'i stobs*) in the discipline (Asanga's *CD*, f. 22a6).

299. In the following pages, Kongtrul makes an extremely brief summary of the last sixty-eight folios (from f. 127b5 to f. 195) of Asanga's *Proclaimer's Stages* which masterfully discusses mental quiescence and insight and their application in attaining awakening. A comprehensive commentary on this summary is beyond the scope of this translation; however, a few notes of explanation will be provided to clarify the general meaning.

300. Latent emotions (*nyon mongs pa'i bag la nyal*): subtle forms of emotions that are not yet manifest and their seeds.

301. The practitioner, motivated to accomplish his goal, respectfully approaches a master to request instruction. A preceptor, tutor, spiritual master, or any experienced meditator may act as his spiritual advisor. The practitioner requests instruction, whereupon the master inquires about his true motivation and encourages him in his quest by explaining the benefits of dedicating oneself to a life of meditation.

Following this, the master asks the beginner the following questions concerned with the four requirements: (1) Have you the desire to follow a non-Buddhist teacher or another object of worship other than the Buddha, his teaching, and his community? (2) Have you maintained pure ethics and have you the correct view needed to engage in the meditation for the sake of attaining liberation? (3) Have you heard and retained much or little of the discourses that expound the four truths and their distinctions, etc.? (4) Have you become a renunciate with an earnest interest in attaining perfect peace and transcending suffering?

If the beginner answers these in a way that shows his aptitude, the master proceeds in examining the four causes or conditions: aspiration, family, capabilities, and tendencies. To examine his aspiration, the following questions are asked: "To which way do you aspire? To the way of the proclaimers, the way of the solitary sages, or the Universal Way?"

Following this, questions are asked concerning his family or affinity, capabilities, and tendencies. If the beginner is intelligent, he will understand the questions and will answer in the correct way. If he is dull, he will not understand well what is being asked and his answers will reflect this. Then, the teacher will ascertain his affinity in this manner: using clear, connected, various, pleasant, and earnest words, the teacher will give a discourse on the proclaimers' way. If the beginner possesses affinity for the proclaimers' way, he will be overjoyed to hear about it and will show great interest. Similarly, he might show affinity for the way of the solitary sages. If he has an affinity for the Universal Way, upon hearing discourses on that way, he will be overjoyed and have sincere interest in it, and will not show any affinity for the ways of the proclaimers or the solitary sages.

Likewise, the teacher tests the capabilities of the beginner by teaching first an easy topic, a medium, and then a profound one. He determines whether the monk is dull, middling, or sharp based on his comprehension, retention, and analytic ability.

The master then tests his tendencies: If the beginner's strongest emotion is attachment, when he hears teaching on faith, he will feel great inclination and his mind will become smooth. If he tends toward anger, he will not like the teaching. If he tends toward ignorance, when he hears a discourse on the transcendence of suffering and the elimination of material things, he will become afraid. If he tends toward jealousy, he will not listen to the teacher's discourse with respect (Asanga's *PS*, ff. 127b6-129b6).

302. Asanga explains that maintaining and creating the conditions for contemplation (*ting nge 'dzin gyi tshogs bsrung zhing bsags pa*) means to be endowed with the ethical vows not to give up the effort to maintain conscientiousness, to practice the points of training in order to bring them to fulfillment, and not to allow the ethics taught by the Buddha to degenerate. This implies not to regress from the path of training in the perfect morality that one has acquired, to attain the path of training that one has not yet attained, to restrain the doors of the senses in accordance with the ethical vows, to be moderate in one's eating, to exert oneself in one's training by renouncing sleep during the latter part of the first and last parts of the night, to be mindful in behaviors, etc. (*PS*, ff. 130a5-139b3).

303. Perfect seclusion (*rab tu dben pa*) has three aspects: most appropriate place

(*gnas phun sum tshogs pa*), most appropriate behavior (*spyod lam phun sum tshogs pa*), and most appropriate seclusion (*dben pa phun sum tshogs pa*). The first refers to an appropriate place for meditation in an isolated environment, be it at the foot of a tree, a charnel ground, a cave, a grass hut, etc. The place should possess the five characteristics of being pleasant, with mild climatic conditions, free from causes for fear, convenient with regard to life's necessities, and in close proximity to spiritual advisors.

The second refers to practicing meditation during the day and during the first part of the night, sleeping during the middle part of the night, and rising early during the latter part of the night; to sit crossed-legged on the type of bed or seat permitted by the Buddha, in other words, to follow the example of the Buddha and his disciples in not undergoing the austerities of non-Buddhists, but to sit straight in a natural way, without contrived attitude, avoiding fogginess and sleepiness, mindful and free of distractions.

The third, most appropriate seclusion, refers to physical and mental seclusion. Physical seclusion (for renunciates) means not staying with laypeople. Mental seclusion means that one eliminates sources for negative emotions, forsakes neutral activities, and engages in meditative absorption on a worthy object, which is attentive meditation derived from the conditions conducive to contemplation (*PS*, ff. 130b3-131b).

304. Intense concentration (*sems rtse gcig pa*): concentration or a one-pointed virtuous mind refers to a stream of consciousness that possesses continuous mindfulness, a concordant focus of meditation, and a steady focusing on it. This concentration lacks unwholesome factors and is joyful.

Such concentration is twofold, pertaining to mental quiescence and insight. The first consists of the nine methods of mental quiescence (setting the mind) (see note 312); the second, to the four aspects of insight (see note 313) (*PS*, f. 132a3-b6).

305. Removing impediments (*sgrib pa rnam par sbyong ba*) means to apply remedies to the four impediments, with the recognition of their nature, causes, and faults.

The four impediments are distress, obstacles, conceptions, and pride. Distress denotes states of mind such as exhilaration, mental distress, disturbance, a polluted desire to pursue meditation or a dislike for it. Obstacles consist of the five kinds of desires, the longing for objects of desire, etc. Conceptions denotes all tainted thoughts such as desire. Pride is feeling satisfied with just a little wisdom or vision, thinking that one has attained a definite level above that of others.

The causes of distress are linked to the actions of previous lives, a weak physical constitution due to illness, excessive exertion, mistaken exertion, unexperienced exertion, emotionality, and not being accustomed to meditation. The cause that creates obstacles, conceptions, and pride is a continuous misapprehension of the factors that lead to these. Misapprehension results from not contemplating "ugliness" and thus becoming drawn to beauty, not developing loving-kindness and thus being subject to anger, not nurturing clarity and thus being subject to obscurity, and not engaging in mental quiescence and thus having restless thoughts.

As a consequence of these states of mind, one's yogic practice weakens, one remains ignorant of what one ought to know, loses the knowledge one has, remains entangled in emotions and suffering, demeans oneself and is degraded by others, and experiences a life in hell after dying.

The remedy to distress is mindfulness which uplifts the mind and removes discouragement. Distress caused by a weak constitution is removed by adjusting one's effort so that it is not too strenuous, and mistaken effort is remedied by having respect. Distress caused by emotionality is remedied by training in meditation on ugliness and other focuses. Not being accustomed to meditation is resolved by understanding the need to practice meditation and encouraging oneself to become familiar with meditation.

The remedy for the remaining impediments is to correct one's wrong thinking and engagement (Asanga's *PS*, ff. 146b3-147b4).

306. The characteristics of mentally oriented contemplation (*yid la byed pa bsgom pa*) are subsumed under single-pointed concentration, forsaking the mistaken approach in removing impediments, and training in the perfect practice. For a beginner, the contemplation entails striving to attain joy in concentration of mind and in the work of abandonment through four types of mental contemplation, beginning with ever-present distress (see note 314) (*PS*, f. 149a2-3).

307. Grossness (*rags pa*) and peacefulness (*zhi ba*). After achieving quiescence (which is the preparation for the first concentration and also considered a kind of beginner's contemplation) (*yid la byed pa las dang po ba*), in order to become free of the desires characteristic of the desire realm, the meditator initially views the desire realm as gross and the first concentration of the form realm as peaceful. To view the desire realm as gross means that one contemplates the faults of the environment and the beings of that realm. To view the first concentration as peaceful means that one views it as lacking the faults of the desire realm (focusing, for example, on the fact that beings in the first concentration are peaceful, lack belligerence, have shame, have less suffering, and live in inestimable mansions, etc.).

To effect freedom from the desires of the desire realm, the meditator first engages in "mental contemplation based on appreciation," derived mainly from learning and reflection. Subsequently, the "mental contemplation of thorough isolation" (so called because the yogi is for the first time separated from the major emotions related to the desire realm) is applied. Then one engages in the "mental contemplation of analysis" (to determine whether or not one still has to forsake emotions related to this realm); lastly, one applies the "contemplation of the final training" (when one attains the uninterrupted path of stopping the obscuring emotions with regard to the desire realm) and subsequently attains the result of the final training, the first concentration, in which the emotions related to the desire realm are temporarily suppressed.

To become free from the attachment to the remaining concentrations within conditioned existence, the same contemplation process is repeated with respect to the second, third, and the other higher states of concentration up to the peak of existence.

Generally speaking, having attained mental quiescence and insight, a practitioner has two choices: to use these attainments in order to advance to a higher state of existence or to use them to escape conditioned existence. If one chooses to attain liberation, one will do so by uprooting the emotions. One will not analyze the faults of the desire realm, and so forth, by discriminating the aspects of grossness and peacefulness. Instead, one will practice the five contemplations just mentioned, switching their focus to the aspects of the four noble truths, impermanence, and so forth.

For an elaborate discussion of these points, see Lati Rinbochay et al., *Meditative States in Tibetan Buddhism* (London: Wisdom Publications, 1983).

308. Worldly paths (*'jig rten pa'i lam*): paths that lead to the attainment of higher status within conditioned existence. To be free from desires with respect to the worldly paths means to have temporarily suppressed the manifest emotions related to these states of existence.

309. See note 181.

310. The eight stages of the proclaimers (*nyan thos kyi sa brgyad*) are as follows:

(1) the stage of full positive sight (*dkar po rnam par mthong ba'i sa*), which corresponds to the path of preparation of the proclaimers, so called because it is a virtue conducive to liberation. "Positive" refers to liberation, and since the focus of this level is the seeking of liberation, it is virtue;

(2) the stage of the affinity (*rigs kyi sa*) that corresponds to the acceptance and highest quality stage of the proclaimers' path of preparation, so called because at that level the practitioner cannot change his affinity to become a solitary sage or a bodhisattva;

(3) the stage of the eighth (*brgyad pa'i sa*), when the practitioner becomes a stream-enterer (see note 184) (eighth when counting the level of abider in the result of the *arhat* state as the first level);

(4) the stage of seeing (*mthong ba'i sa*) in which the practitioner abides in the result of the stream-enterer, so called because the practitioner acquires a direct understanding of all aspects of the four truths (see note 315);

(5) the stage of the subtle (*srab pa'i sa*), when the practitioner has eliminated most, but not all, of the emotions related to the desire realm so that he will be born again once (in the desire realm); thus, he or she is called a once-returner;

(6) the stage free of attachment (*'dod chags dang bral ba'i sa*), when the practitioner has eliminated all kinds of attachment pertaining to the desire realm and will not be born again in it; thus, he is called a non-returner;

(7) the stage of actualization of the deed (*byas pa rtogs pa'i sa*) that corresponds to the attainment of the goal of the arhat, the path of direct realization of the four truths, and liberation;

(8) the level of the proclaimer (*nyan thos kyi sa*), not a level separate from the above seven, but the basis for their differentiation.

See Kongtrul's *IOK*, vol. III, Book IX, pp. 493-494.

311. See note 182.

312. Four mental contemplations (*yid la byed pa bzhi*) of quiescence: (1) forcible engagement (*bsgrims te 'jug pa'i yid byed*); (2) interrupted engagement (*chad cing 'jug pa'i yid byed*); (3) uninterrupted engagement (*chad par med pa 'jug pa'i yid byed*); and (4) effortless engagement (*rtsol ba med par 'jug pa'i yid byed*).

The first contemplation is applied to the initial two stages of achieving mental quiescence: setting and continuous setting of the mind. The second contemplation is applied to the next five stages of achieving mental quiescence: resetting the mind, close setting, disciplining, pacifying, and thoroughly pacifying. The third contemplation is applied to the stage called single-pointed setting. The fourth contemplation is applied to the stage called setting in equipoise (*PS*, f. 131b1).

Concerning the nine methods in achieving mental quiescence (setting the mind) (*sems gnas pa'i thabs dgu*), Asanga states: (1) Setting the mind (*'jog pa*) denotes the initial meditative stabilization that frees the mind from distractions by withdrawing it from all external objects and focusing it on an internal object. (2) Continuous setting of the mind (*yang dag par 'jog pa*) is a meditative stabilization that cuts through the oscillation, coarseness, and movements of the mind by resetting it on the same focus and by making it clearer, thus making the mind more subtle and undistracted. (3) Resetting the mind (*bsdus te 'jog pa*) is a meditative stabilization that draws back the mind which due to forgetfulness has left its settled state and become distracted by an outer object. (4) Close setting (*nye bar 'jog pa*) is a meditative stabilization that causes the mind to remain on its object once set on it so that the mind does not project outwardly in spite of subsequent influences. (5) Disciplining (*'dul bar byed pa*) denotes a meditative stabilization so that when the mind becomes distracted by the perception of a form, sound, etc., or by thoughts of desire, hatred, or stupidity, it is held right from the outset with the awareness of the faults of such objects, not projecting to these objects. (6) Pacifying (*zhi bar byed pa*) is a mental stabilization so that when the mind is disturbed by thoughts or emotions, such as longing for the objects of one's desires, the mind is held from the outset by the awareness of their faults and does not follow these emotions. (7) Thoroughly pacifying (*nye bar zhi bar byed pa*) is a meditative stability so that when due to forgetfulness, thoughts related to outer objects and disturbing emotions arise, the mind is aware of their being sources of suffering and eliminates them. (8) Single-pointed setting (*rgyud gcig tu byed pa*) is a meditative stabilization that is free from interruptions and set continuously in a state of concentration. (9) Setting in equipoise (*ting nge 'dzin du byed pa*) denotes a meditative stabilization in which the mind enters spontaneously an undistracted state of concentration free from mental activity as a result of the habituation of repeated concentration. (*PS*, f. 132b3) See also Hopkins' *ME*, pp. 80-86 and Lati Rinpochay's *Meditative States*, pp. 58-72.

313. Four mental contemplations of insight: analysis of phenomena (*chos rnams rnam par 'byed pa*), clear analysis (*rab tu rnam par 'byed pa*), thorough examination (*yongs su rtog pa*), and thorough investigation (*yongs su dpyod pa*). These four analyses comprise rough and subtle discrimination of the phenomenal and noumenal aspects of the five aggregates and other subjects.

Insight is explained as having three approaches and focusing on six different aspects. The three approaches are insight that simply engages in its object without reflection, examination, or ascertainment; insight that engages in seeking, i.e., reflection, examination, and ascertainment; and insight that engages in discriminative examination of the object sought in such ways [the object here being selflessness].

The six aspects that are investigated in insight meditation are meaning (*don*), entity (*dngos po*), characteristics (*mtshan nyid*), class (*phyogs*), time (*dus*), and reasonings (*rigs pa*). The first involves recognition of the given meaning of an instruction; the second, discrimination as to whether an external or internal entity is meant; the third, determining particular and general characteristics; the fourth, determining its virtuous or unvirtuous nature by examining faults and qualities; the fifth, determining the occurrence of something in the past, present, or future; and the sixth, investigation of the object using four types of reasoning: reasoning of dependence (*ltos pa'i rigs pa*) (the cause); reasoning of functionality (*bya ba byed pa'i rigs pa*); validity (*'thad sgrub kyi rigs pa*); and nature (*chos nyid kyi rigs pa*). (Asanga's *PS*, ff. 134a1-142a6) See also Lati Rinpochay's *Meditative States*, pp. 155-156.

314. Four mental contemplations: ever-present distress (*sems kun du gdung bar 'gyur ba'i yid la byed pa*), moistened mind (*sems mngon par brlon par 'gyur ba'i yid la byed pa*), giving ease (*shin tu sbyangs ba skyed pa'i yid la byed pa*), and purifying pristine awareness and vision (*ye shes dang mthong ba rnam par sbyong ba'i yid la byed pa*).

(1) Ever-present distress is a mental contemplation that turns the meditator away from things that are distressful or conducive to distress (what is tainted and its related factors, wealth, friends, etc.). (2) Moistened mind is a mental contemplation that causes joy in things that are joyful or conducive to joy (the Three Jewels, the basis of the training, one's own fortunate condition, etc.). (3) Giving ease is a mental contemplation that at the right time turns one away from things that are distressful or conducive to distress and causes one to take joy in things that are joyful or conducive to joy. It thereby pacifies the mind inwardly and places it in a meditative stability of single-pointed awareness in which there are no attributes (to apprehend) and no conceptions. These causes and conditions produce satisfaction of body and mind, and ease of body and of mind, which are remedies for physical and mental unworkability.

With ever-present distress, the mind turns away from what is tainted and related factors. With the mind moistened with joy, one is attracted to renunciation, seclusion, and the meditation practice. With the mental engagement that gives ease, the mind settles into a state of quiescence. With the mental engagement that purifies wisdom and vision, one applies the four kinds of analysis of phenomena. (Asanga's *PS,* ff. 149a3-151a6).

315. Sixteen attributes of the four noble truths, four for each truth. The four attributes of the truth of suffering (*sdug bsngal bden pa'i rnam pa bzhi*): impermanence (*anitya, mi rtag pa*) in that phenomena arise and perish moment by moment; misery (*duḥkha, sdug bsngal ba*), the continuous injury caused by the three kinds of sufferings; emptiness (*śūnya, stong pa*), the absence of a permanent, single,

and independent self among the aggregates; and selflessness (*nairātmya, bdag med pa*) in that the aggregates are not the self.

The four attributes of the truth of the source of suffering (*kun 'byung bden pa'i rnam pa bzhi*): the cause (*hetu, rgyu*), the actions and emotions that produce the suffering of cyclic existence; the source (*samudaya, kun 'byung*), the origin of the six types of existence within the three realms; strong production (*prabhava, rab skye*), the cause for the emergence of strong emotions that results in an immediate experience of suffering; and the condition (*pratyaya, rkyen*), the actions and emotions that create the aggregates permeated with suffering in the three realms.

The four attributes of the truth of cessation ('*gog pa'i bden pa'i rnam pa bzhi*): definite cessation (*nirodha, 'gog pa*) of emotions and intentional actions; peace (*śānta, zhi ba*) devoid of any experience of suffering; excellence (*praṇīta, gya nom pa*) in that there will be no future birth and suffering in the three realms; and definite emergence (*niḥsaraṇa, nges par 'byung ba*), the deliverance from cyclic existence and attainment of the state of bliss.

The four attributes of the truth of the path (*lam gyi bden pa'i rnam pa bzhi*): the path (*mārga, lam*) that takes one from the level of an ordinary being to the exalted state; appropriateness (*nyāya, rigs pa*) in that the path is the antidote to the emotions that are inappropriate; achievement (*pratipad, sgrub pa*) or perfect engagement of an unmistaken mind; deliverance (*nairyāṇika, nges par 'byin pa*) or separation from cyclic existence and attainment of the state of perfect peace.

316. The stage of appreciation (*mos pa'i spyod pa'i sa/ mos pa'i sa*) refers to the path of preparation.

317. So called because it is based on hearing and reflection on the teaching.

318. See Hopkins' *ME*, pp. 94-95.

319. Asanga states that the mental contemplation of thorough isolation refers to the mental engagement that possesses the perfect path able to remove the emotions, from the initial direct perception of truth up to the abandonment of the factors to be forsaken on the path of seeing (*PS*, f. 191b3-4).

320. Reading *dpyod pa* for *sbyor ba*.

321. Reading *sdud* for *sdug*.

322. The path of meditation comprises eleven aspects: mental quiescence, insight, meditation on the mundane path, on the supramundane path, on the small path, on the middling path, and on the great path, on the preparatory path, on the uninterrupted path, on the fully liberated path, and on the special path.

(1) Meditation on mental quiescence comprises the nine methods (see note 312); (2) insight comprises the four analyses (see note 313); (3) meditation on the mundane path consists in viewing the "grossness" (faults) of the lower levels and viewing the "peacefulness" (qualities) of the higher ones and becoming free of the attachment to various states of existence up to the one called nothingness (the third of those within the formless realm); (4) meditation on the

supramundane path consists in contemplating the truth of suffering and the truth of the path, and in freeing oneself from attachment to the various states of existence up to the peak of existence; (5) the meditation on the small path consists in forsaking the gross level of emotions; (6) the meditation on the middle, in forsaking the middling emotions; (7) the meditation on the great path, in forsaking the subtle emotions; (8) the meditation on the preparatory path consists in preparation for the training through which the emotions are forsaken; (9) meditation on the uninterrupted path is characterized by the abandonment of these emotions; (10) meditation on the fully liberated path is the path that arises as soon as these have been abandoned; (11) meditation on the special path is characterized by the attainment of the final result, in which no further training is needed. (Asanga's *PS*, ff. 192b1-193a2) See also Hopkins' *ME*, pp. 104-108.

323. Asanga explains that the attainment of adamantine contemplation (*rdo rje lta bu'i ting nge 'dzin*) indicates that all impediments to awakening will be overcome. Just as the diamond is the finest of all precious stones, being harder than pearl, lapis lazuli, coral, etc., and able to cut through others while being itself indestructible, the adamantine contemplation is the best of all meditative absorptions in that it outshines all emotions and is not conquered by them (*PS*, f. 193a6-b1).

324. See note 184. See also Hopkins' *ME*, pp. 106-108.

Chapter III: The Commitments of Awakening Mind

1. Asanga's *Stages of the Bodhisattva* (henceforth cited as *SB*) (*Bodhisattvabhūmi; Byang chub sems dpa'i sa*) (Toh. 4037), f. 9a3-5.

2. Asanga states that the perfect affinity (*rigs phun sum tshogs pa*) refers to an affinity for the Universal Way. This affinity is called *tathāgatagarbha* or buddhanature and in higher Buddhist philosophical and meditational systems is said to exist in every sentient being regardless of his or her status or form of life. Such buddha-nature has two aspects, intrinsic (*prakṛtistha, rang bzhin gyis gnas pa'i rigs*) and evolved (*samudānīta, yang dag par bsgrubs pa'i rigs*). The first has existed since time without beginning by virtue of the very nature of things (*dharmatā-pratilabdha, chos nyid kyis thob pa*); the second is gained as a result of having cultivated what is wholesome in previous lives. The affinity referred to here is the one gained by virtue of the very nature of things (*SB*, f. 2b4).

3. The two aspects of relative awakening mind: the aspiration to awaken and venturing on the path to awakening.

4. *Mahāyānasūtrālaṃkārakārikā; Theg pa chen po'i mdo sde'i rgyan zhes bya ba'i tshig le'ur byas pa* (Toh. 4020), f. 4b5-6.

5. Sthiramati specifies that awakening mind is formed by this factor when the student repeats after the preceptor the appropriate formula for its generation after having understood the significance, benefits, etc., of awakening mind itself as have been explained by the preceptor or master. Such an awakening mind is referred to as a "sacred mind conceived from words." (*Commentary on the Scripture*

Ornament [*Sūtrālaṃkāravṛttibhāṣya; mDo sde rgyan gyi 'grel bshad*] [henceforth cited as *CSO*] [Toh. 4034], vol. Mi, ff. 54b2-55a2.)

6. Vasubandhu states that awakened affinity refers to an affinity for the Universal Way that has awakened from a latent state and become manifest as a person's perceivable qualities. These qualities include spontaneous compassion; interest in the Universal Way; ability to withstand hardships [for others' sake]; and virtuous engagement in the six perfections. (*Explanation of the Scripture Ornament* [*Sūtrā-laṃkāravyākhyā; mDo sde'i rgyan gyi bshad pa*] [henceforth cited as *ESO*] [Toh. 4026], f. 137b4.) Sthiramati states that a mind of awakening may be formed simply through the force of one's affinity for the bodhisattva path (*CSO*, vol. Mi, f. 54b3).

7. Vasubandhu explains that a root of virtue is nurtured as a result of the evolution of one's affinity for the Universal Way (*ESO*, f. 140a1).

8. To hear expositions on various subjects of the Buddhist teachings over and over again (Vasubandhu's *ESO*, f. 140a1). Sthiramati points out that an awakening mind may be formed in this life by having cultivated wisdom in previous lives through hearing, pondering, and making a living experience of the teachings of the Universal Way. For example, a multitude of humans and gods (*deva*) generated awakening mind upon hearing the discourse of the Buddha that later become known as the *Scripture Ornament*, because of having listened to the teachings in their previous lives (*CSO*, vol. Mi, f. 54b4-5).

9. Vasubandhu explains that familiarization means to hear repeatedly the Buddhist teachings, retain their meaning, and preserve them as an experiential understanding throughout one's life (*ESO*, f. 140a2). Similarly, Sthiramati states that an awakening mind can be formed through the strength of familiarity with the Buddhist teachings by listening to expositions given by many spiritual guides and gaining true understanding of them (*CSO*, vol. Mi, f. 54b6).

10. Here, Kongtrul has chosen to present the factors that contribute to the formation of an awakening mind as they are stated in the *Scripture Ornament* rather than in Asanga's *Stages of the Bodhisattva*. The following is a summary of the four factors according to Asanga: (1) Witnessing or hearing about the miracles and powers of the Buddha or of bodhisattvas will generate an earnest interest in the state of enlightenment; based on that, one will make the resolve to awaken. (2) Even if one has not witnessed or heard of these miracles and powers, by studying the collections of the scriptures on the bodhisattva's path that explain the nature of full enlightenment, one will be inspired to attain the pristine awareness of a buddha, and on that basis, one will make the resolve to awaken. (3) Even if one has not studied these scriptures in depth, seeing the approaching decline of the teachings on the bodhisattva's path, one realizes that their preservation would relieve numberless beings from their misery and thereby decides to work so that these teachings may last for a long time. This results in appreciation of the pristine awareness of enlightenment, and on that basis, one will make the resolve to awaken. (4) Even if one does not understand that the bodhisattva teachings are on the verge of declining, one certainly sees that these are degenerate times in which beings are tormented by their emotions. Thus, one realizes

that the resolve to attain the goal of the proclaimers and solitary sages is a difficult one to make; how much more so is the resolve to attain the goal of the bodhisattvas. In order that others follow one's example and in consideration of the difficulty of making such a resolve in these degenerate times, one will make the resolve to attain the full awakening of a buddha. (*SB*, ff. 8a6-9a4).

11. *Abhisamayālaṃkāranāmaprajñāpāramitopadeśaśāstra; Shes rab kyi pha rol tu phyin pa'i man ngag gi bstan bcos mgon par rtogs pa'i rgyan* (Toh. 3786), f. 2b5.

12. See chapter II, note 23.

13. Daṃṣṭrasena: a famous Indian commentator on the *Transcendent Wisdom Scriptures*. Two works are attributed to Damstrasena in the Tengyur, the *Commentary on the Transcendent Wisdom Scripture in One Hundred Thousand Lines* (*Śatasāhasrikā-prajñāpāramitābṛhaṭṭīkā; Shes rab kyi pha rol tu phyin pa 'bum pa rgya cher 'grel pa*) (Toh. 3807) and a commentary on all three, the extensive, medium, and short *Transcendent Wisdom Scriptures* (*Śatasāhasrikāpañcaviṃśatisāhasrikāṣṭādaśasāhasrikā-prajñāpāramitābṛhaṭṭīkā; Shes rab kyi pha rol tu phyin pa 'bum pa dang nyi khri lnga stong pa dang khri brgyad stong pa'i rgya cher 'grel pa*) (Toh. 3808).

14. Worldly paths (*lokamārga, 'jig rten pa'i lam*) here refers to the paths of accumulation and preparation traveled prior to gaining a direct realization of reality; supramundane paths (*lokattaramārga, 'jig rten las 'das pa'i lam*) refers to the paths of seeing, meditation, and no more learning.

15. Abhayakara (Abhayākara, 'Jigs pa'i 'byung gnas): foremost master among the Universal Way succession of teachers at Vikramashila Monastery. He lived during the period of King Ramapala and is said to be the last undisputed Indian Buddhist scholar of both sutra and tantra.

16. Smritijnana (Smṛtijñāna, Dran pa'i ye shes): an Indian scholar who traveled to eastern Tibet where he taught extensively, helped in the translation of the new tantras, and wrote commentaries such as his commentary on *Chanting the Names of Manjushri* (*Mañjuśrīnāmasaṃgīti*). Some believe that after his death he reincarnated in Tibet as the renowned Rongzom Pandita (Rong zom chos kyi bzang po).

17. Earth, which symbolizes awakening mind accompanied by earnest desire; gold, by intention; and moon, by determination.

18. Sagaramegha (Sāgaramegha, rGya mtsho sprin): an Indian scholar who lived at the time of King Shri Dharmapala (765-829). He was instructed by Maitreya in a vision to write a commentary on Asanga's *Stages of the Bodhisattva* (*SB*).

19. Son of a Bengal king, Atisha was inspired by Tara, his tutelary deity, to renounce his kingdom and seek a spiritual goal. He began his quest as a yogin, then became a monk, and subsequently became famous as the greatest scholar and most saintly person of his time, revered by both the Individualist and Universalist monastic communities. Upon receiving a prophecy from Tara and an invitation from a Tibetan king, despite the fact that his life would be shortened, he decided to travel to Tibet to propagate Buddhism. There he taught extensively and died without returning to India. His contribution to the later development

of Buddhism in Tibet is felt up to the present day. For the life of Atisha, see Alaka Chattopadhyaya's study, *Atiśa and Tibet* (Calcutta, 1967).

20. Irreversible (*phyir mi ldog pa*) refers to the awakening mind of a bodhisattva at the stage of acceptance of the path of preparation, at which stage there is no turning back to the path of the Individual Way.

21. The five early masters of the Sakya school of Tibetan Buddhism: Sachen Kunga Nyingpo (Kun dga' snying po) (1102-1158), Sönam Tsemo (bSod nams rtsed mo) (1142-1182), Drakpa Gyaltsen (Grags pa rgyal mtshan) (1147-1216), Sakya Pandita Kunga Gyaltsen (Kun dga' rgyal mtshan) (1182-1251), and Chögyal Pakpa (Chos rgyal 'phags pa) (1235-1280). These words, which Sakya Pandita attributes to the oral teachings of his master (most probably Drakpa Gyaltsen), are found in the *Rite for the Formation of the Awakening Mind according to the Centrist System* (*dBu ma lugs kyi sems bskyed kyi cho ga*) in the *Collected Works of Sakya Pandita* (Beijing: Bod ljongs bdo yig dpe rnying dpe bskrun khang, 1992), vol. II, p. 547.

22. The first aspect refers to a beginner's aspiring mind; the second, to the aspiring mind formed in a ritual; and the third, to preserving the purity of the aspiring mind. The same applies to the three aspects of the venturing mind (H.H. Sakya Trizin, oral communication).

23. The actual title of Shantipa's work is *Commentary on the Mandala Rite of Guhyasamaja* (*Guhyasamājamaṇḍalavidhiṭīkā; gSang ba 'dus pa'i dkyil 'khor gyi cho ga'i 'grel pa/ Zhi brgya lnga bcu pa'i 'grel pa*) (Toh. 1871). The citation is found on f. 69b1.

24. An approximate awakening mind is imputed or formed through indications or words (*brdar btags pa/ rda las 'byung ba*), while the subtle one corresponds to the ultimate (*don dam pa*) awakening mind. "Formed through indications or words" refers to the aspiration to awaken in order to put an end to the suffering of all beings. Because it is first hinted at or suggested by the words of a spiritual master, such an aspiration is said to "arise from indications." Ultimate awakening mind is formed through the force of this aspiration for enlightenment; it is non-conceptual pristine awareness free from all mental fabrications, its focus being the selflessness of all phenomena (Shantipa's *Commentary on the Mandala Rite of Guhyasamaja*, ff. 68b1-69a6).

The awakening mind hinted at by others is formed by repeating after a master the formula for its generation (Ashvabhava's *Commentary on the Scripture Ornament* [*Mahāyānasūtralaṃkāraṭīkā; Theg pa chen po'i mdo sde'i rgyan gyi rgya cher 'grel pa*] [Toh. 4029], f. 54a1). The ultimate awakening mind arises through the cultivation of merit and pristine awareness (Dharmashri's *Commentary on the Three Vows* [*sDom 'grel/ sDom pa gsum rnam par nges pa'i 'grel pa legs bshad ngo mtshar dpag bsam gyi snye ma*] [Chorten Monastery edition, published at Deorali, Gangtok, Sikkim, by Dodrup Chen Rinpoché], f. 34a5).

25. f. 4b2-3.

26. Appreciation (*mos pa*) is based on the confidence one has in the profound and magnificent subjects of the Universal Way (in particular, the subject of emptiness), but not on the direct realization of these subjects (Sthiramati's *CSO*, vol. Mi, f. 52a7).

27. The seven impure stages (*saptāśuddhabhūmi, ma dag pa'i sa bdun*) are the first seven stages of awakening. They are called impure because on these stages bodhisattvas have not yet purified a subtle form of pride. This pride is eventually purified in the last three stages of awakening, which are therefore called the three pure stages (*tri viśuddhibhūmi, dag pa'i sa gsum*).

According to Sthiramati, extraordinary intention (*lhag pa'i bsam pa*) denotes the mind that perceives the equality of oneself and others, which enables the bodhisattva to work for his or her own and others' welfare. Such intention is pure (*dag pa*) in that it is unpolluted by grasping to the reality of apprehended (objects) and the apprehending (mind) (*CSO*, vol. Mi, f. 52b1-2).

28. The awakening mind on the eighth, ninth, and tenth stages of the bodhisattva path is said to be mature because on these stages, non-conceptual pristine awareness is spontaneously present, and as a result, the bodhisattva engages effortlessly in generosity and the other perfections (*CSO*, vol. Mi, f. 52b3-4).

29. The first kind of awakening mind arises from its causes; the second, from pristine awareness; the third, from the elimination of what is to be forsaken on the path; and the fourth, from the realization of the goal, enlightenment (*CSO*, vol. Mi, f. 52b6-7).

30. f. 2b5-6.

31. Reading *glu* for *klu*.

32. The similes for and qualities accompanying the awakening mind at different stages of development are as follows: (1) earth (*sa*), earnest desire (*'dun pa*); (2) gold (*gser*), intention (*bsam pa*); (3) waxing moon (*yar ngo'i zla ba tshes pa*), superior determination (*lhag pa'i bsam pa*); (4) fire (*me*), application (*sbyor ba*); (5) great treasure (*gter chen*), generosity (*sbyin pa*); (6) jewel mine (*rin po che'i 'byung gnas*), ethics (*tshul khrims*); (7) ocean (*rgya mtsho*), patience (*bzod pa*); (8) diamond (*rdo rje*), effort (*brtson 'grus*); (9) the king of mountains (*ri'i rgyal po*), meditation (*bsam gtan*); (10) medicine (*sman*), wisdom (*shes rab*); (11) spiritual friend (*dge ba'i bshes gnyen*), skillful means (*thabs la mkhas pa*); (12) wish-fulfilling gem (*yid bzhin gyi nor bu*), aspiration (*smon lam*); (13) sun (*nyi ma*), strength (*stobs*); (14) beautiful song (*glu snyan*), pristine awareness (*ye shes*); (15) king (*rgyal po*), clairvoyance (*mngon par shes pa*); (16) storehouse (*bang mdzod*), merit and pristine awareness (*bsod nams dang ye shes*); (17) highway (*lam po che*), factors conducive to awakening (*byang chub kyi phyogs dang mthun pa'i chos*); (18) conveyance (*bzhon pa*), mental quiescence and insight (*zhi gnas dang lhag mthong*); (19) spring (*bkod ma'i chu*), memory and eloquence (*gzungs dang spobs pa*); (20) echo (*sgra brnyan*), feast of Dharma (*chos kyi dga' ston*); (21) the current of a river (*chu bo'i rgyun*), sole path (*bgrod pa gcig pa'i lam*); (22) a cloud (*sprin*), the dimension of reality of awakening (*chos kyi sku*).

33. Generosity up to and including pristine awareness make up the ten perfections.

34. Thirty-seven factors conducive to awakening: see chapter II, note 183.

35. The dimension of reality of awakening (*dharmakāya, chos sku*) or the omniscient

mind of a buddha, which is the buddha's pristine awareness (*jñāna-dharmakāya, ye shes chos sku*) and its intrinsic dimension (*svābhāvikakāya, ngo bo nyid sku*) or ultimate nature of emptiness.

36. The small, middle, and great path of accumulation (*sambhāramārga, tshogs lam*).

37. Ten perfections: the six (generosity, ethics, patience, effort, meditation, and wisdom), plus means, aspiration, strength, and pristine awareness. See section below entitled "The Six Perfections in Detail."

38. Ten stages (*daśabhūmi, sa bcu*) of the enhanced realization of a bodhisattva, starting from the attainment of the path of seeing up to the final awakening: Joyful (*pramuditā, rab tu dga' ba*), Stainless (*vimalā, dri ma med pa*), Illuminating (*prabhākarī, 'od byed pa*), Radiant (*arcismatī, 'od phro ba*), Difficult to Conquer (*sudurjayā, shin tu sbyang dka' ba*), Approaching (*abhimukhī, mngon du gyur ba*), Gone Far (*dūrangama, ring du song ba*), Unshakable (*acalā, mi g.yo ba*), Good Discrimination (*sādhumatī, legs pa'i blo gros*), and Cloud of the Teachings (*dharma-meghā, chos kyi sprin*). For a discussion of these stages, see chapter 19 of Gampopa's *Jewel Ornament of Liberation (JOL) (Dam chos yid bzhin nor bu thar pa rin po che'i rgyan*).

39. See note 27.

40. Saint (*arhat, dgra bcom pa*): one who has fully overcome the emotions, more often used to denote the goal of the Individualists, here equivalent to the state of a buddha. The most common Tibetan translation of the Sanskrit term is *dgra bcom pa* (one who has defeated the enemy [of the disturbing emotions]). Another translation of *arhat* is *mchod par 'os pa* (one worthy of veneration), used sparingly by Tibetan translators.

41. The correspondence between each simile and awakening mind is explained in different ways by the commentators on the *Ornament of Realizations*. Vimuktasena, citing extensively the Buddha's discourses, states:

   (1) The awakening mind of a beginner bodhisattva accompanied by earnest interest is like the earth in that it serves as the foundation for the attainment of the Buddha's qualities.
   (2) Awakening mind accompanied by intention, like beautiful gold, is the wish to help and make others happy through the practice of the six perfections, a wish that remains unchanged until the bodhisattva's goal is reached.
   (3) Awakening mind accompanied by superior determination, like the waxing moon, is a strong intention to enhance wholesome qualities to their fullest.
   (4) Awakening mind accompanied by application, like fire, enhances the application of the three knowledges—of the foundation (*gzhi shes*) [the Individual Way's understanding of the selflessness of phenomena], of the path (*lam shes*) [the knowledge directed to the actualization of the "perfect end" of emptiness], and the knowledge of all aspects (*rnam mkhyen*) [the final knowledge that directly comprehends in an instant reality as it is and as it manifests].

(5) Awakening mind accompanied by the perfection of generosity, like a great treasure, satisfies countless beings through the gift of the teachings and material things.

(6) Awakening mind accompanied by the perfection of ethics, like a jewel mine, is a source of limitless good qualities.

(7) Awakening mind accompanied by patience, like an ocean, is never disturbed by the experience of many difficulties.

(8) Awakening mind accompanied by effort, like a diamond, is a firm, undivided mind.

(9) Awakening mind accompanied by the perfection of meditation, like the king of mountains, is unperturbed by distractions.

(10) Awakening mind accompanied by the perfection of wisdom, like a medicine, eliminates all illnesses of emotions and impediments to the attainment of omniscience.

(11) Awakening mind accompanied by the perfection of skillful means, like a spiritual friend, at no time neglects others' welfare.

(12) Awakening mind accompanied by the perfection of aspiration, like a wish-fulfilling gem, accomplishes whatever it aspires to.

(13) Awakening mind accompanied by the perfection of strength, like the sun, brings practitioners to spiritual maturity.

(14) Awakening mind accompanied by the perfection of pristine awareness, like a beautiful song, reveals itself to inspire practitioners.

(15) Awakening mind accompanied by clairvoyance, like a king, accomplishes the welfare of others with unobstructed power.

(16) Awakening mind accompanied by merit and pristine awareness, like a storehouse, accommodates all merit and pristine awareness.

(17) Awakening mind accompanied by the factors conducive to awakening, like a highway, is traversed by the exalted ones, one after the other.

(18) Awakening mind accompanied by the union of mental quiescence and insight, like a conveyance, carries one easily, never leaving one in cyclic existence or in static peace.

(19) Awakening mind accompanied by memory and eloquence, like water from a spring, contains and gives forth unceasingly the teachings retained in the minds of bodhisattvas.

(20) Awakening mind accompanied by the feast of the teachings, like a melodious sound, proclaims the four seals—impermanence, suffering, selflessness, and peace—to practitioners who aspire to liberation. [Kongtrul cites "echo" rather than melodious sound.]

(21) Awakening mind accompanied by the sole path, like the current of a river, is entered spontaneously at the attainment of acceptance of the unborn [reality] and followed undividedly in order to fulfill others' welfare.

(22) Awakening mind accompanied by the reality dimension of awakening, like a cloud, resides in the pure land of Tushita, accomplishing the welfare of others by teaching constantly.

(Vimuktasena's *Commentary on the Ornament of Realizations*, [*Pañcaviṃśatisāhasrikā-prajñāpāramitopadeśaśāstrābhisamayālaṃkāravṛtti; Shes rab kyi pha rol tu phyin pa stong phrag nyi shu lnga pa'i man ngag gi bstan bcos mngon par rtogs pa'i rgyan gyi 'grel pa*] [Toh. 3787], ff. 18a1-21b6).

42. In this case, "beginner" refers to a bodhisattva on the path of accumulation or preparation.

43. The preparatory part of a tantric initiation (*dbang gi sta gon*) and the main part of the initiation (*dbang gi dngos gzhi*).

44. Nagarjuna (Nāgārjuna, Klu sgrub): born in southern India in a Brahmin family, became the pioneer of the Centrist system of philosophy and one of the foremost proponents of the Universal Way. He is said to have been called Nagarjuna ("One who has achieved his goal with the aid of nagas") because nagas presented him with the large *Transcendent Wisdom Scripture* and other scriptures that were hidden in their world.

Asanga (Asaṅga, Thogs med), tutored as a young child in fine arts, grammar, medicine, and debate by his own mother in Peshawar, became a great Buddhist monk and scholar. However, still unable to fathom the message of the *Transcendent Wisdom* scriptures, he devoted himself to Maitreya as his tutelary deity. After a meditation trial that lasted twelve years, legend says that he was taken by Maitreya to the pure land of Tushita, where he listened extensively to the teachings. Upon his return to the earth, he gathered the fruits of his studies into the *Five Works of Maitreya*. He become the second father (after Nagarjuna) of the Universal Way by pioneering the Idealist system of philosophy.

45. Manjughosha, "the Sweet-Voiced" (Mañjughoṣa, 'Jam dbyangs) or Manjushri (Mañjuśri, 'Jam dpal): the bodhisattva who symbolizes transcendent wisdom. Considered to be a source of mystic inspiration and a protector of Centrist philosophers, he is depicted brandishing in his right hand a sword with a flaming tip, and in his left hand, the stem of a lotus on whose corolla rests a scripture. The system for the development of awakening mind derived from Manjughosha is said to be based on the *Flower Array Scripture* (*Gaṇḍhavyūhasūtra; sDong po bkod pa'i do*) (Toh. 44) and the *Akashagarbha Scripture* (*Ākāśagarbhasūtra, Nam mkha'i snying po'i mdo*) (Toh. 260).

46. Aryadeva (Āryadeva, 'Phags pa lha): born in the third century as the son of a Sri Lankan king, he became an ardent follower of the Buddhist teachings, the spiritual heir of Nagarjuna, and promulgator of the Centrist philosophy. His most famous works are the *Experientialist Four Hundred* (*Catuḥśatakaśāstra-kārikānāma; bsTan bcos bzhi brgya pa zhes bya ba'i tshig le'ur byas pa*) (Toh. 3846) on the exoteric aspects of Buddhism and the *Lamp Summary of the Practice* (*Caryā-melāpakapradīpa; sPyod pa bsdus pa'i sgron ma*) (Toh. 1803), a tantric work.

47. Shantideva (Śāntideva, Zhi ba lha): an eighth-century Indian master and follower of the Centrist philosophy. Due to his outstanding accomplishments, particularly his *Guide to the Bodhisattva's Way of Life*, he continues up to the present day to be an inspirational figure for followers of the Universal Way.

48. Punyashri (Punyaśrī, bSod nams dpal): Sakya Pandita, at the beginning of his *Rite for the Formation of the Awakening Mind according to the Centrist System* (*Collected Works of Sakya Pandita*, vol. II, p. 542), mentions him as Punyashrimitra, an accomplished Indian pandita who was inspired by Manjushri. His name appears in the Tengyur as one of the two translators of Bodhibhadra's *Rite for the Commitments of Awakening Mind* (*Bodhisattvasaṃvaravidhi; Byang chub sems dpa'i sdom pa'i cho ga*) (Toh. 3967).

49. See note 21.

50. Maitreya "Loving One" (Byams pa): according to Universalist scriptures, a bodhisattva now residing in the pure land of Tushita, who is to appear in this world as the next buddha when the force of Buddha Shakyamuni's teachings has ended. A source of mystic inspiration and a protector of the magnificent deeds lineage of masters, he is usually depicted seated in Greek fashion, a crystal reliquary adorning his head, holding in his right hand the stem of a flower on whose blossom rests a wheel, and in the left, a stem on whose blossom rests a ritual vase. The system for the development of awakening mind inspired by Maitreya is based on the *Bodhisattva Section Scripture* (*Bodhisattvapiṭakanāmasūtra; Byang chub sems dpa'i sde snod ces bya ba'i mdo*) (Toh. 56).

51. Vasubandhu (dByig gnyen): the younger brother of Asanga, he became a learned scholar and teacher of the Individual Way in Kashmir under the abbot Sanghabhadra. Having failed to grasp the meaning of Asanga's *Stages of Yogic Practice* (*Yogacāryabhūmi*) (Toh. 4035-4037), he made some derogatory statements about his brother. Eventually, however, Asanga managed to convert him to the Universal Way, of which he become a fervent proponent. He wrote more than fifty works explaining both Universalist and Individualist discourses, including the *Treasury of Phenomenology*.

52. Chandragomin (Candragomin) is believed to have been born in the latter part of the sixth century in southern India. He became a lay master of exceptional learning who taught extensively at Nalanda University. He and Shantideva were known as the "two wonderful teachers." He experienced a visionary meeting with Avalokiteshvara, who henceforth served as his source of mystic inspiration.

53. See note 19.

54. The Buddha's Word as Instructions Tradition (*bka' gdams pa*): the earliest of the new schools of Buddhism in Tibet, which originated with Atisha's mission and the teachings of his spiritual heir, Dromtönpa (1005-1064). It continues today as the New Kadampa or Geluk tradition founded by Tsongkapa.

55. Oral Transmission of Gampopa (*dwags po bka' brgyud*): a new school of Buddhism in Tibet which originated with Marpa the Translator (1012-1097) and was formalized by the scholar and saint Gampopa.

56. Daö Shönnu (Zla 'od gzhon nu) or the "Physician from Dakpo" (Dwag po lha rje), better known as Gampopa (sGam po pa) (1079-1153), the most gifted of

Milarepa's disciples. He entered monastic life at the age of twenty-six following the death of his wife, an event that triggered profound renunciation in him. He began his studies within the Kadampa tradition. Upon first hearing the name of Milarepa, who was to become his principal mentor, he was filled with great faith. Milarepa imparted essential instructions and urged him to practice them. After a prolonged practice of meditation, Gampopa experienced the ultimate nature of mind. From his stream of disciples, several schools have emerged that emphasize the practice of the Great Seal (*mahāmudrā*).

57. See note 15.

58. Pawo Tsuklak Trengwa (dPa' bo gtsug lag phreng ba) (1504-1566): a famous scholar and historian of the Kagyu school.

59. Virupa: student of Nagabodhi and foremost among the eighty-four Indian tantric adepts. Virupa became a yogin of great powers upon having a vision of the deity Yamari. While residing at Somapuri Monastery, he regularly engaged in tantric conduct, and one day was discovered by his fellow monks as he was drinking beer and consorting with women. As a consequence, he was punished by expulsion; he used that occasion, however, to demonstrate miracles. He is the source of many instructions that were transmitted in Tibet. See *Masters of Mahamudra*, trans. Keith Dowman (Albany: State University of New York Press, 1985).

Naropa: a renowned scholar of Nalanda University. Inspired by a *ḍākinī* who appeared to him in the guise of an old woman, he became the student of the accomplished master Tilopa. Naropa spent twelve years serving his master while undergoing various trials, and finally transcended mere intellectual learning to attain experiential accomplishment. He become the master of the Tibetan translator Marpa, and for this reason he is considered to be the forefather of the Kagyu school of Tibetan Buddhism. See *Life and Teaching of Nāropa*, trans. Herbert Guenther (Oxford: Clarendon Press, 1963).

60. *Fortunate Eon Scripture* (*Bhadrakalpikasūtra; bsKal pa bzang po'i mdo*) (Toh. 94), citation not found.

61. See chapter II, section "Classification of Personal Liberation Vows with respect to the Person."

62. Mandala: everything in the universe suitable to be an offering is visualized and offered to the master.

63. The seven-branch service in Nagarjuna's and Shantideva's rites for the formation of the awakening mind consists of offering (*pūjam, mchod pa phul ba*), taking refuge (*śarana gamana, skyabs 'gro*), confession (*deśayā, bshags pa*), rejoicing in others' merit (*anumoda, rjes su yi rang ba*), supplication of the buddhas to teach (*samcodāta, bskul ba*), petition for the buddhas to remain in the world (*prāthanā, gsol ba*), and dedication of merits (*parināma, bsngo ba*). In the usual seven-branch service, homage (*namaḥvandana, phyag 'tshal ba*) is the first branch, offering the second, and the taking of refuge is not considered as a separate branch. For a

lengthy description of the rite, see Tsuklak Trengwa's *Commentary on the Guide to the Bodhisattva's Way of Life* (*Byang chub sems dpa'i spyod pa la 'jug pa rnam bshad theg chen chos kyi rgya mtsho zab rgyas mtha' yas snying po*) (Rumtek, Sikkim: Karmapa XVI, 1974), ff. 29b7-30a1.

64. The first verse indicates the way the buddhas and bodhisattvas of the past formed the awakening mind and entered the training. The second verse is the formula for the aspirant to form the aspiring and venturing awakening minds and assume their commitments (Dharmashri's *Commentary on the Three Vows*, f. 139b1-4).

65. Shantideva's *Compendium of Trainings* (*CT*) (*Śikṣāsamuccaya; bSlab pa kun las btus pa*) (Toh. 3940), ff. 38b3-39a3; *Akashagarbha Scripture* (*AS*) (*Ākāśagarbhasūtra; Nam mkha'i snying po'i mdo*) (Toh. 260), ff. 272b4-273a5.

66. The representations of the Buddha's body, speech, and mind may be statues or paintings, scriptures recording his discourses, or reliquaries, etc.

67. To wear the attributes of a monk means to have shaven the head and wear the yellow monastic robes. To harm a monk means to rob him of his robes or cause him to take up the life of a householder, to injure him with weapons, to throw him into prison, or kill him (Shantideva's *CT*, f. 38b7).

68. This enumeration is the one given in Shantideva's *CT*, f. 39a3. According to the *Akashagarbha Scripture* (ff. 273b3-274a1), stealing the property is counted as the first downfall, the four destructions counted as the second, to abandon the teachings as the third, to harm a monk as the fourth, and to commit the five deeds of direct retribution as the fifth.

69. The four castes: royalty (*kṣatriya, rgyal rigs*), brahmin (*brāhmaṇa, bram ze'i rigs*), merchants (*vāiśya, rje'u rigs*), and the menial class (*śūdra, dmangs rigs*).

70. The eighteen crafts or artisans (*bzo rig bco brgyad*): (1) merchant (*tshong pa*); (2) potter (*rdza mkhan*); (3) garland-maker (*phreng mkhan*); (4) wine-seller (*chang tshong*); (5) cattle-seller (*phyugs tshong*); (6) barber ('*dreg mkhan*); (7) presser of sesame seeds to make oil ('*bru mar 'tshir ba*); (8) smith (*mgar ba*); (9) carpenter (*shing mkhan*); (10) fortune-teller (*phya mkhan*); (11) weaver (*tha ga pa*); (12) leather craftsman (*ko pags mkhan*); (13) fisherman (*rkyal chen pa*); (14) dyer (*brtso blag mkhan*); (15) bamboo-weaver (*smyig ma mkhan*); (16) butcher (*bshan pa*); (17) hunter (*gdol pa mkhan*); (18) cart-maker (*shing rta mkhan*). Dg.T. dkar chag, p. 236.

71. *CT*, ff. 39a4-41b7, and *AS*, ff. 274b3-278a2.

72. This infraction is incurred when one explains scriptures that reveal the profound meaning of emptiness and as a result, one's students become frightened, renounce their resolve to attain full awakening, and set as their goal the awakening of the proclaimers (*CT*, f. 39a6-b2).

73. This means to dissuade someone from following the personal liberation system and the morality set forth in the discipline scriptures by saying that once a person has entered the Universal Way and formed the resolve to attain full awakening, any emotionally based physical, verbal, or mental actions will bear no karmic results (*CT*, f. 39b6-7).

74. To claim that the proclaimers' way does not yield great results in future lives, and that by following it, one will not completely overcome one's emotions, but that only the Universal Way eliminates the possibility of all unfortunate rebirths and allows one to swiftly attain complete awakening. If the person who hears such views believes them and comes to profess them, the infraction is incurred by both (*CT*, f. 40a1-4).

75. To praise oneself and belittle other bodhisattvas by saying, for example, "I am a follower of the Universal Way. That person is not!" (*CNPTV*, f. 56b6).

76. This means to teach the scriptures that are concerned with the truth of emptiness after having just memorized or recited them, while claiming, out of desire for wealth, etc., to have attained a direct understanding of the truth. It should be understood that the truth of emptiness is the domain of understanding of outstanding saintly scholars who are firmly grounded in perfect recollection, acceptance, and contemplation, and are well-trained bodhisattvas (*CT*, f. 40b3-4).

77. Contemplative monks (*dge slong bsam gtan pa*) are holy persons worthy of veneration since they lead a life of contemplation and are able to recollect the teachings and understand the truth, while monks who only read scriptures or act as caretakers of the monastery are not so worthy. Contemplative monks are like illuminators and guides for the world; they free others from their karma and passions and place them on the path to perfect peace (*CT*, ff. 41b7-42a2).

78. *CT*, f. 43b3-4.

79. *Condensed Transcendent Wisdom Scripture*, in *Collected Scriptures and Dharani*, vol. sMad cha, f. 28a7-b1.

80. The path of the ten virtues (*dge ba'i las lam bcu*) consists of actions opposite to the ten unvirtuous actions: to protect life, to be generous, to maintain chaste behavior, to speak truthfully, to create harmony, to speak gently, to speak meaningful words, to be content with what one has, to wish for others' happiness, and to believe the words of the Buddha (Tsuklak Trengwa's *Commentary on the Guide to the Bodhisattva's Way of Life*, f. 41b1-2).

81. A person of highest capability should shun all eighteen root downfalls. Practitioners of average or inferior capabilities should safeguard those precepts of the awakening mind that accord with their capacities. Infractions of those precepts that are beyond their capacity to maintain do not lead to the deterioration of their training in the awakening mind since they have not made the promise to train in all the precepts but just in those that suit their capacities (Dharmashri's *Commentary on the Three Vows*, ff. 182b5-183a1).

82. If one has incurred a root downfall, one should first wash oneself, clean one's dwelling, and light incense, and then call the bodhisattva Akashagarbha by name, offer prostrations, and supplicate him to purify one. Following that, if the bodhisattva Akashagarbha does not appear in one's dream or in a vision in his usual form or another manifestation, one should rise in the predawn hours, and

facing east, offer incense. One then requests Akashagarbha (the "aurora deity") to appear in a dream to indicate the means to purify the transgression and to bless one with the Universal Way's skill in means and awareness: "O Akashagarbha, you are possessed of great compassion. Great Fortunate One, as you appear each day in the world, protect me with your kindness. I beseech you to teach me in my dream how to repair my downfall and how to attain the skillful means and discriminative awareness of the exalted bodhisattvas." Returning to sleep, at dawn one will dream of the bodhisattva Akashagarbha who will help to purify the transgression and show the skillful means of the bodhisattvas. As a result, the beginner bodhisattva will attain the contemplation in which awakening mind is never forgotten and will remain firmly grounded in the Universal Way (*CT*, f. 42a-b3).

Pema Karpo's *Extensive Commentary on The Three Vows* (*TV*) (*sDom gsum rgya cher 'grel pa/sDom pa gsum gyi rgyan ces bya ba'i rgya cher 'grel ba*) notes that three times during the day and three times at night, one should recite the *Three-Part Scripture* and purify downfalls by relying on the buddhas and bodhisattvas and by reciting the confession of the bodhisattva's downfalls found in the *Dialogue with Upali Discourse* (*TV*, vol. Nga, ff. 38a6-39a1).

83. *CT*, f. 43b3.

84. *Three-Part Scripture* (*Triskandhakasūtra, Phung po gsum pa'i mdo*) (Toh. 284): so called as it comprises three parts—homage, confession, and dedication.

85. Krishna Pandita (Kṛṣṇa Paṇḍita), author of one of the most respected commentaries to Shantideva's *Guide to the Bodhisattva's Way of Life*. He is not the Krishna (Kṛṣṇācārya) who is counted among the eighty-four accomplished tantric adepts of ancient India. The means for restoration of the commitments is found in his *Ascertainment of the Difficult Points of the Guide to the Bodhisattva's Way of Life* (*Bodhisattvacaryāvatāraduravabodhananirṇaya; Byang chub sems dpa'i spyod pa la 'jug pa'i rtogs par dka' ba'i gnas gtan la dbab pa*) (Toh. 3875), f. 95a7-b3.

86. Krishna states that an inferior practitioner, because of grasping to reality, must confess the downfall in front of another person while expressing regret. The individual can then rise from the downfall after a considerable time by making the promise not to repeat it in the future. The middling practitioner rises from a downfall by receiving pardon from Akashagarbha or another deity of the awareness mantra after having pleased him. The superior practitioner (*dam pa*) needs only the understanding that the transgression itself is [of the same nature as ultimate] awakening mind, as stated in the *Scripture that Demonstrates the Non-Origination of All Phenomena*: "Manjushri! By [understanding] that without action there is no fruitional result, the bodhisattva remains pure from the obscurations of actions" (*Ascertainment of the Difficult Points of the Guide to the Bodhisattva's Way of Life*, f. 95a7-b3).

Dharmashri explains that an exceptional practitioner of highest capability may restore commitments in the following way: first, keeping in mind the illusory or dream-like nature of all things, one verbally confesses the downfall before all buddhas and bodhisattvas pervading space. Then, one examines the nature of the downfall itself and understands it to be without basis, like space. Remaining in contemplation on this nature, one becomes free of any fault (*Commentary on the Three Vows*, f. 189a2-4).

In Nagarjuna's system, if one has incurred a downfall with heavy emotional involvement motivated by a potent hatred toward a special person such as an outstanding bodhisattva, one must confess the downfall in front of ten holders of the awakening mind commitments. When the downfall has stemmed from a particularly harmful ignorance concerning the teachings, one must confess it in front of five holders. Other downfalls motivated by a simple dislike or attachment may be confessed in front of one or two vow holders. If no vow holder is found, one may confess the downfall in front of a representation of the Three Jewels (ibid., f. 195b3-5).

87. *Prayer to the Chief of the Victorious Ones* (*gTso rgyal ma*): an inspiring and eloquent prayer expressed by Shantideva in his *Guide to the Bodhisattva's Way of Life*, (*Bodhisattvacaryāvatāra; Byang chub sems dpa'i spyod pa la 'jug pa*) (Toh. 3871), verses 47 to 53 in the chapter on Confession, *GBL*, ff. 5b6-6a3.

88. The six kinds of remedies are the following: (1) to recite the names of the buddhas and bodhisattvas; (2) to erect representations of the buddha, etc., and stupas; (3) to prostrate before and make offerings to such symbols; (4) to read or recite the profound discourses of the Buddha and the tantras; (5) to mutter the mantras that are praised as being especially effective in purifying unwholesome deeds, such as the hundred-syllable-mantra of Vajrasattva; and (6) to take earnest interest in emptiness, i.e., to try to discover the nature of the downfall, and when one gains certainty that no nature exists, to allow the mind to settle in that state (Dharmashri, f. 195a6-b2). The mantra of the transcendent ones is identical to the one hundred-syllable-mantra of Vajrasattva, except that "tathagata" replaces "vajrasattva" (according to Thrangu Rinpoché).

89. *CT*, f. 9b1-2.

90. *SB*, f. 51a.

91. A league (*yojana, dpag tsad*): about 8000 yards or 7.4 km; an earshot (*krośa, rgyang grags*): five hundred armspans or bows, about 1 km.

92. To take the commitments of the aspiring mind by oneself (provided one possesses the personal strength of an awakened affinity for the Universal Way), one first performs the preliminary parts of the ceremony (as outlined in note 95). Then, in front of a representation of the Buddha, one imagines oneself to be in the presence of all the buddhas of the ten directions and follows the procedure below (note 95), omitting the words of request that address the master. To take the commitments of venturing mind (under the same condition of the awakened affinity), kneeling with the right knee touching the ground in front of the representation of the Buddha while imagining all the buddhas of the ten directions to be present, one repeats three times the following words: "O buddhas and bodhisattvas who have attained the great stages and are dwelling throughout the ten directions, pay heed to me (so and so). I now fully assume the training of the bodhisattvas, the ethics of the bodhisattvas, the ethics of restraint, the ethics of acquiring wholesome qualities, and the ethics of working for the

welfare of all beings which all bodhisattvas of the past have observed, which all bodhisattvas of the future will observe, and which all present bodhisattvas are observing throughout the ten directions" (Pema Karpo's *TV*, vol. Ca, f. 11a5-b6).

93. Bodhibhadra (Byang chub bzang po): Born in Orissa, Bodhibhadra became a noteworthy scholar at the time of King Chanaka. He received spiritual instructions from Avalokiteshvara, his inspirational deity, and eventually succeeded Naropa as guardian of the northern gate of Vikramashila Monastery when Naropa left the monastery to lead a yogin's life under his master Tilopa. Bodhibhadra's assertion that the presence of a master is indispensable in restoring deteriorated commitments is found in his *Revelation of the Difficult Points of the Twenty Verses on the Bodhisattva's Commitments* (*Bodhisattvasaṃvaraviṃśakapañjikā; Byang chub sems dpa'i sdom pa nyi shu pa'i dka' 'grel*) (Toh. 4083), ff. 202b-204a.

94. Kongtrul here alludes to Atisha's *Stages of the Rite for the Formation of Awakening Mind and Its Commitments* (*Cittotpādasaṃvaravidhikrama; Sems bskyed pa dang sdom pa'i cho ga'i rim pa*) (Toh. 3969). Asanga's *Stages of the Bodhisattva* states only the following words to form the mind of aspiration: "Alas! May I attain perfect and full enlightenment. May I work for the benefit of all beings. May I place them in ultimate perfect peace and in the pristine awareness of the transcendent ones" (Pema Karpo's *TV*, vol. Ca, f. 8a4-6).

95. During the preliminary part of this ceremony, while considering the master to be the Buddha, the aspirant repeats three times the following request: "Just as the buddhas, the saintly transcendent ones, and the bodhisattvas dwelling on the higher stages first formed the mind of the unsurpassable awakening, O master, grant me (so and so) the mind of unsurpassable awakening." Following this, one takes refuge with these words: "O master, take heed of me! I (so and so), from this time forward, until I reach the heart of enlightenment, go for refuge to the Buddha, the Blessed One, supreme among humans. O master, take heed of me! I (so and so), from this time forward, until I reach the heart of enlightenment, go for refuge to the teachings that embody peace and freedom from attachment, supreme of all teachings. O master, take heed of me! I (so and so), from this time forward, until I reach the heart of enlightenment, go for refuge to the supreme community of exalted and irreversible bodhisattvas, the supreme of all communities." For the cultivation of merit, one first visualizes Buddha Shakyamuni surrounded by all the buddhas and bodhisattvas of the universe and performs the sevenfold service consisting of homage, offerings, confession, rejoicing, requesting the buddhas to turn the wheel of the teachings, urging the buddhas to remain in the world, and dedication of merit. (Atisha's *Stages of the Rite for the Formation of Awakening Mind and its Commitments*, f. 245a4-b3). See also Shantirakshita's *Commentary on the Twenty Verses on the Bodhisattva's Commitments* (*Saṃvaraviṃśakavṛtti; sDom pa nyi shu pa'i 'grel pa*) (Toh. 4082) (henceforth cited as *CTVBC*), f. 167b onward.

For the central part of the ceremony, the aspirant kneels with the right knee touching the ground and with folded hands repeats three times the following request: "O buddhas and bodhisattvas dwelling in the ten directions, take heed of me! O master, take heed of me! I (so and so), by virtue of the generosity, ethics, and meditation that I have practiced, encouraged others to do, and rejoiced in during this life, and that I will practice in my next lives, just as the buddhas and the great bodhisattvas who perfectly attained the great stages formed the mind of unsurpassable, perfect, and full enlightenment, I (so and so) also, from now until I have reached the final stage of enlightenment, form an awakening mind that aspires to achieve unsurpassable, perfect, and full enlightenment. I will liberate those not liberated [from the impediments to omniscience]. I will release those not released [from cyclic existence]. I will relieve those unrelieved [in unfortunate existences]. I will set in the state of perfect peace those sentient beings who have not transcended suffering." (Atisha's *Stages of the Rite for the Formation of Awakening Mind and its Commitments*, ff. 245b4-246a1).

96. For the preliminary part of the ceremony to assume the commitments of venturing mind, the aspirant touches the feet of the master and makes the following request three times: "O master, respond to my request: Bestow on me the commitments of a bodhisattva. If there is no harm in doing so, I beseech you to heed me with compassion and grant me the commitments."

The master then examines the motivation of the aspirant by posing these questions: "O child of a good family! Will you liberate those not yet liberated? Will you release those not yet released? Will you relieve those who are unrelieved? Will you set in the state of perfect peace those beings who have not yet transcended suffering? Do you desire to uphold the buddhas' lineage? Will you be firm in the mind of awakening or not? Are you taking the commitments in order to compete with someone else? Are you taking the commitments on the insistent request of someone else?"

The aspirant, having been led before an image or painting of Buddha Shakyamuni, imagines being in the presence of Buddha Shakyamuni and all the buddhas and bodhisattvas of the universe. He or she makes the five outer offerings (form, sound, etc.) and prostrates to the buddhas. At this point, the master sits on a high throne. The aspirant prostrates to the master who is considered to be the Buddha himself. With the right knee touching the ground and hands folded, he or she requests the master to bestow the commitments by repeating the following words three times: "O master! I beseech you to grant me as soon as possible the commitments of the bodhisattvas' ethics." Then the master, sitting or standing, inquires whether there are obstacles to the aspirant's acceptance of the commitments: "You (so and so), are you a bodhisattva? Have you resolved to awaken?" If the aspirant answers in the positive, the master accepts him or her as a suitable candidate.

The aspirant sits without speaking, mind filled with joyful anticipation of receiving the commitments of a bodhisattva, the source of the precious qualities of all the buddhas, an inexhaustible, incommensurable, and unsurpassable great treasure of merits. The master introduces the aspirant to the three kinds of ethics: the ethics of restraint, of acquiring wholesome qualities, and of working for the benefit of beings, which comprise all areas of the ethical training of all bodhisattvas and buddhas. The master then asks the aspirant whether or not he or she wishes to follow these. With the positive reply of the aspirant, the master starts the main body of the rite.

"Venerable child of good family, will you (so and so) receive from me, the bodhisattva (so and so), the ethics that form the basis of training and the training itself of all past, present, and future bodhisattvas who dwell in the ten directions of the universe, which consist of the ethics of restraint, the ethics aimed at acquiring wholesome qualities, and the ethics of working for the benefit of all beings?" The master repeats these phrases three times and at the end of each, the aspirant replies, "I will accept them," thus fully assuming the commitments (Atisha's *Stages of the Rite for the Formation of Awakening Mind*, ff. 246b1-247b4). See also Shantirakshita's *CTVBC*.

97. At the conclusion, the master rises and makes three full prostrations to the buddhas and bodhisattvas of the ten directions, and with folded hands, asks the buddhas three times to acknowledge the aspirant's acceptance of the commitments: "I request you (the buddhas), who know clearly all phenomena extending up to the limits of the ten directions, to acknowledge that the bodhisattva (so and so) has now perfectly received from me, the bodhisattva (so and so), the commitments of a bodhisattva's ethics." Master and disciple then stand up. The disciple prostrates, whereupon the master informs the disciple that all the buddhas and bodhisattvas have acknowledged the commitments and that thereafter they will care for the beginner bodhisattva with kindness so that his or her merit and pristine awareness will increase.

The master then says: "You, the bodhisattva (so and so), listen! Do not speak of these bodhisattva commitments to those who lack faith. If you reveal your commitments to them, they will demean them, and thereby create for themselves negative consequences equal in force to all the merits of all the bodhisattvas who abide by those commitments. Since the duty of a bodhisattva is to save others from suffering and turn them away from evil deeds, highly virtuous bodhisattvas should keep their commitments secret." Following this, the master explains to the beginner bodhisattva the root downfalls that damage the commitments, as well as the emotional and non-emotional minor infractions, and gives a brief résumé of Chandragomin's *Twenty Verses on the Bodhisattva's Commitments* and of the chapter on the bodhisattva's ethics in Asanga's *SB*. (Atisha's *Stages of the Rite for the Formation of the Awakening Mind*, ff. 247b4-248b1). See also *CTVBC*.

98. Chandragomin, *Twenty Verses on the Bodhisattva's Commitments* (*Bodhisattvasaṃvaraviṃśaka; Byang chub sems dpa'i sdom pa nyi shu pa*) (Toh. 4081), f. 166b4-5.

99. *SB*, f. 85a6-b4.

100. Emotional involvement is moderate when any one of the branches indicating great emotional involvement is present, but afterwards one feels some degree of shame and embarrassment, and urged by someone else, stops engaging in the infraction. Emotional involvement is slight when afterwards one feels a great measure of shame, and without being urged by anyone else, quickly stops engaging in the infraction. Infractions committed with moderate or slight emotional involvement do not destroy the commitment (Dharmashri's *Commentary on the Three Vows*, f. 197a2-4).

101. Chandragomin's *Twenty Verses*, ff. 166b6-167a5.

102. A practitioner who abides by the commitments of a bodhisattva should make a daily offering, large or small, to the Transcendent One or to reliquaries; to the scriptures in general and to those concerned with the bodhisattva [training] in particular; and to the community of bodhisattvas of the ten directions. The practitioner should at least offer a prostration to the Three Jewels while reciting a verse of praise; or, at the very least, he or she should recollect their qualities with faith. If a day and a night goes by without making such efforts, one incurs a contradiction to generosity. If the neglect is due to irreverence, complacence, or laziness, an emotional contradiction is incurred; if it is a result of forgetfulness, the downfall is non-emotional. A person in a deranged state of mind is not subject to any consequences if he or she neglects to make offerings (*CTVBC*, f. 173a2-5).

103. If a practitioner has great desires, is never content, craves wealth and honor, and seeks to satisfy these desires with great longing, he or she incurs an emotional contradiction. However, if he or she has resolved to renounce these negative traits and strives to apply remedies to them, but while doing so is overpowered by emotions and incurs the contradiction, the contradiction has no significant consequence (*CTVBC*, f. 173a6-b2).

104. If one meets a bodhisattva who is senior to oneself and endowed with good qualities, but out of pride, ill will, or anger, does not stand up respectfully and offer him or her a seat, one incurs an emotional contradiction. The contradiction is non-emotional if incurred out of complacence, laziness, indifference, or forgetfulness (*CTVBC*, f. 173b2-3).

105. If a bodhisattva, feeling pride, ill will, or anger, refuses to answer when asked a question or to converse with someone who wishes to talk, he or she incurs an emotional contradiction. The contradiction is non-emotional if done out of complacence, laziness, indifference, or forgetfulness. The refusal is not a contradiction if one is seriously ill or in a deranged state of mind (*CTVBC*, f. 173b3-6).

106. A bodhisattva incurs an emotional contradiction if he or she, because of pride, ill will, or anger, does not accept an offering of food, drink, or clothing or refuses an invitation to the home of another bodhisattva or layperson or to another monastery. The contradiction is non-emotional when done out of complacence or laziness. No downfall is incurred if it is impossible to accept the invitation because one is ill or in a deranged state of mind, or because the place is too far away or the journey would be full of perils. No downfall is incurred if the refusal is a means to spiritually uplift the host or to change his or her frame of mind to a better one (*CTVBC*, f. 174a2-4).

107. To refuse gifts of gold, silver, pearls, blue beryl, or other valuables due to pride, ill will, or anger constitutes an emotional contradiction since this involves disregard for others. It is non-emotional when due to complacence or laziness. No downfall is incurred if the refusal is based on the understanding that by accepting the goods, one will become attached to them; if one suspects that the

gift was a mistake; if one believes that the giver will regret the gift; or if concerned that the person, by giving away his wealth, will become destitute. Also, no downfall is incurred by not accepting goods if one suspects that they belong to the monastic community, have been stolen, or have been acquired as a result of killing, binding, punishing, or harming another being (*CTVBC*, f. 174a7-b4).

108. Not to give teachings to those who are interested in them due to ill will, anger, or jealousy is an emotional contradiction. The contradiction is non-emotional if incurred due to indolence or laziness. No contradiction is incurred if one refuses to give teachings to non-Buddhists who wish to listen to them in order to find fault with them; or if one is seriously ill or in a deranged mental state. The same is true if the refusal is intended as a way to spiritually uplift someone and to better his frame of mind; if one does not have adequate knowledge of the teachings; or if the listener shows disrespectful manners. Furthermore, it is not a contradiction to refuse to expound the magnificent aspects of the teachings to obtuse students if these students might be intimidated by the profundity of the teachings, generate wayward views or misunderstandings, be harmed, or regress spiritually. There is also no downfall if the refusal is based on the suspicion that the person will then reveal what he has heard to unworthy disciples (*CTVBC*, ff. 174b4-175a1).

109. A bodhisattva incurs an emotional contradiction by rejecting or ignoring a person who is evil or has broken vows if the rejection is due to ill will or anger felt toward the person because his ethics are corrupted. The contradiction is non-emotional if due to complacence, laziness, or forgetfulness. No contradiction is incurred if the rejection is a means to spiritually uplift the other person, to prevent a bad influence from spreading to others, or in order to maintain discipline in the monastic community (*CTVBC*, f. 175a2-6).

110. Shantirakshita's *CTVBC* explains this contradiction based on the original words of Chandragomin's *Twenty Verses on the Bodhisattva's Commitments*, which reads *pha rol dad phyir slob mi byed* (not to observe the training in order to inspire others): A bodhisattva should observe, just as the proclaimers do, all aspects of the disciplinary code as prescribed by the Buddha in order to spiritually inspire those who have no faith, as well as those who do have faith, and to guide them to liberation (f. 175a6-b1).

111. Shantirakshita states that although the Buddha instructed the proclaimers to pursue only a few goals, undertake few activities, and have few worldly aspirations, this advice does not apply to bodhisattvas. If a bodhisattva, motivated by ill will or anger, limits his or her scope of concern and activity, an emotional contradiction is incurred. It is quite appropriate for the proclaimers, who practice for their own welfare alone, to restrict their activities, to strive to achieve only a few goals, and to have few aspirations for the sake of others. However, for a bodhisattva whose aim is to accomplish others' welfare, the same would be inappropriate.

Furthermore, [contrary to the usual monastic code,] it is permissible for a bodhisattva who is a monk to accept thousands of garments from a householder who can afford to make such an offering, provided the bodhisattva is doing so for altruistic purposes. It is also appropriate for a bodhisattva who is a monk to acquire hundreds of silk mats or quantities of gold, silver, etc., if this would benefit others. The same applies to the other aspects of the monastic discipline. In brief, bodhisattvas who follow the monastic discipline should not be bound to the rules as the proclaimers are. Since they maintain two kinds of ethics, that of the proclaimers and that of the bodhisattvas, it is appropriate for bodhisattvas to accomplish their own welfare provided they are thinking ultimately of others' benefit (*CTVBC*, ff. 175b1-176a2).

112. Shantirakshita states that if a bodhisattva commits a deed that is unwholesome in nature, but does so with compassionate skill in means, he or she not only does not incur a fault, but actually cultivates merit. Suppose, for example, that a bodhisattva were to become aware that an evil person, motivated by his desire to acquire material things, was plotting to kill millions of exalted proclaimers, solitary sages, and bodhisattvas. The bodhisattva, understanding that the man was on the verge of committing many deeds of immediate retribution, might decide to kill him before he had the chance to kill many others. The basis for this act would be the compassionate intention to prevent him from killing and subsequently being reborn in hell. This act of killing, performed in such a virtuous frame of mind, would not constitute a contradiction and would increase his merit. Similarly, stealing, sexual misconduct, lying, and all other unvirtuous deeds are permissible for a bodhisattva if the action is motivated by compassion. However, it must be noted that sexual activity of any form is prohibited for a bodhisattva who has monastic vows, as this would be a bad example for other monks and could result in a degeneration of the monastic discipline (*CTVBC*, ff. 176a3-177b2).

113. If a bodhisattva uses material things he or she has acquired through one of the five wrong means of livelihood—flattery, hinting, seeking reward for a favor, pretentious behavior, and hypocrisy—without trying to avoid and renounce these means, he or she incurs an emotional contradiction. No contradiction is incurred if the bodhisattva is making a sincere effort to renounce using such material things, but is overpowered by desire for them (*CTVBC*, f. 177b2-4).

114. A bodhisattva incurs an emotional contradiction by taking pleasure in excited and restless states of mind, engaging in playful activity, becoming involved in and distracted by meaningless jokes, or wishing to excite others. There is no downfall if the bodhisattva plays or jokes in order to dispel the ill will of others or to relieve their sorrow (*CTVBC*, f. 177b4-7).

115. A bodhisattva should not harbor a strong desire to attain the state of perfect peace, but rather should resolve not to enter this state. In addition, he or she should not fear or try to reject emotions. If a bodhisattva resolves to stay three countless eons in the cycle of existence and then enter into perfect peace, he or she incurs an emotional contradiction (*CTVBC*, f. 178a1-6).

116. A bodhisattva should try to dispel negative talk about himself or herself and make known the truth. Not to do so is an emotional contradiction. If what is

being said is actually the truth, not to correct the behavior causing the talk would constitute a non-emotional contradiction. There is no contradiction if a bodhisattva does not dispel the negative talk of non-Buddhists or those who cling strongly to their own opinions, or criticism expressed by others because he adheres to a monastic discipline, lives on alms, or follows a virtuous practice; or words arising from strong anger or misunderstanding (*CTVBC*, f. 178a6-b2).

117. If a bodhisattva, while being aware that a disquieting or violent method (or a peaceful one) would be of benefit to other beings, does not apply it due to fear of displeasing others, he or she incurs an emotional contradiction. No contradiction is incurred by not applying such methods when they would be of little benefit for a person in his present life or would make him greatly upset (*CTVBC*, ff. 178b2-179a2).

118. If one has committed a wrong deed, or is suspected of having done so, and feeling ill will or pride, does not apologize or make amends in a suitable way but ignores the person who is upset with one, one incurs a contradiction. No contradiction is incurred if the refusal to apologize is intended as a means to spiritually uplift the other person; if the other person is a non-Buddhist or improperly insists on having an apology; if to apologize to someone quarrelsome by nature would cause a dispute to augment; or if one is aware that the other person, being meek and forbearing in character, would become embarrassed (*CTVBC*, ff. 178b4-1791).

Bodhibhadra explains this contradiction in the following way: To reject and not to apologize to or ask forgiveness of someone who is angry or upset with one (*Revelation of the Difficult Points of the Twenty Verses on the Bodhisattva's Commitments*, f. 211a2).

119. A bodhisattva who, motivated by ill will or scorn, does not accept the apology of someone who has argued with him or her incurs an emotional contradiction. If the refusal to accept is due to the other person being obnoxious or intolerable, this still constitutes a contradiction, but not an emotional one. No contradiction is incurred if the refusal is a means to spiritually influence the other person; or when the apology would be inappropriate or untimely (*CTVBC*, f. 179a2-4).

120. If a bodhisattva, feeling anger towards someone, clings firmly to the anger, he or she incurs an emotional contradiction. No contradiction is incurred if the bodhisattva makes a sincere effort to get rid of the anger but still comes under its sway (*CTVBC*, f. 179a4-5).

121. If a bodhisattva gathers a circle of followers out of a desire to be honored or materially enriched by them, he or she incurs an emotional contradiction (*CTVBC*, f. 179a5-7). No contradiction is incurred if the bodhisattva accepts honor and services without any self-interest, or gathers students motivated by loving-kindness and receives service or honor incidentally (Bodhibhadra's *Revelation of the Difficult Points*, f. 211b5).

122. The bodhisattva who does nothing to overcome inertia, laziness, or attachment to sleep, lying down, or relaxing at improper times and beyond moderation

incurs an emotional contradiction. There is no contradiction if resting is due to tiredness from a journey or if the periods of relaxation are moderate and occasional (*CTVBC*, f. 179a7-b1).

123. A bodhisattva who passes time conversing with others in social gatherings out of a liking for such diversions incurs an emotional contradiction. No contradiction is incurred if the bodhisattva happens to be in the midst of a conversation and participates briefly while maintaining awareness; nor is there anything wrong in asking or answering questions if the conversation is uplifting or informative (*CTVBC*, f. 179b2-3).

124. If a bodhisattva, although wishing to develop meditative concentration, refuses to seek instructions due to ill will or pride, he or she incurs an emotional contradiction. No contradiction is incurred if the refusal is due to illness or a suspicion that the instructions are not genuine; or if he or she has already been instructed, is learned, or able to settle the mind in equipoise (*CTVBC*, f. 179b3-6).

125. A bodhisattva who is fettered by the impediments caused by craving for objects of desire and does nothing to eliminate them incurs an emotional contradiction. No contradiction is incurred if while striving to dispel such impediments one is overcome by longing. The same is applies to malice, sleepiness, excitement, remorse, and doubt (*CTVBC*, ff. 179b6-180a1).

126. A bodhisattva who believes that another bodhisattva should not hear the proclaimers' doctrine, retain it, or train in it, that it is meaningless for a bodhisattva to listen to it, retain it, or train in it, and verbalizes these beliefs incurs an emotional contradiction. A bodhisattva should be familiar with non-Buddhist treatises; thus, it goes without saying that he or she must also study various kinds of Buddhist scriptures. However, there is no contradiction if a bodhisattva does not study particular scriptures in order to counteract his or her own strong interest in the proclaimers' way (*CTVBC*, f. 180a2-5).

127. If a bodhisattva, while having access to the scriptures that present the bodhisattva's training, does not engage in studying these scriptures, pondering their meanings, and making a living experience of them, but instead disregards them and engages in the study of the scriptures of the proclaimers, he or she incurs an emotional contradiction (*CTVBC*, f. 180a5-6).

128. If a bodhisattva who has access to the Buddhist scriptures does not make an effort to study, retain, and practice these teachings, but instead engages in the study of non-Buddhist treatises, he or she incurs an emotional contradiction. If the bodhisattva is exceptionally brilliant, evolved, and capable of retaining the teachings for long, reflecting on their meaning, and understanding them, and already has a comprehension of the Buddhist scriptures derived from analytical reasoning so that faith in them is unchanging, there is no contradiction if one day out of two he or she studies Buddhist scriptures and on the other day studies non-Buddhist ones (*CTVBC*, f. 180a6-b1).

129. If a bodhisattva who is qualified (see previous note) to become learned in non-Buddhist scriptures does so with great joy and takes great delight in them,

he or she incurs an emotional contradiction (*CTVBC*, f. 180b1-3).

130. A bodhisattva incurs an emotional contradiction if he or she, upon hearing the exclusive message of the bodhisattva scriptures or profound and sublime topics such as the powers of buddhas and bodhisattvas, does not take interest in them due to misconception, and deprecates them (i.e., views the Universalist scriptures as meaningless, untrue, not reflecting the actual words of the Transcendent One, and of no benefit to sentient beings), or causes others to do so.

If a bodhisattva when hearing such profound and sublime topics does not naturally feel interested in them, he or she should make an effort to develop unwavering confidence in them by thinking, "Although I am blind, lacking the eyes to see these profound truths that are seen only by the Transcendent One's eyes, it is not right for me to reject what the Transcendent One knows and has taught," and engage in earnest study of them (*CTVBC*, f. 180b3-7).

131. If a bodhisattva does not attend a discourse on the sacred teachings or a related discussion due to pride, ill will, or anger, he or she incurs an emotional contradiction. There is no contradiction if the bodhisattva does not attend because he or she is ill, suspects that the teaching is not genuine, does not wish to upset the speaker by his or her presence, or is extremely stupid and has weak power of understanding (*CTVBC*, f. 181a3-6).

132. If a bodhisattva, desiring material gain or motivated by anger, praises himself and deprecates another, he or she incurs an emotional contradiction. No contradiction is incurred if the object of deprecation is a non-Buddhist provided one's intention is to make the Buddhist teachings last longer; or if praising oneself and deprecating another would serve as a means to uplift others spiritually, to make non-believers believe, or to lead on the path to liberation those who do have faith (*CTVBC*, f. 181a1-3).

133. If a bodhisattva, out of irreverence or conscious disregard for the meaning of a discourse, scorns or mocks a person who is expounding the teachings, he or she incurs an emotional contradiction (*CTVBC*, f. 181a7). Bodhibhadra states that to fixate on the words of the teaching rather than their meaning with the intention of criticizing the teacher is a contradiction (*Revelation of the Difficult Points*, f. 214a3-4).

134. A bodhisattva who is abiding by the commitments should perform the following activities: caring for the needs of others, helping those who are on a journey, helping others to accomplish their tasks, looking after the belongings of others, reconciling factions, and helping others earn their living or hold festivities. Not to do so out of ill will or anger constitutes an emotional contradiction.

There is no contradiction in not performing these duties in the following cases: when the bodhisattva is unable to help due to illness, has entrusted the responsibility to another capable person, or the other person is able to help himself or has an attendant or guardian to help him; when to help would be dangerous or not in accord with the teachings; when the bodhisattva is busy in other wholesome activities such as meditation; when not helping would be a means to protect many persons, or to uphold the discipline of the monastic community; or when the bodhisattva is unable to expound the teachings due to insufficient study or inferior intellect (*CTVBC*, f. 181b1-4).

135. If a bodhisattva meets a sick person and, out of ill will or anger, does not attend to his needs, he or she incurs an emotional contradiction. There is no contradiction in the following cases: if the bodhisattva himself is sick; if he or she entrusts the duty to someone else; if the sick person has an attendant or can take care of himself; or if the bodhisattva is engaged in other important virtuous deeds and helping would constitute an interference to these (*CTVBC*, ff. 181b5-182a1).

136. If a bodhisattva meets a person who is suffering, and because of pride, anger, or ill will, does not alleviate his suffering but turns his back on him, he or she incurs an emotional contradiction. The contradiction is non-emotional if based on complacence or laziness. No fault is incurred if the bodhisattva himself is suffering (Bodhibhadra's *Revelation of the Difficult Points*, f. 214b5-6). The specifications of the previous notes also apply here.

137. If a bodhisattva meets a person who has entered a path that is mistaken in the sense of being detrimental to his welfare in the present life and in future ones and, out of ill will or anger, does not point out to him the correct path, he or she incurs an emotional contradiction. No fault is incurred in the following cases: when one is unable to help, or has entrusted the responsibility to someone else who is competent; when the person can correct himself or is already under the care of a spiritual guide; when the person to be corrected feels ill will toward oneself, or would take one's advice in the wrong way because of being insubordinate; when the person is wicked and would have no respect or appreciation for the advice; or when aware that to give the advice would be in vain (*CTVBC*, f. 182a2-5).

138. If a bodhisattva, out of ill will or anger, does not repay or even feel inclined to repay help received, he or she incurs an emotional contradiction. No contradiction is incurred if one tries to reciprocate but is unable to do so; or if the other person does not wish to be repaid (*CTVBC*, f. 182a5-b1).

139. If a bodhisattva, out of anger or hatred, does not alleviate the suffering of people close to him or of those who are destitute, he or she incurs an emotional contradiction (*CTVBC*, f. 182b1-2).

140. If a bodhisattva refuses to give others material aid such as food, beverages, or other objects of desire when asked for them because of ill will or anger, he or she incurs an emotional contradiction. No contradiction is incurred if one does not have the objects requested or if one is asked for inappropriate or unsuitable things; or if refusal is necessary to maintain monastic discipline (*CTVBC*, f. 182b3-5).

141. If a bodhisattva, because of ill will or anger, does not provide spiritual care for his or her circle of followers, or does not seek from faithful patrons clothes, food, bedding, mats, medicines, and other necessities for them, he or she incurs an emotional contradiction. No contradiction is incurred if one's students are well-off or capable of taking care of themselves; or if they have already completed their training; or if among one's students, a non-Buddhist has come to

listen to the teachings for an inappropriate reason and there is no chance for him to be converted (*CTVBC*, ff. 182b5-183a3).

142. If a bodhisattva, because of ill will, does not act in accordance with others' wishes, he or she incurs an emotional contradiction. No contradiction is incurred if the other's needs have already been satisfied; if one is unable to; if to act in accordance would jeopardize the discipline within the monastic community; if satisfying the needs of one person would be contrary to the wishes or needs of many others; or if not acting in accordance would convert a non-Buddhist, etc. (*CTVBC*, f. 183a3-6).

143. If a bodhisattva because of ill will does not speak of and praise the good qualities of another or give recognition to someone else for a well-delivered speech, he or she incurs an emotional contradiction. No contradiction is incurred if one knows that that person is naturally modest; if one is unable to; or if one suspects that praising the person would inflate his pride, arrogance, or conceit, or harm him somehow; or if the other person has feigned good qualities or speech (*CTVBC*, f. 183a6-b).

144. If a monk, according to the rules of the monastic discipline, deserves to be put under surveillance, punished, or banished, and the responsible bodhisattva, for some afflicted motive, does not carry out this duty, he incurs an emotional contradiction. No contradiction is incurred in not subjecting the monk to disciplinary measures if the monk is insubordinate, ill willed, or of bad character; if doing so would cause a quarrel or a division in the monastic community; or if the monk, although careless, still has shame and embarrassment and therefore will quickly improve by himself (*CTVBC*, f. 183b3-7).

145. If a bodhisattva is capable of showing powers, performing miracles, and creating emanations, and does not do so before someone who should be intimidated or one who might be spiritually inspired, he or she incurs an emotional contradiction. No contradiction is incurred if the person is extremely opinionated, is a non-Buddhist, deprecates exalted beings, or has wayward views; or when the person is in a highly deranged state of mind or oppressed by suffering, or is not a member of the monastic community (*CTVBC*, ff. 183b7-184a3).

146. Complacence (*snyoms las*) implies that one is well aware that a particular deed is an infraction to the bodhisattva's training but one still engages in it. Shantirakshita and Bodhibhadra, commentators on the *Twenty Verses on the Bodhisattva Commitments*, as well as Asanga, in presenting most of the forty-six secondary infractions, state that an infraction incurred through complacence constitutes a non-emotional infraction.

147. In addition to these conditions for infractions to be of no consequence, Asanga states that if an infraction is committed while tormented by suffering, or by one who has not assumed the bodhisattva commitments, it is of no consequence (*SB*, f. 97a6-7).

148. *SB*, f. 86a3-6.

149. Shantirakshita states that unlike the offenses of a monk, which are categorized

as five types (defeating offenses, partially defeating offenses, downfalls that involve forfeiture or confession alone, offenses to be individually confessed, and minor infractions), transgressions to the bodhisattva's commitments are only of two kinds: factors for a defeat (*pham pa'i gnas lta bu'i chos su gtogs pa*) and factors for a minor infraction (*nyes byas kyi chos su gtogs pa*) (*CTVBC*, f. 173a7).

150. Vow holder (*sdom ldan*). Shantirakshita states that one can confess a transgression committed with moderate or slight emotional involvement to followers of either the proclaimers' or the bodhisattvas' training (*CTVBC*, f. 172a6). Of the same opinion is Atisha; see *Commentary on the Lamp for the Path* (*Bodhimārgapradīpapañjikā; Byang chub lam gyi sgron ma'i dka' 'grel*) (vol. Khi, f. 266b3) (Toh. 3948).

151. "One's own mind" refers to having shame and embarrassment, discipline and pacification, and the intention not to repeat the transgression. When no appropriate person is found, all infractions may be confessed in the imagined presence of the buddhas and bodhisattvas (*CTVBC*, f. 172b5-6).

152. *SB*, f. 86a6.

153. Ten virtuous activities (*chos spyod bcu*): copying the scriptures, making offerings, being generous, listening to the teachings, memorizing and studying the scriptures, expounding the teachings, reciting the scriptures, pondering the import of the teachings, and integrating them into one's life. Dharmashri states that the way to cultivate merit in conjunction with pristine awareness is by performing virtuous activities without conceptualization of the reality of the agent, act, and object (*Commentary on the Three Vows*, f. 154b3).

154. These four black and four white deeds are also presented in the tenth chapter of Gampopa's *JOL*, ff. 88b5-94a6.

155. The ethics of restraint (*sdom pa'i tshul khrims*), of acquiring good qualities (*dge ba chos sdud pa'i tshul khrims*), and of working for the benefit of others (*sems can gyi don byed pa'i tshul khrims*).

156. *JOL*, f. 106a5-6.

157. The ethics of restraint calms one's mind and instills a feeling of well-being in this life. The ethics of acquiring good qualities brings one's enlightened qualities to maturity without physical hardship. The ethics of working for the benefit of others leads others to spiritual maturity (*SB*, f. 101b2).

158. The eight worldly concerns (*'jig rten chos brgyad*) in four pairs: the hope for gain and fear of loss; and likewise, fame and obscurity; praise and blame; pleasure and misery.

159. The opposites of the eightfold noble path (*aṣṭāṅgamārga, 'phags lam yan lag brgyad*): wrong view, thought, speech, effort, livelihood, mindfulness, concentration, and action.

160. Those of evil occupations (*caṇḍāla, gdol pa*) include butchers, hunters, fishermen, and robbers, who were considered outcaste in the caste system of ancient India.

161. Chandragomin's *Twenty Verses*, f. 167a5.

162. As means to help others, even the seven unvirtuous actions of body and speech are permitted in special circumstances. For instance, to save the lives of many people, one may kill their potential murderer; to save a person from dying of hunger, one may steal food from a wealthy person; to save a woman who would die from unsatisfied sexual desire, one may engage in sexual intercourse; to save someone sure to be killed, one may hide him and lie about his whereabouts; to save someone being led to lower forms of life by an evil companion, one may slander one of them in order to divide the two; to relieve someone's sorrow or to lead one who likes to chatter to the true teachings, one may tell stories and engage in other kinds of senseless speech; and to divert someone from doing an evil act, one may use harsh speech. However, since one's state of mind is the crucial factor in determining whether an act is virtuous or not, the three unvirtuous states of mind, covetousness, malice, and wayward views, are never acceptable in any circumstances (Dharmashri's *Commentary on the Three Vows*, ff. 181b5-182b2).

163. *JOL*, ff. 107b6-108a1.

164. Three spiritual paths: those of the proclaimers, solitary sages, and bodhisattvas.

165. The six branches of generosity—the generosity of generosity, the generosity of ethics, the generosity of patience, and so on—stem from the practice of getting others to practice each of the six perfections; the six branches of ethics, from the practice of each of the six perfections unstained by their respective incompatible factors; the six branches of patience, from the practice of each perfection while enduring their respective hardships; the six branches of effort, from the practice of each perfection accompanied by joy; the six branches of meditation, from the undistracted practice of each perfection; and the six branches of wisdom, from the practice of each perfection free of the concepts of act, agent, and object (Dharmashri's *Commentary on the Three Vows*, ff. 61a1-3).

166. This overall description is drawn from the eleventh chapter of Gampopa's *JOL*, ff. 94a6-96b6.

167. Gampopa states that improper intention (*bsams pa ma dag pa*) means to give with the perverse intention of harming someone, with the wish to acquire a good reputation in the present life, or in order to compete with others; or to offer with the inferior motivation of wishing to be free of poverty in the next life, or with the desire to be reborn as a human or a god and to enjoy that life. Improper gifts (*dngos po ma dag pa*) refers to such articles as poison, fire, and weapons, when these can be harmful, or one's father, mother, child, or spouse. Improper recipient (*zhing ma dag pa*) refers to those who wish to practice necromancy, demonic beings, or insane people, to whom a bodhisattva should not give away his or her body or limbs. Improper manner of giving (*thabs ma dag pa*) means to give while angry or upset with the recipient; with scorn or disdain toward a bad person; or to a beggar while rebuking, threatening, or disheartening him (*JOL*, f. 98b2-99b4).

Dharmashri states that the giving of material things is a practice to be done mainly by lay bodhisattvas; the gift of the teachings, by monastic bodhisattvas; the giving of one's country, children, spouse, and limbs, by those who have gained a direct understanding of emptiness (*Commentary on the Three Vows*, f. 163b4-5).

168. This classification of generosity is derived from Asanga's *Synthesis of Phenomenology* (*Abhidharmasamuccaya; Chos mngon pa kun las btus pa*) (Toh. 4049), modified by Gampopa in *JOL*, f. 101a3-4.

169. Nine methods to develop patience: (1) recognize that those who harm us are not masters of themselves; (2) examine the unfitness of our actions; (3) the unfitness of our body; (4) and the unfitness of our attachment to it; (5) understand that faults lie in both oneself and the other; (6) reflect upon the usefulness of harmful persons; (7) think of them as benefactors; (8) repay the kindness the buddhas have shown to us; and (9) realize the chance harmful people give us to attain enlightenment.

The first method is expressed in verse 31 of chapter VI of Shantideva's *Guide to the Bodhisattva's Way of Life* (f. 15b6):

> Everything is governed by something else
> And thus a human being is powerless.
> Having understood this, I should not become angry
> At things which are like a magical spell.

the second method, in verse 42 (f. 16a5):

> Similar harm I did
> Previously to others.
> It is fitting that this harm now be returned
> To me who has been injurious to other beings.

the third method, in verse 43 (f. 16a5-6):

> His weapon and my body
> Are both the cause of my suffering.
> Since he brought forth the weapon and I the body,
> Who shall I angrily blame?

the fourth method, in verse 44 (f. 16a6-7):

> This sore that resembles a human body
> Cannot bear to be touched and is painful.
> If blinded by attachment I cling to it
> With whom shall I become angry when it is injured?

the fifth method, in verse 67 (f. 17a5):

> When some do wrong out of ignorance
> And others ignorantly become angry at that,
> Who can be said to be without fault?
> Who can be said to be at fault?

the sixth method, in verse 48 (f. 16b1-2):

> Depending on them for my patience,
> I purify many evils.

But they depending upon me
Will stay long in a hell of misery.

the seventh method, in verses 107-8 (f. 18b7):

Since he assists me in my awakening
I must be pleased to have an enemy.

Because I train with him,
The fruit of patience
Should be first bestowed on him,
For he is the cause of patience.

the eighth method, in verse 119 (f. 19a7):

Moreover, what way can there be to repay [the buddhas]
Who grant incommensurable benefit
And are reliable friends,
Other than by appeasing sentient beings?

the ninth method, in verse 112 (f. 19a2-3):

The Mighty One has said
That the field of sentient beings is a buddha field,
For many who have appeased them
Have thereby reached perfection.

The identification of the verses that correspond to the nine methods is based on Gampopa's *JOL*, ff. 113a2-114b1.

170. Five thoughts (*'du shes lnga*) to develop patience: the thought of how dear the harmful person may have been in one's previous lives (*sngon gyi tshe rabs su snying du sdug par gyur pa'i 'du shes*); the thought of the harmful person as simply a phenomenon (*chos tsam gyi rjes su 'brang ba'i 'du shes*); the thought of impermanence (*mi rtag pa'i 'du shes*); the thought of misery (*sdug bsngal ba'i 'du shes*); and the thought of fully accepting others (*yongs su bzung ba'i 'du shes*).

Asanga's *Stages of the Bodhisattva* presents the steps to cultivate these five: (1) How does a bodhisattva train in considering how dear a harmful person was in previous lives? By thinking that over the course of many lives, that person may have been one's father, mother, brother, sister, attendant, preceptor, master, or spiritual guide. [The benefit one has received from him] is difficult to fathom. With this correct perspective, the bodhisattva gives up the idea of the person being an enemy, but considers him precious; and does not wish to retaliate, but patiently accepts whatever harm is done.

(2) How does a bodhisattva train in considering the harmful person as just a phenomenon? By thinking that the person harming oneself exists only in dependence upon many conditions, and of many composite factors, simply a phenomenon. Therefore, one can isolate no self, mental substance, life principle, or personality that is abusing, angry, beating, reviling, or finding fault with oneself. With this correct perspective, the bodhisattva dissolves the idea of the

harmful person as a [real] person and sees him as just a phenomenon. Considering the nature of that person to be simply a phenomenon, the bodhisattva does not wish to retaliate, but instead patiently accepts whatever harm is done.

(3) How does a bodhisattva train in considering the impermanence of the harmful person? By thinking that all sentient beings are impermanent and subject to death. The worst harm would be to deprive them of their lives. A wise bodhisattva should never be unaware of the transient nature of beings, not to speak of being so confused as to strike them with one's hand, throw earth, hit them with a stick, or kill them. With this correct perspective, the bodhisattva dissolves the idea of eternalism and substantiality with respect to the harmful person and sees him as transient and essenceless. Considering the transient nature of that person, the bodhisattva does not wish to retaliate, but patiently accepts whatever harm is done.

(4) How does a bodhisattva train in considering the misery of the harmful person? By thinking that even beings in the most excellent of circumstances are subject to the triad of misery: the misery intrinsic to conditioned existence, the misery of change, and the misery of misery. Seeing the constant state of suffering of beings, the bodhisattva resolves to dispel their misery, thinking: "I should not [retaliate] as this would cause the very misery that I must dispel." With this correct perspective, the bodhisattva dissolves the idea of the harmful person as a happy being. Thinking of the suffering of that person, one does not wish to retaliate, but patiently accepts whatever harm is done.

(5) How does a bodhisattva train in the full acceptance of the harmful person? By thinking "Having formed the mind of awakening, I will accomplish the welfare of others." The bodhisattva should treat all beings as a spouse, thinking, "Accepting all beings in this way, I will work for their benefit. To wish to harm them is not proper." With this correct perspective, the bodhisattva dissolves the idea that the harmful person is someone unrelated and fully accepts that person. By doing so, he or she does not wish to retaliate, but patiently accepts whatever harm is done (*SB*, ff. 102b1-103b3).

171. The quest for the teachings entails being strongly inclined to examine the eight topics of spiritual interest: (1) the qualities of the Three Jewels, (2) the meaning of reality (emptiness), (3) the power of the buddhas, (4) the power of the bodhisattvas, (5) the law of causality, (6) the goal one seeks, (7) the means to achieve that goal, and (8) the range of topics to be known to gain that end (*SB*, f. 105a5-6).

172. Armor-like effort (*go cha'i brtson 'grus*), effort applied to the task (*sbyor ba'i brtson 'grus*), and insatiable effort (*chog mi shes pa'i brtson 'grus*). Gampopa designates the first as the perfect motivation, the second as the perfect application, and the third as the perfection of their integration (*JOL*, f. 118b1-2).

173. Fivefold effort in accomplishing what is wholesome: ever-active effort that knows no interruption; devoted effort in acting swiftly in a joyful and interested

state of mind; effort unshaken by the negative effects of one's emotions, preconceptions, and misery; effort not deflected by circumstances although knowing that one can be hurt, treated harshly, or upset by others when seeing the manifestations of their deteriorated views; effort without pride or a feeling of superiority (*JOL*, ff. 119b1-120a2).

174. Meditative concentration by which one rests in a state of ease in the present life (*mthong ba'i chos la bde bar gnas pa'i bsam gtan*), acquires good qualities (*yon tan sgrub pa'i bsam gtan*), and works for the welfare of others (*sems can gyi don byed pa'i bsam gtan*). The meditative concentration (of a bodhisattva) is defined as mental quiescence (which is a virtuous mind resting single-pointedly on worldly or transworldly paths), insight, and the path that unifies both, which have been preceded by listening to and reflecting on the teachings on the bodhisattva path (*SB*, f. 111a2-3).

175. A bodhisattva's meditative concentration has six qualities: (1) free from concepts in that the mind rests in single-pointedness, devoid of the movement [of conceiving] being or not being, etc.; (2) producing physical and mental pliancy in that all kinds of unfitness of mind and body have been eliminated; (3) completely tranquil, a state that is entered spontaneously; (4) without pride, that is, without the impediment of an [afflicted] view; (5) free from attachment to pleasure, that is, without the impediment of worldliness; and (6) free from objectifiable attributes, being devoid of the pleasant experiences of the form realm, etc. (*JOL*, ff. 129b6-130a1).

176. Totalities (*zad par*), masteries (*zil gnon*), and emancipations (*rnam thar*) are forms of concentration (*ting nge 'dzin*). For an explanation of these, see Kongtrul's *Infinite Ocean of Knowledge* (*IOK*) (*Shes bya mtha' yas pa'i rgya mtsho*) (Beijing: Bod mi rigs dpe bskrun khang, 1982), vol. II, pp. 614-618. See also Guenther's *Philosophy and Psychology in the Abhidharma* (Berkeley and London: Shambhala, 1976), pp. 134-141.

177. The concentrations that constitute the ten powers of the Buddha: the power of knowing what is right and not right, knowing the ripening results of actions, knowing the various inclinations of beings, knowing the types of beings, knowing the higher and lower faculties of beings, knowing the destinies of beings, knowing polluted and purified phenomena, knowing previous lives, knowing future lives, and knowing the extinction of afflictions.

178. Common sciences: medicine (*gso ba rig pa*), logic (*gtan tshigs rig pa*), linguistics (*sgra rig pa*), and arts (*bzo rig pa*). The inner science or Buddhist spirituality (*nang rig pa*) is the transmundane science from which arise transmundane types of wisdom.

179. See chapter II, note 13.

180. *Condensed Transcendent Wisdom Scripture*, in *Collected Scriptures and Dhāraṇi*, vol. sMad cha, f. 9a5-6.

181. This section on the six perfections is drawn from *JOL*, ff. 96b6-153b1.

182. The forty-one prayers to cultivate awakening mind: (1) "May I lead all

sentient beings to the citadel of liberation" is the prayer of the bodhisattva when entering a house; (2) "May all sentient beings attain the dimension of reality of a buddha," when going to sleep; (3) "May all sentient beings realize the dream-like nature of things," when dreaming; (4) "May all beings awake from the sleep of ignorance," when waking up; (5) "May all beings attain the form dimensions of a buddha," when getting up; (6) "May all beings wear the robes of conscience and embarrassment," when putting on clothes; (7) "May all beings be secured by the root of virtue," when putting on a belt; (8) "May all beings reach the seat of enlightenment," when sitting down; (9) "May all beings reach the tree of enlightenment," when leaning back; (10) "May all beings exhaust the fuel of the passions," when lighting a fire; (11) "May all beings cause the fire of pristine awareness to blaze," when making a fire blaze; (12) "May all beings come to drink the nectar of pristine awareness," when holding a cup; (13) "May all beings attain the food of meditative concentration," when eating; (14) "May all beings escape from the prison of cyclic life," when going outside; (15) "May I plunge into cyclic life for the sake of all beings," when going down a staircase; (16) "May I open the door of liberation for all beings," when opening a door; (17) "May I close the door to the lower forms of life for all beings," when closing a door; (18) "May all beings set out on the exalted path," when setting out on a path; (19) "May I lead all beings to the higher forms of life," when going uphill; (20) "May I sever the stream of the lower forms of life for all beings," when going downhill; (21) "May all beings meet the Buddha," when meeting someone; (22) "May I walk toward the welfare of all beings," when placing the foot down; (23) "May I lift all beings from out of cyclic existence," when lifting the foot; (24) "May all beings attain the ornaments of the major and minor marks of a buddha," when seeing someone wearing ornaments; (25) "May all beings be endowed with the twelve ascetic virtues," when seeing someone without ornaments; (26) "May all beings be filled with good qualities," when seeing a filled container; (27) "May all beings be without faults," when seeing an empty container; (28) "May all beings take joy in the teachings," when seeing someone joyful; (29) "May all beings be dissatisfied with composite phenomena," when seeing someone sad; (30) "May all beings win the bliss of a buddha," when seeing someone happy; (31) "May all the sentient beings' anguish be alleviated," when seeing someone suffering; (32) "May all beings be free from illnesses," when seeing someone sick; (33) "May all beings repay the kindness of all buddhas and bodhisattvas," when seeing someone repaying another's kindness; (34) "May all beings be unkind to wrong views," when seeing someone not repaying kindness; (35) "May all beings be competent when meeting those who challenge them," when seeing a dispute; (36) "May all beings praise the qualities of all buddhas and bodhisattvas," when seeing someone praise another; (37) "May all beings attain the eloquence of a buddha," when seeing someone discuss the teachings; (38) "May all beings be unimpeded in seeing all the buddhas," when seeing someone meet a representation of the Buddha; (39) "May all beings become monuments of enlightenment," when seeing a stupa; (40) "May all beings attain the seven riches of an exalted being (faith, ethics, learning, liberality, conscience, embarrassment, and discriminating awareness)," when seeing someone engaged in business; (41) "May the crown of the head of all beings be seen (as that of the Buddha) by all the world and the gods," when seeing someone bowing down. Cited from the *Flower Ornament Scripture* (*Buddhāvataṃsaka-nāmamahāvaipūlyasūtra; Sangs rgyas phal po che zhes bya ba shin tu rgyas pa chen po'i mdo*) (Toh. 44) in Dharmashri's *Commentary on the Three Vows*, ff. 176a5-177b1.

183. *CT*, f. 1a4.

184. A practice based on appreciation is performed primarily on the paths of accumulation and preparation. See chapter I, note 26.

185. See chapter I, note 27.

186. *JOL*, f. 72a5.

187. *JOL*, f. 69b3.

188. For a discussion of this viewpoint, see *The Rite for the Formation of the Aspiring, Venturing, and Ultimate Awakening Minds* (*sMon 'jug don dam gsum gyi sems bskyed kyi cho ga yid bzhin nor bu*) in *A Collection of Instructions on Buddhist Practice* by 'Bri gung skyob pa 'Jig rten mgon po.

189. A ritual involving creative imagination performed during a tantric empowerment during which one thinks of oneself as being in the simple form of the deity for which one is empowered. One stands with eyes blindfolded at the entrance of the eastern gate of the deity's mandala. There one takes the refuge, bodhisattva, and mantra vows. At that point, the relative and ultimate minds, together known as the mind of all-encompassing yoga, are generated. One imagines that relative awakening mind takes the form of a moon disc at the heart, and ultimate awakening mind, a five-pronged vajra standing on a moon disc. See Tenzin Gyatso, the Dalai Lama, *The Kalachakra Tantra, Rite of Initiation*, edited and translated by Jeffrey Hopkins (London: Wisdom Publications, 1985), pp. 234-235.

190. Kongtrul here paraphrases the words of Sakya Pandita's verses found in his *Analysis of the Three Vows* in *Collected Works*, vol. II, p. 29, lines 3-6, and p. 17.

191. As explained above, the awakening mind that arises through indications given by a spiritual teacher is a relative one.

192. The *Hundred Rites of Renunciation and Fulfillment* (*sPang skong phyag brgya pa*) (Toh. 267), ff. 1b-5b: according to legend, a scripture that fell from the sky onto the top of Yumbu Lakang Palace (*pho brang yum bu gla sgang*) at the time of the Tibetan King Lha Totori. By saying "it is possible," Sakya Pandita indicates his doubt about the authenticity of this text. Further, in his *Rite of Formation of the Awakening Mind* (*Collected Works*, vol. II, p. 583), he states: "The *Hundred Rites* fell from the sky in Tibet and is not a translation from Sanskrit; therefore, it is difficult for scholars to consider it as an authentic source."

193. The assertion made by followers of Ngari Panchen may be summarized as follows: the tantras *Magical Net* (*Mañjuśrījñānasattvasya-paramārthanāma-saṃgīti; 'Jam dpal ye shes sems pa'i don dam pa'i mtshan yang dag par brjod pa/ 'Jam dpal sgyu 'phrul drva ba*) (Toh. 360), *Vairochana-abhisambodhi* (*Mahāvairocanābhisambodhi-vikurvitādhiṣṭhānavaipulyasūtreindrarājanāmadharmaparyāya; rNam par snang mdzad*

chen po mngon par rdzogs par byang chub pa rnam par sprul pa byin gyis rlob pa shin tu rgyas pa mdo sde'i dbang po'i rgyal po zhes bya ba'i chos kyi rnam grangs) (Toh. 494), Nagarjuna's *Commentary on the Awakening Mind* (*Bodhicitta vivaraṇa, Byang chub sems kyi 'grel pa*) (Toh. 1800), the *Five Stages* (*Pañcakrama; Rim pa lnga pa*) (Toh. 1802) and others, do present ceremonies for the formation of an ultimate awakening mind. These are Secret Mantra procedures that take as their path the pristine awareness of the result. Through such ceremonies, a facsimile of ultimate awakening mind is formed as a means to create the conducive circumstances for the actual attainment of ultimate awakening mind. This facsimile has the nature of the aspiring mind, but is not the actual ultimate awakening mind which can only be formed through the strength of meditation. The statement from the *Hundred Rites of Renunciation and Fulfillment* (*sPang skong phyag brgya pa*) (Toh. 267) refers simply to a promise to form ultimate awakening mind, not to the ultimate mind itself. Otherwise, if one accepts the notion that an awakening mind could be formed through a rite, one would have to endorse the consequence that ultimate awakening mind is born from indications (words). However, this is not the case because, as stated by Kamalashila in his *Stages of Meditation*, such a mind is actualized through the constant cultivation of mental quiescence and insight (Dharmashri's *Commentary on the Three Vows*, ff. 242b1-244a5).

194. Absolute dedication (*yongs 'dzin*), subsequent achievement (*rjes sgrub*), and realization (*rtogs pa*). In the following verse cited from the *Scripture Ornament*, the first aspect is conveyed by the words "well-honored" (*rab mnyes*); the second, by the words "merit and awareness have been thoroughly cultivated" (*tshogs rab bsags*); and the third, by the words "non-conceptual pristine awareness has arisen" (*chos la mi rtog pa'i ye shes*).

195. f. 4b6.

196. In his *Explanation of the Scripture Ornament*, Vasubandhu states that ultimate awakening mind attained on the first stage of a bodhisattva (called Joyful) is a mind of equanimity toward all phenomena that has realized the selflessness of all. It is a mind of equanimity toward all beings that has realized the equality of oneself and others. It is a mind of equanimity toward the activities of beings that wishes the end of all suffering of others just as one wishes the end of one's own. It is a mind of equanimity toward the Buddha that realizes the inseparability of oneself and the sphere of reality (f. 140a7-b2).

197. *GBL*, f. 8a1-2. This is verse 11 of chapter IV.

198. *JOL*, ff. 86b4-87a1.

199. f. 35a4-5.

200. Vasubandhu (*ESO*, f. 247b6) and, likewise, Sthiramati (*CSO*, vol. Tsi, f. 219b2) state that bringing others to spiritual maturity is accomplished on the first to the seventh stages of awakening, on which the bodhisattva converts the unfaithful to the Buddhist teachings, and leads them on the path.

201. According to Sthiramati, the faultless state refers to the first bodhisattva stage. It is called faultless because at that stage the bodhisattva has become free

of the [speculative] adherence to the apprehended (*gzung ba*) and the apprehender ('*dzin pa*) (*CSO*, vol. *Tsi*, f. 219b1).

202. Sthiramati states: "The bodhisattva trains in making the environment of sentient beings appear with a crystal or golden hue" (*CSO*, vol. Tsi, f. 219b4-5).

203. Vasubandhu states that purifying one's own buddha field and attaining non-abiding perfect peace refer to the three irreversible stages (*phyir mi ldog pa'i sa gsum*)—the eight, ninth, and tenth bodhisattva stages (*ESO*, f. 247).

204. Both the *Scripture Ornament* (f. 35) and Vasubandhu's commentary on it (f. 247b7) read *dang* ("and") instead of *lam* ("path") as Kongtrul has. Here we are reading in accordance with Kongtrul's text.

Sthiramati's authoritative commentary (*CSO*, vol. Tsi, f. 219b6) reads *byang chub mchog kyang rnam par ston* ("demonstrating supreme enlightenment") and explains that after awakening, the Buddha enters the womb of the mother, manifests in the world, demonstrates the path to enlightenment, and turns the wheel of the teachings.

205. Lesser path of accumulation (*tshogs lam chung ngu*): the initial stage of this path, the basis for the subsequent middle path and great path of accumulation.

206. The ability of a bodhisattva to create a buddha field (*byang chub sems dpa'i rnams kyi sangs rgyas kyi zhing yongs su dag pa*). The Buddha's exposition on this quality is recorded in *The Holy Teachings of Vimalakirti*, trans. Robert A. F. Thurman (University Park: Pennsylvania State University Press, 1976).

207. See chapter II, note 315.

208. The five aggregates of form, sensation, discernment, mental formations, and consciousness.

209. See chapter II, note 182.

210. See chapter III, note 38.

211. The dimension of reality (*dharmakāya, chos sku*) is the mind of a buddha. The form dimensions (*rūpakāya, gzugs sku*) are the enjoyment dimension (*saṃbhogakāya, longs sku*) and manifest dimension (*nirmāṇakāya, sprul sku*) of a buddha. These are known as the three dimensions of awakening (*kāya, sku*). For further explanation, see chapter 20 of *JOL*.

Chapter IV: The Vows and Pledges of the Secret Mantra

1. The new schools (*gsar ma*), which originated from the later translations (*phyi 'gyur*) of tantras from Sanskrit, refers to the lineages of the Kagyu (bKa' brgyud), Sakya (Sa skya), and Geluk (dGe lugs) traditions. The Kagyu (Transmission of the Oral Teaching) lineage begins with Marpa the Translator (1012-1099); the Sakya (Grey Earth) lineage, with Könchok Gyalpo (dKon mchog rgyal po) (1034-1102); and the Geluk (Virtuous Ones) lineage, with Tsongkapa (1357-1419). The Geluk tradition was rooted in the Kadam (Words of the Buddha as Personal

Instructions) tradition, which began with Atisha (982-1054) and his renowned disciple Dromtönpa ('Brom ston pa) (1004-1064). The main practices of these lineages are based on the tantras translated after the beginning of the eleventh century and during the later spread of Buddhism in Tibet. The pioneer of these translations was Rinchen Zangpo (Rin chen bzang po) (958-1051).

2. The ancient school (*rnying ma*), which originated with the early translations of tantras, was inspired by the mystic activity of the Indian master Padmasambhava in the ninth century. The tantric texts translated from Sanskrit prior to the end of the tenth century and during the early spread of Buddhism in Tibet are known as the tantras of the early translation (*gsang sngags snga 'gyur*).

3. *Two-Part Hevajra Tantra*, f. 27a7 (*Kye'i rdo rje mkha' 'gro ma dra ba'i sdom pa'i rgyud kyi rgyal po*) (Toh. 418).

4. The purificatory fast consists in the observance of eight precepts for a day (Bhavabhadra's *Commentary on the Hevajra Tantra* [*Hevajravyākhyāvivaraṇa; dGyes pa'i rdo rje'i rnam bshad rnam par 'grel pa*] [Toh. 1182], f. 271a1). For details, see chapter II of this work.

The ten areas of training refers to practicing ten forms of virtue (not to kill, etc.,) and renouncing their opposites (Vajragarbha's *Commentary That Epitomizes the Hevajra Tantra* [*Hevajrapindārthaṭīkā; Kye'i rdo rje bsdus pa'i don gyi rgya cher 'grel pa/ rDo rje snying 'grel*] [Toh. 1180], f. 117a3-4). Alternatively, the ten areas of training refers to the ten main vows of a novice (Kongtrul's *Commentary on the Hevajra Tantra* [*dPal dgyes pa rdo rje'i rgyud kyi rgyal po brtag pa gnyis pa'i tshig don rnam par 'grol ba gzhom med rdo rje'i gsang ba 'byed pa*] [Rumtek, Sikkim: Dharma Chakra Centre, 1981], f. 300b6).

5. *Two-Part Hevajra Tantra*, f. 27a7.

6. The four trends of Buddhist philosophical thought. See chapter II, n. 13. Bhavabhadra states that the Analysts' [view] represents the systems of the proclaimers and the solitary sages. Those systems lead to the awakening of the proclaimers, the nature of which is the elimination of emotional impediments, and to the awakening of the solitary sages, the nature of which is the elimination of emotional impediments plus half of the impediments preventing the attainment of omniscience. The Traditionalist view is based on a literal reading of the Buddha's discourses. The Experientialist view maintains that only consciousness is real. The Centrist view is that all that exists is mere convention (*Commentary on the Hevajra Tantra*, f. 271a3-4).

Saroruha states: To elucidate the Analyst philosophy, teach the nature of the five aggregates and so forth. For the Traditionalist view, teach the scriptures of the Universal Way. For the Experientialist view, teach that all is consciousness. And for the Centrist view, teach the emptiness that is devoid of being, not being, etc. (*Commentary on the Difficult Points of the Hevajra Tantra* [*Hevajratantrapañjikāpadmin; Kye'i rdo rje'i rgyud kyi dka' 'grel pad ma can*] [Toh. 1181], f. 172a3-4). See also Vajragarbha's *Commentary That Epitomizes the Hevajra Tantra*, f. 117a4-b3.

7. *Two-Part Hevajra Tantra*, f. 27b1.

8. According to Saroruha, the various levels of mantra are the Action, Conduct, Highest Yoga, and Yogini tantras (*Commentary on the Difficult Points of the Hevajra Tantra*, f. 172a3).

9. Fruition Universal Way (*'bras bu theg chen*) refers to the Secret Mantra, while the Causal Universal Way (*rgyu theg chen*) refers to the Way of the Perfections. The Secret Mantra is known as fruition because its practitioner employs meditative techniques in which he or she imagines having already attained the purities of the fruition stage of a buddha. See Tsongkapa's "The Great Exposition of Secret Mantra," in *Tantra in Tibet* by H. H. the Dalai Lama, Tsong-ka-pa, and Jeffrey Hopkins, (Ithaca: Snow Lion, 1987).
The Secret Mantra comprises two aspects: actual and nominal. Actual mantra is the indivisibility of skillful means and wisdom. Nominal mantra includes deities, mantras [as incantations], seals, sets of ritual activities and contemplations, forms of worship, praises, etc. (Jnanashri's *Dispelling the Two Extremes in the Indestructible Way* [rDo rje theg pa'i mtha' gnyis sel ba] [Toh. 3714], f. 119b3).

10. *gzung 'dzin gyi rnam rtog*: grasping to subject and object as real, the basis of dualistic thought.

11. The propensity for movement (*'pho ba'i bag chags*) refers to the propensity for the emission of the seminal essence (*bindu, thig le*). The seminal essence is the basis for the experience of great bliss; its emission or loss compromises the experience of the pristine awareness of great bliss and perpetuates cyclic life, in the outer sense of initiating the life of another being and in the inner sense of starting the process of dualism. Thus, the Wheel of Time (Kalachakra) and other tantras speak of the propensity for emission of seminal essence as the cause of cyclic life. (Kongtrul's *Commentary on [Rangjung Dorjé's] Profound Inner Reality* [rNal 'byor bla na med pa'i rgyud sde rgya mtsho'i snying po bsdus pa zab mo nang gi don nyung nu'i tshig gis rnam par 'grol ba zab don snang byed], ff. 101a1-102a4.)

12. Pema Karpo states that "awareness" (*vidyā, rig pa*) in awareness-holder vows (*rig 'dzin gyi sdom pa*) refers to the pristine awareness of the union of skillful means and emptiness. To remain in pristine awareness is "to hold" (*'dzin pa*) awareness. The binding of the three doors—body, speech, and mind—effected by remaining in pristine awareness constitutes the "vow" (*sdom pa*). (*Extensive Commentary on the Three Vows* [sDom gsum rgya cher 'grel pa/ sDom pa gsum gyi rgyan ces bya ba'i rgya cher 'grel ba] [henceforth cited as *TV*], vol. Nga, f. 4b6.)

13. *Two-Part Hevajra Tantra*, f. 20b2-3.

14. Ibid., f. 20b3.

15. Kunda (*kun da*): the jasmine flower, often used as a metaphor for the seminal essence in the tantras.

16. Vajragarbha explains that in the Universal Way, awakening mind (*bodhicitta*), the resolve to awaken for others' sake, is considered to be the seed that develops into full enlightenment. In tantra, while retaining this same meaning, awakening

mind is equated with the seminal essence, which is the seed or support of great bliss. The relative aspect of awakening mind is the seminal essence itself, while the ultimate awakening mind is the bliss which is born from it. When bliss arises from union with the lotus of the consort but subsequently ebbs due to loss of the seminal essence, the cycle of life is initiated. When the seminal essence is retained, the experience is one of great bliss. By binding that great bliss with the "chain" of the understanding of reality, one attains the vajra-like dimension of awakening. Such awakening mind or great bliss is formed through the stages of self-blessing involving the descent of the seminal essence located at the crown of the head. As the outflow of the seminal essence is blocked, non-recognition of bliss ceases; the essence is drawn back to the navel, heart, throat, and crown of the head, and is stabilized and absorbed at various places. In this manner, cyclic life (the aggregates and other components) becomes perfect peace. For this reason, the seminal essence (*bodhicitta*) is perfect peace (*nirvāṇa*) and embodies both the relative and the ultimate (*Commentary That Epitomizes the Hevajra Tantra*, f. 98a1-b4).

17. Subhagavajra states that tantra (lit. "continuity") (*rgyud*) comprises two aspects: actual tantra (*don gyi rgyud*) and tantra of words (*tshig gi rgyud*). Actual tantra is threefold: tantra of the ground [or causal tantra] (*gzhi'i rgyud*); tantra of skillful means (*thabs kyi rgyud*); and tantra of the result (*'bras bu'i rgyud*). The tantra of the ground comprises the two truths; the tantra of skillful means, the two phases of tantric practice, creation and completion; and the tantra of the result, the reality and form dimensions of awakening. Tantra (continuity) is so called because the three aspects of the actual tantra are interconnected: based on the ground tantra, the practitioner cultivates the tantra of skill in means, and as a consequence of that, he or she attains the resultant tantra. (*Stages of the Path of the Universal Way* [*Mahāyānapathakrama; Theg pa chen po'i lam gyi rim pa*] [Toh. 3717], f. 193a1-4.)

Kongtrul defines *rgyud* (tantra) as the continuity of natural clear-light awareness (*'od gsal*), the ever-perfect (*samantabhadra, kun tu bzang po*) mind of awakening (*bodhicitta, byang chub kyi sems*) that knows no beginning or end. The clear light's continuity is ever-present from time without beginning and knows no interruption. This continuity has three aspects: the causal continuity (*rgyu'i rgyud*), the continuity of skillful means, and the resultant continuity. The causal continuity refers to the sky-like nature of the mind that does not change in any given state, whether one is a sentient being bound by attachment or a buddha. The skillful means continuity, in general terms, embraces all the stages of the experiential path from practice of the six perfections and the three spiritual ways up to the Yoga Tantra path. More specifically, it refers to the two phases of the Highest Yoga Tantra that have been prepared for through the initiation, along with all the branches of these two phases. The causal continuity freed from all adventitious stains is the result continuity: awakening itself, the dimension of purity (acquired purity and natural purity) and the foundation for actualizing the welfare of others. (*The Infinite Ocean of Knowledge* [*Shes bya mtha' yas pa'i rgya mtsho*] [Beijing: Bod mi rigs dpe bskrun khang, 1982] [henceforth cited as *IOK*], vol. II, pp. 612-615.)

According to Manjushriyashas, the resultant tantra or continuity refers to Buddha Vajradhara. The skillful means continuity refers to the assemblage of the causal conditions of mantra, seals, mandala, etc.; it is also called the continuity of yoga (*rnal 'byor rgyud*) where yoga denotes the union of wisdom and means. As well, the term *tantra* or *continuity* is used to denote the scriptures that record the words of instruction for the yoga. (*Explanation of Root Tantric Downfalls* [*Vajrayānamūlāpattiṭikā; rDo rje theg pa'i rtsa ba'i ltung ba'i rgya cher bshad pa*] [Toh. 2488] [henceforth cited as *ERD*], f. 202b1-3.)

18. For a discussion of the various systems of classifying the tantras and the underlying bases for these classifications, see Kongtrul's *IOK*, vol. II, pp. 572-580.

19. A practitioner imagines himself or herself as the appropriate deity and uses as the spiritual path the joyous bliss that arises from desire caused by looking at the consort, etc.

In the lower sets of tantras, this is not done while observing an external seal [an actual consort], and even in the higher set of tantras [Highest Yoga], it is not taught that such is done [in the lower tantras]; therefore, these should be understood as meditated goddesses, such as Lochana. (Tsongkapa, "The Great Exposition of Secret Mantra," in H. H. the Dalai Lama et al., *Tantra in Tibet*, pp. 160-161.)

20. Common spiritual way (*theg pa thun mong*) here refers to the Way of the Perfections or common Universal Way.

21. The four gross and four subtle forms of grasping to subject and object (*gzung 'dzin gyi rnam rtog phra rags bzhi*): the two very rough (*shin tu ches ba*) and the two rough (*ches ba*) forms of grasping to subject and object as real, and the two subtle (*phra ba*) and the two very subtle (*shin tu phra ba*) forms. The four gross and four subtle propensities for movement (*pho ba'i bag chags phra rags bzhi*) are classified in the same way (Oral communication of Khenpo Chödrak, Tso Pema, H.P. India).

22. Regular confession or sevenfold service (*rgyun bshags / rgyun bshags kyi yan lag bdun pa*) consists of confession of wrong deeds, rejoicing in virtue, formation of the ultimate awakening mind, taking refuge, formation of the awakening mind of aspiration, the venturing awakening mind, and the dedication of merit. See Tenzin Gyatso, the Dalai Lama, *The Kalachakra Tantra: Rite of Initiation* (London: Wisdom Publications, 1985) (henceforth cited as *KT*), pp. 184-185.

23. For an example of the preparatory phase of an initiation (*sta gon*), see *KT*, pp. 167-189. See also Naropa, *Iniziazione Kalacakra* (Milan: Adelphi Edizioni, 1994), (henceforth cited as *IK*), pp. 159-172.

24. Three places (*gnas gsum*): crown of the head, throat, and chest, representing, respectively, body, speech, and mind. At this stage, the master (visualized as the deity) who is bestowing the initiation touches with the vajra the disciples' three places, while they imagine that lights radiating from the master's three places purify their evil deeds of body, speech, and mind, and transform them into the pure entities of the Buddha's body, speech, and mind. See *KT*, pp. 184-189.

25. Outer entry (*phyi 'jug pa*): the stage of an initiation when disciples are led to the front of the closed doors of the mandala of the deity to be prepared for entry

into it. This stage consists of a recitation, after which disciples imagine they have become the deity, take their places at the eastern gate of the mandala, and there take refuge vows, the awakening mind commitments, and the mantric vows. See *KT*, pp. 101-105, 217-235.

26. The phase of the initiation at which the master asks the disciples who they are and what they desire. Disciples reply by declaring themselves to be bodhisattvas who aspire to use great bliss in the path of the Secret Mantra. See *KT*, p. 102 and p. 223.

27. See chapter III, n. 189. See also *KT*, pp. 232-235.

28. Inner entry (*nang 'jug*): the phase of the initiation at which disciples are led beyond the curtains of the mandala (the curtains of the constructed mandala) for the initiation that gives them divine fortune. Disciples (blindfolded) imagine that they are entering the mandala from the eastern door and circumambulating the deities; they promise to honor the pledges; the pristine awareness deities descend and become inseparable from the commitment deity in whose form the disciples visualize themselves; they each cast a flower onto the mandala to determine their affiliation to one of the buddha families while the master invokes the power of truth; they are each empowered with a garland so that they may be spiritually nurtured by the lord of the buddha family to which they belong; and finally, they take off their blindfolds and imagine beholding the deities of the mandala. See *KT*, pp. 101-105, 236-254.

29. See previous note.

30. At this point, the master introduces the disciples to the deities by describing them, and the disciples imagine that they are actually seeing them. See *KT*, pp. 248-254.

31. Vase initiation (*bum dbang*): the first of the four Highest Yoga Tantra initiations. In the system of the Wheel of Time Tantra, this is preceded by seven inferior initiations, and is therefore the eighth. For a discussion of the vase initiation, see Ferdinand D. Lessing and Alex Wayman, *mKhas grub rje's Introduction to the Buddhist Tantric Systems* (The Hague: 1968; 2nd ed. Delhi: Motilal Banarsidass, 1978) (henceforth cited as *IBTS*), pp. 309-317. See also *IK*, pp. 187-190.

32. The higher initiations (*dbang gong ma*) of the Highest Yoga Tantra are the secret initiation (*guhyābhiṣeka, gsang dbang*), the initiation of pristine awareness through wisdom (*prajñājñāna abhiṣeka, shes rab ye shes kyi dbang*), and the word (fourth) initiation (*akṣarābhiṣeka, tshig dbang*). The first empowers speech and purifies the stains and habitual tendencies of speech. It authorizes disciples to practice meditations on energies and channels and enables them to attain the enjoyment dimension of awakening. The second empowers mind and purifies its stains and habitual tendencies. It authorizes disciples to practice meditation on the stage of completion and enables them to attain the reality dimension of awakening. The third empowers body, speech, and mind, and purifies all stains and tendencies of these three aspects of experience. It introduces disciples to the union of the illusory pure body and radiant awareness of a buddha, authorizes

them to cultivate such union, and enables them to attain the natural dimension of awakening. In the Wheel of Time Tantra, which includes two sets of higher initiations, the vase initiation is also considered a higher initiation related to the phase of completion.

For a detailed discussion of these, see *IBTS*, pp. 309-328. See also *IK*, pp. 187-201.

33. The appended (initiation) using symbols of auspiciousness (*mtha' rten gyi dbang*): a part of the vase initiation during which the master encourages and bestows power on disciples by presenting them with the seven royal articles (*rgyal srid sna bdun*) (the precious wheel, jewel, queen, minister, elephant, horse, and general), eight auspicious signs (*bkra shis rtags brgyad*) (parasol, pair of golden fish, treasure vase, lotus, conch shell swirled clockwise, endless knot, banner of victory, and wheel), and eight substances that bring good fortune (*bkra shis rdzas brgyad*) (mirror, *ghiwang* medicine, yogurt, *durva* grass, *bilva* fruit, conch shell swirled clockwise, cinnabar, and white mustard seeds).

34. In the three higher initiations, pristine awareness is induced directly: in the secret initiation as result of self-blessing; in the pristine-awareness-through-wisdom initiation as a result of the bliss arising from the melting of the seminal essence while in union with a consort; and in the word initiation, through the great bliss of non-emission (Dharmashri's *Commentary on the Three Vows* [*sDom 'grel/sDom pa gsum rnam par nges pa'i 'grel pa legs bshad ngo mtshar dpag bsam gyi snye ma*], f. 200b2-5). Moreover, there is a particular manner in which each of the four initiations (vase, secret, pristine awareness-through-wisdom, and word) induces the pristine awareness of great bliss (which "protects" the mind from conceptualization and the propensity for emission of seminal fluid or dispersed bliss): slow, proximate, very close, and swift (f. 201a1-3).

35. Dharmashri states that pledges that are empowered for safeguarding through the central phase of the initiation are assumed with a verbal promise and are nominal (*btags pa ba*) mantric vows. Those pledges assumed with an understanding of pristine awareness while one is being initiated are actual or authentic (*mtshan nyid pa*) mantric vows. One could therefore say that the initiation nurtures and makes powerful the pristine awareness that is naturally present in oneself. With such pristine awareness acting as antidote, one overcomes the factors to be purified that coexist with pristine awareness. Even though pristine awareness may not actually arise during the initiation, the initiation leaves a potency for its manifestation. The placing of such potency is the beginning of the purification of impurities and development of qualities, and as such, is tantamount to the transformation in the mind known as "ripening of the mind," "being initiated," or "assuming the vows and pledges." This aspect of the seed of the mind's virtuous qualities being nurtured through the initiation procedure, being the factor that holds the three secret vajras of all buddhas, is known as "pledge." Being a binding factor for one's own mind, it is known as "vow." (*Commentary on the Three Vows*, f. 202a2-b1).

36. Kongtrul, citing the *Essence of Pristine Awareness*, states that in the Conduct Tantra there are five initiations: water, diadem, vajra, bell, and name. However, the *Vairochana-abhisambhodi Tantra* mentions only the water initiation and the

permissions through the [golden] chirurgical spoon (*gser gyi thur ma'i dbang*), the mirror (*me long gyi dbang*), and the authorization to teach the doctrine (*chos bshad pa'i dbang*) (*IOK*, vol. II, p. 594).

Pema Karpo describes the water initiation and the permissions: Holding a precious vase filled with jewels and medicines, the master initiates disciples with the water of the vase; the disciples imagine they receive the blessings of the bodhisattvas, Samantabhadra, Maitreya, Sarvaranivishkambi, and others. The master, while uttering encouraging words, then holds a golden chirurgical spoon (used to remove cataracts) in front of each disciple's eyes to symbolize that all the buddhas are removing the ignorance of the disciple's mind. Holding up a mirror, the master explains the characteristics of phenomena: "All things are like a reflection, limpid and unpolluted, and cannot be grasped by or expressed in words. Arising from causes and actions, they lack an intrinsic nature and are without stability. Understand all phenomena to be like that, and accomplish unfailingly the welfare of others!" Placing the wheel which symbolizes the Buddhist teachings below the disciple's foot and a fine conch shell in the left hand, the master authorizes the disciple to teach the Conduct Tantra (*TV*, vol. Ca, ff. 50b5-51b4).

37. In the Yoga Tantra, the irreversible initiation (*avaivartikābhiṣeka, phyir mi ldog pa'i dbang*) is known as the vajra-master initiation (*vajrācāryābhiṣeka, rdo rje slob dpon gyi dbang*). It is added to the five initiations of the Conduct Tantra (*IOK* vol. II, Book VI, chapter IV, p. 603).

38. The vase, secret, pristine-awareness-through-wisdom, and word initiation. For a description of these initiations, see *IBTS*, pp. 311-325.

39. *Vajrapani Initiation Tantra* (*Vajrapāṇyabhiṣekatantra; Lag na rdo rje dbang bskur ba'i rgyud chen po*) (Toh. 496), f. 41a1-2.

40. *General Tantra* (*Sarvamaṇḍalasāmānyavidhīnāmaguhyatantra; dKyil 'khor thams cad kyi spyi'i cho ga gsang ba'i rgyud*) (Toh. 806), f. 141a1-2.

41. Irreversible wheel initiation (*phyir mi ldog pa'i 'khor lo'i dbang*): this is also a vajra-master initiation, but it is exclusive to the Yoga Tantra. For different opinions on whether the vajra-master initiation is found in the two lower tantras, see the discussion in *IBTS*, chapter 4, pp. 141-149.

42. Three vajras (*rdo rje gsum*): the adamantine body, speech, and mind of the deity.

43. The water initiation (*toyaseka, chu'i dbang*) is related to the family of Akshobhya; the diadem initiation (*mauliseka, cod pan gyi dbang*), to Ratnasambhava; the vajra initiation (*vajraseka, rdo rje'i dbang*), to Amitabha; the bell initiation (*ghaṇṭaseka, dril bu'i dbang*), to Amoghasiddhi; the name initiation (*nāmaseka, ming gi dbang*), to Vairochana; and the conduct initiation (*vratacāryaseka, spyod pa'i brtul zhugs kyi dbang*), to the vajra master. See *IBTS*, pp. 311-317.

44. The aggregate of form is consecrated as Vairochana; the aggregate of discernment, Amitabha; the aggregate of feeling, Ratnasambhava; the aggregate of volition, Amoghasiddhi; the aggregate of consciousness, Akshobhya; and their reality, Vajrasattva.

45. See note 32.

46. Pema Karpo defines skill in means in this context as the personal experience of immutable bliss (*mi 'gyur ba'i bde ba*), which has the unmodified nature of the Great Seal (*mahāmudrā, phyag rgya chen po*) and transcends conceptual meditations. This immutable bliss cannot be expressed in words; it is free of the conceptual processes of exclusion and restriction to categories of subject and object, shape, etc.

Wisdom, the emptiness comprehensive of all aspects (*shes rab rnam bcas*), refers to the Great Seal which generates immutable bliss. It is the supreme emptiness which, being free of cognizable aspects, is comprehensive of all aspects; it possesses the forms of the universe as mirror divination images, images that are not made of subtle or gross particles but are simply the mind's projections (*TV*, vol. Ca, ff. 178b5-179a1).

Kongtrul notes that although in some tantric systems immutable bliss is posited as relative (*kun rdzob*) since it has to be realized through the relative means of melting the seminal essence, in the uncommon categories of the Kalachakra Tantra (to which Kongtrul is referring here), immutable bliss is termed "ultimate truth" (*don dam bden pa*) because it lacks the fabrication of a perceiver and an object perceived, etc. For this reason, the pledge concerning the immutable bliss is here called the ultimate pledge (*don dam pa'i dam tshig*).

The great seal of empty forms comprehensive of all supreme aspects (*rnam pa kun gyi mchog dang ldan pa'i stong gzugs phyag rgya chen po*) is termed relative truth (*kun rdzob bden pa*) because it is the very nature of every relative phenomenon while its appearances are similar to those of relative phenomena themselves. For this reason, the pledge concerning emptiness is called relative (*kun rdzob pa'i dam tshig*) (*IOK*, vol. III, pp. 218-219).

47. *Two-Part Hevajra Tantra*, f. 16b4-5.

48. Kongtrul explains that this vow is said to be the vow of all buddhas because it has the nature of the inseparability of great compassion and emptiness which is the pristine awareness of all buddhas, the realization of the reality of all things. It is called vow (*saṃvara*, lit. "bound") because supreme bliss, the nature of all things, is perfectly gathered or bound by all buddhas. It is found in the aspect or meaning of *E*, which stands for wisdom, and *VAM*, which stands for skill in means, and it is the great innate bliss which is the aspect or meaning of *EVAM*. It is to be comprehended and realized through initiation in which metaphoric pristine awareness and the actual pristine awareness are experienced (*Commentary on the Hevajra Tantra*, f. 207a3-6).

49. *Continuation of the Guhyasamaja Tantra* (*'Dus pa phyi ma*) (Toh. 443), f. 151b2.

50. *Collected Transmitted Precepts of the Ancient Tradition* (*rNying ma bka' ma rgyas pa*) vol. Nga, f. 2b3 (Kalimpong, India: Dudjom Rinpoche, 1982) (henceforth cited as *NKG*). *Manjushri's Magical Net* is the name used by the Nyingma school to refer to the tantra *Chanting the Names Manjushri* (*'Jam dpal sgyu 'phrul drva ba*) (Toh. 360).

51. The six elements (*khams drug*) are earth (*pṛthivī, sa*), water (*toya, chu*), fire (*agni, me*), wind (*vāyu, rlung*), space (*ākāśa, nam mkha'*), and pristine awareness (*jñāna, ye shes*) (Kalachakrapada's *Expanding on the Brief Discussion of the [Kalachakra] Initiation* [Toh. 1353], f. 6b3). Kongtrul specifies that the element of pristine awareness refers to the emission of the seminal essence (*khu ba ltung ba*) (*IOK*, vol. II, p. 633).

52. This verse from the *Fundamental Tantra of Kalachakra* is cited in Pundarika's *Stainless Light* (Toh 1347) vol. Tha, f. 117b3-4.

53. Oddiyana (*O rgyan*): the land identified by some scholars as the Swat Valley in northern Pakistan, said to have been at one time a sacred land of sky-farers, practitioners of the tantra, and the place from where many tantras were brought to central India. See Dharmashri's *Commentary on the Three Vows*, f. 196b2-6.

54. *Indestructible Peak Tantra* (*Vajraśekharamahāguhyayogatantra; gSang ba rnal 'byor chen po'i rgyud rdo rje rtse mo*) (Toh. 480), f. 210b5-6.

55. Ibid., f. 210b6.

56. *Samvarodaya Tantra*, vol. Kha, f. 302a7.

57. Jnanakara's *Guide to Mantra* (*Mantrāvatāra; gSang ngags la 'jug pa*) (Toh. 3718), f. 196a2.

58. Pema Karpo states that to abandon the correct view on the conventional (belief in the law of causality) is to adopt a nihilistic view. To renounce the Three Jewels amounts to abandoning the Buddhist teachings, while to forsake the conventional (relative) mind of awakening would amount to rejecting the Universal Way. To reject the initiation is to forsake the Indestructible Way (*TV*, vol. Ca, f. 304).

Jnanakara states that the first pledge is not to deny the law of causality and to believe in the ripening results of actions. This pledge is called basic because it is the vow common to both Buddhists and non-Buddhists who wish to attain higher status within cyclic existence. The second pledge is not to venerate deities other than the Three Jewels, a pledge exclusive to those who have entered the Buddhist doctrine. The third pledge forms the special basis for the Secret Mantra. The fourth means not to have received the initiation, or to reject it, in which case one cannot be called a mantric adept (*Commentary on the Guide to Mantra* [*Mantrāvatāravṛtti; sNgags la 'jug pa'i 'grel ba*] [Toh. 3719], f. 206a1-7).

59. *Summary of Pledges* (*Dam tshig thams cad bsdus pa*) (Toh. 3725) (by Ashvaghosha), f. 45a4. Kedrupjé states with reason and finality that this text is wrongly attributed to Atisha (*IBTS*, p. 155).

60. *Susiddhi Tantra* (*Susiddhikaramahātantrasādhanopāyikapaṭala; Legs grub/ Legs par grub par byed pa'i rgyud chen po las sgrub pa'i thabs rim par phye ba*) (Toh. 807), f. 172b4-5. The pledges for the practitioner of the Action Tantra are discussed on ff. 172b3-175b7 of this tantra.

61. According to Kedrupjé, the *Secret Tantra of the General Ritual for All Mandalas* (*Sarvamaṇḍalasāmānyavidhi-nāma-guhyatantra; dKyil 'khor thams cad kyi spyi'i cho*

ga gsang ba'i rgyud) (Toh. 806), the *Susiddhi* (*Susiddhikaramahātantrasādhanopāyika-paṭala; Legs grub/ Legs par grub par byed pa'i rgyud chen po las sgrub pa'i thabs rim par phye ba*) (Toh. 807), the *Questions of Subahu Tantra* (*Subahupariprccha-nāma-tantra; dPung bzang gis zhus pa zhes bya ba'i rgyud*) (Toh. 805), and the *Dhyanottara* (*Dhyānottarapaṭalakrama; bSam gtan gyi phyi ma rim par phye ba*) (Toh. 808) are the four general Action tantras (*IBTS*, p. 135). For a description of their contents, see *IBTS*, pp. 135-137.

62. Ngor chen kun dga' bzang po (1382-1456): the founder of the Ngor sub-school of the main Sakya lineage. A contemporary of Tsongkapa, he had received tantric teachings from him but later openly criticized some of Tsongkapa's views on the tantra.

63. To have faith in the Three Jewels, the Secret Mantra Way, and the Universal Way.

64. Pema Karpo enumerates the five deeds of immediate retribution: to kill a saint, one's father, or one's mother, to create a schism in a harmonious monastic community, and out of malice to cause a buddha to bleed. Five deeds almost as serious as those of immediate retribution are to destroy a reliquary of the Bud-dha, to kill a bodhisattva, to engage a nun who has extinguished her emotions in sexual intercourse, to kill a person who is on the path of training, and to steal the belongings of the monastic community. If the practitioner were to commit any of these, he would be reborn in the hell of Unceasing Torture for an eon. In this life, even if he were to apply himself earnestly to tantric practice to achieve the powers of the Secret Mantra, he would not attain them (*TV*, vol. Ca, f. 31a1-b2).

65. The offense of harming the Three Jewels: to squander or burn scriptures con-taining the teachings of the Joyful One (Buddha), or to throw them into a river out of malice; to reject the reality dimension of awakening; to kill a monk or a nun endowed with all the levels of monastic ordination; to kill a male or female lay practitioner; or to set a temple on fire out of malice (*TV*, vol. Ca, f. 31b2-6).

66. Bodong Panchen or Bodong Choklé Namgyel (Bo dong phyogs las rnam rgyal) (1376-1451): an eminent scholar and tantric master in the Kalachakra lin-eage; also a prolific writer who composed about one hundred volumes of com-mentary. Originally an upholder of the Sakya lineage, he started a school bear-ing his name which has not survived as an independent school. His *General Pre-sentation of Tantras* (*rGyud sde spyi'i rnam bshad*) is found in vol. 24 (b'ha) of the *Collected Works of Phyogs las rnam rgyal*.

67. Jampa Lingpa (Byams pa gling pa): Panchen Jampa Lingpa, an eminent dis-ciple of Tsongkapa. The text alluded to here, *Great Mantra Discipline* (*Byams pa gling pa'i sNgags 'dul chen mo*), is identified by Ven. Jampa Wangyal as Jampa Lingpa's commentary on Tsongkapa's *Stages of the Mantra* called *The Stairways Leading to the State of Union* (*sNgags kyi 'grel chen zung 'jug bgrod pa'i thems skas*).

68. Kongtrul expands on the verses of the *General Tantra* (Toh. 806), ff. 163b-164a.

69. According to the traditional explanation, the common Three Jewels are the Buddha, his teachings, and the spiritual community; the exceptional ones are the master, meditational deities, and sky-farers and guardians of the teaching.

However, commenting on this vow, Pema Karpo does not distinguish between the common and exceptional. The Buddha, he states, refers to awakening and the omniscient ones; the teachings, scriptural transmission and spiritual accomplishment; and the community, the eight great [kinds of] persons (those who abide in the result of stream-enterer, etc.) and bodhisattvas on the irreversible path (*TV*, vol. Ca, f. 15b).

70. Pema Karpo explains these three kinds of "mantra" as follows: Tantras may be classified as six or three. The three classes are secret mantras (*guhyamantra, gsang sngags*), awareness mantras (*vidyāmantra, rig sngags*), and recollection mantras (*dhāraṇi mantra, gzungs sngags*). Secret mantras are primarily the tantras that expound the method aspect or the male deity. Awareness mantras are primarily the tantras that expound the wisdom aspect or female deity. Recollection mantras are part of both secret and awareness mantras as they serve as means to recollect or not to forget the import of these two after one has understood them. Recollection mantras can also be understood as tantra including both male and female aspects of one tantra.

In the ultimate sense, these "mantras" represent the indivisibility of skillful means and wisdom. They are called secret mantras since they represent knowledge of the principle of indestructibility, i.e., indivisible pristine awareness, and since they serve as protection for living beings and one's own mind. They are called awareness mantras because they remove ignorance and thus impart awareness. They are called recollection mantras since they symbolize the tantras of indivisible method and wisdom (*TV*, vol. Ca, ff. 16b5-17a4).

See also *IBTS*, p. 116, n. 18. On the different ways of positing the three mantras, see Jnanashri's *Dispelling the Two Extremes in the Indestructible Way* (*rDo rje theg pa'i mtha' gnyis sel ba*) (Toh. 3714), f. 117a6-7.

71. The master in this case is the one from whom the disciple has received the tantra, who should be regarded as the Buddha himself (*TV*, vol. Ca, f. 18a4-5).

72. Deities whose worship is shared by other practitioners (*thun mong sgrub pa'i lha*) refers to worldly or transworldly deities that are not the specific focus of one's practice, the worldly ones worshiped also by non-Buddhists. (Karma Ngedön Nyingpo's *Commentary on Ngari Panchen's Three Vows* [henceforth cited as *CNPTV*], f. 69b4.)

73. On this pledge, Pema Karpo cites the following from the *Subahu Tantra* (*TV*, vol. Ca, f. 22b1-4):

> Even in fear, one should not worship Indra, Vishnu,
> Or the wrathful Deity of Wind,
> Or rely on their doctrines.
> Do not engage in their ascetic practices, never offer to them.
> Without feeling defiant of their doctrines,
> Never take delight in their activities;
> Do not recite their hymns or incantations.

74. On this pledge, Pema Karpo states: If you are tired of recitation (tantric practice), to purify your past evil deeds, read the scriptures, or in a clean and isolated

place, build reliquaries of the Joyful One. To the relics or the reliquaries housing them, offer with great faith praises, garlands, perfumes, lights, parasols, standards, banners, and music. In these and other ways, a mantric adept should cultivate merit (*TV,* vol. Ca, f. 19a1-5).

75. Sitting with the body straight and unmovingly watching the senses, the adept engages in recitation of mantra. This should not be too fast (in order not to omit syllables), not too slow (not to become distracted), not too loud (a sign of excitement), not too low (a sign of torpor), not while speaking (since the words of the mantras are blessed by the joyful ones; therefore, it is improper to mix them with ordinary speech), not while distracted by some object (other than the form of the deity, the letters of the mantra, or its sound), and not without reverence (for the visualization or sound of the recitation). The *Subahu Tantra* states:

> A man who does not hold the sword properly,
> Grasping it by its edge, will likely cut his hand.
> Likewise, a mantrin who does not recite mantras correctly
> Either attains no result or is defeated.

Setting the mind single-pointedly in a continuous state of awareness, the mantrin should make the mind pliable; with such pliability, he or she will accomplish without obstacles the powers coming from recitation of mantra (*TV,* vol. Ca, ff. 19a4-20b2).

76. Pema Karpo states that to maintain the pledges of the other families means to observe the pledges of the deities of the three [main Action Tantra families], the pledges of their rites, the pledges in relation to attainments reached through these rites, and exclusive pledges particular to an individual, according to the tantras of each [deity] (*TV,* vol. Ca, f. 20b3-5).

77. The seals (*phyag rgya*) in the Action Tantra refer mainly to hand gestures.

78. Pema Karpo explains that to remain peaceful means to transform attachment by viewing the body as impure, to transform anger by using the moisture of love and compassion, and to transform stupidity by applying knowledge of the interdependence of phenomena. To transform attachment when the object is another person, one reflects upon the changing nature of relationships (sometimes, even an enemy may become one's friend; one's friend may become an enemy; similarly, someone who was neutral may become friend or enemy). Setting aside exaggerated liking for friends, a mantric adept should rest the mind relaxedly in a virtuous state and transform emotions by pondering upon the selflessness of phenomena:

> Things do not exist before they arise.
> Neither are they created by Ishvara,
> Nor do they arise without causes.
> Beings arise from actions and emotions.
> Form is composed of the five elements;
> These are not the self, and the self does not possess them.
> There neither is self in form, nor does self have form.
> Form is empty, as are the other aggregates.
> Form is like froth,

And feeling, like bubbles on water.
To see things in this way is the correct view.
Seeing them differently is a perverse view (*TV*, vol. Ca, f. 21a1-b5).

79. The practitioner should eat at the appropriate time, wash three times a day, and offer to the deity garlands of flowers, lights, incense, and perfumes, but not meat or alcohol. Then, sitting on a mat of *kuśa* grass, he engages in meditation. With the knowledge of the purity of the body and assuming the purificatory fast precepts for one, two, or three days, he should fast and dedicate himself to the meditation (*TV*, vol. Ca, ff. 21b5-22a5).

80. Not to invent mantras or rites even for the sake of defeating an evil person (*TV*, vol. Ca, f. 22b4-6).

81. Pema Karpo specifies that a mantric adept should not perform fierce rites with the perverse wish to hinder someone's efforts in performing rites to gain supernatural powers. As part of this pledge, a practitioner should not perform rites that include striking the dagger while reciting fierce mantras in a place that is inhabited by *nāgas* or a similar class of beings (*TV*, vol. Ca, ff. 23a2-24a4).

82. A mantrin must not perform tantric activities to compete with or to injure or kill another (*TV*, vol. Ca, f. 24a4-b2).

83. A master should reveal the mandala, initiate, and transmit the secret instructions, which are the seals of mantra, only to disciples who have made the pledges and can preserve them. Disciples who have not made the pledges are not authorized to see the mandala of the deity or to receive the initiation. If a master were to give them the secret instructions and they to follow them, unfortunate consequences would befall both. Even though they may already know tantric procedures, disciples who do not honor the master are not to be taught the tantras (*TV*, vol. Ca, ff. 44b2-45a).

84. Concerning this pledge, Pema Karpo cites the following words of the *Susiddhi Tantra*:

> Do not eat or destroy
> What resembles [ritual] weapons
> Or, likewise, sentient beings,
> Or resembles tantric symbols.
> Neither should a good mantrin
> Degrade medicines
> By making them dirty
> Or stepping on them,
> Or ride chariots,
> Crush lotus flowers,
> Or touch with the feet
> Leftover food (*TV*, vol. Ca, f. 25a4-b2).

85. Not to be unrestrained in body, speech, and mind with regard to food and behavior. Pema Karpo cites the *Susiddhi Tantra* as follows:

> Even a learned lay practitioner of Mantra
> Should not wear clothes dyed his preferred color.

> Never should he wear continuously
> Old and smelly clothes...

and:

> Or eat food from the back of a leaf.
> A learned practitioner should neither eat foods that cause attachment
> Nor eat while sitting on a bed or seat.
> A wise practitioner should not lie down
> With unclean people,
> Or lie supine or on the back.
> He should not eat repeatedly,
> Too little or too much,
> Nor should he eat too fast,
> Or eat food he has some suspicion about (*TV*, vol. Ca, ff. 25b2-26a2).

86. According to Pema Karpo, these include foods made into unsuitable shapes (a tantric symbol, etc.), meat, alcohol, mountain garlic, garlic, onions, oil from seeds (like mustard oil), sesame, radish, and foods (*torma*) offered to the deity. On this pledge, the *Susiddhi* states:

> A mantrin who wishes to attain powers
> Should abstain from rubbing the body
> With oils from seeds,
> Or eating sesame,
> Radish, onions, salts,
> Any kind of sour drink,
> Gourd or round peas,
> And also cooked beans,
> Sesame dough, and gingerbread.
> A mantrin should also renounce
> All devious foods
> And those [offered] as *torma*,
> Milk rice soup with black sesame and beans,
> Or plain milk rice soup.

The *Subahu Tantra* states:

> I declare that the foods for the mantrin
> Are the three sweet foods [honey, molasses, sugar],
> Roots, stalks, fruits, greens,
> Curd, barley, milk, ghee,
> Oil from unrefined grains, whey, boiled milk, and broths
>   (*TV*, vol. Ca, f. 26a2-b3).

87. Not to feel loving-kindness in particular for those who are suffering and in general toward all creatures (*TV*, vol. Ca, f. 26b5-6).

88. Concerning this vow, Pema Karpo cites the following words from the *Susiddhi Tantra*:

> When engaged in recitation, the wise one,
> Unless there is a specific necessity,

> Should never speak with others
> With the exception of the mantric helper.

and:

> Unless it is to answer [your teacher],
> Do not interrupt recitation of my mantra.

and the *Subahu Tantra*:

> Having started recitation, until the practice is completed,
> To brahmins, royalty, aristocrats, or peasants,
> To women, eunuchs, or small girls,
> The tantric practitioner should never speak.
> If necessary, one may speak to one's tantric helper
> Just a little when [a session of] recitation is over.
> After speaking or having gone to relieve oneself,
> Enter a river and wash (*TV*, vol. Ca, f. 27a2-6).

89. To engage in wrathful rites when the aim to be accomplished is trivial or when angered by a small misdeed of another (*TV*, vol. Ca, f. 27a1).

90. Not to feel contempt or dislike for oneself. Pema Karpo cites the *Subahu Tantra*, which states:

> Just as to cure and heal a wound
> Sick persons are given medication,
> In order that mantrins not suffer from hunger,
> The Buddha said that they should not reject food.

and:

> [However,] the body is [essenceless] as a small banana.
> Thus, do not become attached to foods or to similar things (*TV*, vol. Ca, f. 28a4-b1).

91. Pema Karpo cites the *Subahu Tantra*, which states:

> Do not revile others.

and:

> The wise do not argue
> With the followers of the Universal Way.
> Upon hearing of powerful bodhisattvas,
> They do not disgrace them,
> Or challenge a practitioner of Mantra.

and:

> A mantrin should not quarrel
> With non-Buddhists, etc. (*TV*, vol. Ca, f. 28b1-3).

92. Pema Karpo cites the following lines of the *Subahu Tantra* concerning unworthy actions:

> A mantrin should always shun
> Offensive speech, slander,
> Sexual relations with married women,
> Lying, stealing, killing, injuring another,

And inflicting punishment.

and:

Conquer the eight worldly concerns
Of [hope and fear for] fame and obscurity, gain and loss,
Pleasure and misery, and praise and blame,
Not allowing even their residue since they are wrong.

and:

With the exceptions of monastic attire and ceremonies,
A mantrin should observe all aspects of the discipline
Of the pure ethics of personal liberation
That I, the Victorious One, have taught.

The *Susiddhi Tantra* states:

Out of stupidity, do not blame others.
Do not relax [endeavors in] meditation,
Or fall sway of distractions,
Or have many goals in mind.
Without sexual attachments,
The practitioner should engage in the Mantra (*TV*, vol. Ca, ff. 28b3-29a4).

93. Concerning this vow, Pema Karpo cites the *Subahu Tantra*:

A practitioner should never go
Where young cows and calves are living,
Where people drink alcohol
Or engage in wrongful sex,
Where people eat dog meat during festivities,
Where many people gather,
Or where music is played (*TV*, vol. Ca, f. 29a4-b4).

94. The three Supramundane (or Principal) and the three Worldly (or Auxiliary) families of the Action Tantra: the Supramundane families are the Tathagata Family, the Lotus Family, and the Vajra Family, the highest, middling, and lowest, respectively. The three Worldly families are the Wealth Family, the Ox (*ba glang*), also called Prosperity Family (or Yaksha of Wealth Family), and the Family of Worldlings (*TV*, vol. Ca, f. 39b4-5).

The secret mantras or awareness mantras of buddhas, bodhisattvas, and the different worldly gods are subsumed under three families: the Tathagata, the Lotus, and the Vajra Family, and also under the Wealth Family, the Prosperity Family, and the Family of the Worldlings.

The Tathagata Family represents the knowledge of the ultimate nature of all things and "going the way the buddhas have gone." The Lotus Family represents the compassion of Avalokiteshvara who sees all sentient beings during the six times of the day and night with his eye of compassion undefiled by passions. The Vajra Family represents the protection of the Buddhist teachings and destruction of elements hostile to them.

The Wealth Family represents the elimination of the plague of poverty by Shri Manibhadra and other deities. The Prosperity Family, which is associated with five hundred gems, demonstrates "the play of five dice," which refers to prosperity rites for having children, increase of wealth, etc. The Family of the Worldlings comprise gods, titans, and others, excluding those belonging to the other five families, who bestow their individual mantras and rites; these beings are included in all three principal families. The Wealth Family is included in the Lotus Family; the Prosperity, in the Vajra Family; and the Family of the Worldlings, principally, in the Lotus and Vajra. Only families included in these principal and auxiliary families have arisen from the blessing of the Tathagata (*Commentary on the Questions of Subahu Tantra* [*Subāhuparipṛcchā-namā-tantra-piṇḍārthavṛtti; dPung bzangs kyis zhus pa'i rgyud kyi bsdus pa'i don dgrol ba'i brjed byang*] [Toh. 2673], ff. 101a3-102b1).

95. Reading *rigs* for *rig*.

96. *Unconquerable Vajra That Blazes Like Fire* (*Vajrājitānalapramohani-nāma-dhāraṇī, rDo rje mi 'pham pa me ltar rab tu rmong byed ces bya ba'i gzungs*) (Toh. 752). The actual mantra to be recited is found on f. 4a4-5 of this tantra, which belongs to the "Mother of the Vajra Family" of the Action Tantra.

97. Fire-offering (*homa, sbyin sreg*): the ritual that consists of making offerings to the deity generated in the heart of the fire god, for the sake of appeasing, prosperity, domineering, or destroying activities. The kinds of substances used, the drawing at the base of the platform, as well as its dimensions and the ritual itself, vary according to which of these four purposes one intends to accomplish and the deity associated with the ritual being performed.

98. Entering the mandala by being initiated repeatedly by a master (*TV*, vol. Ca, f. 34a3-4).

99. f. 175b6-7.

100. *Vairochanabhisambodhi Tantra* (*Mahāvairocanābhisaṃbodhivikurvitādhiṣṭhā-navaipulyasūtreindra-rājanāmadharmaparyāya; rNam par snang mdzad chen po mngon par rdzogs par byang chub pa rnam par sprul pa byin gyis rlob pa shin tu rgyas pa mdo sde'i dbang po'i rgyal po zhes bya ba'i chos kyi rnam grangs*) (Toh. 494) is the chief of all the tantras of the Conduct Tantra class.

101. To forsake the scriptural teachings and the teachings as spiritual accomplishment and to be irreverent toward the teachers who expound them (*TV*, vol. Ca, f. 56b6).

102. Pema Karpo specifies that these are pledges of the causal stages [leading to awakening]. First, the vow of the "mind of entering" is to restrain from polluted deeds that are the creative cause of the polluted aggregates of body, speech, and mind, and so forth. Thus, such a vow consists in a promise not to engage in deeds that are the cause of birth in the cycle of existence. The bodhisattva practices the tantra on the basis of such ethics in order to approach the great pledge.

The vow of "abiding [awakening] mind" refers to the formation of the awakening mind in accordance with the very state of awakening, i.e., by remaining in the very nature of one's mind as the experiential path. The bodhisattva engages in the tantra by way of the realization of the equality of all phenomena, as he or she understands that mind is unborn from the beginning, has the nature of emptiness, lacks substance, has no characteristics, location, or impediments, and is beyond all conceptual fabrications.

The vow of the "mind of involvement" refers to the awakening mind that does not remain absorbed in the utterly non-conceptual reality although understanding such reality just as it is, but wishes to guide all beings to the same enlightened state devoid of inherent characteristics, free from all fabrications, and lacking any objective reference, that oneself has attained. This state is itself the great pledge (*TV*, vol. Ca, ff. 52b5-54b1).

103. Pema Karpo states that proclaimers and solitary sages do not train in great compassion or in the wisdom of understanding phenomenal selflessness (*chos kyi bdag med*), and for this reason, are said to lack skill in means and wisdom. Although they are possessed of the skill in means and wisdom spoken of in the way of the perfections, [they lack] the wisdom distinguished by understanding phenomena to be primordially unborn (*chos thams cad gdod ma nas ma skyes pa*). Their skill in means is confined to engagement in the six perfections such as generosity, free from conceptualizing the giver, gift, and giving by viewing them as if they were a magical creation. They lack, however, the skill in means taught in the Conduct Tantra of manifesting oneself in three aspects: the deity as form (*gzugs kyi lha*), deity as letters (*yi ge'i lha*), and deity as symbols (*phyag rgya'i lha*) (*TV*, vol. Ca, ff. 57b4-58a3).

104. The complete recitation is as follows:

> Just as the protectors throughout the three times
> Made their vows to awaken,
> I now form the sacred and unsurpassed
> Resolve to become enlightened.
> To honor the [transcendent family's] pledges
> Of the yoga of the buddhas,
> I will firmly observe the three forms of ethics:
> The ethics of restraint, acquiring good qualities,
> And working for the welfare of all beings;
> Henceforth, I will commit myself
> To the unsurpassable Triple Jewel,
> The Buddha, his teachings, and the community.
> To honor the pledges
> Of the supremely great vajra family,
> I will commit myself to the vajra, bell, seal,
> And also to the master.
> To honor the gracious pledges
> Of the supremely great jewel family,

I will always practice the four kinds of generosity
During the six times of the day and night.
To honor the pledges of the supremely pure lotus family
Born from the great awakening,
I will persevere in the sacred teachings
Of the outer, inner, and secret [tantras] and the three spiritual ways.
To honor the pledges of the supreme great action family,
I will maintain impeccably
All types of pledges
And exert myself in making offerings.
For the sake of all beings
I resolve to attain the sacred
And unsurpassable awakening
And will maintain all vows.
I shall liberate those not liberated [from the impediment to omniscience],
I shall release those not released [from cyclic existence],
I shall relieve those unrelieved [in unfortunate existences]
And set sentient beings in the state of perfect peace.

(Anandagarbha's *Illumination of Reality* [*Sarvatathāgatatattvasaṃgrahamahā-yānābhisamayanāmatantra-tattvālokakarīnāmavyākyā*; *De bzhin gshegs pa thams cad kyi de kho na nyid bsdus pa theg pa chen po mngon par rtogs pa zhes bya ba'i rgyud kyi bshad pa de kho na nyid snang bar byed pa*] [Toh. 2510], vol Shi, f. 115b2-6.)

105. Discussing the five families (*pañcakula, rigs lnga*) in the context of Yoga Tantra, Pema Karpo explains: *Ku* in *kula* is related to *kutsi*, meaning "bad" (*ngan pa*); and *la*, to *laya*, meaning "to enter" (*thim pa*). The families are of two kinds, inferior (*dman pa*) and supreme (*mchog*).

To the inferior families belong beings who have entered (*thim pa*) bad existences (*ngan 'gro*) as a result of their negative emotions. Beings who have good characters and whose emotions are in equal strength belong equally to all the five families. Beings who have a preponderance of attachment (*'dod chags*) belong to the Transcendent or Tathagata family (*tathāgatakula, de bzhin gshegs pa'i rigs*); beings who have a preponderance of hatred (*zhe sdang*), to the vajra family (*vajrakula, rdo rje'i rigs*); beings who have a preponderance of avarice (*ser sna*), to the jewel family (*ratnakula, nor bu'i rigs*); beings who have a preponderance of stupidity (*gti mug*), to the lotus family (*padmakula, pad ma'i rigs*); and beings who have a preponderance of laziness (*le lo*), to the action family (*karmakula, las kyi rigs*).

To the supreme or adamantine (*vajra, rdo rje*) families belong enlightened beings, buddhas, and the bodhisattvas who have transcended lower destinies, are free of the impediments of inferior families, and serve as antidotes to the emotions of the inferior families. These families fit the above etymology because they are the families of those [buddhas and bodhisattvas] who, by the force of their compassion for others, have entered (*thim pa*) bad existences (*ngan 'gro*). The supreme families are those of the five transcendent ones: Vairochana, Akshobhya, Ratnasambhava, Amitabha, and Amoghasiddhi. They are transcendent families because they are of the nature of all the transcendent ones.

The deities who have emanated from these five buddhas to counteract the respective emotions also belong to one of the transcendent (*de gzhin gshegs pa*), vajra (*rdo rje*), jewel (*nor bu*), lotus (*pad ma*), or action (*las*) families (*TV*, vol. Ca, ff. 64a1-65b1).

106. Pema Karpo here enumerates four pledges: of the vajra, of the bell, of the seal, and of the master. The vajra (*vajra, rdo rje*) represents the skillful means (*thabs*) or mind of awakening, and the bell (*ghaṇṭā, dril bu*) represents wisdom knowing reality. Not to forsake skillful means and wisdom and to apply them is the nature of the two pledges. The seal is the great seal (*mahāmudrā, phyag rgya chen po*), which consists in the contemplation of the deity's form as the inseparability of emptiness and vivid appearance.

The word seal (*mudrā, phya rgya*) is related to *modānāta*, "to please," and to *mudrāna*, "to seal" (*TV*, vol. Ca, f. 80a6-b5). Mudra is thus a seal because it "pleases" the deity's mind or because it "seals" by swift accomplishment of the desired goal and benefits by protecting others. Its synonyms are attribute (*mtshan ma*), sign (*rtags*), and proximate characteristics (*nye ba'i mtshan nyid*) (ibid., ff. 85a3-4 and 91a5).

The master (*ācārya, slob dpon*) is the very cause of the pristine awareness of reality (ibid., f. 85a5).

107. The mantra here refers to the tantras and their observances. See note 112 for a discussion of seals.

108. According to Pema Karpo, this refers to eating or stepping over food that is in the shape of the deity's insignia, such as a wheel, vajra, lotus, weapon, etc. (*TV*, vol. Ca, f. 90a5).

109. Not to reveal the contents of the initiation one has received (*TV*, vol. Ca, f. 59b5).

110. See note 112.

111. *Summation of Essential Points* (*Sarvatathāgatatattvasaṃgrahanāma; De bzhin gshegs pa thams cad kyi de kho na nyid bsdus pa*) (Toh. 479). Considered to be the original tantra of the Conduct Tantra class.

112. A reference to the four seals in Yoga Tantra. Padmavajra explains that "seal" (*mudrā*) signifies the power to gladden or to make an impression. It is "gladdening" because of its ability to please the exalted ones; it is a seal because it cannot be erased and swiftly grants the desired goal. It is also called "attribute" (*nimitta, mtshan ma*) since it issues from pristine awareness and is [linked to] the conception of an attribute. It is a "sign" (*liṅga, rtags*) by virtue of having the nature of the great pristine awareness or issuing from its blessing. It is a "proximate characteristic" (*upalakṣaṇa, nye ba'i mtshan nyid*) because it points to pristine awareness or because through it one enters into the state of pristine awareness. (*Explanation of [Buddhaguhya's] Guide to the Purport of the Tantra [Tantrārthavatāra-vyākhyāna; rGyud kyi don la 'jug pa'i 'grel bshad]* [Toh. 2502], f. 94a6-b1.)

The four seals correspond to the awakened dimensions of body, speech, and mind, and activity: the great seal (*kāyamahāmudrā, sku phyag rgya chen po*) which is the body [of the deity], the seal of the pledge (*samayamudrā, dam tshig gi phyag rgya*), the seal of the teachings (*dharmamudrā, chos kyi phyag rgya*), and the action seal (*karmamudrā, las kyi phyag rgya*).

The great seal is the image of the deity's body which reveals the mode of the deity. Since it serves as the pre-eminent ground for vividly contemplating the mode of being of the deity by way of his or her form, it is called the great seal (f. 94b5-6).

The seal of the pledge is the blessing of the seal of pristine awareness possessed with perfect qualifications which reveals the mode of the deity's mind as the seal of the fully liberated mind. Since the deities do not transcend [pristine awareness], it is called the seal of the pledge (f. 95a1-2).

The seal of the teachings comprises the terms used in the teachings such as "indestructible pristine awareness" (*vajrajñāna*), "symbolic being" (*samayasattva*), etc., which are the attributes or signs of pure buddha speech, and reveal the mode of the speech of the deity. This seal imparts the ultimate teachings of the deity's words (f. 95a4-5).

The action seal comprises the deity's actions and reveals the mode of these actions which are of two kinds: bound and imagined. The first has the characteristics of the seal of supreme enlightenment or gesture of the hands separated and forming two "vajra fists" (with the thumbs at the roots of the ring fingers) and other gestures. The second is the four-pronged vajra imagined at one's heart whose nature reveals that at the time of accomplishing a particular deity the enlightened activity of that deity pervades everything (f. 95a6-7).

For an exhaustive discussion of the four seals in the Yoga Tantra system, see *IBTS*, pp. 223-249.

113. See chapter III, note 189.

114. See note 106.

115. By Anandagarbha (*Vajradhātumahāmaṇḍalavidhisarvavajrodaya; rDo rje 'byung ba/ rDo rje dbyings kyi dkyil 'khor chen po'i cho ga rdo rje thams cad 'byung ba*) (Toh. 2516).

116. See chapter III, section entitled "The Fourteen Downfalls that Apply to Acute Practitioners."

117. Pema Karpo cites these lines from the *Indestructible Peak Tantra:*

> Do not take the lives of creatures,
> Or take what is not given.
> Do not commit adultery
> Or speak untruth.
> Abstain from [drinking] alcohol,
> Which causes all defeats for oneself.
> Do not perform any unwholesome deed
> Unless for the sake of guiding someone.
> Devote yourself closely to an authentic master
> And honor the yogin who perseveres in meditation.
> As much as you can,
> Cultivate the three [virtues] of body,

The four of speech,
And the three of mind.
Do not deride gods
Demigods, secretists (*yakṣas*),
Or seals; do not step over [the master's] seat
Or the [deity's] weapons or insignias.
These are explained as the pledges.
You should always honor them (*TV*, vol. Ca, ff. 88b5-89a3).

118. Gods (*deva, lha*): a class of beings (one of the six major classes) who live on the top of Mount Meru and in the sky above it and enjoy high status in conditioned existence. Demigods (*asura, lha ma yin*): a class of beings (one of the six major classes) who inhabit the crevices of Mount Meru and live tortured by jealousy of their superiors, the gods. Yakshas (*yakṣa, gnod sbyin*): semi-divine beings ruled by the god of wealth, Kubera, and inhabiting both divine and human environments.

119. *TV*, vol. Ca, ff. 83b3-95a4.

120. See notes 145, 165, and 168.

121. *Sarvatathāgatakāyavākcittarahasyaguhyasamājanāmamahākālparāja*; *De bzhin gshegs pa thams cad kyi sku gsung thugs kyi gsang chen gsang ba 'dus pa zhes bya ba brtag pa'i rgyal po chen po* (Toh. 442), f. 97b1-2.

122. See note 243.

123. Hand offering (*lag mchod*): visualizing the deities on the palm of one's hand and making offerings to them with the other hand.

124. The emptiness, or primordial nature, of body, speech, mind, and pristine awareness.

125. The action seal (*karmamudrā, las kyi phyag rgya*), seal of the teachings (*dharmamudrā, chos kyi phyag rgya*), seal of the pledge (*samayamudrā, dam tshig gi phyag rgya*), and great seal (*mahāmudrā, phyag rgya chen po*). In the stage of completion of all Highest Yoga tantras, these are the means to accomplish the pristine awareness of the union of bliss and emptiness.

Abhayakaragupta's *Cluster of Secret Instructions* (*Saṃpuṭatantrarājaṭikāmnāyamañjarī; Man ngag snye ma/ dPal yang dag par sbyor ba'i rgyud kyi rgyal po'i rgya cher 'grel pa man ngag gi snye ma*) (Toh. 1198) differentiates the four seals in terms of the phases of creation and completion and their result. Kongtrul provides the following summary of Abhayakara's discussion: In the phase of creation, the action seal is the meditation on the form of a female deity (*devī*). The seal of the teachings is the arrangement of the letter [*HUM*, etc., in one's heart]. The seal of the pledge is the marvelous activity of emanation and withdrawal of light [and the circle of the deities of the mandala from the seed syllable at one's heart], etc. The great seal is the inseparability of appearance and emptiness of the form of the deity.

In the phase of completion, the action seal is a real consort (*vidyā, rig ma*). Since she bestows joy through the act of embracing, etc., she is called "action seal." The great seal is the central channel (*avadhūtī*) since it bestows the special innate joy. The pristine awareness of the inseparability of great bliss and emptiness is the seal of the teachings since it is the mind of unsurpassable awakening. The imaginary consort appearing as a female deity is the seal of the pledge.

At the level of the result, the manifest dimension of awakening is the seal of the pledge. The dimension of great bliss is the great seal. The reality dimension of awakening (*dharmakāya*) is the seal of the teachings, and the enjoyment dimension of awakening is the action seal (*IOK,* vol. II, pp. 687-689).

Pema Karpo defines these four seals based on Naropa's explanations: The action seal is the cause, the undegenerated unborn bliss which arises from the union with a consort. The seal of the teachings refers to meditation with an imaginary consort. After having transformed the ordinary body into the deity's form, the yogin imagines uniting with her. This makes the fire of wisdom blaze, the *HAM* at the crown of the head melt, and the seminal essence flow through the chakras to the tip of the jewel. The yogin's faculties, their objects, etc., become the nature of bodhichitta, unmixed, but of one flavor with great bliss. One should abide in this meditation until the glorious great seal is realized. The great seal is the goal to be attained by embracing the great seal that has the nature of a dream, an optical illusion, etc., until the seal of the pledge is actualized. The seal of the pledge is the spontaneously present, supreme, and unchangeable nature (*TV,* vol. Ca, f. 190b2).

126. The symbolic (*choma, brda*) behavior, consisting in physical and verbal signs, is performed at the time a yogin (or yogini) undertakes the special conduct of awareness so that yogins and yoginis can recognize each other or in order to recognize the consort who will assist one in tantric conduct. Another purpose served is that the adept does not incur the root downfall of "disclosing secrets" during a tantric feast or other activity that may be attended by people who lack the tantric pledges (Kongtrul's *Commentary on the Hevajra Tantra,* ff. 103b3-104a4). For a full discussion, see Kongtrul's *Commentary,* ff. 103b3-108b4; and *The Saṃvarodaya-Tantra, Selected Chapters,* trans. S. Tsuda (Tokyo: Hokuseido Press, 1974) chapter IX.

127. See *Saṃvarodaya-Tantra, Selected Chapters,* chapter XXI.

128. Conduct of the left (*g.yon pa'i kun spyod*) refers to the special observance of Mother tantras of initiating any physical movement or activity with the left side of the body in order to recollect emptiness which, of the two aspects of skill in means (right) and wisdom (left), pertains to wisdom.

129. In discussing the meaning of seminal essence (*bindu, thig le*), Kongtrul writes: Seminal essence (*thig le*), *tilaka* in Sanskrit, means "nucleus or seed of great bliss." Seminal essence comprises two aspects: the conventional (relative) (*kun rdzob*) seminal essence, and the ultimate "seminal essence" of pristine awareness (*don dam ye shes kyi thig le*). In this context, seminal essence denotes the first, which is a substantial seminal essence (*rdzas kyi thig le*), having a white and red part. The main seminal essences number thirty-six, existing throughout the body's channels (*rtsa*), twelve pure (*dvangs ma*) and twenty-four impure (*snyigs ma*); the secondary ones are very numerous. These seminal essences are like wealth owned by the winds.

The pure part of the white (*dkar cha*) substantial seminal essence abides in the upper extremity of the central channel (*dbu ma'i yar sna*) in the nature of the letter *HAM*. The pure part of the red (*dmar cha*) seminal essence abides below the navel at the juncture of the three channels (left, right, and central) in the aspect of a small letter *A* that has the nature of heat. The white part is called glory (*dpyid*) since it yields bliss; and the red part, vital essence (*thig le*) since bliss depends on it. As the seminal essence is the "place" where awakening is actualized, it is called the indestructible seat (*vajrāsana, rdo rje gdan*).

Supported by these pure seminal essences are the impure ones which also have pure and impure components. The pure component produces physical strength and radiance, while the impure part flows out from the orifices (*IOK*, vol. II, pp. 641-644).

130. The mother tantras, in particular the Chakrasamvara, emphasize the practice of wandering throughout special localities known as power places (*pīṭha, gnas*) so that the yogin can summon, meet, and practice with three types of emissaries (*dūtī, pho nya*) who are at different levels of realization. These emissaries are mantra-born (*sngags skyes*), field-born (*zhing skyes*), and innate (*lhan skyes*). The innate are exalted beings who reside in the pure land of Superior (Akaniṣṭha), the enjoyment dimension of enlightenment manifesting in the form of goddesses. The field-born abide in unsurpassable contemplation and manifest as yoginis in the thirty-two power places. The mantra-born are trained in the mantric path and are born in the central region [India] or in other places.

To begin with, the yogin relies on the mantra-born in order to assemble the field-born, and then relies on both. Finally, the yogin can meet the innate emissaries and achieve the highest realization.

A woman can be trained "to be the receptacle for" (to become) the three kinds of emissaries. Such a woman, on whom the yogin relies during the phases of creation and completion of the tantra, should have confidence in the Secret Mantra, be mindful, have been initiated and have assumed the pledges in front of a master belonging to an authentic lineage, and be without attachment to sense pleasures. In addition, she must be able to generate great bliss and act as a condition for the yogin to realize blissful pristine awareness (Kongtrul's *IOK*, vol. III, Book IX, chapter III, "The Tantric Activities Enhancing Realization"; and Kongtrul's *Commentary on the Hevajra Tantra*, ff. 232b-233a2). See *The Buddhist Tantras: Light on Indo-Tibetan Esotericism* by Alex Wayman (New York, 1973; rpt. Delhi: Motilal Banarsidass, 1990), pp. 184-196, for its discussion of the three kinds of emissaries.

131. The tantric conduct of daily service is prescribed in the *Indestructible Tent Tantra* (*Ḍākinīvajrapañjaratantra; mKha' 'gro ma rdo rje gur zhes bya ba'i rgyud*) (Toh. 419), ff. 64b5-65a1.

132. For this tantric conduct, see the *Abhidana Tantra* (*Abhidāna-uttaratantra; mNgon par brjod pa'i rgyud bla ma*) (Toh. 369), f. 333b3.

133. For this tantric conduct, see the *Abhidana Tantra*, f. 333b5-6.

134. The *Abhidana Tantra* states:

Practice with the emissary [of awareness];
Do not, blinded by desire, unite with other [consorts];

> Always be free from attachment to the emissary;
> Never transgressing this pledge, delight in her (f. 333b6-7).

135. For this tantric conduct, see the *Abhidana Tantra*, f. 334a6.

136. The *Abhidana Tantra* states:

> Whoever shows anger to the yogin who is the cause
> Of the accomplishment of all one's desired goals
> Will be reborn as a dog for a hundred lifetimes
> And then as a butcher (f. 334b1-2).

137. The *Abhidana Tantra* states:

> Always wear the five symbolic ornaments
> And skulls as ornaments on your head.
> Carry the skull-cup and the mystic staff,
> And smear your body with ash.
> Always eat the great flesh,
> And drink every kind [of spirit] to intoxication.
> Sit on corpses
> Wearing a pelt as garment.
> Consume the appropriate foods,
> And satisfy yourself with flesh and blood.
> Dwell in towns or isolated places.
> Whenever you wander around,
> Remain always without attachments.
> Continuously enjoy charnel grounds
> Or market gatherings.
> Do not stray into the place of proclaimers, worldly people,
> Or those without good fortune, who are full of ignorance and confusion,
> Or into monasteries where proclaimers live.
> Live like a destitute,
> While leading a bodhisattva's life,
> Enjoying the indestructible dance.
> Always dwelling in cemeteries,
> Consuming feces and the great flesh,
> Drinking intoxicating liquors,
> Chief of the heroes, single-pointedly
> Rest in meditation (f. 251b4).

138. For the remaining lines, see *KT*, p. 231.

139. According to Naropa, they are known as evil (ill deeds) because they chain one to cyclic existence and destroy one's goodness. See *Commentary on the Summary of the [Kalacakra] Initiation (Paramārthasaṃgrahanāmasekoddeśaṭīkā; dBang mdor bstan pa'i 'grel bshad don dam pa bsdus pa zhes bya ba)* (Toh. 1351), ff. 232a4-5.

140. Dharmashri explains why the first four types of killing are listed separately: to clearly refute the view professed by religious extremists that in some cases such killing may be meritorious (to sacrifice cattle to win a higher existence, for example). "To destroy a reliquary" is placed separately not only to refute the

barbaric view that to do this is an authentic spiritual practice but also to emphasize that this is an extremely negative act (*Commentary on the Three Vows*, ff. 267b5-268a4).

141. The vajra or adamantine nature of body, speech, mind, and pristine awareness refers to the primordial nature of these four planes of individual existence. Through the union of special means (great bliss) and pristine awareness (emptiness), the ordinary body, speech, and mind, and their propensities are purified as the enlightened body, speech, mind, and pristine awareness of a buddha.

142. Secrets (*gsang ba*) of body, speech, and mind: their ultimate or primordial nature, or emptiness.

143. Five symbolic bone ornaments (*rus pa'i phyag rgya*): the crown ornament, symbolizing Akshobhya and mirror-like pristine awareness; earrings, symbolizing Amitabha and the pristine awareness of discernment; the necklace, symbolizing Ratnasambhava and the pristine awareness of equality; bracelets and anklets, symbolizing Vairochana and the pristine awareness of the sphere of reality; belt or ashes, symbolizing Amoghasiddhi and the aim-accomplishing pristine awareness.

A variant introduces an additional ornament—the sacred thread worn by brahmins—and points out the correspondence to the six perfections: the necklace represents generosity; bracelets and anklets, ethics; the earrings, patience; the crown ornament, diligence; the sacred thread, meditation; and the belt (or sacred ashes), discriminative wisdom.

Kongtrul explains that these ornaments also symbolize the yogin's or yogini's pledges: the yogin wears the crown ornament on the head in order not to forget to pay homage to the vajra master who is "heavy" with qualities, the master who bestows the instructions, and the favored deity. The yogin wears the earrings as a reminder to not despise the master, etc.; the necklace as a reminder to never stray from the inner and outer mantra recitations which protect the mind from objectifying conceptions; the bracelets and anklets as a symbol of the vow not to kill creatures; the belt to symbolize the binding of the seminal essence by relying on the consort. According to the definitive meaning, the crown ornament symbolizes the fixing of the seminal essence at the crown of the head and at the other focal points of energy (*Commentary on the Hevajra Tantra*, ff. 289b1-290a2).

See Wayman's *The Buddhist Tantras*, pp. 118-122, for a brief discussion of this subject.

144. Quoted from Pundarika's *Stainless Light Commentary on the Kalachakra*, Toh. 1347, vol. Da, f. 145a2.

145. In the Kalachakra Tantra, the five meats (*sha lnga*), known as five lamps (*sgron me lnga*) or "stimulators" of the senses, refer to five outer and five inner meats. The outer meats are cow (*ba glang*), dog (*khyi*), horse (*rta*), elephant (*glang po che*), and human (*mi*). The five inner meats are the five sense organs. The five nectars (*bdud rtsi lnga*) refer to inner and outer nectars. The outer are excrement (*dri chen*), urine (*dri chu*), blood (*khrag*), semen (*rdo rje'i zil pa*), and human flesh (*mi'i sha*). The five inner are the five aggregates. The adept first dissolves the

meats and nectars, purifies them by meditation on non-reality, then has them reappear, and finally transforms them into ambrosia. However, unless the adept has the ability to actually perform this transformation, these substances do not contribute to the attainment of the qualities of awakening (*TV*, vol. Ca, f. 163b5-6).

146. Camphor (*ga pur*): a metaphor for the seminal fluid.

147. Offerings are of two kinds: outer and inner. The outer are the offerings of the five sense objects, visual forms, etc., and the five nectars and the five meats, which satisfy the aggregates and elements of the body. The inner offerings are the offerings of the aggregates, the senses, and their objects purified through the immutable great bliss produced by retention of the seminal essence (*TV*, vol. Ca, f. 164a3-b6).

148. The first seven Kalachakra initiations: water (*toyaṣeka, chu'i dbang*), diadem (*mauliseka; cod pan gyi dbang*), ribbon (*paṭṭaseka, dar dpyangs kyi dbang*), vajra and bell (*vajraghaṇṭāseka, rdo rje dril bu'i dbang*), conduct (*vrataseka, brtul zhugs kyi dbang*), name (*nāmaseka, ming gi dbang*), and permission (*ājñā, rjes gnang*) initiations. See Naropa's *Commentary on the Summary of the [Kalachakra] Initiation*, ff. 237a7-238b2.

To these are added the higher and supremely high initiations: two vase (*kalaśaseka, bum pa'i dbang*), two secret (*guhyaseka, gsang ba'i dbang*), two pristine-awareness-through-wisdom (*prajñājñānaseka, shes rab ye shes kyi dbang*), and the provisional word and the definitive word initiations (a total of fifteen, or eleven if the two last groups of four are counted as only one set of four). See *KT*, pp. 68-69 and 213-214.

149. Single-pronged vajra (*ekasūkavajra, rdo rje rtse gcig*), since its pledge is the one unique cause that produces the victorious ones (*TV*, vol. Ca, f. 163a5).

150. Non-objectifying compassion and emptiness (*mi dmigs pa'i snying rje dang stong pa nyid*): the first refers to unchanging bliss, which is non-objectifying (*mi dmigs pa*) because it is devoid of the dualism of perceiver and perceived; the second, to supreme emptiness comprehensive of all aspects. See notes 156 and 157.

151. See note 164.

152. Empty image (*stong gzugs*) refers to the unique Kalachakra system of tantric practice in which the material components of one's body (seminal fluids, energy winds, and particles) are exhausted (dematerialized) and the empty images of the deities in union are achieved. Thus, the resultant union of bliss and emptiness in the Kalachakra refers to the union of immutable bliss and empty images (the male and female deities). See below, notes 156 and 157. See also Taranatha's *Meaningful to Behold, Practical Instructions on the Indestructible Yoga's Profound Path (Zab lam rdo rje'i rnal 'byor gyi 'khrid yig mthong ba don ldan*), in Kongtrul Lodrö Tayé's *Treasury of Key Instructions (gDams ngag mdzod*) (Delhi: N. Lungtok and N. Gyaltsen).

153. The ten energy winds in the Kalachakra Tantra are divided into five principal and five secondary ones. The five principal ones are vital (*prāṇa, srog 'dzin*), downward-clearing (*apāna, thur sel*), balancing heat (*samāna, me mnyam*), upward-moving (*udāna, gyen rgyu*), and pervasive (*vyāna, khyab byed*); the five secondary

ones, snake (*nāga, klu*), turtle (*kūrma, rus sbal*), chameleon (*kṛkara, rtsangs pa*), gift of the gods (*devadatta, lhas byin*), and victorious through wealth (*dhanañjaya, nor las rgyal*). See Geshé Ngawang Dhargyey, *A Commentary on the Kālacakra Tantra* (Dharamsala: Library of Tibetan Works and Archives, 1985), pp. 117-120.

154. Inner heat (*caṇḍālī*). The Tibetan *gtum mo* is derived from the Sanskrit *caṇḍā*, meaning fierce. *Caṇḍālī* is a female untouchable, which is one of the preferred consorts of the adept. Being "untouchable" symbolizes the "ineffable" nature of pristine awareness. At an inner level, untouchability represents the heat or passion lying below the navel that, once aroused through relying on a consort or imaginatively, melts the seminal essence dormant at the crown of the head.

As an auxiliary technique, "inner heat" (*gtum mo*) refers to a meditation whereby the adept visualizes within his or her body the central, left, and right channels and the focal points of energy (*cakra*). Below the navel is visualized a syllable or a fine shape that is of the nature of fire. Then, in conjunction with the vase breathing that causes the winds of the left and right channels to converge into the central one, the fire of the inner heat rises within the central channel to melt the white seminal essence, which is visualized either in the aspect of the syllable *HAM* or as a seminal point at the crown of the head, causing the seminal essence to flow downward within the central channel to the tip of the sexual organ, where it is then held and its course is reversed.

For a discussion of the elaborate and simple forms of the inner heat techniques, see Taranatha's *Meaningful to Behold*, ff. 135b3-137b2.

155. The great seal of empty image (*stong gzugs phyag rgya chen po*): see notes 156 and 157. On the "nominal causal" relationship between the great seal of empty image and the immutable bliss, see Kongtrul's *IOK*, vol. III, pp. 213-221.

156. Kongtrul states that immutable bliss (*akṣarasukha, mi 'gyur bde ba*) refers to intrinsic awareness, the expanse of blissful pristine awareness free from mental fabrications which is the unity (*gcig tu 'dres pa*) of the changeless nature of reality and the bliss of the non-emitted seminal essence. Since this great bliss ends the suffering of oneself and others, it is called great compassion.

In the Kalachakra system, immutable bliss is termed "ultimate" due to the absence of the conceptual fabrication of perceiver and perceived. The empty image comprehensive of all aspects, the great seal (*stong gzugs phyag rgya chen po*), is termed "relative" because its appearances are similar to relative phenomena. Nevertheless, unchanging bliss and the emptiness comprehensive of all aspects are in fact one unity (*IOK*, vol. III, pp. 217-221).

157. Kongtrul explains that the Kalachakra Tantra teaches the "emptiness endowed with the supreme aspects" (*rnam kun mchog ldan gyi stong pa nyid*) which constitutes the chief view of all the tantras. This emptiness alone is capable of producing supreme unchanging bliss. Of the three aspects of emptiness—that of the ground, the path, and the result—this is an emptiness meditated upon on the path. In the Kalachakra system, the supreme emptiness is called indefinite emptiness (*rnam par ma nges pa'i stong pa nyid*) because the forms in which it manifests are indefinite, being unlimited radiant awareness ('*od gsal*) and multicolored images (*viśvabimba, sna tshogs gzugs brnyan*). This emptiness is revealed

after the manifestation of ten signs which are images of empty images (*śūnyata-bimba, stong nyid kyi gzugs*) produced by the yogas of the day (*nyin gyi rnal 'byor*) and of the night (*mtshan mo'i rnal 'byor*).

This quintessential emptiness has a nature like that of the visions in mirror divination. It has all the appearances (*rnam pa thams cad*) of the three realms of existence, while its own nature is without real characteristics, not being composed of atoms and free of constructive thought. It is direct knowledge. It is the illusory appearance of supremely (*mchog*) radiant pristine awareness. Its quality is expressed in its being the source of great bliss because if one meditates on such emptiness, it has the power to produce the pristine awareness of great bliss.

The image of the supreme emptiness refers to the indivisibility of emptiness and compassion (*IOK*, vol. III, pp. 213-218).

158. On this point, see the discussion in Naropa's *IK*, pp. 76-80.

159. The objects of the ten generosities.

160. The five nectars and the five meats.

161. Five supernatural knowledges (*abhijñā, mngon par shes pa*): miraculous powers (*ṛddhi, rdzu 'phrul*), divine eye (*divyacakṣus, lha'i mig*), divine ear (*divyaśrota, lha'i rna ba*), knowing others' thoughts (*paracittajñāna, gzhan sems shes pa*), and recollection of previous lives (*pūrvanivāsānusmṛti, sngon gnas rjes su dran pa*). A sixth, the knowledge that causes the extinction of all pollutants (*āsravakṣayaka-rajñāna, zag zad mkhyen pa*) in one's mind stream, is commonly included.

162. Bokar Rinpoché explains that according to the tantras, an evil person who throughout his life harbors intense hatred for and constantly injures others, when he cannot be tamed by any other means, should be released (*grol ba*) from the fetters of his evil existence and his consciousness transferred to a pure buddha realm. This release serves the double purpose of saving the evil person from rebirth in hell and relieving others and the world of his harmful presence. The ritual to perform this release can only be performed by a yogin of the highest attainment who meets the following requirements with regard to motivation, action, and result: Regarding the motivation, the yogin must have no self-interest whatsoever and desire only the other person's ultimate good. For the action, the yogin must effect the release through meditative absorption, mudra (hand gestures) and mantra, and never resort to the use of poison or weapons of any kind. In addition, the yogin must be able to resurrect the individual. For the result, the adept, using the power of meditation, must direct the consciousness of the person into a pure realm.

Naropa states that until the yogin has gained the five clairvoyances, he must abstain from all wrathful rites. Why? Because although the person who is the object of the rite may have committed one of the five inexpiable deeds, later on he may engage in virtuous acts. For example, King Ashoka was extremely cruel in the earlier period of his life, but then became a great protector of the Buddhist teachings. If one were to end such a person's present existence, the consequences would be unfortunate. Therefore, to perform wrathful rites without foreknowledge of the karma of that person is prohibited (*Commentary on the Summary of the Kalachakra Initiation*, f. 236a5-7).

Dharmashri, citing the *Shimmering Light on the Pledges*, enumerates ten recipients of the effect of this rite (*zhing bcu*): an enemy of the Three Jewels who causes great harm to the teachings, in particular an enemy of a qualified spiritual master; practitioners who let their pledges deteriorate and do not restore them; those who reject the Secret Mantra after having entered its way; those who despise the master or vajra siblings; those who, though unauthorized, participate in tantric activities with the intention to steal; those who have harmed sentient beings; those who are fierce enemies of practitioners who honor their pledges; those who engage exclusively and continuously in evil actions; and those beings whose evil actions would lead to rebirth in the three lower forms of life or who are currently experiencing the result of these actions in lower forms of life (*Commentary on the Three Vows*, ff. 261b5-262a5).

For a discussion of the provisional and definitive meanings of the pledges of the different families, see *KT*, pp. 349-351.

163. Kongtrul enumerates the twelve stages of awakening (*bhumi, sa*) in the Kalachakra Tantra: Illuminating (*samantaprabhā, kun tu 'od*), the stage at which the darkness of impediments to omniscience are dispelled; Light of Nectar (*amṛtaprabhā, bdud rtsi'i 'od*), the stage associated with the passion of non-emitted bliss; Light of the Sky (*ākāśaprabhā, nam mkha'i 'od*), the stage of seeing all phenomena as space; Adamantine Light (*vajraprabhā, rdo rje'i 'od*), the stage of a firm, altruistic mind, undivided by egoistic thoughts; Gem Light (*ratnaprabhā, rin chen 'od*), the stage of the pristine awareness of the initiation conferred by the deity; Lotus Light (*padmaprabhā, pad ma'i 'od*), the stage of seeing the natural purity of the mind; Worker of the Buddhas (*buddhakarmakarī, sangs rgyas kyi las byed pa*), the stage of enacting the marvelous activity of emanating as buddhas and bodhisattvas; Incomparable (*anupamā, dpe med pa*), the stage of seeing that pristine awareness cannot be described through examples; Example for All Examples (*upamā, dpe thams cad kyi dpe*), the stage of knowing reasons and examples for every phenomenon; Wisdom Light (*prajñāprabhā, shes rab kyi 'od*), the stage of an immense expansion of intelligence with respect to any object of knowledge; Omniscience (*sarvajñatā, thams cad mkhyen pa*), the stage of the elimination of the predispositions of the impediment to universal knowledge; Self-Experienced (*pratyātmavedyā, so so'i bdag nyid rig pa*), the stage of manifestation of the self-experienced pristine awareness.

These twelve stages are simply twelve distinctions in the modes of pristine awareness. They are called stages (*bhūmi, sa*) because they serve as the bases for the gaining of higher realizations. These twelve are essentially the qualities of the buddhas; however, they are attained simultaneously with the initial moment of the path of seeing. That moment corresponds to the end of the so-called twelve lesser stages found in relation to the last branch of the sixfold yoga, contemplation, when the adamantine rainbow body (*'ja' lus rdo rje sku*) is attained. All of these twelve are present on each of the usual ten stages of awakening such as Joyful (*rab tu dga' ba*) and at the stage of a buddha. These twelve stages are qualities undifferentiated from buddha-nature (*tathāgatagarbha, bde gshegs snying po*) and exist spontaneously from the beginning of time. On the path of an exalted adept, these stages pertain to the path that removes impediments and are present in both equipoise and post-equipoise. At the level of a buddha, these primordial stages become actualized (Kongtrul's *IOK*, vol. III, pp. 552-553). See also Naropa's *IK*, p. 335.

164. Naropa's *Commentary on the Summary of the Kalachakra Initiation* defines enlightened speech as the invincible sound that unceasingly manifests as the different languages of infinite creatures, gods, humans, etc., to bestow the nectar of the teachings (f. 237b3); and the sound that imparts the teachings to all creatures by manifesting itself as the sounds of all languages. Thus, the "lie" is the so-called invincible sound existing at the heart (f. 236b6-7).

Naropa adds that the invincible sound is heard after the azure sphere, the last of ten signs of the yoga of the day and night (belonging to the yoga of withdrawal), has appeared. Within that sphere, the image of the manifold enjoyment dimension of awakening, free of objectivity, appears. While the adept sees these images, he or she also hears the invincible sound. Thus, by virtue of the appearances of the image, there exists the manifest dimension (*nirmāṇakāya*); and by virtue of the appearance of sound, the enjoyment dimension of enlightenment (*saṃbhogakāya*) (ff. 250b5-251a7).

165. The first branch of the sixfold yoga (*sbyor ba yan lag drug*) practiced in the completion phase of the Kalachakra Tantra. The sixfold yoga consists of the following branches: withdrawal (*so sor sdud pa*), meditative absorption (*bsam gtan*), control of the breath (*srog rtsol*), retention (*'dzin pa*), subsequent application (*rjes su dran pa*), and contemplation (*ting nge 'dzin*).

Withdrawal (from the Sanskrit *pratyāhāra*, of which *praty* means individually, and *āhāra*, to withdraw) means to stop the interaction between the ordinary sense organs and their objects by withdrawing the mental consciousness from its referent; and to experience the five objects which are of the nature of radiant awareness and the five senses which are of the nature of pristine awareness. In brief, withdrawal means to withdraw the mind from ordinary appearances and engage in the appearances of pristine awareness.

During withdrawal, the adept applies the yoga of the night (*mtshan mo'i rnal 'byor*) and the yoga of the day (*nyin mo'i rnal 'byor*). The yoga of the night is practiced in complete darkness, seated in cross-legged posture. The adept gazes, eyeballs turned upward, on the black space at a height of sixteen fingers above the eyebrows and remains free of any mental activity while mixing mind and winds.

The yoga of the day is practiced in an isolated place, unseen by others, gazing directly into expansive, cloud-free space (in the morning, toward the west, and in the evening, toward the east), with the sun behind the shoulders. The manner of meditation is the same as the one done in darkness. (With some exceptions, the same gaze is adopted in both the withdrawal and concentration parts of the yoga.) As a result of these yogas, the adept sees many indefinite signs of multicolored images (*sna tshogs gzugs brnyan*); and the ten signs (*rtags bcu*) that manifest with defined aspects: the four during the night yoga of smoke, mirage, the luminosity of a very radiant and clear sky, and lamp; and the six during the day yoga of a flame, the moon, the sun, a vajra (here, a black sphere), lightning, and an (azure) sphere. These are called signs because they indicate the ultimate pristine awareness' presence within oneself, and because they constitute the basis for the confidence that by experientially cultivating the path, one will be able to actualize pristine awareness. The signs are not distorted illusions, but images of emptiness (*stong pa nyid kyi gzugs*) perceived directly and unmistakenly.

The second branch, meditative absorption (*dhyāna, bsam gtan*), also employs the yoga of night and day and has the function of consolidating the empty images or images of emptiness experienced in the withdrawal. In this yoga, instead of concentrating on space, the adept focuses on the empty images, without any discursive thought. Meditative absorption has five moments: concentration (*rtse gcig sems*), examination (*rtog pa*), analysis (*dpyod pa*), joy (*dga' ba*), and bliss (*bde ba*). Concentration consists in the wisdom that is one-pointedly concentrated within the radiant awareness of the image of emptiness comprehensive of all aspects. Examination consists in the knowledge of the characteristics of the images of emptiness having the aspects of phenomena and experiencing such characteristics as being simply one's mind. Analysis is the ascertainment or experience of the mind's nature manifesting as the image of emptiness while unmoved by any stain of subject and object, perceiver and perceived. Joy is focused outwardly, a joy likened to an unprecedented sense of satisfaction. Bliss is focused inwardly and derives from the concentration itself manifesting as bliss. As a result of bliss, the body is pervaded by a special bliss of ease.

The special sign of the yoga of meditative absorption is then seen: the vision of multicolored images of manifold form, sound, smell, taste, and tactile sensation marked by spheres endowed with five qualities—emitting light, subtle, bright, quivering, and difficult to destroy. Within these spheres, many buddhas manifest. These are manifestations of the purity of the mind's nature; having such realization, all karmic appearances also manifest as illusions.

The third branch is control of the breath: In the Sanskrit term *prāṇayāma*, *prāṇa* means vital (*srog*) and refers to winds; *ayāma* means to block or exhort (*rtsol*), in the sense of causing the winds to enter the central channel. Control of the breath (*srog rtsol*) is thus performed in order to block the karmic winds from flowing into the right and left channels and to cause them to enter into the central channel and dissolve into the indestructible seminal essence. To do this, the adept first visualizes the three channels in the body and practices the adamantine recitation (*rdo rje bzlas pa*) of exhaling with the sound of the letter *AH*, inhaling with the sound of the letter *OM*, and concentrating on the letter *HUM* at the navel during the pause with the sound of the letter *HUM*. This is to clear the inner channels, after which one adopts the soft breathing ('*jam rlung*) to channel the vital wind into the central channel. Once the wind has entered the channel, through the forceful breathing (*rtsub rlung*) of the vase breathing (*rlung bum pa can*), the vital energy is held in it, and the adept experiences the ten signs within the body and concentrates on the empty images in the body. Through this yoga, the adept also accomplishes the cause for the immutable bliss (which in this system is posited as the great seal of the empty images) and gains control over winds and seminal essences (in particular, the ability to hold and turn back the seminal essence). The scope of breath control is enhanced by other techniques such as that of the inner heat, sexual union with a real consort, and forceful physical exercises.

Retention (from the Sanskrit *dhāraṇā*), the fourth, has a variety of meanings but in this context refers to preventing (holding) the winds from moving. Retention is the yoga using the special vase breathing techniques associated with heart, navel, throat, forehead, and top of the head. The aim of this yoga is to make the seminal essence unmoving and to ignite the inner heat, the seed of the occurrence of special images of emptiness, which can directly bring about immutable bliss. The nature of retention is a concentration related to the dissolution of the winds into the seminal essence within the central channel at the place of the five or six energy focal points (*cakra*); in particular, it causes the dissolution of the winds at the forehead seminal point, where the non-emitted seminal essence is firmly held. Its signs are the appearance of a black line emitting rays, the blazing of the inner heat, and hearing extremely distinctly the indestructible sound.

The fifth, subsequent application (from the Sanskrit *anusmṛti*, where *anu* means subsequent, and *smṛti*, recollection), is a repeated meditation on the great seal of the empty images. The auxiliary aspects of this meditation are related to the channels, winds, and seminal essences; the empty images of the blazing of the inner heat; the five or six seminal essences at the energy focal points, and the melted bliss related to these; training in melting the bliss, etc. The nature of recollection is the contemplation which repeatedly produces the melted bliss through the equipoise on the empty images of the three existences (among which the main is the image of the male and female deity in union) which are appearances of the blazing of the inner heat accompanied or not by the practice of the action or imaginary seals. In this system, it is said, however, that the adept of less capability is unable to experience fully the four joys of the melted seminal essence without relying on an actual consort. When his capability develops, he relies only on the last two seals, the imaginary and the great, and finally, only on the great seal. The signs accompanying this phase of the yoga include the manifestation of one's body as the empty image of a light mandala; and emanation and withdrawal of pure and impure images of the three worlds. As the result of subsequent application, a mandala of light, the effect of one's channels being filled with seminal essence, pervades everywhere, inside and outside; even if one's body is not transformed, one's mind becomes the actual form of the deity; the experience of bliss and emptiness remains constant.

The sixth, contemplation (from the Sanskrit *samādhi*), is to remain in a state of indivisibility of subject and object, free from perceiver and perceived. In this phase of the yoga, the adept trains exclusively with an imaginary consort, practicing for an extended length of time using the vase breathing for each focal point of energy in relation to the descent and ascent of the seminal essence, and remains absorbed in the state of bliss and empty images.

The focus of the concentration is the bliss and the empty images meditated upon to increase the immutable bliss. While doing this, the adept's body is purified and becomes the dimension of pristine awareness. This concentration is extended from the first moment of immutable bliss up to the completion of 21,600 moments, when the body of the adept dematerializes. Its nature is that of a concentration on the images of pristine awareness through the force of the immutable bliss. During the actual contemplation, the adept engages in melting continuously the seminal essence, and externally he or she engages without interruption in the elaborate mode of tantric conduct. Through this contemplation, the adept gradually attains the state of a buddha, the great dimension of non-dual pristine awareness. See Taranatha's *Meaningful to Behold* and Naropa's *IK*. For the position of each branch of the sixfold yoga in relation to the five paths and twelve stages, see Kongtrul's *IOK*, vol. III, pp. 518-524.

166. Here, "meat" refers to the flesh of animals who have died naturally. This pledge applies only in countries where the eating of meat is taboo. Alcohol is consumed as a pledge substance while remaining in control (unintoxicated) (Dharmashri's *Commentary on the Three Vows*, f. 255a4-5).

167. On the correspondence between the nectars and the dhyani buddhas, the *Essence of the Great Seal Tantra* states that Ratnasambhava is blood; Amitabha, semen; Amoghasiddhi, human flesh; Akshobhya, urine; Vairochana, excrement (Pundarika's *Stainless Light Commentary*, Toh. 1347 vol. Da, f. 230a6-7).

168. Dharmasri states that in the definitive sense, to eat the five meats is to bind the pure essences of the five senses; to drink alcohol is to bind in non-emission the descending innate bliss of the melted seminal essence; to eat the five nectars is to bind the essences of the five elements. By binding these, the subtle and gross particles of the melted seminal essence are purified; by enjoying all kinds of objects, the pure essences of feces, urine, and semen are stabilized at the navel by reversing them upward (*Commentary on the Three Vows*, f. 255a6-b2).

169. Immutable (*akṣara, mi 'gyur ba*) bliss is bliss characterized by the arrest of the seminal fluid at the tip of the vajra. The mutable (*kṣara, 'gyur ba*) bliss is characterized by the descent and movement of seminal fluid toward the tip of the vajra.

170. Adamantine bodhichitta (*rdo rje byang sems*). Bodhicitta in the Universal Way is the resolution (*citta, sems*) to attain awakening (*bodhi, byang chub*) for the welfare of others. As such, it is the seed of awakening. In tantra, without losing its original connotation, the term denotes the seminal essence (*bindu, thig le*) residing at the top of the head, which is the basis for the blissful pristine awareness. As such, it is understood as having two aspects: the relative aspect, which is substantial and of a white, moon-like seminal essence; and the ultimate aspect of the pristine awareness of bliss and emptiness.

171. On the control of the winds (*byed bcings kyi sbyor ba*), Taranatha's *Meaningful to Behold* explains that *byed* refers to control over the five winds associated with the sense organs; and *bcings*, to the control of the vital (*prāṇa, srog*) and downward-clearing winds (*thur sel*).

The control of the winds of the sense organs is effected by assuming the face of a wrathful deity: narrowing the gaze to a subtle point, rolling inward the tongue, contracting the lips, nose, and ears; contracting the muscles of the four limbs, contracting inwardly the toes, tightening the vajra fists, assuming the cross-legged posture, and pushing up one's shoulders forcefully.

The control of the vital and descending winds is effected by different forms of breath control (p. 161 lines 1-6).

172. Contemplation (*samādhi, ting nge 'dzin*). See note 165.

173. According to Pema Karpo, who supports his opinion by quoting the Kalachakra and other tantras, the root downfall of expressing anger toward one's spiritual siblings applies to a beginner only in relation to the vajra siblings with whom he or she has assumed pledges from the same master, mandala, and consort. For an experienced meditator, however, this downfall can be incurred even in relation to common spiritual siblings, i.e., all sentient beings (*TV*, vol. Ca, f. 129a5-6).

174. Buddhajnanapada's enumeration of five kinds of vajra siblings or spiritual companions is found in his *Presentation of the Stages* (*Rim pa rnam pa gzhag pa*): (1) All those who have entered the Buddhist teachings or the Indestructible Way; (2) all sentient beings (since pristine awareness is present in all of them); (3, 4, and 5) those who have been initiated by the same master, in the same mandala, and with the same consort, distinguished as close, special, and most special siblings with respect to the four initiations (TV, vol. Ca, f. 128b 3-5).

Lilavajra, in his *Shimmering Light on the Pledges*, distinguishes four kinds of siblings: General (common) siblings are all sentient beings who are none other than a manifestation of one's own intrinsic awareness and thus not to be regarded as "others," and who are future buddhas in that they possess the potential to become buddhas. Distant siblings are all followers of the Buddha's teachings. Close siblings are those who have the same view and conduct in that they lead lives of chastity (*brahamacarya*). Inner (*nang 'dres*) siblings are those with whom one shares the same vajra master, initiatory mandala, and consort in the initiation (*TV*, vol. Ca, ff. 127b5-128a5).

Manjushriyashas distinguishes six kinds: Vajra siblings include all who have entered the same mandala of Guhyasamaja or another. Close siblings include all who have entered the Way of Indestructible Reality. Beautiful siblings include all who have entered the Buddhist teachings. Furthermore, vajra siblings include all sentient beings since all have the nature of Vajrasattva. Special vajra siblings include all those who have received the vase, secret, pristine-awareness-through-wisdom, and the symbolic fourth initiation from the same master and consort. Particular siblings include all those who have received one of these initiations together (*TV*, vol. Ca, f. 128a6-b3).

175. Seven kinds of vajra siblings are mentioned in Dharmashri's *Commentary on the Three Vows*: all sentient beings (general siblings); all Buddhists (extended siblings); all mantrikas (close siblings); and the four kinds of intimate siblings— all those initiated into the same mandala (siblings of the same "mother"); all those initiated by the same master (siblings of the same "father"); all those initiated into the same mandala and by the same master, either at different times (siblings of the same "parents", "younger" or "older") or at the same time (twins); and all those who have received all four initiations together (this last being the deepest of all connections) (f. 259a1-4) The seven vajra siblings referred to in the Kalachakra tantra may possibly correspond to these.

176. Pema Karpo explains that these four refer to abandoning love in a light manner, in a medium manner, in a heavy manner, and in a very heavy manner. The first means abandoning love for just a second and immediately restoring it, like drawing a picture with a stick on the surface of water. The second is compared

to making a drawing on sand which is then erased by the wind. The third refers to a mind that remains long without love, likened to a crack in the earth which needs to be joined by water. The fourth refers to giving up completely one's love for another, likened to a diamond shattered into two which can never be re-united, or a ripened fruit which has fallen to the ground and smashed (*TV*, vol. Ca, f. 130b3).

177. The citation is found in Pundarika's *Great Commentary*, vol. Da, f. 154a7. Here, the relative awakening mind refers to the seminal essence the loss of which prevents the arising of unmoving bliss. The ultimate awakening mind denotes bliss, which relies on the seminal essence, the relative awakening mind (*TV*, vol. Ca, f. 134a3-5).

Bokar Rinpoché explains that an adept who engages in sexual union as a means to deepen realization does so only when complete mastery over the movement of the seminal essence has been achieved so that no emission occurs. The motivation must be the resolve to attain awakening, uncorrupted with lust. During union, which serves as the basis for the generation of the pristine awareness of supreme bliss, yogin and yogini imagine themselves to be in the form of the male and female deities in union; the result consists in the realization of the ultimate awakening mind.

178. Nectar pills (*bdud rtsi ril bu*): pills containing the five nectars to be used during tantric rituals, such as for the inner offerings. Other purposes for which the emission of seminal fluid is permitted include to maintain one's family lineage, and as a means to remove obstacles [to one's own life] (*TV*, vol. Ca, f. 134b2).

179. Here, Kongtrul is referring to Darika's *Explanation of the Kalachakra Initiation* (*Kālacakratantrarājasekaprakriyāvṛtti; rGyud kyi rgyal po dpal dus kyi 'khor lo'i dbang gi rab tu byed pa'i 'grel pa*) (Toh. 1355), f. 50b5.

Darika is numbered among the eighty-four great tantric adepts of ancient India. A king of Pataliputra, he became a disciple of Luipa, who sold him to a prostitute in order to shatter his concept of caste. While serving the prostitute, Darika secretly practiced the instructions of his master and became an accomplished yogin. For details of his life, see Keith Dowman's *Masters of Mahamudra* (Albany: State University of New York Press, 1985).

180. Attainment (*siddhi, dngos grub*), particularly supernatural attainment, is divided into two kinds: supreme attainment (*mchog gi dngos grub*), often equivalent to full spiritual accomplishment; and common attainments (*thun mong gi dngos grub*). The common attainments are generally enumerated as eight: the power of the magic sword of invincibility, the eye elixir that enables one to see other realms, swift walking, invisibility, the elixir of youth, walking in sky, shaping pills of the five meats and five nectars, and moving underground. See *IOK* vol. III, Book X, chapter II.

181. The vase initiation authorizes the practitioner to engage in tantra's phase of creation in which the five aggregates are imaginatively associated with the respective buddhas; the elements, with the consorts of the buddhas; and the sense fields, with the bodhisattvas. The aggregate of form is Vairochana; feeling,

Ratnasambhava; discrimination, Amitabha; composite factors, Amoghasiddhi; and consciousness, Akshobhya.

182. Manjushriyashas states that pure nature (*dag pa'i chos*) means devoid of self (*ERD*, f. 285b4).

183. She who bestows the bliss (*bde ba sbyin pa mo*), the third of these three types of seals: the action seal who gives a moving bliss (*kṣara, 'gyur ba*); the imaginary seal who gives the vibrating (*spanda, g.yo ba*) bliss; and the great seal who gives the immutable bliss, i.e., the great seal that is the supreme emptiness comprehensive of all aspects (*rnam kun mchog ldan gyi stong pa nyid*). See Naropa's *Commentary on the Summary of the Kalacakra Initiation*, ff. 273b3-274a1 and *IK*, pp. 313-315.

184. "Etc." refers to refusing to enter into union with a qualified consort at the times this is required (*TV*, vol. Ca, f. 151b2). Dharmashri states that a yogin's pledges include to keep ritual objects such as vajra, bell, ritual dress, and ornaments; to enjoy foods and drinks such as the inner and outer five meats and nectars; and to dance, chant songs, and enter into union with a qualified consort (*Commentary on the Three Vows*, f. 263a3-6).

185. Kongtrul explains that an actual ritual feast (*gaṇacakra, tshogs kyi 'khor lo*, lit. "wheel of the group") comprises a gathering of yogins and yoginis equal in number to the male and female figures found in the mandala of the tantric deity of which these yogins and yoginis are adepts.

The ritual feast is performed on different occasions, such as the fourteenth, the eighth, and the tenth of the waxing moon, dates on which offerings acquire a special magnitude. Yogins and yoginis gather at night in a suitable isolated place, such as where sky-farers gather, the outskirts of a town, a temple, a cemetery, an empty cave, at the foot of a tree, or at the edge of a forest. Depending on its type and purpose, the ritual feast may last a night, a month, or three years and three fortnights. The purpose may be to offer to worldly and transworldly sky-farers, to perform an initiation rite, or to allow a friendly gathering of tantric practitioners. In terms of its effect on the personal practice of the yogin or yogini, the ritual feast is a way to enhance realization.

Once the place has being chosen (some tantras specify that the hidden ritual feast house be of three stories, below the ground, or one half above, etc.), the mandala is drawn, and the yogins and yoginis take their places on seats of corpses, tiger skins, or other, surrounding the central figure, the yogin or yogini leader of the feast. The offerings, of the five nectars and the five meats, alcohol, etc., are consecrated according to the appropriate ritual and then enjoyed by the congregation as an "inner fire offering" to the deities of the body mandala of each participant. The yogins and yoginis enjoy food and drinks imagining them to pervade all their psychophysical constituents and thereby generating pleasure. During union while in the state of meditative absorption, the yogin and yogini experience the four joys while holding the seminal essence, and remain absorbed in the state of coemergent bliss and emptiness. Arising from the absorption, they see all appearances as illusions, and whatever appears manifests as the form of the deity. Then the yogins and yoginis continue in the enjoyment of the feast while sharpening their senses with reciprocal offerings, dances, music, songs, displays of symbolic language and gestures.

Celebration of heroes (*dpa' bo'i ston mo*) are gatherings of yogins; and celebration of heroines (*dpa' mo'i ston mo*), gatherings of yoginis, predominantly. A ritual feast in which one relies on an imaginary consort and only imaginatively creates the presence of the number of female and male figures of the mandala is a facsimile of a feast and is the style of the ritual feasts of present-day mantra practitioners (*IOK*, vol. III, pp. 552-560). For a discussion of the term *ganacakra*, see Guenther's *Creative Vision*, pp. 120-121.

186. As stated in the tantras, every woman possesses the nature of wisdom and is the embodiment of all adamantine sky-farers (*dākinis*). Nature of wisdom refers to the knowledge of reality. A woman is said to possess wisdom-nature because she is the basis that points to such knowledge or the basis upon which such knowledge can be realized, as the active consort in the third initiation. For these reasons, she should not be disrespected but always revered, as stated by the master Kanha:

> Upon seeing any woman
> Circumambulate her counterclockwise three times,
> Bowing your head
> Supplicate her thrice:
> "O mother, I am your son!
> Thus, from now until awakening,
> Nurture me with the milk
> Of the factors leading to awakening
> That springs from your breast" (*TV*, vol. Ca, ff. 153a4-5; 153b3; 155a1-3).

187. *Indestructible Nucleus' Ornament Tantra* (*Vajrahrdayālamkāratantra; rDo rje snying po rgyan gyi rgyud*) (Toh. 451).

188. Black Yamari tantras (*Krsnayamāritantra; gShin rje gshed nag po'i rgyud* [Toh. 469] and *Yamārikrsnakarmasarvacakrasiddhikaratantra; gShin rje'i gshed dgra nag po'i 'khor lo las thams cad grub par byed pa'i rgyud* [Toh. 473]); Red Yamari tantras (*Raktayamāritantra; gShin rje'i gshed dmar po'i rgyud* [Toh. 474] and *Madraktayamāritantra; gShin rje gshed dmar po'i rgyud* [Toh. 475]).

189. *Indestructible Tent Tantra*, f. 64b3-4.

190. Manjushriyashas presents this in his work called *Essence Ornament of the General Procedure for All Secrets* (*Sarvaguhyavidhigarbhālamkāra; gSang ba thams cad kyi spyi'i cho ga'i snying po rgyan*) (Toh. 2490), f. 234a5-6.

191. Manjushriyashas adds that even if she has the proper qualifications, it is a downfall to rely on her out of attachment or without the wish to attain perfect peace (*ERD*, f. 219a6-7).

192. See note 145.

193. Proclaimers also include solitary sages, who although possessing the view of selflessness are satisfied with the conduct of observing the ethics related to body and speech only, and strive for their own individual freedom (*TV*, vol. Ca, f. 158a3-5).

194. According to the Kalachakra Tantra, the outer (*phyi*) level denotes our world system; the inner (*nang*) level, the adamantine body; and the alternative (*gzhan*) level, the mandala of Kalachakra (*IOK*, vol. I, p. 214).

195. Personal instructions (*slob bshad*): instructions related to the [two or three] higher initiations, which empower the disciple to cultivate the phase of completion of the Highest Yoga Tantra. Collective explanations (*tshogs bshad*): instructions related to the vase initiation, which authorizes one to cultivate the phase of creation of the Highest Yoga Tantra.

On this subject, Kongtrul states that among the six parameters and four styles for expounding the tantras, the following may be taught to an assembly of disciples: the literal meaning or standard terminology (*sgra ji bzhin pa*); non-interpretable meaning (*dgongs pa can min pa*); provisional meaning (*drang don*); explanation of the words (*yi ge'i don*); and general explanation (*spyi'i don*). The following are taught only to jewel-like disciples: non-literal meaning or coined terminology (*sgra ji bzhin min pa*); teachings on the phase of completion that represent the definitive meaning (*nges don*); interpretable teachings (*dgongs bshad*); the hidden meaning (*sbas don*); and ultimate meaning (*mthar thug pa'i don*). Public explanations are therefore restricted to those concerning the phase of creation and related topics, excluding [practices involving] passion which are to be kept secret. Personal instructions are those concerning the phase of completion (*IOK*, vol. II, pp. 722-723). On the six alternatives, see also Shraddhakaravarman's *Commentary on the Seven Ornaments of the Compendium of Pristine Awareness Tantra* (*Ye shes rdo rje kun las btus pa'i rgyud las 'byung ba'i rgyan bdun rnam par dgrol ba*) (Toh. 1789), f. 9b1.

196. The Guyhasamaja Tantra speaks of five types of disciples: the blue-lotus-like person (*ut pa la lta bu'i gang zag*), the white-lotus-like person (*pad dkar lta bu'i gang zag*), the lotus-like person (*pad ma lta bu'i gang zag*), the sandalwood-like person (*can da na lta bu'i gang zag*), and the jewel-like person (*rin po che lta bu'i gang zag*).

The blue-lotus-like person, although capable of apprehending the meanings and words of what is taught, immediately forgets them. Such a disciple is like a blue lotus, fragrant while growing in the water, but losing its fragrance and withering as soon as it is plucked.

The white-lotus-like person, although learned and capable of understanding correctly the meaning of what is taught through intelligent reflection, is like a seed in a vase filled with cotton which cannot sprout. Like a white lotus whose fragrance remains in its bud and does not diffuse, such a one is unable to transmit knowledge to others.

The lotus-like person has compassion and discriminative awareness, and after learning the teachings, is capable of opening another's mind. However, since a thorough experience has not been gained, these qualities do not last. He or she is like a lotus which has a good fragrance but the drop of dew at the center of its bud cannot be held and vanishes as soon as the sun rises.

The sandalwood-like type of disciple has little knowledge but claims to know everything. He or she lacks the foundations of familiarity with reasonings and scriptures, yet speaks a great deal and is incapable of acquiring true qualities.

Just as it is not advisable to get near to a sandalwood tree that bears no fruit and has many thorns as well as a venomous snake coiled around its trunk, it is not advisable for a master to get close to such a disciple.

The jewel-like disciple maintains pure ethics and conduct; wise, perfected in learning, reflection, and meditation, he or she endeavors in what is wholesome, exercises discriminative awareness, demonstrates a naturally sharp intelligence, has an earnest interest only in the Secret Mantra, does not mix the view with that of other systems, and can teach correctly in accordance with the scriptures. He or she is like a jewel that is hard to find, but once found, fulfills one's wishes.

The best disciple is the jewel-like; the other three are middling, and the sandalwood, the least preferred. Among the middling three, the lotus-like is best, the white lotus, middling, and blue lotus, least preferred. The sandalwood-like disciple is hard like matter, but can be taught the collective instructions since he or she is inspired to listen to the tantras and gradually with training will acquire a supreme intelligence. See Pema Karpo's *TV*, vol. Ca, ff. 101a3-102a5; Kongtrul's *IOK*, vol. II, pp. 723-724; Aryadeva's *Commentary on the Clear Lamp* (*Pradīpodyotananāmaṭīkā; sGron ma gsal ba zhes bya ba'i 'grel bshad*) (Toh. 1794), f. 172a1-173b3.

197. Showing secret articles (*gsangs ston*): to show images of tantric deities, volumes of the tantras, symbolic hand gestures, vajra, bell, etc., to someone who has not received the initiation or has no faith.

198. The works of Manjushriyashas referred to here are the *Explanation of Root Tantric Downfalls (ERD)* and the *Essence Ornament of the General Procedure for All Secrets*.

199. Taranatha (1575-1634), whose real name was Kunga Nyingpo (Kun dga' snying po), composed numerous works on tantra and history. Being a direct disciple of Indian mahasiddhas, he became a vital link in the transmission of various meditation instructions and practices. A scholar of exceptional brilliance, possessed of analytical and critical talents, and an outstanding meditation master, Taranatha was, however, the object of criticism by his contemporaries, who apparently could not tolerate his unorthodox view on extrinsic emptiness. His beneficial influence on the development of Tibetan Buddhism is widely recognized and felt even now. He is often referred to as the Lord of Jonang to indicate his affiliation with the Jonang school.

200. This same list of eight secondary downfalls is found in *Yan lag gi dam tshig* (Toh. 2483), author unnamed. It is not found in Garbhapada's *Explanation of Root Tantric Downfalls (rDo rje theg pa'i rtsa ba'i ltung ba'i rgya cher 'grel pa)* (Toh. 2486). These eight are also similarly explained with some elaboration in Lakshminkara's *Explanation of the Fourteen Root Tantric Downfalls (Vajrayānacaturdaśamūlāpattivṛtti; rDo rje theg pa'i rtsa ba'i ltung ba bcu bzhi pa'i 'grel pa)* (Toh. 2485). The text *Elimination of Errors* is unidentified.

201. According to Denma Locho Rinpoché, physical seal (*lus kyi phyag rgya*) refers to seals as symbolic gestures, bodily postures, yogic exercises, etc.

202. See note 126.

203. Two works of Śūra (dPa' bo) or Ashvaghosha contained in the Tengyur (*Vajrayānamūlāpattisaṃgraha; rDo rje theg pa rtsa ba'i ltung ba bsdus pa* [Toh. 2478] and *Sthūlāpatti; lTung ba sbom po* [Toh. 2479]) deal with the fourteen root and the eight secondary tantric downfalls respectively. Following these two, the Dergé Tengyur contains two short works comprised of few lines each (*lTung ba bco lnga pa* [Toh. 2480] and *Yan lag gi nyes pa bdun pa* [Toh. 2481]), the authors of which are not specified, which present respectively the fifteen infractions related to charismatic activity and the seven branch infractions. It could be that Kongtrul considers their author to be Shura or Ashvaghosha. (Tibetan historians consider Ashvaghosha and Shura to be the same person; modern historians believe them to be two different persons.)

The twenty-eight infractions are also discussed in Manjusriyashas's *ERD*.

204. To be irreverent toward one's meditational deity and to make discriminations between one deity and another, without realizing the sameness of all deities, in that all the transcendent ones have gathered into the deities' forms and embody their blessing. This is not an infraction when switching to another deity is done to obey the wish of one's master, to acquire special means of practice, or to perform different kinds of activities in particular situations. It is also not an infraction if one understands the sameness of all deities (*ERD*, f. 221a1-2).

205. This does not constitute an infraction if one does not perform these practices due to being engaged in works for one's master or when sick (*ERD*, f. 221a5).

206. This does not constitute an infraction when done to uplift someone spiritually; when in the presence of one's master [or vajra siblings, etc.]; if one's life would be at risk; or if one has to do so as a form of punishment (*ERD*, f. 221a6).

207. To transgress the directives of the teachings out of attachment to worldly things. This does not qualify as an infraction when done as a means to uplift somebody or for the sake of experiencing great bliss (*ERD*, f. 221b6).

208. The correct time would be when one has reached the spiritual level necessary for that activity. Activities are distinguished as those performed by a beginner, by one who has attained a slight degree of stability, by one who has attained stability, and by one who has attained greater stability (*ERD*, f. 222a1).

209. If one's relationship to the master dissolves, no attainments will result from one's spiritual efforts. There is no infraction if he or she is not an authentic tantric master. A false master is one who has no knowledge of mantric principles, is ignorant of the Universal Way's teachings, lacks compassion, has no faith in or enthusiasm for the teachings, is always engrossed in unwholesome behavior, and despises the tantric treatises (*ERD*, f. 227a7-b2).

210. Desire here stands for the entire range of one's emotions (*ERD*, f. 227b4-5).

211. The Three Jewels include the master and special companions such as vajra siblings (*ERD*, f. 227b6).

212. In order not to incur this infraction, the practitioner should always engage in virtue with the initial motivation of attaining awakening, the final dedication

of the merit for the same aim, and the understanding of the emptiness of merit, dedication, and the goal to which they are dedicated (*ERD*, f. 228a1).

213. To transfer consciousness to higher states when the time of death has come, but not before the signs indicating death are manifest (*TV*, vol. Ca, f. 160a2-3).

On this point, Manjushriyashas says: The transference of consciousness as the yogin (or yogini) dies pertains to the perfection of wisdom. At the time of death, the yogin, viewing all things as an illusion in the mode of the two truths (conventional and ultimate), remains free from attachment and anger, and clearly imagines the mandala of the deity. As the stages of death occur, the yogin absorbs the mandala into intrinsic pristine awareness in the following way. The three worlds are imagined to dissolve into light, which is viewed as the mandala. This then dissolves into the seed syllable in the midst of wisdom and means, and that syllable then dissolves at the heart region along with the light (*ERD*, f. 228a7-b1).

214. The Individual Way, Universal Way, and Way of Indestructible Reality.

215. See chapter I, "The Tantric Master" section.

216. *Red Yamari Tantra* (*Raktayamāritantra; gShin rje'i gshed dmar po'i rgyud*) (Toh. 474), f. 213.

217. The Path and its Fruition (*lam 'bras*): teachings forming a meditational system particular to the Sakya school of Tibetan Buddhism, originally expounded by the Indian saint Virupa.

218. The three realities (*ngo bo nyid gsum*): the aspect or "side" of appearance (*snang phyogs*) of the deity; the aspect or "side" of emptiness (*stong phyogs*); and the union of appearance and emptiness (*zung 'jug gi ngo bo nyid*). Not one of the three realities is a manifestation of unawareness; each is free of mental projections. Thus, the three are of identical natures and are differentiated only categorically. They are posited as a yogin's non-conceptual experience of contemplation. (*The Slob bshad Tradition of the Sa skya Lam 'bras* [*gSung ngag lam 'bras slob bshad chen mo*], [25 vols. Dehra Dun: Sakya College, 1983] vol. Ma (XVI), ff. 88b3-90a1).

Regarding the three realities, H. H. Sakya Trizin explains that in the context of the pledges of the four initiations, equipoise (*mnyam gzhag*) refers to the mundane path linked to the phase of creation when there is no actual pristine awareness; and post-equipoise conduct (*rjes spyod*), to the transmundane path or result of equipoise. The side of appearance refers to the deity appearing by itself, without any effort or conceptual process whatsoever; the side of emptiness refers to the subsiding of the deity in favor of emptiness; and union refers to the indivisibility of appearance and emptiness in the rainbow-like or illusory body of the deity.

219. This refers to the fourteen root tantric downfalls and the eight secondary ones mentioned above.

220. Control of breath and channels (*rtsa rlung*) refers to the retention of the breath (*srog rtsol*) or vajra recitation (*rdo rje'i bzlas pa*), the three branches of exhalation

(*gtong ba'i yan lag gsum*), the two branches of inhalation (*dgang ba'i yan lag gnyis*), and dwelling of the breath inside (*gnas pa*). (*The Slob bshad Tradition of the Sa skya Lam 'bras*, vol. Ma, ff. 99b2-113a1.)

221. Here one speaks of self-existing pristine awareness (*rang 'byung ye shes*) because such pristine awareness arises through the mystic heat practice and without the external aid of a consort. It refers to the experience of the view gained through *caṇḍālī* (mystic heat). (*The Slob bshad Tradition of the Sa skya Lam 'bras*, vol. Ma, ff. 113a1-114b1.)

222. Here mandala circle (*dkyil 'khor 'khor lo*) refers to the practices with a real or imaginary consort. See note 322.

223. See *The Slob bshad Tradition of the Sa skya Lam 'bras*, vol. Ma, ff. 121a1-122a5.

224. The six losses of the seminal essence (*thig le 'dzag pa drug*): loss due to illness (*nad kyis 'dzag pa*); spirits (*gdon*); diet (*bzas*); behavior (*spyod lam*); pleasure (*bde bas*), i.e., abundance of seminal fluid due to passion (*chags pa'i stobs*) or the presence of a wisdom-consort (*rig ma'i stobs*) (verbal communication of H. H. Sakya Trizin).

225. The three waves (*rba rlabs gsum*). Here, "vajra" means adorned by non-conceptual bliss; "waves" refers to dualistic conceptions (*gnyis 'dzin gyi rtog pa*). Waves are of the nature of the ocean and are absorbed back into it; likewise, dualistic conceptions are not beyond the nature of emptiness and bliss and are absorbed into it. They number three as they relate to body, speech, and mind.

The practice related to the three waves is intended to subdue dualistic conceptions: with respect to the body, one practices the vase-breath retention (*kumbhaka*), with respect to the speech, one controls the winds in gentle and forceful techniques; and with respect to the mind, one engages in the wave of contemplation relying on an actual or imaginary consort. (*The Slob bshad Tradition of the Sa skya Lam 'bras*, vol. Ma, ff. 88b3-90b1).

226. Emotional impediments and impediments to knowledge.

227. *Padmini* usually denotes the best of the five types of consorts whose names derive from the *Kamashastra* literature, namely, *mṛgī* (*ri dwags can*), *hastinī* (*glang po can*), *śaṅkhinī* (*dung can*) and *citriṇī* (*sna tshogs can*). Here, however, it seems to be used generally to encompass both good and bad types. *The Slob bshad Tradition of the Sa skya Lam 'bras* speaks of three types of *padminī*. The first and best *padminī* resembles a white bird, has a red channel at the *bhaga* (vagina), a rough body, reddish at the root of the eyes, slim, particularly at the waist, has reddish feet, and good teeth. By relying on her, one achieves enlightenment in the same lifetime. The second and middling has white skin, belongs to an outstanding family, has rough bones, and a large bosom; she behaves outrageously, has a beautiful face, bears only sons, cannot be influenced, and is expert in worldly offerings and activities. By relying on her, if one finds her channel [at the vagina], one attains enlightenment in less than a year. The third and least has a white complexion, is not pleased even if one treats her well, cannot keep tantric

secrets, uses make-up on her body and face, laughs, speaks a lot, has bulging eyes, and is gullible. She is not to be relied upon (vol. Ma, ff. 123a1-5).

228. Citation found in *Samputa Tantra* vol. Ga, f. 158a4-6. Reading *nyid* for *gnyis* (on the basis of Khenpo Apé's handwritten notes to the *Samputa Tantra*).

229. *Indestructible Nucleus' Ornament Tantra*, f. 48a2-5.

230. Naropa defines the different seals: The action seal (*karmamudrā, las rgya*) is a real woman, with breasts and hair; she is the cause for the bliss related to the desire realm (*'dod spyod las rgya*). She is an "action" seal as she performs such actions as kissing, embracing, making contact with the secret parts, etc. She is "seal" as she bestows bliss, in this case a mutable (*kṣara, 'gyur ba*) bliss.

The pristine awareness (*jñānamudrā, ye shes kyi phyag rgya*) or imaginary seal is constructed by one's mind, and consists of various deities, such as Vishvamata. She is the cause for the bliss related to the form realm, which is an unsteady (*spanda, g.yo ba*) bliss.

The great seal (*mahāmudrā, phyag rgya chen po*) is the pristine awareness of an immutable (*akṣara, mi 'gyur ba*) and supreme bliss.

(*Commentary on the Summary of the Kalachakra Initiation*, ff. 273b3-274a1). See also Vajrapani's *Eulogy-Commentary on the Chakrasamvara Tantra* (*Lakṣābhi-dhānāduddhṛtalaghutantrapiṇḍārthavivaraṇa; bsTod 'grel/ mNgon par brjod pa 'bum pa las phyung ba nyung ngu'i rgyud kyi bsdus pa'i don rnam par bshad pa*) (Toh. 1402) (henceforth cited as *EC*), f. 125a7-b5.

231. According to Pema Karpo, to cultivate the pledge in this context refers to enhancing or preserving the four aspects of bodhichitta (seminal essence) which have the nature of the sixteen joys (f. 176b1). See note 243.

232. The *Hevajra Tantra* speaks of four types of consorts: the consort of the vajra family of Akshobhya is a washer woman (*gyung mo*); that of the lotus family of Amitabha, a dancer (*gar ma*); that of the action family of Amoghasiddhi, a dyer (*tshos mkhan ma*); that of the transcendent family of Vairochana, a brahmin girl (*bram ze mo*); and that of the jewel family of Ratnasambhava, an outcaste girl (*gdol pa ma*) (Kongtrul's *Commentary on the Hevajra Tantra*, f. 78a7-b4).

A yogin must rely on a consort who belongs to his own family. For example, if he is of the lotus family, he should rely on a consort of the lotus family. Complexion is a factor clearly indicating the family a consort belongs to. The color of the Vairochana family is white; therefore, a consort of that family would be a qualified brahmin girl or another of white complexion. When a consort of his own family is not found, he may resort to one of another family. A non-human consort, such as a deva or celestial musician (*gandharva*), is also suitable (ff. 93b2-94a3).

233. See following note.

234. Naropa explains that the end of the full moon (*nya'i mthar*) refers to the innate bliss which is correlated to the sixteenth of the month. The waning (dark) phase of the moon (*nag po'i phyogs*) refers to the joy or bliss which has gone beyond the innate one (the sixteenth), i.e., waning due to the outpouring of seminal fluid.

To explain, through the heat or fire of attachment aroused by the imaginary or real presence of a consort, a yogi awakens the seminal essence which rests at the crown of the head. The seminal essence then descends as far as the tip of the organ, where instead of outflowing, it is held and reversed upward to the crown of the head. The descent of the seminal essence is characterized by four stages of increasingly higher delight: initial delight (*prathamānanda*), supreme delight (*paramānanda*), special delight (*viramānanda*), and innate delight (*sahajānanda*). These occur as the seminal essence reaches the four focal points of energy: throat, heart, navel, and secret parts. At the throat, seminal essence is associated with pristine awareness; at the heart, with the mind; at the navel, with the speech; at the secret region, with the body. These are often spoken of as the four seminal essences (*bindu*). Each of the stages of delight has four degrees called delight of body (*kāyānanda*), of speech (*vāgānanda*), of mind (*cittānanda*), and pristine awareness (*jñānanda*).

When the seminal essence is lost and the experience of the four delights which are pervaded by passion (*rāga*) come to an end, there is a period of satisfaction or disgust (*virāga*). This period has four moments characterized by the above four delights but in the reverse order. First is the multiform delight, followed by the supreme delight, then initial delight, and finally a moment of total lack of passion called absence of moon (*naṣṭacandra*).

Such process is paralleled to the waxing and waning phases of the moon, the moon internally being the seminal essence in its fifteen clear and the fifteen dark moments. The seminal essence at the focal point of energy at the crown of the head is the new moon which aroused by passion grows through fifteen moments (*kalā*) to reach its fullness, the full moon, just before emission. The sixteenth day or moment concluding the clear fifteen moments is the innate bliss and that concluding the dark fifteen moments is the absence of moon or dark moon. The task of the yogin in this process is to prevent the outflow of the seminal essence: once it has reached the tip of the organ to reverse its course upward in order to attain immutable bliss (*Iniziazione Kālacakra*, pp. 68-80; 305-308).

235. Reading *bsrub* for *srung*.

236. Female (*mi mo*) refers to wisdom, transcendent (*pha rol tu phyin pa*) and all-good (*kun tu bzang mo*). The conduct (*spyod pa*) of the female is the practice done in order to accomplish altruistic aims (*TV*, vol. Ca, f. 177a1-2; *EC*, f. 138b6).

237. Chastity refers to great bliss; face of the vajra (*rdo rje'i zhal*), to the orifice of the penis (*rdo rje'i sgo*) (*EC*, f. 139b2).

238. Drawing the seminal essence up the channels (*rtsa'i kun tu spyod pa*) (*TV*, vol. Ca, f. 177a3-5; *EC*, f. 139a1-b2).

239. *EC*, f. 139a2.

240. *TV*, vol. Ca, f. 222a2 and following.

241. Ritual articles include vajra, bell, the six kinds of symbolic ornaments of a heruka, the *khaṭvāṇga* (mystic staff) appropriate to one's buddha family, three

kinds of small drums symbolizing the outer, inner, and secret aspects, the skull-cup, the rosary for mantra recitation appropriate to the specific activity one intends to perform, images, the volumes of the tantras, the double-twined cord, the elephant skin, and the tiger skin to be used during ritual feast and other appropriate occasions, articles to be used during the fire offering and other rituals, etc. (*TV*, vol. Ca, ff. 167b5-168a2).

242. These include the five sense objects (form, sound, odor, taste, and tactile objects); the five meats (that of ox, dog, horse, elephant, and human); the five nectars (the white and red bodhichitta, feces, urine, and the pure essence of the great flesh); the five drinks (spirits made from honey, sugar cane, fruit essence, tree sap, and brewed alcohol); the five consorts (belonging to the five families such as the vajra family); and the seventy-two types of meat (of dog, ox, elephant, sheep, goat, deer, donkey, pig, camel, etc.) (*TV*, vol. Ca, f. 168a2-6).

243. Pema Karpo explains the hidden meanings of each of these four: to take life, tell lies, steal, and have intercourse with the spouse of another. To take life means to stop the vital energy within one's body, i.e., to dissolve one's body and all phenomena into the state of clear light. To block the body's vital energy is also explained as to block (stabilize) the seminal essence at the crown of one's head. Moreover, it means to block the flow of the five major winds, the ten subsidiary [winds], and the 21,000 [daily breaths], called "vital [energy]" (*prāṇa, srog*) within the right (*rasanā*) and left (*lalanā*) channels.

With respect to the causal aspect of the practice, to block the vital winds means to exhaust the flow of winds in the central channel as a result of which seminal essence rises to the crown of the head. Also, the *Hevajra Tantra* says:

> By blocking the body
> The vital wind is blocked.
> Firmly blocking the vital wind
> Controls bodhichitta.
> By blocking bodhichitta
> Transmigration is blocked.
> When transmigration is blocked, in that instant
> All yogins become buddhas themselves.

The *Guhyasamaja Tantra* states:

> Vitality indicates the great wind that always moves.
> To block or bind that is to take life.
> It does not mean to kill someone.

To take the life of the vital energy also means to rest in the equipoise in which there is no artificiality as to unfabricated reality. When through such an indestructible practice one attains contemplation in the state of emptiness by understanding the nature of all phenomena included in the aggregates, elements, sense fields and so on, the artificiality with regard to them is destroyed. Also, the *Commentary on the Essence* states:

> Vital energy is mind
> And mind is wind and semen.

To tell lies refers to the indestructible sound or inexpressible word that imparts in the different languages of sentient beings simultaneously the teaching that all inner and outer phenomena, beings and their environment, are not permanent, not made by a creator, but are arising interdependently, like magical illusions.

To steal comprises four pledges. The first is the pledge of the vajra body which refers to the seminal essence that has the nature of the Buddha's body and produces the waking state. Melted by the passion of the wisdom woman, the seminal essence is preserved in lotus (at the secret place). That essence has four aspects: the joy of body, the joy of speech, the joy of mind, and the joy of pristine awareness. To maintain that essence, one consumes the great flesh, where flesh represents the aggregate of mental formations and to consume means to clear it of impediments.

The pledge of the vajra speech refers to the seminal essence that has the nature of the Buddha's speech and produces the dream state. Melted by the passion of the wisdom woman (consort), it is preserved in the lotus of the navel. That also has four aspects, the supreme joy of body, the supreme joy of speech, the supreme joy of mind, and the supreme joy of pristine awareness. Enlightened body, speech, and mind, and pristine awareness are one in the form of the seminal essence at the navel and thus should be protected. That protection occurs with the "unchanging vajra speech," i.e., the bliss of the non-emitted essence of bodhichitta, which is called great since it does not change for an instant. To maintain that essence of vajra speech, one consumes feces and urine, which means to free the aggregate of consciousness from impediments.

The pledge of vajra mind refers to the seminal essence that has the nature of the Buddha's mind and produces deep sleep. Melted by the passion of the wisdom woman (consort), it is preserved in the lotus of the heart. That essence has four aspects: the special joy of body, special joy of speech, special joy of mind, and special joy of pristine awareness. To maintain that essence, one consumes blood and semen, which means to free respectively the aggregate of feeling and that of perception from impediments. In relation to this pledge, it is also stated that with stable conduct, the yogin should always rely on an action seal (consort) without emission of seminal fluid: this means to be endowed with the pledge of the vajra mind.

The pledge of vajra pristine awareness refers to the seminal essence that has the nature of the Buddha's pristine awareness and produces the fourth pivotal state. Melted by the passion of the wisdom woman (consort), it is preserved in the lotus of the throat. It has four aspects: the innate joy of body, the innate joy of speech, the innate joy of mind, and the innate joy of pristine awareness. It is to be maintained by consuming form and other sense objects, the six sense consciousnesses, etc. These are the pledges pertaining to stealing; the pristine awareness of great bliss or the Buddha's pristine awareness is understood by one's own intrinsic awareness and is not dependent on others. In this sense, it is "stolen."

To have intercourse with the woman of another is to be interpreted in relation to the state of union. "Another" stands for Vajrasattva or for "best." The Vajrasattva or best woman is the blessed transcendent wisdom mother, the consort (mother) of all buddhas. That mother, possessing observable attributes, is called wisdom woman, and being supremely endowed with aspects is called emptiness or the great seal. Having intercourse with the woman of another refers to the blissful union with such a "mother" without losing the seminal essence (*TV,* vol. Ca, f. 169a6 onward).

244. In this class of pledges, Pema Karpo also includes the nine pledges concerning conduct taught in the *Abhidhana Tantra* or *Unsurpassable Chakrasamvara Tantra* (f. 183b5) (see above section on "Conduct," page 246), and the six modes of conduct for practitioners who dwell in a constant state of contemplation (f. 184b5), taught in the *Indestructible Tent Tantra* (page 273).

245. *Indestructible Tent Tantra,* f. 64b6. Kongtrul explains that the pristine awareness of experiential warmth (*drod kyi ye shes*) is that of a yogin (or yogini) on the tantric path of preparation of the Highest Tantra. Such a yogin has experienced the phase of completion and thus continually engages in the metaphorical pristine awareness. He has acquired proficiency in the states of bliss, clarity, and non-conceptuality, as indicated by the signs of warmth. The pristine awareness at this stage is known as experiential warmth because it serves as a direct cause that leads to the path of seeing. The signs indicating warmth are lesser, middling, and great. The lesser signs are that a yogin is no longer subject to fear, madness, sorrow, pain, or frustration, and cannot be injured; and the middling, that he is not affected by strong desire, hatred, ignorance, or other emotions that arise through the force of major circumstances. The great signs include clairvoyance and other miraculous powers. These signs concord with the stages of warmth, peak, and acceptance explained in the Way of the Perfections. Once the yogin has experienced these signs, if he enhances his realization through the complex, non-elaborated, and simple tantric practices, he will swiftly reach the path of seeing (*Commentary on [Rangjung Dorjé's] Profound Reality* Rumtek, Sikkim: Dharma Charkra Centre, 1981, ff. 155a3-b3).

The signs that indicate experiential warmth (*drod rtags*) are usually understood as those that indicate the yogin's maturity for special tantric practices that accelerate spiritual accomplishment. As taught in the second book of the *Hevajra Tantra,*

> Fear, madness, and likewise sorrow and pain,
> Frustration and injury,
> Great desire, hatred, and ignorance
> Do not obscure the adept.

In addition, Tibetan masters speak of three degrees of warmth, the best being the understanding of reality; the middling, the leveling of the eight worldly concerns; and the least, the ability to demonstrate magical feats (Kongtrul's *Commentary on the Hevajra Tantra,* f. 93a1-5).

246. Pema Karpo states that in the first two cases, a root downfall is incurred. There is no real failing if the pledge is transgressed because of illness, lack of control, for the sake of others, for a greater scope, when the practitioner has a

stable [understanding of the] unborn nature of things or has attained powers, has been given dispensation, is following the directive of a spiritual master, or to avert an impediment [to one's life] (*TV*, vol. Ca, f. 156a4-6).

247. Manjushriyashas's *Essence Ornament of the General Procedure for All Secrets*, f. 234b6-7.

248. *Dakinisamvara Tantra* (*Ḍākinīsaṃvaratantrarāja; mKha 'gro ma'i sdom pa'i rgyud*) (Toh. 406), f. 243b3-4.

249. These are the first initiations in the Kalachakra system. The first seven of the eleven initiations are the water, diadem, silk ribbon, vajra and bell, conduct, name, and permission initiation. The uncommon vase and the other three (secret, pristine-awareness-through-wisdom, and word) initiations form the first set of higher initiations in the Kalachakra Tantra. See note 148.

250. By Manjushriyashas, ff. 237a7-238b2.

251. The yoga of the seminal essence (*binduyoga, thig le'i rnal 'byor*) here refers to the meditation in which one first transforms oneself into the deity while clearly visualizing the vital points of energy. Then, holding the energies at the navel, one causes the seminal essence or glorious essence (*dpyid thig*) to melt and descend. The subtle yoga (*suksmayoga, phra mo'i rnal 'byor*) refers to the meditation in which one focuses the mind on the subtle implements of the five buddhas visualized in the center of the five points of energy (Dharmashri's *Commentary on the Three Vows*, f. 287b1-2).

These are yogas that are largely part of the phase of completion called self-consecration (*rang byin rlabs*). See Kongtrul's discussion of the different traditions of the completion phase in *IOK*, Book VIII, chapter III, pp. 210-275.

252. Burning black sesame seeds in a ritual for which the main deity is the male Vajradaka (rDo rje mkha' 'gro).

253. See note 185.

254. Vajrasattva (rDo rje sems dpa', lit. "Adamantine Being"): in another context the progenitor of all buddha families, here Vajrasattva stands as the epitome of purification deities. Depicted as a white male deity, holding the vajra at the heart with the right hand and the bell on the hip with the left, he sits on a moon disc placed on a lotus. The methods of meditation and mantra recitation in relation to Vajrasattva vary according to different traditions. For examples, see Geshé Rabten's *The Preliminary Practices of Tibetan Buddhism* (Burton, Washington: Tusum Ling Publications, 1974) and Kongtrul's *Lamp of the Definitive Meaning of the Great Seal* (*Phyag chen sngon 'gro bzhi sbyor dang dngos gzhi'i khrid rim mdor bsdus nges don sgron me*) (dPal spungs: 1844); Reprinted in Rumtek, Sikkim: Dharma Chakra Centre, 1975.

Samayavajra (Dam tshig rdo rje, lit. "Adamantine Pledge"): considered to be an aspect of Vajrasattva specifically linked to the purification of the transgression of tantric pledges.

255. The special higher initiations are the pristine-awareness-through-wisdom initiation and word initiation.

256. Self-blessing or self-consecration (svādiṣṭhāna, rang byin rlabs): meditational practices belonging to the causal phase of completion (rgyu'i rdzogs rim) where the adept focuses on the mystic heat (me), seminal essence points (thig le), or letters (yi ge) within the central channel. Kongtrul explains: It is natural that wherever the mind is directed, right there the winds gather. Thus, through meditation focusing on those [above mentioned] objects, the winds first gather, then remain, and finally dissolve into the middle of the focal point of energy ('khor lo) upon which one's meditation is directed. When the winds dissolve, many special modes of dissolution of the levels of subtle and gross seminal essences and bliss [resulting from] the melting [of seminal essence] are produced (IOK, vol. II, Book VI, chapter IV, pp. 685-686).

The stages of self-consecration generally refer to the relative aspect of the completion phase of the Highest Yoga Tantra that has two aspects, the meditational practices related to the caṇḍālī or mystic heat and those intended for the attainment of the illusory body (sgyu lus). See Kongtrul's lengthy discussion of the various traditions of the completion phase in IOK, Book VIII, chapter III, pp. 210-275.

257. The Ancient Translation School enumerates nine ways of spiritual development (theg pa'i rim pa dgu): those of the proclaimers (śrāvaka, nyan thos), the solitary sages (pratyekabuddha, rang rgyal ba), and the bodhisattvas (bodhisattva, byang chub sems dpa') (which belong to the indicative [mtshan nyid] or causal [rgyu] way); Kriyatantra (bya ba'i rgyud), Upayatantra or Charyatantra (upa'i rgyud, spyod pa'i rgyud), and Yogatantra (rnal 'byor gyi rgyud) (the three outer tantras); Mahayoga (rnal 'byor chen po), Anuyoga (rjes su rnal 'byor) Atiyoga (shin tu rnal 'byor) or Great Perfection (the three inner tantras).

Kriyatantra, Upayatantra, and Yogatantra are known as outer tantras, as their focuses of practice and abandonments, antidotes, and so forth resemble those of the outer Indicative Way. Mahayoga, Anuyoga, and Atiyoga are known as inner since through these ways the very nature of mind spontaneously manifests as the mandala of pristine awareness and its dimensions; thus, perfection is not sought somewhere else but is seen as one's own natural pristine awareness. According to the great perfection system, all paths to freedom fall into these nine ways, and all these nine are encompassed by the Way of Great Perfection.

Because of the swiftness and depth of the techniques of the various systems of tantra, in particular mahayoga, anuyoga, and atiyoga, they are known collectively as the Way of Skillful Means (thabs kyi theg pa).

For a detailed discussion of these nine spiritual ways, see Dudjom Rinpoche's The Nyingma School of Tibetan Buddhism: Its Fundamentals and History (Boston: Wisdom Publications, 1991) (henceforth cited as NSH).

258. Concise Heruka Tantra, in NG, vol. Ra, f. 20b3.

259. See note 316.

260. Lilavajra's *Shimmering Light on the Pledges*, f. 36b1-2. Lilavajra (sGeg pa'i rdo rje) was a disciple of the great master Lalitavajra (Rol pa'i rdo rje) from Oddiyana. He committed to writing the many instructions that his master had brought from that land. Lilavajra was in turn the master of Manjushrishrijnana.

261. On the six masters, or the six roles of a master in the case of a master who performs all roles, Longchenpa explains these five: the master who leads (*'dren pa'i bla ma*) is the preceptor who confers the novice ordination (more generally, the first teacher to encourage and introduce one to the teachings, explain the benefits, give the vows of refuge, etc.).

The master who opens one's mind (*shes rgyud 'grol ba'i bla ma*) is the one who explains the teachings and by doing so breaks the "shell" constraining one's intelligence.

The master who imparts the secret instructions (*man ngag ston cing lung 'pog pa'i bla ma*) is the spiritual friend in the presence of whom one takes the commitments of awakening mind. More generally, it is one who teaches the essence of view, meditation, and action; here, transmission (*lung*) of secret instructions refers to the empowered words spoken by a master of the three lineages (the intentional lineage of the buddhas, the symbolic lineage of the awareness-holders, and the aural lineage of ordinary individuals).

The master who restores infractions (*nyams chags skong ba'i slob dpon*) is the one to whom confession is made.

The master who confers initiation and pledges is the one who initiates one. See *Dispelling Darkness in the Ten Directions* (*Phyogs bcu'i mun sel*) (Published by Dilgo Kyentsé based on Adzon Drukpa [a 'dzom 'brug pa] redaction), a commentary on the Guhyagarbha Tantra, f. 278a1-b1.

On the master who is a leader of all (*spyi'i bla ma*), Dodrup Chen III Jikmé Tenpai Nyima's *General Meaning of the Guhyagarbha Tantra* (*gSang ba snying po spyi don*) (NKG, vol. 35/ci) explains that he is a master revered by all as a holy person, from whom one has received a measure of his kindness. This is a master who is not directly spoken of in the tantras (f. 82b1).

Similarly, Khetsun Sangpo Rinpoché comments: A "leader of all" is a master upon whom all followers of a particular system must rely. The teacher may be remote or close. Buddha Shakyamuni is the "remote master" to be relied upon by all Buddhists, while Garab Dorjé is an example of a remote master to be relied upon by all practitioners of great perfection. An example of the "close teacher of all" would be a universally respected master, such as the present Dalai Lama.

262. Lilavajra's *Shimmering Light*, f. 36b2.

263. Ibid., f. 36b2-4.

264. Ibid., f. 36b7.

265. Jadral Rinpoché explains *mantra* in this context in the following way: *rtsa* means root mantra; *skyed* means generation mantra; and *las sngags*, action mantra. Root mantra refers to one of the root mantras of the five Dhyani Buddhas, *OM HŪM TRAM HRĪ AH*, for example. An example of a generation mantra, so

called because through this the deity is generated, is *OM VAJRA VAIROCANA*. An example of an action mantra is *SARVA SIDDHI HŪM*, or one of the mantras associated with the four charismatic activities: for the pacifying activities, *ŚĀNTIM KURU SVĀHĀ*; for enriching, *PUṢṬIM KURU SVĀHĀ*; for domineering, *VAŚAM KURU SVĀHĀ*; and for fierce, *MĀRAYA* (these last are listed in Aryadeva's *Commentary on the Clear Lamp*, f. 166a5).

266. Lilavajra's *Shimmering Light on the Tantras*, f. 37a2-3.

267. Lilavajra includes among the pledge substances the special offerings to the Three Jewels, food offerings (*torma*) and collective offerings, the skull-cup (the wrathful container), the ritual dagger, the lotus (the peaceful container made of precious substances), secret substances, tantric instruments, and the mandala. Moreover, the sound of the yogin's bell and small drum should not be heard by others (*Shimmering Light*, f. 37a3-4).

268. The indivisibility of the two superior truths (*lhag pa'i bden pa gnyis dbyer med*) refers to the indivisibility of the superior ultimate and superior relative truths as explained in particular in the Mahayoga. To realize such indivisibility means to realize that all appearances are but the very nature of one's mind, i.e., the indivisibility of emptiness and appearances. Here, the two truths are called superior (*lhag pa*) because the way to realize the two truths in Mahayoga is superior to the way taught in the sutras (*IOK*, vol. II, Book VI, chapter IV).

269. This point is elucidated in Kongtrul's *Commentary on the Hevajra Tantra*: The ultimate queen (*btsun mo*) is supreme transcendent wisdom. Her seminal essence or fluid (*śukra, khu ba*) is non-dual pristine awareness. This pristine awareness is not given but "stolen" by the cultivation of the exalted path as the skillful means. The relative queen is the yogin's consort. Her seminal fluid is not given, but is drawn up and "stolen" by the strength of breath control (f. 219a4-5). Of the two types of queens, the ultimate one is emptiness; her "seminal fluid" is the correct realization of the meaning of emptiness (f. 299b5-6). The relative queen is of two types: the consort's body and one's own body. The first refers to the mantra-born and the other kinds of consorts. Her seminal essence or fluid is the white and red seminal essences (*bindu, thig le*) drawn up and stolen by the power of wind control. One's own body, which embodies skillful means, consists in the thirty-two channels of the four focal points of energy (*cakra, 'khor lo*) in the central channel (*avadhūtī, rtsa dbu ma*). The seminal fluid is the bliss experienced as the seminal essence descends through the focal points of energy or the central channel (f. 300a1-3).

270. Five poisons (emotions) (*pañcaviṣa, dug lnga*): desire (*rāga, 'dod chags*), hatred (*dveṣa, zhe sdang*), ignorance (*moha, gti mug*), pride (*māna, nga rgyal*), and jealousy (*īrṣyā, phrag dog*). The *Shimmering Light on the Pledges* distinguishes between the five ordinary and five perfect poisons. The five ordinary poisons are the five negative emotions, just as they are. In this system, these are not to be viewed as enemies, as proclaimers view them. Why is this so? Being empty of any nature, phenomena do not truly exist as objects to be forsaken. Thus, it is pointless to forsake the emotions in the same way that it is pointless to block the water in a mirage.

Further, since the five emotions are primordially the nature of the five pristine awarenesses, they should not to be forsaken [but used skillfully], just as one must first get the seeds if one wishes to produce sesame oil. Each emotion is the pledge of a buddha. For instance, ignorance is the pledge of Vairochana. Why a pledge? Because ignorance is not something to be abandoned. Similarly, intrinsic awareness is not something to be attained. In the sphere of reality these two are of one flavor. (Dharmashri's *Commentary on the Three Vows*, ff. 274b4-275a6). The five perfect poisons are explained in the course of the text itself.

271. The aggregates and the five male transcendent ones are associated in the following way: the aggregate of form (*rūpaskandha, gzugs kyi phung po*) is Vairochana; the aggregate of consciousness (*vijñānaskandha, rnam shes kyi phung po*), Akshobhya; the aggregate of feelings (*vedanāskandha, tshor ba'i phung po*), Ratnasambhava; the aggregate of perceptions (*samjñāskandha, 'du shes kyi phung po*), Amitabha; and the aggregate of volitions (*samskāraskandha, 'du byed kyi phung po*), Amoghasiddhi.

The elemental properties and the five female transcendent consorts are associated in the following way: cohesion (*chu*) is Mamaki (Ma ma ki); solidity (*sa*), Lochana (sByan ma); warmth (*me*), Pandara (Gos dkar mo); movement (*rlung*), Samayatara (Dam tshig sgrol ma); and space (*nam mkha'*), Dhatvishvari (dByings phyug ma).

The five sense organs (*pañcendriya, dbang po lnga*), the eye, ear, nose, tongue, and skin, and the related five sense consciousnesses (*indriyajñāna, dbang shes lnga*) are the male bodhisattvas Manjushri ('Jam dpal dbyang), Maitreya (Byams pa), Kshitigarbha (Sa'i snying po), Akashagarbha (Nam mkha'i snying po), Avalokiteshvara (sPyan ras gzigs), Vajrapani (Phyag na rdo rje), Nivaranavishkambhi (sGrib pa rnam sel), and Samantabhadra (Kun tu bzang po).

The five sense objects (*pañcavisaya, yul lnga*), form, sound, odor, taste, and tactile objects, are the female bodhisattvas Lasya (sGeg pa ma), Gita (Glu ma), Narti (Gar ma), Mala (Phreng ba ma), Dhupi (bDug spos ma), Pushpa (Me tog ma), Aloka (sNang gsal ma), and Ghanda (Dri chab ma).

The five colors and five pristine awarenesses are as follows: blue (for the vajra family) is Akshobhya's mirror-like pristine awareness (*ādarśajñāna, me long lta bu'i ye shes*), white (for the transcendent family) is Vairochana's pristine awareness of the sphere of reality (*dharmadhātujñāna, chos dbyings ye shes*), red (for the lotus family) is Amitabha's pristine awareness of discernment (*pratyavekṣaṇajñāna, so sor rtogs pa'i ye shes*), yellow (for the jewel family) is Ratnasambhava's pristine awareness of equality (*samatājñāna, mnyam nyid ye shes*), and green (for the action family) is Amoghasiddhi's aim-accomplishing pristine awareness (*kṛtyānuṣṭhānajñāna, bya sgrub ye shes*).

See Khenpo Yönten Gyatso (a disciple of Paltrul Rinpoché), *Commentary to [Longchenpa's] Treasury of Enlightned Qualities (Yon tan rin po che'i mdzod kyi 'grel pa zab don snang byed nyi ma'i 'od zer)*, Collected Works of the Nyingmapas (rNying ma bka' ma rgyas pa), vol. Thi (Delhi: Dudjom Rinpoche, 1982-87).

272. Full citation is in Dharmashri's *Commentary on the Three Vows* (f. 267a4-b2).

273. This means, for instance, not to discourage someone from making a large

offering or telling a practitioner of the Universal Way that he should practice the Individual Way (oral explanation by H. H. Dilgo Kyentsé).

274. *dBang rtags kyi phyag rgya.* According to Khetsun Sangpo Rinpoché, this means the signs and symbols, such as implements used in the domineering activity and the other charismatic activities.

275. Khetsun Sangpo Rinpoché explains that "to disturb the yogin's mandala" means to disrupt his inner concentration on the mandala of the deity; externally, it also includes disrupting the outer mandala of colored powders, etc.

276. *Vajrasattva's Magical Net* (Toh. 834), f. 252a6. Kongtrul here paraphrases the original.

277. The ten secrets are presented above as the root pledge of the mind of a buddha in the section entitled "The Extensive Explanation" of vows common to Mahayoga, Anuyoga, and Atiyoga.

278. *Subtle and Extensive Pledges* (*Dam tshig phra rgyas*) is a commentarial text, part of the *Sixty Manuals on Guhyagarbha's Magical Net*, translated from the Sanskrit, the woodblocks for which, prior to the Chinese takeover of Tibet, were preserved at Shechen Monastery in eastern Tibet. As to the title of this text, subtle (*phra*) refers to the root or fundamental pledges, and extensive (*rgyas*), to the secondary or branch pledges (verbal communication of Jadral Rinpoché Sangyé Dorjé).

279. *Secret Nucleus*, f. 252b7.

280. The three existences refers to the three realms: desire, form, and formless. The six worlds are the worlds of the six kinds of beings—gods, demi-gods, humans, animals, starving spirits, and hell beings.

281. Rong zom chos kyi bzang po (1012-1088): an accomplished master and scholar of the Nyingma school. Declared by Atisha to be the reincarnation of the Indian adept Krishnacharya, he maintained many lineages of instructions linked to the sutras, tantras, and the system of the Great Perfection (Dzog-chen).

282. *The Precious Jewel Commentary* (*dKon mchog 'grel*) is another name for Rongzom's *Commentary on the Tantra of the Secret Nucleus* (*gSang snying 'grel pa*) (*NKG*, vol. 25). This citation is Kongtrul's summary of Rongzom's discussion of the sevenfold greatness of the tantric pledges.

283. *Mamo* (*ma mo*): one of the eight classes of spirits—*lha, gshin rje, ma mo, bdud, btsan, rgyal bsren, srin po,* and *klu*. For a detailed classification of these beings, see *NSH,* Glossary of Enumeration, under "Eightfold Groups of Spirits."

Sky-farer (*ḍākinī, mkha' 'gro ma*): this term includes various female beings who may be witches, guardians of the teachings and particularly of the tantras, female practitioners of tantra at certain levels of realization, and fully enlightened beings.

284. Rongzom explains "domain": Since everything is perfect from the very beginning, buddhas never stray from the conduct that is free from acceptance and rejection. However, they do appear in the manifest dimension (*nirmāṇakāya*) and

the enjoyment dimension (*saṃbhogakāya*) of awakening to assure the welfare of others; this is their "domain" (*Commentary on the Tantra of the Secret Nucleus, NKG*, vol. 25, f. 413).

285. Field of Samantabhadra (*kun tu bzang po'i zhing*), according to Rongzom (*Commentary on the Tantra of the Secret Nucleus*), is the state in which there is no acceptance or rejection of anything since all that exists, encompassing cyclic existence and perfect peace, is primordially pure.

286. On the term *samaya* (*dam tshig*), Rongzom states: *sama* means "sameness" and *ya* means "to link up to." It is samaya because it links the adept to the meaning of the very sameness of all things (*Commentary on the Tantra of the Secret Nucleus, NKG*, vol. 25, f. 404).

287. *General Scripture That Gathers All Intentions* (*sPyi mdo dgongs pa 'dus pa* or *'Dus mdo chen po*), the main explanatory tantra of the anuyoga class, in seventy-five chapters and ten sections, translated from *bru sha* (Gilgit) language by Che btsan kyes. Found in Dg.K. rNying rgyud, vol. Kha, ff. 86b-290a (Toh. 929) and in *NG*, vol. Da.

288. Nub Sangyé Yeshé (gNubs sangs rgyas ye shes) (832-943): an eminent master of the Ancient School who attended numerous teachers and traveled to both India and Nepal for his spiritual apprenticeship. In India, he studied with Prakashalamkara (Prākāśālaṃkāra) who at that time was said to be one thousand six hundred years old. Prakashalamkara instructed Sangyé Yeshé to proceed to Gilgit and study the mahayoga *Scripture That Gathers All Intentions* under an Indian master living there at the time. Having freed his mind after nine months of meditation, Nub became a yogin possessed of boundless supernatural powers which he employed to disperse the enemies of the teachings. Among his writings, the *Lamp for the Eye of Contemplation* constitutes one of the most authoritative explanations of the Great Perfection system. Another of his works, from which the explanation of the analogies is likely taken, is *Armor Against Darkness: A Large Commentary on the Scripture That Gathers All Intentions* (*mDo'i 'grel chen mun pa'i go cha*). For details of his life, see *NSH*, pp. 607-614.

289. Yantra yoga (*'khrul 'khor*): systems of physical and breathing exercises aimed at controlling energies and seminal essence in order to allow the natural condition of body, speech, and mind to unfold. For example, see Vairochana's *Union of Sun and Moon*, edited by Chögyal Namkhai Norbu (Merigar: Shang Shung Editions).

290. Possibly a reference to the enemies mentioned in the pledges to conquer the four enemies, discussed below.

291. See note 162.

292. The realm Superior (*Akaniṣṭha, 'Og min*): the ultimate realm where awakening is achieved, which transcends the three worlds and therefore is not a physical place.

293. *General Scripture That Gathers All Intentions, NG,* vol. 11 (Da), f. 215b2.

294. Ibid., f. 215b4-5.

295. Impediments that deviate (*gol grib*) from authentic contemplation.

296. Mystic union with the master (*guruyoga, bla ma'i rnal 'byor*) is the means by which one refreshes one's link to the teaching, the master, and the lineage, and to the transmission and its power.

297. Cutting through (*khregs chod*); direct leap (*thod rgal*): the words of the pledges themselves elucidate the nature of the "cutting through" and "direct leap" practices of the Great Perfection (Dzog-chen) system. For a discussion on this, see *NSH.*

298. Eight similes of illusion: dream, magic, optical illusion, reflections of the moon on water, echo, ethereal city, and phantom. These examples are explained extensively in Longchenpa's *sGyu ma ngal gso,* translated by H. V. Guenther as *Kindly Bent to Ease Us,* vol. III. (Emeryville, CA: Dharma Publishing, 1976)

299. Four visionary appearances (*snang ba bzhi*): the visionary appearance of the direct perception of reality (*chos nyid mngon sum gyi snang ba*), the visionary appearance of increasing contemplative experience (*nyams gong 'phel gyi snang ba*), the visionary appearance of reaching perfected awareness (*rig pa tshad phebs kyi snang ba*), and the visionary appearance in which phenomena cease to be apprehended in reality (*chos nyid zad pa'i snang ba*). See Dudjom Rinpoche's succinct explanation of these in *NSH,* p. 339.

300. See above section "Means to Restore Pledges."

301. Indrabhuti's *Jnanasiddhi* (*Jñānasiddhisādhana; Ye shes grub pa'i sgrub pa'i thabs*) (Toh. 2219), f. 38a5-6.

302. Regarding the suitable kind of gem, different gems represent the various castes and buddha families. See Naropa's *The Commentary on the Summary of the Initiation: Compendium of Ultimate Reality* as translated in *IK,* p. 177.

303. See chapter II, note 278.

304. From the white letter *OM* at the forehead, the red letter *AH* at the throat, and the blue letter *HŪM* at the heart.

305. *All-Gathering Awareness,* the original tantra of the anuyoga class (*Sarvatathāgatacittaguhyajñānārthagarbhakrodhavajrakulatantra-piṇḍārthavidyā-yogasiddha; De bzhin gshegs pa thams cad kyi thugs gsang ba'i ye shes don gyi snying po khro bo rdo rje'i rigs kun 'dus rig pa'i mdo rnal 'byor grub pa'i rgyud*) (Toh. 831).

306. *Emptying the Depths of Hell* (*Na rag dong sprungs*). A ritual focusing on Vajrasattva as the main deity belonging to the transmitted precepts of the Nyingmapa, *NKG,* vol. 13.

307. Subhagavajra, *Stages of the Path of the Universal Way* (*Mahāyānapathakrama; Theg pa chen po'i lam gyi rim pa*) (Toh. 3717), f. 189b4.

308. See note 51.

309. See note 196.

310. See chapter I, section "The Tantric Master."

311. Four styles (*tshul bzhi*) of tantric explanation: disclosing the literal, general, hidden, or final meaning. See Kongtrul's *IOK*, vol. II, pp. 720-722.

312. Three impediments: emotional impediment (*nyon mongs pa'i sgrib pa*), impediment to knowledge (*shes bya'i sgrib pa*), and the propensity for movement (*'pho ba'i sgrib pa*). See note 11.

313. Four states (*gnas skabs bzhi*): wakefulness (*sad pa*), dream (*rmi lam*), deep sleep (*gnyid 'thug po*), and orgasm (*'khrig pa*). See Tenzin Gyatso's *KT*, pp. 120-122.

314. Yoga with signs (*mtshan bcas*) and without signs (*mtshan med*) characterize practices within the Action and Conduct tantras. The yoga with signs takes a conventional aspect such as the body of the deity or the recitation of the mantra as its referent for meditation; the yoga without signs takes as its referent reality or emptiness.

315. The three contemplations (*ting nge 'dzin gsum*)—initial application, triumphant mandala, and triumphant action—are common to both Yoga and Highest Yoga Tantra. In the Highest Yoga Tantra terminology, these three describe the degrees of accomplishment in the phase of creation. In the contemplation called initial union (*prathamaprayoga, dang po'i sbyor ba*) of the deity yoga, the yogin (or yogini) works to create a general appearance of the deities and the mandala; in the second, called the triumphant mandala (*vijayamaṇḍala, dkyil 'khor rgyal mchog*), the yogin works at making such appearance detailed and vivid; and in the third, called the triumphant act (*karmavijaya, las kyi rgyal mchog*), the yogin in the role of the deity enacts enlightened activity, such as purifying sentient beings.

316. Kongtrul presents the four branches of familiarization and attainment (*caturaṅgasevāsādhana, bsnyen sgrub yan lag bzhi*) according to Nagarjuna and the system of the Guhyasamaja tantra. Familiarization (*sevā, bsnyen pa*) consists in familiarizing pristine awareness with its object, emptiness; close familiarization (*upasevā, nye bar bsnyen pa*) comprises the phases of creation of the deity up to the completion of the mandala of the body; attainment (*sādhana, sgrub pa*) consists in realizing one's body, speech, and mind as the body, speech, and mind of the buddhas; great attainment (*mahāsādhana, sgrub chen*) is the state of having become the deity, adorned at the crown of the head with the lord of the family, and performing the activities of a buddha of liberating others, etc. (*IOK*, vol. III, pp. 176-177).

317. Six branches of visualization (*mngon rtogs yan lag drug*) given in the *Adamantine Tent Tantra*:

> The creation of the mandala and resident deities, the branch of Vairochana associated with the body;
> Tasting the ambrosia of the five nectars and the five meats, the branch of Amitabha associated with speech;

Praise, the branch of Ratnasambhava associated with marvelous qualities;
Offerings, the branch of Amoghasiddhi;
Initiation, the branch of Akshobhya;
Affection, the branch of Vajrasattva.

For full explanation of these branches, see Kongtrul's *IOK*, vol. III, pp. 181-182.

318. Kongtrul explains that the phase of completion on the side of appearance (*snang phyogs kyi rdzogs rim*) refers to the form of oneself as the deity and the related signs during the phase of completion. It is subdivided into three: (1) the complete yoga, which is the form of oneself as the deity that vividly appears, with no mental projection (*rnam rtog*), by the force of the meditation on the deity and through the secondary condition of the mind being blessed by the ordinary bliss resulting from the melting of the seminal essence; (2) the self-consecration of the illusory body, the form of oneself as the deity which actually manifests from just energy and mind; and (3) the yoga of signs, the manifestation of signs such as smoke and so forth (*IOK*, vol. II, pp. 704-705).

319. The phase of completion on the side of emptiness (*stong phyogs kyi rdzogs rim*): the direct realization of the mind's natural unpolluted state, i.e., pristine awareness coemergent with the indivisibility of bliss and emptiness [resulting from] the gradual dissolution of the eighty natural conceptions and the three appearances (*IOK*, vol. II, pp. 689-707).

320. The phase of completion with respect to the state of union (*zung 'jug gi rdzogs rim*) refers to the blending of the two sides: the side of emptiness (the pristine awareness of bliss and emptiness [resulting from] the dissolution of winds and mind in the central channel) and the side of appearance (the appearance of the form of the deity and the blessing of that pristine awareness) (*IOK*, vol. II, p. 707).

321. See note 256.

322. The mandala circle (*dkyil 'khor 'khor lo*): meditational practices belonging to the causal phase of completion involving union with a real consort (*karmamudrā, las rgya*) during which the adept causes the winds to simultaneously enter, abide, and dissolve [within the central channel]. This quickly brings about a great bliss from the melting [of the seminal essence] descending within the central channel. As a subsidiary method for stabilizing the blissful pristine awareness, the adept practices with an imaginary consort (*jñānamudrā, ye shes kyi phyag rgya*), also known as the great consort attended by an aspect (*rnam bcas phyag rgya chen mo*) (*IOK*, vol. II, pp. 686-687).

323. Indestructible yoga (*rdo rje'i rnal 'byor*): the meditational practice of the great seal (*phyag rgya chen mo*), the twofold meditation that brings about bliss and the meditation that "channels" seminal essence and conceptual mind. The two stages of meditation are as follows: (1) After having acquired familiarity with the pristine awareness coemergent with the bliss of the melted [seminal essence], the adept remains absorbed in the pristine awareness of bliss and emptiness; such absorption again causes the winds and mind to gather, and the adept thereby experiences repeatedly a special melted bliss. (2) The adept channels the seminal essence into the central channel, and conceptions into clear-light awareness;

doing this, he or she meditates exclusively on emptiness. As a result, the practitioner more effectively blocks the dualistic appearances of subject and object. Self-consecration, the mandala circle, and the indestructible yogas are considered to be the causal phase of completion because they serve as the causes for the pristine awareness of great bliss (*IOK*, vol. II, p. 687).

Alternatively, the indestructible yoga may refer to the sixfold yoga of the Kalachakra system also called indestructible yoga.

324. The "all-shaking avadhuti" (*avadhūti, kun 'dar*) conduct means "shaking off" or casting off dualistic thoughts. It consists of engaging in all kinds of activities that give rise to ordinary excitement: partaking of the five nectars and five meats, union with consorts, etc. It is performed in secret or in disguise (i.e., pretending to be crazy), either to deepen the yoga of the deity or to enhance the experience of clear light. The beginner's level (at which this conduct is practiced) requires having entered the path and having acquired a stable experience of pristine awareness.

The "ever-perfect conduct" (*kun tu bzang po*) means that whatever actions one performs, whether conventionally good or bad, all are inherently perfect. This conduct is performed openly since the yogin has attained stability, and it consists in leading others on the right path by displaying miraculous feats or gathering dakinis through power gazes, etc. The ever-perfect conduct is performed by an experienced practitioner who has experienced the dissolution of manifest conceptual constructions. Thus, it is said that these two conducts, although performed all the way to awakening, are mainly focused on in the lower path of preparation.

The conduct "victorious in all quarters" (*phyogs las rnam rgyal*) means to overcome emotions and to acquire the strength to help others. This conduct entails gathering goddesses, such as the goddess of water, and relying on them as one's tantric consorts to enable one to immediately attain the vision of reality on the path of seeing. This is the main conduct to be performed by an accomplished practitioner, i.e., one who has attained a great degree of warmth [on the path of preparation] indicating that attainment of the actual pristine awareness is close, up until the attainment of full awakening (*IOK*, vol. III, pp. 543, 549-552).

325. Using desire (*'dod 'jug*) refers to the "conduct" performed by the yogin (or yogini) between meditation sessions of enjoying food, drinks, and other pleasures. When this conduct is not directly pervaded by non-conceptual pristine awareness, it is said to be common; when pervaded, it is uncommon (*IOK*, vol. III, p. 536).

326. The common practice of training and enjoying pleasures (*brten slob*) in conjunction with complex (*spros bcas*), unelaborated (*spros med*), and utterly simple conducts (*shin tu spros med*) is principally taught in the father tantras. To train and enjoy pleasures in conjunction with complex conduct means to cultivate a conceptually based meditation in which one imagines whatever appears to one's senses to be the male and female deities and in this way to enjoy all the sense objects one encounters. To train and enjoy pleasure in conjunction with the unelaborated conduct means to cultivate a meditation, only partially conceptually

based, which sees one's faculties and sense objects as those of the deity and to enjoy all sense objects, while understanding that the deity is the appearance of one's own mind. To train and enjoy pleasure in conjunction with an utterly simple activity means to cultivate the meditation on the form of the deity as being the manifestation of bliss and emptiness and to enjoy sense objects with the understanding that deity and pleasures have no reality (*IOK*, vol. III, pp. 536-537).

The three types of conduct (complex, etc.) pertaining to the uncommon conduct of awareness (*rig pa brtul zhugs kyi spyod pa*) are emphasized primarily in the mother tantras. In this system, for complex conduct, the yogin wears the ornaments and attributes of the deity, relies on consorts who number the female deities of the mandala (of his practice), enjoys playful pleasures, such as songs, music, and dances, and makes use of symbolic language. In the unelaborated conduct, the yogin keeps only one or two consorts and uses a lesser degree of elaboration in his enjoyments. A practitioner who engages in the utterly simple conduct dispenses with external elaborations and relies exclusively on a solitary practice of contemplation (ibid., p. 538).

327. Yogins (or yoginis) traversing the two phases of the Highest Yoga Tantra are classified as four types: the beginner yogin (*las dang po ba*); the yogin on whom a little pristine awareness has descended (*ye shes cung zad babs pa*); the yogin who has gained slight mastery over pristine awareness (*ye shes la cung zad dbang thob pa*); and the yogin who has gained thorough mastery over pristine awareness (*ye shes la yang dag par dbang thob pa*). The first is unable to sustain a clear appearance of the coarse mandala and the deities for a considerable length of time; the second is more advanced but meditation is still unclear on the subtle aspects of the mandala and deities; the third has gained the ability to generate a clear appearance of the mandala and the deities in a tiny drop and is therefore on the subtle phase of creation; the fourth has attained the actual clear-light awareness, onward. See Akya Yongdzin (A kya yongs 'dzin), *Presentation of the Grounds and the Paths of Mantra* (*dPal gsang ba 'dus pa 'phags lugs dang mthun pa'i sngags kyi sa lam rnam gshad skal bzang 'jug ngogs*) (Dharamsala: Namgyal Dratsang, 1969).

328. See note 180.

329. The dimension of the deity, i.e., the body that manifests in the absence of conceptualizations (*rnam rtog dang bral ba'i sku*) refers to a body of only mind and energy (*rlung sems tsam gyi sku*). The yogin (or yogini) attains such a body as soon as he arises from absorption into the final metaphoric clear-light awareness of the black vision called "near attainment," entered by relying on the practice with an action seal. This marks the entering of the "peak" stage of the path of preparation (Kongtrul's *IOK*, vol. III, p. 514).

The absence of conceptualization in this context does not imply the suppression of the eighty natural conceptions (as this occurs on the receptivity stage of the path of preparation) or their elimination (that occurs on the path of seeing). Possibly it indicates that at this stage the body of the deity is not conceptually constructed, but actually arises as an illusory body of wind and mind, which is still impure since the path of seeing, on which emotional impediments are eliminated, has not yet been attained.

330. Eighty natural conceptions (*rang bzhin brgyad bcu'i rtog pa*): a classification of conceptions, such as the various degrees of non-attachment (aspects of hatred), attachment, and ignorance. These three groups of conceptions arise in turn from the ordinary minds of the three appearances—white light, red light, and black light. In the final stages of the process of death, these eighty conceptions dissolve.

The natural conceptions associated with radiant white appearance (*snang ba dkar lam pa*) number thirty-three; the first three refer to different degrees of hatred in apprehending an object as unpleasant:

(1) *Small lack of desire,* whose mode of apprehension of the object is slightly unclear;

(2) *Middling lack of desire,* whose apprehension is clear, but being brief and so forth, does not have the power to initiate an action based on it;

(3) *Great lack of desire,* whose apprehension is clear and continuous and is capable of instigating an action based on it;

(4) *Movement of the mind* to an external object and *withdrawal to internal objects,* both denoting intentionality;

(5) *Sorrow,*

(6) *Middling sorrow,* and

(7) *Great sorrow,* which denote different degrees of distress caused by being separated from a pleasurable object;

(8) *Peace,* which denotes a stupor resembling fatigue or exhaustion which is a lack of discriminative alertness;

(9) *Conceptuality,* which denotes a discernment that apprehends attributes by linking [the generic image based on] names with that [derived from a sense perception of] an object;

(10) *Fear,*

(11) *Middling fear,* and

(12) *Great fear;*

(13) *Craving,*

(14) *Middling craving,* and

(15) *Great craving,* which denote degrees of attachment to a pleasurable [object or experience occurring] in the past, present, or future;

(16) *Grasping,* which denotes the wish to engage in what is craved for;

(17) *Hunger* and *thirst,* which denote two kinds of mental unhappiness caused by these two;

(18) *Feeling,*

(19) *Middling feeling,* and

(20) *Great feeling,* which denote different degrees of feelings of pleasure, pain, and indifference;

(21) *Conception of knowing,*

(22) *Conception of a knower,* and

(23) *Conception of an object known,* which denote the mistaken cognitions

that apprehend the actual knowing, the agent of knowing, and object known for what they are not;

(24) *Discriminative examination,* which denotes [a mind] analyzing what is suitable and unsuitable;

(25) *Shame,* which denotes not wanting to be immoral;

(26) *Shunning unwholesome deeds* out of apprehension of others' disapproval. Embarrassment is also included here.

(27) *Compassion,* which denotes the wish to free others from suffering;

(28) *Loving kindness,*

(29) *Middling loving-kindness,* and

(30) *Great loving-kindness,* which denotes different degrees of love for others or wanting their happiness. Alternatively, these three are explained as cherishing a person, wishing his or her happiness, and wishing to protect the person from harm.

(31) *Apprehension* or *qualm,* which denotes an unsteady disposition accompanied by anxiety and doubt;

(32) *Accumulation,* which denotes wanting to gather [possessions] and not to give things away out of avarice;

(33) *Jealousy,* which denotes a mind disturbed by others' excellence.

Forty natural conceptions associated with the spread of the red appearance (*mched pa dmar lam pa*) are as follows:

(1) *Desire* for an object not yet acquired;

(2) *Adherence* to an object acquired;

(3) *Joy,*

(4) *Middling joy,* and

(5) *Great joy,* which denote different degrees of joy upon seeing the pleasant;

(6) *Rejoicing,* which denotes the joy of having achieved the desired goal;

(7) *Rapture* or *intense contentment,* which denotes repeatedly experiencing a desired goal;

(8) *Amazement,* which denotes a high spirit over [having obtained] an object that had not arisen before;

(9) *Excitement,* which denotes being distracted in pursuit of the pleasant;

(10) *Contentment,* which denotes being satisfied by pleasure;

(11) *Embracing* or desiring to embrace, which here denotes the wish to undertake physical and verbal actions motivated by desire for an [animate] object;

(12) *Kissing* or desiring to kiss, which here denotes the wish to repeatedly undertake actions [motivated by] desire;

(13) *Clinging* or desiring to cling, which here denotes the wish not to relinquish the endeavor to undertake actions motivated by desire;

(14) *Stability,* which denotes a discernment that is firm in that it cannot be changed;

(15) *Effort,* an attraction to virtue;

(16) *Pride,* a mind holding oneself higher [than others] based on social status, or for other reasons;

(17) *Activity,* the will not to slack in the effort to complete a task;

(18) *Robbery,* the desire to possess others' wealth, i.e., covetousness;

(19) *Force,* wanting to conquer others;

(20) *Earnest interest,* mind's involvement in ordinary activities;

(21) *Engagement in hardship,*

(22) *Middling engagement in hardship,* and

(23) *Great engagement in hardship,* which denote different degrees of courage in engaging in tasks that are hard to accomplish.

(24) *Vehemence,* which denotes wanting to quarrel and so forth out of anger;

(25) *Flirtation* toward what is beautiful;

(26) *Angry disposition* that harbors resentment;

(27) *Virtue,* which denotes rejoicing in virtue;

(28) *Clear speech,* which denotes the wish to speak so that others can understand;

(29) *Truth,* the wish to speak truthfully;

(30) *Untruth,* the wish to lie;

(31) *Definitiveness,* which denotes having a steady intent;

(32) *Non-appropriation,* not desiring to possess something due to having considered the grief this may cause;

(33) *Giving,* the disposition of a generous person;

(34) *Exhorting,* the desire to urge others into work and action;

(35) *Heroism,* the wish to be free from impediments [to liberation, etc.];

(36) *Shamelessness,* which denotes failure to shun the unwholesome;

(37) *Deceit,* the wish to cheat or mislead others;

(38) *Viciousness,* adherence to the five bad views;

(39) *Rudeness,* scorning others when their living environment, status, health, and possessions decline;

(40) *Dissimulation,* the hypocrisy of hiding one's faults.

Seven natural conceptions are associated with the black culminating appearance (*thob pa nag lam pa*):

(1) *Middling desire,* which denotes an ignorance or mind obscured due to attachment. It is "middling" as its aspect is unclear.

(2) *Forgetfulness,* which denotes a decline in recollection;

(3) *Misapprehension,* apprehending what is big as small, form as sound, and so forth;

(4) *Non-speaking,* disinterest in speaking;

(5) *Discouragement* caused by various circumstances;

(6) *Idleness,* which denotes lack of interest in or enthusiasm for what is wholesome;

(7) *Doubt,* which denotes oscillating between two possibilities (*IOK* vol.II, pp. 697-703).

See also Aryadeva's *Lamp Summary of Practice,* f. 78a3-b3; Lati Rinbochay and Jeffrey Hopkins' *Death, Intermediate State and Rebirth in Tibetan Buddhism* (London: Rider, 1979; rpt. Ithaca: Snow Lion Publications, 1980) (interpretations of some conceptions differ from those given here); and Aryadeva's *Commentary on the Clear Lamp,* ff. 188 onward.

331. Great power places (*yul chen*) refers to outer locations found in India, Tibet, and other Himalayan areas, as well as the inner parts of the body. Kongtrul explains: the yogin who has attained the body of mere energy and mind engages in tantric practice in the twenty-four outer places and assembles an entourage of consorts, such as Vajravarahi, who dwell in these places. Uniting with them, he is able to purify the potentialities of the channels, energies, and seminal essences of the twenty-four inner power places by absorbing them into the central channel.

When the potentialities of the channels, energies, and seminal essences of the inner power places of Pulliramalaya in the head, Jalandhara in the crown of the head, Oddiyana in the right ear, and Arbuda in the upper part of the head bone are purified, the first stage of awakening is attained. When the potentialities of those of Godavari in the left ear, Rameshvara in the eyebrows, Devikota in both eyes, and Malava in the shoulder joints are purified, the second stage is attained. When the potentialities of those of Kamaru in the armpits and Odra in the breasts are purified, the third stage is attained. When those of Trishakuni in the navel and Koshala at the root of the nose are purified, the fourth stage is attained. When those of Kalinga in the mouth and Lampaka in the center of the throat are purified, the fifth stage is attained. When those of Kanchi in the heart and Himalaya in the secret place are purified, the sixth stage is attained. When those of Pretadhivasini in the sex organ and Grihadevata in the rectum are purified, the seventh stage is attained. When those of Saurashtra in the thighs and Suvarnadvipa in the tibias are purified, the eighth stage is attained. When those of Nagara in the toes and Sindhu in the heels are purified, the ninth stage is attained. When those of Maru in both toes and Kulata in the knees are purified, the tenth stage is attained. These ten stages are said to be part of the path of preparation.

The next two stages are called "abstinence from drinking" (*'thung gcod*) and "subsidiary abstinence from drinking" (*nye ba'i 'thung gcod*). "Drinking" refers to the emotions and to their predispositions, and "abstinence" to the actual process by which these are eliminated. "Subsidiary abstinence" refers to the extent to which the emotions have been eliminated. With these, the yogin attains the dimension of the non-dual pristine awareness of the path of seeing, thus making twelve stages of awakening (*sa bcu gnyis*). [These are called provisional as opposed to the thirteenth stage, the vajra stage of a buddha, which is the final.] (*IOK*, vol. III, pp. 514-515, 529).

332. Union that requires no more learning, or union beyond training (*mi slob pa'i zung 'jug*): the union of the pure [i.e., free from emotions and impediments] illusory body and the actual clear light; or union of the form dimension of enlightenment and the dimension of reality. Its characteristics are summarized by Kongtrul in the following way: "...a great union exemplifying highest freedom and realization. Freedom refers to the knowledge that impediments and their predispositions are already exhausted (primordially). Realization refers to the

knowledge, free of conceptual designations, that cognizes all phenomena of cyclic existence and peace, such as the ground, the path, and so forth, as images in a divination mirror." (*IOK*, vol. III, p. 657).

333. State of Vajradhara with the sevenfold features of [male and female deity] facing each other (*kha sbyor yan lag bdun ldan rdo rje 'chang*): (1) enjoyment: possessing thirty-two major and eighty minor marks of a buddha; (2) embrace: union with the consort that is a manifestation of one's [pristine awareness]; (3) great bliss: abiding in the essence of innate bliss; (4) unreality: abiding in the essence of emptiness devoid of mental fabrications; (5) compassion: always permeated by non-objectifying compassion for all living beings; (6) unending stream: an eternal unfolding of the dimensions of awakening and pristine awareness; (7) continuous presence: freedom from interruptions with respect to the mind's absorption in cessation without any form and with respect to the form dimensions of awakening (*IOK*, vol. III, p. 658).

334. *The Key to Initiation* (*dBang gi lde'u mig*). Text not identified.

335. Vibhutichandra's *Stream of Light on the Three Vows* (*Trisaṃvaraprabhāmālā; sDom gsum 'od kyi phreng ba*) (Toh. 3727), f. 54b1-56b7. Vibhutichandra, a master of the sixfold yoga of the Kalachakra, was invited to Dingri (Tibet) from Nepal by Kodrakpa Sonam Gyaltsen (1182-1261), with whom he had a reciprocal teacher-disciple relationship. He is said to have received the instructions on the sixfold yoga in Nepal from the great saint Shavari, who arrived in front of him disguised as a simple yogin dressed in black. Roerich's *Blue Annals* (Calcutta, 1949; 2nd ed. Delhi: Motilal Banarsidass, 1976), p. 727.

336. Gampopa's followers include the masters of the four main Kagyu schools which originated from his disciples: Barompa ('Ba' rom pa) founded by Barom Darma Wangchuk ('Ba' rom dar ma dbang phyug); Pakdru (Phag gru) founded by Pakdru Dorjé Gyalpo (Phag gru rdo rje rgyal po); Kamtsang (Kam tshang) founded by Dusum Kyenpa (Dus gsum mkhyen pa), the first Karmapa; the Tsalpa (Tshal pa) founded by Zhang Tsalpa Tsöndru Drakpa (Zhang tshal pa brtson 'grus grags pa), and the Dakpo Kagyu (Dwags po bka' brgyud), itself continued by other disciples of Gampopa (Kongtrul's *IOK*, vol. I, pp. 529-530).

337. The eight minor Kagyu subsects, traditions originating with Pakmo Drupa (Phag mo gru pa): the Drigung ('Bri gung pa), which was founded by Drigung Kyobpa ('Bri gung skyob pa, 1143-1217); the Taklung (sTag lung), founded by Tangpa Trashi Palwa (Thang pa bkra shis dpal ba, 1142-1210); the Tropu (Khro phu), founded by Drogön Gyaltsab ('Gro mgon rgyal tshab, 1173-1228); the Lingré (Kling ras), found by Lingré Pema Dorjé (Kling ras pad ma rdo rje, 1128-88); the Martsang (sMar tshang), founded by Marpa Drubtob (sMar pa grub thob); the Yelpa (Yel pa), found by Yeshé Tsekpa (Ye shes brtsegs pa); the Yazang (gYa' bzang), founded by Zarawa Yeshé Sengé (Zwa ra ba ye shes seng ge); and the Shukseb (Shug gseb), founded by Nyipu Gyergom Chenpo (sNyi phu gyer sgom chen po) (*IOK*, vol. I, pp. 530-531).

338. Uncle and nephew (*khu dbon*): Drakpa Gyaltsen (1147-1216) is referred to as the uncle of Sakya Pandita (1181-1251), the greatest scholar of the Sakya school.

339. Pema Wangyal, *Treatise that Ascertains the Three Vows* (*sDom gsum rnam par nges pa'i bstan bcos*), NKG, vol. 37, f. 39a5.

340. Riwo Gedenpa (*ri bo dge ldan pa*), lit. the "Virtuous Ones of the Mountain," a name for the Geluk school of Tibetan Buddhism. "Mountain" refers to the site where Tsongkapa founded Ganden, the first monastery of this school, a natural and scenic amphitheater situated on an isolated mountainside in central Tibet.

341. *mKha' 'gro ma'i gsang mdzod.* Text not located.

Bibliography of Works Cited
by the Author

SCRIPTURES

Abhidana Tantra
Abhidāna-uttaratantra
mNgon par brjod pa'i rgyud bla ma
Dg.K. rGyud 'bum, vol. Ka, ff. 247a-370a (Toh. 369)

Advice to the King Scripture
Rājāvavādakasūtra
rGyal po la gdams pa'i mdo
Dg.K. mDo sde, vol. Tsha, ff. 207a-210a (Toh. 221)

Akashagarbha Scripture (AS)
Ākāśagarbhasūtra
Nam mkha'i snying po'i mdo
Dg.K. mDo sde, vol. Za, ff. 264a-283b (Toh. 260)

All-Gathering Awareness
Sarvatathāgatacittaguhyajñānārthagarbhakrodhavajrakulatantrapiṇḍārtha-
vidyāyogasiddha
Kun 'dus rig pa'i mdo/ De bzhin gshegs pa thams cad kyi thugs gsang ba'i
ye shes don gyi snying po khro bo rdo rje'i rigs kun 'dus rig pa'i mdo rnal
'byor grub pa'i rgyud
Dg.K. rNying rgyud, vol. Kha, ff. 1b-110a (Toh. 831)
NG, vol. Na

Amoghapasha Scripture
Amoghapāśahṛdayasūtra
Don yod zhags pa'i snying po'i mdo
Dg.K. rGyud 'bum, vol. Ba, ff. 278b-284a (Toh. 682)

Analysis of Discipline Scripture
Vinayavibhaṅga
'Dul rnam 'byed
Dg.K. 'Dul ba, vols. Ca, ff. 21a-292a; Cha, ff. 1b-287a; Ja, ff. 1b-287a; Nya, ff. 1b-269a (Toh. 3)

Beholding the Qualities of the Spiritual Master Tantra
Bla ma'i yon tan yongs bzung gi rgyud
Not identified

Biography of Shri Sambhava
dPal 'byung gi rnam thar
The life story of Śrī Saṃbhava forms the fiftieth chapter of the *Flower Array Scripture*, which is the third part of *The Flower Ornament Scripture* (*Buddhāvataṃsakasūtra*).
Dg.K. Phal chen, vol. A, ff. 278b-288b (Toh. 44)

Biography of the Lay Practitioner Achala
dGe bsnyen ma mi yo ba'i rnam thar
The lifestory of Achala forms the nineteenth chapter of the *Flower Array Scripture*.
Dg.K. Phal chen, vol. A, ff. 35b-43a (Toh. 44).

Black Yamari Tantras
Sarvatathāgatakāyavākcitta kṛṣṇaya mārināmatantra
De bzhin gshegs pa thams cad kyi sku gsung thugs gzhin rje gshed nak po
Dg.K. rGyud 'bum, vol. Ja, ff. 134b-151b (Toh. 467)

Kṛṣṇayamāritantra
gShin rje gshed nag po'i rgyud
Dg.K. rGyud 'bum, vol. Ja, ff. 164a-167b (Toh. 469)

Yamārikṛṣṇakarmasarvacakrasiddhikaratantra
gShin rje'i gshed dgra nag po'i 'khor lo las thams cad grub par byed pa'i rgyud
Dg.K. rGyud 'bum, vol. Ja, ff. 175a-185b (Toh. 473)

Bodhisattva Section Scripture
Bodhisattvapiṭakanāmasūtra
Byang chub sems dpa'i sde snod ces bya ba'i mdo
Dg.K. dKon brtsegs, vols. Kha, ff. 255b-294a; Ga, ff. 1b-205b (Toh. 56)

Brahmana Vyasa Scripture
Brāhmaṇavyāsasūtra
gNas 'jog pa'i mdo
Dg.K. mDo sde, vol. Sa, ff. 263b-268a (Toh. 333)

Chakrasamvara Fundamental Tantra/Chakrasamvara Tantra
Cakrasaṃvaramūlatantra/ Tantrarājaśrīlaghusambara
bDe mchog rtsa ba'i rgyud/ rGyud kyi rgyal po dpal bde mchog nyung ngu
Dg.K. rGyud 'bum, vol. Ka, ff. 213b-246b (Toh. 368)

Chanting the Names of Manjushri
Mañjuśrijñānasattvasya-paramārthanāma-saṃgīti
'Jam dpal ye shes sems pa'i don dam pa'i mtshan yang dag par brjod pa
Part of the *Secret Nucleus*
Also known as *Manjushri's Magical Net* ('*Jam dpal sgyu 'phrul drva ba*) and
   considered a tantra of the enlightened body (*sku'i rgyud*) associated with
   Manjushri; cycle of teachings.
Dg.K. rGyud 'bum, vol. Ka, ff. 1b-13b (Toh. 360)
Trans. A. Wayman, *Chanting the Names of Mañjuśrī*. Boulder: Shambhala, 1985.

Cluster of Jewels
Mahāratnakūṭadharmaparyāyaśatasāhasrikagranthetrisaṃvaranirdeśa-
   parivarta
dKon mchog brtsegs pa chen po'i chos kyi rnam grangs le'u stong phrag
   brgya pa las sdom pa gsum bstan pa'i le'u
Dg.K. dKon brtsegs, vol. Ka, ff. 1b-45a (Toh. 45)

Collected Scriptures and Dhāraṇī
gZungs bsdus/ mDo sngags gsung rab rgya mtsho'i snying po sdud pa
2 vols. Dharamsala: Bod gzhung shes rig khang, 1976; second edition 1977.

Collection of Spontaneous Utterances
Udānavarga
Ched du brjod pa'i tshoms
Dg.K. mDo sde, vol. Sa, ff. 209a-253a (Toh. 326)

Condensed Heruka Tantra
He ru ka 'dus pa'i rgyud
NG, vol. Ra, ff. 1-60

Condensed Transcendent Wisdom Scripture
Prajñāpāramitāsañcayagāthā
Shes rab kyi pha rol tu phyin pa sdud pa tshigs su bcad pa
Dg.K. Shes phyin, vol. Ka, ff. 1b-19b (Toh. 13)
Also in: *Collected Scriptures and Dhāraṇī* (*gZungs bsdus/ mDo sngags gsung rab
   rgya mtsho'i snying po sdud pa*). 2 vols. Dharamsala: Bod gzhung shes rig
   khang, 1976; second edition 1977.

Continuation of the Guhyasamaja Tantra
'Dus pa phyi ma
Dg.K. rGyud 'bum, vol. Ca, ff. 148a-157b (Toh. 443)

Dakinisamvara Tantra
Ḍākinīsaṃvara-tantrarāja
mKha 'gro ma'i sdom pa'i rgyud
Dg.K. rGyud 'bum, vol. Ga, ff. 242b7-244a7 (Toh. 406)

Display of Miracles Scripture
Buddhabalavardhanaprātihāryavikurvāṇanirdeśasūtra
Sangs rgyas kyi stobs skyed pa'i cho 'phrul rnam par 'phrul ba bstan pa'i mdo
Dg.K. mDo sde, vol. Tsa, ff. 143b-158a (Toh. 186)

Emptying the Depths of Hell
Na rag dong sprugs
A rite of the one hundred peaceful and wrathful deities focusing on
Vajrasattva.
NKG, vol. 13

Essence of the Great Seal
Mahāmudrātilakanāmamahāyoginītantrarājādhipati
Phyag rgya chen po'i thig le zhes bya ba rnal 'byor ma chen mo'i rgyud kyi
rgyal po'i mnga' bdag
Dg.K. rGyud 'bum, vol. Nga, ff. 66a-90b (Toh. 420)

Essence of Pristine Awareness
Jñānatilakayoginītantrarājaparamamahādbhuta
Ye shes thig le rnal 'byor ma'i rgyud kyi rgyal po chen po mchog tu rmad du
byung ba
Dg.K. rGyud bum, vol. Na, ff. 96b-136b (Toh. 422)

Essence Ornament of the General Procedure for All Secrets
Sarvaguhyavidhigarbhālaṃkāra
gSang ba thams cad kyi spyi'i cho ga'i snying po rgyan zhes bya ba
Dg.T. rGyud, vol. Zi, ff. 232b-243b (Toh. 2490)

Flower Array Scripture
Gaṇḍhavyūhasūtra
sDong po bkod pa'i mdo
Part of *The Flower Ornament Scripture.*
Dg.K. Phal chen, vols. Ga (end) and A (Toh. 44)

Flower Ornament Scripture/ Great Bounteousness of the Buddhas Scripture
Buddhāvataṃsakanāmamahāvaipūlyasūtra
Sangs rgyas phal po che zhes bya ba shin tu rgyas pa chen po'i mdo
Dg.K. Phal chen, vols. Ka, ff. 1b-393a; Kha, ff. 1b-396a; Ga, ff. 1b-396; A, ff.
1b-363a (Toh. 44)
Trans. T. Cleary, *The Flower Ornament Scripture*. 3 vols. Boulder: Shambhala, 1984.

Fortunate Eon Scripture
Bhadrakalpikasūtra
bsKal pa bzang po'i mdo
Dg.K. mDo sde, vol. Ka, ff. 1b-340a (Toh. 94)

General Scripture That Gathers All Intentions
Sarvatathāgatacittajñānaguhyārthagarbhavyūhavajratantrasiddhiyogāgama-
samājasarvavidyāsūtramahāyānābhisamayadharmaparyayāvyūhanāma-
sūtra
sPyi mdo dgongs 'dus/ 'Dus pa mdo /De bzhin gshegs pa thams cad kyi
thugs gsang ba'i ye shes don gyi snying po rdo rje bkod pa'i rgyud rnal

'byor grub pa'i lung kun 'dus rig pa'i mdo theg pa chen po mngon par
rtogs pa chos kyi rnam grangs rnam par bkod pa zhes bya ba'i mdo
Dg.K. rNying rgyud, vol. Kha ff. 86b-290a (Toh. 829)
Also in: *NKG*, vol. Pha; *NG*, vol. Da.

*General Tantra/ Secret General Tantra/ Secret Tantra of the General Ritual of All
Mandalas*
Sarvamaṇḍalasāmānyavidhīnāmaguhyatantra
dKyil 'khor thams cad kyi spyi'i cho ga gsang ba'i rgyud
Dg.K. rGyud 'bum, vol. Wa, ff. 141a-167b (Toh. 806)

Great Mindfulness Scripture
Saddharmasmṛtyupasthāna
Dam pa'i chos dran pa nye bar gshag pa
Dg.K. mDo sde, vols. Ya, ff. 82a-318a; Ra, ff. 1b-307a; La, ff. 1b-312a; Sha, ff.
1b-229b (Toh. 287)

Guhyasamaja Tantra/ Glorious Guhyasamaja
Sarvatathāgatakāyavākcittarahasyaguhyasamājanāmamahā-kālparāja
De bzhin gshegs pa thams cad kyi sku gsung thugs kyi gsang chen gsang ba
'dus pa zhes bya ba brtag pa'i rgyal po chen po
Dg.K. rGyud 'bum, vol. Ca, ff. 90a-148a (Toh. 442)

Hevajra Tantra/ Two-Part Hevajra Tantra
The *Two-Part Hevajra Tantra (brTag gnyis)* which comprises the Hevajra Tantra
is composed of the following two books:
Kye'i rdo re zhes bya ba rgyud kyi rgyal po
Hevajratantrarājanāma
Dg. K. rGyud 'bum, vol. Nga, ff. 1b-13b (Toh. 417)

Kye'i rdo rje mkha' 'gro ma dra ba'i sdom pa'i rgyud kyi rgyal po
Dg.K. rGyud 'bum, vol. Nga, ff. 13b-30a (Toh. 418)

Trans. D. Snellgrove, *Hevajra Tantra, A Critical Study.* London: Oxford University Press, 1959.

Indestructible Garland
Vajramālābhidhānamahāyogatantrasarvatantrahṛdayarahasyavibhaṅga
rNal 'byor chen po'i rgyud dpal rdo rje phreng ba mnon par brjod pa rgyud
thams cad kyi snying po gsang ba rnam par phye ba
Dg.K. rGyud 'bum, vol. Ca, ff. 208a-277b (Toh. 445)

Indestructible Nucleus' Ornament Tantra: see *Nucleus' Ornament*

Indestructible Peak Tantra
Vajraśekharamahāguhyayogatantra
gSang ba rnal 'byor chen po'i rgyud rdo rje rtse mo
Dg.K. rGyud 'bum, vol. Nya, ff. 142b-274a (Toh. 480)

Indestructible Tent Tantra
Ḍākinīvajrapañjaratantra
mKha' 'gro ma rdo rje gur zhes bya ba'i rgyud
Dg.K. rGyud 'bum, vol. Nga, ff. 30a-65b (Toh. 419)

Inspiring Universal Responsibility Scripture
Adhyāśayasañcodana sūtra
Lhag pa'i bsam pa bskul ba'i mdo
Dg.K. dKon brtsegs, vol. Ca, ff. 131a-135b (Toh. 69)

Kalachakra Tantra: see *Wheel of Time Condensed Tantra* and *Wheel of Time Fundamental Tantra*

Key to the Initiation
dBang gi lde'u mig
Not identified

Kilaya Wrathful Anger Tantra
Phur pa zhe sdang khros pa'i rgyud
Not identified

King of Contemplations Scripture
Sarvadharmasvabhāvasamatāvipañcitasamādhirājanāmamahāyānasūtra
Chos thams cad kyi rang bzhin mnyam pa nyid rnam par spros pa ting nge
'dzin gyi rgyal po zhes bya ba theg pa chen po'i mdo
Dg.K. mDo sde, vol. Da, ff. 1b-170b (Toh. 127)

Magical Net Tantra: see *Secret Nucleus*

Manjushri Fundamental Tantra
Mañjuśrīmūlatantra
'Jam dpal gyi rtsa ba'i rgyud
Dg.K. rGyud 'bum, vol. Na, ff. 88a-351a (Toh. 543)

Manjushri's Magical Net: see *Chanting the Names of Manjushri*

Nucleus' Ornament/ Indestructible Nucleus' Ornament Tantra
Vajrahṛdayālaṃkāratantra
rDo rje snying po rgyan gyi rgyud
Dg.K. rGyud 'bum, vol. Cha, ff. 36-58 (Toh. 451)

Paramadya Tantra/ Glorious Paramadya
Paramādyamantrakalpakhaṇḍa
mChog dang po'i sngags kyi rtog pa'i dum bu
Dg.K. rGyud 'bum, vol. Ta, ff. 173a-265b (Toh. 488)

Personal Liberation Scripture/ Personal Liberation Discourse
Prātimokṣasūtra
So sor thar ba'i mdo
Dg.K. 'Dul ba, vol. Ca, ff. 1b-20b (Toh. 2)

Possessing Pure Ethics Scripture/ Proclamation of the Doctrine Scripture
Śilasaṃyuktasūtra
Tshul khrims yang dag par ldan pa'i mdo/ Chos bsgrags kyi mdo
Dg.K. mDo sde, vol. Sa, ff. 127a-127b (Toh. 303)

Precious Palm Scripture
Ratnolkānāmadhāraṇisūtra
dKon mchog ta la la'i gzungs zhes bya ba'i mdo
Dg.K. mDo sde, vol. Pa, ff. 34a-82a (Toh. 145)

Proclamation of the Doctrine Scripture: see *Possessing Pure Ethics Scripture*

Questions of Kashyapa Scripture
Kāśyapaparivartanāmasūtra
'Od srung gi le'u zhes bya ba'i mdo
Dg.K. dKon brtsegs, vol. Cha, ff. 119b-151b (Toh. 87)

Questions of Ratnachuda Scripture
Ratnacūdapariprcchasūtra
gTsug na rin po ches zhus pa'i mdo
Dg.K. dKon brtsegs, vol. Cha, ff. 210a-254b (Toh. 91)

Questions of Sagaramati Scripture
Sāgaramatipariprcchasūtra
Blo gros rgya mtshos zhus pa'i mdo
Dg.K. mDo sde, vol. Pha, ff. 1b-115b (Toh. 152)

Questions of Subahu Tantra
Subāhupariprcchātantra
dPung bzang gis zhus pa'i rgyud
Dg.K. rGyud bum, vol. Wa, ff. 118a-140b (Toh. 805)

Red Yamari Tantras
Raktayamāritantra
gShin rje'i gshed dmar po'i rgyud
Dg.K. rGyud 'bum, vol. Ja ff. 186a-214b (Toh. 474)

Madraktayamāritantra
gShin rje gshed dmar po'i rgyud
Dg.K. rGyud 'bum, vol. Ja, ff. 215a-244b (Toh. 475)

Reunion of Father and Son Scripture
Pitāputrasamāgamanasūtra
Yab dang sras mjal ba'i mdo
Dg.K. dKon brtsegs, vol. Nga, ff. 1b-168a (Toh. 60)

Sacred Primordial Buddha's Tantra
Dam pa dang po'i rgyud/ Dam pa dang po'i sangs rgyas kyi rgyud
See the *Wheel of Time Condensed Tantra*

Samputa Tantra
Samputatantra
Yang dag par sbyor ba zhes bya ba'i rgyud chen po
Dg.K. rGyud 'bum, vol. Ga, ff. 73b-158b (Toh. 381)

rGyud kyi rgyal po chen po dpal yang dag par sbyor ba'i thig le
Dg.K. rGyud 'bum, vol. Ga, ff. 158b-184a (Toh. 382)

Samvara Tantra/ Samvarodaya Tantra
Mahāsamvarodayatantrarāja
sDom 'byung/ bDe mchog 'byung ba zhes bya ba'i rgyud kyi rgyal po chen po
Dg.K. rGyud 'bum, vol. Kha, ff. 265a-311a (Toh. 373)
Trans. S. Tsuda, *The Samvarodaya-Tantra, Selected Chapters*. Tokyo: Hokuseido
   Press, 1974.

Scripture on the Subtle Matters of Discipline
Vinayakṣudrakavastu
'Dul ba phran tshegs kyi gzhi
Dg.K. 'Dul ba, vols. Tha, ff. 1b-310a; Da, ff. 1b-333a (Toh. 6)

Scripture Revealing the Inconceivable Secrets of the Transcendent One
Tathāgatācintyaguhyanirdeśa
De bzhin gshegs pa'i gsang ba bsam gyi mi khyab pa bstan pa
Dg.K. dKon brtsegs, vol. Ka, ff. 100a-203 (Toh. 47)

Secret Moon Essence Tantra
Candraguhyatilakatantra
Zla gsang thig le zhes bya ba rgyud
Dg.K. rGyud 'bum, vol. Ja, ff. 247b-303a (Toh. 477)
Also in: *NG*, vol. Na, pp.188a-272a

Secret Nucleus/ Secret Nucleus of the Magical Net
Guhyagarbhamayajalatantra
gSang ba snying po de kho na nyid nges pa/ dPal gsang ba snying po sgyu
   'phrul drva ba
A tantra of the enlightened speech (*gsungs kyi rgyud*) associated with the deity
   Hayagriva (rTa mchog rol pa); Part of the *Secret Nucleus* cycle of teachings.
Dg.K. rNying rGyud, vol. Kha, ff. 198b-298b (Toh. 834)

Secret Tantra of the General Ritual of All Mandalas: see General Tantra

Skill in Means Scripture
Upāyakauśalyasūtra
   Thabs mkhas pa'i mdo
Dg.K. mDo sde, vol. Za, ff. 283b-310a (Toh. 261)
Trans. M. Tatz, *Sutra of Skill in Means*. Delhi: Motilal Banarsidass, 1994.

Stories of Buddha's Former Lives
Jātakanidāna
sKyes pa rabs kyi gleng gzhi
Dg.K. Shes phyin, vol. Ka, ff. 183a-250a (Toh. 32)

Summation of Essential Points
Sarvatathāgatatattvasaṃgraha
De nyid 'dus pa/ De bzhin gshegs pa thams cad kyi de kho na nyid bsdus pa
Dg.K. rGyud 'bum, vol. Nya, ff. 1b-142a (Toh. 479)

Susiddhi Tantra
Susiddhikaramahātantrasādhanopāyikapaṭala
Legs grub/ Legs par grub par byed pa'i rgyud chen po las sgrub pa'i thabs
rim par phye ba
Dg.K. rGyud 'bum, vol. Wa, ff. 168a-222b (Toh. 807)

Tantra of Consecration
Supratiṣṭhatantrasaṃgraha
Rab gnas kyi rgyud
Dg.K. rGyud 'bum, vol. Ta, ff. 146b-150a (Toh. 486)
Not identified with certainty

Ten Qualities Scripture
Daśadharmakasūtra
Chos bcu pa zhes bya ba'i mdo
Dg.K. dKon brtsegs, vol. Kha, ff. 164a-184b (Toh. 53)

Three-Part Scripture
Triskandhakasūtra
Phung po gsum pa'i mdo
Dg.K. mDo sde, vol. Ya, ff. 57a-77a (Toh. 284)
Translated as *The Sutra of Three Heaps* in *Mahayana Purification*. Dharamsala:
Library of Tibetan Works and Archives, 1980.

Transcendent Wisdom in Eight Thousand Lines
Aṣṭasāhasrikāprajñāpāramitā
'Phags pa shes rab kyi pha rol tu phyin pa brgyad stong pa
Dg.K. Shes phyin, vol. Ka, ff. 1b-286a (Toh. 12)

Two-Part Hevajra Tantra: see *Hevajra Tantra*

Unconquerable Vajra That Blazes by Fire
Vajrājitānalapramohanī-nāma-dhāraṇī,
rDo rje mi 'pham pa me ltar rab tu rmongs byed ces bya ba'i gzungs
Dg.K. rGyud 'bum, vol. Wa, ff. 1-4 (Toh. 752)

Union of Joyful Ones, Peaceful Tantra
bDe 'dus zhi rgyud/ bKa' brgyad bde gshegs 'dus zhi ba'i rgyud
The tantra of the *Cycle of the Eight Transmitted Precepts (bKa' brgyad bde gshegs
'dus pa'i chos skor)* rediscovered by Nyangrel Nyima Özer (Nyang ral nyi
ma 'od zer); found in the *Ngagyur Nyingme Sungrab*, vols. 75-87. Published
by Sonam T. Kazi, Gangtok, Sikkim, 1978.

Unsurpassable Chakrasamvara Tantra
bDe mchog mngon brjod bla ma
See *Abhidana Tantra*

Vairocanabhisambodhi Tantra
Mahāvairocanābhisaṃbodhivikurvitādhiṣṭhānavaipulyasūtreindrarāja
nāmadharmaparyāya
rNam par snang mdzad chen po mngon par rdzogs par byang chub pa rnam
par sprul pa byin gyis rlob pa shin tu rgyas pa mdo sde'i dbang po'i rgyal
po zhes bya ba'i chos kyi rnam grangs
Dg.K. rGyud 'bum, vol. Tha, ff. 151b-260a (Toh. 494)

Vajrapani Initiation Tantra
Vajrapāṇybhiṣekatantra
Lag na rdo rje dbang bskur ba'i rgyud chen po
Dg.K. rGyud 'bum, vol. Da, ff. 1b-156b (Toh. 496)

Vajrasattva's Magical Net
Vajrasattvamāyājalaguhyasarvādarśa
rDo rje sems dpa'i sgyu 'phrul drva ba gsang ba thams cad gyi me long
A tantra of the enlightened mind (*thugs kyi rgyud*) associated with the deity
Vishuddha (*Yang dag*); part of the *Secret Nucleus* cycle of teachings
Dg.K. rNying rgyud, vol. Kha, ff. 132b-198a (Toh. 833)

Valuable for Monks Scripture
Bhikṣupriyasūtra
dGe slong la rab tu gces pa'i mdo
Dg.K. mDo sde, vol. Sa, ff. 125a-127a (Toh. 302)

*Wheel of Time Condensed Tantra/ Great King of Tantras issued from the Sacred
Primordial Buddha, the Glorious Wheel of Time*
Laghutantra/ Paramādibuddhoddhṛtaśrikālacakranāmatantrarāja
bDus pa'i rgyud/ mChog gi dang po'i sangs rgyas las phyung ba rgyud kyi
rgyal po dpal dus kyi 'khor lo
Dg.K. rGyud 'bum, vol. Ka, ff. 22b-128b (Toh. 362)

Wheel of Time Fundamental Tantra
Kālacakramūlatantra
Dus 'khor rtsa rgyud
Not extant

White Lotus of the True Doctrine Scripture
Saddharmpuṇḍarikasūtra
Dam pa'i chos pad ma dkar po'i mdo
Dg.K. mDo sde, vol. Ja, ff. 1b-180b (Toh. 113)

Yamantaka Tantra: see *Black Yamari* and *Red Yamari* tantras

Yoga of General Cleansing: The Faultless King of Confessions Tantra
rNal 'byor spyi khrus dam tshig thams cad kyi nyams chag skong ba'i lung
bshags pa thams cad kyi rgyud dri ma med pa'i rgyal po
NKG, vol. 13, ff. 5-128
Also in *NG*, vol. Pha, under the title *Dri med bshags pa'i rgyud.*

TREATISES

Abhayākaragupta
Cluster of Secret Instructions
Saṃputatantrarājaṭikāmnāyamañjari
Man ngag snye ma/ dPal yang dag par sbyor ba'i rgyud kyi rgyal po'i rgya
cher 'grel pa man ngag gi snye ma
Dg.T. rGyud, vol. Cha, ff. 1b-316a (Toh. 1198)

Ānandagarbha
Illumination of Reality
Sarvatathāgatatattvasaṃgrahamahāyānābhisamayanāmatantratattvāloka-
karināmavyākyā
De bzhin gshegs pa thams cad kyi de kho na nyid bsdus pa theg pa chenpo
mngon par rtogs pa zhes bya ba'i rgyud kyi bshad pa de kho na nyid
snang bar byed pa
Dg.T. rGyud, vol. Li, ff. 1b-352a; Shi, ff. 1b-317a (Toh. 2510)

Indestructible Source
Vajradhātumahāmaṇḍalavidhisarvavajrodaya,
rDo rje 'byung ba/ rDo rje dbyings kyi dkyil 'khor chen po'i cho ga rdo rje
thams cad 'byung ba
Dg.T. rGyud, vol. Ku, ff. 1b-50a (Toh. 2516)

Āryadeva
Experientialist Four Hundred
Catuḥśatakaśāstrakārikānāma
bsTan bcos bzhi brgya pa zhes bya ba'i tshig le'ur byas pa
Dg.T. dBu ma, vol. Tsha, ff. 1b-18a (Toh. 3846)

Āryasūra
Garland of Former Lives of the Buddha
Jātakamālā
sKyes pa'i rabs kyi rgyud
Dg.T. sKyes rabs, vol. Hu, ff. 1b-135a (Toh. 4150)

Asaṅga
Compendium of Discipline (CD)
Vinayasaṃgraha
'Dul ba bsdu pa
Dg.T. Sems tsam, vol. 'I, ff. 1b-22a (Toh. 4040)

Proclaimers' Stages (PS)
Śrāvakabhūmi
Nyan thos kyi sa
Dg.T. Sems tsam, vol. Dzi, ff. 1b-195a (Toh. 4036)

Stages of the Bodhisattva (SB)
Bodhisattvabhūmi
Byang chub sems dpa'i sa
Dg.T. Sems tsam, vol. Wi, ff. 1b-213a (Toh. 4037)

Synthesis of Phenomenology
Abhidharmasamuccaya
Chos mngon pa kun las btus pa
Dg.T. Sems tsam, vol. Ri, ff. 44b-120a (Toh. 4049)

Aśvaghoṣa
Fifty Verses on Devotion to the Master
Gurupañcāśikā
Bla ma lnga bcu pa
Dg.T. rGyud, vol. Tshu, ff. 10a-12a (Toh. 3721)

Summary of Pledges
Dam tshig thams cad bsdus pa
Dg.T. rGyud, vol. Tshu, ff. 44a-59b (Toh. 3725)
Wrongly attributed to Atisha

Buddhaguhya
Sequence of the Path/ Sequence of the Path of the Magical Net
Pathakrama/ Māyājālapathakrama
Lam rim/ sGyu 'phrul lam rim
Also known as *Buddhaguhya's Sequence of the Path.*
NKG, vol. 23, ff. 5-133. A shorter work of the same title and by the same author is found in vol. 23, ff. 135-157.

Candragomin
Twenty Verses on the Bodhisattva's Commitments
Bodhisattvasaṃvaraviṃśaka
Byang chub sems dpa'i sdom pa nyi shu pa
Dg.T. Sems tsam, vol. Hi, ff. 166b-167a (Toh. 4081)
Trans. M. Tatz, *Twenty Verses on the Bodhisattva Vow* in *Difficult Beginnings.* Boston: Shambala, 1985.

Candrakīrti
Analysis of the Five Aggregates
Pañcaskandhaprakaraṇa
Phung po lnga'i rab tu byed pa
Dg.T. dBu ma, vol. Ya, ff. 239b-266b (Toh. 3866)

Dārika
Explanation of the Kalachakra Initiation
Kālacakratantrarājasekaprakriyāvṛtti
rGyud kyi rgyal po dpal dus kyi 'khor lo'i dbang gi rab tu byed pa'i 'grel pa
Dg.T. rGyud, vol. Pa, ff. 40b-71b (Toh. 1355)

Dharmamitra
Great Commentary on the Summary of Discipline
Vinayasūtraṭīkā

mDo rtsa'i 'grel chen/'Dul ba'i mdo'i rgya cher 'grel pa
Dg.T. 'Dul ba, vols. 'U, ff. 1b-388a; Yu, ff. 1b-390a (Toh. 4120)

Ḍombipa
Ten Essential Points
Daśatattva
De kho na nyid bcu pa
Dg.T. rGyud, vol. Nya, ff. 37a-41a (Toh. 1229)

Garbhapāda
Extensive Explanation of Root Tantric Downfalls
rDo rje theg pa'i rtsa ba'i ltung ba'i rgya cher 'grel pa
Dg.T. rGyud, vol. Zi, ff. 185a-192b (Toh. 2486)

Guṇaprabha
Fundamental Summary of Discipline (SD)
Vinayasūtra
'Dul ba'i mdo
Dg.T. 'Dul ba, vol. Wu, ff. 1b-100a (Toh. 4117)

One Hundred Formal Procedures (HFP)
Ekottarakarmaśataka
Las brgya rtsa gcig pa
Dg.T. 'Dul ba, vol. Wu, ff. 100b-259a (Toh. 4118)

Indrabhūti
Jnanasiddhi
Jñāsiddhisādhana
Ye shes grub pa'i sgrub pa'i thabs
Dg.T. rGyud, vol. Wi, ff. 36b-60b (Toh. 2219)

Indranāla
Commentary on Buddhasamayoga Tantra
Śrisarvabuddhasamayogaḍākinimāyāsaṃbaratantrārthodaraṭikā
mNyam sbyor 'grel pa
Dg.T. rGyud, vol. Ra, ff. 245a-389a (Toh. 1659)

Jetāri
Ceremony for the Acceptance of the Sacred Commitments
Bodhicittotpādasamādānavidhi
Byang chub kyi sems bskyed pa dang yi dam blang ba'i cho ga
Dg.T. dBu ma, vol. Gi, ff. 241b-245a (Toh. 3968)

Jñānākara
Guide to Mantra
Mantrāvatāra
gSang sngags la 'jug pa
Dg.T. rGyud, vol. Tsu, ff. 194a-196b (Toh. 3718)

Kṛṣṇa
Ascertainment of the Difficult Points of the Guide to the Bodhisattva's Way of Life
Bodhisattvacaryāvatāraduravabodhananirṇaya
Byang chub sems dpa'i spyod pa la 'jug pa'i rtogs par dka' ba'i gnas gtan la
     dbab pa
Dg.T. dBu ma, vol. Sha, ff. 90b-159a (Toh. 3875)

Līlāvajra
Shimmering Light on the Pledges
Dam tshig gsal bkra/ sPyi'i dam tshig mdor bsdus pa
Dg.T. rGyud, vol. Tshu, ff. 36a-41a (Toh. 3723)

Maitreya
Ornament of Realizations
Abhisamayālaṃkāranāmaprajñāpāramitopadeśaśāstra
Shes rab kyi pha rol tu phyin pa'i man ngag gi bstan bcos mngon par rtogs
     pa'i rgyan
Dg.T. Shes phyin, vol. Ka, ff. 1b-13a (Toh. 3786)

Scripture Ornament/ Ornament of the Scriptures of the Universal Way
Mahāyānasūtrālaṃkārakārikā
Theg pa chen po'i mdo sde'i rgyan zhes bya ba'i tshig le'ur byas pa
Dg.T. Sems tsam, vol. Phi, ff. 1b-39a (Toh. 4020)

Mañjuśrīyaśas
Essence Ornament of the General Procedure for All Secrets
Sarvaguhyavidhigarbhālaṃkāra
gSang ba thams cad kyi spyi'i cho ga'i snying po rgyan
Dg.T. rGyud, vol. Zi, ff. 232b-243b (Toh. 2490)

Explanation of Root Tantric Downfalls (ERD)
Vajrayānamūlāpattiṭīkā
rDo rje theg pa'i rtsa ba'i ltung ba'i rgya cher bshad pa
Dg.T. rGyud, vol. Zi, ff. 197b-231b (Toh. 2488)

Mātṛceta and Dignāga
Interwoven Praises
Miśrakastotra
sPel mar bstod pa
Dg.T. bsTod tshogs, vol. Ka, ff. 181a-193b (Toh. 1150)

Nāgārjuna
Ceremony for the Formation of the Awakening Mind
Bodhicittotpādavidhi
Byang chub tu sems bskyed pa'i cho ga
Dg.T. dBu ma, vol. Gi, ff. 237a-239a (Toh. 3966)

Five Stages
Pañcakrama
Rim pa lnga pa
Dg.T. rGyud, vol. Ngi, ff. 45a-57a (Toh. 1802)

Jewel Garland
Rājaparikathāratnamālā
rGyal po la gtam bya ba rin po che'i phreng ba
Dg.T. sPring yig, vol. Ge, ff. 107a-126a (Toh. 4158)

Letter to a Friend
Suhṛllekha
bShes pa'i spring yig
Dg.T. sPring yig, vol. Nge, ff. 40b-46b (Toh. 4182)
Trans. Geshe Lobsang Tharchin and A. B. Engle, *Nagarjuna's Letter.* Dharamsala:
   LTWA, 1979.

Prajñendraruci
Means of Accomplishment of the Glorious Blazing Jewel King of Tantras
Ratnajvalasādhana
Rin chen 'bar ba zhes bya ba'i sgrub pa'i thabs
Dg.T. rGyud, vol. Nya, ff. 214a-241b (Toh. 1251)

Praśāntamitra
Indestructible Nucleus Commentary
Vajramaṇḍalālaṃkāramahātantrapañjikā
rDo rje snying po'i rgyan gyi rgyud chen po'i dka' 'grel
Dg.T. rGyud, vol. I, ff. 313a-362a (Toh. 2515)

Puṇḍarika
Stainless Light Commentary on the Kalachakra/ Commentary by the Bodhisattva
Vimalaprabhānāmamūlatantrānusāriṇidvādaśasāhasrikālaghukāla-
   cakratantrarājaṭikā
bsDus pa'i rgyud kyi rgyal po dus kyi 'khor lo'i 'grel bshad rtsa ba'i rgyud
   kyi rjes su 'jug pa stong phrag bcu gnyis pa dri ma med pa'i 'od
Dg.K. Dus 'khor 'grel bshad, vol. Shri, ff. 1b-469a (Toh. 845)
Also: Dg.T. rGyud, vols. Tha, ff. 107a-277a; Da, ff. 1b-297a (Toh. 1347)

Ultimate Familiarization
Paramārthasevā
Don dam pa'i bsnyen pa
Dg.T. rGyud, vol. Na, ff. 1b-20a (Toh. 1348)

Pūrṇavardhana
Commentary on the Treasury of Phenomenology
Abhidharmakoṣaṭikālakṣanānusāriṇi
Chos mngon pa'i mdzod kyi 'grel bshad mtshan nyid kyi rjes su 'brang ba
Dg.T. mNgon pa, vols. Cu, ff. 1b-347a; Chu, ff. 1b-322a (Toh. 4093)

Ratnākaraśānti
Jewel Lamp Commentary on Yamantaka, the Black Enemy
Kṛṣṇayamārimahātantrarājapañjikāratnapradīpa
gShin rje dgra nag po'i rgyud kyi rgyal po'i chen po'i dka' 'grel rin po che'i
   sgron ma
Dg.T. rGyud, vol. Bi, ff. 124a-172b (Toh. 1919)

Śākyaprabha
> *Luminous Commentary on the Three Hundred Stanzas on the Novitiate (CTHSN)*
> Mūlasarvāstivādiśrāmanerakārikāvrttiprabhāvati
> 'Od ldan/ gzhi thams cad yod par smra ba'i dge tshul gyi tshig le'ur byas
>   pa'i 'grel ba 'od ldan
> Dg.T. 'Dul ba, vol. Shu, ff. 74a-162b (Toh. 4125)

> *Three Hundred Stanzas on the Novitiate*
> Mūlasarvāstivādiśrāmanerakārikā
> gSum brgya pa/ gzhi thams cad yod par smra ba'i dge tshul gyi tshig le'ur
>   byas pa
> Dg.T. 'Dul ba, vol. Shu, ff. 63a-74a (Toh. 4124)

Śāntideva
> *Compendium of Trainings (CT)*
> Śikṣāsamuccaya; Śikṣāsamuccayakārikā
> bSlab pa kun las btus pa; bSlab pa kun las btus pa'i tsig le'ur byas pa
> Dg.T. dBu ma, vol. Khi, ff. 1a-3a (Toh. 3939); ff. 3a-194b (Toh. 3940)

> *Guide to the Bodhisattva's Way of Life (GBL)*
> Bodhisattvacaryāvatāra
> Byang chub sems dpa'i spyod pa la 'jug pa
> Dg.T. dBu ma, vol. La, ff. 1b-40a (Toh. 3871)
> Trans. S. Batchelor, *A Guide to the Bodhisattva's Way of Life*. Dharamsala: LTWA,
>   1979.

Śāntipa
> *Commentary on the Mandala Rite of Guhyasamaja/ Four Hundred and Fifty Lines*
>   *Commentary*
> Guhyasamājamaṇḍalavidhiṭikā
> gSang ba 'dus pa'i dkyil 'khor gyi cho ga'i 'grel pa/ bZhi brgya lnga bcu pa'i
>   'grel pa
> Dg.T. rGyud, vol. Ni, ff. 59a-130a (Toh. 1871)

Subhagavajra
> *Stages of Path of the Universal Way*
> Mahāyānapathakrama
> Theg pa chen po'i lam gyi rim pa
> Dg.T. rGyud, vol. Tsu, ff. 183a-194a (Toh. 3717)

Vajragarbha
> *Commentary That Epitomizes the Hevajra Tantra/ Vajragharbha's Commentary*
> Hevajrapindārthaṭikā
> Kye'i rdo rje bsdus pa'i don gyi rgya cher 'grel pa
> Dg.T. rGyud, vol. Ka, ff. 1b-126a (Toh. 1180)

Vajrapāṇi
  Eulogy-Commentary on the Chakrasamvara Tantra (EC)
  Lakṣābhidhānāduddhṛtalaghutantrapiṇḍārthavivaraṇa
  bsTod 'grel/ mNgon par brjod pa 'bum pa las phyung ba nyung ngu'i rgyud
    kyi bsdus pa'i don rnam par bshad pa
  Dg.T. rGyud, vol. Ba, ff. 78b-141a (Toh. 1402)

Vasubandhu
  Principles of Elucidation
  Vyākhyāyukti
  rNam par bshad pa'i rigs pa
  Dg.T. Sems tsam, vol. Shi, ff. 29a-134b (Toh. 4061)

  Treasury of Phenomenology
  Abhidharmakoṣakārikā
  Chos mngon pa'i mdzod kyi tshig le'ur byas pa
  Dg.T. mNgon pa, vol. Ku, ff. 1b-25a (Toh. 4089)

Vibhūticandra
  Stream of Light on the Three Vows
  Trisaṃvaraprabhāmālā
  sDom gsum 'od kyi phreng ba
  Dg.T. rGyud, vol. Tshu, ff. 54b-56b (Toh. 3727)

Viśākhadeva
  Stanzas on the Discipline/ Garland of Flowers
  Vinayakārikā
  'Dul ba tshig le'ur byas pa/ Me tog phreng rgyud
  Dg.T. 'Dul ba, vol. Shu, ff. 1b-63a (Toh. 4123)

TIBETAN WORKS

Bodong Panchen Choklé Namgyal (Bo dong pan chen phyogs las rnam
    rgyal)
  General Presentation of the Tantras
  rGyud sde spyi'i rnam bshad
  In: *Collected Works of Phyogs las rnam rgyal*, vol. 24 (of 137 volumes). Repro-
    duced by photographic process by Tibet House Library Publications, Ti-
    bet House, 16 Jor Bagh, New Delhi, 1971.

Butön Rinchen Drub (Bu ston rin chen grub)
  General Presentation of the Classes of Tantra
  Three works of this name are found in the *Collected Works of Bu-ston*, a me-
    dium, extensive, and short work:

rGyud sde spyi'i rnam par gzhag pa rgyud sde thams cad kyi gsang ba gsal bar byed pa (vol. 15/Ba, ff. 2a-152a)

rGyud sde spyi'i rnam par gzhag pa rgyud sde rin po che'i mdzes rgyan (vol. 15/Ba, ff. 152a-304a)

rGyud sde spyi'i rnam gzhag bsdus pa rgyud sde rin po che'i gter sgo 'byed pa'i lde mig (Vol. 14/Pha, ff. 2a-86a)

Collected Works of Bu-ston. 28 vols. Edited by Lokesh Chandra. New Delhi: International Academy of Indian Culture, 1969.

Dharmashri, Lochen (Lo chen dharma shri)

Commentary on the Three Vows/ The Commentary that Ascertains the Three Vows, The Wish-Fulfilling Cluster of Good Explanations

sDom 'grel/ sDom pa gsum rnam par nges pa'i 'grel pa legs bshad ngo mtshar dpag bsam gyi snye ma.

Commentary on Ngari Panchen's *Three Vows*.

Published at Chorten Monastery, Deorali, Gangtok, Sikkim, by Dodrup Chen Rinpoché.

Also published at Rong phu mdo sngags gling Monastery, Nepal, based on the original woodblocks of Mindroling Monastery. Also found in *NKG*, vol. 37, ff. 41-675.

Drikung Kyobpa Jikten Gönpo ('Bri gung skyob pa 'jig rten mgon po)

The Rite for the Formation of the Aspiring, Venturing and Ultimate Awakening Mind

sMon 'jug don dam gsum gyi sems bskyes kyi cho ga yid bzhin nor bu

Collection of Highly Esoteric Instructions on various aspects of Buddhist practice, comprising parts sealed with secrecy of the collected writings of 'Bri gung skyob pa 'jig rten mgon po. Vol. 1. Reproduced from a rare manuscript from the library of the Ven. Togden Rinpoche (rTogs ldan rin po che) of sGang snong Monastery by Tsering Dorma Gheleg. New Delhi, 1975.

Gampopa (sGam po pa Dvags po lha rje)

Jewel Ornament of Liberation (JOL)

Dam chos yid bzhin nor bu thar pa rin po che'i rgyan

Rumtek, Sikkim: Dharma Chakra Centre, 1974

Jampa Lingpa, Panchen (Byams pa gling pa)

Great Mantra Discipline

sNgags 'dul chen mo/ sNgags kyi 'grel chen zung 'jug bgrod pa'i thems skas (*The Extensive Commentary on [Tsongkapa's Stages of the] Tantric Path, the Stairways Leading to the State of Union*) (identification of long title by Ven. Jampa Wangyal). Text not located.

Karma Trinlepa (Karma phrin las phyogs las rnam rgyal)

Chariot of Karma

Karma shing rta

Not located

Longchenpa (Klong chen pa)/ Longchen Rabjampa (Klong chen rab byams pa)
Treasury of Wish-fulfilling Jewels
Theg pa chen po'i man ngag gi bstan bcos yid bzhin rin po che'i mdzod
Published by Yeshe De Project (1991) based on the A'dzom and sDe dge
editions.

Mikyö Dorjé, the Eighth Karmapa (Mi bskod rdo rje)
*The Great Commentary on Discipline/ A Detailed Commentary on the Vinayasutra
and Buddhist Monastic Discipline*
'Dul ti ka chen po/ 'Dul ba mdo rtsa ba'i rgya cher 'grel spyi'i don mtha'
dpyad dang bsdus don sa bcad dang 'bru yi don mthar chags su gnyer ba
bcas 'dzam bu'i gling gsal bar byed pa'i rgyan nyi ma'i dkyil 'khor
Reproduced from prints of the dPal spungs Monastery blocks. New Delhi:
Karmapa XVI, 1973

Pema Karpo, Drukpa ('Brug pa padma dkar po)
Extensive Commentary on The Three Vows (TV)
sDom gsum rgya cher 'grel pa/ sDom pa gsum gyi rgyan ces bya ba'i rgya
cher 'grel ba
vols. Nga and Ca of the *Collected Works of Pema Karpo.* Thimphu, Bhutan:
Acharya Shedup Tenzin and Lama Dhondup Tharchen, 1991

Pema Wangyal, Ngari Panchen (mNga' ris pan chen padma dbang rgyal)
Three Vows
sDom gsum/ Rang bzhin rdzog pa chen po'i lam gyi cha lag sdom gsum
rnam par nges pa zhes bya ba'i bstan bcos
Published by Rong phu mdo sngags gling Monastery, Solokumbu, Nepal
Also found in *NKG*, vol. 37, ff. 5-41.

Rangjung Dorjé, the Third Karmapa (Rang byung rdo rje)
Ocean of Pledges
Dam tshig rgya mtsho
Not located

Rongzom Pandita (Rong zom pandita)
Precious Jewel Commentary/ Commentary on the Tantra of the Secret Nucleus
mKon mchog 'grel/ gSang ba'i snying po'i 'grel pa
NKG, vol. 25

Sönam Tsemo (bSod nams rtse mo)
Gateway to the Doctrine
Chos la 'jug pa'i sgo zhes bya ba'i bstan bcos
Collected Works of Sonam Tsemo (bSod nams rtse mo'i bka' 'bum), vol. 2/Nga, ff.
263a-317a, contained in the *Complete Works of the Great Masters of the Sakya
Sect of the Tibetan Buddhism.* Compiled by Sönam Gyatso (bSod nams rgya
mtsho). Tokyo: Toyo Bunko, 1968.

Taranatha (Ta ra na tha)
Elimination of Errors
'Khrul spang
Not located

Tsuklak Trengwa (gTsug lag phreng ba)
Commentary on the Guide to the Bodhisattva's Way of Life
Byang chub sems dpa'i spyod pa la 'jug pa rnam bshad theg chen chos kyi
    rgya mtsho zab rgyas mtha' yas snying po
Rumtek, Sikkim: Karmapa XVI, 1974

Wönkarma, Karma Ngelek Tendzin (dBon karma, Karma nge legs bstan 'dzin)
The Essential Bountiful Vase of the Three Vows
sDom gsum rnam par bstan pa nyer mkho'i bum bzang
Dergé, Tibet: dPal spungs thub bstan chos 'khor gling Monastery

Reference Bibliography

INDIC TEXTS

Āryadeva
Commentary on the Clear Lamp
Pradīpodyotananāmaṭīkā
sGron ma gsal ba zhes bya ba'i 'grel bshad
Dg.T. rGyud, vol. Khi, ff. 155a-205a (Toh. 1794)

Lamp Summary of Practice
Caryāmelāpakapradīpa
sPyod pa bsdus pa'i sgron ma
Dg.T. rGyud, vol. Ngi, ff. 57a-106b (Toh. 1803)

Asvabhāva
Commentary on the Scripture Ornament
Mahāyānasūtrālaṃkāraṭīkā
Theg pa chen po'i mdo sde'i rgyan gyi rgya cher 'grel pa
Dg.T. Sems tsam, vol. Bi, ff. 38b-174a (Toh. 4029)

Aśvaghoṣa
Fifteen Downfalls
lTung ba bco lnga pa
Dg.T. rGyud, vol. Zi, f. 180a3-5 (Toh. 2480)

Serious Downfalls
Sthūlāpatti
lTung ba sbom po
Dg.T. rGyud, vol. Zi, ff. 179b-180a (Toh. 2479)

Seven Secondary Infractions
Yan lag gi nyes pa bdun pa
Dg.T. rGyud, vol. Zi, f. 180a6-7 (Toh. 2481)

Summation of Tantric Downfalls
Vajrayānamūlāpattisaṃgraha
rDo rje theg pa rtsa ba'i ltung ba bsdus pa
Dg.T. rGyud, vol. Zi, ff. 179a-179b (Toh. 2478)

Atiśa
Commentary on the Lamp for the Path
Bodhimārgapradīpapañjikā
Byang chub lam gyi sgron ma'i dka' 'grel
Dg.T. dBu ma, vol. Khi, ff. 241a-293a (Toh. 3948)
Trans. R. Sherburne. *A Lamp for the Path and Commentary.* London: George
    Allen & Unwin, 1983.

Instruction on Taking Refuge
Saraṇagamanadeśanā
sKyabs su 'gro ba bstan pa
Dg.T. dBu ma, vol. Khi, ff. 297b-299a (Toh. 3953)

Lamp for the Path
Bodhipathapradīpa
Byang chub lam gyi sgron ma
Dg.T. dBu ma, vol. Khi, ff. 238a-241a (Toh. 3947)
Trans. R. Sherburne. *A Lamp for the Path and Commentary.* London: George
    Allen & Unwin, 1983.

Stages of the Rite for the Formation of Awakening Mind and Its Commitments
Cittotpādasaṃvaravidhikrama
Sems bskyed pa dang sdom pa'i cho ga'i rim pa
Dg.T. dBu ma, vol. Gi, ff. 245a-248b (Toh. 3969)

Bhavabhadra
Commentary on the Hevajra Tantra
Hevajravyākhyāvivaraṇa
dGyes pa'i rdo rje'i rnam bshad rnam par 'grel pa
Dg.T. rGyud, vol. Ka, ff. 173b-275a (Toh. 1182)

Bodhibhadra
*Revelation of the Difficult Points of the Twenty Verses on the Commitments of Awak-
    ening Mind/ Bodhisattva's Commitments*
Bodhisattvasaṃvaravimśakapañjikā
Byang chub sems dpa'i sdom pa nyi shu pa'i dka' 'grel
Dg.T. Sems tsam, vol. Hi, ff. 184b-217b (Toh. 4083)

Rite for the Commitments of Awakening Mind
Bodhisattvasaṃvaravidhi
Byang chub sems dpa'i sdom pa'i cho ga
Dg.T. dBu ma, vol. Gi, ff. 239a-241b (Toh. 3967)

Buddhaguhya
Guide to the Purport of the Tantra
Tantrārthāvatāra

rGyud kyi don la 'jug pa
Dg.T. rGyud, vol. 'I, ff. 1b-91b (Toh. 2501)

Candrakīrti
Commentary on the Experientialist Four Hundred
Bodhisattvayogācāracatuḥśatakaṭīkā
Byang chub sems dpa'i rnal 'byor spyod pa bzhi brgya pa'i rgya cher 'grel pa
Dg.T. dBu ma, vol. Ya, ff. 30b-239a (Toh. 3865)

Guide to the Middle Way
Madhyamakāvatārābhāṣya
dBu ma la 'jug pa'i bshad pa
Dg.T. dBu ma, vol. A', ff. 220b-348a (Toh. 3862)

Lucid Exposition: A Commentary on [Nagarjuna's Fundamental Text on] Wisdom
Mūlamadhyamakavṛttiprasannapadā
dBu ma rtsa ba'i 'grel pa tshig gsal ba
Dg.T. dBu ma, vol. A', ff. 1b-200a (Toh. 3860)

Collected Tantras of the Ancient Tradition (NG)
rNying ma rgyud 'bum
36 vols. Thimpu, Bhutan: Dilgo Khyentse Rinpoche, 1973

Collected Transmitted Precepts of the Ancient Tradition (NKG)
rNying ma bka' ma rgyas pa
Kalimpong, India: Dudjom Rinpoche, 1982

Commentary on the Fifty Verses on Devotion to the Master (CFVD)
Gurvārādhanapañjikā
Bla ma'i bsnyen bkur gyi dka' 'grel
Dg.T. rGyud, vol. Tshu, ff. 12a-36a (Toh. 3722)
Author unknown

Commentary on the Questions of Subahu Tantra
Subhāhuparipṛcchānāmatantrapiṇḍārthavṛtti
dPung bzangs kyis zhus pa'i rgyud kyi bsdus pa'i don dgrol ba'i brjed byang
Dg.K. rGyud, vol. Thu, ff. 100b-116b (Toh. 2673)
Author unknown

Daṃṣṭrasena
*Extensive Commentary on the Large, Medium, and Short Transcendent Wisdom
Scriptures*
Śatasāhasrikāpañcaviṃśatisāhasrikāṣṭādaśasāhasrikāprajñāpāramitābṛhaṭ
ṭīkā
Shes rab kyi pha rol tu phyin pa 'bum pa dang nyi khri lnga stong pa dang
khri brgyad stong pa'i rgya cher 'grel pa
Dg.T. Shes phyin, vols. Pha, ff. 1b-292b (Toh. 3808)

Extensive Commentary on the Transcendent Wisdom in One Hundred Thousand Lines
Śatasāhasrikāprajñāpāramitābṛhaṭṭīkā
Shes rab kyi pha rol tu phyin pa 'bum pa rgya cher 'grel pa
Dg.T. Shes phyin, vols. Na, ff. 1b-331a; Pa, ff. 1b-252a (Toh. 3807)

Ḍhaṅkadāśa
Utterly Stainless Union, Commentary on the Hevajra Tantra
Śrihevajratantrarājaṭikāsuviśadasampuṭanāma
rGyud kyi rgyal po dpal kye'i rdo rje'i 'grel bshad kha sbyor shin tu dri ma
    med pa
Dg.T. rGyud, vol. Kha, ff. 61a-294a (Toh. 1184)

Haribhadra
Illumination of the Ornament of Realizations
Aṣṭasāhasrikāprajñāpāramitāvyākhyābhisamayālaṃkārāloka
Shes rab kyi pha rol tu phyin pa brgyad stong pa'i bshad pa mngon par rtogs
    pa'i rgyan gyi snang ba
Dg.T. Shes phyin, vol. Cha, ff. 1b-341a (Toh. 3791)

Jinaputra
Explanation of the Synthesis of Phenomenology
Abhidharmasamuccayabhāṣya
Chos mngon pa kun las btus pa'i bshad pa
Dg.T. Sems tsam, vol. Li, ff. 1b-117a (Toh. 4053)

Jñānākara
Commentary on the Guide to Mantra
Mantrāvatāravṛtti
gSang sngags la 'jug pa'i 'grel pa
Dg.T. rGyud, vol. Tsu, ff. 196b-208a (Toh. 3719)

Jñānaśri
Dispelling the Two Extremes in the Indestructible Way
Vajrayānakoṭidvayāpoha
rDo rje theg pa'i mtha' gnyis sel ba
Dg.T. rGyud, vol. Tsu, ff. 115a-120a (Toh. 3714)

Kālacakrapāda
Explanation Expanding on the Brief Discussion of the [Kalachakra] Empowerment
Sekoddeśaṭikā
dBang mdor bstan pa'i rgya cher 'grel pa
Dg.T. rGyud, vol. Pa, ff. 1b-27b (Toh. 1353)

Kuladatta
Compendium of Activities
Kriyāsaṃgraha
Bya ba bsdus pa
Dg.T. rGyud, vol. Ku, ff. 227b-362a (Toh. 2531)

Kṛṣṇasamayavajra
Revealing the Difficult Points of the Five Stages
Pañcakramapañjikā
Rim pa lnga'i dka' 'grel
Dg.T. rGyud, vol. Chi, ff. 157b-187a (Toh. 1841)

Lakṣmīkara
Elucidation of the Five Stages
Pañcakramavṛttārthavirocana
Rim pa lnga'i don gsal bar byed pa
Dg.T. rGyud, vol. Chi, ff. 187b-277a (Toh. 1842)

Explanation of the Fourteen Root Tantric Downfalls
Vajrayānacaturdaśamūlāpattivṛtti
rDo rje theg pa'i rtsa ba'i ltung ba bcu bzhi pa'i 'grel pa
Dg.T. rGyud, vol. Zi, ff. 181a-185a (Toh. 2485)

Maitreya
Five Works of Maitreya
Byams chos sde lnga'i rtsa ba phyogs bsdebs
Sarnath, India: Kargyud Relief and Protection Committee, Central Institute
    of Higher Tibetan Studies, 1984

Nāgabodhi
Jewelled Garland
Rim pa lnga pa'i bshad pa nor bu'i phreng ba
Dg.T. rGyud, vol. Chi, ff. 14a-157a (Toh. 1840)

Nāropa
*Commentary on the Summary of the [Kalachakra] Initiation: Compendium of Ulti-
    mate Reality*
Paramārthasaṃgrahanāmasekoddeśaṭīkā
dBang mdor bstan pa'i 'grel bshad don dam pa bsdus pa zhes bya ba
Dg.T. rGyud, vol. Na, ff. 220b-289a (Toh. 1351)
Trans. R. Gnoli and G. Orofino in *Iniziazione Kalacakra*. In Italian. Milan:
    Adelphi Edizioni, 1994.

One Hundred Rites of Renunciation and Fulfillment
sPang skong phyag brgya pa
Dg.K. mDo sde, vol. Ya, ff. 1b-5b (Toh. 267)

Padmavajra
Explanation of the Guide to the Purport of the Tantras
Tantrārthavatāravyākhyāna
rGyud kyi don la 'jug pa'i 'grel bshad
Dg.T. rGyud, vol. 'I, ff. 91b-351a (Toh. 2502)

Sāgaramegha
Explanation of the Stages of the Bodhisattva
Bodhisattvabhūmivyākhyā
Byang chub sems dpa'i sa'i rnam par bshad pa
Dg.T. Sems tsam, vol. Yi, ff. 1b-338a (Toh. 4047)

Śāntirakṣita
Commentary on the Twenty Verses on the Commitments of Awakening Mind/
   Bodhisattva's Commitments (CTVBC)
Saṃvaravimśakavṛtti
sDom pa nyi shu pa'i 'grel pa
Dg.T. Sems tsam, vol. Hi, ff. 167a-184b (Toh. 4082)

Saroruha
Commentary on the Difficult Points of the Hevajra Tantra
Hevajratantrapañjikāpadmin
Kye'i rdo rje'i rgyud kyi dka' 'grel pad ma can
Dg.T. rGyud, vol. Ka, ff. 126b-173a (Toh. 1181)

Śraddhākaravarman
Commentary on the Seven Ornaments of the Compendium of Pristine Awareness Tantra
Ye shes rdo rje kun las btus pa'i rgyud las 'byung ba'i rgyan bdun rnam par
   dgrol ba
Dg.T. rGyud, vol. A, ff. 8b-10a (Toh. 1789)

Sthiramati
Commentary on the Scripture Ornament (CSO)
Sūtrālamkāravṛttibhāṣya
mDo sde rgyan gyi 'grel bshad
Dg.T. Sems tsam, vols. Mi, ff. 1b-283a; Tsi, ff. 1b-266a (Toh. 4034)

Tripiṭakamala
Lamp of the Three Modes
Nayatrayapradīpa
Tshul gsum gyi sgron ma
Dg.T. rGyud, vol. Tsu, ff. 6b-26b (Toh. 3707)

Vajragarbha
Commentary That Epitomizes the Hevajra Tantra/ Vajragarbha's Commentary
Hevajrapiṇḍārthaṭīkā
Kye'i rdo rje bsdus pa'i don gyi rgya cher 'grel pa/ rDo rje snying 'grel
Dg.T. rGyud, vol. Ka, ff. 1b-126a (Toh. 1180)

Vasubandhu
Explanation of the Scripture Ornament (ESO)
Sūtrālamkāravyākhyā
mDo sde'i rgyan gyi bshad pa
Dg.T. Sems tsam, vol. Phi, ff. 129b-260a (Toh. 4026)

Vimuktasena
Commentary on the Ornament of Realizations
Pañcaviṃśatisāhasrikāprajñāpāramitopadeśaśāstrābhisamayālamkāravṛtti
Shes rab kyi pha rol tu phyin pa stong phrag nyi shu lnga pa'i man ngag gi
   bstan bcos mngon par rtogs pa'i rgyan gyi 'grel pa
Dg.T. Shes phyin, vol. Ka, ff. 14b-212a (Toh. 3787)

Viśeṣamitra
Summary of Discipline
Vinayasaṃgraha
'Dul ba bsdus pa
Dg.T. 'Dul ba, vol. Nu, ff. 88a-268a (Toh. 4105)

Viśvāmitra
A Drop in the Ocean of Secret Instructions on the Tantra of Guhyasamaja
gSang ba 'dus pa'i rgyud kyi man ngag gi rgya mtsho thigs pa
Dg.T. rGyud, vol. Ji, ff. 53b-161b (Toh. 1844)

TIBETAN WORKS

Butön (Bu ston)
History of Buddhism
Chos 'byung
Beijing: Bod kyi shes rig dpe bskrun khang, 1988
Trans. E. Obermiller. *The History of Buddhism in India and Tibet.* Delhi: Sri
  Satguru, 1986.

Gendun Drubpa, the First Dalai Lama (dGe 'dun grub pa)
Commentary on Vasubhandu's Treasury of Phenomenology
Dam pa'i chos mngon pa'i mdzod kyi rnam par bshad pa thar lam gsal byed
Sarnath, India: Elegant Sayings Press, 1973

Jikmé Tenpai Nyima, the Third Dodrupchen (rDo grub 'jigs med bstan pa'i nyi ma)
General Meaning of the Guhyagarbha Tantra
gSang ba snying po spyi don
NKG vol. 35/ci, pp. 377-490

Karma Ngedön Nyingpo (Nges don snying po)
Commentary on [Ngari Panchen's] Three Vows (CNPTV)
Rang bzhin rdzogs pa chen po'i lam gyi cha lag sdom pa gsum rnam par
  nges pa'i bstan bcos kyi tshig don legs pa'i 'grel pa 'jam dbyangs dgyes
  par zhal lung
Edited by Dudjom Rinpoche, Kalimpong

Kongtrul Lodrö Tayé (Kong sprul blo gros mtha' yas)
Commentary on the Hevajra Tantra
dPal dgyes pa rdo rje'i rgyud kyi rgyal po brtag pa gnyis pa'i tshig don rnam
  par 'grol ba gzhom med rdo rje'i gsang ba 'byed pa
Rumtek, Sikkim: Dharma Chakra Centre, 1981

Commentary on [Rangjung Dorjé's] Profound Inner Reality
rNal 'byor bla na med pa'i rgyud sde rgya mtsho'i snying po bsdus pa zab
  mo nang gi don nyung ngu'i tshig gis rnam par 'grol ba zab don snang byed
Rumtek, Sikkim: Dharma Chakra Centre, 1981

Infinite Ocean of Knowledge (IOK)
Shes bya mtha' yas pa'i rgya mtsho
Beijing: Bod mi rigs dpe bskrun khang, 1982
Palpung Monastery: dPal spungs thub bstan chos 'khor gling, 1844

Longchenpa (Klong chen rab byams pa)
Dispelling Darkness in the Ten Directions: A Commentary on the Secret Nucleus
gSang snying 'grel chen phyogs bcu'i mun sel
Published by Dilgo Khyentsé based on Adzom Drukpa (A'dzom 'brug pa) redaction.
NKG, vol. 26.

Ngawang Kunga Tendzin, the Third Kamtrul (Kham sprul gsum pa ngag dbang kun dga' bstan 'dzin)
Foundations of the Great Seal Precepts
Phyag rgya chen po lhan cig skyes sbyor gyi sngon 'dro'i khrid yig
New Delhi

Sakya Pandita (Sa skya pandita)
Analysis of the Three Vows
sDom pa gsum gyi rab tu dbye pa'i bstan bcos
Collected Works of Sakya Kunga Gyaltsen. Beijing: Bod ljongs bdo yig dpe rnying dpe bskrun khang, 1992 vol. III

Rite for the Formation of the Awakening Mind according to the Centrist System
dBu ma lugs kyi sems bskyed kyi cho ga
Collected Works, vol. II

Sönam Drakpa, Panchen (bSod nams grags pa)
Sun Illuminating the Discipline with Reasons and Scriptures (SID; SID 16)
So thar tshul khrims kyi pad tshal rgyas byed pan chen bsod grags kyis mzad pa'i 'dul ba'i legs bshad lung rigs kyi nyi ma
Two vols. Woodblock print. Library of Geshé Puntsok Jinpa, Sonada, W.B. India.

Sönam Lha'i Wangpo (bSod nams lha'i dbang po)
Jewel Lamp Illuminating the Cluster of Gems of Parables
dPe chos rin chen spungs pa'i gsal byed rin po che'i sgron me'am gtam brgyud rin chen phreng mdzes
Dharamsala: Department of Religious and Cultural Affairs

Sönam Tsemo (bSod nams rtse mo)
Presentation of the Sets of Tantras
rGyud sde spyi'i rnam par gzhag pa
Gangtok, Sikkim: Ngor Monastery. Woodblock print.

Taranata (Ta ra na tha)
History of Buddhism in India
Dam pa'i chos rin po che 'phags pa'i yul du ji ltar dar ba'i tshul gsal bar ston pa dgos 'dod kun 'byung
Sarnath, India: Elegant Sayings Press, 1984
Trans. Lama Chimpa and A. Chattopadhyaya, *History of Buddhism in India.* Calcutta: K.P. Bagchi and Co., 1970.

Meaningful to Behold: Practical Instructions on the Indestructible Yoga's Profound Path
Zab lam rdo rje'i rnal 'byor gyi 'khrid yig mthong ba don ldan
In: Kongtrul Lodrö Tayé's *Treasury of Key Instructions* (*gDams ngag mdzod*),vol.
Ba, pp. 133-232. Delhi: N. Lungtok and N. Gyaltsen.

Tsonapa Sherab Zangpo (mTsho sna ba shes rab bzang po)
Sunlight Illuminating [Gunabrapha's] Root Summary of Discipline (*SIRD*)
'Dul ba mdo rtsa'i rnam bshad nyi ma'i 'od zer legs bshad lung gi rgya mtsho
Two vols. Woodblock print. Library of Geshé Puntsok Jinpa, Sonada, W.B.

Tsongkapa (Tsong kha pa)
*Commentary on the Fifty Verses on Devotion to the Master: Fulfilling the Aspira-
tions of Disciples*
Bla ma lnga bcu pa'i rnam bshad slob ma'i re ba kun skong
In the *Collected Works of Tsongkapa*, vol. Ka. 36 vols. Dharamsala: Shree
Publications.

Vairocana (Bai ro tsa na)
Union of Sun and Moon
Nyi zla'i kha 'byor
Edited by Chogyal Namkhai Norbu
Merigar, Italy: Shang Shung Edizioni

Yonten Gyatso, Khenpo (Yon tan rgya mtsho)
Commentary to [Longchenpa's] Treasury of Enlightened Qualities
Yon tan rin po che'i mdzod kyi 'grel pa zab don snang byed nyi ma'i 'od zer
Collected Works of the Nyingmapas (*rNying ma bka' ma rgyas pa*), vol. Thi. Delhi:
Dudjom Rinpoche, 1982-87.

OTHER WORKS AND TRANSLATIONS

Allen G. F. *The Buddha's Philosophy: Selections from the Pali Canon*. London: George
Allen and Unwin Ltd., 1959.

Atiśa. *A Lamp for the Path and Commentary*. Translated by Richard Sherburne.
London: George Allen & Unwin, 1983.

Butön (Bu ston). *The History of Buddhism in India and Tibet*. Translated by Eugene
Obermiller. Heidelberg: 1932; rpt. Delhi: Sri Satguru, 1986 (Bibliotheca Indo-
Buddhica no. 26).

————. *The Jewelry of Scripture of Bu-ston*. Translated by Eugene Obermiller.
1931; rpt. Delhi: Sri Satguru, 1987 (Bibliotheca Indo-Buddhica no. 42).

Candragomin. *Difficult Beginnings: Three Works on the Bodhisattva Path*. Translated by Mark Tatz. Boston: Shambhala Publications, 1985.

Chattopadhyaya, Alaka. *Atiśa and Tibet*. Calcutta, 1967; rpt. Delhi: Motilal
Banarsidass, 1996.

Dhargyey, Geshe Ngawang. *A Commentary on the Kālacakra Tantra*. Translated by
Alan Wallace. Edited by Ivanka Vana Jakic. Dharamsala: Library of Tibetan
Works and Archives, 1985.

Dowman, Keith, trans. *Masters of Mahamudra: Songs and Histories of the Eighty-Four Buddhist Siddhas.* Albany: State University of New York Press, 1985.

Dudjom Rinpoche, Jikdrel Yeshe Dorje. *The Nyingma School of Tibetan Buddhism: Its Fundamentals and History (NSH).* Translated and edited by Gyurme Dorje and Matthew Kapstein. 2 vols. Boston: Wisdom Publications, 1991.

Dutt, Nalinaksha. *Early History of the Spread of Buddhism and the Buddhist Schools.* London, 1926; rpt. Delhi: Rajesh Publications, 1980.

————. *Early Monastic Buddhism.* 2 vols. Calcutta, 1941-1945.

Edgerton, Franklin. *Buddhist Hybrid Sanskrit Grammar and Dictionary.* 2 vols. New Haven: Yale University Press, 1953; rpt. Delhi: Motilal Banarsidass, 1970.

Gampopa (sGam po pa). *The Jewel Ornament of Liberation (JOL).* Translated by Herbert V. Guenther. London: Rider, 1959; rpt. Berkeley: Shambhala, 1971.

Guenther, Herbert V. *The Creative Vision: The Symbolic Recreation of the World According to the Tibetan Buddhist Tradition of Tantric Visualization Otherwise Known as the Developing Phase.* Novato, CA: Lotsawa, 1987.

————. *Meditation Differently.* Delhi: Motilal Banarsidass, 1992.

————. *Philosophy and Psychology in the Abhidharma.* Berkeley: Shambhala, 1976.

————, trans. *The Life and Teaching of Nāropa.* Oxford: Clarendon Press, 1963; rpt. Oxford: Oxford University Press, 1971.

Gyatso, Tenzin (bsTan 'dzin rgya mtsho), Dalai Lama XIV. *The Kalachakra Tantra: Rite of Initiation for the Stage of Generation (KT).* Edited and translated by Jeffrey Hopkins. London: Wisdom Publications, 1985.

Hazra, Kanai Lal. *Constitution of the Buddhist Sangha (CBS).* Delhi: B.R. Publishing, 1988.

Holt, John C. *Discipline: The Canonical Buddhism of the Vinayapitaka.* Delhi: Motilal Banarsidass, 1981.

Hopkins, Jeffrey. *Meditation on Emptiness (ME).* London: Wisdom, 1983.

Kongtrul Lodrö Tayé. *Myriad Worlds: Buddhist Cosmology in Abhidharma, Kalacakra and Dzog-chen.* Translated by the International Translation Committee. Ithaca: Snow Lion Publications, 1995.

Lessing, Ferdinand D., and Alex Wayman, trans. *mKhas grub rje's Introduction to the Buddhist Tantric Systems.* (IBTS) The Hague: 1968; 2nd ed. Delhi: Motilal Banarsidass, 1978.

Lati Rinbochay, Denma Locho Rinbochay, and Panchen Sonam Drakba. *Meditative States in Tibetan Buddhism: The Concentrations and Formless Absorptions.* Translated by Leah Zahler and Jeffrey Hopkins; edited by Leah Zahler. London: Wisdom Publications, 1983.

Lati Rinbochay and Jeffrey Hopkins. *Death, Intermediate State and Rebirth in Tibetan Buddhism.* London: Rider, 1979; rpt. Ithaca: Snow Lion Publications, 1980.

Longchenpa (Klong chen rab 'byams pa). *Kindly Bent to Ease Us*. Translated by Herbert V. Guenther. Emeryville, CA: Dharma Publishing, 1976.

Monier-Williams, Sir Monier. *A Sanskrit-English Dictionary*. Oxford: 1899; rev. ed. Delhi: Marwah Publications, 1986.

Nāgārjuna. *Nāgārjuna's Letter: Nāgārjuna's "Letter to a Friend" with a commentary by the Venerable Rendawa, Zhön-nu Lo-drö*. Translated by Geshe Lobsang Tharchin and Artemus B. Engle. Dharamsala: Library of Tibetan Works and Archives, 1979.

Namkhai Norbu, Chögyal. *The Precious Vase*. Translated from Italian by John Shane. Merigar, Italy: Shang Shung Edizioni, 1994.

Naropa. *Iniziazone Kālacakra (IK)*. Edited and translated by Raniero Gnoli and Giacomella Orofino. In Italian. Milan: Adelphi Edizioni, 1994.

Rabten, Geshe. *The Preliminary Practices of Tibetan Buddhism*. Translated by Gonsar Tulku and edited by George Driessens. Burton, Washington: Tusum Ling Publications, 1974.

Rahula, Walpola, trans. *Le Compendium de la Super-Doctrine (Philosophie) (Abhidharmasamuccaya) d'Asanga*. Paris: École Française d'Extrême-Orient, 1971; 2nd ed. 1980.

Roerich, George N., trans. *The Blue Annals*. Calcutta, 1949; 2nd ed. Delhi: Motilal Banarsidass, 1976.

Sakaki, R., ed. *Mahavyutpatti*. Tokyo: Suzuki Research Foundation, 1962.

Shantideva, Acharya. *A Guide to the Bodhisattva's Way of Life*. Translated by Stephen Batchelor. Dharamsala: Library of Tibetan Works and Archives, 1979.

Smith, E. G. *Introduction to Kongtrul's Encyclopedia of Indo-Tibetan Culture (Shes bya kun khyab)*. Delhi, India: Lokesh Chandra, 1970.

Snellgrove David L., trans. *Hevajra Tantra, A Critical Study*. Part I: Introduction and Translation. London: Oxford University Press, 1959.

Tārānatha. *History of Buddhism in India*. Translated by Lama Chimpa and Alaka Chattopadhyaya; edited by Debiprasad Chattopadhyaya. Calcutta: K. P. Bagchi & Company, 1970.

Thubten Legshay Gyatsho. *Gateway to the Temple: Manual of Tibetan Monastic Customs, Art, Building and Celebrations*. Translated by David Paul Jackson; edited by H. K. Kuloy. Bibliotheca Himalayica, series III, vol. 12. Kathmandu: Ratna Pustak Bhandar, 1979.

Thurman, Robert, A. F., trans. *The Holy Teaching of Vimalakīrti: A Māhāyana Scripture*. University Park: Pennsylvania State University Press, 1976; rpt. Delhi: Motilal Banarsidass, 1991.

Tsong-ka-pa. *Tantra in Tibet: The Great Exposition of Secret Mantra*. Translated by Jeffrey Hopkins. London: George Allen & Unwin, 1977; rpt. Ithaca: Snow Lion Publications, 1987.

Tsuda, Shinichi, trans. *The Saṁvarodaya-Tantra, Selected Chapters*. Tokyo: Hokuseido Press, 1974.

Ui, Hakuju; Munetada Suzuki; Yensho Kanakura; and Tokan Tada, eds. *A Complete Catalogue of the Tibetan Buddhist Canons (Bkaḥ-ḥgyur and Bstan-ḥgyur)*. Sendai, Japan: Tohoku Imperial University, 1934.

Wayman, Alex. *The Buddhist Tantras: Light on Indo-Tibetan Esotericism*. New York, 1973; rpt. Delhi: Motilal Banarsidass, 1990.

————, trans. *Chanting the Names of Mañjuśrī*. Boston: Shambhala, 1985.

Index